Improving Business Communication Skills

FOURTH EDITION

Deborah Britt Roebuck, Ph.D.

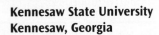

Kennesaw State University
Kennesaw, Georgia

Assisted by
Mary Ann McKenney, Student

PEARSON
Prentice
Hall

Upper Saddle River, New Jersey 07458

D1385230

Library of Congress Cataloging-in-Publication Data
Roebuck, Deborah Britt.
    Improving business communication skills / Deborah Britt Roebuck; assisted by Mary Ann
McKenney—4th ed.
        p. cm.
    Includes bibliographical references index.
    ISBN 0-13-118459-8 (alk. paper)
    1. Business communication. I. McKenney, Mary Ann. II. Title.
    HF5718 .R634 2005
    658.4'5—dc2
        200500877

Director of Production and Manufacturing: Bruce Johnson
Senior Acquisitions Editor: Gary Bauer
Editorial Assistant: Jacqueline Knapke
Development Editor: Deborah Hoffman
Marketing Manager: Leigh Ann Sims
Managing Editor—Production: Mary Carnis
Manufacturing Buyer: Ilene Sanford
Production Liaison: Denise Brown
Full-Service Production: Heather Willison/Carlisle Publishers Services
Composition: Carlisle Communications, Ltd.
Manager of Media Production: Amy Peltier
Media Production Project Manager: Lisa Rinaldi
Interior Cartoon Illustrations: Don Martinetti
Senior Design Coordinator: Christopher Weigand
Cover Design: Eve Ruutopold
Cover Printer: Phoenix Color
Printer/Binder: Banta Harrisonburg

Pearson Education Ltd.
Pearson Education Singapore Pte. Ltd.
Pearson Education Canada, Ltd.
Pearson Education—Japan

Pearson Education Australia Pty. Limited
Pearson Education North Asia Ltd.
Pearson Educatión de Mexico, S.A. de C.V.
Pearson Education Malaysia Pte. Ltd.

10 9 8 7 6 5 4 3
ISBN: 0-13-118459-8

This textbook is dedicated to Dr. Eduardo Montana who continually encouraged my heart both while a student in our Physician Executive MBA program and as a member of our Executive Programs Advisory Board. He was a special individual who truly cared about others.

CONTENTS

CHAPTER 6

Writing Memos, E-Mails, and Short Reports 118

CHAPTER 7

Making Business Letters and Documents Look Attractive on Paper and on the Computer Screen 154

CHAPTER 8

Writing Formal Reports, Business Plans, and White Papers   176

CHAPTER 9

Learning the Three P's of Oral Presentations: Preparation, Practice, and Presentation   219

CHAPTER 10

Using Technology to Communicate Within Virtual Teams 267

CHAPTER 11

Communicating in Meetings and by Telephone 290

CHAPTER 12

Searching for Your Career 337

CHAPTER 13

Composing Cover Letters and Résumés 356

CHAPTER 14

Preparing for and Surviving the Interview   389

CHAPTER 15

Understanding the Challenge of Ethical Communication   418

PREFACE

This fourth edition of *Improving Business Communication Skills* continues to deliver the foundation on which to build and improve all of your communication skills. The book was written with you, the student, in mind. The short, easy-to-read chapters teach you how to interact with others, either through written or spoken communication. You can immediately apply the principles you learn to your professional and personal life, although most application scenarios in the book ask you to assume the role of a manager communicating with employees, clients, or customers. This text delivers practical and vital communication skills you need to be successful in your career and personal life.

People learn best when they show interest in the topic and can involve themselves in a creative, self-directed fashion. This text furnishes you that opportunity. It involves you in the learning process so that you can understand and immediately apply the principles. As Confucius said, "I hear and I forget, I see and I remember, I do and I understand." To give you the opportunity to *do and understand,* this text allows you to apply theory and to learn from your own experiences.

IMPACT OF TECHNOLOGY AND THE INFORMATION HIGHWAY

In their book *It's Alive,* Christopher Meyer and Stan David state that in 1940 the maximum speed for connection was 1,000 bits per second. By 2000 it had risen to 10 trillion bits per second. The number of Internet hosts (possible places to search for information) is over 100 million. In 2002, the number of mobile phones worldwide had reached one billion. It is no wonder that nearly two-thirds of workers in the United States are employed in the service sector, and "knoweldge" has become the most important product." More information has been produced in the last 30 years than during the previous 5,000 years. Remarkably, this information supply doubles every three years.

¹*http://www.ipsos-insight.com/tech/tech_facts.cfm.*

The United States has the highest level of Internet usage among 12 countries surveyed by The Face of the Web tracking study: 72 percent of the American adult population reported having gone online at least once in the past 30 days. Canada is in a strong second place. South Korea, the United Kingdom, Japan, Germany, and France all registered significant percentage-point increases in Internet usage over the last two years, but their populations still trail behind Americans' widespread acceptance of the medium. Over one-quarter (28 percent) of the American population aged 12 and over have now downloaded a music or MP3 file off of the Internet.[1] Technology has revolutionized the way we learn, work, and live our lives. The marriage of information technology and the Internet has created a networked world in which everyone is connected to everyone else. The Internet is the fastest-growing telecommunication system ever—outpacing even the telephone system! You can communicate with colleagues around the world regardless of the time difference. Virtual organizations, e-business, and e-commerce are gaining momentum every day, as the electronic highway has transformed communication, collaboration, and commerce.

An interesting transition is taking place as we appear to be shifting from the "knowledge era" to the "communication era." Knowledge is critical, but if you can't communicate that knowledge, then it serves no purpose. Therefore, individuals must learn how to effectively communicate knowledge through traditional methods of communication as well as the technology-driven communication mediums.

WRITTEN, ORAL, AND INTERPERSONAL COMMUNICATION

One of the most surprising features of the information revolution is that the momentum has turned back to the written word. Writing well is a valuable skill often lacking among employees at all levels. The *Wall Street Journal* has reported that, of 443 companies surveyed, 80 percent cited poor writing as their biggest skill problem. In a more recent *Wall Street Journal* article entitled "What Recruiters Want," 89 percent of the recruiters rated communication skills as very important attributes for students and business schools. Within this article, investment banker Darren Whissen was quoted as saying, "I have found that many seemingly qualified candidates are unable to write even the simplest of arguments. No matter how strong one's financial model is, if one cannot write a logical, compelling story, then investors are going to look elsewhere." This quote highlights the critical role of written communication.

With technological advances, you have many communication mediums from which to choose. However, most studies still show that spoken, face-to-face communication is preferred in many situations. Studies show conflict may escalate when people use e-mail to try to solve an interpersonal problem. These studies have found that one five-minute telephone conversation can sometimes clear up e-mail messages that have gone back and forth for days. So the challenge for you, as a communicator, is to know your audience and thus determine whether to use the written or oral channel.

The knowledge era has created new organizations. The organizations of the twenty-first century are made of virtual teams, remote teams, far-flung teams, and networks. The network, not the pyramid, will become the conceptual model for how people work together to achieve goals. In addition to oral and written communication skills, individuals will need to sharpen their interpersonal communication and teaming skills to succeed in this type of organizational structure.

If you realize the importance of oral, written, and interpersonal communication skills, and you are willing to invest time and energy to improve these skills, you will have a real advantage in the workforce. Whether you are pitching a business proposal, leading a team, or justifying a budget, the quality of your communication skills will determine your success or failure.

SKILLS BUILT ON ORGANIZATION

Because the world of work demands effective oral, written, and interpersonal skills, the text emphasizes these skills. The convenient text-workbook format combines *learning, analysis, practice,* and *application.* The book features short chapters with cartoons and checklists emphasizing the major points, followed by exercises that explore and analyze effective and ineffective communications. Assignment Options encourage you to practice applying a competency in a work-like situation and to transfer your learning to real-life situations. This format will help you improve your communication skills by giving you numerous opportunities to practice and to develop your confidence. This is an all-in-one learning package; you have to purchase only one text that can serve as a reference handbook after class ends.

Improving Business Communication Skills develops communication skills in a carefully planned design. Chapter 1 lays a foundation by presenting the paradigm shift created by the information explosion and how it has impacted the way we communicate. It also discusses the importance of communication and causes of miscommunication. Chapter 2 provides the mechanics of business writing whether writing on paper or on the computer screen. Chapters 3 through 6 introduce the writing strategies based upon your audience's reaction and helps you apply these strategies to different settings including international audiences. You will learn how to write e-mail messages, letters, memos, and reports, employing the direct and indirect writing strategies. Chapter 7 shares how to create business letters and electronic documents that will get read. Chapters 9 through 11 teach more strategies, including making presentations, working in virtual teams, and leading meetings. Chapters 12 through 14 apply all the strategies to help you successfully complete a job search. Extremely important topics covered here include résumés, cover letters, and thank-you letters. Information on conducting the job search and interviewing enhances your success at finding the right job. Chapter 15 helps you understand the challenges of ethical communication, with a special emphasis on global and technological issues.

Each chapter of the text begins with a thought-provoking statement to sharpen your focus on the upcoming content. The cartoons and checklists encourage students—even those who do not normally read a text—to pick this one up. Virtually every chapter provides Web addresses for resources and references on the Internet. The exercises break down the writing process into simple, manageable pieces so that you achieve success before you write an entire document. The options allow you to sometimes rewrite "real business documents," thus again achieving success before you must compose your own documents. Finally, most assignments allow you to write "real" memos, letters, and reports instead of responding to fictional, unfamiliar cases.

EASY REFERENCE

Appendix A includes a checklist of the most common business communication errors, classified by the 7 Cs. An explanation and illustration of errors helps you overcome troublesome writing difficulties. Students and professors alike find this a useful tool throughout the course. Professors can mark a number on a student's page instead of writing the same comment, time and time again. Appendix A includes all the strategies for effective business writing. Appendix B includes over 100 website addresses for websites relating to business communication. Appendix C provides a list of all checklists found in the text.

STUDENT CD

Included with the textbook is a CD entitled "Student CD," which contains all the Exercises and Assignments at the end of each chapter in the textbook chapters, as well as additional Exercises and Assignments. You can copy the material from the CD to your computer system instead of having to key them from the text. Having the Exercises and Assignments on the CD encourages you to edit and write at your computer instead of just transferring handwritten documents to a computer.

INSTRUCTOR'S TOOLS

An *Annotated Instructor's Edition* provides instructors with an easy-to-use, all-in-one manual. The CD with the *Instructor's Edition* includes Answers to Exercises and Applications, PowerPoint files and a True/False and Multichoice Test Bank.

CONCLUSION

I sincerely hope, through your use of *Improving Business Communication Skills,* you will learn the important role business communication plays in your life. So buckle your seat belt and hang on. You are in for the communication ride of a lifetime!

ACKNOWLEDGMENTS

I wish to acknowledge and thank the following individuals for their assistance in completing this fourth edition:

My graduate student assistant, Mary Ann McKenney, and my administrative assistant, Nancy Barnes, who spent endless hours with me editing, proofing, and rewriting. I could not have completed this revision without them.

My sister, Rebecca Britt Warlick, who also spent much time helping me edit and revise this edition.

My students, who let me use their work. I would especially like to thank Dr. Eduardo Montana, Sr., MD; Carol Joy; and Tom Rogers.

My husband, Rob, who did not question where I was going when I headed downstairs to my office.

My daughter, Hillary, who would ask: "What are you doing? Aren't you done with that book yet?"

The rest of my family, from whom so much time was taken, for their support, encouragement, and patience!

Special thanks to the reviewers of this text: Melynda Barks, Mineral Area College in Park Hills, MO and Charles Kuehl, University of Missouri at St. Louis, MO.

Deborah Britt Roebuck

CHAPTER 1

Experiencing Communication in Today's Technology-Enabled World

*J*ust as the personal computer revolutionized the workplace throughout the 1980s and 1990s, recent developments in information and communication technology are on the verge of creating a new revolution in the coming decade. Technology is converging to forge the foundation of a new workplace.[1]

Anthony Townsend, Samuel M. DeMarie, and Anthony R. Hendrickson

LEARNING OBJECTIVES

After reading this chapter, you should be able to:

☞ Discuss how technology has changed the way we communicate.

☞ Understand the importance of communication.

☞ Describe the communication process.

☞ List the causes of miscommunication.

☞ Explain the tips for giving feedback.

☞ Distinguish between sensory and normative perception.

☞ Give examples of external and internal noise.

☞ Identify ways to become a better listener.

☞ Explain how personality, gender, and intercultural differences can affect communication.

[1] Anthony Townsend, Samuel M. DeMarie, and Anthony R. Hendrickson, "Virtual Teams: Technology and the Workplace of the Future," *Academy of Management Executive*, Volume 12, Issue 3, pp. 17–29, August 1998.

The Paradigm Shift the Information Explosion Has Created

The Internet revolution and the expansion of the World Wide Web have combined with faster and lower-cost personal computer products to create an explosion of growth in new networks and network services. **The World Wide Web has revolutionized the way we learn, work, and live our lives.** In the early part of this century, approximately one billion Internet users will be online. Internet traffic has increased by as much as 15 percent a month, making the Internet the fastest-growing telecommunication system ever—even outpacing the telephone system.[2]

Today, nearly two-thirds of U.S. workers are employed in the service sector, and "knowledge" is becoming the most important "product." We live in a networked world in which everyone is connected to everyone else. You can communicate with colleagues around the world regardless of time differences. Virtual organizations, e-business, and e-commerce are gaining momentum every day, as the electronic highway has transformed communication, collaboration, and commerce. This marriage of communication, technology, and business has created a fourth economy that is changing the way that people communicate.

EVOLUTION IN TECHNOLOGICAL COMMUNICATION TOOLS

E-Mail. Ten years ago, businesses began to use e-mail as a means of communication—and five years ago it began to take on a life of its own. Today, it is rare that someone doesn't have e-mail, even someone who is not technically inclined. Not having an e-mail address has become akin to not having a telephone 40 years ago. In fact, e-mail is the primary communication mechanism for most businesses. Of 387 business-technology professionals surveyed by Meta Group in April 2003, 80 percent preferred e-mail to the telephone for their daily business communication.[3]

Two surveys indicate that these trends seem to be worldwide. First, a survey conducted in the United Kingdom found that 83 percent of businesses polled did not think they could last longer than one week without e-mail. A further 12 percent said that they would not be able to last one day without it, while only 2 percent said they could survive for a whole month. Finally, 7 percent said they could last indefinitely.[4]

In addition, a survey conducted by the Swedish company Netsurvey found that using e-mail, as well as connecting to the Internet and an intranet, were the preferred third-generation services among Swedish companies.[5]

Cell Phones. Cell phones offer another example of the evolution in communication. These little devices have become a means of instant access that people now demand. An employer may think, "I pay for cell phones for my staff so I expect to be able to reach them all immediately." Mary Ann McKenney has stated:

> E-mail has become such a powerful and persuasive component of our communication toolbox that we can hear people type while they use it to communicate with us.
>
> Source: "Being Heard in the Age of E-mail," William Arruda, retrieved from *http://www.stickysauce.com/articles/maillistsarticles/being_heard_in_the_age_of_e-mail.htm*

---

[2] N. Chinna Natesan, "Computer-Mediated Business Communication in the Classroom," in *Tested Teaching Ideas for Business Communication,* edited by Courtland L. Bovee and John V. Thill (New York: McGraw-Hill, 1995), pp. 45–46.

[3] Roma Nowak, "Behind the Numbers: E-mail Beats the Phone in Business Communication," *Information Week,* Issue 940, p. 66, May 19, 2003.

[4] "Star Internet Survey Shows Increasing Dependence on E-mail in the UK," *Telecomworldwire,* p. 1, February 17, 2004.

[5] "Swedish Companies Prefer E-mail and Internet to Other 3G Services," *Telecomworldwire,* p. 1, February 25, 2004.

Five years ago, I provided 24/7 technical support worldwide via beeper. I'd get a call and I was expected to return the call within a half hour. Now, employees are expected to be available immediately, which gives employers a new vision of their employees. [Personal Interview]

Wireless phones are among the most important tools we have, as their portability enables us to work from anywhere. An employee is no longer strapped to his or her desk while waiting for that all-important call. When using cell phones, the etiquette associated with telephones has changed as well. People seem to think nothing of talking about personal things in public, in tones anyone can hear. *Reader's Digest* talks of another phenomenon called time slippage, in which people are no longer late for meetings, as they can call the other attendees and change the time of the meeting.[6]

In a recent poll, a majority of Americans said the cell phone is the invention they most hate but can't live without. "Cell phones are a really profound technology," says William Gibson, science fiction author (*Neuronmancer*) and futurist who coined the term "cyberspace." "I don't think we understand what it's done to us already," he adds. "I think that's the nature of emergent technologies—we don't understand them."[7]

PDAs. As prices have declined, another increasingly important device, the PDA (personal digital assistant) or handheld computer, is becoming more popular. This system allows you to synchronize your key organizational elements with your desktop or laptop computer. In a small handheld system, you have your entire contact list, your calendar, and your "to do" list. These devices further blur the line between work and leisure time, as many of the units allow you to send and receive e-mails anywhere so you are never "out of touch."

Instant Messengers. Another communication mechanism that enables you to stay in touch in "real time" is instant messengers (IM). These programs or communication services let you communicate with someone else who is using the same program. Within the last year, instant messenger services have connected millions of Americans through the Internet using pagers, cell phones, televisions, computers, PDAs, and handheld PCs. A recent report concludes that 53.8 million Americans used instant messaging from their homes in 2001 while another 13.8 million used it at work. Forecasts indicate that the growth rate of instant messaging will exceed that of any other Internet-based communication method. Unlike e-mail, instant messaging is real-time communication, allowing immediate response to critical situations.[8]

"You get to see that the other person is there. You don't see that with e-mail or phone," EXP.com president Mark Benning said at the Internet World Conference in Los Angeles. "It's real-time, it's immediate—you expect an answer back immediately." "We see it as a fundamental e-business capability," IBM's John Patrick said. "On the surface, people think it's a large number of teenagers having chats, but in a business context, it facilitates more productive business dialogue. So attorneys can negotiate, and at the same time they are exchanging instant messages under the table with their partners."[9]

> "Instant messaging is becoming a critical technology for corporations wanting to increase collaborative efforts and improve productivity," said Giga Information Group analyst Rob Endele. "It represents one of the strongest opportunities to apply technology in a way that makes companies more competitive."
>
> Source: Jim Herman, "Instant Messaging's Gonna Get You," *Business Communications Review*, Volume 33, Issue 10, pp. 16–17, October 2003.

[6] Peter Griffith, "When Time Stands Still Only in America," *Reader's Digest*, p. 19, March 2004.

[7] Phil Kloer, "Can You Hear Us Now?" *The Atlanta Journal-Constitution*, Sunday Living, L1 and L2, March 7, 2004.

[8] "IM Used Within a Business Is a Great Way to Reach and Include Remote Workers. E-Commerce Web Sites Such as Lands' End and 800.com Use Instant Messaging as an Alternative to Phone Calls and E-Mail to Communicate with Customers," retrieved from *http://www.imsecurity.com/instantmesg.htm*.

[9] Wylie Wong and Troy Wolverton, "Instant Messaging Latest Trend in E-commerce Software," CNET News.com, April 6, 2000. Retrieved from *http://patrickweb.com/inthenews/messaging-iws2000.html*.

Experts agree that instant messaging will revolutionize communication in the coming decade.

Pagers.   While pagers have been around for a long time, with the addition of text and two-way paging they have experienced a rebirth. Pagers are no longer just a one-way device; now you can get your e-mail and reply to the person that pages you. Karen Regno, a BellSouth employee, shares the following story about how she effectively used her i-pager when she had to travel out of town.

> I was supposed to fly to Greensboro on Monday, June 2. I stopped by the office on the way to the airport and ended up missing my flight due to a crisis that had to be handled by 9:30 A.M. Monday. The Audit team required a response and no one was available who could answer, except me. My co-worker had not stopped by the office and had boarded the plane at 8:35. I had all of the information—the office address, the car rental info, the hotel address—because she did not want to carry any extra information or papers with her. Now, she is on the plane; I am in the office and the next plane is at 12:15 P.M. Since neither of us had a cell phone, we used the i-pager to work through this issue. I paged her with directions to the office and hotel and the car rental information. She paged me with the phone number of the car rental desk so I could add her as a second driver and provide them my credit card number. I then paged her when I landed and she met me at the airport. Without the i-pager, passing the information and getting back together would have been extremely difficult. She thought I was on the plane and she had just not seen me board. Before she could realize that I was not there, I had provided her with all of the information she needed to carry on without me present. This was her first trip for Bell-South, so she was already nervous about traveling. The messages helped her relax. [Personal Interview]

Fax machines provide the easist and quickest way to send a document that exists in hard-copy form.

SOURCE: Pearson Education/PH College. Photograph by Brian Waring.

Facsimile.   The fax is an important business tool for quick communication and sharing of documents with others. With some fax machines, the faxes can be forwarded to an e-mail address, while other faxes can be viewed on the Internet. Incoming faxes can be sent to several e-mails at once, which is helpful if you need to ensure an individual has received your document or if being responsive to several individuals is key. For companies sending many faxes that must originate as paper, a simple scanner or existing fax machine can be used for outgoing paper faxes. However, for many businesses, electronic faxes eliminate the need for a dedicated fax line, or can free-up a voice line for voice or dial-up without having to choose whether to be online or to send/receive faxes. Along these lines, nearly all of today's modems are actually fax-modems; in effect, they are fax machines built into the computer. Even if users don't want their computers to stay on and connected to a live phone line to receive faxes, the fax-modem is a convenient technology for sending faxes. And, it's already paid-for.[10]

Faxing remains a popular means of communication and has kept up with the changes in the technological world by merging old-style fax-to-fax with e-mail. The practical side of the fax machine makes it a viable communication medium. Although doing business over the Internet is a growing trend, when it comes to transmitting printed forms and signed documents as well as working with smaller companies that don't have e-mail or Internet access, the fax remains the technology of choice. The fax also provides an easy and quick way to transmit a document existing only in hard-copy form. In addition, you know your receiver received the fax

---

[10] "Technology for the Record—Use Existing Technology to Simplify Your Life," *The Daily Record*, p. 1, February 20, 2004.

Today through the power of the Internet, you can retrieve more information than you ever imagined.

because you receive a confirmation. Many predicted that faxes would die out with the advent of e-mail, but that has not happened as faxes seem as popular as ever.

THE TECHNOLOGICAL EVOLUTION HAS IMPACTED BUSINESS PRACTICES, WORK PRACTICES, AND WORK LOCATIONS

The information explosion and the paradigm shift it has created have impacted where and how business is transacted and where and how individuals within organizations work, meet, and communicate to manage their job responsibilities.

As a result, e-business, telecommuting, audioconference, and videoconferences are all on the rise.

E-Business. E-business, also known as e-commerce, involves doing business over the Internet, and allows smaller, entrepreneurial businesses to compete with larger companies. Doing business online allows organizations to expand into new markets, operate around the clock, and boost their profits without making major investments or incurring extra overhead.

The World Wide Web has spawned a new culture with its own rules of interaction, its own language, and its own **netiquette** (Net + etiquette; proper manners on the Net) rules. See Box 1.1 for six basic netiquette guidelines for using the electronic highway.

Many organizations use e-business for internal organizational needs as well. For example, IBM uses the Web for approximately 30 percent of its training and education. Educational establishments use the Internet to allow distance learning and on-demand learning, so that you can gain access to material anywhere at any time.

Because of the enormous popularity of the Internet, many companies and organizations have adapted state-of-the-art Internet technologies into internal networks, or *intranets,* to facilitate communication and **knowledge management.** Mary Ellen Guffey writes, "Knowledge management involves the conscious creating, organizing, and sharing of an organization's collective wisdom and knowledge to further its goals."[12]

It aids communication across all organizational boundaries, enabling the entire company to work together. Senders and receivers are linked across geographical and departmental boundaries through e-mail listserves, newsgroups, electronic bulletin boards, intranets with chat rooms, department pages, and expert lists with contact information. In *Information Week,* Jeff Angus and colleagues noted:

> . . . corporate communications are tools used by managerial craftspeople much as carpenters use saws, planes, and hammers. Managers should

1. Refrain from flaming, typing in ALL CAPS, and getting carried away with the message, sometimes to the point of using profanity.[11]
2. Wait for a while before posting messages to a new discussion group.
3. Do not ask questions that have been asked a million times. Refer to a list of FAQs (Frequently Asked Questions).
4. Describe the topic of your message in the subject line.
5. Keep public messages brief in discussion groups.
6. Do not use profanity or exhibit hostile behavior.

BOX 1.1 ☛ **Netiquette Guidelines**

SOURCE: Susan C. Herring, Associate Professor of Linguistics, University of Texas at Arlington.

[11] Lyle Sussman, Peggy Golden, and Renee Beauclair, "Training for E-Mail," *Training and Development Journal,* p. 70, March 1991, p. 70.

[12] Mary Ellen Guffey, "The Latest in Business Buzzwords: A Primer on Knowledge Management," *Business Communication News,* South-Western College Publishing, Number 18, p. 1, Fall 1999.

know which tools to use and how to use them to achieve productive and profitable results. To give employees access to each other and to facilitate information flow, knowledge managers must create communication channels for employees to reach each other. In large corporations, simply encouraging employees to visit one another's cubicles may be a step, but it will fall drastically short of supplying the necessary channels for senders and receivers to transfer messages. Companies, particularly larger decentralized ones, need to physically provide technological channels, through which knowledge can be shared, because technology is what facilitates the practice of knowledge management.[13]

Federal Express found that its Internet website was a cost-saving solution for customer service, so the company decided to try out the technology on an internal basis. The firm now operates over 60 intranet websites among 30,000 worldwide office employees.[14]

Telecommuting. Telecommuting, the practice of allowing employees to work from an office at home or from a mobile office in the field, has increased as a result of the communication revolution. Telephony helps keep mobile workers and telecommuters connected by combining the telephone with the computer. Internet technology has created advanced e-mail systems, unified messaging, and the ability to make phone calls over the Internet through a process called Voice Over Internet Protocol (VOIP). With cell phones and the Internet, it is possible to do business without ever having a physical office. And it would be impossible for people to notice a difference, unless they came to see you. In 1998, International Data Corporation, a Framingham, Massachusetts-based market research firm, estimated that, in 9.9 million households, at least one person worked at home for an employer three days a month during normal business hours. That number was up from 9.1 million households in 1997, and is expected to grow at an 8.8 percent rate annually over the next few years. IDC attributes the increase to advances in technology and companies' continuing efforts to meet employee needs in a tight labor market.[15]

In addition, there are approximately 24 million home-based businesses. Technology makes it possible for entrepreneurs and employees to make a seamless transition from a traditional business setting to a home office.[16]

Telecommuting is an increasingly international trend as well. According to the University of California at Davis, the first telecenter, a private and public venture designed to accommodate 100 employees, opened in France's Marne Valley in 1981. Meanwhile, a study funded by the U.S. Department of Transportation and California's Department of Transportation identified 60 telecommuting ventures in a dozen nations. Sweden even experimented with an "office train" in 1986, paying about 20 Swedish managers for work completed during their commutes to and from their offices in Stockholm.[17]

Telecommuting offers the advantages of skipping the daily commute and not having to worry about a dress code. Telecommuters can work on the road, from home, from headquarters, or from a foreign subsidiary. Often, telecommuters find themselves working more hours, as work more easily creeps into their leisure time

---

[13] Jeff Angus, Jeetu Patel, and Jennifer Harty, "Knowledge Management: Great Concept But What Is It?" *Information Week,* 673, pp. 58–70, March 16, 1998.

[14] Deborah L. Duarte and Nancy Tennant Snyder, *Mastering Virtual Teams* (San Francisco: Jossey-Bass Publishers, 1999), p. 17.

[15] George Alexander, "Is Telecommuting Right for You?" *Black Enterprise,* 29, 11, pp. 61–62, June 1999.

[16] Tim McCollum, "A High-Tech Edge for Home Offices," *Nations Business,* 86, 12, pp. 52–54, December 1998.

[17] Jenny C. McCune, "Telecommuting Revisited," *Management Review,* 87, 2, pp. 10–16, February 1998.

and technology makes it easier to keep working. They can also find themselves missing the face-to-face contact with other employees.

"Good communication between the telecommuter and those in the office is essential for effectiveness," explains Roy You, director of Flexible Resources' Los Angeles office. "We recommend that the home-based worker be very creative in communicating with bosses and colleagues. Lunch dates, regular telephone calls, and e-mail are keys to preventing an out-of-sight, out-of-mind situation."[18]

Workplace flexibility in which full-time workers have more control over their schedules and can choose to work part time without penalty is another outcome of the impact of technology. The concepts promoted by the proponents of workplace flexibility are detailed in Box 1.2.

Audio- and Videoconferencing. Two other means of communication that advances in technology enable are audioconferencing and videoconferencing.

- **Flexible schedules for full-time work.** A number of companies already allow workers some flexibility in when they start and stop their workdays. For example, they take a break in the late afternoon and early evening to be with their families and finish their work at night.

- **More and better part-time work.** Many individuals advocate giving an employee who works three-quarters time 75 percent of the pay and benefits of a full-time worker—and eligibility for promotions at three-fourths the speed.

- **Career flexibility.** Many professions today have what some describe as "relatively rigid" probationary up-or-out paths for those trying to enter them. It can be difficult for workers to advance after having cut back, for example, to care for a baby.

- **Better planning.** Most organizations assume employees will sometimes get sick. But many don't acknowledge other demands on employees' time: children's doctor's appointments, helping care for elderly parents, and parental leave.

- **Cost.** Two part-time workers may require more work space, equipment, and supervisors' time than one full-time worker. Some companies may balk at this extra cost, though others have said that it's worth it.

- **Management.** Many employers say that if they allow some workers to work from home or at odd hours, they will have to let everyone do it. "For a people manager, the essence of his or her job is to direct work and lead other people," said Cheryl Hannon, vice president of human resources at iManage in Foster City, California. "That means you've got to be available to them."

- **Client demands.** The bottom line is that work still has to get done. You can lay out plans and can do everything, but that doesn't preclude a client calling and saying, "I've got an emergency." Then employees have to be flexible as well.

We need to redefine the "ideal worker" because, according to Jeffrey Pfeffer, professor of organizational behavior at the Stanford Graduate School of Business, employers use a worker's willingness to work long hours as a measure of loyalty. "They want people who are willing to devote themselves body and soul to the company." Experts say the flexibility dilemma will probably be solved differently by different people. Even when employers have the best of intentions, not all jobs lend themselves to flexible schedules.

BOX 1.2 🖝 **Balancing Work and Life**

SOURCE: "Flexibility: Balancing Work, Families Difficult," *The Atlanta Journal-Constitution*, Sunday, February 8, 2004. Section R, pp. 1–3. Reprinted with permission of Knight Ridder/Tribune (KRT).

[18] George Alexander, pp. 61–62.

There has been a drop in the cost of audioconferencing. This cost savings, paired with less travel following 9/11, has led to companies choosing to do teleconferencing at the drop of a hat in order to resolve problems. Videoconferencing still has a cost factor and a complexity for scheduling that causes it to be used less often than audioconferencing, but it is more cost effective and cheaper than getting the parties together via airlines.

Regardless of the changes the information revolution has brought to this techno-charged era of evolving communications tools and business practices, one universal truth about communication remains the same. People prefer to get information face-to-face, and they want their manager/supervisor to be the person who delivers it. In a recent OfficeTeam survey of executives of the 1000 largest U.S. companies, 44 percent preferred face-to-face meetings.[19]

For example:

LEXIS/NEXIS: "Most people here are very busy and working long hours, so they're looking for substance in communications from management. They don't want platitudes and they don't want messages that lack clear direction. What they do want—what they welcome, in fact—are face-to-face forums with managers and supervisors that offer the opportunity for question and answer sessions."

IBM LOTUS: "This is a company that communicates almost obsessively. We send each other around 40,000 e-mail messages a day. But as much as we rely on e-mail, I'd say face-to-face communication is still the most effective. I totally buy into the theory that communication should be put into the hands of supervisors; should be delivered by the people who are working on a daily basis with the teams and individuals directly affected."

NCR: "The whole point of cascade communication is to move top-level messages down to the workforce in such a way that they'll be believed, clearly understood and acted upon with commitment, efficiency and appropriateness. We've found that the best way to do that at NCR is to channel executive material down to the managers and team leaders who are working directly with the front-line people for whom the message is intended."[20]

The Importance of Communication

When a former president of Shell Oil Company said, "This business of communicating has become as important as finding more oil," he stated a belief held by many.[21]

Watson Wyatt studied 267 U.S. companies and found that those that communicate most effectively provided a 26 percent return to shareholders from 1998 to 2002. Those with the least-effective communication provided a return of 15 percent. Those with more effective communication also had less employee turnover.[22]

So, whatever type of organization you work in, now or in the future, your success and your organization's success hinges on the ability to communicate *effectively*.

Studies have found people spend 70 to 85 percent of their work time deliberately communicating through writing, reading, speaking, and listening. In a sur-

[19] Chaim Yudowsky, "E-mail Dependent," *Cybersense*, Vol. 18, Issue 23, Pagination 24, ISSN: 0896467X.

[20] Carol Kinsey Goman, "Face-to-Face Communication," retrieved from *http://www.iamawiz.com/communication/face2face.htm.*

[21] Robin D. Willits, "Company Performance and Interpersonal Relations," *Industrial Management Review*, Volume 7, pp. 91–107, July 1967.

[22] Elizabeth Frick, *The Text Doctor*, P.O. Box 9376, North St. Paul, MN 55109, *http: www.textdoctor.com.* Personal Communication.

vey of 480 companies and public organizations by the National Association of Colleges and Employers, the ability to communicate ranked first among personal qualities of college graduates sought by employers.[23]

Henry Mintzberg discovered that chief executives spend "almost every minute" of their days communicating.[24]

In a recent article entitled "The Future of Work" in *Business Week,* Peter Coy states that jobs will require subtle and frequent interaction with other people, often face to face.[25]

These statements support the claims that communication is the lifeblood of any organization.

In an organization, people communicate in many ways. Face-to-face communication takes place during one-on-one discussions, in informal groups, and during meetings. When individuals communicate face-to-face, they experience the most effective form of communication. Both nonverbal cues and verbal communication supply immediate feedback. Individuals also communicate orally on the telephone, by videoconference, during presentations, and in writing using desktop computers or terminals to compose letters, e-mails, memos, and reports. Recently, 24 executive MBA students at Kennesaw State University were asked to identify the three most important skills for their current job. Communication skills were listed 36 times, thus illustrating the continued importance of effective communication at work. Because communication influences organizations in major ways, the communication process must be examined in greater detail.

In today's world, you can communicate from virtually anywhere.

The Communication Process

To increase your effectiveness as a communicator, you must be aware of the various components of the communication process. Each part plays a vital role. Exhibit 1.1 depicts the basic communication process.

[23] "Work Week," *Wall Street Journal,* Volume CCXXII, Issue 126, p. A1, December 26, 1998.

[24] Henry Mintzberg, *The Nature of Managerial Work* (New York: Harper & Row, 1973), p. 38.

[25] Peter Coy, "The Future of Work. Flexible, Creative, and Good with People? You Should Do Fine in Tomorrow's Job Market," *Business Week,* pp. 50–52, March 22, 2004.

EXHIBIT 1.1

The communication process.

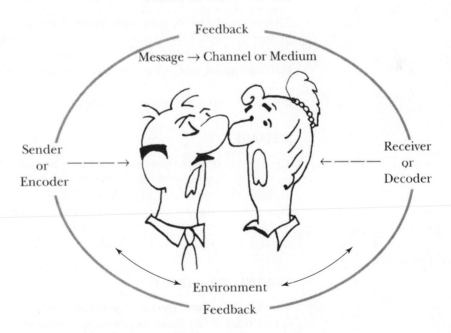

SENDER OR ENCODER

The sender initiates a communication and determines the intent of the message, how to send it, and what, if any, response is required. The sender bears the burden in this process, communicating not only the content of the message, but information about history and attitude toward the receiver as well.

RECEIVER OR DECODER

Receivers comprise the target audience of a message transmitted by the sender. The message the sender encodes may not be the message received, as receivers interpret messages based upon their frame of reference. This frame of reference includes their life experiences, cultural background, and the values and beliefs they hold. Because these filters may adversely affect the intent of the sender, some feedback must occur to prevent misunderstandings.

MESSAGE

The message contains ideas expressed to other individuals. The message must be transmitted in a form that receivers can understand. Messages generally take one or more of three forms: *to inform, to persuade,* or *to take action.* Informative messages share information or describe something to the receivers; persuasive messages attempt to change receivers' attitudes, beliefs, or perceptions; and action-oriented messages motivate receivers to do a task.

CHANNEL OR MEDIUM

The channel conveys the message to the receiver, either verbally and face-to-face (air provides the medium), or in another mediated fashion (by telephone, written memo, videotape, or electronic mail). The medium can distort the message positively or negatively, so the sender must choose the best medium for assuring effective communication. In considering which medium to choose, here are some options:

- Face-to-face meetings allow communication on all levels: verbal, vocal, and visual. This "human moment" is the best way to build trust and consensus in a group and help others work through resistance to new ideas. Face-to-face meetings continue to be the first choice among executives.[26] The downside: Time constraints and travel costs are often obstacles.

- Videoconferencing simulates live, face-to-face interaction, although people attending the "meeting" may be thousands of miles apart. The downside: Participants miss the energy provided by sharing space, and there is always the threat of technological glitches.

- Telephone calls enable you to pick up a lot of important information including the tone and energy in the other person's voice. The downside: Participants miss the information provided from the visual aspect of communication.

- Voice mail is great as long as it's used with respect. Keep voice messages clear, concise, and action-oriented. The downside: Your message may be misinterpreted.

- E-mail is rapidly becoming the most common form of business communication. E-mail is very effective for providing detail and as a record of information, allowing readers to reference it later. The downside: The sender has no control over when and if the recipient reads or forwards the message. E-mail does not provide the best medium for sensitive or negative messages.

The critical question for you to ask in making this choice is, "What is my objective?" If you want to motivate others to support a new idea, face-to-face communication is your best option. It enables you to communicate your ideas through your words, your voice, and your body language. It encourages spontaneous exchange and clarification. The next choice would be videoconferencing, followed by live telephone and then voice mail. If your objective is to transfer detailed information, then e-mail is the ideal choice. It provides a written record and can be saved and referred to later. For a quick "heads up" message, voice mail may be the most efficient and effective option. Sometimes, however, a combination of vehicles is the best choice.[27]

FEEDBACK

Feedback reports back to the sender that the receiver (the decoder) received and understood the message. When the receiver responds to the sender, the communication process starts over. Feedback makes communication a two-way process, allowing the sender to become a receiver and vice versa. Here is a list of tips for improving feedback:

Immediate feedback is best.

Supervisory feedback complements work-related behavior.

Positive feedback produces the best results, but negative feedback can be better than no feedback.

Verbal feedback accompanies and supports or verifies nonverbal signals.

Workers remember what they hear first and last in a message.

Feedback allows us to learn how people think and feel about things.

[26] "High Touch in the Midst of High Tech," *Making the Spoken Connection,* II, p. 1, Winter 1998.

[27] "How Do I Communicate with Thee? Let Me Count the Ways," *Making the Spoken Connection—Decker Newsletter,* VI, p. 2, Spring 1999.

Feedback comes in many different forms. Three of the most common types of feedback include interpretive feedback, descriptive feedback, and evaluative feedback. Interpretive feedback ascribes interpretation or motives to behavior. An example would be: "You are angry with me." Descriptive feedback shares observations and descriptions of the behavior to which you are reacting. For example, "You are frowning and your fists are clenched." Evaluative feedback means you are passing judgment on another person's behavior or imposing your own standards. An example would be: "You shouldn't speak so fast." Generally, it is best to avoid giving evaluative feedback and focus on a description of the feedback without presenting a judgment.

About 80 percent of our feedback should focus on positive behavior. To encourage this, one model entitled "BET" can be used to give positive feedback.

- *Behavior*—Exact, Specific, Detailed "When you come to class on time . . . ."
- *Effect*—Concrete Result of that Behavior " . . . the effect is that class can start on time."
- *Thank You*—"Thank you for being considerate of others."

About 20 percent of our feedback should be suggestions for improvement. To assist in this process, Patti A. Wood, a communication consultant, has created the ERASER model, a step-by-step process to script out your message and word it in such a way as to lessen conflict and defensiveness in the other person. Ideally, it will ERASE the offending behavior.

When using the ERASER model, it is important to only use the script to ask for a change in one offending behavior. If you wait and serve up a laundry list of complaints, the individual is certain to become defensive. Also, you must take an honest look and decide whether this behavior is the other person's problem or yours. Start by examining his or her behavior. Is there a pattern to it? Look at it as a journalist would a news story. Stand away, look objectively, and ask yourself, "What is the behavior?" "When does the behavior occur?" "Where does the behavior occur?" and, "How often does the behavior occur?" Then begin to follow the steps of the ERASER model.

STEP E **Be Exact.** Describe the offensive behavior on paper, then answer the "W" questions noted above regarding the behavior.

You should express your concerns in exact terms and not use generalizations such as, "Every time you. . . " or "You never. . . " or "You always. . . ." And, you should not guess at or express an opinion as to why they do what they do. For example, "If you weren't so busy with _____, you would. . . ." Some examples of constructive ways to word your concerns follow:

"Five times in the past three weeks, you have been at least 15 minutes late for work."

"I've noticed that the last four times you have taken a message for me, the full name of the caller and the phone number were not written down."

Sometimes you may ask for a response back from the person such as "Is that accurate?" Be careful about asking people why they did what they did. It is almost certain to create defensiveness. You need to decide how much dialogue you want. If it's difficult for you to give this kind of message, you may need to ask the other person if you can go straight through the ERASER script and then talk about it.

STEP R **Know the Result.** Ask yourself, "What is the concrete result of the offending behavior?"

After you've described the behavior, the person may still not understand why he or she should change the behavior. You may need to provide a result, (i.e., tell them what happens as a result of the behavior). For example:

> "When you are not at your desk at 9:00 A.M., Ann or Mike must take your calls and they cannot make their sales calls."

> "Because I did not have a last name or phone number, I could not return the call and we lost a $10,000 booking."

Remember when you were little and your mom asked you to do something? Didn't you almost always ask, "Why should I?" When we grow up, we still want to know.

STEP A Create Awareness.   When appropriate, state how you feel in response to the individual's behavior.

There are times when it's obvious from the steam escaping from your ears that a person's behavior is upsetting to you. At other times it is not so obvious, especially to the offending person. Clue that person in. Notice what emotion the behavior arouses in you and communicate it to him or her. Examples include:

> "When you are late, I feel anxious that the work won't be done."

> "I was frustrated when I did not have a way of returning the call."

Notice these statements are worded carefully. Absent are statements such as "You made me angry." By using an "I" statement, you avoid arguments. No one can argue with an "I" statement, as it's pretty difficult for someone to tell you how you do or don't feel about something. Your feelings are your feelings. There are times when this step is very significant.

For example, I once told two friends that I got upset when they teased me about my posture. They individually apologized and said they would stop. They didn't know it was bothering me. For them, knowing their behavior bothered me was sufficient motivation for them to stop the behavior.

Granted, there are people who only need to know what really aggravates you to be motivated to continue the behavior! Fortunately, those people are rare. You might just as well skip this step with them. Why throw gasoline on the fire? You may need to have other forms of conversation with an individual who fits this mold.

STEP S Switch the behavior.   Suggest and recommend the behavior you would like to see occurring in place of the current offensive behavior.

If you've ever tried to stop a habit, you know how difficult it can be. Something that can make it easier is to replace the old, negative habit with a new, positive habit. This technique makes a return to the old habit less likely. So, why not help the offending person out by providing a new, less offensive behavior to switch to? Suggest an alternative behavior that would work for you and for him or her!

> "I would like to see you sitting at your desk at 9:00."

> "Could you please put the full name and phone number down on the pink slip?"

STEP E Evidence.   Establish and agree on the behavior change.

If you're concerned that people may backslide into an old behavior, or it is critical that they do something a certain way, you may wish to add an evidence step to your script. Outline what will happen or stop happening as a result of the behavior modification. Support it with an expressed agreement as to what the change will look like. Perhaps you can give them a time frame when you will be observing the behavior, or a specific number of times you would like to see the behavior.

> "I would like to see you sitting at your desk at 9:00 A.M. for the next three weeks."

"Please try to completely fill out the pink slips for the next two days. See how people respond to your asking them to give their full name and telephone number."

Remember, you may want to open up some dialogue here and ask them what the evidence would look like.

STEP R **Reward good behavior.** Some people are motivated by rewards; some are persuaded through the prospect of punishment. Think about what motivates people. Would it be helpful to provide a specific reward if they erase the old behavior and switch to a new one? What punishment could you present as a possibility if they don't? Caution—make sure it's something you absolutely, positively will do. If you won't carry through on this step, it's powerless. People must know you mean business.

"If you are 10 minutes early for three weeks, you can leave at 4:00 P.M. the third Friday."

"If you take complete messages and it results in a booking this week, we'll go out to lunch on me."

After you've finished your script, look it over and make sure all the necessary steps are included. Edit out any generalizations or ambiguous terms like "good" or "bad." If it is difficult for you to give criticism, practice the ERASER script with a friend. Have your friend respond as the offending person might, and ask for suggestions. If you're still nervous, it may help to preamble your conversation by telling him or her you are practicing a new method of communicating and solving problems. Then, do the most important part—deliver the communication! No communication—no result.[28]

ENVIRONMENT

The environment in which the communication process occurs may influence the probability of success or failure. The environment includes room color, temperature, lighting, furniture, and timing, as well as organizational climate and superior–subordinate and peer relationships. Effective organizational communication depends on how successfully the communicator takes these environmental factors into account. Even when communicators consider all factors, miscommunication can still occur.

Causes of Miscommunication

Because people come from diverse family backgrounds or from various parts of the country or different countries, they sometimes have difficulty communicating with each other. This section addresses inferences, word-meaning confusion, differing perceptions, information overload and timing, nonverbal messages, noise, listening, personality differences, gender differences, and intercultural differences.

INFERENCES

When you make an inference, you draw a conclusion based on facts. The process works as follows: You observe something and, as a result, gain information. You then analyze the information and draw a conclusion about what you have ob-

---

[28] Patti Wood, "The E.R.A.S.E.R. Method," retrieved from *http://www.PattiWood.net.*

served. Your conclusion, or inference, may be correct or incorrect. Let's consider some examples.

1. The meeting participants were smiling.
2. The meeting participants were smiling; therefore, every participant was satisfied with the outcome.

The first statement contains a fact; you can easily verify it. You can see the participants smiling as they come out of the meeting. The second statement, an inference, involves drawing a conclusion based on more than what you observe.

As a communicator, you must be conscious of the inferences you make. Be careful to label your inferences as such. Your audience must be able to distinguish between what you know and what you think, assume, believe, or judge to be true.

WORD-MEANING CONFUSION

When a sender and receiver give the same word different meanings or give different words the same meaning, word-meaning confusion occurs. Words have both *denotative* and *connotative* meanings: Denotative meanings are the ones found in the dictionary, while connotative meanings come from the meanings people add to words. For example, if you look up the word "cube" in the dictionary, you probably would find a definition of a solid with six equal, square sides. However, in some business environments, "cube" refers to an open work space in the office. In another example, if you look up the word "ill" in the dictionary, you probably would find a definition meaning sick; but in the southern region of the United States, "ill" could refer to a misbehaving child.

The 500 most commonly used words in the English language have 14,070 dictionary meanings. That's an average of more than 28 meanings per word. The word "set," for example, has 194 different meanings. Words themselves don't contain the meaning—people supply the meanings depending on past experiences. Consider the following example. An administrative assistant needed to place an order for stationery. She told the inexperienced sales representative her boss wanted something different. The representative showed her several samples. Finally, she found one she felt would do the job. She concluded her transaction with the representative and said, "Let's keep it simple. Put the name in the center." When the first ream of stationery arrived, the secretary found the company's name placed exactly in the middle of each sheet, instead of centered at the top as she had intended.

To avoid word-meaning confusion, consider the person with whom you communicate, ask questions, and paraphrase important statements.

DIFFERING PERCEPTIONS

Look at the picture in Exhibit 1.2. What do you see? Do you see an old lady, a young girl, or both? People perceive things differently. The image is truly in the eye of the beholder.

Your perceptions provide your view of reality, but they depend on how you interpret what you see and hear. Perceptions are influenced by a variety of factors, including personal background, education, age, and experiences. Two categories of perception exist: sensory perception and normative perception.

Sensory Perception. This type of perception provides your view of physical reality. When a supervisor says, "Log the incoming mail on the mail register in the office," the clerk knows which mail register the supervisor means (unless several exist) because the clerk can refer to the register. Still, sensory perception can cause communication problems because employees do not always perceive what employers literally present to them. You must ask not only *whether* a person understands, but also *what* a person understands.

Normative Perception. Normative perception involves your interpretation of reality. When individuals express their opinions, normative perception occurs. As a communicator, you interpret the situation.

Miscommunication based on normative perception occurs when you attempt to communicate with others and you assume they interpret data the same way you do. You must be careful, because we all view the world differently. To avoid miscommunication based on differing perceptions, make your message specific, clarify important points, and seek feedback.

INFORMATION OVERLOAD AND TIMING

Information overload happens frequently in the business world today. Advances in technology have increased the amount of paper you must handle. Technology has made it easy to send a fax, make a copy, or print a report. The global nature of to-

EXHIBIT 1.2

Older woman or young woman?

day's businesses is enhanced by technology that allows individuals to communicate outside normal business hours. This requires the recipient to check for and respond to messages received since the close of the previous day's business. Unfortunately, you have only a limited capacity to handle and process these communications. Because so much information must be processed, some of it gets lost. You can prevent such information loss by becoming concerned more with the *quality* of your communication than with its *quantity*. The need for clear, concise communication is essential in the face of information overload. Keep your communications short and to the point.

Similarly, when communicating with employees, whether face-to-face or over the telephone, effective communicators always check their timing. If an individual rushes in, interrupts, and demands time, the receiver may feign listening or listen halfheartedly. This behavior could be costly to an organization if it results in miscommunication and wrong action.

NONVERBAL MESSAGES

Senders sometimes forget the importance of nonverbal messages, but, as a communicator, you should pay careful attention to the nonverbal communication of the sender and listen for the message "between the lines." According to Albert Mehrabian, 93 percent of the total impact of any given message occurs from nonverbal factors, as shown in Table 1.1.

TABLE 1.1 ☛ **Nonverbal communication.**

MESSAGE IMPACT	TYPE OF COMMUNICATION
7%	Words
38%	Tone and way the words are spoken
55%	Body position, gestures, and facial expressions

SOURCE: Albert Mehrabian, "Communication Without Words," *Psychology Today*, pp. 53–55, September 1968. Reprinted with permission from *Psychology Today* magazine. Copyright © 1968.

Actions Speak Louder Than Words

Listening Takes Practice!

Nonverbal and verbal communication usually happen simultaneously, as part of a total situation. When assessing nonverbal messages, be careful not to place too much importance on a single, isolated nonverbal behavior; instead, look for several nonverbal cues. If the verbal and nonverbal cues disagree, you can usually believe the nonverbal ones because they tend to be spontaneous and less controlled. Nonverbal actions provide a key to a person's true feelings and attitudes.

NOISE

Noise can interfere with every aspect of the communication process. Noise may be external or internal.

External Noise.   External noise comes from your surroundings. Some examples of external noise include a phone line crackling with static, a telephone ringing, a landscaping crew mowing the yard, or associates laughing in the cubicle next to yours.

Internal Noise.   This type of noise comes from within and could include such factors as dislike of your receiver, distraction by another problem, prejudice against a person, closed-mindedness on an issue—even lack of interest. If individuals neglect getting to know their subordinates, colleagues, and associates, they may not structure their communication properly for maximum effectiveness. Such neglect does not necessarily signal an uncaring attitude, but it contributes to noise in both the encoding and decoding process.

LISTENING

To be an effective communicator, you must learn to actively listen.

Most people use only about 25 to 30 percent of their listening potential. This inefficiency results in many problems. For example, immediately after listening to a 10-minute oral presentation, the average person understands and remembers no more than half of what was said. One to two days later, less than one-fourth of what was said is remembered.

According to Hamilton and Kleiner, when your eyes wander, your retention of what has been said is affected.[29]

If you focus too hard on little facts, you can miss the overall message. If you assume the speaker or subject to be uninteresting, you may miss out; and if you pretend to listen, you may get caught! You can use the following six guidelines by Hamilton and Kleiner to improve your listening skills.

1.   Look at the person speaking to show interest.

2.   Ask questions to help clarify what the speaker said.

---

[29] Cynthia Hamilton and Brian H. Kleiner, "Steps to Better Listening," *Personnel Journal,* pp. 20–21, February 1989.

3. Don't interrupt the speaker without reason.

4. Don't change the subject, because the speaker may have no thoughts on the new subject.

5. Control your emotions about the subject matter.

6. Be responsive and let the speaker know he or she has communicated effectively.

Another listening barrier occurs because we have different rates of listening and speaking. Speakers generally talk at about 125 to 150 words a minute, while receivers can listen to about 400 to 500 words per minute. This difference in ability allows for ample daydreaming, which in turn leads to miscommunication. Receivers must work at listening and try to avoid becoming distracted.

To be an effective manager, you must be an effective listener. Most managers have many activities putting them under stress and time pressure. Sometimes listening to employee problems gets pushed aside. Within an organization, your role as manager often requires you to speak rather than listen. Many managers have not learned the important role listening plays within the business. Another difficulty can arise when managers view listening as a lack of control.

According to Longenecker and Liverpool,[30] the following behaviors display poor listening skills: looking out the window or at your watch while someone talks; continuing to work during the conversation; appearing rushed during a conversation; walking away from a person who is speaking; continually playing with pens, papers, and other items; finishing another person's sentences; answering incoming phone calls; inserting humorous remarks in response to serious problems; and looking at a person other than the individual speaking. Longenecker and Liverpool state the first step to becoming a better listener involves identifying your shortcomings and then applying these suggestions:

- If you do not have time to interact properly with an employee, postpone the meeting.
- Show the employee you want to listen.
- Do not prejudge the employee.
- Empathize with the employee.
- Be patient with the employee.
- Resist arguments and criticisms.
- Ask questions and show understanding.

When you show your employees you will listen and interact with them, their morale increases. Employees typically generate more ideas and feel less discouraged when they know they can make a contribution to the organization. Effective listening makes not only a superior manager, but also a better organization. We can become better listeners. Tests at the University of Minnesota show individuals can improve listening skills from 25 to 42 percent with coaching.

PERSONALITY DIFFERENCES

No two people are exactly alike. We are a combination of genes and environment, and the experts are still debating which has more of an influence on our lives. The latest thinking is that both are equally important to defining who we are and how we interact with others. Sometimes when people do not respond or behave as you feel or think they should, you might take it personally by thinking they did not like

---

[30] Clinton O. Longenecker and Patrick R. Liverpool, "Making Yourself All Ears," *Management World*, pp. 22–23, September/October 1988.

you or respect your point of view. The truth is that they are just responding based upon their preferred communication style. Dalton has classified eight behavioral types that can be found in the workplace and provides some tips and suggestions for interacting with these behaviorial types.[31]

1. **Commanders.**   Commanders are individuals who thrive on control. They are often seen as demanding, domineering, and bossy. When they communicate, they are abrupt as they speak in crisp, direct, and hard-hitting tones without worrying about being tactful. They don't mean to come across as rude, but they are often mentally engaged in some issue and don't perceive that the softer side of human interaction is important. They are uncomfortable with talking about feelings. So, when you communicate with a commander remember to avoid any talk of feelings. Focus on the desired results or outcome without telling him or her what to do.

2. **Drifters.**   These individuals are easygoing, impulsive, disorganized, and have short attention spans. They often don't pay attention to the details, forget to follow up, or miss deadlines. They are often perceived as warm and friendly individuals who enjoy life and are creative. They are flexible and enjoy working on a variety of tasks. When communicating with drifters, tell them how the task will help you personally and keep the communication exchange short. Let them know that you value their "out of the box" thinking.

3. **Attackers.**   Attackers will appear angry, hostile, cynical, and grouchy. They can be perceived as highly critical, demeaning, and condescending while viewing themselves as superior to their peers. Attackers interpret feedback as a sign of disrespect; therefore, a more indirect approach may be more effective in communicating with these individuals. One strategy to employ when interacting with an attacker is to begin by asking questions such as: "What do you believe to be the most important characteristic of teamwork?" or "How do you plan to evidence these over the next review period?" You should let them know that you appreciate their resilience and their willingness to do the unpopular tasks that no one else wants to do.

4. **Pleasers.**   The pleasers are thoughtful, pleasant, and helpful individuals who are easy to get along with. They seek the approval of others, often agree to maintain harmony, and have difficulty telling others "no" to requests. In fact, they will not even complain when they are treated badly or taken advantage of by others. To them, their peers are their family, and therefore, they often remember special occasions such as birthdays and anniversaries. Giving feedback to a pleaser is done most effectively through the sandwich approach in which you provide constructive feedback in between two positive comments. You begin and end your conversation with praise.

5. **Performers.**   Performers may come across as flamboyant, loud, jovial, and entertaining. They make people laugh and seem to find humor in all things. They desire recognition and will often volunteer and then not be able to complete the task because they have taken on too much. They build relationships with others because of their sense of humor and wit. When giving feedback, an indirect approach seems to work best. You might begin by telling a story in which an undesirable behavior is assigned to someone you worked with in another organization. The performer will quickly perceive your intent and discern that your message was meant for him or her.

---

[31] Francie M. Dalton, "The Eight Classic Types of Workplace Behavior," *HR Magazine,* pp. 1–4, September 2000.

6. Avoiders.   These quiet and reserved individuals prefer to work alone. When working on a team, they will speak only in superficial terms, in clichés or to validate what someone else has already said. Fear often prevents them from taking initiative. They shun both recognition and increased responsibility because both would require increased interaction and visibility. They focus on doing their jobs and will do them right. When interacting with avoiders, it is important not to threaten them and to assure them that their jobs are not at risk. They prefer detailed instructions in writing and will meticulously follow your instructions.

7. Analyticals.   Analyticals are perceived to be cautious, precise, and diligent. They tend to overanalyze situations and tasks, and will often challenge new ideas. They are more comfortable with data than people. For them understanding emotions is difficult because they thrive on logic. They can see several steps ahead and anticipate potential risks. When giving feedback, you should have examples of the behavior you're criticizing since, without examples, the analytical will perceive your allegation as invalid. You must show respect for the details that analyticals bring forth and express appreciation for the fact that you can rely on them for any explanations needed.

8. Achievers.   Achievers are content, peaceful, and pleasant individuals that others enjoy being around. They are self-confident without appearing arrogant. They have an inner focus and self-discipline. They have no hidden agendas and hold themselves accountable for their results. They are interested in hearing the thoughts of others and actively seek feedback. Achievers focus on what is best for the organization. When interacting with these individuals, you should validate their objectivity and ability to interact with all behaviorial styles.

The previous descriptions are generalized, and you may see individuals fitting into more than one category. As a communicator, you will need to adjust your style and use your judgment when communicating with others as there are no absolutes. When it comes to people, there truly are no simple or easy answers.

GENDER DIFFERENCES

Women and men see the world differently, which often causes breakdowns in communication. Women tend to learn conversational rituals that focus on the rapport dimension of relationships whereas men tend to learn rituals that focus on the status dimension. In general, when women are young, they tend to play with a single best friend or in small groups, where much time is spent in conversations. Young women use language to negotiate how close they are; they learn to downplay ways in which one is better than the other and emphasize ways in which they are all the same. Thus young women learn to talk in ways that balance their own needs with those of others—to save face for one another in the broadest sense of the term.

In contrast, young men tend to play very differently. They usually play in larger groups in which more young men can be included, but not everyone is treated as an equal. Young men with high status in their group are expected to emphasize rather than downplay their status, and usually one or several young men will be seen as the leader or leaders. Young men generally don't accuse one another of being bossy, because the leader is expected to tell lower-status boys what to do. Young men learn to use language to negotiate their status in the group by displaying their abilities and knowledge, challenging others, and resisting challenges. Giving orders is one way of getting and keeping the high-status role. Another is taking center stage by telling stories or jokes.

For the most part, these childhood play groups are where men and women learn their conversational styles. In this sense, they grow up in different worlds. The result is that women and men tend to have different habitual ways of saying what they mean, and conversations between them can be like cross-cultural communication. You can't assume that the other person means what you would mean if you said the same thing in the same way. These patterns of behavior are learned while individuals are young and then they are carried into the workplace.[32]

What does this mean for you? If you understand the differences between the conversational styles, you can learn to be more adaptive and flexible when communicating with others. Communication is the lifeblood of an organization and understanding that people have different ways of communicating will make it possible for you to take advantage of the talents they bring to the workplace. As Stephen Covey, author of *The 7 Habits of Highly Effective People,* states, you should seek first to understand and then to be understood.

Typical gender differences that affect the way men and women communicate are as follows:

Women, in general:

- Tend to ask more questions.
- Are more tentative when answering questions.
- Attach tag questions to the ends of statements.
- Emphasize feelings and emotions rather than tasks.
- Wait to be noticed and promoted.
- Are better at decoding nonverbal cues.
- Are seen as more supportive of others.
- Work harder to maintain discussions.
- Gather more data through the way something is said as opposed to the content of the message.
- Tend to be indirect with their speech patterns (e.g. "might," "would").
- Are touched more.
- Receive less praise and attention.

Males, in general:

- Talk more often and longer, answer more questions, and interrupt more often.
- Stop conversations by responding with "um" or "uh-huh," and use more personal space.
- Talk primarily about "task-related" topics, and speak directly ("can" or "will").
- Use sports and military language and expect others to use this language.
- Focus on goals, plans, or accomplishments, and are assertive at getting accomplishments noticed.
- Are considered by others to be more credible and authoritative.
- Are more likely to be offered interviews based on their resumes.

INTERCULTURAL DIFFERENCES

Individuals from different cultures bring different perceptions, value systems, and languages to the workplace. This makes the task of communicating even more difficult. For example, holidays and vacation schedules vary from country to country. Employees in one country may be unaware that an office in another country is

---

[32] Deborah Tannen, "The Power of Talk: Who Gets Heard and Why,"*Harvard Business Review,* Product Number 9977, 2002.

closed on a given day or that vacations may be taken at different times of the year. The way a particular culture responds to deadlines and timing is often different. To be successful in business dealings, you must be aware of and sensitive to cultural differences, use appropriate language, correctly interpret nonverbal communication, and value individual and cultural differences.[33]

Being Aware and Sensitive.   You must be aware that an individual's background and experience can affect his or her interpretation and perception of a message. Check to see if you have any hidden biases and see if you have formed an opinion about how people of a certain sex, religion, or race appear, think, and act based simply on their belonging to a particular group. Prejudging people as a group may make it difficult to communicate with them as individuals. Try to avoid stereotyping and the use of sexist, racist, or ethnic remarks.

Using Appropriate Language.   Remember, the same word may mean different things to people from other countries. Some words may have different meanings in other languages. For example, the word "sensible" means *sensitive* in French and the word "he" means *she* in Hebrew. Use feedback to clarify your message. By asking questions, you can usually determine whether or not the individual understood your message as you intended. Use the guidelines presented in Table 1.2.

Interpreting Nonverbal Communication.   Almost 70 percent of our communication occurs nonverbally, and each culture interprets and displays body language differently. Certain nonverbal signs can be clues that the receiver does not understand and is trying to save face. For example, excessive nodding, inappropriate laughter,

TABLE 1.2 🖋 **Communicating with people from different cultures.**

WHEN SPEAKING:	WHEN ASSESSING HOW WELL YOU DID:
Construct your sentences carefully and precisely.	Watch for nonverbal signs.
Don't shout.	Notice a lack of interruptions.
Speak slowly and distinctly.	Notice employees' efforts to change the subject.
Avoid pidgin English.	Notice the complete absence of questions.
Emphasize key words.	Notice inappropriate laughter.
Allow pauses.	Invite questions in private and in writing.
Let the worker read your lips.	Allow enough time for questions.
Use visual aids.	Be alert to the "yes" that means "Yes, I hear your question" not "Yes, I understand."
Organize your thoughts.	
Use handouts.	Be alert to a positive response to a negative question.
Use nonverbal signals.	Be aware of the tone of your voice.
Use familiar words.	Be alert to a qualified "yes" in response to the question: "Do you understand?"
Repeat and recap frequently.	Have the listener repeat what you said.
Take care not to patronize.	
Check often for understanding.	
Don't cover too much information at one time.	
Be careful when translating.	
Choose interpreters carefully.	
Use bilingual group leaders.	

SOURCE: Adapted and reprinted with the permission of Lexington Books, an imprint of Simon & Schuster, from *Bridging Cultural Barriers for Corporate Success: How to Manage the Multicultural Workforce,* by Sondra Thiederman, Ph.D. Copyright © 1991 by Sondra Thiederman, Ph.D.

[33] Eleanor Davidson, "Communicating with a Diverse Workforce," *Supervisory Management,* pp. 1–2, December 1991.

tentative "yes" answers, silence, and lack of initiative all point to a breakdown in communication. In Japan, nodding to the speaker does not necessarily mean agreement, but denotes an acknowledgment of the understanding of the verbal communication. Personal space differs in various parts of the world. In the United States and other English-speaking cultures, an arm's length is considered an appropriate separation between two individuals engaged in conversation. Conversely, in some Latino cultures, closer contact is standard practice.

When an individual has difficulty speaking English, you should closely observe the nonverbal communication. The body language may tell you what the words don't.

Valuing Differences.   As an effective communicator, you must learn to value, appreciate, and accept individual differences. As the workforce becomes more culturally diverse, employees need to understand and welcome the opportunities presented through interaction and interdependence. The continually changing employee population presents opportunities for personal growth and improvements in global understanding.

The Diversity Game, a board game similar to Trivial Pursuit, allows you to test your knowledge of different cultures.[34] The game requires teams to answer multiple-choice questions about anything from societal trends to cultural differences. Your company will have a competitive advantage if its employees understand and appreciate cultural diversity.[35]

Review the tips in Box 1.3 for additional guidance on international communication.

Avoid using your own slang across borders and do not use another country's colloquialisms unless checked out by someone in that country.

Remember that things such as currencies, house values, power references, building specifications, and weights and measures need to be translated into their equivalents.

Minimize mistakes by always asking nationals of a country who are living there to check the translation, because of their experience and familiarity with the local scene.

When translating a message into another language, using words that create pictures to get inside the minds of audiences may be more effective than using a literal word-for-word transcription.

Always adjust the message for the variety of cultures and customs involved. Public holidays and national occasions in various countries, for example, seldom match.

What is simply written in one language may become convoluted in another. Again, ask a national to check the readability of the copy.

Gerry Mulholland offers the best tip of all: "When we communicate internationally, we should think more about getting, and paying for, the help and cooperation of our professional colleagues in other countries."

BOX 1.3 ☞ International Communication Tips

SOURCE: Norm Leaper, "Ahh . . . the Pitfalls of International Communication," *Communication World,* Volume 3, Issue 6, pp. 58–60, June/July, 1996.

[34] Melissa Wahl, "Diversity Training—The Fun Way," *Executive Female,* p. 20, March/April 1993.

[35] Robert Kreitner and Angelo Kinicki, *Organizational Behavior,* 3rd ed. (Chicago: Irwin, 1995), pp. 60–62.

Conclusion

Technology has revolutionized the way we communicate and conduct business. Yet, the most vital element of communication remains the continued development of an organization's most valuable resource—its people. In this new century, you will deliver your messages to increasingly splintered and diverse audiences using new and emerging technologies. As a communicator, you need to be careful not to let technology take over and become the end rather than the means. Communication is a process, not an event. Ongoing communication requires an infrastructure that is focused on building relationships with audiences. As a sender, you must strive to transmit messages your receiver can correctly understand. As a receiver, you must realize the important role listening plays. Your success as a communicator truly hinges on your ability to play both important roles. Face-to-face communication is the primary vehicle, with support from a variety of channels, including electronic and print.

By the year 2010, face-to-face interaction in business may be largely unnecessary.[36] The ability to see each other through our telephones and send documents from anywhere could easily render face-to-face meetings and business travel redundant. Although technology continues to change, people will determine the future. The written word, judgment, and common sense will never be replaced by hardware.

Exercises

EXERCISE 1 FINDING OUT ABOUT YOU

Directions: Answer the following on a separate piece of paper.

> Name the first television show you remember watching.
>
> Name your favorite actress or actor.
>
> List your career goals.
>
> Explain briefly why you enrolled in this class.
>
> Detail your hobby and why you enjoy it.

After writing this information, form a circle with five other people. Begin the exercise with a member of your circle sharing his or her name, an adjective describing him or her, and answers to the foregoing questions. For example, "Hello, I'm Hillary—as in Happy Hillary." Appoint a timekeeper and limit each introduction to one or two minutes. After all the members of your circle have made their introductions, appoint one person to introduce the group to the entire class. Your appointed leader will introduce your group members using the descriptive adjectives and first names. After all group leaders finish their introductions, the instructor will form new groups. You will then identify the members of your new group using the descriptive adjectives and first names.

This exercise allows you to learn the names of your classmates in a fun way while polishing your listening skills.

---

[36] Christopher Bunting, "International Communication Toward 2010," *Communication World,* Volume 11, Issue 1, pp. 44–45, January/February 1994.

EXERCISE 2 WHAT DOES THE STORY TELL?

Directions: Read the following story. Don't try to memorize it; you can look back at it at any time. Then read the numbered statements about the story and decide whether you consider each one true (*T*), false (*F*), or questionable (*?*). Circling the *T* means definitely true; *F* means definitely false; *?* means you cannot tell. If you feel doubtful about any part of the statement, circle the question mark.

   Answer the questions in turn, and do not go back to change any of your answers. Do not reread any of the statements after you have answered them.

Story: The owner of the Salem Manufacturing Company entered the office of one of her foremen where she found three employees playing cards. One of them was Carl Black, brother-in-law of foreman Henry Giles. Giles, incidentally, often worked late. Company rules did not specifically forbid gambling on the premises, but the president had expressed herself forcibly on the subject.

Statements:

T F ? 1. Briefly, the story concerns a company owner who found three men playing cards.

T F ? 2. The president walked into the office of one of her foremen.

T F ? 3. Company rules forbade playing cards on the premises after hours.

T F ? 4. While the card playing took place in Henry Giles' office, the story does not state whether Giles was present.

T F ? 5. Giles never worked late.

T F ? 6. Gambling on the premises of the Salem Manufacturing Co. was not punished.

T F ? 7. When the president walked in, Carl Black was not playing cards.

T F ? 8. Three employees were gambling in a foreman's office.

T F ? 9. The card players were surprised when the owner walked in, but the story does not clearly state whether or not they will be punished.

T F ? 10. Henry Giles happens to be Carl Black's brother-in-law.

T F ? 11. The president opposes gambling on company premises.

T F ? 12. Carl Black did not take part in the card game in Henry Giles' office.

T F ? 13. A corporation owner found three employees playing cards.

EXERCISE 3 HOW MANY SQUARES DO YOU SEE?

Directions: Count the squares in the following picture. After you have individually decided on the total number of squares, form a group with five other classmates and decide the total number of squares.

Individual Count _____

Team Count _____

Do these two totals differ? Why or why not?

EXERCISE 4 THINKING ABOUT GENDER

Directions: Reflect and record your answers for each of the questions that follow.

- ☛ How do men and women perceive nonverbal cues differently? Does eye contact, body language, stance, dress, and so forth, convey more than "co-worker" status or individual "style"?
- ☛ Do men compete more/less with women than with men? Do women compete more/less with men than with women? Do women assume caretaking roles with men, even if their work status is equal?

EXERCISE 5 FEEDBACK

Directions: Read the problem and then consider the different solutions presented. Please mark each solution choice as "accept" or "reject." Justify each response by describing what type of feedback was used and why it is that type of feedback.

Problem 1: Your team member mumbled when he gave his presentation. You'd like to give an oral comment and point this out. What is an appropriate response?

- a. You talked funny, kind of like Donald Duck. You didn't convey confidence very well.
- b. You sound bored, like you're uninterested.
- c. You should open your mouth and move your lips more!
- d. Because I couldn't hear you well, I missed some of the points you made.

Problem 2: Joe gave his speech with great enthusiasm. However, you couldn't follow his organization because his main points were not evident to you. What's an appropriate comment to make to him?

- a. I feel as though something is not quite right about your speech.
- b. You shouldn't be so disorganized. I had no idea as to what your main points were.
- c. Your speech was good. You had a great enthusiasm!
- d. Your enthusiasm about your topic was contagious. But I'm not sure what your main points were.

Problem 3: Mary didn't employ much pitch variety and your attention faded during her presentation. What would be an appropriate feedback to give Mary?

- a. You looked depressed and sounded bored while giving your speech.
- b. You shouldn't use a monotone.

c. Your speech will put the class to sleep!

d. To maintain your audience's attention, I suggest you vary your tone and pitch.

Problem 4: Sue reacts to Charles' oral evaluation during team time by saying, "If that's the way you feel about my presentation, forget it! I hope I'm never asked to work with you again." What's an appropriate response for Charles?

a. I don't think I phrased my comments correctly. I'm sorry. . . . May I start over?

b. I'm sorry. I didn't know you were so upset!

c. I'm sorry, but you're a hopeless case.

d. But . . . your presentation was ineffective. Let me tell you how to change it, okay?

EXERCISE 6 LISTENING AND SMALL GROUP COMMUNICATION SKILLS

Directions: Your group will be assigned one of the following questions to answer, after which you will report your findings to the class.

How do you know when someone is listening to you?

How does it make you feel to know that a person is listening to you?

What adjectives describe a person who listens to you?

How do you know when a person is ignoring you?

How does it make you feel to know that a person is ignoring you?

What adjectives describe a person who is ignoring you?

What characterizes a meeting at which you've experienced warm hospitality?

What characterizes a meeting at which you've not felt welcome?

What characterizes a meeting where you believe your participation is welcome?

What characterizes a meeting where you felt your participation was not welcome?

What characterizes a meeting about which you felt strong enthusiasm?

What characterizes a meeting at which you felt very little enthusiasm?

Exercise provided by Thomas Clark, Ph.D., Department of Management, Xavier University, Cincinnati, Ohio.

EXERCISE 7 HOW DO YOU RATE AS A COMMUNICATOR?

Directions: Answer the following questions to find out if you are an effective communicator.

1. Do you frequently have to explain your letters with follow-up correspondence or telephone calls?

2. Do you favor short, direct words over multisyllabic ones . . . or do you erroneously believe that your position dictates the use of gobbledygook?

3. Are you dissatisfied with your correspondence until it says precisely what you want it to say?

4. Do you state your ideas within a familiar context? (Compare and contrast the new with what your reader already knows so the reader can grasp it more quickly?)

5. Do you present your ideas and the facts to back them up in a logical sequence?

6. Do you recognize that listening is an active, not passive, communication skill?

7. Do you watch speakers for nonverbal clues to their meanings?

8. Before answering a speaker, are you usually certain that you have taken in his or her point of view?

9. When giving instructions, do you frequently assume more knowledge on the part of your employee than he or she actually possesses?

10. Do you break complicated procedures down to more easily understood substeps?

11. Do you speak clearly without slurring or mispronouncing words?

12. Do you talk too quickly or too slowly for comprehension?

SOURCE: Ted Pollock, "A Personal File of Stimulating Ideas and Problem Solvers," *Supervision,* Volume 53, Issue 7, pp. 24–26, July 1992.

CHAPTER 2

Writing for the Business World Electronically and on Paper

*O*ne study estimates that unclear writing costs United States business more than $1 billion annually.[1]

Randall S. Hansen, *Marketing News*

LEARNING OBJECTIVES

After reading this chapter, you should be able to:

- Discuss the role of business writing.

- Explain the importance of determining your purpose and analyzing your audience.

- Compare and contrast the jot list and the idea bubble for organizing your thoughts.

- Distinguish between the different approaches for establishing a logical order.

- List and explain the 7 Cs.

- Define technical jargon.

- Demonstrate how to make writing nonsexist.

- Identify three common grammatical mistakes.

- Change passive writing to active writing.

- Cut out wordy expressions and trite phrases when writing.

- Define "you attitude."

- List the tips for proofreading.

[1] Randall S. Hansen, "Clear, Concise Writing Is Especially Important for Marketers," *Marketing News*, Volume 27, Issue 19, p. 20, September 13, 1993.

The Importance of Business Writing

Where once medieval monks toiled for a lifetime over handwritten manuscripts, today's electronic technology allows us to zap our words around the globe in seconds, but it hasn't made us better writers. Arguably, the opposite has occurred. In deference to speed, our writing has often become increasingly terse and sloppy as we sacrifice quality to communicate faster.[2]

Professionals devote approximately 25 percent of their time to producing written documents. These letters, memos, e-mails, and reports carry your company's name and image to customers, competitors, and employees. If you are to make a valuable contribution to your organization, you want these documents to deliver a positive impression of you and your organization. In addition, managers often rank writing skills as "essential" or "important" to job advancement. To climb the corporate ladder, you need to learn how to write effectively.

In the past, millions of communications that would have been more effective as written documents went by the telephone to save time. However, with the arrival of the information highway, the pendulum has swung back to the written word. In fact, according to Russell Galen, the inability to write an effective document will doom those who wish to gain the attention of others.[3]

A recent issue of the *Wall Street Journal* reported that of the 443 companies surveyed, 80 percent cited poor writing as their biggest skill problem.[4] Why do some individuals find creating documents easy, while others stare at blank screens or pages for hours? Many individuals suffer because they do not understand the basic techniques of writing. Applying the techniques in this chapter should help make your writing easier and better suited for the business environment. The writing process consists of these steps: determining your purpose, analyzing your audience, organizing your thoughts, establishing a logical order, constructing your draft, and editing and polishing your writing using the 7 Cs. You may want to visit these websites to help with your writing: *www.owl.english.purdue.edu,www.write101. com* and *http://www.mapnp.org/library/commskls/cmm_writ.htm.*

> "One of the most surprising features of the information revolution is that the momentum has turned back to the written word," says Hoyt Hundson, vice president of IS at InterAccess, an Internet service provider in Chicago. "Someone who can come up with precise communication has a real advantage in today's environment."
>
> Source: Paula Jacobs, "Strong Written Skills Essential for Success, Even in IT," *InfoWorld,* Volume 20, Issue 27, p. 86, Jul 6, 1998.

Determining Your Purpose

Before you write, ask yourself these questions:

What goal do I want to accomplish?

How do I want to achieve it?

Once you have determined the specific goal of your communication, then you can decide what to say and how to say it. To communicate effectively, your writing must have a clear purpose. Besides maintaining goodwill and creating a favorable impression of your organization, you want to accomplish a particular goal.

WEB WRITING TIP: When writing for the Web, your purpose is often to communicate as quickly and efficiently as possible.

---

[2] Edwin Powell, "Ten Tips for Better Business Writing," *Office Solutions,* Volume 20, Issue 6, pp. 36–38, November/December 2003.

[3] Russell Galen, "How to Write Persuasive Query Letters," *Writer's Digest,* pp. 31–33, April 1992.

[4] "Business Writing: A Foolproof System for Getting Started," *Hospital Material Management Quarterly,* Volume 20, Issue 4, pp. 88–89, May 1999.

The following examples present general objectives of business writing with specific examples.

General Objectives	Examples of Specific Objectives
Seek ideas or facts	Request information on a proposed zoning change
Obtain action	Get a customer to buy your product
Send ideas or facts	Provide a copy of a report on traffic congestion
Direct action	Persuade a potential customer to call for a demonstration
Instruct	Give instructions on how to prepare a job announcement
Persuade	Switch to your product
Promote goodwill	Send congratulations on the birth of a new child

Before writing, answer the following questions:

Does the purpose seem realistic?

Have I chosen the right time to deliver this message?

Am I the right person to deliver the message?

Will the organization find the purpose acceptable?

Analyzing Your Audience

Your purpose becomes even clearer when you try to see the situation from your reader's point of view. What does your reader want or need to know? Answering this question can help you clarify your thinking. As our workplace becomes increasingly more global, you may need to consider your audience's cultural background. What are considered good manners in the United States can be considered shockingly bad manners in other cultures. For example, American directness is seen as rude when communicating with people from Japan. Germans often require more detail in their communications than do Americans. Answering the following questions will help you in developing your audience profile:

What do I know about the reader?

What do I know about the reader's experience and knowledge base?

Do I know the reader's cultural background?

What kind of relationship do I have with the reader?

Do I need to be more formal or can I be informal?

Should I be impersonal or personal?

What position does the reader take on this issue?

Do I need to be detailed and thorough or short and direct?

Will the reader's response be positive, negative, or indifferent?

In this profile, you must consider the reader's background, reading level, interests, feelings, and knowledge of the subject matter. Knowing your audience helps you know not only what to say, but also what not to say. You can make the common error of assuming your audience knows more or cares more than they do. When in doubt about differing cultural issues, consult with someone who has more experience in dealing with people from the relevant culture.

The importance of relating to your reader is emphasized in Box 2.1.

The biggest stumbling block, believe it or not, isn't a matter of technique or writing ability. It's a matter of mental attitude. The reason most people do not write better is because they are too self-centered. Self-centeredness is the curse of effective writing.

In writing of any kind, the important thing is to plant an idea in the reader's mind or to stimulate feelings or emotions. In all effective writing, one person and only one person is important—*the reader.* Yet, what happens when the average person sits down to write a letter or report? Somewhere in his or her conscious or unconscious mind an insidious thought raises its head: *What will the reader think of me?* The more that thought interferes with concentrating on the reader, the poorer the writing will be.

Why do so many executives, lawyers, scientists, and engineers sound like executives, lawyers, scientists, and engineers in everything they write? Because they would not want people to think of them in any other way. They are more concerned with the impression they are making than they are about the message.

And what happens when an executive comes along who isn't trying to impress anybody, who's just trying to get his or her ideas across in the simplest, clearest fashion to the reader? More often than not, this person impresses far more than those who are striving to be impressive.

Perhaps you work for the largest, most powerful organization in the world. If so, when you start to write, forget it! Your corporation consists of pleasant, friendly people. So get politely to the point, wrap it up, and wish your correspondent well. Write to him or her in the same language you would use if you were carrying on a conversation across the desk. "Stay loose!" as my old baseball coach used to say.

BOX 2.1 ◼ **The Secret of Good Communication**

SOURCE: John L. Beckley, "The Secret of Good Communication," *Bits and Pieces,* The Economics Press, Inc., Fairfield, NJ 07004–2565, 1–800–526–2554, pp. 10–12, August 22, 1991.

Organizing Your Thoughts

Once you decide your purpose and analyze your audience, put your thoughts on paper. Just like an individual who builds a house, you need a blueprint or organizational plan. Majors[5] presents two techniques for thinking on paper: the jot list and the idea bubble.

The **jot list** works for sequential thinkers: individuals who think easily in linear, logical order. Their ideas seem to emerge in the planning stage already organized. The **idea bubble** helps tangential thinkers. These individuals think in creative, tangential bursts of ideas. Their thoughts often come in random, loosely connected order. Notice in Exhibit 2.1 how the two forms of outlines reflect these two ways of thinking.

Establishing a Logical Order

Your points should follow in a logical order to produce the result you want. Because different documents generate different results, no advice can cover all or even most situations. But one rule seems to work: Organize your message for your

[5] Randall E. Majors, *Business Communication* (New York: Harper & Row, 1990).

EXHIBIT 2.1

Jot List (Sequential)

Idea Bubble (Tangential)

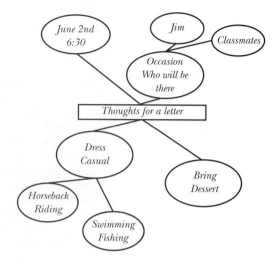

Thoughts for a letter

Purpose: invitation to a party

Occasion: end of school year

Time: 6:30 p.m., Saturday, June 2

Place: my house, address

What to wear: casual

Activities: swimming, horseback riding, and fishing

Who will be there: classmates and guests

What to bring: dessert

Special note: Jim will be there

SOURCE: From *Business Communication* by Randall E. Majors. Figure 4.1: Two Forms of Preliminary Outlines. Copyright © 1990 by Harper & Row Publishers, Inc. Reprinted by permission of HarperCollins Publishers, Inc.

reader's sake, not yours.[6] You can use any of the following approaches to establish a logical order.

1. **Priority:** Start with the most important item and finish with the least important. Priority places emphasis on the most important item, which most likely will be read and remembered.

2. **Reverse Priority:** Start with the least important item and finish with the most important. If you must persuade, you will find this order effective. Usually, the receiver remembers the last item read.

3. **Chronological:** Start with first occurrence and work to the most recent occurrence. When you explain a process or procedure, use this order.

4. **Reverse Chronological:** Start with the most recent occurrence and work backward in time to the first occurrence. This order emphasizes the current situation.

5. **Comparison:** Indicate similarities among the issues under consideration on a series of criteria.

6. **Contrast:** Show differences among the issues under consideration on a set of criteria.

7. **Spatial:** Discuss an element according to some physical order, for example, left to right or top to bottom. This emphasizes the relationship of one part to another.

When working on your first draft, don't worry about perfection.

[6] F. Stanford Wayne and David P. Dauwalder, *Communicating in Business: An Action-Oriented Approach* (Burr Ridge, IL: Irwin, 1994), pp. 40–41.

Constructing Your Draft

When working on your first draft, don't worry about perfection.

Once you have determined your order, put your ideas into paragraphs. Plan to write several drafts. Becoming an effective business writer does not happen in just one day! E. B. White in *The Elements of Style* (website address: *http://bartleby. com/141/strunk101.html*) stated, "Few writers are so expert that they can produce what they are after on the first try."[7]

Individuals who write effectively for the business world will tell you they have had lots of practice. After you feel more confident, you may encounter occasions when you can get it right the first time. But for most writers, getting it right takes time. To improve your writing requires rewriting, rewriting, and rewriting. In the drafting stage, do not worry about perfection. As Mario Puzo said, "It's all in the rewrite." Review the tips below as well as the tips to overcome writer's block that you will find in Box 2.2.

Here are tips to help you approach your writing:

- Break your material down into pieces.
- Write the easiest section first.
- Ask for a second opinion.
- Read more—people who enjoy reading become effective writers.

Here are some constructive tips to overcome writer's block.

- Start in the middle—where you usually have plenty to say. Write your introduction last, so you will know what to emphasize to readers up front.

- Write anything down—no matter how rough you think it is. Consider it to be a written brainstorming session. You can always polish it later.

- Circle what you don't like and keep going. It's easier to rewrite anything than it is to start from scratch.

- Think out loud. Explain your ideas to a coworker. You'll be surprised at how easily the words flow in conversation. Listen carefully for feedback that might give you a new perspective.

- If you can't find a friendly ear, talk into a tape recorder. Then play it back and borrow some of your own ideas.

- Write a letter to someone explaining the topic you're trying to write about. It could be to a friend, a relative, or someone you're simply comfortable with. Use this as your first draft.

- Decide on a reward to give yourself if you write a page. When you get to the end of the page, give yourself the reward.[8]

- Visit this website: *http://www.sft.net/people/LisaRC/* and *http://Ks.essortment.com/tipsovercoming.*

BOX 2.2 🖝 **Writer's Block**

---

[7] William Strunk, Jr. and E. B. White, *The Elements of Style,* 3rd ed. (New York: Macmillan, 1979), p. 72.

[8] *How to Write Right!* Published by Alexander Hamilton Institute, 800-879-2441.

Editing and Polishing

Once you have completed your draft, you must edit the document, applying the principles of effective business writing. A survey of professional writers found most of them spent about 50 percent of their time on planning and organizing, 20 percent on writing, and 30 percent on editing and revising. Effective business writing takes practice and hard work.

Occasionally, you can express your ideas correctly the first time, conveying your message as you would speak it. But editing and polishing your work enhances your credibility. Use the 7 Cs of completeness, clearness, concreteness, correctness, conciseness, courtesy, and character to make sure your message says exactly what you intended it to say.

COMPLETENESS

To write a complete document, you need *all* the facts surrounding the situation. Gather all the information before you start to write. You write completely when you include only necessary details. Ask yourself the following questions to check for completeness:

Who?	Why?	Where?
What?	How?	When?

CLEARNESS

Clear writing is a direct reflection on you and your organization. Whether writing an article for your website, a business letter to a key prospect, or an informational article for a trade publication, it is important to know what to say and how to say it to hold the attention of the right people.[9]

When you clearly understand your purpose for writing, you can write a clear letter. An individual once said, "If you can't write your idea on the back of my business card, you haven't got a clear idea!" Clear writing grows out of clear thinking. Clearness includes using familiar words, avoiding technical jargon, and making documents readable. See Box 2.3 for examples of how to make your writing clearer.

Clearness stems from clear thinking. When you write clearly, you use familiar words, avoid "technical talk," and make documents readable.

1. The prudent avis which matutinally deserts the comfort of its abode will ensure a vermiculate create.

   Translation: The early bird catches the worm.

2. It is recommended that you should avoid shedding drops of liquid secreted by lachrymal glands merely because some lacteal fluid has been allowed to dissipate itself upon the ground.

   Translation: Don't cry over spilled milk.

3. Surveillance should precede saltation.

   Translation: Look before you leap.

4. Opting on the part of mendicants must be interdicted.

   Translation: Beggers can't be chosers.

5. Scintillate, scintillate, asteroid minific.

   Translation: Twinkle, twinkle, little star.

BOX 2.3 🖙 **Writing Clearly**

---

[9] T. J. Tedsco, "Write It Right: Helpful Tips for Creating Clear Copy," *High Volume Printing,* Volume 21, Issue 1, p. 56, February 2003.

Familiar Words.   Familiar words help your reader understand your document. People like to read things they can comprehend quickly and easily, and using conversational words allows them to do so. When you write clearly, your writing leaves no doubts in your reader's mind. Test your sentences by asking yourself: "Would I say it this way in conversation?" If the answer is "no," rewrite your sentence. Readers find short, simple words easier to understand than longer, complicated words. Some examples follow.

Don't Say:	Say:
Prior to	Before
Subsequent to	After
Accomplish	Do
Reimburse	Pay
Determine	Find out
Transmit	Send
Advantageous	Helpful
Utilize	Use
Cognizant	Aware
Necessitate	Require

Technical Jargon.   Technical jargon, a verbal shortcut, allows specialists to talk together. For example, doctors, lawyers, accountants, and computer experts use special words specific to their occupations. When individuals use jargon, they make the assumption that specialists in their discipline share a similar level of knowledge. Therefore, jargon can save time and achieve understanding. The problem occurs when a specialist uses jargon to communicate with someone who does not share the same background knowledge. For example, to a banker the term *CD* means a certificate of deposit, but to a stereo buff or a computer user it means compact disc.[10]

WEB WRITING TIP: Web writers should avoid using Web jargon such as "Click here," "follow this link," and "this website." Generally, if the words or phrases are specific to Web use, they are words you should probably avoid.

The longer specialists work within their chosen fields, the more inclined they become to use jargon with everyone else, as illustrated in Box 2.4; when that happens, misunderstandings and frustrations inevitably follow.[11]

Writing clearly means avoiding jargon. Why didn't she just say, "All the flowers are limp"?

---

[10] Scott Ober, *Contemporary Business Communication* (Boston: Houghton Mifflin, 1992), pp. 64–65.

[11] John Morkes and Jakob Nielsen, "Concise, Scannable, and Objective: How to Write for the Web," 1997. Retrieved from *http://www.useit.com*.

It is in process.	It is so wrapped in red tape that the situation is almost hopeless.
We will look into it.	By the time the wheel makes a full turn, we assume you will have forgotten about it.
We will advise you in due course.	If we figure it out, we will let you know.
We are aware of it.	We had hoped that the fool who started it would have forgotten about it by this time.
It is under consideration.	Never heard of it.
It is under active consideration.	We are looking in the files for it.
We are making a survey.	We need more time to think of an answer.
Let us get together on this.	I am assuming you are as confused as I am.
Please note and initial.	Let us spread the responsibility for this.

BOX 2.4 ☛ **What Does That Familiar Phrase Really Mean?**

The following examples illustrate technical jargon.

interface	user-friendly	input/output
network	access	viable
per diem	disconnect	eom (end of message)

Here are some definitions of high-tech jargon.

Disconnect—Always used as a noun, as "We had a disconnect on the HTML issue."

Facemail—Technologically backward means of communication, clearly inferior to voice mail or e-mail, that involves actually walking to someone's office and speaking to him or her face-to-face.

Generating content—Writing, as in "We'll need to hire some content providers to generate content by Milestone 1."

Nonlinear—Becoming nonlinear means becoming irrationally angry. "When he found out the R.T.M. date was slipping, Ed went totally nonlinear."

Own—To take responsibility for an issue. Ownership is even more serious than drivership; you can drive an issue without owning it, but it's unlikely that you would own it without also driving it.[12]

Steer clear of another form of jargon—slang. Two decades after the song "Valley Girl" popularized the word "like," a fresh effort is afoot to stamp out this liguistic quirk. The generation that grew up saying "like" is hitting adulthood and the workforce. As a result, the word is now in the lexicon of investment bankers, doctors, and even teachers, where it can sound especially jarring. "I'm sure I say 'like' a lot," says Liza Sutherland, 28, a sixth-grade humanities teacher in New York. In a

---

[12] Steven Greenhouse, "Braindump on the Blue Badge: A Guide to Microspeak," *New York Times,* p. D1, August 13, 1998.

- Colleges are not schools, they are learning institutions.
- Problems do not have answers, they have viable solutions.
- People don't spend money, they reallocate resources.
- Newspersons do not use tipsters, they rely on informed sources.
- Speakers do not make speeches, they give oral presentations.
- Bosses do not set quotas, they just indicate objectives.
- Workers do not take orders, though they implement directives.
- Machinery cannot break down, but components can malfunction.
- A court does not command, it just issues an injunction.
- Programs do not have failures, they have qualified successes.
- And jargon doesn't hurt you—it just constantly distresses!

BOX 2.5 🖝 **Readability Gap**

University of Alberta study, which involved 30 Americans ranging in age from 14 to 69, a couple of the participants used the word more than 100 times in a half-hour conversation. The study found that while younger people used it more often, all age groups employed the Valley-girl-type "like."[13]

So when writing in business, avoid jargon unless you know the reader will understand it. For a review of the problems jargon causes, review Box 2.5.

Readability. Long words and sentences make your documents difficult to read. Hard-to-read documents add to the cost of doing business because they make management and administration more complicated. Denmark states:

> There is an apparent conviction of many executives and writers that stilted, archaic language reflects their own level of achievement. There is a widespread tendency for managers to adopt the "prevalent business style," a style making even a simple announcement of the office Christmas party read like a proclamation from the Great Industrial Potentate. This style wastes the reader's time by being much more difficult to understand than the subject matter warrants.[14]

You can write any idea, no matter how simple, so complicatedly that your reader will not begin to understand it. To write well, you do not draw attention to style.

During the late 1940s, individuals developed mathematical formulas to judge the degree of complexity of written material. Robert Gunning developed one of these formulas, known as the Fog Index.[15]

Gunning's Fog Index gauges the grade level of written material. By determining the grade level, the writer knows how educated the receiver must be to understand the document. It works best with text of at least 200 words. The Fog Index does not work on letterheads, inside addresses, or other similar items. You interpret the Fog Index by converting it to a grade level. For example, if the index comes out to 6, then the writer wrote at the sixth-grade level. Gunning states that anyone who writes at a level higher than 12 invites misunderstanding.

---

[13] Andrea Peterson, "The Campaign Against Like," *Personal Journal in The Wall Street Journal*, pp. D1, D4, February 3, 2004.

[14] Michelle J. Denmark, "The Language of Big Business: Is It Too Big for Its Britches?" *Secured Lender*, Volume 46, Issue 4, pp. 12–16, July–August 1990.

[15] Robert Gunning, *The Technique of Clear Writing* (New York: McGraw-Hill, 1952), p. 38.

The *Flesch Reading Ease* and *Flesch-Kincaid Grade Level* are two other commonly used indices to measure readability. The *Flesch Reading Ease* rates the text on a 100-point scale. If your document has a high score, the reader will find your document easy to understand. For most standard documents, you should aim for a score of approximately 60 to 70. The *Flesch-Kincaid Grade Level* rates text on a U.S. grade-school level similar to the Gunning Fog Index. For example, a score of 8 means that an eighth-grade student should be able to read and understand your document.

The following tips provide suggestions for clearer writing. Many of the ideas directly influence readability.

Tips for Clearer Writing

Keep sentences short. Aim for an average of 20 words or fewer. Newspaper editors often tell their writers to keep lead sentences shorter than 25 words! Make sure your sentences do not ramble, connected by a string of "ands," "buts," "whiles," or "becauses."

Choose the simple over the complex; this suggestion applies to sentences, words, and thoughts.

Familiar words work best.

Avoid unnecessary words. Read what you wrote. Then leave out words that do not mean anything.

Use action verbs; avoid the passive voice.

Write the way you talk, with a conversational tone.

Use concrete terms your reader can picture.

Write for your reader.

Vary your words, sentence length, and sentence construction to sustain interest.

Sentences and paragraphs must logically hang and flow together. Each sentence or paragraph must be logically connected to the previous one. If it is not logically connected, you force your reader to make the transition for you—an act of poor writing.[16]

Give the reader frequent breaks.

Use transitions to connect sentences and paragraphs so they flow together. They serve as stepping-stones to guide the reader along. Transitions can be one or two words, such as "therefore" or "however," or entire sentences.

Write to express ideas, not to impress the reader.

Position the most important information at the beginnings or ends of sentences and paragraphs.

Emphasize important words and ideas by setting them apart into short sentences.

Be careful of overusing capital letters. Research has shown readers find lowercase letters easier to read.

Review Box 2.6 for an example of one writer's challenge to create an acceptable company report.

WEB WRITING TIP: When writing for the Web, standard fonts such as Times and Arial are best for most Web browsers and are recommended for their readability. Italics can be very difficult to read on a computer screen and should be avoided.[17]

---

[16] Robert E. Cason, *Writing for the Business World* (Upper Saddle River, New Jersey: Prentice Hall, 1997), p. 232.

[17] Gate Matthew Stoner, "Effectively Communicating Via the Web," 2001. Retrieved from *http://www.u.arizona.edu/~gstoner/effectiveweb.html*.

One of our editors spent 20 years as head of corporate communications for a large company. One of his first jobs involved writing the company's annual report. After he completed the report, he discovered he needed the approval of a long-standing 15-member committee. He sent copies of the text to the committee members and began meeting with them. Engineers, accountants, and lawyers made up the committee.

The committee first pointed out that when referring to the company in the report, only the full name could be used or, in second reference, *The Company*. They emphasized the latter had to have a capital T and a capital C. Never, they said, could the personal pronoun *we* be used when referring to the company. When our editor friend asked why, they explained it had never been done before. They began referring to the report snidely as "the we-we report."

In subsequent meetings, the committee criticized the frequent use of short words and short sentences. Such writing was for kindergarten books, they said. Longer words and longer sentences were more dignified, they said. They were more businesslike.

At the end of the third day, the committee was only up to page 5 of the text. Six weeks later, when the final meeting was held, our friend did not recognize his text. The committee members did because it read the same as it did the year before.

The following year, our friend made an end run around the committee. He took the text of the annual report directly to the CEO. The CEO liked it. Encouraged, our friend showed the CEO examples of how the committee had massacred his text the year before and asked the committee to be confined to checking the report for accuracy and not for editorial content. The CEO went him one better. He abolished the committee.

Our friend prevailed because short words and short sentences are easier to understand than long ones. Personal references make reading more interesting.

If you want to be your own editor, you can follow a few simple rules to make your writing more readable. They apply to business letters, annual reports, memos, or speeches.

Readable prose contains sentences averaging about 17 words. In every hundred words, you should have only about 150 syllables. It also helps to have about six personal references per 100 words. Go easy on the adjectives and adverbs. Other rules, of course, exist, but these are basic. Try them. You do not have to count every word and syllable. Just keep these guidelines in mind as you write and you will be pleased to see how much your writing improves.

BOX 2.6 📌 **Creating an Acceptable Company Report**

SOURCE: *Bits and Pieces,* The Economics Press, Inc., Fairfield, NJ 07004–2565, 1–800–526–2554, December 10, 1992, pp. 4–5.

As countries compete globally, clear communication becomes even more vital. Since English is used for most international written messages, it becomes critical that your message be as clear as possible. International English is English for businesspeople that either deal with other cultures whose native language is not English or for whom English may be a second language; it is limited to the 3,000 to 4,000 most common English words. The following are guidelines when writing for an international audience.[18]

📌 Use only the most common meaning of words or words that have singular rather than multiple meanings. The word "high" has 20 meanings; the word "expensive" has one.

---

[18] Lillian H. Chaney and Jeanette S. Martin, *Intercultural Business Communication,* 2nd ed. (Upper Saddle River, NJ: Prentice Hall, 2000), p. 130–131.

- Select action-specific verbs and words with few or similar alternative meanings. Use *cook* breakfast rather than *make* breakfast; use *take* a taxi rather than *get* a taxi.

- Avoid redundancies (*interoffice memo*), sports terms (*ballpark figure*), and words that draw mental pictures (*red tape*).

- Avoid using words in other than their most common way, such as making verbs out of nouns (*impacting* the economy and *faxing* a message).

- Be aware of words with a unique meaning in some cultures; the word *check* outside the United States generally means a financial instrument and is often spelled *cheque*.

- Be aware of alternate spellings in countries that use the same language; for example, *theatre/theater, organisation/organization, colour/color,* and *judgement/judgment.*

- Avoid creating or using new words; avoid slang.

- Avoid two-word verbs such as to *pick up;* use *lift.*

- Conform carefully to rules of grammar; be particularly careful of misplaced modifiers, dangling participles, and incomplete sentences.

- Use more short, simple sentences than you would ordinarily use; avoid compound and compound-complex sentences.

- Adapt the tone to the reader; for example, use unconditional apologies if that is expected in the reader's culture.

- Try to capture the flavor of the language when writing to someone whose cultural background you know.

- Avoid acronyms (e.g., ASAP) and emoticons.

Some countries have started a push for *plain English.* For example, in Australia the courts have signaled they will penalize any organizations whose documents are difficult to understand. They want organizations to use plain English. The courts have stated that business documents should convey a simple, direct, and clear message.[19]

Official letters from the government of the United Kingdom now talk to the reader as "you," not as "persons who have recourse to. . . . " The move for a simpler writing style has occurred because of the international use of English as a means of communicating between countries and because English is the language of the Web. The simplified style provides a more efficient way of exchanging information.

Some real-life examples show the need and importance of clear writing.

An Australian banking client was excused from having to pay under a guarantee because none of the barristers in the case could explain the guarantee's first sentence to the judge. The sentence was over 1500 words long, and there was no punctuation.

A New Zealand insurer who won a case had to pay the loser's legal costs simply because the insurer's documents were so unintelligible.

An English court found that a solicitor's letters of advice were so unclear that the solicitor had to pay its client nearly $300,000 to compensate the client for losses suffered because the client misunderstood the advice.[20]

CONCRETENESS

You write concretely when you paint a clear and definite picture in the reader's mind. Skillful business writers avoid both vague words and words creating disagreeable mental pictures.

---

[19] Mike Whale, "Plain English Documents," *Chartered Accountants Journal of New Zealand,* Volume 74, Issue 2, pp. 50–52, March 1995.

[20] Christopher Balmford, "The Write Stuff," *Australian CPA,* Volume 73, Issue 8, pp. 44–45, September 2003.

Creating Clear Mental Pictures. Write using specific, concrete language and avoid generalities. Compare the following two examples.

Abstract: You will have a fine vacation here. You can rest. Things are quiet and conducive to peace.

Concrete: When you spend your vacation here, you will have all about you the magic of the woods. You will hear the rhythmic beating of the surf. You can swim under the watchful eyes of our trained lifeguards, or you can just drowse in the sun. At night, when you wander along the paths, you can see the stars through the pines. You will return to your room for a night of sound, uninterrupted sleep.

The writer in the second example creates a vivid image in the mind of the reader and makes the vacation getaway seem much more desirable.

Readers can be confused by unclear references in your writing. What does *that* or *they* mean? What *thing, object,* or *matter* do you mean? Be as precise as you can and use pronouns or general nouns only when constant repetition of the main word becomes awkward. Even then, try to use more precise substitute words such as *product, campaign,* or *process.* Vague, general words may have different meanings to you and your receiver. What does it mean when you say you read a "good" book? What was *good* about the book? We don't know until we get specific. Some vague words to avoid include:

a few	low	nice	slow	a small number	very
many	quick	small	high	more	
several	soon	large	most	short	

The word "very" causes problems for many writers. Review Box 2.7 for ideas to boost your vocabulary.

Avoiding Disagreeable Mental Pictures. Because you want to get a result, you need a positive attitude. You strive to create desire for, not opposition to, your writing. Therefore, don't say: "*You failed to pay,*" "*You are wrong,*" or "*You cannot return.*" Avoid using words that antagonize your reader. Some other words you should use with caution include *careless, for instance, weak, foolish, but,* or *misguided.* The word "*but*" is an "eraser" word that undoes all the good work in the previous thought, as in: "You're a terrific manager, but we have a few suggestions."

Using sexist language may create negative mental images. You can offend both men and women when using such language. Whether sexist language offends you or not, someone in your audience could be offended. Well-educated women *and* men prefer nonsexist language.

Huseman et al.[21] provide ways to remove sexist language from your writing.

Ways to Avoid Sexist Writing

1. Use the word "*person.*"

   Sexist: When you schedule a meeting with a businessman, be aware of the importance of his time.

   Nonsexist: When you schedule a meeting with a businessperson, be aware of the importance of time.

2. Use plurals.

   Sexist: An employee will be promoted based on his ability and seniority.

   Nonsexist: Employees will be promoted based on their ability and seniority.

> Avoid using language that could be interpreted as a slight against a particular gender, ethnic group, or other segment of the population.

---

[21] Richard C. Huseman, James M. Lahiff, and John M. Penrose, Jr., *Business Communication* (Chicago: Dryden Press, 1991), p. 65.

This quiz will help you escape the very trap you fall into when you combine "very" with another word. You usually can say it just as easily with one word. See if you can boost your vocabulary by thinking of a one-word substitute for each of the following:

1. very stupid
2. very far
3. very near
4. very large
5. very hot
6. very pretty
7. very weak
8. very small
9. very strong
10. very quiet

Note: If you come up with a one-word substitute that's not listed below and you believe the word qualifies, give yourself a point.

Scoring:
9–10 very, very good
5–8 very good
3–4 very bad
0–2 very, very bad

Answers:
1. dense, moronic, idiotic
2. distant, remote
3. adjacent, close
4. enormous, immense, huge, spacious, vast
5. torrid, scorching, fiery
6. gorgeous, beautiful
7. exhausted, frail, flimsy, inadequate
8. tiny, puny
9. powerful, potent, forceful
10. still, silent

BOX 2.7 🖙 **Can You Come Up with a Better Word?**

3. Use the word "you" or "your."

   Sexist: An employee should punch his time card promptly each morning.

   Nonsexist: Punch your time card promptly each morning.

CORRECTNESS

Henry Ford has been credited with saying, "Paying attention to the simple little things that most men disregard as unimportant makes a few men rich." More individuals should listen to Henry Ford! Too many people feel the little things do not count, and they do! The fourth **C** involves the format of the document (letter and memo formats are discussed in Chapters 6 and 7), spelling, grammatical usage, punctuation, and active writing.

Correcting errors costs money. If you send documents containing errors, you may become embarrassed. Your reader may laugh at you instead of with you. The content and mechanics must both be correct. Spelling and grammatical mistakes have cost companies more than mistakes in engineering. Develop the dictionary habit. Visit this website to explore the different dictionaries available for your use: *http://www.dictionary.com/.*

You may want to visit an online writing lab, otherwise known as OWL, if you have questions about effective and appropriate writing. Many universities have OWLs you can access. For example, try these Web addresses:

http://www.webgrammar.com/commonmistakes.html
http://www.cs.utexas.edu/users/ethics/Other/writing_skills1.html
http://owl.english.purdue.edu/

Carelessness reaps heavy damage as thousands of letters never reach their intended destination. The following sections present common grammatical mistakes and guidelines for active writing.

Grammatical Mistakes. Written communication can often be understood in spite of grammatical errors. However, correct grammar improves your credibility as a writer. Even if you have great ideas, if you use incorrect grammar many readers will discount your ideas because the grammar detracts from them. Advertisers know the package often sells the product. You will find that many businesspeople feel the same way about documents written using incorrect grammar.

To help you overcome costly errors, develop the dictionary habit and use the spelling and grammar checker on your word processing package. Taking such actions will pay you dividends in the end. It's important to remember that word processing tools and computer programs can identify potential grammatical mistakes, but the writer must know how, when, and what rules of grammar to apply to the situation. Electronic scans of word processing documents are aids to a writer and must not be construed as authorities on usage.

It's important to understand which parts of a grammar checker's advice to ignore and which parts to accept. Grammar checkers do good things, bad things, and stupid things.

Grammar checkers usually tell you not to use contractions. That's because there's no serious writing expertise underlying the rules grammar checkers use. When a grammar checker cautions you on something, let yourself be the judge.

Here are four positive things grammar checkers do:

- Tell you your average sentence length (words per sentence).
- Tell you how hard your words are to read (characters per word).
- Tell you the percentage of your sentences that use passive voice.
- Give you a number that rates the overall readability of your writing (readability index).

The numbers almost always confirm our own subjective view of whether a piece of writing is hard or easy to read.[22]

For more help and guidance on grammatical mistakes, visit these websites:
http://www.ccc.commnet.edu/grammar
http://www.chompchomp.com
http://newark.rutgers.edu/~jlynch/Writing/a.html

[22] Edward P. Bailey, "Writing and Speaking at Work," *A Practical Guide for Business Communication.* Prentice Hall, Upper Saddle River, New Jersey 07458, page 23.

Three grammatical mistakes business writers consistently make involve dangling modifiers, parallel structure, and subject/verb agreement. Examples of each follow.

Dangling Modifiers. Modifying words or phrases should be placed as close as possible to the words or phrases they modify. Adjective participial phrases often cause problems when they open the sentence. Opening participial phrases can be taken to modify the noun, but when the noun does not appear in the sentence, then the phrase does not make sense.

Incorrect: Loudly protesting, the puppy was taken from the man.
(The first word has been left out so the introductory phrase does not complement what follows.)

Correct: The man protested loudly when his puppy was taken from him.
(Now the reader knows the man was protesting.)

A second problem occurs when a phrase or word in a sentence is too far from the idea it modifies.

Incorrect: A dependable vehicle, the family decided to buy the sports utility car.
("A dependable vehicle" should be placed closer to "the sports utility car.")

Correct: The family decided to buy a sports utility car, a dependable vehicle.
(Now the modifying phrase is placed next to the idea it modifies.)

Parallel Structure. To tie together components of a sentence, you can use coordinate structures having the same grammatical form. Parallel structure requires the writer to compose lists, series of words, phrases, or clauses in the same grammatical form. Use all verbs, participles, or infinitives, not one of each. For example:

I like *eating* more than *cooking*.
(A gerund is paired with a gerund.)

I like to eat more than to cook.
(An infinitive is paired with an infinitive.)

The main results of the university's curriculum reform were: class size decreased, more multicultural courses were offered, and students were allowed to choose a pass or fail option.
(All three items in the series are noun clauses.)

When the structures are parallel in form and length, readers comprehend the written word more swiftly.

Correlative ideas are formed with correlative conjunctions such as either-or, neither-nor, not only-but also, both-and, whether-or, and as-as. The structure after the second part of the pair should be exactly parallel in form to the structure after the first part. Some examples follow.

*He made up his mind either to study or to drop out of school. (*To study *follows* either; *therefore, an infinitive,* to drop out, *should follow* or.)

He loves both swimming competitively and playing ball. (An ing *word (gerund) follows* both; *therefore, an* ing *word (gerund) should also follow* and.)

For a proper idiom, place the correlative conjunction immediately before the parallel terms:

Incorrect: Bob has *both* experienced the sweet taste of success and the bitterness of defeat.
(A correlative conjunction is misplaced.)

Correct: Bob has experienced *both* the sweet taste of success and the bitterness of defeat.
*(*Both, *the correlative conjunction, is placed before* sweet taste of success *and* the bitterness of defeat.)*

Incorrect: Linda completes her tasks with patience, hard work, and takes pride in her work.

(The series consists of a noun, a noun phrase, and a participle phrase all acting as objects of the preposition with.*)*

Correct: Linda completes her tasks *with* patience, hard work, and pride.

(All three items in the series are nouns serving as objects of the preposition with.*)*

Incorrect: To do well in school, you should have excellent team skills, demonstrating outstanding oral and written communication skills and be hardworking.

(The series mixes compound verbs with a verbal form.)

Correct: To do well in school, you should demonstrate excellent team skills, show skill in oral and written communication, and be hardworking.

(All three items are compound verb forms.)

To increase understanding, strive to make the words, phrases, and clauses approximately the same length.

Subject/Verb Agreement. A singular subject takes a singular verb while a plural subject takes a plural verb. The subject and the verb must also agree as to person: A first-person subject takes a first-person verb.

Incorrect: AirTran Airlines serve only customers in the southeast.

Correct: AirTran Airlines *serves* only customers in the southeast.

Rule: Even though company names or titles may appear to be plural, they are singular and require singular verbs.

Incorrect: Becky and her boss works at Perimeter Mall.

Correct: Becky and her boss *work* at Perimeter Mall.

Rule: When one subject joins another by the word "and," the subject is plural and needs a plural verb.

Incorrect: Neither the manager nor the employee know the answer to the question.

Correct: Neither the manager nor the employee *knows* the answer to the question.

Rule: When two subjects are joined by "or" or "nor," the verb should agree with the closer subject.

Incorrect: Everybody in the office have a two-week vacation.

Correct: Everybody in the office *has* a two-week vacation.

Rule: Some indefinite pronouns are always singular, others are plural. Refer to the following list for guidance.

Always Singular	Always Plural
anyone, anybody, anything	both
each, either, every, everyone	few
everybody, everything	many
neither, nobody, nothing, someone	several
somebody, something	

Active Writing. In active writing, the doer of the action is the subject of the sentence. Usually you put the *subject* or *doer* up front, and then the verb tells what happens. Note the following example: The manager (the subject or doer) approved (the action) the request. This sentence clearly states who does what.

Generally writers want to write actively because this approach decreases wordiness and brightens the action. Writing actively involves using action verbs. If you use action verbs, your writing becomes more powerful and exciting. To write actively, eliminate the weakest verb form, *is,* from your writing. You can do this by using your word processing package's search-and-replace feature. Every time your word processing feature finds one of these forms, ask yourself where the action really resides. Try to think of an action verb to replace the weaker verb form. You can also use your electronic thesaurus to help you think of other action verbs. Sometimes when you write, you oversue the same verb. Looking at the thesaurus allows you to use different words. An example of passive writing versus active writing follows:

Passive: The horses were watered by Hillary.

Active: Hillary watered the horses.

Passive: These guidelines have been changed by the director.

Active: The director changed these guidelines.

Passive writing can be your enemy because it requires more words. When you write passively, your writing becomes vague, denies responsibility, and creates an artificial distance between you and your reader. It makes your writing sound clumsy and increases wordiness. According to many software editorial aids, if your letters, memos, or reports contain more than 25 percent passive writing, your writing style appears dry, wordy, and uninteresting. Your goal should be to have no more than 10 percent passive writing in any document. Review Box 2.8 for more insight into passive writing.

Use simple action verbs to cut down on inefficient words and to add more impact to your documents. The following examples illustrate how you can eliminate wordiness while making your document more active.

Take into consideration	Consider
Make an announcement	Announce
Send an invitation	Invite
Bring to a conclusion	Conclude
Make your selection	Select

Incorporate the following tips to change your passive writing to active writing:

1. Turn the sentence around.

   Passive: After the total amount has been determined, the discount percentage will be calculated.

   Active: We will calculate the discount percentage after determining the total amount.

2. Change the verb.

   Passive: A list of clients can be found in Attachment A.

   Active: Attachment A lists our clients.

3. Rethink the sentence.

   Passive: A meeting should be set up so that the problem can be dealt with.

   Active: We should get together to solve this problem.

Visit these websites for additional help with active writing:

http://fisher.osu.edu/~ryan3/ugd/activewriting.htm
http://owl.english.purdue.edu/handouts/grammar/g_actpass.html

Sometimes you want to use passive voice to soften the message. You should use passive voice when you need to:

1. Deemphasize the doer of the action.

   Active: You must analyze all data before you make a decision.

   Passive: All data must be analyzed before a decision is made.

Nothing, really, is wrong with passive writing. However, it gets entangled in some business writing and strangles everything in sight. It cuts off the action, adds extra words, and hides the "Who did what?", sort of like those weeds that choke your garden, slow down growth, and conceal blooming flowers.Active voice, however, untangles sentences and clears out the underbrush. It helps your reader know exactly "Who's doing it?", such as "Stocks rose 16 points today" or "When the board meets on October 10, architects will present their final design."

In English, we usually put "the subject" or "doer" up front for all to see (like petunias along the patio) and then write "the predicate" to tell what happens: "The supervisor did not approve the increase" or "Tomorrow, our lawyers will study the environmental plan and check the requirements." These subjects act! They DO it—and clearly and quickly. There's no beating around the proverbial bush.

Check your last memo or report and see who is active in your sentences. Have you written, "The talk will be given by the president when the quarterly meeting of the board is held in September?" If so, the "talk" gets the emphasis or the action, the verb is passive, and the "president" or doer dangles at the end. Why not write, "The president will speak at the September board meeting"? It gives the same information with half the words, and is called pruning the passive.

Most experts list three disadvantages of passive voice.

1. It uses more words and takes longer to understand.
2. If the doer is not stated, readers aren't clear about who's responsible.
3. Too many passive verbs make writing ponderous and often boring.

   Passive voice does, however, have its place.

1. Use it to emphasize the "who" or the "what" when the receiver is more important than the doer is: "Your request was carefully studied by the district manager." "Additional discounts will be yours this weekend."
2. Choose passive voice when tact suggests not mentioning the doer. "The item numbers were not included in your recent order." Don't point your finger! Or "Coffee cups were found again in the corporate lounge." Who wants the blame for that one?
3. When the "Who did it" is not known or not important, use a passive verb. "These forms were printed 10 years ago." "Changing the schedule was approved earlier this year." The doer is really no longer important.

Because passive voice can be awkward and somewhat lifeless, competent writers seek a more natural, forceful, yet economical style. They "offer, fulfill, propose, continue, announce, include, decide, send, and build." Few verbs such as "is being announced, are considered, was sent, were adjusted, will have been decided" flourish in their writing. They pull such weeds and prune the dead branches. Accenting the action, they make things happen—just like the best of gardeners.

BOX 2.8 🖝 **What's Wrong with Passive Writing?**

SOURCE: Phyllis M. Taufen, "What's Wrong with Passive Voice," *Business Communication Forum*, Fall 1992.

2. Deemphasize the receiver of the action.

   Active: The department store accepted the application.

   Passive: The application was accepted.

3. Avoid personal, blunt accusations.

   Active: You didn't include your check for payment.

   Passive: The check for payment was not included.

4. Present bad news.

   Active: You will not receive any bonus money.

   Passive: The bonus money will not be distributed.

5. Make a smooth transition from one sentence to the next.

   Active: To simplify maintenance requirements, we started using a different kind of machine.

   Passive: A different kind of machine was installed to simplify maintenance requirements.

WEB WRITING TIP: Conventional business writing guidelines also apply to web writing such as carefully organizing the data so that important information is easy to find, using words and categories that make sense to the audience, using topic sentences, limiting each paragraph to one main idea, and providing the right amount of information.

CONCISENESS

When you write concisely, you say what you want to say in the fewest possible words. You write concisely when you avoid filler words such as:

Replying to your inquiry, we would say

We have your inquiry, and in reply will say

Referring to your inquiry

In reply to your letter

These openings just take up space and add nothing of value to your document. Do not rehash an earlier letter from your reader, who already knows what was said. Plunge right into the subject of the letter, unless you must deliver unpleasant news.

Writers can often omit the word *that* without distorting the meaning of a sentence. In fact, to improve the conciseness of a sentence, some writing authorities recommend the word *that* be deleted in most situations in which it functions as a subordinating conjunction.

Deciding whether to delete *that* from a sentence is largely a writer's option. However, when writers physically delete *that,* it is still part of the sentence, much like the understood *you* subject in sentences such as, "Do not overload the elevator!" That is, in most instances, a dependent clause still exists, even if *that* is not physically in the sentence.

In general, writers can eliminate the wordy *that* in the following situations:

1. When *that* is used to introduce a subordinate clause functioning as the object of a verb.

   With: Henry says *that* he is poor.

   Without: Henry says he is poor.

2. When *that* is used to introduce a subordinate clause stating a fact, wish, reason, or cause.

   With: Jack hopes *that* he will win the race.

   Without: Jack hopes he will win the race.

3. When *that* is used to introduce a subordinate clause modifying an adverb or adverbial expression.

   With: The homeless will sleep anywhere *that* they can.

   Without: The homeless will sleep anywhere they can.

4. When *that* is used to introduce a subordinate clause that is joined to an adjective or noun subjective complement.

   With: Bonnie is positive that she is right.

   Without: Bonnie is positive she is right.

5. When the subject of a relative clause is different from the referent of the phrase preceding the clause.

   With: Carl has the novel that I was reading.

   Without: Carl has the novel I was reading.

6. When a sentence contains more than one *that.*

   With: I told Marshall that the guidelines that he prepared meet with my approval.

   Improved: I told Marshall that the guidelines he prepared meet with my approval.

   Without: I told Marshall the guidelines he prepared meet with my approval.

As a person's writing proficiency increases, he or she can make intelligent decisions about when to include *that* in a sentence. Two reasonable tests to help a writer decide whether to include or to delete *that* are:

1. Is *that* used as a subordinating conjunction to introduce a dependent clause?

2. Does the sentence sound right when *that* is deleted?[23]

A concise writer avoids wordy expressions, trite phrases, and useless repetition. The following sections present these ideas.

Wordy Expressions. Wordy expressions create dead weight in a sentence. Many wordy sentences begin with *there are, it is,* or *there is.* You can say the same thing without these slow-starting phrases; they stand for nothing! When you use them to begin a sentence, they often mask the true subject of the sentence and they add extra words. Eliminate them whenever possible. Use the global search and replace tool on your word processor to identify and eliminate these weak beginnings.

Don't Say:	Say:
There are three fine restaurants on Broad Street.	Broad Street has three fine restaurants.
It is important that all employees read the handbook.	All employees should read the handbook.

Use the following examples to make your writing more concise.

Why Say This	When You Can Say This?
at all times	always
at the present time	now
costs the sum of	costs
due to the fact that	because
enclosed herewith for your	enclosed
first of all	first
in the amount of	for
in the month of June	in June
we would ask that you	please
in the neighborhood of	approximately

[23] Ted D. Stoddard, R. DerMont Bell, and Max L. Water, "THAT—Often an Extraneous Word," *Business Communication Forum,* Spring 1993.

PLEASE NOTICE:

You may have noticed the increased number of notices for you to notice. Some of our notices have not been noticed. This is very noticeable. It has been noticed that the responses to the notices have been noticeably unnoticed.

This notice is to remind you to notice the notices and to respond to the notices because we do not want our notices to go unnoticed.

THE MANAGER

BOX 2.9 ☛ **How Much Notice Do You Need?**

Useless Repetition. Writers sometimes repeat ideas for emphasis and to make an impression in the reader's mind. For example, persuasive advertisements repeat information to help customers remember their products and services. Yet sometimes writers use useless repetition of the same idea, which just creates a longer document. See Box 2.9 for an example of how to overuse a word.

Here are some examples of useless repetition.

Attempting to Qualify a Term That Can't Be Qualified:

absolutely free	finish up
absolutely complete	reduce down
true facts	past experience
human volunteer	continue on
exactly identical	cancel out

Needlessly Qualifying a Term:

second in sequence	during the year of 1987
audible to the ear	first began
for a period of one month	stockbroker by occupation
rectangular in shape	frown on her face
for the month of July	for the purpose

Redundant Couplets:

thought and consideration	immediately and at once
permanent and lasting	full and complete
opinion and belief	if and when
anxious and eager	hope and trust

Trite Phrases. A cemetery monument manufacturer wrote to a customer to thank him for an order. His letter closed, "We hope to serve you again in the future—and often." Many times writers use trite phrases carelessly, without really thinking. They come across sounding pretty silly.

Trite phrases are phrases that have been used for so long they have lost their meaning and really contribute nothing to a document. If you use them in your letters, you sound stuffy and stereotyped. You can eliminate some trite phrases completely, and use more current replacements for others. Review the following examples.

Instead of:	Try:
Per your request	As you requested
Under separate cover	By UPS (or whatever)
Enclosed please find	Enclosed
This writer	I
The undersigned	I or me
Pursuant to your request	As you requested
Copy of said report	Copy of the report
Kindly advise	Please tell us
Permit me to say	(Simply say it!)
We wish to say	(Simply say it!)
At your earliest convenience	(Give a time frame)

The following examples show some commonly used expressions and how the receiver might react.

Saying	Reaction
I wish to state	Why wish? Just say it!
We beg to state	Get off your knees!
Kindly place your order	Must I be kind?
We would like to thank you for	Just do it!

WEB WRITING TIP: Being concise is important when writing for the Web, as most Web readers do not like long, scrolling pages and prefer the text to be short and to the point. Documents intended for online reading should rarely be longer than 1000 words. A good target to aim for is 600 to 700 words.[24]

Conciseness is important for Web writing. One person said, "Websites are too wordy. It's hard to read a lot of text on the screen." While looking at a news story, another person said, "I like that short style. I don't have time for gobbledygook. I like getting the information fast." One guideline states that you should write no more than 50 percent of the text you would have used in a hard copy publication, as reading from computer screens is about 25 percent slower than reading from paper. Most individuals seem to agree that people's attention spans shorten when they go online and they can click away at any second. If you write paragraphs with more than 50 words, you may want to cut your paragraphs down as well as keep your sentences short and simple.[25]

A study of five different writing styles found that a sample website scored 58 percent higher in measured usability when it was written concisely.[26]

When writing for the Web, if at all possible, avoid repetition and excess verbiage. Watch the overuse of adjectives and adverbs. You can use lists rather than paragraphs so that your reader can pick out information more easily. Providing your information in precise segments called chunking also helps keep documents concise. However, you do have to be careful not to over-subdivide your information. If you break it up too much, your readers will get frustrated by too many choices and you will find it difficult to create a coherent narrative if the information chunk is too specific to make sense out of context.[27]

---

[24] Gerry McGovern, "The Web Content Style Guide Excerpt: Writing for the Web: Part 2, retrieved from *http://www.gerrymcgovern.com/guide_write_02.htm.*

[25] John Morkes and Jakob Neilsen, "Be Succinct!" 1998. Retrieved from *http://www.useit.com.*

[26] John Morkes and Jakob Nielsen, "Concise, Scannable and Objective: How to Write for the Web," 1998. Retrieved from *http://useit.com/alertbox9710a.html* and *http://www.useit.com/papers/webwriting/writing.html.*

[27] Sarah Horton, "Writing for the Web," in *Web Teaching Guide,* 2000. The Chronicle of Higher Education: Information Technology. Retrieved from *www.chronicle.com.*

- Do not allow your personal feelings and attitudes to interfere with your message.
- Use a style you would enjoy reading.
- Prepare a blueprint of your finished product before you start writing.
- Carefully select the right nouns and verbs to set the tone of your writing.
- Be prepared to rewrite, as rewriting results in better writing.
- Use logic and evidence to convince your reader.

BOX 2.10 🖝 **Helpful Hints for Developing a "You Attitude"**

COURTESY

When your writing contains courtesy, it expresses an attitude of friendliness and goodwill. You have probably visited a business establishment where people made you feel they cared about you. You will return to that store, theater, or restaurant because of that customer service. To establish positive relationships, you must employ courtesy when writing. Expressing courtesy means using a "you attitude" and positive words.

Web Writing Tip: When writing for the Web, you want to write conversationally as if you were talking to the readers.

"You Attitude." Courtesy includes using a "you attitude," which means putting yourself in the reader's place. See Box 2.10 for some hints for developing a "you attitude."

A business document written with this attitude shows empathy and understanding of the situation and stresses the reader's point of view or interest. The letter or memo talks about the receiver's convenience instead of the company's convenience. When you write letters using a "you attitude," your documents are courteous and sincere. Notice the difference in tone between the "we" and "you" letters in Box 2.11.

An insurance company mailed two differently worded messages when it wanted to update its address files. Half the policyholders received a card with this wording:

> Since we haven't written you in some time, please help us bring your records up-to-date by filling in and returning the other half of this card.

The other half of the policyholders received a card with this wording:

> So that your dividend checks, premium notices, and other messages of importance may reach you promptly, please fill out and return the other half of this card.

After several weeks, the first card motivated only 3 percent of the policyholders to respond. In contrast, the second card generated a *90 percent* return in less than a week. What accounted for such a dramatic difference in the effectiveness of the two cards? Simply writing most sentences from the "you the customer/employee/reader" point of view rather than the "I" and "we" perspective automatically increased reader involvement.[28]

---

[28] Barbara Lou, "Adding Instant Readership Appeal to Your Business Correspondence," *NRECA Management Quarterly*, pp. 13–15, Summer 1989.

BOX 2.11 ☛ **"We" Letter versus "You" Letter**

Positive Words. The final component of courtesy focuses on the positive, not the negative. You want to create a pleasant climate and produce goodwill for your organization. You do so by using words such as "please," "thank you," and "appreciate." As much as possible, you should avoid using the following negative words.

delay	can't	impossible	inconvenience	will not
trouble	blame	sorry	fault	unable
disagree	damaged	failure	prejudiced	complaint
unfortunate	wrong	mistake	difficult	failed
never	regret	neglect	no	prohibit
hesitate				

The following examples show how to turn negative sentences around.

Negative: Please do not hesitate to call me when you arrive in town.

Positive: Please call me when you arrive in town.

Negative: You neglected to give the size so it is impossible to fill your order.

Positive: Please send us the size you need and we will promptly fill your order.

Negative: Don't wait until the last minute to get your shopping done.

Positive: Get your shopping done early.

CHARACTER

The final **C,** character or personality, combines all principles of effective business writing. Character lifts your document above the drab and commonplace. Your business document should be your original creation. Never try to copy the writing style of someone else; it just will not work.

Your document contains character when it holds no stereotyped words or worn-out clichés and when it breathes the spirit of consideration for your reader. Your memo or letter gains character when you use concrete language, and when courtesy shines through the words, sentences, and paragraphs. Character shows clearly the writer thought about the needs, wants, and interests of the reader. As you can see, character encompasses all the other six **Cs.**

Richard Lanham[29] has developed what he calls the **"Paramedic Method."** This method allows you to edit your writing to make sure you have included all the elements of effective business writing. His simple method includes the following steps:

1. Circle all the prepositions. Then determine which prepositional phrases add extra words you can leave out.
2. Circle the *is* forms. Replace forms of *is* with stronger action verbs.
3. Ask yourself these questions: "Where's the action?" "Who's kicking whom?" Did you write using active or passive writing?
4. If your document contains passive writing, change to active writing. Put your "kicking" action into a simple active verb.
5. Start fast—no slow windups that use delayers or extra words.

Here's an example of how the Paramedic Method works.

Original Sentence: After we have carefully reviewed your present proposal, we are of the opinion that we are not in the position at this time to accept your offer.

Revision: We cannot accept your offer now.

WEB WRITING TIP: The 7 Cs of effective business writing also apply to writing for the Web. Any Web writing should be carefully organized while using simple words that make sense to the audience. In addition, Web writing should use topic sentences in paragraphs that have one main idea. It becomes imperative that you maintain and update Web content, as having accurate, relevant, and error-free content is a direct reflection on you and your organization.

Always take the time to proofread as a document with errors sends the message that you do not care.

Proofreading

Too often individuals forget to proofread their work or say they just do not have the time. Communication consultant Sara Reynolds considers the problem to be a failure to see proofreading as time well spent. She has seen documents with spelling and typographical errors—documents that made no sense. When she tells writers something needs to be proofread, they say they meant to go back, but never had the time. Managing the writing process includes paying attention to consistency of format; checking for punctuation, spelling, and grammar errors; and

---

[29] Richard Lanham, *Revising Business Prose,* 3rd ed. (New York: Macmillan, 1992), p. 8.

Read this sentence:

Fewer Fatal Failures are the Result of Years of Scientific Study Combined with the Experience of Years.

Now count the Fs in the sentence only once—do not go back and count them again.
For the answer, go to page 57.

BOX 2.12 🖝 **Can You Proofread?**

For those who think "almost" or "nearly" are acceptable words in the search for perfection, we've uncovered some alarming facts. In each case, if 99.9 percent is acceptable, then . . .

- 22,000 checks will be deducted from the wrong bank accounts in the next 60 minutes.
- 12 babies will be given to the wrong parents each day.
- 2,488,200 books will be shipped in the next 12 months with the wrong cover.
- 18,322 pieces of mail will be mishandled in the next hour.
- 20,000 incorrect drug prescriptions will be written in the next 12 months.
- 114,500 mismatched pairs of shoes will be shipped this year.
- 107 incorrect medical procedures will be performed by the end of the day today.
- 315 entries in *Webster's Third New International Dictionary of the English Language* will turn out to be misspelled.

BOX 2.13 🖝 **When 99.9 Percent Isn't Good Enough**
SOURCE: Adapted from "Strive for Perfection—OR ELSE!" *Working Communicator*, p. 6, Summer 1992.

double-checking numbers for accuracy.[30] See if you can correctly proofread the sentence in Box 2.12.

Always take the time to proofread, as a document with errors sends the message that you do not care. If you compose a 99-percent error-free document, the offending 1 percent could still destroy your document's value, waste your time, and seriously damage your credibility. When you sign your name at the bottom of a letter or initial your memo, you demonstrate you have read and approved your work. You indicate that you want it to represent not only you, but also your organization. If you send out sloppy work, it hurts not only you, but also your company. See Box 2.13 for an example of when 99.9 percent isn't good enough.

Sending a document with mistakes communicates that you do not care enough to take the time to proofread your work. Do you really want to send that message? If not, use the following tips to eliminate errors.

[30] Louise E. Boone and David L. Kurtz, *Contemporary Business Communication* (Englewood Cliffs: Prentice Hall, 1994), p. 160.

TIPS FOR PROOFREADERS

Most routine documents require light proofreading. Print out a rough draft copy of your document. Your document will look different on paper than on your computer screen. When you see the hard copy, you may decide to change the format or spacing if, for example, your page breaks do not occur where you planned them.

People forgive spelling errors the least because of the resources we have available to prevent them. Dictionaries, reference materials, and computerized grammar and spelling checker programs help identify spelling errors. However, do not depend on the computer spell checker without proofreading; the following poem by an anonymous author illustrates why.

I have a spelling checker;

It came with my PC.

It plainly marks four my revue,

Mistakes I cannot sea.

I've run this poem threw it,

I'm sure your please too no;

It's letter perfect in this weigh—

My checker tolled me sew.

For extremely important or complex documents, try to develop a partner system. A **partner system** allows you to receive help and also to give help. Have your partner read the final draft, while you follow along on the receiver's copy. Read the message at least twice—once for word meanings and once for grammar and mechanics. For an extremely long document, read it a third time to verify consistency in formatting. When proofreading, reduce your reading speed and concentrate on individual words rather than ideas.

If you do not have a partner, try reading the material backward so you won't get caught up in the sense of the document and overlook errors. Look for errors your spelling checker won't catch, such as *to* for *too*.

Note the type sizes and styles you have used. Make sure you have consistently used the same formatting throughout your document. If you have used any figures, illustrations, or graphics, make sure you have properly located and identified them.

Check for errors in spacing between words and sentences. Leave one space between words and two spaces at the end of sentences. Make sure you do not have any paragraphs with only one line or part of a line left at the top or bottom of your page—called *orphans* and *widows*. You must have at least two lines to start or finish a paragraph at the top or bottom of a page.

You may be one of the fortunate individuals who has a secretary to check and proofread your documents. But even when you have a secretary, you should know the fundamentals of correct format and check your document for errors before you sign your name!

For example, before you sign your letter, look at it closely to make sure it meets several important requirements. Ask yourself:

Have I positioned it property on the page?

Did I spell all names correctly?

Will it make a favorable impression on the recipient?

When you can answer "yes" to these questions, sign and include any enclosures. Keep a copy of your letter. Keep either a hard copy or electronic copy of your letter and file it with any previous correspondence, just in case your original does not reach its destination. See Box 2.14 for further proofreading and editing tips.

WEB WRITING TIP: For Ten Tips for Proofreading Online Writing, visit this website: *http://www.clickz.com/experts/archives/design/onl_edit/article.php/838051*

- Read it out loud and also silently.
- Read it backward to focus on the spelling of words.
- Read it upside down to focus on typology.
- Use a spell checker and grammar checker as a first screening, but don't depend on them.
- Have others read it.
- Read it slowly.
- Use a screen (a blank sheet of paper to cover the material not yet proofed).
- Point with your finger to read one word at a time.
- Don't proof for every type of mistake at once—do one proof for spelling, another for missing or additional spaces, consistency of word usage, font sizes, and so forth.
- Keep a list of your most common errors (or those of the writers you are proofing for) and proof for those on separate "trips."
- If you are editing within Word, use the "track changes" or "mark changes" function to make your comments apparent to other reviewers (additions and deletions can be set to appear in different colors).
- Print it out and read it.
- Read down columns in a table, even if you're supposed to read across the table to use the information. Columns may be easier to deal with than rows.
- Use editor's flags. Put #s in the document where reviewers need to pay special attention, or next to items that need to be double-checked before the final proof print. Do a final search for all # flags and remove them.
- Give a copy of the document to another person and keep a copy yourself. Take turns reading it out loud to each other. While one of you reads, the other one follows along to catch any errors and awkward-sounding phrases. This method also works well when proofing numbers and codes.
- First, proof the body of the text. Then go back and proof the headings. Headings are prone to error because copy editors often don't focus on them.
- Double-check fonts that are unusual (italic, bold, or otherwise different).
- Carefully read type in very small fonts.
- Be careful that your eyes do not skip from one error to the next obvious error, missing subtle errors in between.
- Double-check proper names.
- Double-check little words: *or, of, it,* and *is* are often interchanged.
- Double-check boilerplate text, like the company letterhead. Just because it's frequently used doesn't mean it's been carefully checked.
- Closely review page numbers and other footer and header material for accuracy and correct order.
- Reading aloud is perhaps the most powerful tool available for polishing and proofreading. Read aloud with feeling, if your work is meant to have an emotional impact. Saying a word many times tends to make it lose meaning to the person saying it. Rereading many times does the same thing. When this happens, the writer tends to scan rather than address each word and sentence the way a new reader would. Reading aloud puts some distance and freshness back into the process by encouraging the writer to say and hear every word (and error). Reading aloud with feeling allows the writer to feel the emotion in the words (and more importantly, to miss it if it's not there). Reading aloud is tedious, but exceptionally powerful.

BOX 2.14 ☞ **Further Proofreading and Editing Tips**

SOURCE: James A. Ayers and Criscadian Editorial Services, *Crisadian's Active Voice,* 1996, 1997.

Writing for an International Audience

When you write international letters, remember to study the cultural conventions of your receiver's country.

Let's face it, we know English is a difficult language, and the following sentences illustrate why it is so hard to learn.

- The bandage was wound around the wound.
- The farm was used to produce produce.
- The dump was so full that it had to refuse more refuse.
- We must polish the Polish furniture.

As a hybrid language, English seems illogical in structure to non-English speakers. In addition, international audiences are frequently confused by the imprecise nature and ambiguity of written English. If General Motors had relied on a good editor before launching its Chevy Nova ad campaign in Mexico, sales might have been better: Spanish speakers interpreted the billboards as a warning because, to them, "Chevy Nova" means "Chevy doesn't work (no go)." A Middle Eastern businessman, threatened with termination if he failed in an assignment, assumed that he was to be shot. A Chinese student sat by the phone for two days after receiving a letter from an American contact that said he would call him soon. Editing for an international audience requires particular care and precision.

The following suggestions may help when preparing material for individuals for whom English is a second language.[31] You can find additional tips for global writing in Box 2.15.

SYNTAX AND STYLE

Some basics apply when writing for international audiences, such as:

- Keep sentences short and simple. Emphasize strong transitional words and phrases. Use key terms or phrases consistently.

Few businesspeople know the rules of international correspondence, says Mary A. De Vries, author of *Internationally Yours: Writing and Communicating Successfully in Today's Global Marketplace* (Houghton Mifflin). Some tips include:

1. Before you write anything, research the other country's customs and business practices.
2. Keep your document clear and precise. Everything you write may be translated literally.
3. Businesspeople in other countries are often multilingual. You'll earn the respect of your overseas colleagues by learning some of their language.
4. Don't get too friendly too fast. It's better to be more formal than you'd be with colleagues at home.
5. Avoid confusion on business cards by eliminating abbreviations. Better yet, print one side of your card in English and the other side in your client's language.
6. Beware of unintentional racial and ethnic biases.

BOX 2.15 🖝 **Six Tips for Global Writing**

SOURCE: Taken from Elizabeth Janice, "Foreign Exchange: The Rules of Global Letter Writing," *Black Enterprise*, December 1995, via http://www.missjune.org/2002badcultural.html (accessed 11 June 2002).

[31] "Editing for an International Audience," retrieved from *http://www.editexpress.com/article_intl-audience. html*.

- Convert passive voice to active voice whenever possible. Avoid the introductory subordinate clause.
- Use visual clues (indentation, bullets, symbols) to increase comprehension.

LANGUAGE

Jargon, slang, euphemisms, and clichés cause particular difficulties for the international reader. Generally, you should substitute a single word or more explicit term for:

- Industry jargon such as "decision tree," "bubble chart," "preventive health care," "body language," and "fast track." If you will visualize your terms when making a decision whether or not to use a phrase, it will help you determine if it would be appropriate for your audience. If it is difficult to paint a "learning curve" in the mind, then the term would probably be difficult for your reader.
- Words that have acquired an accepted secondary usage in English but not in other languages. Examples are "tailored," "geared," "dedicated," and "submit." If in doubt, check for primary meanings in a conservative dictionary.
- Nouns that have recently acquired limited acceptance as verbs include "task," "impact," "leverage," and "network".
- Compound words or terms, generally. "Cost-effective," "labor intensive," "breakthrough," "multichain," and "market-driven" are terms or concepts that do not occur in other languages. A good rule of thumb to determine a term's appropriateness for an international audience is to look it up in the English-French or English-German section of a reliable dictionary. If it doesn't appear, make a substitution.

CONVENTIONS AND COURTESIES

This section presents some differences in U.S. conventions and international audiences and reminds us of the importance of courtesy.

- **Money.** Many nations use the "$" symbol. Distinguish $US from Can$, $A, and $Mex. "$Mex" is actually Mexican for pesos, not dollars.
- **Geography.** It's courteous to include the states as well as the city. "New York" has universal recognition; "Chicago" or "Houston" needs a more specific location.
- **Telephone numbers/time zones.** Include area codes with telephone numbers. Beware of "800" numbers; add time zones if appropriate.
- **Decimal points.** Europeans would express "100,000" as "100.000"
- **Special offers.** When editing material prepared primarily for a U.S. audience, check that any prices or special offers (hot-lines, 24-hour service) are applicable internationally. Many companies have lost money by failing to state "U.S. only."
- **Dates.** Typically dates are written with the day of the month coming first. For example, 2/1/05 would be January 2, 2005 in other countries.
- **Tone.** Generally, international communications observe a more formal and polite convention than is typical in the United States. "Submit entries by December 2" could offend an international reader. More acceptable would be "Please send completed forms before December 2."

PRODUCTION

You will need to remember that:

- Foreign language adaptation or translation of material will result in text expansion (25 percent expansion for Romance languages, 30 percent for Germanic languages). Design and layout should account for the expansion with adequate white space.

- If you are working electronically, make sure your word processing software or desktop publishing system and printer support the foreign-language character sets you need.

The following suggestions by Janet K. Winter[32] can be valuable aids in formulating a business message communicating across cultures:

- Study the context of communication for the relevant cultures. Consider the directness and degree of accuracy considered important to writers of that culture. For example, Japanese business exchanges begin with simple courtesies and pleasantries, appearing extremely positive and apologetic, while German writing tends to be direct.

- Keep the message *concise* without sacrificing adequate explanation and courtesy. Use simple sentence structure and familiar words.

- Make sure you create a *clear* message, using easily understood sentences with transition and emphasis techniques to guide the reader through the message in an easy-to-follow format.

- Include all appropriate details to have *complete* information that avoids misinterpretation, confusion, and the need for further exchanges to clarify details. Use metric designations to indicate quantities.

- Ensure your structure and mechanics are *accurate* but simple (to avoid the possibility of misinterpretation if the message is translated verbatim). Avoid using slang, acronyms, two-word verbs (e.g., put off), and words with more than one meaning.

- Exercise *patience* when presenting complicated explanations and details. If a concept may be difficult to understand, explain it in different ways; however, be careful to avoid sounding patronizing when using detailed, simple explanations. Whenever possible, include graphic aids to illustrate a point.

- Maintain a *positive* tone throughout the message to show concern for the listerner's or reader's feelings and personal dignity. Exhibit a commitment to service even if such assistance consumes extra personal time.

- Show a *tolerant* attitude by avoiding any suggestions of prejudice or stereotyping. Attempt to communicate naturally within the context of the culture.

- Use *active writing* to indicate involvement in the situation and to enhance understanding. Employ passive writing to avoid negativity, accusations, and egotistical emphasis on the writer (I, we, our).

- Encourage *interactive* communication by providing opportunities for responses from the receiver of the message and by asking specific questions, both open- and closed-ended.

- Exhibit a *courteous* attitude and show respect for the recipient's country, culture, and beliefs.

- Another valuable idea is to simply remember the Use Swiss Cheese™ rule. (*Use Short Words in Short Sentences.*) For example, say "help me" instead of "lend me your assistance." However, not all short words will make sense to

[32] Janet K. Winter, "Writing for Effective Business Communication," in *Tested Teaching Ideas for Business Communication,* edited by Courtland L. Bovee and John V. Thill (New York: McGraw Hill, 1995) pp. 40–42.

a non-native English speaker. Words such as "ad" for "advertisement" may not be understood. Contractions, such as "don't" or "he'll," may also be confusing. If in doubt, spell out the words. This shortness rule goes for paragraphs as well. Non-English thinkers can be put off by long paragraphs—three to four sentences are sufficient.[33]

WEB WRITING TIP: As of 1998, the Web became truly international. English will remain the leading language on the Web, and Americans will still form the largest single concentration of Web users, but they will not be as dominant as in the past. Keep two factors in mind with the increased number of overseas users: First, all Web content should be written so that it is understandable for second-language speakers of English; therefore, slang and jargon should be avoided. Second, puns and plays on words can definitely cause problems among people whose first language is not English and who will be confused or misled by them. You should make sure all icons and graphics are acceptable for internationals.[34]

Conclusion

Now that you know the basics, you are better prepared to write a clear and concise business letter, memo, or report. You can only improve your writing if you take every opportunity to write and practice the techniques presented in this chapter. When you start to write, break down the document into pieces; write the easiest section first; remember to write to express, not to impress; ask for a second opinion; practice; and read other well-written documents. When you read other well-written documents, you learn and can improve your writing. Remember to keep these tips in mind: Write actively; never use several words when one will do; write as you would talk; keep the sentence length short; and divide your work into paragraphs to give your reader a break.[35] Then, you will be on your way to writing effectively for the business world. The principles in Box 2.16 summarize essential points in this chapter.

- Proofread carefully.
- Trim unnecessary words. Think of words as your daily food intake—make sure you get all the essential vitamins and minerals, but trim off the excess fat and calories.
- Simplify your language. The ability to convey a thought in a pointed, direct manner takes practice. Simple writing requires putting ego aside, but it gains you more appreciation.
- Make passive sentences active, when appropriate.
- Search for mechanical errors and communication errors.
- Aim for a final professional document that clearly communicates your message.

BOX 2.16 ☛ **Principles of Effective Style**

SOURCE: Taken from Elizabeth Janice, "Foreign Exchange: The Rules of Global Letter Writing," *Black Enterprise*, December 1995, via http://www.northernlight.com (accessed 11 June 2002).

---

[33] Priscilla Richardson, M.A., JD., "When in Rome: 5 Surefire Tips for Communicating Over Borders," The Center for Association Leadership, Center Collections, November 2001. Retrieved from *http://www.centeronline.org/Knowledge/whitepaper.cfm?ID=643&ContentProfileID=122135&Action=searching*.

[34] Charles Morris, "Cut It Down and Open It Up," July 5, 1999. Retrieved from *http://wdvl.internet.com/Internet/Writing/cut.html*.

[35] Liz Fisher, "The Write Idea," *Accountancy*, Volume 123, Issue 1270, p. 46, June 1999.

Use the 7 Cs checklist in Table 2.1 and the document evaluation checklist in Table 2.2 to proofread your document. If you can answer "yes" to every question, you have created an effective business document.

TABLE 2.1   7 Cs checklist.

	YES	NO
Checking for Completeness		
Have you given all the facts?	❏	❏
Have you covered all the essentials?	❏	❏
Have you answered all the questions?	❏	❏
Have you organized your writing?	❏	❏
Checking for Clearness		
Have you used familiar words and short sentences?	❏	❏
Have you presented only one idea in a sentence?	❏	❏
Have you avoided unfamiliar business or technical terminology?	❏	❏
Have you written in the reader's language?	❏	❏
Checking for Concreteness		
Have you written with crisp, exact details?	❏	❏
Have you used words that paint a picture and make the facts vivid?	❏	❏
Have you avoided using sexist language?	❏	❏
Have you eliminated vague words?	❏	❏
Have you presented positive images?	❏	❏
Checking for Correctness		
Have you checked all facts?	❏	❏
Have you spelled all words correctly, including names?	❏	❏
Have you verified all numbers and amounts?	❏	❏
Have you written actively?	❏	❏
Have you used the grammar checker in your word processing package?	❏	❏
Checking for Conciseness		
Have you identified immediately the subject of the message?	❏	❏
Have you avoided rehashing the reader's document?	❏	❏
Have you avoided needless "filler" words or phrases?	❏	❏
Have you avoided useless repetition?	❏	❏
Checking for Courtesy		
Will the writing win goodwill?	❏	❏
Have you used positive, pleasant words?	❏	❏
Have you used *please, thank you,* or I *appreciate* somewhere in your writing?	❏	❏
Have you used titles before names?	❏	❏
Checking for Character		
Have you put the reader's needs first?	❏	❏
Have you highlighted the reader's interest?	❏	❏
Have you spoken the reader's language?	❏	❏
Have you incorporated all the **C**s into your document?	❏	❏

TABLE 2.2 ☞ **Document evaluation checklist.**

	YES	NO
Tone and Effective Word Use		
1. Did you use a courteous, conversational tone?	❑	❑
2. Does your writing reflect a "you attitude"?	❑	❑
3. Did you use positive words and expressions?	❑	❑
4. Did you use correct and nonsexist words?	❑	❑
5. Did you avoid clichés, jargon, and redundancies?	❑	❑
6. Did you use active writing?	❑	❑
Sentences and Paragraphs		
7. Did you avoid sentence fragments and choppy or run-on sentences?	❑	❑
8. Did you vary the sentence structure, but keep avarage sentence length between 17 and 24 words?	❑	❑
9. Did you use transitional words to connect sentences and paragraphs?	❑	❑
10. Did you avoid shifts in voice, tense, person, and number?	❑	❑
11. Did you avoid misplaced modifiers and maintain parallel structure?	❑	❑
12. Do your paragraphs appear to be the appropriate length?	❑	❑

Rate Your Overall Impression of Your Document

❑ Excellent   ❑ OK   ❑ Poor

Exercises

EXERCISE 1 LOGICAL ORDER

Directions: For each sentence, identify the correct logical order: priority, reverse priority, chronological, reverse chronological, comparison, contrast, or spatial.

1. You must prepare a status report to account for daily activities.

2. You examine how three companies solved the same problem.

3. You must write a report to discuss your department's major projects.

4. You develop a set of instructions for an on-the-job training manual.

5. You attended a meeting representing your boss, and you are now writing a memo to your boss about what happened.

6. You evaluate a new employee relations program just before implementation.

7. You must find out why policy manuals are not being read and recommend some changes.

8. You examined two pieces of equipment and must determine which one will cost less to operate.

EXERCISE 2 CLEARNESS

Directions: Applying the principles of clearness discussed in the chapter, make the following statements clearer.

Not Clear: Security personnel need not detain packages when the claimant presents a green pass signed by the manager.

Clear: _____

Not Clear: We are appreciably cognizant of your esteemed order for 10 dozen computer diskettes.

Clear: _____

Not Clear: Illumination is required to be extinguished on these premises after nightfall.

Clear: _____

Not Clear: I acknowledge receipt of your letter and I beg to thank you.

Clear: _____

Not Clear: My thinking has evolved to the significant point where a concept has emerged.

Clear: _____

Not Clear: Our facilitator will interface with the new employees.

Clear: _____

EXERCISE 3 CONCRETENESS

Directions: Applying the principles of concreteness, make the following ineffective sentences effective.

Ineffective: Your passbook savings account will earn the highest possible interest.

Effective: _____

Ineffective: The majority of our shareholders voted for the new plan.

Effective: _____

Ineffective: You failed to enclose a check with your order; therefore, it is impossible to send you the merchandise.

Effective: _____

Ineffective: There can be no exceptions to this policy.

Effective: _____

Ineffective: The salesman made $10,000 in commissions in one day.

Effective: _____

Ineffective: The typical businessperson spends four hours each day in meetings.

Effective: _____

EXERCISE 4 CORRECTNESS

Directions: Applying the principles of correctness, improve the following incorrect sentences.

Incorrect: Smelling of liquor, the policeman arrested the driver.

Correct: _____

Incorrect: The purposes of the meeting was: (1) to communicate personnel policies; (2) encouragement of participation in in-service training programs; and (3) introducing several new employees.

Correct: _____

Incorrect: The report was intended for Fred and I, not for John and Susan.

Correct: _____

Incorrect: A $35 price discounted by 10 percent is $3.15.

Correct: _____

Incorrect: A refund will be sent to you.

Correct: _____

Incorrect: It was both a long meeting and very tedious.

Correct: _____

Incorrect: Business used to be taught by the textbook method, while today the practical experience method is used.

Correct: _____

Incorrect: When the ship arrives, you must take two steps: (1) Telephone the Customs House broker immediately. (2) The other is to alert the Missouri factory.

Correct: _____

EXERCISE 5 CORRECT SPELLING

Directions: Place a check mark in the blank before the correctly spelled word in each pair.

_____	1. arrangment	_____	arrangement
_____	2. maladjusted	_____	malajusted
_____	3. temperament	_____	temperment
_____	4. questionaire	_____	questionnaire
_____	5. acommodate	_____	accommodate
_____	6. jepardy	_____	jeopardy
_____	7. precede	_____	preceed
_____	8. disimilar	_____	dissimilar
_____	9. inadvertent	_____	inadvertant
_____	10. mediocer	_____	mediocre
_____	11. reluctent	_____	reluctant
_____	12. prevalent	_____	prevelant
_____	13. irresistible	_____	irresistable
_____	14. strategy	_____	stratagy
_____	15. jubilent	_____	jubilant
_____	16. emminent	_____	eminent
_____	17. iradicate	_____	eradicate
_____	18. deficit	_____	defecit
_____	19. remeniscent	_____	reminiscent
_____	20. debatable	_____	debateable

EXERCISE 6 CONCISENESS

Directions: Applying the concepts of conciseness discussed in the chapter, improve the following sentences.

Not Concise: The two cars were exactly identical.

Concise: _____

Not Concise: With the extension of the scheduled date, there exists the possibility that Marketing may exceed staffing limitations.

Concise: _____

Not Concise: It would be my recommendation that we request a firm completion date for this project.

Concise: _____

Not Concise: It is of utmost importance that these reports be printed.

Concise: _____

Not Concise: I spoke with MIS, and they informed me that there will be no problem completing the special runs by Friday.

Concise: _____

Not Concise: Thank you very much for the very thoughtful gift.

Concise: _____

Not Concise: There was a general difficulty in printing from the PC software packages because we were not using a standard PC printer. Still, it was the consensus of all present that the packages were superior to our current software.

Concise: _____

Not Concise: We are not in a position to comment on this job you contemplate or in a position to assist you in drawing up your resume, but it is our opinion that your professor would be in a position to provide an answer to these questions.

Concise: _____

Not Concise: A more or less obvious type of pattern among those stores with declining volume of sales is a nature to indicate need for some kind of refresher course for each of the managers with this type of sales trend.

Concise: _____

Not Concise: Subsequent to the time of the governmental survey of forests apparently under condition of state ownership through cession of one kind or another, the land office found 50 of the titles of a questionable nature with the consequence of mandatory negotiations and purchases on an individual basis from one hundred heirs.

Concise: _____

EXERCISE 7 COURTESY

Directions: Improve the following sentences using the principles of courtesy.

Ineffective: We didn't receive a check.

Effective: _____

Ineffective: mployees who are late three days with no excused reason will be dismissed.

Effective: _____

Ineffective: We've mailed a check.

Effective: _____

Ineffective: Our savings accounts pay 6 percent interest.

Effective: _____

Ineffective: I want to express my appreciation.

Effective: _____

Ineffective: We have in stock a wide selection of fabrics.

Effective: _____

Ineffective: We are pleased to announce our new 800 customer service telephone number.

Effective: _____

Ineffective: To help us improve our production schedule, we would appreciate your placing your orders two weeks in advance of the date that you need the merchandise.

Effective: _____

Ineffective: You failed to submit your receipts for your travel expenses; consequently, we cannot process your request for travel reimbursement.

Effective: _____

Ineffective: If in the future you will address your inquiries to this office instead of the Atlanta office, you will not experience the delays about which you complained.

Effective: _____

EXERCISE 8 USAGE

Directions: Read each item below and circle or fill in the correct answer.

1. The _____ of studying can be to _____ your grades in college.
   a. affect/effect
   b. effect/effect
   c. effect/affect
   d. affect/affect

2. Circle the letter of the correct sentence.
   a. The president pledges not to raise taxes, which would be harmful to the economy.
   b. The president pledges not to raise taxes that would be harmful to the economy.

3. Choose the correct sentence.
   a. Was 23 July 19XX the date of the basketball game?
   b. On July 23, 19XX I graduated from college.
   c. On July 23, 19XX, I'm leaving to go to Florida.

4. Choose the correct phrase.
   a. An historic date.
   b. A historic date.

5. The boss can _____ all the files _____ the ones we mailed today.
   a. except/except
   b. accept/except
   c. accept/accept
   d. except/accept

6. I would _____ you to follow the _____ of your professor.
   a. advice/advise
   b. advise/advice
   c. advise/advise
   d. advice/advice

7. We were _____ to leave when Mrs. Williams asked us if we had _____ been given a copy of the schedule.
   a. all ready/already
   b. already/already
   c. all ready/all ready
   d. already/all ready

8. Complete each sentence using either *capitol* or *capital.*

    a. Atlanta is the _____ of Georgia.

    b. The company tried to raise enough _____ to buy new computers.

    c. The first word in a sentence should begin with a _____ letter.

EXERCISE 9 CHARACTER

Directions: Apply the 7 **C**s of effective business writing to this letter. Then write a better letter.

Dear Sir:

We have at hand your recent letter in which you make request for delivery of merchandise that you ordered. We are more than willing to help you in said matter, but your order—if we received it—is buried in the depth of our new computer. In order to assist us we would desire some additional information than that contained therein in your letter of December 1, mentioned above (copy of which is enclosed for your convenience), secondly, the manner in which your order was submitted by you to us, and the name of the salesman, agent, or other individual who received your order. As soon as we receive your letter we will investigate same. Address undersigned as indicated hereunder in the Adjustment Department. Hoping and trusting that this meets with your approval and assuring you of our earnest desire to be of service to you at all times, we remain.

                                    Yours very truly,

EXERCISE 10 DEBATE

This exercise was provided by Sana Reynolds, Associate Professor: Management Communication, Stern School of Business, New York University, 40 West Fourth Street, Suite 202C, New York, New York 10012–1118 Telephone: 212–998–0091 (business), Facsimile: 212–995–4213, E-Mail: **sreynold@stern.nyu.edu**

Directions: This activity will require your class to debate whether others should adapt to the American way or we, as Americans, should adapt to their way. Come prepared to debate either side of this issue to increase sensitivity to issues of acculturation and ethnocentricity.

EXERCISE 11 CULTURAL VALUES REVEALED IN EVERYDAY ACTIVITIES

Directions: This exercise increases your awareness of cultural differences by understanding how cultural values are revealed in mundane, repetitive actions.

    You are asked to describe a typical day from waking until bedtime. Then you will analyze and write how cultural values govern your actions. Bring your thoughts to class to share with your team members.

Action	Value
Brush teeth, take shower, apply deodorant	Personal odors are considered offensive in the United States.
Put on jeans and t-shirt	Personal comfort and informality are prized.

EXERCISE 12 THE MYSTERY OF CULTURAL BEHAVIORS

Directions: This exercise allows you to share knowledge already owned by your team and to develop a class dynamic in which questions and dialogue are handled respectfully. Each team member should think of examples of a cultural behavior that he or she does not understand that have caused misunderstanding. Ask teams to discuss the behaviors to see if they can arrive at an explanation. Come to class prepared to discuss your team's thoughts with the other teams in the class.

Assignment Options

OPTION 1: INTERNATIONAL INTERVIEW

Directions: Find a businessperson who communicates internationally, in writing, as part of his or her job. Interview that person about the following topics. Then write up your findings in a memo addressed to your professor.

a. What international business writing do you do? With whom do you communicate? What is the context? What is the mode? What is the message?

b. How much of your business communication is in writing? What are the advantages and disadvantages of writing? How much of your business communication is international? How has the amount of international business writing in your job changed?

c. What strategies have you used to become a more successful international business writer?

d. What stages have you gone through in becoming a more successful international business writer? What have you learned along the way?

e. What variations have you found in the way communication is conducted in different cultures? What have been the implications of those variations for your business writing?

f. What variations have you found in the way people balance individual and collective interests in different cultures? In the way people deal with gender differences? In the way people deal with authority? What have been the implications of those variations for your business writing?

g. What variations have you found in what causes people to change in different cultures? In how people feel about change? In how people think about time? What have been the implications of those variations for your business writing?

OPTION 2: TEAM PANEL PRESENTATION

This assignment was provided by Sana Reynolds, Associate Professor: Management Communication, Stern School of Business, New York University, 40 West Fourth Street, Suite 202C, New York, New York 10012–1118 Telephone: 212–998–0091 (business), Facsimile: 212–995–4213, E-mail: **sreynold@stern.nyu.edu**

Directions: You are a team of outside consultants working with a company that would like to expand internationally. (You select both the company and the country.) The management of the company has little background or knowledge of intercultural communication or international business writing. What does the company need to know about that country's economic system, history, religion, core values, culture, business practices, and communication patterns to conduct business successfully? Prepare a presentation to brief company management.

Your team will present a panel discussion that will be videotaped. This panel presentation will empower you to learn more about culture(s) from a business perspective and to anchor the knowledge you acquire by sharing information with the class. Panels should present useful (rather than merely theoretical) information in an organized manner using concrete examples.

Below you will find some suggestions for this presentation. Once your team has chosen its topic, please inform your professor. You may come up with your own topic, but you should seek approval from your professor before preparing your presentation.

- How does the concept of management differ from culture to culture? What do these differences mean? How do they play out in the way business is conducted, in relationships with clients, and in interactions with managers and coworkers? Support your presentation with concrete examples.

- Strategies for negotiation vary from culture to culture. Select and discuss, using examples, the negotiation strategies used by two or three countries.

- Roger Axtell in *Do's and Taboos of Doing Business around the World,* Robert Moran in *Managing Cultural Differences,* and others have identified a number of translating problems in marketing/advertising campaigns. Some examples:

    General Motors failed to market the "Nova" automobile in Latin America because "no va" means "doesn't go" in Spanish.

    Pepsi's "Come alive with Pepsi" was translated in Taiwan as "Pepsi brings your ancestors back from the grave."

    The advertising campaign used by Electrolux, the Swedish vacuum manufacturer, failed in the United States. The slogan used in Europe was "Nothing sucks like Electrolux."

    Sales of Big Macs and Coke plummeted during the 1994 World Cup when both McDonald's and Coca-Cola reprinted the Saudi flag including the quote from the Koran—"There is no God but Allah, and Mohammed was his prophet." Muslims were appalled that those words sacred to them would be used to sell a product or be put on something that is thrown away.

- Think of a product you would like to sell, distribute, or represent internationally. How would you alter your marketing approach or advertising campaign to succeed in a given country/culture?

CHAPTER 3

Learning to Write Directly Electronically and on Paper

*W*riting effective letters ranks among the top abilities of people in business. Adecca Personnel Services surveyed 908 personnel executives and found that "despite the increase in office automation, 36 percent of managers spend three or more hours a day on routine paperwork."[1]

Elys McLean-Ibrahim, *USA Today*

LEARNING OBJECTIVES

After reading this chapter, you should be able to:

- Discuss the importance and advantages of writing directly.

- Explain the role of the audience's reaction to the message.

- List the three steps to writing directly.

- Explain the action step.

- Identify situations in which you should write directly.

[1] Elys McLean-Ibrahim, "Paperwork Is Here to Stay," *USA Today*, Sec. B, p. 1, C1, January 9, 1989. Reprinted by permission of the publisher.

The Importance of Writing Directly

Letters, e-mails, and memos convey an impression of you. Sometimes your written documents are the only link you have with your receiver. Therefore, to appeal to your reader, you must properly organize your writing.

In deciding how to write your documents, you must consider the audience's reaction to what you will be stating. You need to put yourself in the reader's place and decide whether your message will be favorably received, unfavorably received, or resisted. Given this information, you will have a better idea of how to write.

If you think your information will be favorably received, you can usually take the *direct* approach, called bottom-lining. However, if you think the reader will be unhappy or need persuasion, approach your writing using the *indirect* approach, discussed in Chapter 4.

Use the chart in Table 3.1 to help you decide how you should approach your writing. Just put yourself in your reader's shoes.

Good news strengthens rapport and maximizes goodwill. Neutral messages keep communication channels open until improvement of circumstances makes good news possible.

Direct Writing

Approximately 90 percent of the documents in Anglo-American business situations follow the direct style. Good-news documents written directly include: goodwill, congratulations, adjustments, approvals on claims, routine requests, credit extensions, credit approval, and order acknowledgments. Some examples of routine correspondence are making routine claims, requesting routine information, requesting credit, and placing orders.

To write directly, arrange your ideas with the most important news first. Many readers never read beyond the first few lines of most documents; therefore, you must make those lines count! Do not "bury the lead," a newspaper term for making your reader wade through several paragraphs before getting to the most important news.[2] Many times writers use a subject line to save the reader's time by establishing the positive news and the nature of the letter. Whether you use a subject line or not, your first paragraph should contain a specific main idea. The second paragraph provides secondary details, and the third paragraph ends the document with a positive close.

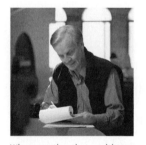

When creating that positive message, remember to begin with the main point.

DELIVER THE NEWS OR MAKE THE REQUEST

Because you know your audience will be favorably disposed to your news, present your main idea immediately—in the first sentence, if possible. You want the reader

TABLE 3.1 Direct versus indirect messages.

THE ANTICIPATED AUDIENCE REACTION TO THE MESSAGE	
(DIRECT) WHEN THE AUDIENCE FEELS:	(INDIRECT) WHEN THE AUDIENCE FEELS:
Eager—Excited—Interested—Pleased— Neutral	Displeased—Disappointed—Uninterested— Unwilling

[2] Therese Dyer-Caplan and Jane Gurin "Business Writing: A Foolproof System for Getting Started," *Hospital Material Management Quarterly,* Volume 20, Issue 4, pp. 88–89, May 1999.

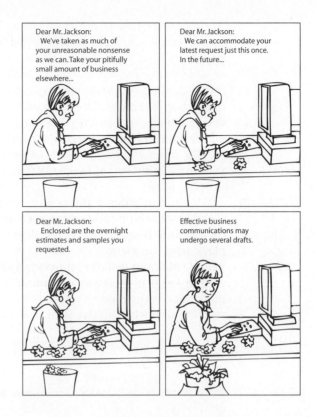

to know your topic. If you cannot open with your main idea in the first sentence, you must include it by the end of the first paragraph.

By placing your good news in the opening, you create a shorter document and one your reader will be more likely to read. Your reader will appreciate your getting to the point.

INCLUDE DETAILS OR EXPLANATIONS

The second paragraph should explain or further elaborate on the main point. For example, in responding to a request letter, if you can fulfill the request, then present the details. You may discuss such factors as when the request will be granted and how. If you acknowledge someone's order, the explanation might include when the items will be shipped and how.

When you present the details, put yourself in your readers' place and try to think of every question they may have. Try to anticipate their questions or concerns. You want to tell your readers all they need to know, not all the information you have available! Get to the point and keep your document brief.

Depending on the situation, you may need to divide the details or explanation into two paragraphs. Certain types of good news and neutral documents might require more explanation.

CLOSE POSITIVELY WITH THE ACTION STEP

This paragraph closes the message. You have an opportunity to reinforce the goodwill of your organization. Typically, you want to maintain a working relationship with the receiver. An appropriate close could suggest you wish to continue your relationship. You want to leave the customer, client, vendor, or coworker with a positive feeling toward you, your department, and your organization.

When ending, avoid worn-out clichés such as "Do not hesitate to call me," or "I look forward to hearing from you." Remember, these clichés have lost their meaning and only add dead weight to your letter.

You should have no difficulty writing good or neutral news documents like the ones shown in Box 3.1. Your message will be favorably received and your reader will be pleased.

As you can see, the direct approach to writing has many advantages. It improves comprehension, as your readers can assimilate and comprehend content more easily when they know the purpose immediately. You can withhold your conclusion until the end if you are writing a mystery story, but a busy executive may resent every minute he or she spends trying to determine your main point.

The direct approach focuses on the audience as it emphasizes the results of your analysis. It saves your audience time, as they can understand the message with little rereading.

You may wonder, if this approach has so many benefits, why it is not used more? For one thing, most communicators find it is easier to write or speak the way they think, although it is harder on their readers or listeners. In addition, most people learned the indirect structure in their formal schooling. Therefore, they are more comfortable with that approach. Others perceive that they need to build suspense to keep their audience's attention. In reality, doing so may cause the reader to put the document aside. Others want their audience to appreciate all the effort they went through, when, in fact, such an approach may lead to unnecessary confusion

ABC Communication Consultants
106 Jaywood Drive
Woodstock, GA 30188

May 10, 20XX

Ms. Phyllis Brown, Training Coordinator
Callao Community Bank of Macon County
P.O. Box 1146
Smyrna, GA 30081

Dear Ms. Brown:

Main Point

Thank you for allowing me to present the "Effective Business Communication" seminar to the personnel at Callao Community Bank. The involvement of the seminar participants shows a strong commitment to improving their writing skills.

Secondary Details

I've enclosed copies of the program evaluation forms and a summary of the numerical evaluations. This information should give you feedback regarding how the participants responded to the seminar.

Positive Close

Thank you for allowing me to work with your bank. Please call if you have any questions concerning this or future seminars.

Sincerely,

Rebecca Britt
Rebecca Britt
President

BOX 3.1   An Effective Direct Letter and an Effective Direct Memo

To: Teresa Finch, CFO
From: Cheryl T. Hayes, Director of Admissions *ch*
Date: February 22, 20XX
Subject: CER for Emergency Department Registration Renovation

Main Point

The attached documents present my plans to refurbish the registration and adjacent work area in the Emergency Room. Cox Interiors completed these plans last fall and estimated the cost of this project to be $19,573.00.

Secondary Details

The plan calls for new registration booths, an information desk, and a financial counseling office. We also asked for an improved pass-through window to the triage nurse office. The work area includes lockers for the employees and a storage closet for work supplies with bi-fold doors. Aesthetically, Susan is calling for installation of carpeting and new base cover for the work area as well as some paint and artwork.

Positive Close

Please review the attached plans and quotes. I'll touch base with you in two days to see if you have any questions. Thank you for helping us improve our "face" to our Emergency Department customers.

C: Ellie Post, RN, Director of Critical Care Nursing

Attachments

BOX 3.1   (continued)

rather than understanding. Your goal as a communicator should always be to put yourself in your receiver's shoes to determine the best writing approach.

This direct approach is also preferred for Web writing. Research has shown that Web readers like summaries and the direct approach. Research participants stated that they preferred a conversational, informal writing style so that they could read fast. They stated that they did not like reading every word as is necessary when a more formal style is used. Researchers recommend that you start your page with the conclusion as well as a short summary of the remaining contents. In addition, each paragraph should contain one main idea and you should use a second paragraph for the second idea or secondary information, as users tend to skip any second point when they scan over the paragraph. If you make it easy for your readers to find information, they will thank you. If you make it hard to find by burying what you actually want to communicate in the second or third paragraph, no one may read your document. Research shows that Web readers scan pages before they read anything, meaning they may scan right past your document if it doesn't have a straightforward heading or introduction that includes key words about your topic.[3]

Since readers don't scroll, they very frequently read only the top part of an article. Melinda McAdams' case study of the *Washington Post*'s Digital Ink notes that online newspapers allow articles to remain available online for years. This means that you can click back to old articles instead of having to summarize background information in every article. It seems the Web is a linking medium; hypertext theory states that writing for interlinked information spaces is different than writing linear flows of text. Therefore, Web writers often split their writing into smaller, coherent pieces to avoid long, scrolling pages.[4]

[3] John Morkes and Jakob Nielsen, "Applying Writing Guidelines to Web Pages," 1998. Retrieved from *http://www.useit.com/papers/webwriting/rewriting.html*.

[4] John Morkes and Jakob Nielsen, "Concise, Scannable, and Objective: How to Write for the Web," 1997. Retrieved from *http://www.useit.com/papers/webwriting/writing.html*.

The direct approach is also an appropriate approach in some countries such as Canada, Australia, Great Britain, New Zealand, and Northern Europe. But it would not necessarily be the best writing style for countries like Asia, Africa, South America, and much of the Middle East that are considered high-context cultures, where this approach might seem rude and abrupt. If you used the direct approach in these high-context countries, you might be perceived as unfriendly or unwilling to get to know the reader on a more personal basis.[5]

Direct Openings

Writers often experience difficulty getting started. Therefore, this section provides some sample openings to help you get your documents flowing.

Getting Information

Please answer the following questions regarding the new guidelines you helped us adopt.

Please complete the enclosed application form and return it in the envelope provided.

Seeking Help

Please meet with our planning committee to set up an employee fitness program similar to the one you introduced last year at Jones, Inc.

Making a Request

Please credit account #76543 for $50, the price of a carton of computer paper. We recently received a bill for two cartons of computer paper; however, we received only one carton.

Placing an Order

Please send me: 1 ream of 20 lb. bond paper, 12 HP printer cartridges, and 1 box of 20 folders.

Asking for Credit

Please consider my credit application for a loan with your bank.

Expressing Thanks

Thank you for your outstanding work. Your hotel staff did an excellent job, and we admire your special attention to all details, large and small.

Congratulating Others

Congratulations on your selection as Marketing Agent of the Year. You deserve this award!

Telling a Decision

The Board of Directors decided to accept your proposal.

Making a Recommendation

The committee recommends the purchase of a new fax machine.

---

[5] Linda Beamer and Iris Varner, *Intercultural Communication in the Global Workplace* (New York: McGraw-Hill/Irwin, 2001), p. 131.

Direct Responses

Many times you have to respond to requests. The following are examples of how to open these documents.

Sending Information

The following paragraphs provide additional information on the new company guidelines.

Offering Help

I will meet with you on Friday, October 10, to discuss the procedure for starting an employee fitness program. I have several helpful techniques to share with you.

Granting a Request

Your account #76543 has been credited for $50, the price of one box of computer paper.

Filling Orders

Your February 10 order was shipped immediately. You should receive it by February 16.

Granting Credit

Your horse trailer loan has been approved. Please stop by our office to sign the loan agreement and pick up your check.

Soliciting Feedback

We did not retain you as a customer. Please let us know how we could have better served you.

In Box 3.2, you can find how one company solicited feedback to maintain and encourage customer relationships.

Using the Direct Approach to Write to Government Officials

When writing to government officials, follow these six tips whether writing on paper or electronically.

1. Always copy your letters to your senators and representatives if you're writing to federal agency officials, or copy federal agency officials if you're writing to your legislators.
2. Ask for a specific response so that you'll not receive a form letter answer.
3. Be straightforward, factual, and to the point; keep your letter to one page.
4. Avoid personal attacks.
5. Ask to be placed on an agency's/legislator's list of interested parties on the issue so that you can have the opportunity to comment formally whenever the issue is the subject of proposed federal regulations, and to be a witness on the issue should the agency hold hearings in your area.
6. Organize with other businesspeople in your area who have to deal with the same issue and write a "group" letter; work with your state and national associations if they are in agreement on an issue.[6]

[6] Larry Silvey, "The 'Write Stuff'," *Aftermarket Business*, Volume 113, Issue 11, p. 12, November 2003.

BOX 3.2 🖛 Soliciting Feedback and Maintaining Customer Goodwill

Conclusion

Many business writing tasks involve routine matters in which you must convey either positive or routine information. These situations call for a direct organizational plan. Use the checklist in Table 3.2 to help you write effective documents using the direct approach. You can also visit this website for further guidance on the direct writing style: *http://planet.tvi.cc/ba122/Letters%20and%20Memos/Routine%20and%20good%20news.htm*.

Favorable News

TABLE 3.2 📨 **Checklist for writing directly.**

	YES	NO
1. Did you give the purpose or good news in the first sentence or first paragraph?	❏	❏
2. Does your second paragraph contain the secondary details?	❏	❏
3. Does the document provide all necessary information the reader may need?	❏	❏
4. Does your document meet all the characteristics of effective business writing?	❏	❏
5. Does it have a clear and appropriate introduction, body, and conclusion?	❏	❏
6. Does the document have transitions? Does it lead the reader along?	❏	❏
7. Does the letter leave a positive impression with the reader?	❏	❏
8. Can you read it easily?	❏	❏
9. Does the letter close with a positive ending paragraph? (*This does not mean the complimentary closing, but a closing paragraph.*)	❏	❏

Exercises

EXERCISE 1 DIRECT SENTENCES

Directions: From the receiver's point of view, choose the statement that presents the most direct and positive news.

_____ 1. We have received your resume.

_____ 2. We have received your completed application form.

_____ 3. Thank you for applying with us.

_____ 4. We'd like to have you visit our office for an interview.

_____ 5. You have a nice resume.

_____ 6. You appear to be quite well qualified.

_____ 7. You have a high grade point average.

EXERCISE 2 OPENING STATEMENTS FOR FAVORABLE MESSAGES

Directions: Using the guidelines from this chapter, improve the following openings. Response to computer repair request:

Ineffective: We're sure you'll like the modern features of our computers.
Effective: _____
Response to a request for a copy of a speech:

Ineffective: I was sorry to hear you missed my presentation at the conference due to an illness.
Effective: _____
Response to a request for a speaking engagement:

Ineffective: Speaking techniques should be understood by everyone, especially potential managers.
Effective: _____
Request for a repair:

Ineffective: On April 17, I purchased one X-L-T Computer at your Peachtree Street Store; on April 18, it stopped working.
Effective: _____
Request for a copy of a speech:

Ineffective: I had looked forward to hearing your presentation at the annual conference but became ill at the last minute.
Effective: _____
Request for a speaking engagement:

Ineffective: I was fortunate to be in the audience at the Toastmasters' meeting when you spoke on Speaking Techniques.
Effective: _____

EXERCISE 3 CRITIQUING A GOOD-NEWS LETTER

Directions: The following letter, addressed to Mr. Jerry Caltrider, concerns an audit performed by Habersham Accountants. Read this letter, then edit, revise, and produce a better letter.

Habersham Accountants
8013 MILLCREEK ROAD, N.E.
WASHINGTON, D.C. 20101

July 12, 20XX

Mr. Jerry Caltrider
Municipal Electric Authority of Georgia
1470 Riveredge Parkway, N.W.
Atlanta, GA 30328-4640

As you are well aware, two and one-half months ago you contacted us to conduct an audit of your organization's books. Since then, we have reviewed your financial records, including balance sheets and income and expenditure records. We have contacted selected customers and suppliers to determine the accuracy of certain figures.

Our auditors carried out these activities in a fashion consistent with regularly accepted accounting principles. As Certified Public Accountants, Habersham Accountants prides itself on the exhaustive and high-caliber work it does.

Your books appear to be in excellent order. We found no problems at all. We are preparing a formal statement and report of your financial status for the period covered by the audit. You should receive this document by the end of next week.

Attached to the report we are sending you will be an invoice for $5,000. This is the amount we agreed on for this audit. Now that we are familiar with your organization, I believe we can conduct next year's audit for $3,000.

Sincerely,

Hank Habersham

Hank Habersham, Partner

EXERCISE 4 CRITIQUING AN INFORMATIONAL LETTER

Directions: The following form letter discusses a doctor's move to a new location. Read this letter, then edit, revise, and produce a better letter.

Dear Ms. _____

I am sending this letter because I do believe you are a valuable patient to us and I do want you to have good health care. I have recently located my main office at 883 Johnson Mill Road, Building A, Suite 51, New Cambria, Missouri. Our phone number here will be 891-4567. It is across the street from Southside Hospital. A map is included on the back of the business card enclosed in this letter. However I still maintain my work at Missouri Baptist office and Missouri Baptist Hospital.

The Southside office location is very convenient to a lot of my patients due to the fact that it is very close to Highway 36. And it is close to a very good hospital, Southside Hospital, who I worked in for over six years. Both the office and the hospital are very well equipped for the care I would like for you to have. If you have any further questions please call us we are here to be of good help to you and your family.

Sincerely,

Magdi M. DoLot, M.D.

Magdi M. DoLot, M.D.

EXERCISE 5 USING THE DIRECT APPROACH

Directions: Give an example of how you might directly approach a candidate for a job position you posted in the paper to let him or her know you would like to set up an interview. Let the candidate know you have received his or her resume and application.

Assignment Options

OPTION 1—PRODUCT LETTER

Think of a product or service you would like to buy. Think of some questions about its features, price, guarantee, local availability, or anything else you might like to know. Write to the company or organization offering the product and ask four questions. Be sure to include enough background information so the reader can answer your questions satisfactorily.

OPTION 2—REPRESENTATIVE LETTER

For this assignment, you must write to a local, state, or federal representative. You may write to request information concerning a topic in which you have an interest, ask how the legislator stands on a certain issue, or offer your support for the actions the legislator has taken.

OPTION 3—SPRING BREAK LETTER

For spring break, you and your friends want to visit Walt Disney World in Orlando, Florida. You need information about overnight lodging and admission costs, and general tourist information about the surrounding area. Go to the Web to obtain the e-mail address of the Chamber of Commerce in Orlando, Florida, and write an e-mail message requesting information. Bring a copy of your e-mail to class for the instructor to evaluate.

OPTION 4—LETTER TO THE EDITOR

Write a letter to the editor of the college newspaper expressing your opinion about an issue. Provide a copy of your letter to the instructor for grading. If the newspaper prints your letter, bring the newspaper to class.

CHAPTER 4

Learning to Deliver Bad News

*G*enerally, the letter that gives us pause is the "bad news" or refused request letter. It requires tact and a strategy that attempts to maintain goodwill while rejecting a point of view or a request.[1]

Minerva Neiditz, Institute of Writing, University of Connecticut

LEARNING OBJECTIVES

After reading this chapter, you should be able to:

- ☛ Discuss the importance of writing indirectly.

- ☛ Identify the principles of saying no.

- ☛ List and explain the steps in transmitting bad news.

- ☛ Describe the approaches to opening a bad-news letter.

- ☛ Clarify when you should offer a counterproposal.

- ☛ Explain why you end on a positive note.

- ☛ Relate words or expressions to avoid when presenting bad news.

[1] Minerva Neiditz, *Business Writing at Its Best* (Burr Ridge, IL: Irwin, 1994), p. 72.

The Importance of Writing Indirectly

Sometimes you must break unpleasant news to nice people. Nobody likes to be wrong. When you must tell people they have made a mistake, give them every benefit of the doubt and help them save face. Your purpose in writing a bad-news message is first to convey the bad news and second to maintain the customer's, associate's, or client's goodwill.

When you give bad news, allow conciseness and directness to be secondary to diplomacy. Empathize with your reader and consciously write using a "you attitude." When choosing your words, select positive, courteous ones. Don't use qualifiers or euphemisms to avoid accepting responsibility. For example, a company president wrote to her employees: "It is necessary to resize our operation to the level of profitable market opportunities." What did she mean? She meant the company must lay off staff.[2]

When you write indirectly, be considerate, but do not be too subtle. Otherwise, you may mislead your readers into believing their requests will be granted. Even when you offer your employees criticism, deliver it in a positive way. The memos in Box 4.1 illustrate the importance of tone, positive words, and tact in delivering unfavorable news.

"Before" Memo

TO: Jack Jones

FROM: Janet Salem *js*

DATE: February 20, 20XX

SUBJECT: Denial of Your Request

I regret to inform you that your request to transfer to our Sandy Springs location has been denied. At this point in time, there are no positions open for which you are qualified. Thank you for your understanding.

"After" Memo

TO: Jack Jones

FROM: Janet Salem *js*

DATE: February 20, 20XX

SUBJECT: Response to Your Request

After we spoke yesterday, I checked on your transferring to our Sandy Springs location. With the merger taking place, many changes are occurring.

Mr. Myers, the Sandy Springs manager, stated they have positions available only in their Marketing Department. Employees from the other firm will be filling any accounting positions.

Because of your hard work and dedication, I will keep your request on file. Thank you for being a valuable part of our team.

BOX 4.1 ☛ "Before" and "After" Bad-News Memos

---

[2] Susan L. Brock, *Better Business Writing* (Menlo Park, CA: Crisp Publications, 1988), p. 37.

Note the difference in tone between the two memos in Box 4.1. Both clearly deny the transfer, but the "before" version sounds mechanical, stuffy, and cold. Although you want to be clear and concise in your business writing, you do not want to sacrifice kindness. *Concise* and *brief* do not mean the same thing. When you must give bad news to important employees or customers, take the time to select tactful and kind words.

Saying No

Some examples of when you must say no include: adjustment refusals, credit refusals, problem orders, and favor refusals. This unpleasant task can be made significantly less painful for both parties involved if you apply a few basic principles.

- Put yourself in the shoes of the reader. Empathy allows you to see the impact this news will have on your reader.
- Develop a system for skillfully delivering the disappointing news.
- Be conscious of your attitude.

In responding to complaints, the same principles apply. The customer has either a legitimate gripe or a misunderstanding of the facts. In either case, the customer feels upset. Your answer will have a major impact on the outcome of the situation.

Whether to Use the Direct or Indirect Approach

Whether you chose to use the direct or indirect writing approach will be determined by your relationship with your reader. A first step to help you determine which approach to use is to read the sender's original message. If the original message was written in the direct style, the sender may have considered it a routine request, and you would be safe in answering in the direct style. If the original message was written in the indirect style, the sender probably considered it a persuasive request and you should consider answering in the indirect style. It is important to note that often messages written to your superior are written in the direct style.

For example, an e-mail message telling employees that the cafeteria will be closed for one day to permit installation of new equipment can be written directly. A message telling these employees that the cafeteria will be closed permanently, thus requiring the employees to go outside for lunch and possibly pay higher prices, may require you to use the indirect approach.

WHEN TO USE THE DIRECT APPROACH

Many times writers simply want a yes or no decision and desire to hear it in a direct manner. Often with an issue that will not generate an emotional response, the direct approach is appropriate. The direct plan for bad-news messages is basically the same plan used for good-news or neutral messages discussed in Chapter 3. To help your readers accept your decision when using the direct plan, you should give a brief rationale in the first paragraph along with the bad news. Follow your opening paragraph with any needed explanation and end with a positive close.

Some examples of situations where you could use the direct approach in presenting bad news include:

- The bad news involves a small, insignificant matter and can be considered routine.

- The reader prefers directness or the organization suggests it.
- The writer wants to emphasize the negative news. For example, you may have already refused the request once and the reader writes a second time. A forceful "no" may be appropriate for this situation.
- The receiver may overlook the bad news. With the amount of information received daily, many readers skim messages and only look at the opening. This is especially true with reading online messages.

A message organized using the direct plan may not be any shorter than one organized using the indirect approach. Direct messages are often shorter than indirect messages because the direct approach is often used for simpler situations, which require little explanation or background information.[3]

WHEN TO USE THE INDIRECT APPROACH

When you want to give your audience a chance to "buy into" ideas they agree with or a problem they need to solve, before you present your solution, you should use the indirect approach. This approach softens your audience's resistance, arouses their interest, and increases their tendency to see you as fair-minded. It allows you to spell out your support first and to finish with your generalization or conclusion. Begin your opening paragraph with a neutral statement, then explain the denial and present the refusal in your second paragraph; close your document with a third paragraph providing a positive, goodwill ending.

Begin with a Neutral Statement.   Use the indirect sequence to present your ideas. Your reader will be more likely to read and understand your decision. Open with a neutral comment and acknowledge the problem politely in a way that leads to agreement. The following examples provide approaches to opening bad-news letters.

Appreciation: Thank your reader for a check, information, or whatever.

Compliment: Try to compliment your reader on something good about his or her record or request.

Good News: If you can grant any part of the request and you think your reader will be pleased, begin with the good news.

Neutral Courtesy: Keep the opening paragraph noncommittal.

Explain the Denial.   You should explain and give reasons in a positive manner while being specific, but not using the words *company policy*. The customer probably won't feel sympathetic to that excuse. Carefully lay out the logic of your side of the issue so your reader can understand your company's actions. If you outline your reasoning process slowly, your reader can reach the disappointing conclusion and understand.

Sometimes you do not even have to give the news; a simple statement of fact will make the refusal clear. For example, company recruiters need to tell job applicants they do not meet the requirements. They can include a statement such as: "For this position, the applicant must have five years of full-time job experience." Recruiters do not have to say directly, "You do not have the necessary requirements for this job."

Present the Refusal and Offer an Alternative.   You do want the reader to understand that you are refusing, so you should not be vague in your denial. The reader should not need further communication with you to understand the refusal clearly.

Ideally, the bad news should flow logically from the reasons. If you explained your reasons well, your reader can probably infer a refusal even before reading it.

[3] Scot Obert, *Fundamentals of Contemporary Business Communication* (Boston: Houghton Mifflin Company, 2004), pp. 183–184.

Whenever you have to relay bad news up the line, prepare yourself ahead of time and investigate exactly what happened and why it happened. Then you should honestly present the facts. The sooner you identify what's going on, the easier the problem will be to handle. It's easier to present bad news if you have some idea of what to do about it.

Source: MBA: Management By Averbach, Management Tips from the Leader of One of America's Most Successful Organizations, (May 1, 1994, New York, NY: Collier Books, Red Averback and Ken Dooley).

When you do actually state your refusal, de-emphasize the bad news. Avoid putting it at the beginning or end of a paragraph. Additionally, to help soften unpleasant ideas, use positive words and avoid using words that convey negative feelings. Box 4.2 presents some phrases to avoid.

If you can offer an alternative or make a counterproposal, do so. You might be able to offer an alternative product or service, suggest a substitute, or make a compromise. For example, you might say, "I cannot schedule your two weeks' vacation in July, but I can give you one week in July and one week in August."

End on a Positive Note. Close your document with a positive statement to preserve the established goodwill of the customer. You want your readers to feel favorably disposed toward you and to feel you care about them. Whatever you write, do not bring up the bad news again.

In any negative letter, move carefully and constantly while keeping goodwill in your plan. You want to get the reader on your side by establishing some common ground and by using a positive tone.

These websites provide further guidance and some practice exercises: *http://planet.tvi.cc/ba122/Letters%20and%20Memos/Bad%20News.htm, http://www.prenhall.com/pauline/Episode11.html, and http://www.du.edu/~nhightow/badnews.html.*

1. Expressions such as: *you say, you claim, you assert, you complain,* and *you neglected.* These statements do not help your reader understand, but they do irritate.

2. Negative statements such as: *we fail to understand, we are at a loss to know,* and *you failed to state.* These statements tend to belittle your reader.

3. The phrase *no doubt.* This phrase may be interpreted as sarcasm.

4. The expression *our records* or *our records show.* The reader interprets this to mean: The company makes no mistakes.

BOX 4.2 ☞ **Avoid the Following Word Choices**

SPECIFIC INDIRECT OPENINGS

The following examples provide guidance for beginning bad-news documents. Use these ideas to help you get started in similar situations.

Saying No   Your study of executives' communication skills sounds interesting. The type of information you report could be useful in determining norms for different industries.

Dealing with Problems   Thank you for your December 9 order for one Talking Elmo doll. We did not expect Elmo to be this popular.

Refusing Claims   Of course, you have the right, Mr. Britt, to expect the best possible service from MFA. Every MFA product comes from years of experimentation. We blend each chemical under the most careful controls possible.

Disallowing Claims   When we received your request for reimbursement, we immediately contacted our insurance carrier.

Declining to Extend Credit Terms   We understand your desire to purchase the new Ford Explorer. As a result, we processed your application for a new car loan when we received it.

Rejecting Changes in Policies or Procedures   Thank you for your suggestion for improving our company's sales reporting process.

Boxes 4.3, 4.4, and 4.5 show examples of how to present bad news. Note the steps included.

Using the Indirect Approach with International Audiences

Indirect writing is often used within many global settings. This indirect style is often accompanied by deliberate ambiguity so that the writer can diffuse responsibility and save face. Even in routine situations, such as a request for information, indirectness saves face in case the request is denied or ignored. Indirectness signals the

Paula Holcomb Morris
132 Aspen Court
Marietta, GA 30061

October 15, 20XX

Mr. Steve Mastinson
The Backyard Restaurant
145 South Main Street
Woodstock, GA 30188

Dear Mr. Mastinson:

Neutral Statement

I have frequented your restaurant since it opened last spring. Woodstock certainly needed an eating establishment of your caliber.

Explanation of Bad News

Typically, during my visits, I have received outstanding, prompt service and fine food. Last Friday, I experienced something different. My friends and I were promptly seated. After a delay of 10 minutes, our waiter came to the table and took our drink order. Our drinks arrived promptly, but after that, we did not receive any attention from our waiter. We waited 20 more minutes for our dinner order to be taken. We watched other customers have their orders taken and dinners delivered. After we summoned help from another waiter, our waiter finally approached our table. In dismay, we watched the waiter pass us by and take a drink order from the people sitting at the table adjacent to ours. He totally ignored us!

The waiter's behavior infuriated us, so we decided to leave. We explained what happened to the cashier, but he seemed flustered and offered no compensation for the way we were treated. We paid for our drinks and left in disgust!

Positive Close

I trust you appreciate my concern and will make adjustments. Please contact me with any questions.

Sincerely,

Paula Holcomb Morris
Paula Holcomb Morris

BOX 4.3 ☛ **A Customer Presents Bad News**

writer's intention to be careful so that the reader does not lose face, which is critical in many countries. Using ambiguity means that words are chosen for their ability to mean more than one thing, and patterns of words can have more than one interpretation. This also serves to reveal the subtlety and sophistication of the writer. What is not said may be as important, or more important, than what is said. Writing with indirectness and ambiguity means using a style that favors circumlocution rather than straightforwardness. Sentences may seem to ramble because ideas are developed in relation to each other. Metaphors are preferred because they infer a context of concepts and principles while suggesting possibilities. Indirectness may also mean digression or what may be termed side-conversations and ramblings by

Learning to Deliver Bad News   **91**

East Cobb Pediatrics and Adolescent Medicine

Diplomats, American Board of Pediatrics
Comprehensive Pediatric Services
from Birth through Age 21

August 1, 20XX

Mario Herbert, M.D.
145 Church Street
Marietta, GA 30068

Dear Mario:

Main Point

We have just completed a critical evaluation of our clinical staffing needs with our consultants. This evaluation found that we currently have too many pediatricians for the current and projected number of patients we serve. Based upon this report, we must cut down the number of pediatricians employed in our practice. Unfortunately, this affects you.

Secondary Details

According to your contract, we must give you a 30-day notice that we must end your services. You will receive a full 30-day paycheck at the end of the month.

Positive Close

We have reluctantly made this difficult business decision. We perceive your personal and clinical qualities to be outstanding. We will be happy to send any letters of recommendation for you. We, the partners, wish you nothing but the best.

Sincerely,

Eduardo Montana, Sr., M.D.
Eduardo Montana, Sr., M.D.
Medical Director

C: Personnel records

Main Office:
1121 Johnson Ferry Road • Suite 200
Marietta, Georgia 30068
Voice (770) 977-0094 • Fax (770) 5099463

Kennesaw Office:
3895Cherokee Street • Suite 160-170
Kennesaw, Georgia 30144
Voice (770) 795-1553 • Fax (770) 795-1513

BOX 4.4 🖝 **A Physician Delivers a Difficult Message**

results-oriented cultures such as the United States. These added bits of circumstance and situational description help develop a context for business communication for members of relationship-oriented cultures such as Romania.[4]

---

[4] Linda Beamer and Iris Varner, *Intercultural Communication in the Global Workplace,* 2nd ed. (New York: McGraw-Hill/Irwin), 2001, pp. 132–133.

ING

FINANCIAL SERVICES INTERNATIONAL
NORTH AMERICA

February 11, 20XX

Mr. George Smythe
600 Howard Avenue
Germantown, MD 20878

Dear Mr. Smythe:

Neutral Opening

We received your inquiry about job opportunities at Unger North America Insurance Corporation. We have over 8,000 employees in the Unites States in 15 locations.

Explanation

Within our organization, employment screening and interviewing is done by the site hiring manager and not by a centralized human resource function. When new positions become available elsewhere in the country, we ask applicants to inquire about that opportunity directly to the business location. At this time, your qualifications do not match any of our open position profiles in Atlanta. You may contact our other 14 locations to see if they have any openings.

Positive Close

We appreciate your interest, and we wish you every success in achieving your objective.

Sincerely,

Carol Joy
Carol C. Joy
Human Resource Administrator

ING North American Insurance Corporation
5780 Powers Ferry Road, NW   Tel: 770-980-3300
Atlanta, GA 30327-4390   Fax: 770-980-3301

BOX 4.5 ▶ **A Company Delivers Bad News Indirectly**

Indirect Writing Tips

Most people find writing bad-news documents difficult, because no one likes to receive a negative message. These special documents require you to be tactful but honest. Apply the following *do's* and *don'ts* to help you write these kinds of documents.

Opening the Correspondence

Do: Open with a neutral comment.

Begin with a thought on which both reader and writer can agree.

Don't: State or imply the unfavorable news.

Imply a yes response to the reader's request.

Start with irrelevant statements.

Restate what the reader said originally.

Explaining the Bad News

Do: Devote most of the letter to the explanation.

              Use positive language.

              Emphasize that you carefully considered the request.

Don't: Justify the refusal with "It's company policy."

Stating the Bad News

Do: Minimize the negative language.

              Provide a counteroffer if appropriate.

              Imply the refusal when possible.

Don't: Start or end the paragraph with the bad news.

              Be so vague the decision won't be understood.

Closing the Correspondence

Do: Be positive.

              Emphasize goodwill.

              Use the reader's viewpoint.

Don't: Repeat the bad news.

              End with an insincere statement: "When we can be of further help. . . ."

              Close with a suggestion of further trouble: "When this problem occurs again. . . ."

              Express doubt that the decision will be accepted: "We hope you'll agree. . . ."

              Imply fear of losing the customer: "We hope you'll continue shopping with us, though. . . ."

              Leave the matter open for further discussion: "If you want to discuss this further, just call us."

              Use words such as "therefore," "however," or "consequently." Typically, these words signal rejection or bad news.

Use the guidelines presented in Table 4.1 to help you write effective indirect messages.

TABLE 4.1 ☞ **Checklist for writing indirectly.**

	YES	NO
1. Does the document open with a buffer making clear the reason for writing?	❑	❑
2. Does the buffer lead naturally to the next paragraph?	❑	❑
3. Does the writer precede the bad news with you-oriented and convincing details and explanations?	❑	❑
4. Did the writer omit all apologies?	❑	❑
5. Did the writer omit all references to company policy?	❑	❑
6. Did the writer clearly and diplomatically state the decision?	❑	❑
7. Did the writer include a counterproposal, if appropriate?	❑	❑
8. Does the letter contain a positive statement and tone to preserve the established goodwill of the customer or client?	❑	❑
9. Does the document omit negative words like "however," "although," "but," and "consequently"?	❑	❑
10. Is the document easy to read, sincere, and positive?	❑	❑

Conclusion

As can be noted, as a writer, you must at times deliver unpleasant news. Whether you use a direct or indirect approach will be dictated by your relationship with the receiver and the seriousness of the situation. As the writer, you must determine which approach is the best for you, the writer, your receiver, and the circumstances.

Exercises

EXERCISE 1 IDENTIFYING DIRECT AND INDIRECT WRITING STRATEGIES

Directions: The following sentences will open a letter or memo. Identify the writing strategy used. (Write *D* for *direct* and *I* for *indirect*.)

_____ 1. We are processing your application.

_____ 2. Thank you for purchasing the computer we discussed.

_____ 3. I accept your decision.

_____ 4. Thank you for your letter about your shopping experience at Polks.

_____ 5. We have attached our committee's recommendations for an on-site day care facility.

_____ 6. The marketing study shows a decline in the use of our product.

_____ 7. We suggest closing the Main Street Branch.

_____ 8. We will review your recommendations.

EXERCISE 2 POSITIVE WRITING STRATEGIES

Directions: The following sentences paint negative images in the mind. Reword them to paint a more positive picture.

Negative: You do not have the qualifications for the position.

Positive: _____

Negative: You neglected to give the shoe size so it is impossible to fill your order.

Positive: _____

Negative: Don't wait until the last minute to schedule your appointment.

Positive: _____

EXERCISE 3 OPENING STATEMENTS FOR UNFAVORABLE MESSAGES

Directions: Using the guidelines from this chapter, improve the following openings.

Ineffective: We regret to inform you that your application for employment as marketing director with our company has been rejected.

Effective: _____

Ineffective: Because our tax consulting firm is entering its most busy season, we are unable to provide the free counseling service for the residents of the Lochhaven Rest Home.

Effective: _____

Ineffective: Our community service funds for this year have been earmarked for specific projects so we cannot contribute to your scholarship fund at this time.

Effective: _____

EXERCISE 4 CRITIQUING A JOB REFUSAL

Directions: This letter deals with a job refusal. Read the letter and answer the questions.

Moondust Studios
1719 Moondust Way
Anaheim, CA 93755

January 7, 20XX

Ms. Trisha Impressive
2 Stardom Lane
Hollywood, CA 93810

Dear Ms. Impressive:

Congratulations on a fine acting audition last Friday! Your performance thrilled my assistant producer and me. After narrowing down the field to you and two other actresses, we have finally decided whom to cast as Susan St. Jones in our upcoming video production of *Beauty*.

Unfortunately, you did not get the job. We wanted a slightly thinner girl, and despite your wonderful talent, we decided to go with Cindy Woods. It was a close decision! There are, however, some supporting roles left over. We will notify your agent about the audition dates for those.

We are really sorry we couldn't cast you in a starring role this time. With your talent, there will certainly be other roles in your future. Good luck in your career.

Sincerely,

Marko Vicko

Marko Vicko, Producer

1. What was your immediate reaction to this message? Why?
2. Were you satisfied with the explanation? Why or why not?
3. What was the overall tone of the letter?
4. How did the writer handle the bad news?

EXERCISE 5 CRITIQUING AN E-MAIL MESSAGE

Directions: Read, edit, and rewrite this e-mail message.

Postal Services strive to provide the best possible mail pick-up and delivery service to all campus departments. I know that we often fall short of that goal, but we honestly do attempt to excel. This Valentine's Day we have had several deliveries of flowers, intended for campus sweethearts, brought to Receiving due to incomplete addresses.

Unfortunately, the delivery of flowers is not in our scope of responsibilities. Rather than return the flowers, we have been accepting them, and calling the intended recipients, to inform them that they need to pick up a personal item, which we are not permitted to deliver. I know that this spoils an intended surprise gift, even though we don't reveal what the item is. I suppose it isn't too hard to guess, considering the occasion.

The negative feedback that I have received has forced me to reconsider my policy. I regret that unless future deliveries of flowers are properly addressed (if they come here, they are not), then I have no choice other than to refuse delivery.

EXERCISE 6 CRITIQUING A BAD NEWS-LETTER

Directions: Read, edit, and rewrite the following letter.

Massey & White, Inc.
2543 Tell's Road
Macon, MO 63552

March 23, 20XX

Mr. Bob Wyatt
1978 Riverrun
Bevier, MO 63534

Dear Mr. Wyatt:

In the future, please give us *at least* 24 hours' notice when you are unable to make a scheduled appointment.

I had reserved that specific block of time for you on our schedule for weeks. The practice is very busy and I have patients whose appointments have been delayed because there was no room on the schedule. We had one hour of schedule reserved for you.

A $25 missed appointment charge has been added to your account.

The intention of this letter is not to make you angry, but to let you know that we must fill every hour of our schedule in order to pay the employees and our overhead costs (which, in turn, keeps our fees from rising).

Please call us to reschedule your appointment.

Thank you. Know that we appreciate you.

Sincerely,

Steve Black

Steve Black, Office Manager

Assignment Options

OPTION 1—BAD-NEWS LETTER OR MEMO

Think of a situation in your job in which you must communicate bad news. Perhaps you cannot grant a certain type of customer request or must discontinue providing a service. Write a tactful bad-news letter, memo, or e-mail message.

OPTION 2—DENIAL LETTER

Think of an organization to which you belong. Identify a request that should be denied or a procedure that should be changed or discontinued. Then write a tactful bad-news document.

OPTION 3—POOR QUALITY AND PERFORMANCE LETTER

Perhaps you have bought something recently. Now you feel disappointed in its quality and performance. Write to the manufacturer or the store where you bought the item and present your bad news.

OPTION 4—NEW SMOKING-POLICY MEMO

Write a bad-news memo informing all employees of Atlanta Bell Systems they will no longer be allowed to smoke in the building. Can you offer the employees any alternatives or any incentives to quit smoking?

OPTION 5—POOR SERVICE LETTER

If you have recently visited a fast-food establishment, restaurant, movie theater, or store where you feel you received poor service, write a letter detailing what happened.

OPTION 6—PROBLEM-SOLVING LETTER

You work as Meter Reading Superintendent of Callao Electric Membership Corporation. One of your meter readers has reported she cannot read a customer's meter because of overgrown shrubs. Write to the customer, present the bad news, and ask for assistance in solving the problem. The customer lives at 1594 Jeb Wheeler Road, Roswell, Georgia 30071.

OPTION 7—CASE ANALYSIS

You received the following letter from an upset parent. How would you reply?

Robert and Deborah Roebuck
1594 Hendon Road
Woodstock, GA 55555
404-555-8176

November 10, 20XX

Ms. Donna Shirley
Johnston Elementary School
Woodstock, GA 55555

Ms. Shirley:

Let me begin by stating how much Rob and I admire and support Hillary's teachers. We were somewhat concerned about moving from Cobb County to Cherokee two years ago, but have been delighted. Hillary has been fortunate to have excellent teachers and a wonderful school. She has always loved school.

I come from a family of teachers. My mother will retire this year after 30 years of elementary and middle school teaching. My father was a high school teacher, and I teach in the School of Business at Kennesaw State. I know the stress of teaching and the little reward one receives from teaching. I know that I teach because I enjoy seeing individuals succeed.

We have tried to teach Hillary to always be respectful of her teachers because we know firsthand how difficult it is to be a teacher. Teachers are overworked and underpaid. I know this is an extremely difficult year because of the large classes due to budget cuts.

Something happened last Thursday that upset Hillary terribly for the entire day and evening. From what she told us, she forgot a paper and received a warning for detention.

Last week was a difficult and busy week for us. We had commitments every night. I know that Hillary completed the paper because she did her homework while I fixed supper before we left Wednesday evening.

When she came home last Thursday, she was crying and stated she had the worst day of her life. She explained what happened and we tried to talk with her and comfort her. I tried to explain to Hillary that everyone makes mistakes because that is the way we learn. If we were perfect, we wouldn't have anything to learn. Nevertheless, she was upset all evening. At bedtime she realized that she had not completed her book for reading. She was absolutely scared to death that she would get detention. She cried so much she could not go to sleep and was afraid to go to school on Friday.

Since Hillary was so upset and afraid to go to school on Friday, I did not make her go. She stayed home to finish a few pages of her 161-page reading book. I am not sure what detention is, but it has scared Hillary.

We expect a lot of Hillary because we both work. She is an only child and we depend on her. She has to help take care of five horses every evening. This includes cleaning stalls, feeding, and watering them as well as bringing them in from the pasture. She is also responsible for her room and completing her homework.

It concerns me that Hillary was afraid to go to school Friday. This is the first time in her formal education that she has not wanted to go to school.

I remember when I was in sixth grade, my teacher's husband was the principal. I was afraid all that year that I would get sent to the Principal's office because Mr. Grimshaw was Mrs. Grimshaw's husband. I know that sounds silly, but at the time, it was frightening. I am now 39 years of age and still can remember how I felt then.

I do not want Hillary to be afraid to go to school or feel like she is a failure. I feel Rob and I are somewhat to blame for this incident because of our hectic schedule last week. According to Hillary, this is the only assignment she has failed to turn in. Her grade card was all A's as it has always been, so I feel she is probably telling me the truth.

I did not sleep well last Thursday because Hillary was so upset. I'm sure this experience will stay with her for a long time. I feel confident that she will not forget her paper again.

Because of the impact this warning has had on Hillary, is there any way that you can talk with Hillary? Maybe she has not turned something in or done something else which caused the warning. I do not think she could have been more upset. I told her a warning for detention might not be as serious as she seems to think it is. To her, nothing could be worse.

I was downtown last Friday at a conference. I had hoped to get by to talk with you then, but unfortunately, did not get home in time.

If you feel that a student, parent, and teacher conference is needed, please call me. I would appreciate either talking with you or hearing from you. I just want to understand the situation better. Thank you.

Sincerely,

Deborah Roebuck

Deborah Roebuck

CHAPTER 5

Writing Persuasively on Paper and in Electronic Formats

The fool tells me his reasons, but the wise man persuades me with my own.

Aristotle[1]

1 John J. Hagedorn, "Mastering the Gentle Art of Persuasion," *The Star*, March 9, 1998. Retrieved from http://mqv.min.edu.my/Newspaper/9803/9803136.htm.

LEARNING OBJECTIVES

After reading this chapter, you should be able to:

- Explain when to use the indirect persuasive writing approach or the direct approach.

- Detail the role of credibility.

- Define and explain AIDA.

- Describe a "hook."

- Compare and contrast emotional and logical appeals.

- List the different stages of the collection campaign.

- Describe how to increase the effectiveness of your writing.

The Importance of Persuasive Writing

In business, you will encounter situations requiring you to persuade others to take some specific action or support a particular position or person. Some examples might include (1) persuading others to replace outdated furniture, (2) trying to implement a clean air policy, or (3) recommending a certain individual for a job opening.

Your persuasive message can take the form of a letter, a memo, an e-mail, a proposal, an advertisement, or a presentation. Whatever form you choose, you want to persuade individuals to take action or to change their behavior. Therefore, you should know the rules of effective persuasion.

Persuasive writing requires you to show benefits to the reader. In other words, don't say to your reader: "I'm great, use me!" Instead, say: "Here's how your business will increase and improve if you use me." Your readers must be convinced of the benefits of accepting your proposals. Ask yourself this question: "*What's in it for the person I'm trying to influence?*"

As a persuasive writer, you must be viewed as credible. Readers must respect your ideas if they decide to "buy in" to your request to change their behavior. Your credibility as a writer hinges on these questions:

Do you appear trustworthy?

Do you have expertise and knowledge?

Do you appear dynamic and excited about your proposal?

Will your reader identify with your message?

WEB WRITING TIP: Credibility seems to be an important issue for Web writers, as visitors desire to know who the publisher of a particular site is and the source of the information found on that particular website. Your reader will want to know if your website is a reputable source and if they can trust the information you have placed there. The quality of your website's content will influence your users' evaluation of your credibility. One way to increase your credibility is by using outbound links, as they allow your reader to judge whether what you said was, in fact, true.

Writing Persuasively

When you write persuasively, you try to sell, convince, motivate, or create interest in your products, services, or ideas. If you wrote a persuasive message using the direct approach, you would begin with the most important idea, your request, followed by the persuasive information. Your reader would likely quit reading before you provided the facts and details—your persuasion. For example, a salesperson does not ask you to buy something without first telling you about its features and why you need it.

The indirect approach works best for persuasion because you want to explain before presenting the main point, known as the *hook*. The term "hook" comes from the advertising and public relations fields, where presenters have only a few seconds to make a point. When you write persuasively, you have only a few seconds to grab your reader. To write persuasively, follow the *AIDA* approach: *attention, interest, desire,* and *action.* See if Box 5.1 grabs your attention.

Dear Occupant:

Junk Mail!

Are you tired of receiving mountains of unwanted mail every year? You can, of course, stop such invasion of your privacy. And we can help you!

We can make sure your name never appears on another mailing list. You will never again be bothered with unwanted correspondence. To learn more, just complete the addressed card and mail it back.

You'll be glad you did!

Sincerely,

BOX 5.1 🖙 **A Convincing Form Letter**

ATTENTION

Why did you read the form letter in Box 5.1? Probably because it grabbed your attention. When you open with an attention-getting statement, you capture your readers' attention. You want your readers to keep reading, so you try to "hook" them with your first sentence. Wayne and Dauwalder[2] offer the following techniques to use in your attention-getting start:

1. Make an unusual, suspenseful, or startling statement.
2. Refer to a familiar event or timely concern.
3. Use a rhetorical question.
4. Use a quote.
5. Tell a story.
6. State a problem and promise to solve it.
7. Relate to readers' product or service needs.

Read in Box 5.2 a story about one of the most successful attention-getting starts to a persuasive document.

One of the most successful direct-mail marketing campaigns in history produced some unexpected results. Mailed out by *Reader's Digest,* the letter began: "If thou hast two pennies, spend one for bread and the other to buy hyacinths for the soul …" Two pennies were enclosed with each letter: one for bread, and one to be returned to reserve a subscription to the soul-satisfying *Reader's Digest.*

It was a great marketing ploy, but it required 100 million pennies. For a while, the U.S. Mint was worried that all the cents in New York City would end up at the *Reader's Digest*. The magazine's executive solved that problem by having 60 million pennies shipped in from around the country, but management's troubles weren't over yet. As the pennies piled up, the floor of the *Digest's* warehouse buckled under the weight. Nevertheless, the campaign continued, and the letters proved to be worth their weight in new subscriptions.

BOX 5.2 🖙 **An Innovating Idea**

SOURCE: Adapted from Milton Moskowitz, Michael Katz, and Robert Levering, Eds, *Everybody's Business: The Irreverent Guide to Corporate America* (San Francisco: Harper & Row, 1980). p. 400.

[2] F. Stanford Wayne and David P. Dauwalder, *Communicating in Business* (Burr Ridge, IL: Austin Press, Irwin, 1994), pp. 265–266.

INTEREST

Once you have captured your reader's attention, you must maintain that interest. Introduce your major selling point by stating a benefit, filling a need, or showing a distinct advantage. Your product, service, or idea has a specific appeal, such as financial security, convenience, safety, recreation, or dependability. Determine your appeal and explain how your product or service will satisfy the reader's needs.

DESIRE

At this stage, you build up the reader's desire to act. You move your reader from "I'd like to have that" to "I really need that." The desire you create will make the reader feel a need for your product or service. You can choose either an emotional or a logical appeal.

Emotional Appeal. If you sell your product or service to the public, use an emotional appeal aiming at the heart or ego. You may want your readers to desire your product because "everyone else" has one. Try to stir up various types of feelings within your reader with an emotional appeal. As Bert Decker says in his book, *You've Got to Be Believed to Be Heard,* "You must make emotional contact with your audience. You must reach the hearts as well as the minds of your listeners."[3]

Logical Appeal.   Writers use the logical appeal for business transactions. In business settings, decision makers make choices based on cost versus benefits. When employing this appeal, use logic emphasizing high benefits for relative low cost.

The following examples present different ways to appeal to your reader:

Gaining a sense of satisfaction

Giving comfort or convenience

Saving time, money, effort, or merchandise

Creating and maintaining goodwill

Increasing health benefits

Adding prestige, exclusiveness, or distinction

Gaining attractiveness

Adding taste or wholesomeness

Gaining safety or security

Typically, you de-emphasize the cost of the product, service, or idea, unless price happens to be your major selling point. You learned that in writing bad-news documents, you explain the reasons before presenting the bad news. The same principle applies to persuasive writing. You want your reader to value what you offer and believe that the benefits outweigh the costs.

WEB WRITING TIP: When you write for the Web, you want to sell your reader on the benefits of your product or service. Your readers should know why that benefit is important to *them*. You will need to determine if a logical or emotional appeal is appropriate in describing your benefits.[4]

ACTION

The last paragraph presents the main message. At this stage, you want your reader to take some kind of action, so you make doing so easy, specific, and clear. The clos-

---

[3]Bert Decker, "You've Got to Be Believed to be Heard," (New York, NY: St. Martin's Press, 1992), p. 4.

[4] Joe Robson, "How to Win the Sales Copy Writing Game," retrieved from: *http://www.successfulminds.com/copywriting/sales-copy-game.html.*

ing allows you to stress any timely connection and to reaffirm your hook. You can also connect the action with a reward to encourage the reader to act quickly. You can use the 6 W's to write persuasively:

- What are you trying to persuade? Who is your audience?
- Why do they need your product or service?
- What are the benefits and features of your product or service?
- How do they know you are the right person or company and that it is the right product or service?
- What is the next step?
- When do they need to make a decision?[5]

Box 5.3 shows a letter using this AIDA approach.

WEB WRITING TIP: The action step is critical when you write for the Web. You must determine what you want a reader to do after visiting your website. One way you can lead your reader through the content of your site is by using action-oriented headings that clearly indicate to the readers what they should do.[6]

Persuasive messages can also be used to sell ideas. The letter in Box 5.4 illustrates how a writer used persuasion to sell an idea.

To write persuasively, you must know your product or service, your market, and the sales situation. Your letters will be read if you follow the AIDA plan and apply the principles listed in Box 5.5.

WEB WRITING TIP: When a reader visits your website, you want to persuade him or her to respond in some way. Use the following 14 tips to help you get the response you want.

1. Always focus on the needs, wants, and desires of your readers.
2. Grab attention in the first line.
3. "Chat" on paper to someone you know. Don't write to people in general.
4. Concentrate on the benefits (not the features) of your solution, service, or product.
5. Give specific, relevant information and don't be vague.
6. Use action verbs and write conversationally.
7. Be concise, but say what is necessary.
8. Provide a guarantee.
9. Keep your sentences short. (Maximum of 16 words on average)
10. Keep paragraphs short. (Maximum of five lines)
11. Tell your readers exactly what they need to do.
12. Always include a postscript with an incentive to act now.
13. Bold your headlines, use white space, and align your text to the left.
14. Ask someone to read your text aloud. If they frown, hesitate, or stumble, rewrite.[7]

The American List Council (ALC) has created an impressive website that houses many publications related to business writing and marketing: *http://www.*

---

[5]Kris Mills, "The 6 W's of Writing Persuasive Proposals," March 6, 2003. Retrieved from *http://www. ecomhelp.com/KB/ career/kb_the-six-ws-of-writing-persuasive-proposals.htm.*

[6] Jeannine Gailey, "Writing for the Web: Create Appealing Online Content," posted February 11, 2002. Retrieved from *http://www.microsoft.com/office/previous/frontpage/columns/sbcolumn04.asp.*

[7] "Tips for Persuasive Writing," *Quality Web Content,* retrieved from: *http://www.webpagecontent.com/ arc_archive/42/5/.*

IBM Credit Corporation

200 Harbor Drive
P.O. Box 10399
Stamford, CT 06904-2399
203/973-5100

April 20, 20XX

Mr. Robert Waterhouse
Data Processing Manager
New England Mail Rite
160 Southampton Street
Boston, MA 02118

Dear Mr. Waterhouse:

Attention

Accelerating technology, intensifying financial pressures and more aggressive competition are forcing your business to adapt more rapidly than ever. With this in mind—and based on feedback from our customers—BMI Credit has changed to be more responsive to your needs in these challenging times.

Interest

First, we broadened our cost-effective, flexible financing to cover your entire information technology investment—large systems or personal computers; hardware, software, maintenance and services; domestic or international; new or refurbished; sourced from IBM, other manufacturers or remarketers. You do not need to tie up your capital with large front-end investments or look for multiple financing sources.

Desire

Second, we created innovative services and lease features to make our financing even more valuable to you. You capture the benefits of rapidly improving technology, maintain tight control of your computing budget, avoid obsolescence and minimize equipment disposal issues with our technology upgrade options, version-to-version software upgrades and fixed-rate financing. You can even manage your entire information technology investment using AssetNet (TM), our proprietary asset-tracking system.

Action

This letter cannot do justice to the many ways we can help you. To learn more, please indicate your interests on the enclosed card and drop it in the mail. For your future reference, I have also enclosed a business card of the IBM Credit customer financing executive responsible for our business with you.

Sincerely,

John Callies
John E. Callies
General Manager, End-User Customer Financing

/lam

BOX 5.3 👉 **Selling a Service**

TO: Eloise Hambert, President

FROM: Janson Brawley, Sales Manager

DATE: June 3, 20XX

SUBJECT: Parking Lots

Our employee parking lots tell their own story. They let customers know how much confidence we place in our product.

Whenever individuals from the automobile industry visit our plant, they park in Parking Lots 1 and 2. When they park their cars, they see approximately 33 percent foreign-made cars.

I realize many factors impact an individual's choice in buying an automobile. However, nearly all of our business comes from the American automobile industry. A visitor from one leading American automobile company asked me last week, "How can you expect us to support you, when you don't support us?"

I would like to request we build a separate visitor parking lot close to the building. Visitors then would not notice what the employees drive. I have researched the feasibility of constructing a visitor parking lot and have determined it will take approximately four to six weeks to complete.

I would like to announce your approval of this new plan at our quarterly meeting to be held on July 8. Please let me know your thoughts within the next week.

BOX 5.4 🖝 **Selling an Idea**

- Use a strong, interesting, and hard-hitting opener to get the reader's attention. Limit the use of *I*. Don't begin a letter with "Thank you"; the reader may think you have nothing more to say and stop reading.
- Present the company and the product or service as a benefit or solution. Don't just list a product's features. Instead, tell how the reader benefits from each of them.
- Keep your letter short. Put extra information on an attachment sheet.
- Make a prompt call to action. Use the P.S. for important selling or benefit points.
- Keep a file of direct-mail letters you have received that attracted your attention and prompted a favorable response. Use them to give you ideas about writing your own persuasive documents.

BOX 5.5 🖝 **Tips for Better Sales Letters**

amlist.com/Knowledge/articlelist.asp. For example, one article, "Power Words Add Punch to Your Writing," lists words that add pizzazz to your direct mailings, one form of persuasive writing. The article suggests that for a positive appeal, you use the words "make money" or "own business." For a negative appeal, use "work less" or "worry less." Power words such as "free" or "discount" also move the reader to take action. This website offers over 50 articles related to every aspect of direct mail.[8]

[8] "Web Can Help You with Business Writing," *Link-Up,* Volume 13, Issue 4, pp. 24–25, July/August, 1996.

E-Mail Sales Messages

Today, many individuals are overwhelmed by the amount of unsolicited junk e-mail or spam that they receive. Unsolicited e-mail creates ill will instead of goodwill. If you chose to write online persuasive documents, follow these techniques.[9]

- Be selective. Make sure you have permission to send e-mail marketing messages.
- Use the receiver's name.
- Write a strong subject line. Your subject line should tell your readers what the message is about before they open it.
- Keep the message short, conversational, and focused on one or two central selling points.
- Never begin with "Thank you." You only have a few seconds to grab the reader's attention. Start strong. Make your point in the first few words of the first paragraph, then repeat, rephrase, and reiterate.
- Make a strong offer. Be sure you know your audience so that you can tailor the offer to the buying behavior, needs, and concerns of your readers. Highlight the offer in the subject line or first sentence. Focus on benefits.
- Motivate a response. Make it easy to respond. If you want them to visit your website, provide a hot link or a reward for clicking your way. Give a discount or gift for an immediate response.
- Provide a means for being removed from the mailing list. It's polite and a good business tactic to include a statement that tells readers how to be removed from your mailing database.
- Do not give prospects reasons to disqualify you. Speedy does not mean sloppy. Every e-mail you write reflects on your professionalism and credibility. Spell check and proofread.[10]

Collection Letters

On occasion, customers fall behind in paying their bills. When this happens, the company usually wants to receive payment but also retain the customer. Through a collection campaign, the company's representatives carefully persuade the customer to pay.

Collection letters require a strategy all their own. The process, called the *collection campaign,* occurs over several months. The collection campaign usually includes four steps: *friendly reminder, stronger reminder, discussion letter,* and *urgent appeal.*

FRIENDLY REMINDER

The friendly reminder assumes customers have just forgotten or overlooked paying. The writer uses a friendly, nonaccusing approach. Depending on the relationship between the customer and the company, several friendly reminders may be sent. The friendly reminder gently urges customers to pay. Box 5.6 presents a sample of a friendly reminder.

---

[9] Mary Ellen Guffey, *Essentials of Business Communication,* 6th edition (Mason, OH: Thomson-South-Western, 2004), pp. 185–187.

[10] Nancy Flynn, "The ePolicy Handbook, Writing Effective E-Mail, and E-Mail Rules," Spring 2003. Retrieved from *http://www.epolicyinstitute.com.*

> If we help you, you must help us! By pulling together, we can help each other through this period of temporary difficulty. But first, we must have a clear understanding of the problem.
>
> Have you overlooked paying your bill of $75.43? If so, please use the enclosed, addressed envelope to mail it today!

BOX 5.6 ☛ **Body of a Friendly Reminder**

STRONGER REMINDER

At this stage, you still assume customers will pay, but have just overlooked the debt again. In the stronger reminder, you tell receivers of the value of the products or services. You remind them of their value to the organization.

DISCUSSION OR INQUIRY LETTER

At this stage, the company wants to know why customers have not responded. No longer does the company consider the nonpayment an oversight. Something has definitely caused customers not to pay. Now you want to know why they have not paid, so you ask for an explanation. If a person has been a good customer, he or she likely will pay.

In this letter, appeal to such things as pride, equality, and self-interest. State that the customers will feel a sense of pride in knowing they have honored their financial obligation. In appealing to equality, state that the company has lived up to its obligation and now they must live up to theirs. In appealing to self-interest, remind customers of the valuable role credit plays in our lives. If they want to continue to use credit, they must pay to preserve their credit rating. Note how the writer has composed the body of the discussion letter presented in Box 5.7.

> In a few days, we must audit our accounts. At that time, we must make a decision on those accounts that are seriously past due.
>
> As you might imagine, we struggle over when to place an account with a collection agency. We weigh the advantages and disadvantages with a great deal of care—especially in your case.
>
> Your goodwill, after all, has always been important to us. We truly do not want to take any action that might jeopardize your credit standing and cause you embarrassment or added expense. Our contract states you will be held responsible for collection and legal fees.
>
> Yet I think you will agree we have been fair. We have offered to extend you credit based on your promise to pay according to our terms. Since then, we have contacted you numerous times without response, and now we must consider the possibility of placing your account with our collection agency.
>
> Still, we hope you will act promptly and pay your overdue account today. We will wait 10 days from the date of this letter before we take action.
>
> We must hear from you within those 10 days. If not, we will have to make a decision that neither of us wants.

BOX 5.7 ☛ **Body of Discussion Letter Appeal**

It says, "Dear Taxpayer, If you do not pay your back taxes immediately, we will seize your home and car, drain your bank accounts, sell your personal property, and probably put you in jail. We hope this does not inconvenience you."

You can offer alternatives, such as allowing customers to make a partial payment, setting up a schedule of smaller payments, or extending the deadline. You want a response from the customers. Usually you have to write only one letter at this stage. Most organizations send this type of letter when the account becomes more than 90 days past due.

URGENT APPEAL

If customers do not respond to the discussion letter, the company must move to a stronger approach. At this stage, the account may be as much as 120 days past due. You must impress on the customer the seriousness of the situation. Do not make threats; simply state facts. You can, however, refer to the possibility of legal action.

Your tone becomes stronger and more demanding in this letter. You emphasize that the customers must pay and that you have already discussed all the reasons why they should pay.

Specific Persuasive Openings for Letters and Memos

The following are examples of how to write persuasively. Note the attention-getting start in each example.

SOLICITED AND UNSOLICITED APPEALS TO BUY GOODS OR SERVICES

Riches are where you find them—in a sunset, in autumn leaves, in memories, in people's hearts, in thoughts, or—best of all—in your pockets!

MEMOS SELLING A SERVICE OR IDEA

A new employee must often overcome the difficult problem of fitting into a team. Fortunately for Wards' employees, this problem doesn't exist because of our extensive Team Building Program.

SPECIAL REQUESTS FOR INFORMATION OR ASSISTANCE

In recent weeks, several companies have had lawsuits brought against them for sexual harassment. The people taking action were not clients of those companies, but employees. Williams and Williams could easily become a target for similar lawsuits if we are not extremely careful in handling employees' complaints.

REQUESTS TO GRANT COMPLEX CLAIMS

On October 3, I purchased a silk dress at your Main Street store. To achieve a good fit, extensive alterations had to be made. I left the dress, intending to pick it up in a week. Before the week was over, I was involved in an automobile accident that caused me to spend the next 35 days in the hospital. Since then, I've lost several pounds and the dress now doesn't fit.

APPEALS FOR DONATIONS OR CONTRIBUTIONS

Friday, May 19, Tim Wyatt had no desire to leave his warm bed at 2 A.M. Yet, when the fire monitor sounded in his bedroom, Tim dressed quickly and drove four miles to join his fellow volunteer firefighters in combating a house fire. Within 30 minutes, the fire was under control; Tim got home at 5:45 A.M., in time to shower and dress for his regular job.

APPEALS TO PAY DEBTS

When you first applied for a credit line with our firm, the people who gave references were very complimentary. They used phrases such as "excellent worker," "reliable and responsible," and "a person who can be counted on." At present, your account is past due, and we are concerned.

Superior/Subordinate Messages: Using the Direct Approach for Some Situations

According to Scott Ober, most superiors prefer to have messages from their subordinates organized in the direct writing approach. When your persuasive messages travel up the organizational ladder, the direct approach saves time and immediately satisfies your reader's curiosity about why you are writing. To get your reader's acceptance, you should present your recommendation along with the criteria or a brief explanation in your opening paragraph. Some situations that may call for the direct approach include:

- You are writing to superiors within your organization.
- Your audience is predispoed to listen objectively to your request.
- The proposal does not require strong persuasion as no major obstacles exist.
- Your proposal is long or complex so your reader may become impatient if you don't get to the point quickly.
- You know your reader prefers the direct approach.[11]

[11] Scott Ober, *Fundamentals of Contemporary Business Communication* (Boston: Houghton Mifflin Company, 2004), pp. 208–209.

Effective Writing Strategies

Follow the principles of effective business writing to increase the chances of your document being read. You can increase its effectiveness by following these suggestions: Choose effective, colorful words; write effective, readable sentences; use appropriate paragraphs; and emphasize your ideas.

CHOOSE EFFECTIVE, COLORFUL WORDS

A Yale University study identified the 12 most persuasive words in the English language.[12] These words are: "you," "health," "money," "safety," "save," "love," "new," "discovery," "results," "proven," "easy," and "guarantee." Most of these words appeal to us because they refer to a personal need. Draw your readers into accepting your proposal by using words that help them imagine themselves using your product or services.

Another simple persuasive technique involves personalizing your documents by frequently using the receiver's name. This strategy makes the message seem more real to the receiver.

Use positive, accurate words to create the right impression. Do not use technical words, which create confusion for your reader. Review Table 5.1 for words people like and dislike.

WRITE EFFECTIVE, READABLE SENTENCES

As you learned in previous chapters, short, simple sentences help focus attention on key ideas. Do not bury your main idea in long, complex sentences. Instead, emphasize the important points to help the reader process your message.

TABLE 5.1 ☞ **Liked and disliked words.**

Most People Like These Words

advantage	ease	integrity	responsible
appreciate	economy	justice	satisfactory
benefit	effective	kind	service
capable	efficient	loyalty	success
confidence	energy	please	superior
conscientious	enthusiasm	popularity	useful
cooperation	genuine	practical	valuable
courtesy	helpful	prestige	vigor
dependable	honesty	progress	you
desirable	honor	reliable	yours

Most People Dislike These Words

abuse	decline	ignorant	squander
alibi	discredit	imitation	superficial
allege	dispute	implicate	tardy
apology	exaggerate	impossible	timid
beware	extravagance	misfortune	unfair
blame	failure	negligent	unfortunate
cheap	fault	opinionated	unsuccessful
commonplace	fear	prejudiced	waste
complaint	fraud	retrench	worry
crisis	hardship	rude	wrong

SOURCE: Ted Pollock, "A Personal File of Stimulating Ideas and Problem Solvers," *Supervision,* Volume 46, Issue 2, February 1984, p. 25.

[12] *CBS College Publishing,* The Dryden Press, Holt, Rinehart, and Winston, Saunders College Publishing, 383 Madison Avenue, New York, NY 10017. Copyright © 1985 CBS College Publishing.

Use complex sentences to tie together features and benefits. Complex sentences also allow you to match up negatives with positives. Emphasize the positives by putting them in the independent clauses of the sentence.

USE APPROPRIATE PARAGRAPHS

As in all writing situations, short paragraphs help emphasize key ideas. In persuasive documents, use long paragraphs to explain your services, products, or ideas. However, keep your closing action paragraph relatively short so your reader can easily determine what action needs to be taken.

EMPHASIZE YOUR IDEAS

If you have important ideas to emphasize, consider using dashes, bullets, numbers, arrows, underlines, or italics to set them off. Do not use all of these techniques in one document; rather, pick out two or three techniques you think will best represent your ideas. Overusing these techniques can distract your reader.

When using dashes, bullets, numbers, and arrows, check your items to make sure they are parallel in their structure.

Underlines or italics call attention to words or phrases. You can also use pictures or diagrams to emphasize an important point visually.[13]

The letter in Box 5.8 encompasses the principles presented in this chapter.

East Cobb Pediatrics and Adolescent Medicine

Diplomats, American Board of Pediatrics
Comprehensive Pediatric Services
from Birth through Age 21

February 12, 20XX

Editor
Physician's Journal
704 N. Rush St.
Chicago, IL 60611

Dear Editor:

I find your magazine informative and timely. John Hope's article, "Armchair Ed," that appeared in your September 1999 issue was read and discussed in class at Kennesaw State University as part of the MBA Program for Physician Executives (MBA-PE).

BOX 5.8 🖙 **Presenting New Ideas**

---

[13] F. Stanford Wayne and David P. Dauwalder, *Communicating in Business* (Burr Ridge, IL: Austin Press, Irwin, 1994), pp. 272–274.

Editor
Page 2
February 12, 20XX

Having practiced pediatric medicine in the Atlanta area for 30 years, I consider myself a true "armchair Ed" (not quite a "rocking chair Ed"). Until I enrolled in Kennesaw State's unique MBA program, I would have agreed with colleagues who said, "I just want to practice medicine, and let someone else worry about the business." This way of thinking could result in costly mistakes.

If physicians and their organizations are to succeed in the modern health care environment, they must learn the language of business. Dr. Timothy Mescon, Dean of the Cole School of Business, summarized the concepts of the MBA-PE Program as follows: "… knowledge gained today can solve today's problems, but only the critical capacity to seek knowledge can solve the challenges to come."

Some of the unique features of the MBA-PE Program are:
- The program was conceived five years ago as the brainchild of a former cardiologist, Dr. Robert Lipson, MD, MBA. Dr. Lipson and other physicians in his group, the Promina Northwest Health System in Atlanta, GA, partnered with KSU to develop the original 18-month program.
- The program, now in its fifth year with almost 100 students, adds a new dimension to the concept of distance learning through a Lotus Notes platform. Through laptop computers, the virtual classroom brings knowledge, research, instruction and discussion with other physicians directly to the participants. The need to physically attend classes on campus is limited to once a month.
- Dr Lipson wrote in *Health System Review,* "The program is taught in a team environment simulating the workplace. Individuals who complete the program become adept Physician Executive leaders and managers with fresh ideas, broadened perspectives, increased awareness of technology and an expanded business and health care network."
- The program is less expensive than other MBA programs. The tuition, $24,000, is payable in four installments.

Physicians frequently complain that we are losing control of the business side of medicine. How about joining those of us who believe that the stethoscope, the medical chart, the spreadsheet, and the laptop are not mutually exclusive.

Sincerely,

Eduardo Montana, Sr.
Eduardo Montana, Sr., M.D.

Main Office:
1121 Johnson Ferry Road • Suite 220
Marietta, Georgia 30068
Voice (770) 977-0094 • Fax (770) 5099463

Kennesaw Office:
3895 Cherokee Street • Suite 160-170
Kennesaw, Georgia 30144
Voice (770) 795-1553 • Fax (770) 795-1513

BOX 5.8 ☞ (continued)

Using the Persuasive Approach with International Audiences

When writing to international audiences, you must first determine if your receivers are from low- or high-context countries. In a high-context country, status is extremely important and facts become more subjective and personal as the words and arguments are not separated from the writer. In these cases, the indirect persuasive approach may not work. However, when writing to individuals from low-context countries, where the meaning is trusted almost entirely to words, you can use the indirect persuasive writing approach. Once again, these two examples highlight the fundamental truth of knowing your reader and the culture from which he or she comes.[14]

Conclusion

This chapter presented strategies and techniques for writing persuasive documents. Persuasive writing requires practice, because you must sell a product, a service, or an idea. The AIDA (attention, interest, desire, and action) approach will help you win your reader. With practice, you can get the action you seek for yourself and your organization. Use the checklist in Table 5.2 as you develop your persuasive letters and memos. Visit this website for additional ideas on writing persuasively: *http://home.comcast.net/~garbl/writing/action.htm#persuasively*.

TABLE 5.2 Checklist for writing persuasively.

	YES	NO
1. Does the first paragraph capture the reader's attention?	❏	❏
2. Does it state why this document has been created (the hook)?	❏	❏
3. Does the second paragraph gain the reader's interest?	❏	❏
4. Does the third paragraph create desire for your product or service?	❏	❏
5. Does the document use the correct appeal (emotional or logical)?	❏	❏
6. Does the last paragraph make the reader want to take action?	❏	❏
7. Have you made taking action easy to do?	❏	❏
8. Did you use effective, colorful words?	❏	❏
9. Did you write effective sentences and appropriate paragraphs?	❏	❏
10. Did you emphasize your ideas by using some kind of signposting (using numbers, bullets, headings, tables, or lists)?	❏	❏

[14] Linda Beamer and Iris Varner, *Intercultural Communication in the Global Workplace* (New York: McGraw Hill/Irwin, 2001), pp. 133–135.

Exercises

EXERCISE 1 OPENING STATEMENTS FOR PERSUASIVE MESSAGES

Directions: Create more attention-getting openings.

Request to participate in United Way Campaign:

Ineffective: Can you think of any reason you shouldn't participate in the annual United Way Campaign?

Effective: _____

Request for a donation of a television set to a senior retirement home:

Ineffective: A recent study showed most senior citizens who are in a retirement home watch television as their major source of entertainment.

Effective: _____

Persuade employees to donate blood:

Ineffective: Please stop by the lunch room to donate blood next week.

Effective: _____

Persuade reader to buy a horse magazine:

Ineffective: A saddle, a bridle, a blanket, a horse—these are things that make up an enjoyable afternoon.

Effective: _____

EXERCISE 2 COLLABORATIVELY COMPOSING A SALES LETTER

Directions: Invent a product or service college students need to survive. If you cannot invent something, use an existing product or service. Persuade your classmates to buy your product or service. For two class periods, you will work in teams developing a sales letter. Then you will make copies of your letters. After the class reads all the letters, they will vote for the best.

Assignment Options

OPTION 1—COLLECTION CAMPAIGN

As credit manager for a large hardware store in Woodstock, Georgia, you often allow customers to purchase appliances on credit. A year ago, Mike and Mary Salsman used store credit to purchase a washer and dryer for their new home. The set cost $913 and the Salsmans were to make monthly installments of $50 or more. Both individuals have steady jobs. Mike works as a contractor and Mary teaches school.

For six months, the Salsmans have made regular monthly payments (for a total of $300), but they have not made the current month's payment. Write them a friendly reminder.

Now, three months have passed. You have received no payments from the Salsmans, though you have sent them a courteous reminder. You suspect they may have become overextended with their new home. Write an appropriate inquiry or discussion letter.

Two more months have passed and you have still received no news from the Salsmans. Yet one night you see them dining at the Steak Palace, Woodstock's most expensive restaurant. Write an urgent appeal to Mike and Mary Salsman.

OPTION 2—WILL THEY CHANGE?

Several longtime customers of Bank Company have had regular passbook accounts for years. These sizable accounts could be earning more money in other programs you have available.

These conservative individuals like having their money where they can get it quickly without penalties, if the necessity arises. They are concerned primarily with security.

You have been asked to prepare a persuasive letter informing them of the benefits of changing to one of the higher-interest-bearing accounts.

CHAPTER 6

Writing Memos, E-Mails, and Short Reports

*T*he first written reference to a "memorandum" appeared in 1433 in Britain's Rolls of Parliament. In 1465, a written communication to one Thomas More began "Memorandum to Thomas More that because ye myzt foryete myne errand to Maister Bernay, I pray you rede hym my bille."[1]

Hal Fahner

[1] Hal Fahner, "The 10 Commandments of Memo Writing," *Sales & Marketing Management,* October 1990, p. 85.

LEARNING OBJECTIVES

After reading this chapter, you should be able to:

- Describe situations in which you would write a memo.

- List the advantages of the memo.

- Detail the heading of a memo.

- List the characteristics of successful memos.

- Explain conversational tone.

- Define signposting.

- Distinguish between short and long reports as well as between informal and formal reports.

- Compare and contrast a progress report, a periodic report, an executive memo report, and a justification report.

- Explain what a feasibility report investigates.

- Discuss when to use a proposal.
- List the standard parts of a proposal.
- Describe a policy.
- Present an example of a procedure.
- Distinguish between rules and guides.
- List the guidelines for writing policies and procedures.
- Explain why you should not use *shall* and *will* in policies and procedures.
- List reasons why you should use e-mail.
- State the guidelines for electronic mail.
- Explain flaming and how to control it.

The Importance of Writing E-Mails and Memos

E-mails and memos are the most widely used type of written communication. Not surprisingly, electronic mail has become the main communication channel for millions. Both educational establishments and the business world recognize the benefits of using electronic mail. The public sectors, such as government and health, are also taking advantage of new technology.[2] Problems occur with e-mail when senders assume no one else can read their messages.

E-mails and memos share some of the same characteristics while differing in others. One major difference between e-mail and memos is that memos are used only for communication within an organization. Within an organization, some of the niceties of letter writing (see Chapter 7) are sacrificed for the sake of conciseness. However, since e-mail is used both inside and outside of the organization, salutations and closings are typically employed when using e-mail to communicate outside of the organization.

E-mails and memos typically request information, reinforce agreements, clarify previous messages, or deliver short reports about daily organizational problems.[3] In some cases, e-mail memos are taking the place of the traditional paper memo as organizations rapidly move toward paperless correspondence. E-mail allows organizations, employees, and clients to communicate on a global basis at virtually any time and any place. You can visit this website to measure your EQ (E-mail Quotient): *http://www.ewriteonline.com/test/.*

Advantages of E-Mails and Memos

E-mails and memos have three distinct advantages: You can send one document to many individuals simultaneously, you have a written record for review, and you can transmit complex information.

---

[2] "E-Commerce Is the Great Enabler," *Management Today,* March 1999, p. 5.

[3] Anita S. Bednard and Robert J. Olney, "Communication Needs of Recent Graduates," *The Bulletin of the Association for Business Communication,* December 1987, p. 22.

MANY RECEIVERS

E-mails and memos quickly and efficiently deliver information to one employee or several employees. You can send an e-mail memo almost immediately to another computer, whether in the next cubicle or around the world.

WRITTEN RECORD

In the workforce, you must often "put it in writing," that is, document a transaction or a situation. You can refer to the written e-mail or memo later to jog your memory as your e-mail message can be printed, edited, stored, deleted, or forwarded to someone else.

COMPLEX INFORMATION

E-mails and memos provide a way to send complex information and follow up on oral conversations. If you only *tell* an employee rather than follow-up with an e-mail or written memo, the employee may forget how to complete a project. Instead of asking you for help, the individual may try to remember and thus make a major mistake. If you simply write the employee an e-mail or written memo, it will provide a record of all the necessary details to ensure accurate completion of a task.

Format of E-Mails and Memos

Typically e-mail programs use the standardized memo format of: *to, from, date,* and *subject. This heading helps readers identify immediately who is the recipient of the message, who wrote the message, when it was sent, and why it was written.* By adhering to this format, you can ensure certain types of information always appear in the same place.

Within the body of an e-mail message that is going outside of the organization, the writer should include a salutation that can simply state the individual's name, can use "Dear" and the individual's name, "Hi," or "Greetings." You should use a colon, not a comma, after the salutation. Some appropriate closings include "Good Wishes" or "Best Regards." Then you type or enter an electronic signature at the end of your message so that your reader can identify you. At a minimum, you should include your name, title, and organization within the signature line.

In some organizations, e-mail writers will use salutations and closings internally as well as externally. Because the rules for electronic communication are still evolving, you will see variations in style and format, so the key for you is to be consistent. Box 6.1 provides an example of a memo and an e-mail.

Note that in some organizations, the four basic elements may appear in a different order. However, the key for any organization is to develop and use a consistent format. As the writer (*From*), show your title or position unless the reader knows this information. Usually, *Miss, Mrs.,* or *Ms.* do not appear before the receiver's name (*To*) in a memo, although you can include them if you prefer. However, *Mr.* is never used before a man's name. To show that you, the writer, proofread your memo, place your initials beside your name (either written in paper correspondence or by using a script font if the memo will be sent electronically). Because you normally do not sign a memo, the complimentary close is omitted.

Single-space the body of your memo and double-space between paragraphs. You may block or indent your paragraphs, but most writers use block paragraphs to save time. Side margins should be approximately one inch. Do not center the memo vertically; instead, place the memo heading one inch from the top of the page.

TO: All Toys Be Us Associates

FROM: Tom Bergage *tb*

DATE: October 4, 20XX

SUBJECT: Tobacco-free work facility

Our Human Resources Department has shared that six out of ten employees hospitalized last year had a tobacco-related illness. Studies published recently in the *Journal of Public Health* showed tobacco-free workplaces lead to declining employee tobacco use, which translates into better health.

Many of you have contacted me to express your concerns about cigarette butts being scattered around the entrances to our building. When our customers see this litter, they do not form a favorable impression of our facility.

In the past few years, we have made great strides in eliminating tobacco usage in our work areas. Beginning next month, our entire facility will become a tobacco-free environment. Making this change will allow us to take more pride in our workplace and enjoy a healthier environment.

Because we value you as an employee, we have set up a special program to assist anyone who would like help to stop smoking. We pledge to keep all inquiries concerning this program confidential. In addition, you can contact the American Lung Association at 800-586-4872 or *www.lungusa.org,* or the American Cancer Society at 800-227-2345 or *www.cancer.org.*

We hope you will agree that a tobacco-free environment will result in better health for all of us.

"David Shepherd"
<dshepher@kennesaw.edu>   To:<Deborah_Roebuck@coles2.kennesaw.edu>
                           cc:
07/10/2004 09:51 PM   Subject: National Collegiate Sales Competition-
                           Delegated

Dear Deborah:

This past weekend the Kennesaw State University Center for Professional Selling hosted the National Collegiate Sales Competition. Students and faculty from a total of 32 universities from California to Georgia Southern to University of Connecticut to ITSM of Monterey, Mexico, were here for the competition. Also, 22 sponsoring businesses were here to meet the students and help in the competition. It was an amazing success! In particular, I would like to note that over 120 of our students volunteered and played a very important role in making the competition a success. Also, I am extremely happy to note that our team (Rhonda Fleming and Heather Riemer) finished second in the team competition. In fact, Rhonda was the overall Champion! Please join me in congratulating Rhonda and Heather.

BOX 6.1 ☞ **Memo Format**

The 20XX National Collegiate Sales Competition was truly a team effort and a team success! Please join me in thanking Terry Loe for Directing the NCSC, Mary Foster for doing an amazing job supporting the competition, Randy Stuart for overseeing the critical judging process, Gary Selden for chairing our golf tournament, and Keith Tudor and Tim Mescon for their continued support of this wonderful student learning experience.

Additionally, thanks should go to Karl Aldag and PTD for their awesome support of the competition, Leslie Clark-Matzhan and Teri Ray for coordinating the many events involved in the competition, and Sodexho for preparing the wonderful meals. Finally, thanks also go to Moe Wortham for the outstanding job Facilities and Plant Operations did in making our building and facilities look beautiful.

On a final note, please join me in congratulating Randy Hinds on receiving the Center for Professional Selling Leadership Award for his leadership and support in the development of our Center, which is widely acknowledged as the technological leader in sales education at the university and corporate levels.

Best Regards,

C. David Shepherd

C. David Shepherd, Ph.D.
Professor of Marketing & Director,
Center for Professional Selling
Kennesaw State University
Department of Marketing & Professional Sales
1000 Chastain Rd. #0406
248 Burruss BLDG. #4, Rm. 248
Kennesaw, GA 30144–5591
(770) 423–6405
(770) 499–3261 fax
david_shepherd@coles2.kennesaw.edu

BOX 6.1 ☛ (continued)

---

1. Be specific with your request for action. When and how should the receiver of the message follow up?
2. Refer to only one subject per e-mail message. That way, receivers can respond easily and file the message under the appropriate topic for future reference.
3. If the e-mail is urgent and you are unsure when the receiver will check for messages, leave a "heads up" voice-mail message directing that person to his or her e-mail for the details.

BOX 6.2 ☛ **Tips for Writing Effective E-Mail Messages**

SOURCE: Making the Spoken Connection—Free Newsletter: *http://www.joshhunt. com/Decker/vol3winter.html.*

If a memo requires a second page, use a second-page heading. List the receiver's name, the date, and the page number. Center or block this information, depending on whether you indented or blocked your paragraphs. Be consistent throughout your document.

As in all business writing situations, the appearance of a memo paints a picture of you and your organization. A neat, attractive document will be read! Now that you know how to set up your e-mail memo, refer to the tips in Box 6.2 to get results.

Characteristics of Successful Memos, E-Mails, and Electronic Documents

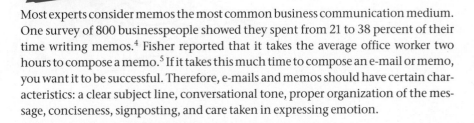

Most experts consider memos the most common business communication medium. One survey of 800 businesspeople showed they spent from 21 to 38 percent of their time writing memos.[4] Fisher reported that it takes the average office worker two hours to compose a memo.[5] If it takes this much time to compose an e-mail or memo, you want it to be successful. Therefore, e-mails and memos should have certain characteristics: a clear subject line, conversational tone, proper organization of the message, conciseness, signposting, and care taken in expressing emotion.

CONTAINS A CLEAR SUBJECT LINE

Because people feel flooded with e-mails, memos, and reports, you need to make your purpose for writing clear. The subject line tells the recipient the purpose of the message. It can be the most important part of your message as it may help determine if an individual will open your e-mail or not. If your readers have difficulty deciding the purpose of your e-mail or memo or why they received it, they probably will not continue to read.

The subject line needs to be specific enough to differentiate the message from another on the same subject. The subject line should clearly state your reason for writing. Study the following examples:

E-Mail Subject Too General: Training Session

Better E-Mail Subject: Dates of 20XX Training Sessions

or

Evaluation of Training Sessions on Conducting Interviews

or

Should We Schedule a Short Course on Proposal Writing?

E-Mail Subject Too General: Business Communication Conference in Romania

Sounds like a conference announcement and would likely be deleted unread by somebody who doesn't plan to travel to Romania any time soon.

Better E-Mail Subject: Invitation—Keynote Speaker at Romanian Business Communication Conference

E-Mail Subject Too General: Your Computer Order

Too general and might appear as spam; in all likelihood, the message will be deleted rather than read.

Better E-Mail Subject: Hard Drive Shipped Today from Computer Land

This example starts with an information-carrying word and is more precise.

[4] Neil Chesanow, "Re: The Office Memo," *New Woman,* February 1987, p. 7.

[5] Liz Fisher, *Accountancy,* Volume 123, Issue 170, June 1999, p. 46.

People who get a lot of e-mail, especially people who do not know you, will use it to decide what to do with your message. A message with a blank subject line or a general subject like "Question" will likely receive a low priority. If you are forwarding an e-mail or replying, change the subject to make it more accurate. Mark things *urgent* or *routine* in the subject line, but use *urgent* cautiously.

Try to make your subject lines brief—no more than 10 words, and often only 3 to 7 words. Note the following examples:

Wordy: Survey of Student Preferences in Regard to Various Pizza

Better: Students' Pizza Preferences

or

The Feasibility of a Cassano's Branch on Campus

or

What Students Like and Dislike about Giovannia Pizza

If you cannot make the subject line both specific and short, be specific.

HAS A CONVERSATIONAL TONE

When you write your memo, use simple language as if you were speaking to the reader.

When you communicate through an e-mail or memo, you usually know your receiver. Therefore, you write informally, using contractions, ordinary words, and first-person pronouns. Use simple language, as if you were speaking to the reader. After you have written your e-mail or memo, read it aloud to see if you would speak the way you have written. If your e-mail or memo sounds pompous, consider revising it!

IS ORGANIZED

When you write an e-mail or memo, include only what is necessary to convey your message and cover only one topic. E-mails and memos effectively deliver simple, routine messages that cover one issue so that your reader can clearly follow your memo without becoming distracted by other issues.

About 90 percent of the time, you put your most important information first to capture your readers' attention. You want to get to the heart of the issue. Start with the conclusion or action you want the reader to take and use the rest of the memo to support your conclusion and convince the reader to agree with your finding.

Within your e-mail, you can create a section entitled "Background" where you spend a few minutes summarizing the situation before launching into a recommendation or asking recipients to share their opinions. Taking this action helps build your credibility and make the most of the e-mail as a way to communicate and build consensus.

After you present the main point, include a transitional statement enumerating the major topics to follow. These major points become headings throughout the body. Within the body, present clear, logical information, details, or explanations.

If you want your readers to take action after reading your e-mail or memo, make it easy for them to do so. Conclude with your action step and make sure you word the action positively, pleasantly, and clearly. Do not leave any doubt in your readers' minds about what action to take and when it needs to be done.

HAS A CONCISE MESSAGE

Eliminate any wordiness or passive writing and keep your sentences short and simple. For best results, try to use 20 words or fewer in each sentence. Use frequent paragraph breaks to help your readers.

> "While e-mail is easy to use," cautions journalist and teacher Lawrence Jeziak, "it increases the competition for an individual's attention. It is, therefore, even more important to make e-mail attractive to the reader in content as well as style."
>
> Source: Jan McDaniel, "E-tiquette: How to Write E-Mail That Brings Results," *Link–up*, Volume 17, Issue 1, Medford, Jan/Feb 2000, p. 14.

Usually the e-mail format makes it necessary for you to use short sentences and smaller paragraphs. You should get to the point, be brief, and be clear. Put the key information up front and tell them the who, what, when, why, and how. If you've got a lot of information to share, consider writing a summary and attaching a longer document. People will not read a long e-mail.

In addition, use white space generously. If you are sending more than two sentences in your e-mail memo, make them separate paragraphs with blank space between them so the reader can skim quickly. You'll get a better response when people can skim what you have to say. One large paragraph may not get read as it looks like too much to read. So, to make the right impression, make it easy for your reader to read, understand, and respond to your message.[6]

If you keep most memos to one page or less, your readers will have no difficulty reading them and will likely take action on your request. Remember, your documents compete with every other document crossing your readers' desks. Make yours stand out from the crowd!

USES SIGNPOSTING

To get your ideas noticed and to make your documents easy to read, use numbers, bullets, headings, tables, lists, and other signposting techniques. Signposts highlight key elements of the document and enable readers to navigate the text more easily. By using these techniques, you increase the chances of your memo being read quickly because they help your readers follow the structure of your doument and allow them to skim the document for the main ideas. Your reader will find complicated material easier to understand when you format it in bullets or lists. Bullets both organize and emphasize the points you are making. Make sure you construct the bulleted sentences in parallel structure; that is, they should all be similarly constructed sentences or all start with a similarly constructed phrase. The same principle should be followed when preparing bulleted points for presentation visuals. See the following examples.

Incorrect Parallel Structure:

Joe Notes should not take the order because:

- 12-cavity molds are required.
- Possible $400,000 loss.
- Must reorganize workers in quality department.
- Engineers continually working on process.

[6] Jann Javons, *"Your Communication Style Makes You or Breaks You."* Retrieved from *http://www.communication-software.com/your-communication-style-makes-you.htm.*

TO: BA 308 Students

FROM: Mrs. Nancy Prochaska *np*

DATE: January 1, 20XX

SUBJECT: Guidelines for Memo Writing

This memo presents guidelines for sharing information within an organization. Asking yourself some questions, making a plan, using the appropriate format, and applying correct mechanics will make your memo writing more effective.

Before you write your memo, ask yourself the following questions: Do I need to send this memo? Would a meeting better serve my needs? What do I hope to accomplish? Who will read this memo? What will the audience's reaction be to this memo?

Outline your message and summarize your points first. Then follow with the details, but remember to be brief. Format can make the message clearer. Use ample paragraphs and consider using bullets to lead the reader through your memo.

Your message will lose all its value if you soil it with mechanical mistakes. Carefully proofread your memo for any spelling, punctuation, or grammar errors.

BOX 6.3 ☛ **Memo without Headings**

Correct Parallel Structure:

Joe Notes should not take the order because:

- ☛ 12-cavity molds are required.
- ☛ A $400,000 loss could result.
- ☛ Quality department workers must be reorganized.
- ☛ Engineers are continually working on the process.

Each line of a bulleted list should be indented. If your bulleted list appears like the following one, it will not make the reading easier. For example:
*These bullets aren't easy to find and don't really provide emphasis.
*The text of the bullets is lined up with the rest of the paragraph.[7]

Headings allow your readers to scan the document quickly for main ideas or to pick out certain sections to read first. Headings also spread your text out and give your document breathing space. If it looks easy to read, your readers will pick it up. If not, your document will probably be tossed in a "To Read Later" pile! Boxes 6.3 and 6.4 show the same memo with and without headings. Which document would you prefer to read?

Did you notice that the headings and the checkmarked list in Box 6.3 guided your reading? Research has shown readers prefer to read documents with headings and other signposting techniques. Typically, readers find listed information easier to comprehend and understand than blocks of prose.

[7] Janell Heineke, "Note on Business Writing," *Boston University, School of Management,* January 1995.

TO: BA 308 Students

FROM: Mrs. Nancy Prochaska *np*

DATE: January 1, 20XX

SUBJECT: Guidelines for Memo Writing

This memo presents guidelines for sharing information within an organization. Asking yourself some questions, making a plan, using the appropriate format, and applying correct mechanics will make your memo writing more effective.

ASKING YOURSELF THE IMPORTANT QUESTIONS

Before you write your memo, ask yourself the following questions:

- ✔ Do I need to send this memo?
- ✔ Would a meeting better serve my needs?
- ✔ What do I hope to accomplish?
- ✔ Who will read this memo?
- ✔ What will the audience's reaction be to this memo?

MAKING A PLAN

Outline your message and summarize your points first. Then follow with the details, but remember to be brief.

USING APPROPRIATE FORMAT

Format can make the message clearer. Use ample paragraphs and consider using bullets to lead the reader through your memo.

APPLYING CORRECT MECHANICS

Your message will lose all its value if you soil it with mechanical mistakes. Carefully proofread your memo for any spelling, punctuation, or grammar errors.

BOX 6.4 ☞ **Memo with Headings**

USES CAUTION WHEN EXPRESSING EMOTIONS

One researcher found that e-mail writers used "much more emotional language than when they communicated in other ways, up to and including language used in locker rooms."[8] Users have developed their own substitute images, called *emoticons,* to accompany electronic words. Read and interpret the examples in Table 6.1 by turning them clockwise 90 degrees.

Humor and irony can easily be misinterpreted when your receiver cannot see a grin or hear a chuckle. You also have greater ability to *flame.* You "flame" when you allow your anger or emotions to affect your message negatively. According to authors Lyle Sussman, Peggy Golden, and Renee Beauclair, "flaming" means you get carried away with the message, sometimes to the point of using profanity.[9]

[8] Marya W. Holcombe, "Wisdom or Information? Managerial Writing in the Office of the Future," in *The Handbook of Executive Communication,* edited by John L. DiGaetani (New York: Dow Jones/Irwin, 1986), p. 261.

[9] Lyle Sussman, Peggy Golden, and Renee Beauclair, "Training for E-Mail," *Training and Development Journal,* March 1991, p. 70.

TABLE 6.1 📝 Emoticons used on e-mail.

:-)	Happy, smiley	>:>	Devilish	\<g>	Grin
;-)	Winking, smiley	:-D	Laughing	:-[	Really sad face
:-(	Sad, frowning	:-@	Screaming	:-e	Disappointed
%-)	Confused	:-/	Skeptical	:-O	Yell
>:<	Angry	:-P	Nyahhh!	((((name))))	Sending your reader a hug

SOURCE: From *Business Communication, Process and Product* 1st edition by GUFFEY. © 1994. Reprinted with permission of South-Western, a division of Thomson learning: www.thomsonrights.com. Fax 800-730-2215.

The e-mail message contained in Box 6.5 is an actual e-mail message that was sent. This writer certainly allowed his anger and emotion to affect the message that he communicated, and it led to unexpected results.

In their book, *The Elements of E-Mail Style: Communicate Effectively via Electronic Mail,* authors David Angell and Brent Heslop provide guidelines to control your flame:

- Before you send an e-mail message, ask yourself, "Would I say this to the person's face?"

- Wait until you have a chance to calm down before responding to an offensive message. Like slipping a letter through the slot in a mailbox, once you send an e-mail message, you are committed to it.

- Read your message twice before you send it, to make sure you did not write something that might be misinterpreted.

- Do not use abusive or obscene language.

- Do not assume every outrageous message is a flame. Flaming is not always a fighting match. If you think that a message is totally outrageous, it might be a joke waiting for you to add the punch line.

- Avoid flaming in public forums. If you disagree, respond to the originator of a message directly. Others often do not appreciate or want to participate in your debate.

- When you flame, indicate to the recipient that you are knowingly blowing off steam by constructing your message as follows: Flame on: *message text* Flame off.[10]

Principles of E-Mail Etiquette

E-mail has some specific rules that are important to know. If you pay attention to these principles, your e-mail communication will be more effective.

KEEP THE LINE LENGTH REASONABLE

Try to keep your line length under 60 characters, because not all e-mail programs wrap lines. You want your message to be displayed on any screen, so use the return key at the end of lines. That way your message does not become one extremely long line. Avoid writing e-mail messages that comprise more than five or six lines; they can be difficult to read on the screen.

---

[10] David Angell and Brent Heslop, *The Elements of E-Mail Style: Communicate Effectively via Electronic Mail,* (Reading, MA: Addison-Wesley Publishing Company, 1994), p. 5.

A Stinging Office Memo Boomerangs

By EDWARD WONG

The only things missing from the office memo were expletives. It had everything else. There were lines berating employees for not caring about the company. There were words in all capital letters like "SICK" and "NO LONGER." There were threats of layoffs and hiring freezes and a shutdown of the employee gym.

The memo was sent by e-mail on March 13 by the chief executive of the Cerner Corporation, a health care software development company based in Kansas City, Mo., with 3,100 employees worldwide. Originally intended only for 400 or so company managers, it quickly took on a life of its own.

The e-mail message was leaked and posted on Yahoo. Its belligerent tone surprised thousands of readers, including analysts and investors. In the stock market, the valuation of the company, which was $1.5 billion on March 20, plummeted 22 percent in three days.

Now, Neal L. Patterson, the 51-year-old chief executive, a man variously described by people who know him as "arrogant," "candid", and "passionate," says he wishes he had never hit the send button. "I was trying to start a fire," he said. "I lit a match, and I started a firestorm." That is not hard to do in the Internet age, when all kinds of messages in cyberspace are capable of stirring reactions and moving markets.

Late last year, for example, a young California investor pleaded guilty to criminal charges that he made $240,000 by sending out a fake news release that resulted in a sharp drop in the stock of Emulex, a communications equipment manufacturer. But in this case, Mr. Patterson was certainly not trying to manipulate the market; he was simply looking to crack the whip on his troops. That sometimes requires sharp language, he said, and his employees know how to take it with a grain of salt.

Business professors and market analysts apparently need more convincing. They are criticizing not only Mr. Patterson's angry tone, but also his mode of communication. Mr. Patterson ran afoul of two cardinal rules for modern managers, they say. Never try to hold large-scale discussions over e-mail. And never, ever, use the company e-mail system to convey sensitive information or controversial ideas to more than a handful of trusted lieutenants. Not unless you want the whole world looking over your shoulder, that is.

In Mr. Patterson's case, this is what the world saw: "We are getting less than 40 hours of work from a large number of our K.C.-based EMPLOYEES. The parking lot is sparsely used at 8 A.M.; likewise at 5 P.M. As managers, you either do not know what your EMPLOYEES are doing; or you do not CARE. You have created expectations on the work effort which allowed this to happen inside Cerner, creating a very unhealthy environment. In either case, you have a problem and you will fix it or I will replace you.

"NEVER in my career have I allowed a team which worked for me to think they had a 40-hour job. I have allowed YOU to create a culture which is permitting this. NO LONGER."

Mr. Patterson went on to list six potential punishments, including laying off 5 percent of the staff in Kansas City. "Hell will freeze over," he vowed, before he would dole out more employee benefits.

BOX 6.5 🖝 **How Not to Send an E-Mail**

A Stinging Office Memo Boomerangs
page 2

The parking lot would be his yardstick of success, he said; it should be "substantially full" at 7:30 A.M. and 6:30 P.M. on weekdays and half full on Saturdays.

"You have two weeks," he said. "Tick, tock."

That message, management experts say, created an atmosphere of fear without specifying what, if anything, was actually going wrong at the company. Moreover, it established a simplistic gauge of success; measuring worker productivity by the number of cars in a parking lot is like judging a book by its word count.

"It's the corporate equivalent of whips and ropes and chains," said Jeffrey Pfeffer, a professor at the Stanford University Graduate School of Business. "It puts you at war with your employees and with your basic tendencies in human nature."

But the more costly error was releasing such an inflammatory memo to a wide audience. Whenever a company does that these days, it is practically inviting a recipient to relay it to friends or even corporate rivals. At that point, a message of even the mildest interest to others will start churning through the farthest corners of the Internet.

"Sadly, there is a tendency to overuse e-mail," said E. Ralph Biggadike, a professor at the Columbia University Graduate School of Business. "I would not advocate the use of e-mail for a problem-solving discussion. E-mail does not really promote dialogue."

For Cerner, it apparently promoted a market upheaval. On March 22, the day after the memo was posted on the Cerner message board on Yahoo, trading in Cerner's shares, which typically runs at about 650,000 a day, shot up to 1.2 million shares. The following day, volume surged to 4 million. In three days, the stock price fell to $34 from almost $44. It closed at $30.94 yesterday.

"While the memo provided some much-needed laughter on Wall Street after a tough week, it probably got overblown as an issue," said Stephen D. Savas, an analyst with Goldman, Sachs, who rates the stock a market performer, which is relatively low. "But it did raise two real questions for investors. One: Has anything potentially changed at Cerner to cause such a seemingly violent reaction? And two: Is this a C.E.O. that investors are comfortable with?"

Mr. Patterson said that the memo was taken out of context and that most employees at Cerner understood that he was exaggerating to make a point. He said he was not carrying out any of the punishments he listed. Instead, he said, he wanted to promote discussion. He apparently succeeded, receiving more than 300 e-mail responses from employees.

Glenn Tobin, chief operating officer at Cerner, said he had read several. "Some people said, 'The tone's too harsh, you've really fouled this one up,'" he said. "Some people said, 'I agree withyour point.'"

Mr. Patterson, who holds an MBA from Oklahoma State University and worked as a consultant at Arthur Andersen before starting Cerner with two partners in 1979, attributes his management style to his upbringing on a 4,000-acre family wheat farm in northern Oklahoma. He spent day after day riding a tractor in the limitless expanse of the fields with only his thoughts for company, he said,

BOX 6.5 ☛ **(continued)**

and came to the conclusion that life was about building things in your head, then going out and acting on them. "You can take the boy off the farm," he said, "but you can't take the farm out of the boy."

And his directness with subordinates is not necessarily a management liability. Cerner is a fast-growing company that had $404.5 million in revenue last year and met earnings projections for the last five quarters. The company said recently that it expected to meet analysts' earnings projections of 15 cents a share for the first quarter. It made *Fortune* magazine's lists in 1998 and 2000 of the 100 best companies to work for in America.

"He has opinions," Mr. Tobin, Cerner's No. 2 executive, said. "He gives his opinions. He can have a blunt style with people who he thinks don't get it, who don't understand the challenges they're facing."

March 13 began like any other day. Mr. Patterson said he woke up at 5 A.M. and did some work at home. Then he drove the 30 miles to Cerner's corporate campus, seven brick-and-glass buildings surrounded by 1,900 parking spaces atop a hill in northern Kansas City. In the elevator, he spoke with the receptionist, a woman who had been with the company for 18 years. She remarked that the work ethic had been declining at the company, he said, reinforcing his own fears.

At 7:45 A.M., he walked into his sixth-floor office and typed up a draft of the memo. He met with a client downstairs, then had two managers and his assistant read over the memo. At 11:48 A.M., he sent it.

It went up on the Yahoo message board a week later. Analysts began getting calls from investors. They in turn called Cerner to verify the authenticity of the memo, then exchanged a flurry of calls and e-mail messages, trying to divine the tea leaves of Mr. Patterson's writings.

"The perception was that they have to work overtime to meet their quota," said Stacey Gibson, an analyst with Fahnestock & Company, who rates the stock a buy and was among the first to post a warning on Thomson Financial/First Call about the memo. "Whether that's true or not, I don't know. This is how it was taken on the Street."

Some analysts say that other factors could have contributed to the drop in the stock price. The overall market was shaky. There were investors who wanted to sell the stock short, betting that it was ready for a fall. One analyst was especially bearish about the company. But even Mr. Patterson acknowledged that his memo "added noise" to what was already out there.

At the end of the week, as the stock fell, Mr. Patterson sent out another e-mail message to his troops. Unlike the first memo, it was not called a Management Directive, but rather a Neal Note. It was both an apology to those he offended and a confirmation of the work-ethic problem within the company.

It began this way: "Please treat this memo with the utmost confidentiality. It is for internal dissemination only. Do not copy or e-mail to anyone else."

BOX 6.5 🖙 **(continued)**

SOURCE: Copyright 2005 by the New York Times Co. Reprinted with permission.

USE APPROPRIATE TYPE STYLE, SIZES, AND COLORS

Each typeface has its own personality, connoting everything from business-like (Arial or Times New Roman) to play (Braggadocio or Bengguiat Frisky). Look at each typeface offered and decide whether it signals the tone you are trying to convey. Increasing the size of the type can add importance to a phrase, while decreasing typeface size can send a message of demoting a particular thought or section. Colors can also influence people's perception. For most business situations, you should stay with black, but colors in our e-mails can create moods. Blue can connote serenity, green signals "go" and "money," while black has a "bottom-line" concreteness to it. Red, of course, can imply passion, danger, or stop.[11]

USE BOTH UPPERCASE AND LOWERCASE LETTERS

Using only uppercase letters makes it appear as if you are shouting and will mark you as heavy-handed or rude. Use uppercase letters only to emphasize special information. Never use all lowercase letters. Readers will have a difficult time reading what you wrote because the uppercase letters typically signal a new sentence. A new sentence allows the reader to pause briefly before reading the next one.

KNOW WHERE YOUR MESSAGE IS GOING BEFORE YOU SEND IT

Look at the "To:" and "Cc:" lines, especially when replying to a message sent to a discussion list or listserv. You might want to send your reply only to the person who posted the message, not the whole list. The "Reply All" option may not be appropriate in all situations. Think before you click; you may create an annoying or even embarrassing situation if your message reaches the wrong party.

RESPOND TO YOUR E-MAILS

Be careful and don't let your e-mail sit too long in your in-basket. Typically, you should try to respond within 24 to 48 hours. If you do not respond to an e-mail, it can be perceived as just as rude as not returning a telephone call and can also create distrust in the person with whom you are corresponding.

USE BLIND COPY WHEN SENDING MASS MESSAGES

When you send a message to a long list of people, use the blind copy (bcc) feature of your mail program rather than exposing all the addresses to all the recipients. Otherwise, a cascade of messages can result when some recipients reply to everyone. The blind copy feature also allows you to discreetly send your message to someone who should be aware of a situation but does not need to respond or act. In other words, the bcc allows you to keep someone else in the information loop.

DO NOT SEND PEOPLE THINGS THEY CANNOT READ

Unless you've checked that the recipient's mail program can handle something fancier, stick to plain text.

Unfortunately, most of the files you're likely to want to send to someone (word processed documents, graphics, programs, compressed files, and so on) are not *text files* but *binary files,* meaning that they contain codes that aren't part of

---

[11] Gary Blake, "E-Mail with Feeling," *Research Technology Management,* Volume 42, Issue 6, Washington, Nov/Dec. 1999, pp. 12–13.

the ASCII set. To be sent by e-mail, a binary file must be converted to text at the sender's end and converted back to a binary file at the recipient's end. The encoding and decoding are handled by software that is usually built into the e-mail program.

Three encoding schemes are in widespread use for Internet e-mail: UUencode, BinHex, and MIME (Multipurpose Internet Mail Extensions). UUencode was first used on Unix computers (the "UU" stands for "Unix-to-Unix") but has since spread to PCs and even Macintoshes. BinHex is most common in the Macintosh world. MIME is the newest of the three schemes, and most modern e-mail programs handle it. (S/MIME, or Secure MIME, is an extended version of MIME that adds special encryption features.)

As with the simple letter-to-number conversion, it does not really matter which scheme you use, as long as you and your correspondents use the same one. To find out what encoding methods your e-mail software can handle, look in your manual, go online for help, or ask your technical support staff.

MAKE WEB ADDRESSES EASY FOR RECIPIENTS TO USE

If you put a Web address in your message (in your signature, for example), include the http:// at the beginning. Many programs will recognize it as a Web address and make it clickable.

DO NOT OVERQUOTE

When you quote the message you are replying to, include only the parts that are relevant to your reply. Be sure to identify quoted text. The usual way is to mark the quoted text with a greater-than sign (>) at the beginning of each line.

DO NOT SEND JUNK

Everyone who uses e-mail daily has been annoyed by chain letters, virus alerts, and even the jokes that circulate by e-mail (which often turn out to be copyrighted material with the attributions omitted). If you're worried about a virus alert, don't forward it to everyone in your address book; instead, check Computer Virus Myths (*http://www.vmyths.com*) or ask your technical support staff.

Junk e-mail, known as *spam,* makes enemies more frequently than it attracts customers. According to an article in the *Atlanta Journal-Constitution,* spam costs approximately 15 percent of a user's average monthly Internet access bill.[12] Some people compare junk e-mail to junk paper mail. But junk e-mail is more like junk faxes, which have been outlawed, because it costs the sender hardly anything and uses recipients' resources instead. With e-mail, sending 100,000 messages is not much harder than sending 100. Dealing with a couple of junk messages a day isn't much of a burden, but nothing prevents that number from increasing to a couple of thousand a day if spam continues to proliferate. Junk e-mail makes it difficult to pick out the messages from friends, relatives, business contacts, and other people you do want to hear from. It also overloads mail servers (the computers that handle e-mail) and other parts of the network infrastructure. For information on junk e-mail and suggestions for fighting it, as well as links to other antispam sites, see Fight Spam on the Internet! (*http://spam.abuse.net*) and Junkbusters (*http://www.junkbusters.com*), which also addresses other forms of intrusive advertising.

Bright Light Technologies has developed a new product, Brightmail, a free subscription service available at *http://www.brightmail.com.* Brightmail sifts through

E-mail security companies estimate that between one-third and two-thirds of unwanted messages are relayed unwittingly by PC owners who set up software incorrectly or fail to secure their machines.

Source: "New Loophole: Poorly Guarded Home Computers," Retrieved February 18, 2004, from *http://www. cnn.com/2004/TECH/ptech/02/1 7/spam.zombies.ap/.*

According to Stephen Wilbers, forgetting to attach the attachment is one of the more common reasons for having to resend a message.

Source: "Follow E-Mail Etiquette to Avoid Being Annoying," *Star Tribune,* Minneapolis, October 20, 2000, p. 2D.

---

[12] Gavin Herlihy, "Deliver Me from Spam," *The Atlanta Journal-Constitution,* September 26, 1999, p. P1, P12.

your mailbox looking for spam by matching offending messages with a database of known spammers, and then removes them from sight. The best advice is for you to not reply to spam or even the "unsubscribe" line, as most spammers will take your "unsubscribe" response as proof of a live site and add your address to their list.

BE SURE TO ATTACH FILES PROPERLY

Often when you send an e-mail message, you attach other files containing documents, pictures, charts, or spreadsheets. Your **attachment** is sent separately, alongside your message, and the recipient can open it by clicking an icon in the message. Many e-mail packages have simplified this process for you by automatically decoding your attachment when it arrives. Other mail programs may not automatically decode, in which case, your recipient will need to have a decoding program. Some companies prohibit the opening of attachments, so check with your receiver to determine whether to attach or put the information within the body of the e-mail message.

Downloading (copying a file online to your computer) attachments can be a slow process for your receiver. When you send graphics as an attachment, they take more space on the screen and more space on the hard drive, thus slowing the copying process. Color graphics take up considerably more space than simple black-and-white line drawings. You can reduce the number of colors or change the format to reduce the file size. Pictures typically come in two file formats: *GIF* (Graphics Interchange Format) or *JPEG* (Joint Photographic Experts Group). The names of GIF files typically have a .gif extension; those of JFIF files (also called JPEG files) typically end in .jpeg or .jpg. Refer to the Guidelines by Adobe Systems at *http://www.adobe.com* to help you decide which format to use. Typically, GIF works best for line drawings and images with large blocks of solid color; JPEG works best with photographs and other images with many different shades. When in doubt, save your image in both formats and chose the one that results in the smaller file size.[13] Another website that may help you with graphics is *http://www.boutell.com/ faq/space.htm*.

CHECK, READ, AND PROOF YOUR MESSAGE BEFORE SENDING IT

As recommended already, do not send anything you will regret later. Take time to read and proof your message to make sure it communicates what you want to say. Follow the guidelines presented in Chapter 2 for effective business writing. Once you send your message, you cannot undo your action.[14] Always take the time to proof for grammatical errors and misspelled words. Some messaging systems provide a tool to help you check for spelling and grammar errors, and others do not. Remember, your e-mail messages are a reflection on you. If time permits, do your final editing on hard copy. You typically catch more errors on paper than on the computer screen. You may want to ask a colleague to read your message and then ask that individual to describe the point of your message. If he or she cannot state the point, rewrite your message.

Consider Carefully What You Write.   Remember, e-mail is a permanent record and can be easily forwarded to others. Just because you delete a message, that does not mean the message is deleted from the system. If confidentiality is an issue, choose another medium as there is truly no privacy in cyberspace. In addition, never write

[13] Keith C. Ivey, "Untangling the Web: Using Graphics on the Web," EEI Press, *eve@eeicom.com*, 1997, 66 Canal Center Plaza, Suite 200, Alexandria, Virginia 22314–5507.

[14] Ed Krol, "E-Mail: A User's Guide: The Whole Internet User's Guide and Catalog," in *Business Communication: Concepts and Applications in an Electronic Age,* edited by Randolph H. Hudson and Bernard J. Selzer (Los Angeles: Roxbury Publishing Company, 1994), pp. 59–61.

anything you wouldn't feel comfortable saying in person. Hundreds of sexual harassment and racial discrimination lawsuits have resulted from improper e-mail messages that were intended as private jokes.[15]

Use Care When Using Acronyms.   Some acronyms such as BTW (by the way) or IMHO (in my humble opinion) should be used with care. Your reader may not know this jargon and may not want to admit his or her confusion.

DELETE OLD MESSAGES

You can delete by sender, topic, or date. If you do not want to delete a certain message, you can create a folder to save it in. Your e-mail in-box can become overloaded. At some point, you need to delete unnecessary e-mails, to refer those that need input by others, to act on others that make requests and require decisions or to file those that just provide reference materials. Some messaging systems allow you to set up a data parameter to automatically discard all messages prior to a predetermined date. Other systems allow you to download your e-mail messsages directly to a file on your hard drive.

The Importance of Short Reports

Organizations cannot function without information, and much of that information can be found in reports. The term "report" covers anything from computer images, preprinted forms, informal letters and memos, and electronic reports, to formal three-volume manuscripts.[16] Individuals use reports to communicate with internal as well as external stakeholders in the organization. Reports serve as a vital link among many different audiences.

Reports monitor progress, provide information, guide decision making, help implement organizational changes, and document work. Reports can be classified as *short* or *long. Short reports,* sometimes referred to as *informal reports,* are typically used in the day-to-day operations of the organization, while *long reports* or *formal reports* require some type of data analysis and recommendations. Long reports are discussed more fully in Chapter 8.

The following sections discuss some commonly used short reports: progress, periodic, justification, and feasibility reports; executive memo reports; proposals; and policies and procedures.

PROGRESS REPORTS

A progress report informs a manager of your progress on a certain assignment and when it will be completed. In the report, present a brief background of the assignment, the details of the work completed, a summary of the work completed most recently, and an evaluation of the progress made. The report concludes with a summary of what needs to be finished and projects a time for completion.

PERIODIC REPORTS

Employees regularly send out periodic reports, whether weekly, monthly, or daily. The periodic report provides routine information and keeps managers and others

---

[15] Nancy Flynn, "Fifteen Secrets to Super-Effective Electronic Sales Letters," The ePolicy Institute, 2003. Retrieved from *http://www.epolicyinstitute.com.*

[16] Courtland L. Bovee and John V. Thill, *Business Communication Today,* 4th ed. (New York: McGraw-Hill, 1995), p. 410.

informed so they can monitor performance and make any necessary modifications. Some periodic reports, such as for accounting and sales, primarily present figures such as sales volume, shipments, accounts receivable, or accounts payable. More challenging periodic reports, such as the sample report in Box 6.6, discuss and describe activities. Because you present information, you can write in the direct style. Therefore, start with a summary of activities for the period covered (the most important information), and follow with a detailed discussion of those activities.

JUSTIFICATION REPORTS

A justification report justifies some action you, the writer, want to take. Whether you want a change in a procedure or approval to purchase new equipment, you must provide a rationale for the request. Present recommendations first, followed by statements explaining how you arrived at this conclusion. Provide your readers with all the information they need to know. Readers should know from the start why you made the request.

FEASIBILITY REPORTS

This report investigates the chances of success of one solution or alternative over another.[17] It analyzes a situation and shows why one solution or alternative may be better than another. Begin indirectly with background information about the situation, and then state the concern that led to your investigation of potential solutions. Next, present the possible solutions, describing their advantages and disadvantages. Then suggest the best solution and provide a plan for carrying it out.

EXECUTIVE MEMO REPORTS

Since most managers have more to read than they have time for, they need a method of receiving information quickly. An executive memo can fulfill this purpose while also allowing subordinates to communicate with their superiors. Write an executive memo either directly or indirectly, as determined by your purpose. If you write your memo directly, place the recommendations at the beginning. If you choose the indirect method, place your recommendations at the end of the memo. Typically, the purpose of this memo is to present the most information possible in an abbreviated and condensed fashion. Eliminate lengthy, detailed explanations and present only the main points. See Box 6.7 for an example of an executive memo report.

PROPOSALS

In a proposal, you make a request to do a particular job or you ask for money to complete a project. A proposal requires the persuasive, indirect approach. Your goal should be to demonstrate your ability to solve the client's problem. Ask yourself the following three questions: Why should they choose my proposal over all others? What does the client need? How can I satisfy those needs?[18] Many organizations require a particular format when submitting proposals. These organizations typically send out an RFP (Request for Proposals) outlining the procedure you should follow. To avoid having this happen to your proposal, include the following:

1. An *introduction,* briefly explaining the reasons for the proposal and identifying key issues. For example, in Box 6.8 the writer focused on a key benefit the training could provide.

(continued on page 142)

According to one report, government evaluators who award federal contracts say that incoming proposals are routinely rejected as technically noncompliant, when the real reason is unintelligible writing.

Source: "Total Quality Business Writing," *Journal for Quality & Participation,* Volume 18, Issue 6, October/November 1995, pp. 34–37.

When writing proposals, you must often follow the guidelines sent out in the RFP (Request for Proposal).

[17] Stanford Wayne and David P. Dauwalder, *Communicating in Business* (Burr Ridge, IL: Austin Press, Irwin, 1994), p. 400.

[18] DeTienne, Kirsten Bell and Alder, G. Stoney, "Developing Winning Proposals," *Mechanical Engineering,* Volume 116, Issue 6, June 1994, pp. 65–66.

TO: Dr. Deborah Roebuck

mj   *ll*   *cn*   *dp*

FROM: Maggie Johnson, Lisa Lake, Carl Neher, Debra Pollack, and John Wichman *jw*

DATE: November 10, 20XX

SUBJECT: Group Self-Evaluation of Dry-Run Video

This memo highlights the team's activities for the week ending November 8. The team spent this week preparing and practicing for the dry-run presentation. This memo provides the results of our practice oral presentation. The following paragraphs detail the strengths and weaknesses of the group as well as the strengths and weaknesses of each member.

GROUP CRITIQUE—STRENGTHS

The group felt positive about the overall outcome. Each member attended the filming dressed in appropriate business attire. The group had voted to wear black or gray clothing and suits, if possible. By following this dress code, the group appeared coordinated and professional.

Each member proved to be a strong and accomplished speaker. No one showed signs of nervousness or anxiety, which may not be the case on the day of the presentation. Although some members spoke too rapidly, their voices were loud and clear.

GROUP CRITIQUE—WEAKNESSES

While the group agreed that specific problems existed, all could be corrected before the actual performance. The group observed the following problems while reviewing the dry-run video:

1. We should not repeat the entire text of our written report. The group must edit the report to decide what to leave in and what to omit.

2. The information must be stated so the audience can relate to the topic. We must place ourselves "in" the situation.

3. For the most part, performers read their scripts, causing them to look down too much. Our presentation must be more extemporaneous; the members will practice their parts independently.

4. Only two of five speakers identified themselves in their opening. Speakers should identify themselves and their topics.

5. Several visual aids need revision.

6. The group left the visual aids on the screen too long. Each performer should decide when to turn the overhead projector on and off.

7. The group must choose a better cue for the projector operator than simply saying, "Visual, please."

8. All negative references to Kenya should be removed or rephrased.

9. The group should decide on the use of the music tape. If used, we must create a better method for fading the music in and out of the program.

10. The group could not settle on where each member should be positioned to ensure a smooth flow of performers.

BOX 6.6 ☛ **Sample Periodic Report**

The group unanimously decided to stay after class on Monday, November 11, to practice their parts. They will then have another dry-run during the meeting scheduled for Wednesday, November 13.

INDIVIDUAL CRITIQUES—STRENGTHS AND WEAKNESSES

Individual members of the group realized while reviewing the video that they needed work on specific areas. The following is a breakdown of strengths and weaknesses of each person.

Maggie Johnson

Maggie presented a professional performance. She handled the visual art well by getting it on and off the screen in a timely fashion. Maggie related her facts to the audience. Maggie felt she talked too fast at times and will work on slowing down her delivery. She must remember to introduce herself before beginning her delivery.

Lisa Lake

Lisa appeared comfortable with her delivery style. She exhibited a personable and enthusiastic personality. She introduced herself and successfully addressed her speech to the audience as if they were leaving for Kenya tomorrow. Lisa felt she should glance at her notecards more often to prevent stumbling. She will practice using her hands in a more animated fashion.

Carl Neher

Carl made some eye contact but will improve on it by not reading his script. He will practice giving his part more extemporaneously. He needs to slow down his rate of speech and use more hand gestures. Carl also needs to introduce himself to the audience before beginning his talk.

Debra Pollack

Debra seemed comfortable at the podium. Debra needed to learn her part better to avoid reading it. She personally felt she had a problem using her hands and found it bothersome to know what to do with them. Debra must introduce herself to the audience instead of jumping right into the subject.

John Wichman

John displayed a comfortable presence on stage and introduced himself before beginning. He projected a professional appearance, and maintained eye contact with the audience. John noted he needed to polish his transition lines and tie his visual aids into the text more efficiently. He also felt he depended too much on his notes.

CONCLUSION

At first, we questioned the usefulness of the dry-run video, but the need for it became painfully apparent to us when we filmed our presentation. We now realize if we had not made the dry-run video, these glitches would have marred our final presentation. Each member now appreciates the usefulness of this required assignment.

BOX 6.6 ☛ (continued)

Date: January 10, 20XX

TO: Managing Directors

FROM: Carol Joy *cj*

SUBJECT: Customer Surveys

This report reviews our present offering of distinctive products, services, and systems as described in customer surveys collected during the final quarter of 20XX.

Future Customer Desires

Our customers told us that to be a valued supplier we need to:

1. Be quality oriented:
   - Provide quality products.
   - Provide quality service.
   - Provide quality information.

2. Be distinctive:
   - Offer products, services, and information not currently available from our competitors.

3. Be aware of our customers' needs:
   - Continually monitor the desire for product change and the specifics of that change.

4. Be educationally oriented:
   - Constantly educate and train the distributors to represent the merchandise and its potential use.

Current Customer Perceptions

1. Our product is the highest quality, our service is dependable, and our information is reliable … although not always current.

2. We are not distinctive in our products and information. The same merchandise is available from our competitors. The only area of distinction is our reliable and friendly service.

3. We are fairly good about maintaining an awareness of our customers' needs. More frequent drop-by visits, however, can ensure that this awareness remains high.

4. Better education of our distributors is needed. They know the product and price, but they do not adequately convey our heartfelt philosophy.

5. We are rapidly losing ground on the best price advantage. Currently, many of our prices are higher than those of our competition. In fact, our competitors are using pricing as their primary sales tool.

Recommendations

Our philosophy is sound. We must ensure that every person who represents us understands and follows our philosophy of providing the best products, service, and information. It is especially important that we meet with distributors more often, after monthly training sessions, to keep them up-to-date on product changes and to furnish the most current information available.

The work that production is doing on the Quality Management Program will improve our inventory control and costing and pricing problems. This must be monitored closely to ensure that problems are truly solved. Such a resolution should enable us to reduce prices in graduated stages to meet those of our competition by the second quarter of 2010.

BOX 6.7 📝 **Executive Memo Report**

DB Roebuck Associates
1356 Hendon Road
Woodstock, GA 30188
(770) 591-8176

August 30, 20XX

Mr. Tom Flaig
Training and Development Specialist
Macon Electric Cooperative
145 Main Street
Macon, MO 63552

Dear Mr. Flaig:

Thank you for speaking with me about training opportunities at Macon Electric. This letter sets out how I propose to assist in meeting your needs for training to improve employee writing skills. I will first review my understanding of the issues, then present my proposal, discuss timing and responsibilities, provide the arrangements for my services, and state the benefits of this training.

My Understanding of the Issues

Macon Cooperative has faced unprecedented changes and increased competition in the electric utility industry. Macon Cooperative understands the vital role employees play and how they affect its ability to succeed in this competitive environment. Therefore, Macon Cooperative has made a commitment to train and empower its most valuable resource.

As Training and Development Specialist, you have conducted interviews with managers to identify needs. Through your interviews, you have learned that managers desire improved communication skills. You realize the critical role communication serves within an organization and know communication training would benefit not only employees but managers as well.

Proposed Plan

On the basis of our discussion on August 25, I propose to work with you to develop a training program. My role will be that of trainer, coach, and facilitator. I will work with your employees to improve their written communication skills. I will assist Macon Cooperative in its efforts to provide quality, relevant training.

Within 60 days, I will custom-design and deliver an intensive eight-hour Effective Business Writing seminar. This seminar will deliver practical guidance for all employees whose duties require written communication. Participants will sharpen their business writing techniques, resulting in clearer, more concise, and more effective communication. They will learn how to select the right words to say exactly what they mean, eliminate wordiness and jargon, and use proofreading techniques as a final check to make sure their work presents a positive image of the organization. This skill-building seminar benefits all employees by helping them improve their memos, letters, reports, and proposals.

BOX 6.8 ☞ **Proposal**

Participants will learn each component of effective business writing and apply their newly learned skills. They will analyze and critique samples of effective and ineffective business writing. Then, individuals will compose work-related documents and receive feedback from the trainer on their efforts.

All participants will receive a Reference Handbook that will become a valuable desktop companion. They will be able to use this handbook long after they have completed the seminar.

Timing and Responsibilities

Based on our preliminary discussion, October seems to be the best time to deliver this training. I will perform all the preparatory work and deliver the program myself. I will report directly to you and to any other member of management you may designate.

I recommend you provide the training over two half-days. Participants benefit from the opportunity to apply their skills in a homework setting.

Arrangements for My Services

My professional fees include two days of preparation time at $100 per hour. The seminar will be customized to meet your needs. Each participant will receive a Reference Handbook. The cost will be $125 for each participant with a minimum of 10 students.

For your review, I have enclosed a biographical sketch of my experience and qualifications.

Benefits

This critical communication training will help Macon Cooperative maintain a competitive edge in the electric utility arena. Investing in Macon Cooperative's most valuable resource will ensure the company's distinctive competence and successful growth in the twenty-first century.

This training endeavor will also allow you to work with me to determine if I am the right agent to assist you in the long term on other training needs. I look forward to building a professional relationship with Macon Cooperative.

I will call you within the next few days to answer any questions you or your staff may have and to determine how we should proceed. If you agree to this proposal, please sign the enclosed copy of this letter and return it to me so that I might begin my work. Thank you again for allowing me to propose this project.

Sincerely,

Deborah Britt Roebuck
Deborah Britt Roebuck, Ph.D.
Principal

BOX 6.8 ☛ (continued)

(continued from page 136)

2. A *background section* identifying the problem and discussing the goals or purposes of the project. Persuade the reader you understand the problem completely.

3. A *proposal section* in which you discuss how you will solve the problem and what you will do for the company. This can be tricky because you do not want to tell them too much. Just tell them in general terms what you propose to do and how it will benefit them.

4. A *timing and responsibilities section* in which you discuss when the project will start and end. Set tentative deadlines for completion of certain aspects of the project. Also, state who will be working on the project and what their responsibilities will be.

5. An *arrangements for services section* in which you propose costs associated with the project. Once you set your fees, you cannot raise them later, because your proposal represents a contract. You can itemize hours and costs or present a total sum only. Provide evidence of your qualifications to show you can complete the project successfully.

6. A *final section* persuading the organization of the *benefits* they will gain by accepting your proposal. Motivate them to take action by making it easy for them to do so.

After you have completed your proposal, look over your work and ask yourself these questions:

1. Do I need to put additional or supporting information in an appendix?

2. Have I been generous with white space? (Remember, you wrote a persuasive document. The more pleasing the layout, the more likely your reader will continue reading and the more likely you will receive a favorable response.)

3. Could I add graphics to make my examples clearer and more interesting? (Visuals help clarify information. Colorful charts and graphs attract and retain readers' interest and attention.)

4. Have I supported all my claims and arguments? (Remember, saying something without evidence to back you up tells your reader you didn't do your homework.)[19]

POLICIES AND PROCEDURES

Organizations must have certain guidelines to conduct business. You may be called on to write a report detailing company policies and procedures. Such guides help managers know how to handle routine and crisis situations.

Policies. A policy acts as a general guide to decision making. Business employees write policy statements to be consistent with organizational objectives. Policies help managers enforce company rules and provide employees with a feeling of fair treatment. Policies help prevent conflict and thereby save time. You may find it difficult or impossible to write a policy for every issue, but you can revise and add policies as needed. The example in Box 6.9 shows how policies help employees know what to do.

A large organization in the South did not have a bad-weather policy. To be honest, the organization had never considered it necessary, but one winter made them change their minds. During this particular winter, the weather seemed worse than normal for Georgia. Ice and snow were being forecast daily. Some employees would try to get to work regardless of the weather, while others would

---

[19] Susan Brock, *Writing Business Proposals and Reports* (Menlo Park, CA: Crisp Publications, 1992), p. 68.

Objective

ABC company will provide employees with paid vacation in a fair and systematic manner.

Policy

All employees of the ABC Company will be eligible for paid vacation upon completion of the six-month probationary period.

a. Employees with three years and less work experience will be allowed five working days (one week) vacation.
b. Employees with the company three years but less than five years will receive ten working days (two weeks) vacation.
c. Employees with the company more than five years will receive fifteen working days (three weeks) vacation.

Procedures

1. Obtain form V-007 from the Human Resources Department to request vacation time.
2. Fill the form out completely, have it signed by your immediate supervisor, and return it to the Human Resources Department.
3. Expect confirmation of the vacation within three working days of receipt of the completed form V-007.
4. Write your name on the Scheduling Board under approved dates when you receive your confirmation letter from the Human Resources Department.

BOX 6.9 🖝 **Company Vacation Objective, Policy, and Procedures**

stay home. Soon conflict arose between the employees who came to work and those who stayed home. The employees who came to work felt the employees who stayed home took advantage of the situation. The managers did not know how to handle the situation because no written policy or procedure existed. If a bad-weather policy had been in place, employees would have known exactly what they should do. After this incident, the company developed a bad-weather policy.

Procedures. A procedure tells specifically how the policy will be implemented. Two types of procedures are used. When procedures allow managers to use their judgment, we call them *guides*. An example of a guide is: "When a customer returns merchandise, check it carefully to make sure all pieces have been returned." Managers have some discretion as to how closely they check the merchandise. The second type of procedure, called *rules*, do not allow managers any decision-making power. They simply implement the rule. An example of a rule is: "To receive a refund, the customer must sign the refund slip." The manager must have the customers sign the refund slips. If customers do not sign the refund slips, the manager will not give their money back.

Writing Policies and Procedures. When you write policies and procedures, follow these suggestions: cover all possible questions, follow a consistent format and orient the message to your receivers.[20]

Cover all possible questions. As you write, try to think of all the questions a reader might ask. Remember to ask who, what, when, where, why, and how. Put yourself

[20] Richard Huseman, James M. Lahiff, John M. Penrose, and John Hatfield, *Business Communication, Strategies and Skills,* 2nd ed. (Chicago: Dryden Press, 1985), pp. 330–335.

in the reader's place, and determine whether you would know exactly what to do. Also, let the readers know how important the policies are and how they will benefit them.

Follow a consistent format. You can organize your document to list all policies first, then the procedures; or you can list procedures, step by step.[21] Occasionally, you will find that more than one policy applies to a procedure. When that happens, you list all policies first, then follow them with procedures. When you write procedures, organize them step-by-step and number them. If you have more than 10 steps, group them into a smaller number of processes to avoid overloading people's short-term memory. You can also give each group a heading. Make sure each step in the procedure requires a different action.

Orient the message to the receivers. Policies and procedures should be written so every employee within an organization can read and understand them. Within many organizations, employees have difficulty reading their company's policies and procedures. A student once told me a story about going to her boss to seek guidance on a certain policy. Her boss read the policy and did not clearly understand it herself. Therefore, she went to her boss, and her boss went to her boss, and so on! No one really had a clue about what that particular policy meant. Many individuals who work for companies can probably relate to that story. Unfortunately, people often have no idea what their policies and procedures really mean.

For policies to be effective, they must be complete, clear, and concise. They must incorporate the 7 Cs of effective business writing. When you write, include action verbs and talk directly to the reader. Tell your reader exactly what to do. If necessary, justify the steps so your reader will understand the purpose and necessity of the policy.

---

[21] Linda S. Flower, John R. Hayes, and Heidi Swarts, "Revising Functional Documents: The Scenario Principle," *Technical Report No. 10* (Washington, D.C.: Document Design Project, 1980), pp. 5, 20, 22, 27, and 29.

Use tact when writing these statements. Do not use imperial words such as "will" and "shall." Using such words paints a picture of the company's superiority. When writing about unpleasant topics such as dismissal or discipline, avoid using *you.* Do not point a finger at an employee.

Policies and procedures are easier to read if you construct a scenario that takes your reader through the document. People read rules not to remember them, but to find out how to do something correctly. To help your readers get the information they need:

Lay out a path your readers can follow.

Present action stories or scenarios with human agents.

Highlight important information.

Use operational definitions to describe meanings in practical terms.[22]

Conclusion

You will probably write more memos and e-mails than any other type of organizational document in the course of your employment. If you incorporate the guidelines presented in this chapter, your memos will get read! Organizations use short reports on a daily basis. If you, as the writer, compose these types of documents effectively, they will communicate for you. Keep the suggestions in Box 6.10 in mind as you write and use the checklist in Table 6.2 when you review your memo or short report.

---

1. Keep your reader in mind when you write. Ask yourself these questions: What does the reader know? What does the reader need to know? Outline the points to be covered, and then start writing.
2. State the purpose clearly and concisely.
3. Make the report objective and not personal. Managers want reports to present both sides of a problem.
4. Be exact with details and support your facts.
5. List the facts in sequence and use headings to ease reading.
6. Use attachments for extra information not needed within the body.
7. Keep paragraphs short. Remember, you want your reader to read the report.
8. Use bullets, boldface, and underscores to emphasize important information.
9. Make your memo inviting to read by positioning the information attractively. Don't crowd too much information on one page.
10. Conclude with a brief summary of key points and offer recommendations.

BOX 6.10 ☞ **Specific Guidelines for Writing Short Reports**

---

[22] Kitty O. Locker, *Business and Administrative Communication,* 2nd ed. (Homewood, IL: Irwin, 1992), p. 368.

TABLE 6.2 ☞ **Memo and short report checklist.**

	YES	NO
1. Did you determine your purpose?	❏	❏
2. Did you write a specific and clear subject line stating your purpose?	❏	❏
3. Did you list specific information within the body?	❏	❏
4. Did you state what action you desire? Did you state this action clearly in the last paragraph?	❏	❏
5. Did you check to make sure you placed "To" before "From"?	❏	❏
6. Did you use a courtesy title if your memo is going up the chain of command?	❏	❏
7. Did you use the complete date: month, day, and year?	❏	❏
8. Did you single-space the body of your memo?	❏	❏
9. Did you use one-inch margins?	❏	❏
10. Did you omit any widows (partial lines) or orphans (any paragraphs with only one line or part of a line left at the top or bottom of your page)?	❏	❏
11. If your memo or report comprises two or more pages, did you include a second-page heading?	❏	❏
12. Did you use a grammar checker and spell checker?	❏	❏
13. Did you make sure you did not use sexist language or faulty parallelism?	❏	❏
14. Did you use complete sentences and make sure each paragraph has at least two sentences?	❏	❏
15. Did you try to keep your passive writing to under 10 percent?	❏	❏

Exercises

EXERCISE 1 IMPROVING SUBJECT LINES

Directions: Make the following subject lines more specific and concrete.

Ineffective: Quality Service

Effective: _____

Ineffective: Summary Report

Effective: _____

Ineffective: Agents in Southeast Customer Service Area

Effective: _____

Ineffective: Office Telephone Usage

Effective: _____

Ineffective: Recommendation for Training

Effective: _____

Ineffective: Self-Regulated Team Problems

Effective: _____

Ineffective: Trip Report

Effective: _____

Ineffective: Concern

Effective: _____

EXERCISE 2 IMPROVING A MEMO

Directions: Edit and revise the following memo.

TO: All Employees
FROM: Mr. Madd
DATE: May 1st, 20XX
SUBJECT: Job Applicants

PLEASE STOP SENDING YOUR FRIENDS, RELATIVES, AND ANYBODY ELSE YOU CAN THINK OF TO THE PERSONNEL OFFICE TO ASK FOR ME.

I am covered up—and these people walking in at all hours of the day, unannounced and unscheduled, are just slowing down the hiring process. I don't think you realize that some of these folks DEMAND to be seen just because you told them they would be. We have a process by which we do our hiring. AND part of that process is checking references before people are interviewed.

If you have someone in mind for a job—JOT IT DOWN, and send it to me! When I get a chance, I will look for their application—BUT I will not consider anybody who argues with me about when I can see them.

EXERCISE 3 IMPROVING A MEMO

Directions: Edit and revise the following memo.

Memorandum

DATE: October 13, 20XX
TO: All KeyPad Personnel
FROM: Peter West, Executive Vice President, Operations
RE: Issuance of Parts Numbers

It has come to my attention that part numbers are still being distributed incorrectly.

I want to make it clear to everyone that no part numbers will be issued or received from another source and distributed without Stephanie Free's knowledge and approval! A breach of this directive should be considered job-threatening!

fed

EXERCISE 4 UNDERSTANDING OBJECTIVES, POLICIES, AND PROCEDURES

Directions: Identify the following statements as company objectives, policies, or procedures. If you identify the statement as a procedure, state whether it represents a rule or a guide.

_____ 1. Every Form 1202 must be signed by your supervisor.

_____ 2. Keep the employees informed.

_____ 3. If the fire alarm sounds, direct your subordinates to the nearest exit.

_____ 4. Make a profit.

_____ 5. After seven years of full-time teaching, the instructor will be promoted or terminated.

_____ 6. ABC Company seeks to maintain positive relations with the union.

_____ 7. The promotion steps for a secretary include: Secretarial Assistant, Secretary, and Senior Secretary.

_____ 8. Employees should offer suggestions to improve the company.

_____ 9. Clock in at 8:00 A.M. sharp.

_____ 10. Complaints must be sent to the manager, who will determine if the complaint should be sent to the Grievance Board.

_____ 11. Students must make up their work within three days of being absent.

_____ 12. Employees must wash their hands before leaving the restroom.

_____ 13. Make the customers happy.

Assignment Options

OPTION 1—LETTER AND MEMO COLLECTION ASSIGNMENT

Collect at least five letters or memos for this assignment. Each document should reflect either direct, indirect, or indirect persuasive writing. The letters or memos do not have to be addressed to you. You may white-out any names or important information to retain confidentiality.

Proofread and edit the letters, applying the concepts of effective business writing. Mark your corrections on the letters or memos using proofreader's symbols. Complete the analysis sheets beginning below. Upon completing the checksheets, write a two- to three-page memo summarizing your findings. Discuss each letter or memo separately, detailing whether you think the writers achieved their goals. In your conclusion, discuss what you learned about business communication, critique the assignment, and make suggestions for improving the assignment. Submit your analysis sheets, your memo, the edited letters, and the edited memos for evaluation.

ANALYSIS SHEET FOR LETTERS

	Letter 1	Letter 2	Letter 3	Letter 4	Letter 5
Stationery					
Regular size	_____	_____	_____	_____	_____
Executive size	_____	_____	_____	_____	_____
Other	_____	_____	_____	_____	_____
Letter Style					
Block	_____	_____	_____	_____	_____
Modified Block	_____	_____	_____	_____	_____
Simplified	_____	_____	_____	_____	_____
Semiblock	_____	_____	_____	_____	_____
Other	_____	_____	_____	_____	_____
Punctuation Style					
Open	_____	_____	_____	_____	_____
Mixed	_____	_____	_____	_____	_____
Other	_____	_____	_____	_____	_____

	Letter Number				

Readability Level or Fog Index _____ _____ _____ _____ _____

Number of Misspelled Words _____ _____ _____ _____ _____

Number of Grammar Problems _____ _____ _____ _____ _____

Letter Number

	1	2	3	4	5

Letter centered on the page _____ _____ _____ _____ _____

Letter parts properly organized _____ _____ _____ _____ _____

Letter written tactfully _____ _____ _____ _____ _____

Any examples of sexist language?

Letter 1 _____

Letter 2 _____

Letter 3 _____

Letter 4 _____

Letter 5 _____

Letter complete _____ _____ _____ _____ _____

Letter clear _____ _____ _____ _____ _____

Any examples of technical jargon?

Letter 1 _____

Letter 2 _____

Letter 3 _____

Letter 4 _____

Letter 5 _____

Letter concise _____ _____ _____ _____ _____

Any examples of wordy or trite expressions?

Letter 1 _____

Letter 2 _____

Letter 3 _____

Letter 4 _____

Letter 5 _____

Letter Number

	1	2	3	4	5

Letter written actively_____ _____ _____ _____ _____

Any examples of passive writing or delayers?

Letter 1 _____

Letter 2 _____

Letter 3 _____

Letter 4 _____

Letter 5 _____

Letter using "you attitude"	_____	_____	_____	_____	_____
Letter concrete and paints a definite picture	_____	_____	_____	_____	_____
Letter contains a positive tone and courtesy	_____	_____	_____	_____	_____

Classify the Letter

Circle the approach used.

Letter One   Direct   Indirect-Bad News   Indirect-Persuasion
Appropriate approach? Why or why not?

Letter Two   Direct   Indirect-Bad News   Indirect-Persuasion
Appropriate approach? Why or why not?

Letter Three   Direct   Indirect-Bad News   Indirect-Persuasion
Appropriate approach? Why or why not?

Letter Four   Direct   Indirect-Bad News   Indirect-Persuasion
Appropriate approach? Why or why not?

Letter Five   Direct   Indirect-Bad News   Indirect-Persuasion
Appropriate approach? Why or why not?

	Memo 1	Memo 2	Memo 3	Memo 4	Memo 5
Stationery					
Regular size	_____	_____	_____	_____	_____
Executive size	_____	_____	_____	_____	_____
Other	_____	_____	_____	_____	_____
Readability Level or Fog Index	_____	_____	_____	_____	_____
Number of Misspelled Words	_____	_____	_____	_____	_____
Number of Grammar Problems	_____	_____	_____	_____	_____

	Memo Number				
	1	**2**	**3**	**4**	**5**
TO shown before FROM	_____	_____	_____	_____	_____
Courtesy title used if upward communication	_____	_____	_____	_____	_____
Date shown in full	_____	_____	_____	_____	_____

    Any examples of incorrect dates?

    Memo 1 _____

    Memo 2 _____

    Memo 3 _____

    Memo 4 _____

    Memo 5 _____

SUBJECT LINE specific
and brief   _____   _____   _____   _____   _____

    Any examples of problems with subject lines?

    Memo 1 _____

    Memo 2 _____

    Memo 3 _____

    Memo 4 _____

    Memo 5 _____

Pen-written initials
shown with the
writer's name   _____   _____   _____   _____   _____

Number of signatures versus
pen-written initials:

    Memo 1 _____

    Memo 2 _____

    Memo 3 _____

    Memo 4 _____

    Memo 5 _____

Top and side margins
approximately
one-inch   _____   _____   _____   _____   _____

Any widow or
orphan lines?   _____   _____   _____   _____   _____

If two-page
document, does it
contain proper
second-page heading?_____   _____   _____   _____   _____

Memo properly
organized   _____   _____   _____   _____   _____

Memo complete   _____   _____   _____   _____   _____

Memo clear   _____   _____   _____   _____   _____

    Any examples of technical jargon?

    Memo 1 _____

    Memo 2 _____

    Memo 3 _____

    Memo 4 _____

    Memo 5 _____

Memo concise   _____   _____   _____   _____   _____

    Any examples of wordy or trite expressions?

    Memo 1 _____

    Memo 2 _____

    Memo 3 _____

    Memo 4 _____

    Memo 5 _____

	1	2	3	4	5
Memo written actively	_____	_____	_____	_____	_____

Any examples of passive writing or delayers?

    Memo 1 _____

    Memo 2 _____

    Memo 3 _____

    Memo 4 _____

    Memo 5 _____

	1	2	3	4	5
Memo using "you attitude"	_____	_____	_____	_____	_____
Memo concrete and paints a definite picture	_____	_____	_____	_____	_____
Memo contains a positive tone and courtesy	_____	_____	_____	_____	_____

Classify the Memo

Circle the approach used.

Memo One   Direct   Indirect-Bad News   Indirect-Persuasion
Appropriate approach? Why or why not?

Memo Two   Direct   Indirect-Bad News   Indirect-Persuasion
Appropriate approach? Why or why not?

Memo Three   Direct   Indirect-Bad News   Indirect-Persuasion
Appropriate approach? Why or why not?

Memo Four   Direct   Indirect-Bad News   Indirect-Persuasion
Appropriate approach? Why or why not?

Memo Five   Direct   Indirect-Bad News   Indirect-Persuasion
Appropriate approach? Why or why not?

OPTION 2—INDIVIDUAL PROGRESS REPORT

Write an individual progress report at the midpoint of your class. The content of this report will include: (1) a purpose statement of your report; (2) work completed—what you have learned and done so far in the course (the exact tasks you have completed, how much time you have spent so far, and problems you have encountered); (3) present work—what you are presently working on; and (4) work to be completed—what remains to be done, what problems you anticipate, and what you hope the results will be.

    Use standard memo format and keyboard your report.

OPTION 3—PROPOSAL

Choose one of the following topics for a research project, or create your own topic. Use the information from your research to identify a problem or a need. Then develop a proposal for solving the problem. Bring five copies to class to share with classmates; get reactions and receive advice. Follow the guidelines given in the chapter for proposals, and keyboard your report.

Describe a problem in an organization familiar to you.

Survey alumni in business and industry to determine how well college has prepared him or her for present business writing tasks.

Interview local businesspeople to determine the kinds of writing they do on the job and discuss any writing difficulties they encounter.

Survey personnel directors of local companies to learn their style preferences for résumés and letters of application.

Survey the local business community to find out whether an interest exists for a college-sponsored business writing seminar.

Analyze some aspect of college life, such as parking, registration, student night life, or safety.

Gather information on a business topic of your choice, such as problems of two-career families, the characteristics of the job market, or small-business opportunities in your community.

OPTION 4—INTERVIEW

Conduct informal interviews with several businesspeople about the kinds of reports they prepare on their jobs. Ask the following questions: To whom do they send various kinds of reports and what information do they contain? How are the reports used? Discuss your findings in a short report and write thank-you letters to the interviewees.

OPTION 5—JUSTIFICATION REPORT

Go to the library to review at least three current business periodicals in your chosen career area. Analyze the journals for possible adoption by your current employer. Then write a justification report to your manager, stating why your office should receive the magazine (whichever you choose). Keep the report to approximately 600 words.

Some criteria to keep in mind as you review the journals and magazines include:

1. Cost and frequency of publication.
2. Content (subject matter of articles featured in the issue you analyze and a list of regular features, usually called *departments*).
3. The style or technicality of the writing.
4. Information about the advertisements (specific goods, services, and companies).

OPTION 6—OBJECTIVE, POLICY, AND PROCEDURES

Prepare a general objective, a policy, and 10 procedural rules or guides for the following case. Present this information in a memo directed to your professor.

Using the classroom building used for this class, prepare the college objective, policy, and procedures identifying how to evacuate the building in case of emergency. These statements should be suitable for publication in the college newspaper and for posting throughout the building.

Consider the number of people using available exits, priorities for exiting the building, what constitutes an emergency, what to do if the water or electricity fails, what to do if you have students with special needs, and who should (and how they should) contact the appropriate college and emergency officials.

CHAPTER 7

Making Business Letters and Documents Look Attractive on Paper and on the Computer Screen

*V*isual appearance (letters that are awkwardly positioned, badly typed, or have smudges will not impress anyone, much less produce any business) and stationery (does the quality fit the recipient and the sender?) count. Remember, you don't make sales calls in blue jeans and sneakers.[1]

Donald Austerman

LEARNING OBJECTIVES

After reading this chapter, you should be able to:

- Discuss the importance of appearance for letters.

- List what can be found on a letterhead.

- Identify the standard parts of a business letter.

- List appropriate courtesy titles.

- Explain the optional parts of a letter.

- Differentiate between open and mixed punctuation styles.

- List the parts of a second-page heading.

- Describe the differences between full block, semiblock, modified block, and simplified letter styles.

[1] Donald Austerman, "Writing Sales Letters That Really Sing," *Sales & Marketing Management*, February 1989; 141, 2; Research Library, pp. 40–44.

- Explain how to fold letters and address an envelope.

- Explain why some American customs will not work when writing international letters.

- Understand that various online documents look different.

- Become aware of the formatting tips to use for online documents.

The Importance of Appearance

Too often, businesspeople overlook the importance of appearance in written communication. They spend hours developing a logical and coherent message, and then pay no attention to how they present their information. First impressions will make or break a document. If readers find the document favorable, they will start reading; but before they begin to read, they will react to the feel of the paper, the design of the letter, the letter arrangement, and the appearance of the type.

Although the content of your message is most important, an appropriate appearance increases the chances your reader will read the message. For a written message to be read and seriously considered, it must meet certain expectations. This chapter focuses on those expectations and what you should do to meet them. Since you want your message read, your document's appearance should not call attention to itself. Instead, the appearance of your message should simplify communication. The following paragraphs describe the characteristics of stationery and the basic elements found on any letterhead.

Stationery

The standard business stationery measures 8 × 11 inches in the United States, Canada, and Mexico. In most other countries the ISO Standard called A4 is used. The ISO paper sizes are based on the metric system and measure 210 mm × 297 mm[2]

Some executives use monarch-size sheets of 7 × 10 inches. For brief internal messages such as memos or notes, you can use half sheets measuring 8 × 5 inches.

Business stationery is usually 16- to 20-pound paper. The weight of the paper refers to the weight of a ream of 17- × 22-inch paper (a standard printer's measure). If lighter than 16 pounds, the stationery appears too fragile, while paper heavier than 20 pounds is too bulky, hard to fold, and expensive.

White continues to be the standard color, although writers are making greater use of light colors than ever before. Colored paper is often used for sales documents.

Many companies personalize their stationery with a watermark identifying the company. You see the watermark as a faint design when you hold the paper up to the light. The paper manufacturer imprints the company logo or other identifying symbols on the paper during production.

---

[2] Retrieved from *http://www.paper-paper.com/A4–1.html* and *http://www.cl.cam.ac.uk/~mgk25/iso-paper.html*.

Letterhead

Companies use letterhead stationery to legitimize their business organization. Your letterhead can be a powerful means of portraying your organization's image. The basic elements found on any letterhead include the company name, address, and zip code. Additional items may include telephone number, cell phone numbers, e-mail addresses, company symbol, picture, slogan, and website. In years past, letterheads included such things as branch offices, names of directors, or even pictures of the headquarters building. Today, businesses take a much simpler approach so as not to detract from the contents of the letter. Usually the letterhead occupies approximately the top two inches of the stationery.

Layout of the Letter

To avoid sending letters with an unattractive or disorganized appearance, you must plan your layout. The placement of the letter on the page determines a pleasing appearance.

If you balance your letter on the page, your document appears more attractive. You can achieve a picture-frame effect by surrounding your message with ample margins. If you vary the top and side margins based on the message length, you can produce a letter with eye appeal. Use the guidelines in Table 7.1 to help you set up your letter.

If the company logo is flush left in block style at the top of your letterhead and the logo is at least 1 inch from the left edge of the paper, the left margin of the body of the letter should line up with the margin of the logo.

Standard Parts of a Business Letter

If you compare business correspondence from a variety of companies, you will notice obvious differences. Although diversity occurs in stylistic features, writers agree on the standard parts of a letter. A letter should contain seven basic parts: the letterhead, the date, the inside address, the attention line, the salutation, the body, and the signature block.

LETTERHEAD

The letterhead contains the company name and address as its minimum elements. With the increased use of fax machines, many organizations now include their fax numbers as part of the letterhead.

TABLE 7.1 ☛ Guidelines for establishing line lengths using the picture-frame method.

LENGTH OF LETTER	NUMBER OF WORDS	SIDE MARGINS
Short	Under 100	2 inches
Medium	100–200	1 inch
Long	200–300	1 inch
Two pages	Over 300	1 inch

DATE

You should date all documents to tell your reader when you wrote the document. The month should be spelled out, and never abbreviated. You should use numerals for the day and the year, but do not add the indications for ordinal numbers *(st, nd, rd, th)* to the day of the month. Also, you should not condense the year with an apostrophe, giving just the last two numbers. Write dates like this:

October 12, 20XX   July 4, 20XX   11 November 20XX

INSIDE ADDRESS

The inside address includes the receiver's name, title, address, and possibly fax number. Single-space this information at the left margin. Use the all-capitalized, two-letter state abbreviations shown in Table 7.2.

Be precise in the way you keyboard a company name and address. Keyboard the information exactly as it appears on the company's letterhead.

Keyboard the name of the person addressed just as it appears on the incoming letterhead or below the signature. In addressing both a company and a person, follow the printed name when it differs from the keyboarded or handwritten version.

Keyboard titles on the same line with a person's name. However, if the title makes the line too long, place the title on a separate line. You can keyboard a title on the line with a company name, separating the two with a comma. When you think the name of a company looks too long on one line, you can make two lines of it. But you should never divide a person's name in an address, no matter how long.

Always be sure to use the appropriate *courtesy title* of Mr., Mrs., Ms., Dr., and so on in an address. If you do not know the marital status of a female, address her as Ms.

TABLE 7.2 ☞ **Recommended abbreviations for state, district, and territory names.**

Alabama	AL	Montana	MT
Alaska	AK	Nebraska	NE
Arizona	AZ	Nevada	NV
Arkansas	AR	New Hampshire	NH
California	CA	New Jersey	NJ
Colorado	CO	New Mexico	NM
Connecticut	CT	New York	NY
Delaware	DE	North Carolina	NC
District of Columbia	DC	North Dakota	ND
Florida	FL	Ohio	OH
Georgia	GA	Oklahoma	OK
Guam	GU	Oregon	OR
Hawaii	HI	Pennsylvania	PA
Idaho	ID	Puerto Rico	PR
Illinois	IL	Rhode Island	RI
Indiana	IN	South Carolina	SC
Iowa	IA	South Dakota	SD
Kansas	KS	Tennessee	TN
Kentucky	KY	Texas	TX
Louisiana	LA	Utah	UT
Maine	ME	Vermont	VT
Maryland	MD	Virgin Islands	VI
Massachusetts	MA	Virginia	VA
Michigan	MI	Washington	WA
Minnesota	MN	West Virginia	WV
Mississippi	MS	Wyoming	WY
Missouri	MO		

When you write to several persons at different locations, include the name and the address of each person and list the names alphabetically. For more than three persons, use the following style instead of keyboarding all names and addresses at the left margin.

Mrs. Mary S. Britt
145 South Seventh Street
Chicago, IL 67327

Mrs. Marilyn Griffith
3607 Highland Court
Kansas City, MO 66121

Mr. John T. Matlik
235 Sheridan Drive
Atlanta, GA 30327

Mr. Harry E. Roebuck
2910 Glenridge Circle
Birmingham, AL 32508

When you write to several persons who know each other well, you may omit the number, street, and city and include only each name. If the list becomes long, keyboard the names alphabetically in two or three columns above the body of the letter.

Occasionally, you must write a letter not addressed to any named person. When you do, use an attention line or subject line.

ATTENTION LINE

The attention line names the specific person who should read the letter. Place it between the inside address and the salutation. However, if you are using an attention line, do not keyboard the individual's name in the inside address; address the letter only to the company. Also, you can use the attention line in place of the salutation, while either the attention line or the salutation may be used with or without a subject line. See the following example.

Show-Me Farm

1594 Hendon Road

Marietta, GA 30066

Attention: Ms. Hillary Roebuck

Subject: Insurance Plans for Horses

Some writers use an attention line when they know the receiver's name but do not know the receiver's sex. For example:

Show-Me Farm

1594 Hendon Road

Marietta, GA 30066

Attention: H. G. Roebuck

SALUTATION

The most frequently used salutation is: Dear Mr., Ms., or Mrs. Some writers now leave off *Dear* as part of their salutations because they do not feel comfortable addressing someone they do not know personally in this manner.

If you know the correspondent, you may be more informal. However, you should not use the individual's first name until you receive permission to do so.

In the past, writers employed such salutations as Gentlemen, Sirs, or Madam. Do not use these terms unless you know the sex of the receiver. Instead, use a job title or a subject line.

Some recipients have titles and expect you to use those titles in the salutation. Use Table 7.3 to determine the appropriate salutation.

When you write to a company, a partnership, or a group, use the salutation "Gentlemen and Ladies." An alternative would be to omit the salutation and use a subject line.

TABLE 7.3 ☞ **Forms of address for dignitaries.**

PERSON	NAME IN ADDRESS	SALUTATION
President of United States	The President	Dear Mr. or Madam President
Cabinet Member	The Honorable *(first & last name)*	Dear Mr. or Madam Secretary
Attorney General	The Honorable *(first & last name)*	Dear Mr. or Madam U.S. Attorney
Senator	The Honorable *(first & last name)*	Dear Senator *(last name)*
U.S. Representative	The Honorable *(first & last name)*	Dear Mr. or Ms. *(last name)*
Governor	The Honorable *(first & last name)*	Dear Governor *(last name)*
State Senator or Representative	The Honorable *(first & last name)*	Dear Mr. or Ms. *(last name)*
Mayor	The Honorable *(first & last name)*	Dear Mayor *(last name)*
Judge	The Honorable *(first & last name)*	Dear Judge *(last name)*
Lawyer	Mr. or Ms. *(first & last name)*	Dear Mr. or Ms. *(last name)*
University President	Dr. *(first & last name)*, President	Dear Dr. *(last name)*
Dean	Dr. *(first & last name)*, Dean of *(school)*	Dear Dr. *(last name)*
Professor	Professor *(first & last name)*	Dear Professor *(last name)*
Rabbi	Rabbi *(first & last name)*	Dear Rabbi *(last name)*
Protestant Clergy	The Reverend *(first & last name)*	Dear Dr., Mr., or Ms. *(last name)*
Roman Catholic Priest	The Reverend Father *(first & last name)*	Dear Father *(last name)*
Roman Catholic Nun	Sister *(name)*	Dear Sister

BODY

The body contains the main message of the letter. Begin the body of the letter two lines below the salutation or subject line. With longer letters or those keyboarded on monarch stationery, single-space between lines and double-space between paragraphs. Research has shown readers find single-spaced letters easier to read, and writers save money on stationery.

The body of the letter should convey the necessary information without leaving significant questions unanswered. Do not fill an entire sheet when a shorter message will accomplish your purpose. The body should be no longer than necessary.

Paragraphing has much to do with the readability of a letter and, therefore, with its success. A paragraph should be a statement or a group of related statements expressing a unit of thought in the development of an idea. All sentences in a paragraph should relate to a single idea, topic, or unit of thought. Yet all sentences relating to a single idea do not have to be put in the same paragraph.

Vary your paragraph length. Short paragraphs make it easy for a reader to scan a letter and identify important points. Longer paragraphs make the letter more difficult to read.

Be careful not to keyboard too near the bottom of the page and not squeeze in the signature. Instead, use a second page and carry over at least a full paragraph of text, not just the complimentary close and signature. On letters of more than one page, leave at least an inch, and preferably a little more, margin at the bottom of the first page.

SIGNATURE BLOCK

Keyboard your name and title on separate lines, four or five lines below the complimentary close. When keyboarding, try to keep both name and title from extending beyond the center of the page.

Optional Parts of a Letter

A letter can also contain optional parts. The optional parts include: subject line, complimentary close, reference initials, enclosures, copies, and postscripts.

SUBJECT LINE

The subject line briefly explains the major issue of your document. The placement of the subject line depends on the style you have chosen. The block style and the simplified style place the subject line at the left margin, while the modified block style can center this line or place it at the left margin.

COMPLIMENTARY CLOSE

Place the complimentary close two lines below the last line of the letter. Depending on letter style, the closing can start at center or be flush with the left margin. Modified block starts the closing at center, while block style places the closing at the left margin. Simplified style omits the closing completely. Capitalize only the first letter of the first word. Common closings include: Sincerely, Respectfully, and Cordially.

Scott Meredith Literary Agency, a top New York agency that publishes the bimonthly *New York Overheard* column, offers a new addition to the list of complimentary closings. Their writers end letters with "All best wishes." The agency feels this provides a small but sincere sense of informal warmth.

REFERENCE INITIALS

If you work in an organization and someone else keyboards your documents, you will need to know who did the keyboarding. By noting the initials, you can usually determine who keyboarded your document. Reference initials appear at the left margin, a double-space below the last line of the signature block. Usually the writer does not capitalize the reference initials.

ENCLOSURES

When you have something to enclose with a letter, place an enclosure notation at the left margin a double-space below the reference initials. Identify each important enclosure. If you want an enclosure returned, say so. If you include more than one enclosure, say how many. Note the following examples:

Enclosure: Cert. CK. $2000

Enclosure: Check No. 12345

Enclosure: Proof of Payment—Please Return

Enclosures (2)

COPIES

If someone other than your intended audience receives a copy, identify that person at the end of your letter. List the names of those who are to receive copies after the single letter *c* with a colon. Keyboard this information one or two spaces below the signature block, reference initials, or enclosure notation. The following examples illustrate how to use the copy notation correctly.

C: N. Prochaska

c: N. Prochaska

You may send *blind* copies of letters to someone without your receiver knowing. Note such action by placing **bc** only on the copy.

POSTSCRIPTS

A postscript, or an afterthought, belongs after reference initials, enclosure notations, or copy notations. Be careful when using a postscript because it may indicate you did not organize your thoughts before you put them on paper. You can use a postscript as a reminder in a persuasive document, because its position can make the reader notice it. Do not label postscripts as **P.S.** or **PS,** and do not sign or initial them.

Important Aspects of Format

This section describes two other important components of format: punctuation style and second-page headings. You can choose which punctuation style to use, but you must use a second-page heading if your document exceeds one page.

PUNCTUATION STYLE

There are two punctuation styles to choose from in punctuating the salutation and the close of a letter. With *open punctuation,* no punctuation follows the salutation or the close. *Mixed punctuation* requires a colon following the salutation and a comma following the complimentary close. See the following examples.

Open:	Dear Mrs. Williams	Sincerely
Mixed:	Dear Mrs. Williams:	Sincerely,

SECOND-PAGE HEADING

When the body of a letter requires more than a single page, use a second-page heading. You can choose from three common headings, as shown in Box 7.1.

The date appearing in the heading of the second page should match the date on the first page. This reinforces the fact that these pages belong together. Of course, you should use the receiver's name in the heading.

On letters of more than one page, leave at least a one-inch margin at the bottom of the first page. Unless you have room for two lines, do not start a paragraph

Show-Me Farm   -2-   May 14, 20XX

or

Mr. Frank Smith, July 31, 20XX, page 2

or

Ms. Taylor Matlik
March 15, 20XX

BOX 7.1 ☞ **Second-Page Heading Formats**

near the end of the page. You should not divide the last word or name on the bottom of a page. Instead, carry it over to the next page. Do not carry over a partial line, called a *widow*. If you must divide a paragraph, carry over at least two lines to the next page. If you are at the end of your letter, do not leave just a partial paragraph on the last page. In that case, do not divide your last paragraph; instead, carry it over. You should have at least one complete paragraph plus the complimentary close and the signature on a second page.

Letter Styles

This section describes the four widely used letter styles: full block, semiblock, modified block, and simplified.

FULL BLOCK STYLE

In full block style, every line begins at the left margin including the date, close, and signature block. Because you focus on the left margin, you make few adjustments on the computer, thus saving time. Box 7.2 presents this letter style.

In Print Magazine
Suite 207
Miami, FL 33101

Date Line

June 3, 20XX

Inside Address

Mr. Robert Wyatt
1356 Hendon Road
Woodstock, GA 30188

Double-Space
Salutation
Double-Space
Subject Line
Double-Space

Dear Mr. Wyatt: (mixed punctuation)

Subject: Letter Format (if used, always following salutation)

This illustration covers practically all the points explained in the preceding directions concerning format and style of letters. The following paragraphs emphasize vital facts.

Body

Remember, your letters represent you; therefore, take pride in them, for you play an important role in your organization.

This two-page letter illustrates several points in the handling of correspondence. The second page shows: (1) how to use the second-page heading, (2) how to conclude a letter, (3) how to indicate copy notations, and (4) how and where to place a postscript.

Double-Space
between Paragraphs

Note the pleasing appearance of this letter. The satisfactory effect comes from attention to details such as even margins and effective paragraphing. Both add not only to the appearance of keyboarded matter, but to the ease of reading. If the recipient finds your letter easy to read, you will likely get a prompt response.

BOX 7.2 ☞ **Full Block Format**

Mr. Robert Wyatt   Page 2   June 3, 20XX

The reputation of your company depends largely on the impression you make on your customers, clients, and associates. Sometimes your only contact with an individual is by letter. Therefore, you should write every letter with utmost care.

Before you sign a letter, proofread it and check the spelling carefully for mechanical and typographical errors. Check, too, to make sure it says everything desired. You want your letter to make a favorable impression for you and your company.

Complimentary close,

John Doe

Name and Title of Signer

Enclosure

Copy

(Remember that a package sells the product!)

BOX 7.2 🖙 **(continued)**

Remember, a two-page, full block-style letter uses mixed punctuation and a return address. The letter looks like a picture in a frame. On multiple-page letters, leave a margin of at least an inch, and preferably a little more, at the bottom of the first page.

SEMIBLOCK STYLE

The two differences between full block and semiblock style are the indention of paragraphs within the body of the letter, and that the date, closing, and signature begin to the right of center. Paragraphs are indented five spaces.

MODIFIED BLOCK STYLE

In modified block style, the date begins at the center of the page. Align the close and the signature block with the date. All other parts stay the same as in full block style. See Box 7.3 for an example.

SIMPLIFIED STYLE

In the simplified style developed by the Administrative Management Society, you do not use a salutation or a close. A subject line replaces the salutation and all lines begin at the left margin. See Box 7.4 for an example.

Merchants Business Park
1279 Peachtree Road • Lenox Twin Towers • Suite 102
Atlanta, GA 30309

June 3, 20XX

Mrs. Mary Britt
2203 Ridgewood Court
Marietta, Georgia 30066

Dear Mrs. Britt:

This letter illustrates the modified block style. Remember, when you write a short letter, you can move the date line down. This provides more white space at the top of your letter.

Be sure to single-space the address in block form. With the modified style, you have the option of indenting or not indenting the first line of each paragraph five spaces.

Unless otherwise instructed, address letters to individuals rather than to companies, corporations, or partnerships.

Complimentary close,

Joe McGuinn

Joe McGuinn
Sales Manager

dmr *(reference initials)*

Enclosure

Copies: 1

Date line begins at center of page

Close and signature block begin at center of page (space for signature)

BOX 7.3 📝 **Modified Block Format**

Most of the business letters you send or receive will represent one of these four placement styles, although writers sometimes devise special formats to get their readers' attention. They may use devices such as unusual margins, color, or boxes to enclose important information.

Templates and Wizards

Templates and wizards are generally accepted standard formats of a company and are frequently included in software packages. Companies often adapt these standardized formats and make one their own. Consistency is the key for communication with customers and clients. Be careful when using templates; check to see if they are correct or outdated.

4 spaces here

Use subject line
instead of saluation

No complimentary
closing

BOX 7.4 ☞ **Simplified Letter Style**

Folding and Inserting Enclosures

Sloppy folding can spoil an otherwise excellent letter. Fold the standard or monarch letterhead horizontally about one-third of the way up from the bottom, and then fold the upper third down from the top, leaving an eighth or quarter of an inch uncovered. Folding your letter in this fashion makes it easy to open. Make sure both folds are parallel with the top and bottom edges of the letterhead.

You can use a No. 10 envelope for standard letterhead, or you may choose to send your letter in a large manila envelope to keep it flat. Occasionally, you might use a No. 6 envelope. Fold your document in half and then in thirds. For monarch stationery, you must use a No. 9 envelope. Study the illustration in Exhibit 7.1.

When you put papers held with a paper clip in an envelope, make sure you place the document so the fastener will be at the bottom of the envelope and on the far side from the postage corner. This protects the papers from possible damage from metering and canceling machines or from automatic letter openers.

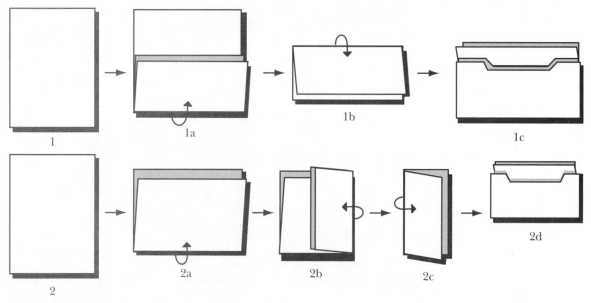

EXHIBIT 7.1

Letter folds for standard-size and monarch letterhead.

Make sure you use the two-letter state abbreviation for zip codes.

SOURCE: Dorling Kindersley Media Library.

When sending letters to international locations, you must make sure your addresses conform exactly to the prescribed format. For example, Canada and Germany will not even attempt to deliver mail that does not meet their format.

Source: Wesley L. Brook, "How to Ensure Your Mail Reaches Its Targets," Target Marketing, Volume 20, Issue 6, June 1997, p. 45.

Addressing Envelopes

When addressing your envelope, start the first line of the address slightly to the right of the center of the envelope. For long addresses, start farther to the left. The United States Postal Service recommends keyboarding addresses in all capital letters with no punctuation.

Keyboard special mailing instructions three lines above the address, using all capital letters, and underscoring if you wish. When required, keyboard *Attention, Please Forward, Hold for Arrival, Personal,* and so on in the lower left quarter of the envelope, and underscore the word or phrase. On envelopes to foreign countries, keyboard the name of the country in all capital letters as the last line of the address.

Keyboard the sender's name above the return address on the envelope. Then, any piece the post office sends back can be routed to the person who mailed it.

If the address has a street address and a post office box, keyboard only the post office box number. Spell out *Company* and *Corporation* unless the organization abbreviates either term. Corporations sometimes use the abbreviations *Inc.* and *Ltd.* Note the proper way to address envelopes in Exhibit 7.2.

International Letters

In the United States, businesspeople appreciate efficient and straightforward letters. Moreover, letters in the United States tend to be informal and conversational. However, international readers may look upon such directness and informality as inappropriate, insensitive, and abrasive. As you read the international letter presented in Box 7.5, compare and contrast it to a business letter you would receive in the United States.

Harris Motor Lodge
Omena, Michigan 49074

SPECIAL DELIVERY

MR ARNOLD C EVANS
2110 CRESTVIEW ROAD
SALT LAKE CITY UT 84116

The Lawrence Book Company
209 West Third Street
Chicago, Illinois 60610

TOWNSEND PAPER COMPANY
1532 LEXINGTON AVENUE
ST. LOUIS MO 63109

Please forward to Mr. John A. Manning

TOWNSEND PAPER COMPANY
1532 LEXINGTON AVENUE
ST. LOUIS MO 63109

<u>Attention</u>: Mr. John A. Manning

EXHIBIT 7.2

Envelope formats.

Typically, when composing a letter to an international colleague, you will use a more formal tone and include maximum punctuation to assure clarity in your international documents. If you have not personally met the individual to whom you are writing, you should not use his or her first name in the salutation. Salutations, for example, in German letters would be the English equivalent of "Very Honored Mrs. Jones" and in Latin American countries, "My Esteemed Dr. Greem." The complimentary closing would often be the English equivalent of "Very respectfully yours."

The Japanese have a traditional format beginning with the salutation followed by a comment about the season or weather. As you can see, it becomes critical that you understand your receiver and his or her culture when writing international letters.[3]

When you write international letters, your work should conform to the organizational format and cultural conventions of the receiver's country. You must do some research before writing your letter. For example, letters in Germany start with a long, formal lead-in, such as, "Referring to your kind inquiry from the 31st of the month, we take the liberty to remind you with this letter. . . . "[4]

Italian business letters may refer to the receiver's family and children, while French correspondents would consider it rude to begin a letter with a request before

> I noticed with interest when my Romanian colleagues would introduce me, they would introduce me as Professor Dr. Deborah Roebuck, as titles are extremely important in Romania.

---

[3] Lillian H. Chaney and Jeanette S. Martin, *Intercultural Business Communication,* 2nd ed. (Upper Saddle River, NJ: Prentice Hall, 2000), pp. 132–133.

[4] Wolfgang Manekeller, as cited in Iris I. Varner, "Internationalizing Business Communication Courses," *The Bulletin of the Association for Business Communication,* p. 10, December 1987.

Dear Debby!

Thank you very much for your nice letter! It is really exciting, that people from both sides could get so much impressions from the relative short visit.

It was very nice for me, too, and I look forward to organise the next meeting—either here or in Atlanta! I believe, there are much possibilities to meet again. I have to re-arrange my own time, I think. I spent enormous time last year for the organisation of the students' projects for companies (research of Eastern-European markets) and international exchange with Belarus. It is all very nice, but at the end you have no time even for your daughter. . . . So I have to define my priorities, and one of the first place will be development of programs with Atlanta.

Currently I stay in contact with Joe Bocchi, WebMBA director, with whom we have primarily the contact about the online projects. I have heard that one faculty member from Kennesaw has been here, but I didn't know this, since he was invited by the MBA International Trade program, leaded by Conny Scott. (The group of Kennesaw students will come here on the week 23-30 May). As you know, I asked Conny Scott to take care of the contacts with Kennesaw, while I will continue the project with WebMBA. It seems, it will run forward!

We will start from 1st of October the new system of bachelor and master here, so we would not have diploma any more. I see that on this way we will have more possibilities for international programs cooperation.

In Germany it is very strong winter, the weather is really unstable and it is very dangerous to drive by car long distances. But, I use to drive every day from Bernburg to campus, because it is a good practice.

My daughter has got the half-year certificate for 9th grade, and it is the best in the class. She is very glad to this (but I glad even more . . .). So she tries to socialize herself in the life of small town, and I think there are some advantages: small towns are more secure. I drive home (I mean to Minsk) for two last February weeks, my father has 70th celebration, so I would like to meet my family.

I wish you very much positive emotions, interesting work and enough time for yourself! You are very nice and an optimistic person, therefore you, shall have luck in all your initiatives and matters!

I will be very glad to keep our communication.

With All My Best Wishes,

Elena Kashtanova

BOX 7.5 🖙 **International Letter from Germany (Verbatim)**

you explain the situation. Finnish writers assume more shared knowledge between the writer and the reader, and therefore write shorter and more direct letters.[5]

International letters may also use different formatting techniques. Some countries, such as France, still use the indented letter style, where each paragraph is indented with closed punctuation. The French also place the name of the originating city before the date and sometimes place the date after the inside address. In their letters, the inside address is typed on the right side with the zip code preced-

---

[5] Mary Ellen Guffey, *Business Communication* (Belmont, CA: Wadsworth, 1994), pp. 160–161.

ing the name of the city (74010 PARIS). In Germany, the inside address is formatted so that the title is placed on the first line; the full name on the second line; the street name followed by the street number on the third line; and zip code, city, and state on the last line. In German letters, the company name is placed below the complimentary close and the writer signs the letter, but the writer's name and position are not typed in the signature block. The street number also follows the name of the street in Mexico and South America. In Japan and China, the surname is placed before the given or first name. You should be careful and try to format your outgoing letters and envelopes exactly as they are shown on the incoming correspondence.[6]

In the United States, you typically keyboard and single-space your letters, while in other countries they may hand write and single- or double-space their letters.

When writing the date, spell out the name of the month rather than indicating the months in dates. In the United States, *2/1/05* means *February 1,* but in most of the rest of the world it means *January 2.* Some other unambiguous formats include *1 Feb 05, 01 February 2005* and *Feb. 1, 2005.* Also spell out other abbreviations. You may know that MO means Missouri and PQ means Quebec, but your international audience may not.

Another formatting difference occurs with telephone numbers. The standard international format starts with a plus sign and includes the country code, city or area code, and local number, in that order; spaces (not hyphens) serve as delimiters. For example, a fax number would look like this: +1 703 683 4915. The country code for the United States (along with Canada and parts of the Caribbean) is 1. Within the United States, you dial 1 for long distance as well, so the number is what most people would write normally except for the plus sign and the spaces. For other countries, the long-distance prefix and the country code are not the same. For example, the phone number for the African National Congress headquarters in Johannesburg, as listed on its website *(http://www.anc.org.za),* is (011) 330 7000. In an international document it should be written as +27 11 330 7000, dropping the long-distance prefix (0) and adding the country code for South Africa (27) and the plus sign.

Include your country within your letterhead. Someone looking for a local vendor might want to know if your company resides in Birmingham, Alabama, or Birmingham, West Midlands, U.K. Besides the capital of New Zealand, the city of Wellington can be found in Kansas, Ontario, and New South Wales.[7]

Since 1994, a course in *international business* writing has been taught simultaneously at institutions in Belgium, Finland, and the United States. The course, which grew out of earlier shorter-term activities involving Belgian and U.S. students, has three components: (1) instruction; (2) a simulation in which students exchange business documents internationally; and (3) case studies of businesspeople who communicate internationally in writing.

Student performance in the **instructional component** of the course is evaluated by examinations and writing assignments. In the United States, for example, students write five letters and memos: one describing their international, business, and writing experience; one characterizing U.S. culture; one characterizing Belgian or Finnish culture; one advising a reader how to write for a high-context audience; and one advising a reader how to write for a collectivist audience.

The simulation component uses English as the common language for all students. The simulation is carefully structured to give students authentic experience in initiating and responding to written communication with their counterparts in the other two countries.

An American graduate student learned a great lesson when she wrote a letter, in French, to a Paris museum asking for permission to do research. She did not receive a response, so she took her letter to her French tutor. He quickly said, "No, no, Mademoiselle! It will never do. It must be more respectful. You must be very careful of individuals' titles. Let me show you." When she wrote a second time, she won the desired permission. The moral of the story—always know your audience!

Source: Janet K. Winter, "Writing for Effective Intercultural Business Communication," in Tested Teaching Ideas for Business Communication, edited by Courtland L. Bovee and John V. Thill (New York: McGraw-Hill, 1995), pp. 40–42.

[6] Lillian H. Chaney and Jeanette S. Martin, *Intercultural Business Communication,* 2nd ed. (Upper Saddle River, NJ: Prentice Hall, 2000), pp. 134–135.

[7] EEI Press, *eye@eeicom.com,* 66 Canal Center Plaza, Suite 200, Alexandria, Virginia 22314–5507, USA Phone +1 703 683 0683; fax +1 703 683 4915, *webmaster@eeicom.com,* 1998.

While the primary purpose of this project is instructional, it has also led to some interesting findings about cross-cultural differences in business writing presented elsewhere. In previous studies, U.S. students wrote long letters that described their supporting arguments in detail, while Flemish students wrote shorter and more direct letters. Finnish students were expected to write more like Flemish students. However, these cross-cultural expectations were not confirmed in this course. Instead, the students from Belgium, Finland, and the United States seemed to write in a fairly similar manner. Most letters were one page long; U.S. students wrote less and Belgian students wrote more than in the earlier study. The Finnish students wrote letters similar to those for the other two groups. One can speculate that the final letters represent an "international style" of letter writing, which contains fewer national features so that it can be received well globally.[8]

> Studies have found that approximately 79 percent of Web users scan pages and do not read word-by-word.
>
> Source: John Morkes and Jakob Nielsen, "Concise, Scannable, and Objective: How to Write for the Web," 1997. Retrieved from http://www.useit.com.

Format Principles for Online Documents

Web readers basically scan online text and often print off documents so that they can read them later in a more comfortable setting, as looking at a computer screen for hours on end can become tiring. Also, Web readers typically do not read a page from start to finish on the computer screen, but rather scan a site looking for relevant items, and then print pages that contain the information they seek.

By using headings, lists, and bullets, you can guide your Web reader. Some experts state you should highlight about three times as many words as you would when writing for print. Colored text or colored background can also be used for highlighting, but writers should not use blue for words as that color is reserved for hyperlinks.

Most often, Web readers pick out a few sentences or even parts of sentences to get the information they want. One user stated: "Give me bulleted items as I find them easy to read." Web research has shown that bullets and numbered lists slow down the scanning eye and can draw attention to important points. You can, however, include a greater number of lists on a Web page than on a printed page. Consider using the following formatting tips to grab the attention of your online reader.

- **Use a headline.**   Condense your most important point down to a one- or two-line headline.
- **Split into Different Pages.**   The unit of text on the Web is called a chunk, which is a screen's worth of information that includes links to other chunks.[9] See Box 7.6 for an example of chunking.
- **Don't Make Your Topics Linear.**   Readers can jump into a website at any page. Therefore each page should be written so that it can stand alone, which is certainly different from traditional writing.
- **Use plenty of subheads.**   People skim headings looking for specific topics—so use subheads liberally.
- **Format headings.**   As separate lines—or as a lead-in sentence to a paragraph.
- **Bold or highlight text to make it stand out.**   It's best to use it sparingly, such as for lead-in headings at the *start* of a paragraph. Bold words scattered inside the text can be confusing.
- **Use italics for *emphasis*.**   Italics help your reader *hear* the same emphasis you *intended*. Italics can help make your text *sound* more conversational.

[8] Ulla M. Connor, Kenneth W. Davis, Teun De Rycker, Elisabeth Margaretha Phillips, and J. Piet Verckens, *Business Communication Quarterly*, Volume 60, Issue 4, Dec. 97, pp. 63–74.

[9] Retrieved from "Writing for the Web," *http://crofsblogs.typepad.com/ckbetas/adapting_print_to_web.doc.*

- **Employment and Unemployment**
- **Prices and Living Conditions**
- **Compensation and Working Conditions**
- **Productivity and Technology**
- **Employment Projections**
- **International Programs**

EMPLOYMENT AND UNEMPLOYMENT

- **Labor Force Statistics from the Current Population Survey** - national data on employment, unemployment, earnings, and other labor market topics by demographic characteristics.

- **Nonfarm Payroll Statistics from the Current Employment Statistics (National)** - monthly national data by detailed industry on employment, hours, and earnings of workers on the payrolls of nonfarm establishments.

- **Nonfarm Payroll Statistics from the Current Employment Statistics (State&Area)** - monthly data on employment, hours, and earnings by industry and geographic area.

- **Quarterly Census of Employment and Wages** - comprehensive employment and wage data by industry and geographic area for workers covered by State Unemployment Insurance laws.

- **Occupational Employment Statistics** - annual data on employment and wages for about 750 occupations and 400 nonfarm industries for the nation, plus occupational data by geographic area.

- **Local Area Unemployment Statistics** - monthly and annual employment, unemployment, and labor force data for Census regions and divisions, States, counties, metropolitan areas, and many cities, by place of residence.

- **Mass Layoff Statistics** - reports on mass layoff actions that resulted in workers being separated from their jobs.

- **National Longitudinal Surveys** - several surveys gathering information at multiple points in time about the labor market and life experiences of six groups of American men, women, and youth.

- **Job Openings and Labor Turnover Survey (JOLTS)** - a new monthly study that has been developed to address the need for data on job openings, hires, and separations.

- **American Time Use Survey (ATUS)** - will collect information on how people living in the United States spend their time. First annual estimates expected to be published in mid-2004.

- **NEW Business Employment Dynamics** - quarterly data series of job gains and job losses statistics, generated from the Quarterly Census of Employment and Wages program.

- **Survey of Employer-Provided Training** - provides detailed information on training by major industry division and by size of establishment from surveys conducted in 1993 and 1995.

PRICES & LIVING CONDITIONS

- **Consumer Price Indexes** - monthly data on changes in the prices paid by urban consumers for a representative basket of goods and services.

- **Producer Price Indexes** - monthly data on changes in the selling prices received by domestic producers of goods and services.

BOX 7.6 ☛ **Illustration of Chunking**

SOURCE: Website: U.S. Department of Labor at www.bls.gov.

- **Import/Export Price Indexes** - monthly data on changes in the prices of imported and exported nonmilitary goods traded between the U.S. and the rest of the world.

- **Consumer Expenditure Survey** - data on the buying habits of American consumers, by socioeconomic characteristics.

COMPENSATION AND WORKING CONDITIONS

- **National Compensation Survey** - designed to integrate data from separate BLS compensation surveys.

   -- **Benefits** - comprehensive data on incidence and provisions of selected employee benefit plans.

   -- **Compensation Cost Trends** - quarterly indexes measuring change over time in labor costs and quarterly data measuring level of average costs per hour worked.

   -- **Wages** - data on occupational wages for localities, broad geographic regions, and the nation.

- **Safety and Health Statistics** - data on illnesses and injuries on the job and data on worker fatalities.

- **Collective Bargaining Agreements** - data on major work stoppages (lockouts and strikes) and a file of collective bargaining agreements.

PRODUCTIVITY AND TECHNOLOGY

- **Quarterly Labor Productivity** - quarterly indexes of labor productivity and related costs measures for major sectors of the economy, including business, nonfarm business, and manufacturing.

- **Multifactor Productivity** - annual indexes for industries and major sectors of the economy that relate output to labor, capital, and--in some cases--other inputs.

- **Industry Productivity** - annual indexes of productivity for detailed industries.

- **Foreign Labor Statistics** - comparative information by country on productivity and unit labor costs; compensation; labor force, employment, and unemployment; and consumer prices.

EMPLOYMENT PROJECTIONS

- **Employment Projections** - projected estimates on the labor market and economy 10 years into future, and career information such as *Occupational Outlook Handbook*.

INTERNATIONAL PROGRAMS

- **Foreign Labor Statistics** - comparative information by country on productivity and unit labor costs; compensation; labor force, employment, and unemployment; and consumer prices.

- **Import/Export Price Indexes** - monthly data on change in the prices of imported and exported nonmilitary goods traded between the U.S. and the rest of the world.

- **International Technical Cooperation** - conducts training in labor statistics for international participants and coordinates international requests for BLS services including technical experts and short-term visits to BLS.

Last Modified Date: February 3, 2004

Frequently Asked Questions | Freedom of Information Act | Customer Survey
Privacy & Security Statement | Linking to Our Site | Accessibility

U.S. Bureau of Labor Statistics
Postal Square Building
2 Massachusetts Ave., NE
Washington, DC 20212-0001

Phone: (202) 691-5200
Fax-on-demand: (202) 691-6325
Data questions: **blsdata_staff@bls.gov**
Technical (web) questions: **webmaster@bls.gov**
Other comments: **feedback@bls.gov**

BOX 7.6 ☞ (continued)

For example, when you read the sentence on page 170, you emphasized the word "sound" because it was in italics. That can make a big difference in the meaning of what you write. While italics can be overused, in general, it helps ensure that people read things the way you *intended* (or the way *you* intended). Notice how the italic changes the meanings of the following sentences:

- *I* said I liked it.
- I *said* I liked it.
- I said *I* liked it.
- I said I *liked* it.
- I said I liked *it*.

- **Use bullets.** Much like traditional business writing, you should keep your average text sentence length at 20 words or shorter.

- **Repeat your most important quotes.** Using pull quotes—quotes set larger and often in a different typeface.

- **Use white space generously as it greatly improves clearness.**

- **Update frequently.** On the main page, have the date of creation or the last update.[10]

- **Use pale, cool colors (blue, green, gray, earth tones) to express conservative, reserved attitudes.** Use bright colors like red and yellow to express energy and movement. Be careful about sending a mixed message where you mix hot and cool colors. Some colors like bright yellow can skew the whole design of a website or document.[11]

- **Use sans serif headlines rather than serif text.**

- **Have a link where readers can print out your document. See Box 7.7 for an example of how one website provided a link to printing version.**

Some additional websites that offer further guidance for online writing:

http://www.netmechanic.com/ news/vol4/design_no10.htm

http://www.microsoft.com/office/ previous/frontpage/columns/ sbcolumn04.asp

http://www.gooddocuments.com/ homepage/homepage.htm

http://www.sun.com/980713/ webwriting/

http://www.dhark.com/wfw.html

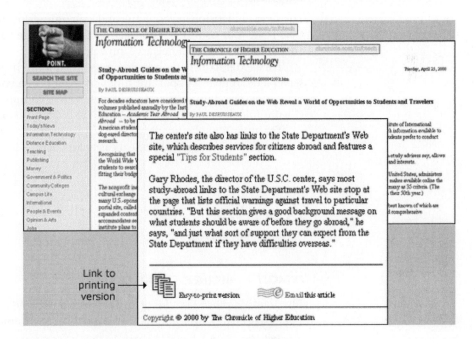

BOX 7.7 ☛ Example of Link to Printing Version

SOURCE: Copyright 2005, the Chronicle of Higher Education. Reprinted with permission.

[10] Retrieved from "Writing for the Web," *http://www.eldis.org/tales/writing/pyramid.htm.*

[11] Retrieved from "Writing for the Web: Adapting Print to the Web," *http://crofsblogs.typepad.com/ckbetas/ adapting_print_to_web.doc.*

TABLE 7.4 🖝 **Checklist for letter format.**

	YES	NO
1. Did I attractively center my letter on the page?	❑	❑
2. Is my letter pleasing to the eye?	❑	❑
3. Did I single-space my letter with extra space between paragraphs?	❑	❑
4. Are my margins neat and uniform?	❑	❑
5. Did I omit any widows or orphans?	❑	❑
6. Did I remember to avoid splitting names or words?	❑	❑
7. On my two-page letter, did I note the receiver's name, page number, and complete date in my heading?	❑	❑
8. Did I use one of the four accepted letter styles?	❑	❑
9. Did I include all required letter parts?	❑	❑
10. Did I use the complete date in the date line?	❑	❑
11. Did I use a courtesy title in the inside address and salutation?	❑	❑
12. Did my return address and inside address show the capitalized, two-letter state abbreviation?	❑	❑
13. Did I remember to sign my letter?	❑	❑
14. Did I use one of the two punctuation styles: open or mixed?	❑	❑
15. Did I make sure I had no spelling, punctuation, grammar, or capitalization errors?	❑	❑
16. Did I check for parallel sentence structure?	❑	❑
17. Did I omit all sexist language?	❑	❑
18. Did I exclude all abbreviations except for courtesy titles and routinely abbreviated words?	❑	❑
19. Did most of my paragraphs begin with words other than *I* or *We*?	❑	❑
20. Did I use complete sentences and make sure every paragraph has at least two sentences?	❑	❑

Conclusion

The visual dimension of your letter and your online documents can enhance or detract from your company's image. You should realize the importance of appearance and the positive or negative impact it makes.

For a letter to be complete, you must include all the standard parts. Each part serves a definite and important function. To increase your credibility as a writer, make sure you set up your letter in one of the four commonly accepted letter styles. Use the guidelines presented in Table 7.4 to double-check your work.

For an online document, remember to use formatting tips that help to grab your reader's attention and make it easier for your reader to scan your documents.

Exercises

EXERCISE 1   BUSINESS STATIONERY

Directions: Collect samples of business stationery and bring them to class. Write a one-page analysis of the similarities and differences among these samples.

EXERCISE 2   MAILING ADDRESSES

Directions: Write the mailing addresses for the following individuals:
    a.   Director of the Better Business Bureau
    b.   Local Air Force recruiter

c. President of your college
d. A minister, priest, or rabbi
e. Your city's mayor

EXERCISE 3 CORRECTION AND REVISION

Directions: Correct and revise the following letter, incorporating what you learned from Chapters 2 and 3. What could you do to make the letter more attractive and inviting to read? Give *at least* six suggestions. Where and how would you implement your suggestions?

June 23, 20XX
Miss Joanne Adams
1070 Mondi Drive
Woodstock, GA 30088

Dear Mrs. Adams

On the date of January 25, a shipment of a crate of seventy-five of our Zippy Posture Chairs to Trust-Us Insurance Company in the city of Houston, was made by Mr. Mark Lamb who is your shipping agent. Six days subsequent to the above date, damage to a vast majority of the chairs was sustained when one of your Phoenix crane operators dropped the crate.

February 16 was the date that a Freight Damage Claim in the amount of the sum of $3500.00 was sent by mail by men at my office to Mrs. Dorothy Richards, in your Claims division in your Phoenix office. Writing me in return, I was advised that she would give my claim special attention and the settlement, no doubt, being received by me at my office at the earliest possible date.

A period of two months passed by and on April 17, I sent an inquiry in regards to the claim to Mrs. Dorothy Richards in your Claims Division in your Phoenix office. A form postcard came by mail to me advising me, three weeks subsequent to my inquiry to your Phoenix office, that the processing of my claim was underway and that my patience would be appreciated. That was two months before the writing of this letter, and no further contact has been made or any remittance sent either.

It is my personal opinion that it ought to be brought to your attention that replacement of our Zippy Posture Chairs had to be made to our customer, Trust-Us Insurance Company in the city of Houston. And, the cost of repairing sixty-eight of the damaged chairs was absorbed by our company. Therefore, it was necessary to get rid of these repaired chairs at prices that were greatly reduced and that caused a loss to our company.

Very soon, I would like to have your reply as to your action; or better yet, it would be greatly appreciated if you would send a check for the amount of $3,800.00 in remittance of your damage caused by your Phoenix crane operators.

Very truly yours,

Sam Jones

Sam Jones, Vice-President of Corporate Affairs, Southside Division, ABC Corporation

dmr

Enclosures

P.S. Please hurry!

CHAPTER 8

Writing Formal Reports, Business Plans, and White Papers

*R*eports must be written so that managers can easily understand the problem, logic, and recommendations. Information should be factual, complete, and objective. The writer must present it in an organized format.[1]

Robert W. Rasberry and Laura Lemoine Lindsay

[1] Reproduced from Robert W. Rasberry and Laura Lemoine Lindsay, *Effective Managerial Communication*, 2nd ed. (Belmont, CA: Wadsworth, 1994), p. 495, with the permission of South-Western College Publishing, a division of International Thomson Publishing Inc. Copyright © 1994, Wadsworth Publishing, Inc. All rights reserved.

LEARNING OBJECTIVES

After reading this chapter, you should be able to:

- Distinguish between term papers and formal reports.
- Compare and contrast primary and secondary research.
- List and discuss the parts of a formal report.
- Describe the differences between a bibliography and a list of works cited.
- Explain the role of headings in a formal report.
- Differentiate between past and present tense and know when to use each in a formal report.
- Compare and contrast MLA and APA styles of attribution.

- Explain the difference between tables and figures.
- List the guidelines for preparing tables.
- Define pie chart, line chart, horizontal bar graph, and vertical bar graph.
- Become acquainted with some guidelines for writing a business plan.
- Learn how and when to write a white paper.

The Importance of Formal Reports

Stephanie Winston, author of *The Organized Executive,* suggests that you look at reports in terms of the bottom line: If you were the reader, would you pay to receive this report? If your answer is yes, go ahead and write.

Source: Brad Cleveland, "Reporting Call Center Activity," *Call Center,* December 1, 2003, p. 36.

In an educational setting, you often write term papers. These papers appear similar to formal business reports, but they differ in a number of ways. First, formal business reports use headings to identify sections of the report. Headings improve readability and allow you either to read straight through or to skip around within the report. Second, business reports rely mainly on *primary research* such as surveys, interviews, experiments, and other methods, while term papers use *secondary research,* which means going to the library or the web and documenting work from other authors. In formal business reports, you often incorporate secondary research to back up primary research findings.

Parts of a Formal Report

A long report may have the following parts: cover; title page; letter of authorization; letter of transmittal; table of contents; list of illustrations; executive summary or abstract; body, including introduction, findings, and conclusion; appendices; and bibliography or works cited. The following sections discuss each of these report parts.

COVER

The cover, of course, holds the report together and protects the contents. A professional cover presents a first impression of your work. The cover can influence whether an individual will read your report.

TITLE PAGE

The title page identifies the name of the report, your name and title, and the date of submission. It may include the name of the individual who will receive the document.

LETTER OF AUTHORIZATION

This letter authorizes the writer to conduct the research necessary to complete the report. It justifies the time and effort necessary to undertake the project.

LETTER OF TRANSMITTAL

The letter of transmittal formally transfers the report to the individual who authorized you to undertake the project. In this letter, you provide an overview of the report, the major findings, and recommendations. Because this letter follows the direct approach, end it on a positive note.

TABLE OF CONTENTS

The table of contents lists the major headings found within the body. Additionally, it details subsections and gives the page number in which each section begins.

LIST OF ILLUSTRATIONS

If you use any graphics within your report, list them in this section, by title and accompanying page number. Graphics include tables, charts, diagrams, and other forms of visually displayed information.

SUMMARY, ABSTRACT, EXECUTIVE BRIEF, EPITOME, OR SYNOPSIS

A one-page summary document highlights the major sections and findings of the report and gives the busy reader an overview of the report. It includes the purpose, methodology (how you collected your data), conclusions, and recommendations (if any).

Executive summaries demand special attention. The first sentence must grab and hold the reader. You cannot afford to start your executive summary with any of the following:

- the purpose of the report,
- the problem question, or
- background to the report.

INTRODUCTION

The introduction presents an overview of the report. The introduction to the body includes the background and problem, scope, limitations, data collection and methodology, and organization of the report.

Background and Problem. Within the background section, present general information necessary for the audience to understand the problem. State the problem as a question, as shown in the following:

Not: This report was completed to accomplish this purpose.

But: This report discusses the results of an investigation conducted to solve the following problem:

or

The problem addressed answers the following question:
What role does . . . ?

Scope of the Report. The scope specifies the depth and breadth of the report. It states how broadly or deeply your report covers these subjects, and it clarifies the boundaries of your report by defining what you have included or excluded.

Limitations of the Report. Limitations include any barriers or problems you faced in completing the report. Make the reader aware of problems or factors limiting the validity of your recommendations. Often, time and money are given as limitations to a report.

Sources and Methods of Data Collection. In discussing your research methodology, briefly tell how you collected the data. (For example, how many questionnaires did you administer? What companies or individuals did you survey or interview?) If you relied heavily on a few secondary sources, mention them here. Cite these and other sources appropriately in the text of the report and include a works cited or bibliography section at the end of the report. This allows the reader to judge the quality of your work and to gather like data, if necessary.

The executive summary demands your best thinking. Because many managers read this section first, make sure it answers the following questions:

- What are its conclusions and recommendations?
- What are the implications for me or my organization?
- What is the report about and who wrote it?
- What does it contribute?

Source: Ted Pollock, "A Personal File on Stimulating Ideas and Problem Solvers," *Supervision,* Volume 53, Issue 7, July 1992, pp. 24–26.

Often when writing a formal report, you must solicit information from others.

Organization of the Report. Following the sources and methods of data collection, "frame" the report. Mention the major divisions or organization to follow. The opening paragraphs of each section should briefly highlight the sections to follow. This practice makes your readers aware of the organization of your subject, so they can easily follow your discussion. The introduction includes a transition to the heart of the report, the body.

BODY OR FINDINGS

The body presents the findings of your investigation. This section allows you to describe and explain what you did. The body or findings form the basis for the conclusions and recommendations that follow. An organized, objective, concrete, and interesting presentation of information in the body adds credibility to your conclusions and recommendations. Review Box 8.1 for some words to avoid in the body of your report.

CONCLUSION AND RECOMMENDATIONS

You base your conclusions and recommendations on the findings. No new data should appear in this section. The conclusion makes an inference based on your

---

When you start to write sections of the report, especially the findings, words may confound you. Look out for these weasel words—most of the meaning is sucked out of them:

    most

    some

    several

    many

    majority

The previous words don't carry much impact. They are usually placed there to fill space. Look at this sentence: "Most employees believe a dress code would be appropriate within the firm." How many? What ages or years of experience? Questions remain when you use weasel words in the findings. People understand *majority* means over 50 percent, which is sometimes defined as 50 percent plus one. Therefore, if you insist on using the weasel word *majority*, please clarify by placing the number and percentage in parentheses after the word; for example, majority (17 people, 60 percent).

BOX 8.1 ⬛ **Weasel Words Need to Be Avoided**

SOURCE: Dr. Jay's "Write" Home Page, *http://www.csun.edu/~vcecn006/*.

findings and should not be a summary, as your abstract has already served that purpose. The recommendations evolve from your conclusions and state what action should be taken. The word "should" will likely appear in your recommendation statements. Since the recommendations ask for specific action, allow each recommendation to stand alone to emphasize the recommended action.[2]

APPENDICES

The appendices contain additional useful information about the report, but is material that might slow down the reader if it appeared in the text. Typical examples include sample questionnaires, interview forms, or other types of documentation used during your research.

BIBLIOGRAPHY OR WORKS CITED

Whether you call your reference section a *bibliography* or *works cited* depends on your attribution style. If you use footnotes or endnotes, include a bibliography. Your bibliography contains a list of all sources you used in writing your report. If you choose internal attribution, such as Modern Language Association (MLA) or American Psychological Association (APA) style, list only sources you cited in the body of the report.

Whether you use a bibliography or works cited, list your sources alphabetically. Type your entries in a hanging indented form, with the second and subsequent lines of each entry indented five spaces from the first line. This placement highlights the first word of each entry, enabling your reader to locate specific entries quickly. Single-space bibliographic entries and double-space works cited entries. Consult an appropriate reference manual when completing this section of your report. Keep the information that follows about style and format in mind when you prepare your report.

A few search engine tips: It is important to know exactly what you are looking for. When typing in key words in search engines, use words that are precise but not overly restrictive. Key phrases might yield more accurate results. Using wild cards to truncate key words in an appropriate manner also helps. Use the search engine and the navigational tools within the site, and perhaps modify the URL of the site to help you in your search.

Source: Anjana Srikanth, "Effective Business Writing: The White Paper," *Writers Write,* September 2002. Retrieved from *http://www.writerswrite. com/journal/Sep02/Srikanth.htm.*

Style and Format

The following ideas relate to style and the way you present ideas. In this section, headings, paragraphs, impersonal style, transitions, and tense are discussed.

HEADINGS

When you write your report, use headings to divide the sections and make the report easy for your reader to follow. At least one sentence of text should follow each heading. Never place two levels of headings together without text separating them. The same principle applies to titles and headings. Box 8.2 explains different levels of headings used in formal reports. You will probably never use all six levels of headings discussed, but most reports use at least three levels. The levels you select do not have to be the top three; however, your choices must be logical to your reader.

PARAGRAPHS

As you write, include sufficient white space to break up your discussion. Vary the lengths of your paragraphs to keep the reader's interest.

---

[2] Robert W. Rasberry and Laura Lindsay, *Effective Managerial Communication,* 2nd ed. (Belmont, CA: Wadsworth, 1994), p. 336.

BOX 8.2 🖝 **Different Levels of Headings**

Write your paragraphs in deductive style (placing the topic sentence at the beginning), unified (relating the entire discussion to the topic sentence), and with coherence (making ideas flow together smoothly).

IMPERSONAL STYLE

Because a report should be factual and objective, use an impersonal style. Avoid using *I, you,* and *we,* as the following examples illustrate.

Not: I found Delta had a net profit last year.

But: Delta had a net profit last year.

An analysis of Delta revealed . . .

TRANSITIONS

Use transitions between the major divisions within the body to tie ideas together and to keep your reader moving along. Place transitions at the beginning of major divisions to serve as mini-introductions to the next section and to outline in detail what the division will discuss. Transitions can also serve as summaries of the ideas presented in the previous section.

TENSE

When writing your report, be careful to use the proper tense in each section. Use *past tense* when discussing your analysis, since you have to complete it before you can discuss it. For example: "The profit and loss statement *was* analyzed. . . ."

Use *past tense* also when discussing historical data or findings from other studies. For example: "General Motors Corporation *had* net sales in 1980 that were greater than. . . ." Use *present tense* to discuss other parts of your study or conclusions from your or other studies. For example:

The next section includes *the statistics.*

International Business Machines prepares *for the future.*

Attribution

Proper attribution gives your report credibility. The reader knows you have based your report on other studies and have not just presented one person's opinion.

When creating your report, you will take information from a variety of sources to answer your problem statement. You must document source material carefully. For example, statistical information of any kind requires documentation. Enclose direct quotations in double quotation marks. *You must give credit to all your sources; anything you read and paraphrase must be documented.*

Use an ellipsis to indicate an omitted part of a direct quotation. Show the omission with three spaced dots for omissions at the beginning of a sentence or within it. Use four spaced dots to show an omission at the end of a sentence. (The first dot appears immediately after the final letter of the last word. It also serves as terminal punctuation for the sentence.)

Example: "We all know merely to understand and accept a principle. . . ."

Example: ". . . merely to understand . . . will not do."

Finally, use the proper form of attribution. Three commonly used types include footnotes (at the bottom of each page), endnotes (on a separate page following the last page of text), and internal attribution (author and year, or numbers in text).

Internal attribution has increased in popularity; most business journals employ this type of attribution. The parenthetical reference directs the reader to a list of complete references in the works cited section. Two popular methods are MLA (Modern Language Association) style and APA (American Psychological Association) style.

MLA

The Modern Language Association (MLA) recommends that you cite references with a brief note within the text, such as (Roebuck 245). This parenthetical comment consists of the author's last name and the page on which you can find the reference. If you do not know the author's name, use an abbreviated title to identify the reference. For detailed information on this system, see the *MLA Handbook for Writers of Research Papers,* 6th ed., by Joseph Gibaldi (New York: The Modern Language Association). Visit the MLA website at: *http://www. mla.org/main_stl.htm.*

APA

The American Psychological Association (APA) developed its own system of referencing. When you use APA style, you cite the author's last name, the year of publication, and pertinent page number(s), such as (Roebuck, 1994, p. 4). Because you will use the World Wide Web for much of your research, some basic guidelines for referencing these sources can be found in the following text. For more complete information on this system, consult the *Publication Manual of the American Psychological Association,* 5th ed. Visit the APA website at: *http://www. apastyle.org/elecref.html.*

Citing E-Mail and Interview Communications. Authors—not journal editors or copy editors—should ensure the accuracy of all references, which includes verifying the source of e-mail communications before citing them as personal communications in manuscripts.

E-mail communications and interviews from individuals should be cited as personal communications, as noted in APA's *Publication Manual* (5th ed.). An example follows: (J. Smith, personal communication, August 15, 2001). According to APA, personal communications are not included in the reference list.

Citing a Website. To cite an entire website (but not a specific document on the site), give the address of the site in the text. For example, Kidpsych serves as a wonderful interactive website for children (*http://www.kidpsych.org*). You need not make a reference entry.

Citing Specific Documents on a Website. Web documents share many of the same elements found in print documents (e.g., authors, titles, dates). Therefore, the citation for a Web document often follows a format similar to that for print, with some information omitted and some added. You will find some examples of how to cite Web documents posted on APA's own website.

An action alert posted by APA's Public Policy Office:

American Psychological Association. (1995, September 15). *APA public policy action alert: Legislation would affect grant recipients* [Announcement]. Washington, DC: Author. Retrieved January 25, 1996, from the World Wide Web: *http://www.apastyle.org*.

An article from the journal *American Psychologist*:

Jacobson, J. W., Mulick, J. A., & Schwartz, A. A. (1995). A history of facilitated communication: Science, pseudo-science, and antiscience: Science working group on facilitated communication. *American Psychologist, 50*, 750–765. Retrieved January 25, 1996, from the World Wide Web: *http://www.apa. org/journals/jacobson.html*.

An article from the *APA Monitor* (a newspaper):

Sleek, S. (1996, January). Psychologists build a culture of peace. *APA Monitor*, pp. 1, 33. Retrieved January 25, 1996, from the World Wide Web: *http://www. apa.org/monitor/peacea.html*.

An abstract:

Rosenthal, R. (1995). *State of New Jersey v. Margaret Kelly Michaels:* An overview [Abstract]. *Psychology, Public Policy, and Law, 1,* 247–271. Retrieved January 25, 1996, from the World Wide Web: *http://www.apa.org/journals/ab1.html*.

All references begin with the same information you would provide for a printed source (or as much of that information as is available). Then, place the Web information in a retrieval statement at the end of the reference. Be sure to give the date of retrieval, because documents on the Web may change in content, move, or be removed from a site altogether.

Citing Articles and Abstracts from Electronic Databases. APA now recommends a retrieval statement that identifies the date of retrieval (omitted for CD-ROMs) and the source (e.g., DIALOG, WESTLAW, SIRS, Electric Library), followed in parentheses by the name of the specific database used and any additional information needed to retrieve a particular item. For Web sources, a URL should point to an "entry page" for the database.

The basic retrieval statement for CD-ROM databases and examples of references follow:

> Retrieved from [source] database ([name of database], CD-ROM [release date], [item no.—if applicable])

The basic retrieval statement for online databases:

> Retrieved [month day, year] from [source] online database ([name of database], [item no.—if applicable])

The basic retrieval statement for databases accessed via the Web:

> Retrieved [month day, year] from [source] database ([name of database], [item no.—if applicable]) on the World Wide Web: [URL].

Examples

> Federal Bureau of Investigation. (1998, March). Encryption: Impact on law enforcement. Location: Publisher. Retrieved from SIRS database (SIRS Government Reporter, CD-ROM, Fall 1998 release).

> Schneiderman, R. A. (1997). Librarians can make sense of the Net. *San Antonio Business Journal, 11*(31), pp. 58+. Retrieved January 27, 1999, from EBSCO database (Masterfile) on the World Wide Web: *http://www.ebsco.com.*

> Kerrigan, D. C., Todd, M. K., & Riley, P. O. (1998). Knee osteoarthritis and high-heeled shoes. *The Lancet, 251,* 1399–1401. Retrieved January 27, 1999, from DIALOG database (#457, The Lancet) on the World Wide Web: *http://www.dialogweb.com.*

> Davis, T. (1992). Examining educational malpractice jurisprudence: Should a cause of action be created for student-athletes? *Denver University Law Journal, 69,* 57+. Retrieved [month day, year] from WESTLAW online database (69 DENULR 57).

> Bowles, M. D. (1998). The organization man goes to college: AT&T's experiment in humanistic education, 1953–1960. *The Historian, 61,* 15+. Retrieved [month day, year] from DIALOG online database (#88, IAC Business A.R.T.S., Item 04993186).

Web Citations in Text.   Follow the author and date format described in the APA's *Publication Manual.* To cite specific parts of a Web document, indicate the chapter, figure, table, or equation as appropriate. For quotations, give page numbers (or paragraph numbers) if available. If page or paragraph numbers are not available (i.e., they are not visible to every reader), you can omit them from the in-text citation. Using most browsers, readers will still be able to search for the quoted material.

Your bibliography or works cited page must follow the correct attribution guidelines. Carefully study a current style manual to help you organize this part of your report.

Graphics

Graphics present information in tables, charts, and other visuals to allow your reader to understand your written word. Computers have made generating visual support easy. Graphics, which have become commonplace in written and oral reports, visually summarize the data. Normally, a table or a figure illustrates an idea more clearly than could be done without such an illustration. To choose the appropriate graphic for your purpose, you need to understand the differences between tables and figures.

TABLE 8.1 🖙 **Number of errors by category in written assignments.**

CATEGORY	FREQUENCY
Spelling	25
Capitalization	21
Grammar	20
Punctuation	15
Organization	10

SOURCE: D. B. Roebuck, K. W. Sightler, and C. C. Brush, "Organizational Size, Company Type and Position Effects on the Perceived Importance of Oral and Written Communication Skills," *Journal of Managerial Issues,* Vol. VII, No. 1, Spring 1995.

TABLES

Tables include a title, column headings, and data. Sometimes they include totals, footnotes, source information, and a caption. Table 8.1 illustrates the correct presentation of a table.

Use the following guidelines to help you prepare your tables. [3]

1. Keep tables simple. If a table becomes too complicated, consider breaking it into two or more tables.

2. Enumerate tables by inserting arabic numerals above each one.

3. Give each table a descriptive name.

4. Place units of time in a row rather than a column.

5. Present the data in a logical fashion.

6. Employ appropriate design techniques, such as using ample white space, bold type, and shading.

7. Use the word "source" and follow it with a bibliographical citation if the data come from a source other than your own primary research.

FIGURES

Figures summarize information, add clarity, illustrate relationships, or add vividness. The most popular types of figures are graphs, charts, and maps.

Graphs show trends, comparisons, and sometimes a combination of both. Writers commonly use pie, line, and bar graphs to illustrate their findings.

A *pie chart* (see Exhibit 8.1) must always add up to 100 percent. Do not include more than six slices. Start at 12 o'clock with the largest slice, and move clockwise in

EXHIBIT 8.1

Pie chart.

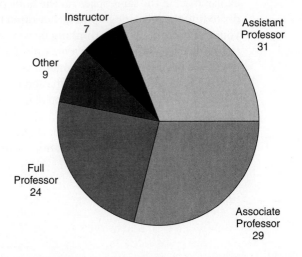

Instructor
7

Assistant
Professor
31

Other
9

Full
Professor
24

Associate
Professor
29

[3] John M. Penrose, Jr., Robert W. Rasberry, and Robert J. Myers, *Advanced Business Communication* (Belmont, CA: Wadsworth, 1993), pp. 38–46.

EXHIBIT 8.2

Line chart.

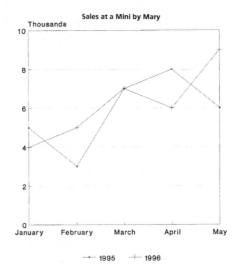

descending size. If using colors, make sure you shade each slice a different color. Use the lightest color for the largest slice and move to progressively darker, smaller slices.

A *line chart* shows trends over time. Color may be used to distinguish between two different trends. Differentiate between multiple lines by using different techniques such as solid, dashed, or dotted lines. Use solid lines for the primary data and dashes for the secondary data. Try not to use more than four lines, or your readers will become confused. Label both the *x* and *y* axes to identify the individual items on the axis. Make sure you include a legend or key to assist in understanding the chart. Exhibit 8.2 presents a line chart.

A *horizontal* or *vertical bar graph* shows comparisons. The bars should be wider than the space between them, and a logical progression should occur. Hold the maximum number of bars to 12 and make all bars the same width. Grid lines or tick marks can be helpful to your reader, but do not overuse them as they can become distracting. Study the examples in Exhibits 8.3 and 8.4.

In summary, remember that graphics should support your report, not replace it. Keep your graphics simple so they help clarify the written text. Be sure to give each of your graphics a number and a title and place the graphic on the page where you present the information. Readers prefer to have graphics and related textual explanation in the same space on the same page. If readers must go to the appendix to find the relevant graphics, they often become lost. Instead, make it easy for your reader to follow your thinking by wrapping the text around the graphic. Try to keep imbedded graphics to a maximum of 25 percent of the page. Remember, when you add a visual to a document, you still need to provide the reader with a textual explanation. If your information came from a published source, provide a source note (in footnote form) immediately below the table or graph. Note the example in Table 8.1.

Box 8.3 provides a formal report that illustrates the writing principles discussed in this chapter. Read this example carefully.

EXHIBIT 8.3

Bar graph.

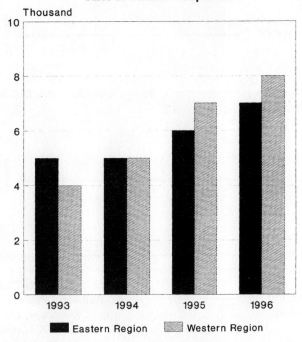

Sales of Cellular Telephones

EXHIBIT 8.4

Bar graph.

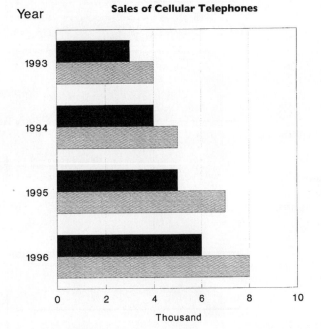

Sales of Cellular Telephones

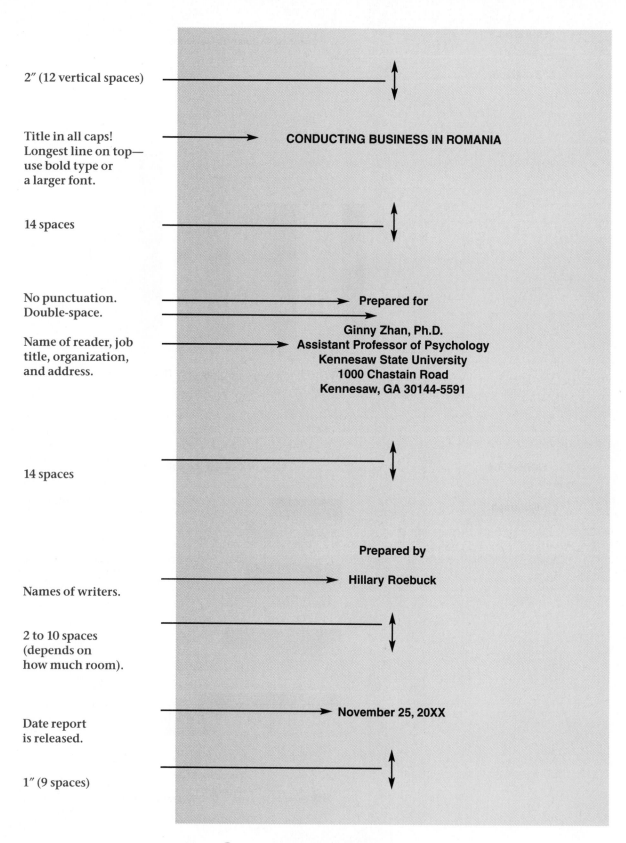

2″ (12 vertical spaces)

Title in all caps!
Longest line on top—
use bold type or
a larger font.

CONDUCTING BUSINESS IN ROMANIA

14 spaces

No punctuation.
Double-space.

Prepared for

Name of reader, job
title, organization,
and address.

Ginny Zhan, Ph.D.
Assistant Professor of Psychology
Kennesaw State University
1000 Chastain Road
Kennesaw, GA 30144-5591

14 spaces

Prepared by

Names of writers.

Hillary Roebuck

2 to 10 spaces
(depends on
how much room).

Date report
is released.

November 25, 20XX

1″ (9 spaces)

BOX 8.3 ☞ **Format of a Formal Report**

Michael J. Coles College of Business
Department of Management and Entreprenuership

August 31, 20XX

Ms. Hillary Roebuck
President
The Research Group
145 South Main Street
Woodstock, GA 30188

Dear Ms. Roebuck:

As I explained this morning, I want your team to research, analyze, and report on conducting business in Romania. As more Americans conduct business abroad, we must prepare our students for such endeavors.

Please direct research, both formal and informal, to present recommendations. I will ask you to make a formal oral report of your findings.

I need your report by the end of November. Do let me know if you encounter any problems or have any questions.

Sincerely,

Ginny Zhan

Ginny Zhan, Ph.D.
Assistant Professor of Psychology

BOX 8.3 (continued)

The Research Group
145 South Main Street
Woodstock, GA 30188

November 25, 20XX

Dr. Ginny Zhan
Associate Professor of Psychology
Kennesaw State University
1000 Chastain Road
Kennesaw, GA 30144-5591

Dear Dr. Zhan:

My team has completed the report you requested. The report researches conducting business in Romania.

The report details Romanian culture, the role of nonverbal communication, the business meeting, and effective communication. We have enjoyed this most interesting project. At your request, I will discuss the report with you.

Sincerely,

Hillary Roebuck
Hillary Roebuck, President

(Transferring the report back to the reader)

BOX 8.3 ☞ (continued)

Table of Contents does not list itself.

Lowercase roman numerals for preface material.

TABLE OF CONTENTS

Indent subheadings.

Line up right margin.

BOX 8.3 ☞ (continued)

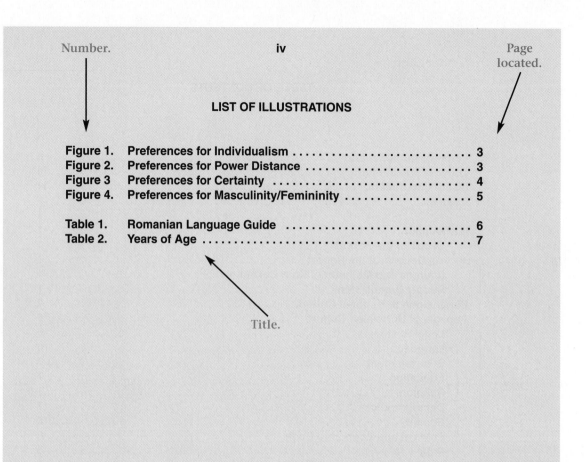

Number.

iv

Page
located.

LIST OF ILLUSTRATIONS

Title.

BOX 8.3 ☞ (continued)

v

Should
not exceed
one page. ————————→ **ABSTRACT**

When conducting business in Romania, cultural differences can affect interaction during negotiations. For American business professionals to succeed, they must know about these differences. Although American and Romanian business practices have many similarities, some differences exist; for example, Americans view conflict as a positive feature while Romanians avoid conflict. Another major cultural difference exists in business dress. While Americans are increasingly dressing more casual, Romanians still are expected to dress in conservative business apparel. To understand the variations in Romanian communication, one must be aware of Romanian culture. Knowledge of Romanian culture gives the American business professional the insight to conduct business successfully in Romania.

[Report in miniature—should not exceed one page.
Helps reader understand content of report.]

BOX 8.3 ☞ (continued)

Title centered 2 inches from top of page.

CONDUCTING BUSINESS IN ROMANIA

This research report contains information helpful to the American professional planning to conduct business in Romania. Successful business transactions depend on communicating clearly and understanding cultural differences. Sebenius (2002) stated "Cultural differences can influence business negotiations in significant and unexpected ways, as many a hapless deal maker has learned" (p. 4). In a recent study that sought to understand the role of leadership in international business interactions, nearly half of the respondents Single-space text. (44 percent of 100 respondents) found cultural differences to be the biggest challenge in working across the globe. Forty-five percent of the respondents felt the ability to identify cultural differences to be the most important skill in cross-cultural communication. According to The Center of Creative Leadership, when managing across cultures, leaders must realize that the interactions become complex because of norms, beliefs, values, and attitudes that distinguish one cultural group from another ("Leading Across Cultural Differences," 2002).

Although Romanians and Americans share many similarities, one must recognize differences that occur because of culture. This paper addresses the following research problem: What do American businesspeople need to know about the cultural differences between Romania and the United States to conduct successful negotiations in Romania? The next sections of the introduction discuss the scope, limitations, sources and methods of data collection, as well as the organization of the report.

Scope of the Report

This report provides an overview of Romanian history, national culture, and cultural aspects that affect how Romanians choose to conduct business matters. The report does not provide specifics of actual cross-border negotiations. The report presents a preliminary look at differences between the two countries. It does not provide all information necessary to do business with a particular Romanian company.

Limitations of the Report

The researcher encountered some challenges in finding printed data about some aspects of Romanian business practices and etiquette. The researcher also lacked time to cover all necessary aspects.

Sources and Methods of Data Collection

The report used both primary and secondary data sources. The researcher conducted two face-to-face interviews with Romanian professors and one face-to-face interview with an American professor. In addition, information was sought from the Web, from individuals who had visited and lived in Romania, and from local libraries.

Report Organization

The report has two major sections. The first section discusses National Culture and provides insight into the Romanian culture. Culture is a complex concept and has been given many definitions. Social scientists have spent decades trying to understand how cultures differ. Dalton, Ernst, Deal, and Leslie (2002) have stated, "To understand the influence of culture within or across countries,

First page number at bottom.

1

BOX 8.3 (continued)

social scientists have had to stand back from individuals and consider people as a group, a society, an average, a whole" (p. 3). One well-known expert on culture, Edward Hall (1966), has written "Culture [is] those deep, common, unstated experiences which members of a given culture share, which they communicate without knowing, and which form the backdrop against which all other events are judged" (p. 3). Geert Hofstede, author of international communication research on culture, refers to it as "the software of the mind," which is more of the operating system of the mind, that is, the environment that controls specific circumstances.

The second section focuses on Romanian business conduct. It specifically addresses aspects such as nonverbal communication, the business meeting, and effective communication.

DIMENSIONS OF NATIONAL CULTURE

Geert Hofstede, a Dutch management scholar, has extensively researched national culture through his study of thousands of IBM employees in more than 40 countries. From his research, he distilled four basic dimensions of work-related values, which he termed individualism/collectivism, power distance, uncertainty avoidance, and masculinity/femininity (Rosenzweig, 1994).

Individualism/collectivism is the degree to which action is taken for the benefit of the individual or the group. In individualistic cultures, such as the United States, see Figure 1, people are concerned with personal achievement, individual rights, and independence. In collectivistic cultures, such as Romania, people tend to see themselves first as part of a group, and typically are more concerned about the welfare of the group than about individual welfare.

Introduce graphics before they appear.

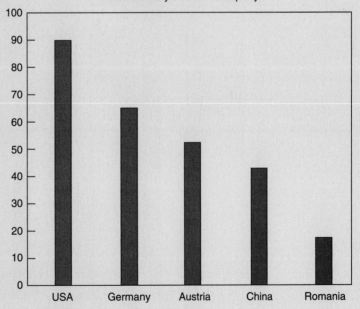

Preferences for Individualism
Individual Style versus Group Style

Number consecutively.

Figure 1. Preferences for Individualism, Individual Style versus Group Style
Source: Reprinted with permission of ITAP International (268 Wall Street, Princeton, NJ).

BOX 8.3 ☛ **(continued)**

Collectivistic cultures value harmony and equality above personal achievement. They may be more concerned about obligations and duties to other members of the group than about individual rights.

Many Kennesaw State University executive-MBA students found this to be true when they worked on their international virtual teams with their Romanian colleagues. The Romanians wanted to build to a relationship before starting on the task.

Team 16, in their international process paper, stated the following about their experiences of working together.

> The importance of the initial face-to-face meeting and interactions with the group should not be underestimated, as this is the time that trust and respect are established and commitment to the project is built. These initial interactions were valuable in the establishment of relationships needed to carry the team during difficult and stressful times. We also learned that cultural differences should be assessed during these initial interactions and provisions made to accommodate them. (Ciliege, Covaciu, Finch, Georgevici, Ilie, Ionascu, Panturu, & Raineri, 2003, p. 2)

Power distance is the degree to which inequality or distance between those in charge and the less powerful (subordinates) is accepted. In high-power cultures, such as Romania (see Figure 2), a wide gap is perceived to exist among people at different levels of the hierarchy. Subordinates accept their inferior positions, show proper respect, and defer to their superiors.

Superiors give orders instead of asking subordinates to participate in decision making. Gscu has stated "Romanians are not too quick to act against authority.

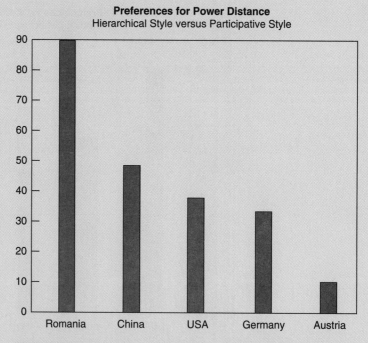

Preferences for Power Distance
Hierarchical Style versus Participative Style

Figure 2. Preferences for Power Distance, Hierarchical Style versus Participative Style
Source: Reprinted with permission of ITAP International (268 Wall Street, Princeton, NJ).

BOX 8.3 ☞ (continued)

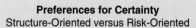

Preferences for Certainty
Structure-Oriented versus Risk-Oriented

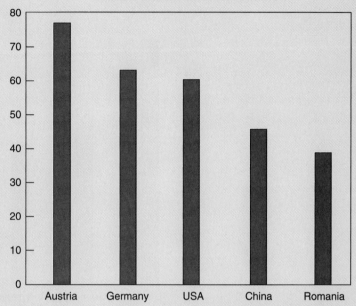

Figure 3. Preferences for Certainty, Structure-Oriented versus Risk-Oriented
Source: Reprinted with permission of ITAP International (268 Wall Street, Princeton, NJ).

They are more laid back and expect that somehow, somewhere somebody will do something and things will miraculously improve. 'Let others do it,' 'Don't get involved,' 'It might be too risky,' are all mottoes of Romanians" (para. 12 and 13, "How I," n.d.). In countries where power distance is low, such as the United States, superiors are more collaborative and less concerned with status. Often, organizational structures are flatter and more team-based. Typically, employees are more vocal and openly express their thoughts and feelings. Some faculty and executive-MBA students from Kennesaw State University have shared that their Romanian colleagues waited for them to take the leadership role as well as to start the virtual dialogue.

Uncertainty avoidance is the extent to which people seek to avoid or feel threatened by ambiguous or risky situations. Cultures with high uncertainty avoidance may not try new ways of doing things or form new working relationships, change jobs, or welcome outsiders. They prefer the here and now, which provides stability. In low uncertainty avoidance cultures, individuals embrace change more readily, show more initiative, and are more accepting of different views and new ideas.

As can be noted from Figure 3, the national culture of the United States is a bit stronger in its desire for structure versus Romania, but it appears that Austria has the strongest ability to embrace change and to take risks.

Masculinity/femininity represents a culture where achievement, assertiveness, and material success is desired. Femininity describes a culture that places greater importance on maintaining relationships, on caring for members, and on a high quality of life. In a masculine or task-oriented country, such as the United States (see Figure 4), work-related values tend to favor achievement

BOX 8.3 ☞ **(continued)**

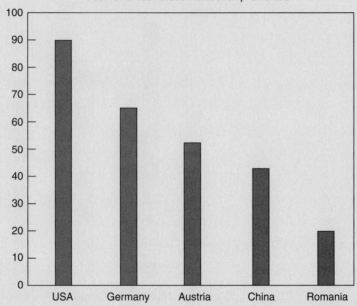

Figure 4. Preferences for Achievement, Task-Oriented versus Relationship-Oriented
Source: Reprinted with permission of ITAP International (268 Wall Street, Princeton, NJ).

and competition. In a more feminine or relationship-oriented country such as Romania, individuals are more concerned for the well-being of the members with an emphasis on the overall welfare of their people rather than bottom-line performance (Rozenzweig, 1994).

In some of the international virtual executive-MBA Romanian-United States teams, the Romanian team members perceived the American members to be more focused on the task instead of wanting to build a relationship. For some teams, the Romanian team members were more interested in developing life-long partnerships than in completing the assigned tasks.

Mirela Florescu, a Romanian student who participated in the international virtual teaming with students from Kennesaw State University, had this to share about some differences between the American students and the Romanian students.

> The American students were complaining about some of my colleagues that during our common project they had some tasks and these should have been fulfilled in order to meet the schedule proposed, but for the reason that "it is my weekend and in spite of everything, I am not going to work on my weekend" they postponed the tasks and did not meet the deadlines. It is very "European" to keep the weekend as something very precious. (M. Florescu, personal communication, January 12, 2004)

In general, Romanians are very friendly, hospitable, courteous, openly affectionate, and very curious about people from other countries. They love to laugh and tell jokes. They are an open people who share all aspects of their lives. Most Romanians will freely disclose how much they earn (Centre for

BOX 8.3 ☞ (continued)

Intercultural Learning, 2000b). They are not, however, confrontational or risk takers. After the fall of communism, Tin (2004) has stated that she felt the Romanians were great survivors.

ASPECTS OF ROMANIAN CULTURE

Now that the national culture of Romania has been explored, it is important to understand the various aspects of the culture such as the legal system, language, education, religion, demographics, political and economic goals, daily life, traditions, and superstitions, which may influence the way that Romanians conduct business transactions.

Legal System

Romania operates a bicameral parliamentary political system where the Romanian Senate has 140 seats and the Assembly of Deputies has 345. Both chambers are directly elected from 41 multimember constituencies comprising 40 counties and the municipality of Bucharest, which is the capital of Romania. Romania has a republican form of government and is considered a democratic state. The principal law is the Romanian Constitution, which guarantees that the national sovereignty belongs to people and is exercised through its representative bodies. The current Constitution, which was adopted in 1991, guarantees the rights of national minorities to preserve, develop, and express ethnical, cultural, linguistic, and religious identity.

In 2003, a new labor taxation law determined the level of social, health care, and other special funds contributions that can be paid by the employer and the employee. In addition, the New Labor Code also became effective in 2003; this code regulates relationships between the employer and the employee, aiming to create a more comprehensive framework and to assure protection to the employee. Meanwhile, this code is imposing substantial restrictions regarding layoffs and costly administrative procedures to employers, and extended industry-wide collective agreements to nonparticipating employers, to the detriment of small- and medium-size enterprises (Doru, 2004).

Language

Romanian, the official language, is considered a romance language and is mainly based on Latin. It is considered a phonetic language and the grammar can be difficult, as words change depending upon whether they are singular or plural, masculine or feminine. Verb endings change according to who performed the action (Gscu, n.d.). Table 1 provides some examples of Romanian words.

Table 1. Romanian Language Guide

English	Romanian
Hello	Buna
Good morning	Buna dimineaja!
Good bye	La revedere!
How are you?	Ce mai facejti?
Please	Va rog
Thank you	Multumesc
You're welcome	Cu placere

Source: From: Ghid de conversatie ENGLEX-ROMAN, Polirom, 2001.

BOX 8.3 ☞ **(continued)**

English and French are taught and have now become the second and third most frequently used languages in Romania. There are also minority languages, for example, Hungarian, German, Turkish, Serbo-Croatian ("MSN Encarta," n.d.).

Entertainment

High-quality opera and classical music concerts occur almost weekly and are very affordable. In Bucharest alone, there are over 40 museums (Roussos, 2004). Soccer is the favorite sport in contrast to golf, where there are only two courses in all of Romania. During the winter, skiing is an obvious attraction. Eating out is easy and most Romanians go out at night after work. The nightlife is vibrant with dozens of dance clubs and casinos (Centre for Intercultural Learning, 2000a).

Education

Prior to the fall of Communism, education was based on practical training and technical learning. As Dr. Marcel Duhaneanu noted in a personal interview, management, business, and social studies have been added since 1989 and are very well-liked (M. Duhaneanu, personal communication, May 19, 2004).

School is free for children between the ages of 7 and 14, and there are five types of secondary education that include general education, vocational, art, physical education, and teacher-training schools. For individuals wanting to continue to further their education, there are eight universities in Romania: the University of Bucharest, the Al. C. cuza University, the Babes-Bolya University, the University of Craiova, the University of Ploiesti, the Dunarea de Jos University of Galati, the University of Timisoara, and the Transylvania University of Brasov ("MSN Encarta", n.d.).

In addition to the above universities, Romania has eight technical schools and many other institutes of higher education. One such example is the Institute of Business and Public Administration (ASEBUSS), where Dr. Marcel Duhaneanu is Rector.

Religion

Approximately 90 percent of the population belongs to the Romanian Orthodox Church. The rest of the population is Roman Catholic, Jewish, Calvinist, Islamic, or atheist (Morrison, Conawy, & Borden, 1994). Romanians have the right to have any religious affiliation.

Demographics

Romania's projected population for 2004 is 22.4 million and the life expectancy is 67.63 years for males and 74.82 years for females (CIA, 2004). A breakdown of age groups appears in Table 2.

Table 2. **Years of Age**

	Years of Age								
Population	0–9	10–19	20–29	30–39	40–49	50–59	60–69	70–79	>80
22,435,205 100%	2,363,092 10.5%	3,396,766 15.1%	3,762,162 16.8%	3,122,707 13.9%	3,187,201 14.2%	2,383,227 10.6%	2,329,651 10.4%	1,489,861 6.7%	400,538 1.8%

Source: From: Institute for World Economy.

BOX 8.3 ☛ (continued)

Annual population growth is estimated at a negative 0.11 percent and the birth rate is 10.69 births for every 1000 individuals. Median age is 36.1 years with males at 34.7 and females at 37.5. Life expectancy at birth for the total population is 71.12 years with females projected to live slightly longer at 74.82 years to males 67.63 years (CIA, 2004).

Equality

The Romanians share a Latin heritage and hold many of the same values of equality and humanitarianism as other Latin cultures. A discernable hierarchy of classes has evolved, from the peasant to the bureaucratic elite. Although egalitarianism is favored, some resentment is still found among the various ethic and social groups. The Hungarian and German minorities are very distinct, with their own languages, and present potential social and political problems. The European Romanians and the Roma or Gypsies as they are called have had a difficult relationship. The gypsies are often considered second-class citizens and appear to be a disadvantaged group in Romanian society. They can frequently be seen begging along the side of streets and roads or driving their horses and wagons.

As far as marriage, both spouses have equal rights and their roles are not clearly differentiated. Dr. Oana Firica, Professor of Quantitative Techniques at the Institute for Business and Public Administration, has stated that in the work-place women find it more difficult to move up into the higher positions and there are few women in business, politics, and in higher-level positions. However, women have made gains in this area in the last decade (O. Firica, personal communication, May 19, 2004). Women do receive a two-year maternity leave from work and women are gaining respect in the workplace (Tin, 2004). With regard to gender, there is little or no discrimination against women. Women have the right and access to the same education, work, and political arenas as men. Women are considered to make an important contribution to the general development of Romanian society.

Political and Economic Goals

The 2007 integration into the European Union is Romania's main political and economic goal for the coming three years. There is a public clock in the centre of Romania's capital that counts the days until 2007—the year when the country hopes to join the European Union ("Don't count," 2004).

Until recently, Romania's macroeconomic performance has been weak and characterized by boom and bust cycles, driven by loose fiscal policy and weak financial discipline in state-owned enterprises (SOEs). Since mid-2001, a combination of budget restraint, ambitious energy price adjustments, and prudent monetary policy have moderated domestic demand and reduced the current account deficit. At the same time, export and GDP growth were among the highest in the region, reflecting the fruits of private investments in export-oriented consumer goods industries over the last few years and the gains in competitiveness from the 1999 adjustment in the real effective exchange rate ("IMF reviews," 2004).

Daily Life

With the transition to a free-market economy, daily life has truly become more difficult. Food prices are high relative to the country's low minimum wage, and few Romanians can afford luxuries. In an interview, a Romanian executive-MBA student stated:

BOX 8.3 ☞ (continued)

If a Romanian, who was in his or her fifties, was asked to draw a comparison between business practices under Communism and the last ten years, they might surprisingly say, probably 95 percent of them, that Romanian Capitalism has brought about instability and insecurity. They prefer a system in which people have a low salary, but they go to work every day without fearing tomorrow (meaning the fear to be fired or the bankruptcy of the company). Fortunately, the mentality of the younger people is changing, and the new generation comes with fresh and realistic ideas. A 25–45-year-old Romanian would put a lot of effort into getting a good job with a multinational, that individual would work hard for a promotion, and on the whole, would partner with his or her employer to make the company more profitable and to be successful personally. (M. Florescu, personal communication, January 10, 2004)

One-family houses are common in Romania's villages, while most city dwellers live in one-family apartments. Most apartment buildings were built during the Communist period and are cramped with minimal facilities. In Romania there are 139 passenger cars and 194 telephones for every 1000 inhabitants.

Popular Romanian foods include mititei (seasoned grilled meatballs) and mamaliga (a cornmeal porridge that can be served in many different ways). Wine and a plum brandy called tuica are popular beverages among Romanians, and placinta (turnovers) are a typical dessert ("MSN Encarta," n.d.).

Traditions

Romanians, like all cultures, have some unique traditions. For example, when going to a restaurant, it is expected that a man will generally enter first and then allow the women to enter.

When offering flowers, an individual should always give an odd number as even number bouquets are given at funerals. When giving flowers, the flowers are frequently held upside down. One should never give carnations as they are acceptable only for funerals, and red roses are reserved for romantic occasions ("Romania's cultural," n.d.).

When visiting a Romanian home, the guest should always bring a small present, eat and drink what is presented, and be prepared to stay quite some time as the Romanians tend to stay up late (Tin, 2004).

Superstitions

Every country has its superstitions and Romania has a few. First, if a bird defecates in an individual's hair, or if an individual accidentally steps in it, good luck will come to that person. Second, if an individual always sits at a corner of a table, that individual may never get married. Third, if an individual sits on a cold slab, that person will get sick (Tin, 2004). Fourth, open windows should always be shut because a draft can make an individual sick (O. Firica, personal communication, May 19, 2004).

Cultural factors have a significant influence on the business environment. Understanding Romanian culture facilitates a comfortable working relationship between American and Romanian business professionals. The next section focuses specifically on business conduct.

BOX 8.3 ☞ **(continued)**

ROMANIAN BUSINESS CONDUCT

Unlike other countries who may want to protect themselves from "outsiders," Romania wants to form alliances with the United States. In fact, in December 2003, Romania gave a $2.5 billion contract to an American company, Bechtel, for what some perceived to be a hardly needed motorway across Transylvania. This was touted as an extravagant gesture to buy American friends ("Don't count," 2004).

Because of Romania's desire to join the European Union in 2007, they are very open to forming alliances and partnerships with other free market economies. Romania, as a country, has always desired independence even when it was under Communist rule.

When conducting business, Romanians are a friendly and outgoing people. Because they like to do business face-to-face, they consider e-mails and faxes too impersonal and a difficult medium in which to build trust, be open, and show sincerity. They much prefer to get up close and personal.

The ethnic Romanians do not hide their emotions and tend to express their intentions, feelings, and opinions freely. They often speak loudly in a singsong manner. They have a lively tone and sometimes people from other countries think individuals are arguing among themselves. Tempers can and do flare easily, and as stated earlier, nothing is hidden as all emotions are openly displayed ("Don't be scared," 2004).

Romanian gestures tend to be expansive and they often "talk" with their hands. They enjoy shaking hands and will do so when introduced, when leaving, and every time they meet. No matter how many times they run into each other during the day, they will shake hands each time. Protocol dictates that men should wait for a woman to extend her hand first. In meetings, women may find they do not receive a handshake but only a nod or a kiss. Some older Romanians will kiss a woman's hand while both men and women openly kiss each other on both cheeks upon meeting.

<u>Entertaining and Giving Gifts</u>

The Romanian people will do the majority of entertaining when visitors come, and the Kennesaw State University executive-MBA students found this to be true when they visited Romania. Their international colleagues would take them to different places every night and would always pay for all things.

If a visitor is invited to a Romanian home and if the visitor decides to bring wine, it should be of the finest vintage. More than one bottle should be brought, as there should be some wine left for the host after the guest has gone.

For business dealings, inexpensive gifts such as pens, calculators, or lighters printed with company names can be given to celebrate holidays or the signing of a contract. When visiting Romania, guests should bring some gift items from their home country as it is expected even if the Romanian counterpart has not offered one yet. Gifts are expected for social events, especially to express thanks after someone has been invited to a dinner party at a home. These gifts are usually opened at the time they are given and received. The easiest way to please Romanians is to treat them to something they cannot get themselves. However, there are some gifts that should be avoided: towels or handkerchiefs, as these items are associated with funerals; gifts wrapped in black paper, as these are

BOX 8.3 ☞ (continued)

traditionally the colors of mourning; and gifts wrapped in purple, as purple is considered a symbolic baby color for little girls ("Romania's cultural," n.d.).

<u>Maintaining Relationships</u>

Once a relationship is established, it requires frequent visits and contact to maintain the partnership. Written communication, planning, and respecting deadlines are not always taken seriously so staying in contact is important. To maintain the relationship means more than just tasks, as Romanians would enjoy visiting his or her partner's home, going out on the town, or participating in other activities outside of work. Again, gift giving helps to cement a good long-term relationship.

NONVERBAL COMMUNICATION

Mehrabian has estimated nonverbal communication comprises 93 percent of all communication. Birdwhistle, another theorist, has stated nonverbal accounts for 65 percent of all communication. Whatever the correct percentage, nonverbal communication figures prominently in interaction with others at the business or social level. For business professionals to be successful in their communication attempts, they must be aware of the power of nonverbal communication. Several areas of importance must be considered when communicating nonverbally with Romanians. These areas include the use of space, touch, eyes, and movement.

<u>The Use of Space</u>

Romanians desire to be close when interacting with others. Romanians shake hands up close and do not move away. They typically communicate at only half-an-arm's length ("Don't be scared," 2004).

<u>The Use of Touch</u>

Sid Jourard, a Canadian psychologist, noted how many times people touch each other in one hour in different cultures. Individuals touched 180 times in Puerto Rico, 102 times in France, 2 times in Florida, and 0 times in England (Phillips-Martinsson, 1981). Romanians do touch a great deal and frequently, as was noted earlier with their handshakes (Don't be scared," 2004). Once Romanians have established a relationship with an individual, it seems touching when speaking is considered a normal part of the conversation. However, they do expect people from other countries to be somewhat more reserved (Centre for Intercultural Learning, 2000b).

<u>The Use of Eyes</u>

As a people, Romanians are considered to have wandering gazes when they speak. They often tend to focus less on the person to whom they are speaking, which may give the impression that they are not paying attention. Trying to maintain constant eye contact may be awkward, but it is not considered offensive (Centre for Intercultural Learning, 2000b). Romanians do perceive eye contact to be very important when communicating and interacting.

<u>The Use of Movement</u>

Romanians generally move at a slower pace than people from the United States. Some might overinterpret this as laziness, indifference, or arrogance,

BOX 8.3 ☞ (continued)

204

but the behavior really only represents their manner of moving. Life in Romania is not as fast paced or hectic as in the United States.

An awareness of nonverbal differences and similarities between Romanians and Americans will help the American business professional communicate his or her message more effectively in the business meeting.

THE BUSINESS MEETING

The following information includes recommendations on how to conduct a business meeting in Romania. In this section, dress, introductions and greetings, time, decision making, and meeting settings are discussed.

Dress

Romanians, as a people, follow a casual western-style, and jeans can be seen everywhere. However, businesspeople are still expected to dress in conservative business apparel. Men wear dark suits except in the summer. During the summer, short-sleeved shirts with ties are acceptable. In addition, women in business are expected to wear suits and heels. It was noted when visiting Dr. Duhaneanu, Rector, and Dr. Adrian Manaicu, Financial Auditor, at the Institute for Business and Public Administration that they would always be dressed in business suits. The higher up someone is in the organization, the more formal the clothing. "Casual Fridays" do not exist in Romania. Romanians expect foreigners to dress well for meetings, for they are quite fashion conscious. In fact, younger professionals can increase their demeanor by dressing more traditionally. Wearing designer clothing signals that an individual has climbed the corporate ladder (Tin, 2004).

Introductions/Greetings

Romanians take little time to open up to strangers and they typically greet others with a kiss on the check and a warm hug. Romanians do consider titles important; therefore, when introducing any Romanian professional, that person should be addressed by his or her title (Doctor, Engineer, Professor, and so forth) and surname. First names are rarely used unless people are well known acquaintances. Generally, people call one another by "Mr. X" ("domnule X" in Romanian) or "Mrs. Y" ("doamna Y" in Romanian). An individual should wait to be invited to use first names. Some older Romanian women will invite individuals to address them as "tante," which is the Romanian equivalent to "auntie" (Centre for Intercultural Learning, 2000c).

Traditionally when Romanians enter into a business meeting, they will bring flowers if the meeting is with a woman. A person should always present a business card after being introduced and the reverse side should be translated into Romanian (Tin, 2004). All advanced degrees as well as titles and positions should be noted on both sides as Romanian businesspeople want to know that they are dealing with important individuals ("Romania's cultural," n.d.).

Romanians like to talk about things that touch their lives such as personal, political, economic, or international situations rather than talking about new subjects, which follows their national culture of security and stability. Talking about work and asking where people are from are good icebreakers as is talking about the weather. Often, the Romanians will want to know what visitors think about their country (Centre for Intercultural Learning, 2000b).

BOX 8.3 ☞ (continued)

Time

When scheduling Romanian meetings, one must consider many factors, as punctuality is not always adhered to. Being a half an hour late is seen as normal and is known as the "academic half hour," which is very acceptable (Centre for Intercultural Learning, 2000c). However, visitors should arrive on time and be prepared to wait before their Romanian counterpart may appear ("Romania's cultural," n.d.).

Meetings should only be scheduled during normal working hours, and individuals should avoid scheduling any meetings coinciding with holidays, weekends, or during July and August. Romanians take their off hours more seriously than do Americans. Due to the shortness of summer, most Romanians take their vacations during July and August; therefore, most firms close during at least the month of August.

Romanians take a more casual approach to time, punctuality, deadlines, absenteeism, and productivity. People show up for work, but lateness, long coffee or smoke breaks, and missed deadlines are common and part of the normal working environment.

Decision Making

As was noted in the national culture of Romania, the Romanians have a strong power orientation; therefore, many Romanian organizations follow a very totalitarian style of leadership and are very centralized. Directors and super-visors do most of the decision making; however, informal relations play an important role in information sharing, the creation of ideas, and decision making. Decisions are made based on the context, the influences at play, and personal interests. There are few established decision-making procedures and final decisions can be slow and protracted, taking several months to a year as risk-taking is very low (Centre for Intercultural Learning, 2000c).

Meeting Settings

Meetings can be held in either formal or informal settings depending on the meeting's purpose. Romanians enjoy conversation and interacting, which can make it difficult to keep the meeting on track and to follow an established agenda. Meetings occur in many places besides a formal meeting room and frequently occur over lunch. Romanians do enjoy heavy lunches as well as wine and hard liquor. A typical Romanian luncheon meeting can last three hours. Clara Moraru, Managing Director of Outsourcing Partners Ltd. (and Romania's unofficial ambassador to FirstTuesday networking), provided useful insights about the etiquette to observe when doing business in her country:

> Romanians are very traditional; pride, honour and "saving face" are important, as are respectful behavior, formal dress and punctuality. Once you've avoided all the social minefields and earned their respect, though, they are very friendly and generous, especially with their food and "tuic" (wine), which flows copiously at business lunches that often last all day long. (para. 8, "Don't be scared," 2004)

EFFECTIVE COMMUNICATION

Many differences exist in the way Romanians and Americans negotiate in business. In fact, these two cultures use opposite styles of negotiation. The following section explains the Romanian use of language and negotiating style.

BOX 8.3 ☞ **(continued)**

Language

Americans have an advantage when doing business with Romanians as they speak English when negotiating. However, Americans will have a greater advantage if they have someone who speaks Romanian on their team. Romanians tend to communicate in Romanian during negotiations without realizing this could appear impolite to their American associates. One person stated, "One thing that often surprised me was the passionate way my Romanian friends and colleagues spoke among themselves. At first, I often mistook normal conversations for conflict" (Centre for Intercultural Learning, 2000b, para. 17).

Americans should consider that Romanians converse in the British English, not American English, so some words may sound unfamiliar. During negotiations, one must limit or avoid using informal expressions or jargon and keep in mind Romanians do not fully understand the nuances of American slang. Americans will impress their Romanian counterparts if they learn a few key phrases in Romanian.

Although Romanians speak fairly fluent English, they may not fully understand the intricacies of a contract or negotiation. Americans should encourage understanding by incorporating charts, diagrams, and other visual aids in their business interactions.

Patience is necessary in establishing business contacts in Romania, but once the connection is established, one can expect to do business with the Romanians for a very long time.

Negotiating Style

In Romanian culture, people are traditionally expected to behave with a sense of decorum and formality at all times. This concept is known as "prima impresie" ("beautiful figure") and refers to the ability to put on a good performance or to present oneself well. The goal for the initial meeting should be to cultivate feelings of respect and trust between the parties. Given that Romanians tend to be guided by their feelings, they will decide whether to do business with an individual based upon whether they like that individual and perceive they can trust him or her ("Romania's cultural," n.d.).

Romanians work toward fairness in their negotiations and like things to go smoothly. Romanian businesspeople want to avoid conflict more than do their American counterparts. Romanians generally prefer to do business with only the most important people in any organization ("Romania's cultural," n.d.). An understanding of the differences between American and Romanian use of language and style of negotiating will eliminate misunderstandings. Attention to these differences will promote mutual understanding and successful business negotiations. As International Team 15 stated in their process paper:

> International virtual teaming was new to most of the team members. We had a strong, positive start, but because of our inexperience, had challenges too. We worked through our difficulties and learned some important lessons along the way. We are wiser and better prepared than we were before. We realize that we (Romanians and Americans) have a lot in common, while in some areas we have different ways of approaching issues. These differences caused tensions among the team members during the two months of working together, but all tensions were minor and forgotten in the end. We feel that we produced a functioning team and a

BOX 8.3 ☛ (continued)

top-quality document. Considering all of the above, we are glad for the opportunity we have had to work with brilliant people from whom we could learn a great deal. This is a once-in-a-lifetime opportunity to develop lasting friendships with individuals from another culture. (Dragomir, Esanu, Necsulescu, Rousseau, Tosto, Vamesu, Vior, Walker, 2003, p. 6)

CONCLUSIONS AND RECOMMENDATIONS

The findings of this report suggest the American business professional will find it easy to conduct business successfully in Romania. Although differences exist in business practices, becoming aware of these differences will help the American businessperson. This understanding leads to successful business negotiations. Therefore, the following recommendations are made.

1. An American business professional should study the culture of the Romanians.

2. An American business professional should exhibit extreme caution when dealing with the Romanians to avoid any communication misunderstanding.

3. An American business professional should never underestimate communication problems or cultural differences.

BOX 8.3 ☛ (continued)

Alphabetic
order.

Only works
referenced
in paper.

WORKS CITED

Central Intelligence Agency. (2004). *The world factbook.* Retrieved July 21, 2004, from *http://www.cia.gov/cia/publications/factbook/index.html.*

Centre for Intercultural Learning. (2000a, August). *Cultural insights: Romania, cultural context.* Retrieved July 19, 2004, from *http://www.dfait-maeci.gc.ca/ cfsi-icse/cil-cai/inter-source/cc-en.asp?iso=ro.*

Centre for Intercultural Learning. (2000b, August). *Cultural insights: Romania, first contact.* Retrieved July 19, 2004, from *http://www.dfait-maeci.gc.ca/cfsi-icse/cil-cai/inter-source/cc-en.asp?iso=ro.*

Centre for Intercultural Learning. (2000c, August). *Cultural insights: Romania, workplace.* Retrieved July 19, 2004, from *http://www.dfait-maeci.gc.ca/cfsi-icse/cil-cai/inter-source/cc-en.asp?iso=ro.*

Ciliege, J., Covaciu, A., Finch, C., Georgevici, A., Ilie, I., Ionascu, A., Panturu, S., & Raineri, K. (2003). *International virtual teaming process paper.* Unpublished research paper, Kennesaw State University, Kennesaw, GA.

Dalton, M. A., Ernst, C. T., Deal, J. J., & Leslie, J. B. (2002). Success for the new global manager. San Francisco: Jossey-Bass Wiley, p. 3.

Dragomir, M., Esanu, C., Necsulescu, A., Rousseau, C., Tosto, P., Vamesu, V., Vior, D., & Walker, M. (2003). *International virtual team group work process paper.* Unpublished research paper, Kennesaw State University, Kennesaw, GA.

Don't be scared of getting close to Romanians. (2004). *PaperJam.* Retrieved on July 23, 2004, from *http://www.paperjam.lu/c/articles/9542.html.*

Don't count your chickens. (2004). *The Economist.* Retrieved July 22, 2004, from *http://www.economist.co.uk/displayStory.cfm?story_id=2598913.*

Doru, R. M. (2004). Romania's new tax code. *The Romanian Digest, IX, 1,* 1–6.

Ellis, W. S. (1975, November). Romania: Maverick on a tightrope. *National Geographic,* 148, No. 5 688–713.

Gscu, S. (n.d.). *How I came to immigrate to America.* Retrieved July 23, 2004, from *http://members.aol.com/simonagscu/romania.html.*

Gscu, S. (n.d.). *Some background information on Romania.* Retrieved July 23, 2004, from *http://members.aol.com/simonagscu/romania.html.*

Hall, E. T. (1966). *The hidden dimension.* New York: Anchor Press/Doubleday.

BOX 8.3 (continued)

IMF Reviews Romania's Performance Under Past Fund-Supported. (2004). *International monetary fund, public information notice (PIN) No. 04/44.* Retrieved July 24, 2004, from *http://www.imf.org/external/np/sec/pn/2004/pn0444.htm.*

Leading Across Cultural Differences Survey. (2002, October). *Center for Creative Leadership E-Newsletter.* Retrieved July 19, 2004, from *http://www.ccl.org/CCLCommerce/news/newsletters/enewsletter/2002/OCTseptsurvey results.aspx?CatalogID=News&News.*

Morrison, T., Conaway, W. A., & Borden, G. A. (1994) Kiss, Bow, or Shake Hands. Holbrook, Massachusetts: Adams Media Corporation, pp. 308–313.

Parliament of Romania. (n.d.). *Chamber of deputies.* Retrieved July 24, 2004, from *http://www.cdep.ro/pls/dic/site.page?id-10&idl=2.*

Phillips-Martinsson, J. (1981). *Swedes as others see them.* Sweden: Studentlitteratur.

Romania. (2004). *Geography.* Retreived July 24, 2004, from *http://www.geo-strategies.com/romania/geography.htm.*

Romania. (n.d.). *In MSN Encarta.* Retrieved July 22, 2004, from *http://encarta.msn.com/encyclopedia_761559516_152/Romania.html.*

Romania's cultural do's and don'ts in business. (n.d.). *Cross cultural business correspondence.* Retrieved July 23, 2004, from *http://www.2cbc.net/2002/introductions/dos/dos_and don'ts.pdf.*

Roussos, P. (2004). There is so much more than Dracula. . . . *New Bucharest Express, 6,* 9.

Rosenzweig, P. M. (1994). National culture and management. *Harvard Business Review, 9-394177,* 1–13.

Sebenuis, J. K. (2002). The hidden challenge of cross-border negotiation. *Harvard Business Review, R0203F,* 4–12.

Tin, K. M. (2004, January). *Romania 2001–2003: My perspective.* PowerPoint presentation given in classroom lecture at Kennesaw State University, Kennesaw, GA.

BOX 8.3 ☞ **(continued)**

SOURCE: Reprinted with permission of Hillary Roebuck.

Business Plans

You may be asked to write a special type of formal report called a business plan. According to the Small Business Administration, a business plan defines your business, identifies your goals, and serves as your organization's resume.[4] The business plan helps you allocate your resources, handle unforeseen complications, and make appropriate business decisions. Your business plan will be used by banks and financial institutions to decide whether to loan you money for your business. In addition, you and your employees will use this plan to gauge your company's success.

Business plans are used for both new business startups and established businesses. In any business loan package, you will be asked to include a business plan because it provides specific, organized information about you and your company.

Your business plan can be the most important persuasive document you ever write. So before you begin, consider these questions:

- What service or product does your business provide and what needs does it fulfill?
- Who are the potential customers for your product or service and why will they use your product or service over someone else's offering?
- How will you reach your potential customers?
- Where will you get the financial resources to start your business?[5]

Each year, MBA students from business schools around the world compete in the Moot Corp. Competition, which according to *Business Week* is a "Super Bowl of Business Plan Competition." This competition gives business students an opportunity to become skilled at analyzing, writing, and presenting business plans to potential investors.

Source: "Moot Corp. Competition, The Super Bowl of Business Plan Competition." Retrieved from *http://www.businessplans.org/businessplans.html*.

Parts of a Business Plan

You should tailor your business plan for a specific purpose. However, the following parts are usually found within any business plan.

TITLE PAGE

Your title page should include your name, address, e-mail address, and telephone number. Next, you should include a paragraph describing your company and the nature of your business. You should also include a confidentiality statement to protect your business endeavor.

"Write the executive summary last. It's just a page or two of highlights."

Source: Tim Berry, "A Standard Business Plan Outline," July 20, 2004, Bplans.com, *http://www.bplans.com/dp/article.cfm/26*.

EXECUTIVE SUMMARY

You should write your executive summary so that it introduces your business strategy and highlights your key points. This summary communicates with potential investors, employees, and customers. As you write this section, you should focus on what your audience will want to learn. Key points you should include are a brief description of the business concept, data that supports your concept, how you will pursue this opportunity, and highlights of how you can achieve your results.

COMPANY DESCRIPTION

In this section, you explain how the business began or how you plan to begin it once you receive funding. Begin the section with your vision and mission statements that

---

[4] "Business Plan Basics." Retrieved July 26, 2004, from *http://www.sbaonline.sba.gov/starting_business/planning/basic.html*.

[5] Retrieved from *http:www.sbaonline.sba.gov/starting_business/planning/basic.html*.

describe your business and what you hope to accomplish. Information about your management team, such as their backgrounds and responsibilities, should be included. You may want to also include an organizational chart where you indicate the lines of authority so that investors know who controls the organization and how people interact with one another. You should summarize any achievements and the performance of the company to date. You can include an analysis of the strengths, weaknesses, opportunities, and threats for the company, which is known as a SWOT analysis.

PRODUCT/SERVICE OFFERING

The next section of your plan should include a specific and detailed description of your business concept. You will need to describe how your product or service differs from others on the market and what makes it special. You should discuss the profile of your potential customer and why he or she would want the product or service.

MARKETING PLAN

In this section, you describe how the products or services will be distributed, priced, and promoted. You include how much you plan to spend on marketing and promotion of your product or service. Generally speaking, potential investors regard the marketing plan as critical to success of the business.

FINANCIAL PLAN

This section determines the investment needed and indicates whether your business plan is truly feasible. It should summarize the forecasted sales and expenses for the first three years. You should provide the cash flow figures for the first three years and the first year's projections provided by month. The projected balance sheet should show the financial condition of the business at a specific point in time.

APPENDIX

Your appendix will contain any backup material not included in the text of the document. Some examples of items that could be found here include: letters from customers, distributors, or subcontractors; secondary or primary research data; and additional financial data.

Visit the following websites to obtain additional guidance on writing a business plan.

Bplans.com
http://www.bplans.com/
> A website dedicated to the small business startup. It includes business plan examples and other advice for a new business owner. This site also sells Business Plan Pro, a commercial product to assist in the development of business plans. However, much of the site's content is available free of charge.

Business Plans Basics (Small Business Administration)
http://www.sbaonline.sba.gov/starting_business/planning/basic.html
> This site was developed by the Small Business Administration (SBA) and provides a comprehensive discussion of the core elements found in a business plan. While it does not include sample plans, it does provide a self-paced tutorial/worksheet to assist the business plan writer and numerous other useful SBA links. The website is also available in Spanish.

CCH Business Owner's Toolkit
http://www.toolkit.cch.com/tools/buspln_m.asp
> You can find downloadable samples and plans. In addition, the site provides a discussion on each required section of a business plan.

TABLE 8.2 📝 **Business plan writing tips.**

When writing your business plan, you should:
- Avoid unnecessary jargon
- Economize on words
- Use short, crisp sentences and bullet points
- Check spelling
- Concentrate on relevant and significant issues
- Break text into numbered paragraphs or sections
- Relegate detail to appendices

SOURCE: "Writing a Business Plan, Section 7, When You Write." Retrieved from http://www.planware.org/bizplan.htm.

The term "white paper" apparently arose in the early twentieth century in England to distinguish shorter government position papers bound in white covers from longer, more detailed reports bound in blue covers called "blue books."

It also derives from the proverbial "clean sheet of paper," on which was written an unbiased and independent set of observations. In its earliest form, the white paper was part of an academic exercise of information sharing.

Source: Manual Gordon and Gordon Graham, "The Art of a White Paper," July 2003, Retrieved from *www.gordonand gordon.com/downloads.html.*

"A white paper is considered to be a standard marketing tool today. Statistics show that decision makers in organizations use them as their first external source of information."

Source: Anjana Srikanth, "Effective Business Writing: The White Paper," *Writers Write,* September 2002. Retrieved from *http://www.writerswrite. com/journal/Sep02/Srikanth.htm.*

More Business: Business and Marketing Plans
http://www.morebusiness.com/templates_worksheets/bplans/
You will find many templates and examples of business and marketing plans.

Small Business Plan Guides
http://www.smbtn.com/businessplanguides/
You will find a large number of guides designed to assist the new business owner. These guides are downloadable as pdf files.[6]

As you write your business plan, be sure to follow the tips given in Table 8.2.

White Papers

Another type of formal report is the white paper. The goal of your white paper may be to educate or inform. In many cases, you may write a white paper to highlight the presence of your organization in the marketplace, to overshadow your competition, or to create a sense of thought leadership. Most often, you write to persuade your reader. Therefore, if you make your purpose clear in the beginning, you can present the evidence, deliver your persuasive arguments, and provide support for them with facts and examples.

Usually white papers are about 10 pages in length but they can vary from 4 to 24 pages. If the white paper is 20 pages or more, a table of contents can help your reader refer quickly to the pages of greatest interest. Most white papers include tables and graphs to supplement the text. Often they can be downloaded from the Web.

Parts of a White Paper

A white paper follows many of the principles of formal report writing and has the following parts: a title page, an executive overview that serves as the introduction, a body, and a conclusion. If the report is bound, you may find information included on the inside front cover as well as the back cover.

TITLE PAGE

The title page includes the title and subtitle of the paper, the name of the author, often the name of the editor, and the name of the organization. One difference is that

---

[6] Deborah Lee, "Sample Business Plans, Selected Internet Sites," created on 3/12/03. Retrieved from *http://www.chronica.msstate.edu/csrc/BusPlans.asp#edd.*

the abstract may be included on the title page instead of being a separate page. Some white papers contain an inside front cover with copyright information.

EXECUTIVE OVERVIEW OR INTRODUCTION

Your white paper begins with an executive overview that is approximately one to two pages. You state the problem, describe the contents of the white paper, and then present an overview of the solution.

BODY

Within the body, your information should support the executive overview and provide enough details to support your conclusion and recommendations. You may begin with a description of the broadest issues and trends and then move into discussing your specific recommendations or solution.

CONCLUSION AND RECOMMENDATIONS

Within the conclusion and recommendations, state how your recommendations can be employed and why they are better than those of your competitors. You should summarize what you expect your reader to do. Remember, this is the most important part of your paper because it is the "sales pitch" that you have been leading up to. Therefore, you need to make your argument clear and persuasive while calling your reader to action. Help your reader by outlining the steps that he or she should take.[7]

The inside back cover can include biographies of the author and organization, as this is a critical element of the overall authority and credibility of the white paper. The back cover can be used as an advertisement, a sales message, and for testimonials.

Conclusion

Formal reports including business plans and white papers can help organizations study problems and provide recommended solutions. The following points summarize the report process.

Analyze the report problem and purpose.

Anticipate the audience and issues.

Prepare a work plan.

Collect data.

Document data sources.

Interpret and organize the data.

Prepare graphics.

Compose a first draft.

Revise and proofread.

Evaluate the product.

After you write your report, business plan, or white paper, use the checklist in Table 8.3 to review your work.

---

[7] Gordon Turner, "Writing White Papers 101," *The Willamette Galley, A Bi-Monthly Newsletter,* Volume 4, Issue 4, September 2001. Retrieved from: *http//www.stcwvc.org/galley/0109/b4.htm.*

TABLE 8.3 ☞ Formal report checklist.

	YES	NO
1. Did I include the background material?	❏	❏
2. Did I state the problem correctly?	❏	❏
3. Did I include the scope of the report?	❏	❏
4. Did I include any limitations?	❏	❏
5. Did I identify major sources and my methods of data collection?	❏	❏
6. Did I provide the major divisions of the report?	❏	❏
7. Within the body, did I clearly define the factors?	❏	❏
8. Did I tie data to sources?	❏	❏
9. Did I discuss the data fully?	❏	❏
10. Does my conclusion appear to be a summary? (Remember to infer a conclusion from the findings.)	❏	❏
11. Did I make any recommendations (if necessary)?	❏	❏
12. Did I include graphics or tables within the body?	❏	❏
13. Did I number graphics and tables?	❏	❏
14. Did I give the sources of graphics or tables?	❏	❏
15. Did I use headings properly within my report?	❏	❏
16. Did I remember not to capitalize prepositions and conjunctions in headings?	❏	❏
17. Did I avoid using *I, We,* or *You*?	❏	❏
18. Did I consistently use one style (endnotes, footnotes, or internal) of attribution?	❏	❏
19. Did I include page numbers for direct quotes?	❏	❏
20. Did I document paraphrased ideas with their sources?	❏	❏
21. Did I use transition to guide the reader?	❏	❏
22. Did I use past tense to discuss my analysis?	❏	❏
23. Did I use past tense to discuss historical data or findings?	❏	❏
24. Did I use present tense to discuss other parts of the study or conclusions from my study or other studies?	❏	❏
25. Does my cover look professional?	❏	❏
26. Is the title page complete?	❏	❏
27. Is the table of contents complete?	❏	❏
28. Did I include a letter of transmittal?	❏	❏
29. Did I include a bibliography or works cited section?	❏	❏
30. Did I check the grammar and spelling?	❏	❏

Exercises

EXERCISE 1   UNDERSTANDING GRAPHICS

Directions: Use your local newspaper or *The Wall Street Journal* to locate one example of a table, a pie chart, a line chart, and a horizontal or vertical bar graph. Bring copies of these graphics to class. On a scale of 1 to 10, with 10 being high, rate the effectiveness of each visual. Then provide a rationale for your rating.

EXERCISE 2   CREATING AN OUTLINE

Directions: Construct an outline with at least three levels of headings and bring it to class for discussion.

EXERCISE 3   JUDGING WHITE PAPERS

Directions: Go to this website: *http://research.mwjournal.com/data/detail?id=1047588039406&type=RES&x=413499797*

Once you are at the website, click on the link "view this document." It should take you to the document entitled "Writing White Papers for the US IT Market, A

Global Business Skills White Paper." Read this document and then complete the section starting on page 53 entitled: "A White Paper Critique—You Be the Judge."

EXERCISE 4 LEARNING MORE ABOUT BUSINESS PLANS

Directions: Go to this Web address: *http://www.sba.gov/hotlist/businessplans.html*. Complete the SBA's Online Classroom presentation on business plans.

Assignment Options

OPTION 1: GROUP REPORT—DEVELOPING A FORMAL REPORT

This assignment will give you some experience in completing a formal research report. While completing this assignment, you will become familiar with library sources of business information; gain experience in organizing and interpreting data; learn about collaborative writing; refine oral presentation skills; and gain further practice in group communication.

Steps Involved in Producing a Business Report

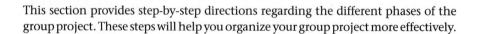

This section provides step-by-step directions regarding the different phases of the group project. These steps will help you organize your group project more effectively.

STEP ONE

Your group should discuss the following possibilities for your report. Pick out two or three alternatives, as your group may not get its first choice. Groups will draw numbers to determine who gets first choice. This list contains possible topics. If your group has other creative topics, discuss them with your instructor.

Nonverbal Communication	Listening
The Grapevine	Ethics
Business Dress	Time Management
Telephone Techniques	Successful Meetings
Communication Technology	Conflict Management
Crisis Communication	Gender Communication
Intercultural Communication	Communication Styles
Communication Climate	Perception
Semantics	Metacommunications
Groupthink	Communication Channels
Communication Networks	Power and Persuasion
Negotiation	Communication Training
Managing Your Boss	Legislative Communication
Total Quality Management	Rightsizing

Organizational Culture	Teamwork and Leadership
Managing Change	Reengineering Workers
Managing the Internet	Emotional Intelligence

STEP TWO

Once you have selected your topic, address the problem. Your research problem should answer the following question:

What role does _____ play in an organization?

You will need to identify the quantity and quality of the resources to be used. Include both theoretical and applied information.

When collecting data for your written report, remember that the body should have a minimum of six sources. Be sure to document your sources, use correct attribution, and employ a suitable style manual. Remember when quoting sources, you must give them credit so document your sources carefully.

STEP THREE

After you have completed your research, develop your collaboratively written report. Follow the guidelines given in this chapter for developing your report and make sure you include all necessary parts. Use the checklist in Table 8.3 to guide your team.

OPTION 2: COLLABORATIVE RESEARCH REPORT

You are to research the topic of virtual teams to educate your audience about the challenges or opportunities of this type of teaming. Each member of your team is to collect at least three articles, summarize those articles into a short report, and make a presentation to your team regarding the findings.

OPTION 3: BUSINESS PLAN

You will use the following business plan guidelines to create your business plan. Guidelines for this assignment were provided by Debbie L. Davidoff of the The Davidoff Group.

Major Segments of the Business Plan

⇒ Vision and Mission

⇒ Opportunity—Goal is to describe the market opportunity as significant and worth pursuing. (**Approximately 4 pages**)

- ○ This section would include the research that identifies the need for the invention
- ○ Target market attributes / customer dynamics
- ○ Market size and growth, as well as market trends, are identified
- ○ Identification of competitors

⇒ Specific Market Strategy—What we are going to do to take advantage of the opportunity we just identified. (**Approximately 6 pages**)

- ○ Product
  - • How will we position it?
  - • How will we price it?
  - • How will we package it?
- ○ Sales and Distribution
  - • Targeted channels . . . the "two-pronged approach"

⇒ Sales Strategy
  ○ Marketing
    • Advertising and PR
    • Public relations and trade shows
⇒ Specific Business Strategy—How will we build the business and how it will make money? (**Approximately 4–6 pages**)
  ○ Business Model—key part of this section
    • Top level revenue streams—where will this come from?
    • Top level profit margins—how profitable will each revenue stream be?
    • Market share—what will our share be for each revenue stream?
    • Growth
  ○ Strategic Initiatives
    • Partners/acquisitions
    • Expansion
  ○ Timeline

Note: Elements of the above will be included in the Business Plan Report

⇒ Organization and Operations (**Approximately 6 pages or less**)
  ○ Organization Structure
  ○ Key Operations
    • Copyrights and patents
    • Product development
    • Distribution
    • Sales
    • Marketing
    • Finance and accounting
    • HR
  ○ Management
    • Senior management team
    • Board of directors
    • Key advisors
    • Strategic investors
  ○ Core Competencies and Competitive Challenges—Summarizes unique competitive advantages in summary fashion.
  ○ Projected Financials
    • Revenue projections
    • Current and projected income statements
    • Balance sheet
    • Cash flow projections
⇒ Appendixes—Optional

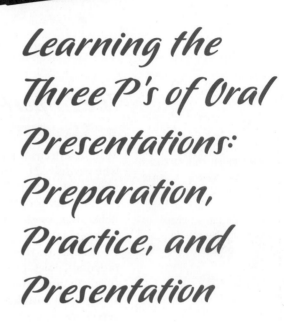

Learning the Three P's of Oral Presentations: Preparation, Practice, and Presentation

*A*lthough in our daily work, we speak more often than we write, many of us have not overcome the fear of having to speak to a group. If this applies to you, you have many friends who feel like you do![1]

Patricia M. Fandt

[1] Patricia M. Fandt, *Management Skills, Practice and Experience* (Minneapolis: West Publishing Company, 1994), p. 156.

LEARNING OBJECTIVES

After reading this chapter, you should be able to:

- Understand why so many people fear oral presentations.

- State the three *P*s of oral presentation.

- List and explain the three general purposes of presentations.

- Relate how you analyze your audience.

- Discuss how to organize your presentation.

- Distinguish between different patterns for forming the main ideas.

- Explain the different kinds of supporting material.

- Identify how you construct the introduction and conclusion.

- Outline a basic presentation.

- Describe how to develop visual aids.
- Spell out how to use a pointer.
- Explain ways to use up nervous energy.
- Report actions to use during the introduction and the body of the presentation.
- List the guidelines for making team presentations.
- Recount how to handle the question-and-answer session.
- Explain when to use a multimedia presentation.

The Importance of Oral Presentations

A quotation from *American Salesman* stated: "If you're more afraid of speaking in front of people than financial difficulties, illness—or even death—you are a . . . victim of America's leading fear."

Source: "The Unspeakable Fear," *American Salesman*, September 1990, pp. 13–15.

Most Americans fear speaking in front of others. In a survey of 2,500 Americans who were asked to rank their greatest fears, speaking before a group of people was ranked before death.[2]

Why do people fear public speaking? Table 9.1 represents the findings of Robert Flax, president of Motivational Systems. In his survey of 12,000 people, he uncovered the top six reasons for being afraid to speak in public.

People use their oral presentation skills to make informal reports, in-house proposals, sales proposals, recommendations, and informal briefings. People spend approximately 30 percent of their time each day communicating orally.[3] A survey completed for the *American Journal of Small Business* ranked perceived success characteristics of successful entrepreneurs. Bank loan managers who were responsible for giving loans to beginning entrepreneurs ranked oral communication skills as number one.[4] Refer to Box 9.1 to see how oral communication skills impacted Charles Schwab's career.

"From the chairman of the board to the assistant manager of the most obscure department, nearly everyone in business speaks in public or makes a speech at some time or other."

Source: "The Science of Speechmaking," *Duris Review and Modern Industry*, December 1962, p. 32.

Oral communication must be clear and concise because misunderstandings can cost both time and money. Oral presentations by a firm's representatives affect its reputation and competitive position.[5] Oral presentations cost money. After a systematic analysis, one aerospace company came up with a minimum annual estimate of over $1.5 million spent on oral presentations within the company.[6] With continued research done to rank oral presentation needs and importance, the

TABLE 9.1 Reasons for being afraid of public speaking.

Fear of making embarrassing mistakes	(81%)
Fear of damaging career or reputation	(77%)
Fear of forgetting or freezing, of not being able to say anything at all	(63%)
Fear of being dull or boring	(58%)
Fear of looking nervous or petrified	(52%)
Fear of being stared at	(45%)

SOURCE: Edward Wakin, "Speaking Frankly about Speech Phobias," *Today's Office*, Volume 25, Issue 5, October 1990, p. 50.

[2] Retrieved from *http://www.jseminars.com/anxiety.htm*, Lenny Laskowski "Overcoming Speaking Anxiety in Meetings and Presentations."

[3] Cynthia Hamilton and Brian H. Kleiner, "Steps to Better Listening," *Personnel Journal*, Volume 66, Issue 2, February 1987, pp. 20–21.

[4] Ray V. Montagno, Donald F. Kuratko, and Joseph H. Scarcella, "Perception of Entrepreneurial Success Characteristics," *American Journal of Small Business*, Volume 10, Issue 3, Winter 1968, pp. 25–32.

[5] Michael F. Warlum, "Improving Oral Marketing Presentations in the Technology-Based Company," *IEEE Transactions on Professional Communication*, Volume 31, Issue 2, January 1988, pp. 84–87.

[6] George T. Vardaman, *Making Successful Presentations* (New York: AMACOM, 1981).

In 1982, Charles Schwab sold the discount brokerage firm that bears his name to Bank of America. The price tag: $50 million. Schwab was living the American dream. Starting from scratch, he built a thriving corporation out of his own ingenuity and hard work. When he sold it, he was living on top of the world—or he should have been. Instead, Schwab felt like he had to start a whole new phase of his career. Why? "As a kid I was good at a lot of things, but I could never remember in sequence. I think a lot of it goes back to the fact that I was dyslexic. I only found out I was dyslexic a few years ago, because when I was younger, no one knew how to diagnose dyslexia. No one knew what my problem was. I just knew there were things I could not do that other kids could do with ease, such as memorizing a passage of poetry. In those days, they taught public speaking in a rote, memorized way. So I had no confidence in that area and was unable to get up and speak in front of people." Schwab was never a poor student. As a child, he exhibited the mental acuity and talent that would one day propel him into the ranks of America's top executives. However, because of an undiagnosed problem that hampered his ability to decode and use language, he was slow in sequential thinking and reading while good in the abstract. Nevertheless, abstract thinking was not (and is not) rewarded in our school system. Therefore, the young Charles Schwab shunned any speaking because he felt inadequate in front of the class. His own experience has given him empathy for others with dyslexia. "My son is dyslexic and my sister is dyslexic," he says. "I set up a foundation for the parents of dyslexic kids, because these kids need parents who are trained to understand, accept and deal with the problem. And the parents need their own support, too." Schwab, who overcame his early limitations and became one of the most successful businessmen in America, recalls with irony the day shortly after he sold his company for $50 million. "Soon after the company was sold," he remembers, "one of my most trusted officers—he'd been with me since the beginning—came up to me and said, 'Chuck, you need help.' I was amazed and frankly a little upset. Here we had just reached our dream, were on a new plateau with the backing to expand our business, and I was being criticized by one of my most trusted. "But he was right. If we were to succeed at this new level—this higher profile—I did need help in becoming more of a public figure. We used still photos extensively and effectively in our advertising campaigns, but I had always shied away from any engagements that required me to communicate—to speak. He was just saying that I had to change." And Charles Schwab did change—he did do something about his communicating. He still feared speaking and it was a high stressor for him. But he knew that to achieve success as a person he needed to have that capability. He said, "It was sheer force of will that got me in front of an audience. I was stressed about it for days on end. Of course, what has happened is that with training, video feedback, and the understanding that I have now, my stress level has gone down 99 percent." Today you often find Charles Schwab in front of an audience, looking relaxed and confident. He does not pretend to enjoy it, but he knows he is effective as a speaker. In his commercials for Charles Schwab and Co, he is believable, likable, and persuasive—the ideal spokesperson for his company. Charles Schwab was not always a natural communicator. But today he is one of the most effective speakers on the American business scene because he made a decision to do something about his personal impact.

BOX 9.1 ☞ "He Said I Needed Help"

SOURCE: Bert Decker, *You've Got to Be Believed to Be Heard* (New York: St. Martin Press, 1992), pp. 25–27.

company could lower those costs by more than $300,000 annually. With costs so high, companies want their decision makers to be well trained and confident in their oral presentation abilities.

A widespread fear of public speaking results from people believing they must be natural-born speakers to be effective. However, through a systematic approach to the entire process of public speaking, you can overcome fear. By removing the uncertainty surrounding speaking and replacing it with a planned approach, individuals can conquer fear. This planned approach includes preparation, practice, and presentation.

Preparation

People usually do not make an effective presentation just out of the blue. They must spend some time setting a clear purpose. If they do not, they appear to wander aimlessly through their presentation. In the words of a popular poster, if you don't know where you are going, you're likely to wind up somewhere else. In oral presentations, that is very true.[7] Careful preparation makes a successful presentation.

To be effective, you must begin by determining the general and specific purposes of your presentation.

DETERMINING THE GENERAL PURPOSE

Finding the purpose of your speech involves two steps. First, you must determine the general purpose; only then can you follow-up by choosing the specific purpose. Most authorities recognize three general purposes: informing, persuading, or entertaining.

Informing. When you try to teach listeners or explain something to them, you inform. You may acquaint listeners with something completely new. You seek to promote understanding.

Persuading. Persuasive speeches range from those seeking to change listeners' beliefs or attitudes to those attempting to get listeners to act in a certain way. Persuasive presentations must inform as well as persuade. Being an effective persuasive speaker depends on providing facts and logical evidence, being credible, and understanding the psychological needs of your listeners.

Entertaining. When you entertain, you want your listeners to enjoy your presentation. Enthusiastic speakers who enjoy sharing about their subjects usually entertain their listeners. Others can entertain through their flair for drama or picturesque language.

Remember to analyze your audience to make emotional contact with your listeners.

CHOOSING THE SPECIFIC PURPOSE

Although you have only three general purposes for making a public presentation, your choices for specific purpose can be infinite. Design your specific purpose with both the subject and the audience in mind.

Although the general purpose may remain the same, the specific purpose varies according to the audience. Few speeches inform, persuade, or entertain entirely; most combine more than one purpose.[8] After you decide your purpose, you need to analyze your audience.

[7] Roy M. Berko, Andrew D. Wolvin, and Ray Curtis, *This Business of Communicating,* 5th ed. (Madison, WI: WCB Brown & Benchmark Publishers, 1993), p. 286.

[8] Zane K. Quible, Margaret H. Johnson, and Dennis L. Mott, *Introduction to Business Communication,* 2nd ed. (Englewood Cliffs, NJ: Prentice Hall, 1988), p. 484.

ANALYZING THE AUDIENCE

You must find out as much information as possible concerning your audience in order to tailor the message. If you make an internal presentation, you must know the makeup of the group. Which departments will attend your presentation? What level of employees or managers will attend? If you address an external group, the audience's backgrounds, attitudes, biases, sympathies, and opinions should be determined. You need to know whether any factions or cliques will be in the audience, agreeing or disagreeing with one another. If possible, try to find out the average age of the audience or the age range, the sexual breakdown of the audience, racial and ethnic groups represented, occupations represented, religious groups present, the political orientation of the group, and the socioeconomic composition of the group.

You must figure out the group's knowledge base. What knowledge do they already possess? You do not want to bore them with something they already know, nor do you want to talk over their heads. Use the telephone, e-mail, and interviews to help learn more about your audience. Find out what the audience wishes to know. You can accomplish this by doing some research in advance.

As more audiences within the United States become diverse and as more individuals from the United States travel internationally to conduct business, it becomes critical to understand different cultural backgrounds. When speaking to international audiences, it is important for you to get to know who your audience will be and to learn what works in that country, since what works in the United States may not be appropriate in another country. For example, French people employ dramatics and emotions in their presentations.

Generally, you must be more formal outside of the United States. Americans love to be extemporaneous; they take pride in being able to think on their feet. For effect, they often mark flip charts or overheads, and welcome audience input. International audiences see these behaviors as unprofessional, and they wonder why the speaker did not prepare or rehearse the presentation. Therefore, you must learn how your audience prefers to receive information. For example, many Europeans historically have preferred to receive information in detail with lots of supporting documentation. They want to hear speakers build their points in the presentations. Japanese audiences follow a similar pattern. American and Canadian audiences tend to prefer a faster pace and a more bottom-line oriented presentation. They prefer speakers who speak from a point rather than build step-by-step toward a point.

If you are issuing a call for action through your presentation, you should make sure you have given a realistic timetable. What is realistic in one culture may not be realistic in another.

When speaking in English, make sure you use simple, neutral language and avoid any jargon or sports terms. Also remember that many English words have different meanings when translated to another culture. For example, in the United States "mad" means you are angry; to a British audience it can mean "insane." Another example is in Australia, where break out sessions are called syndicates. If you were making a joke that used the word "syndicate," you may totally confuse the audience. People from most countries will not relate easily if you mention miles per gallon or miles per hour. You should avoid talking about seasons, sports figures, or celebrities that don't have worldwide name recognition.

You should keep in mind that protocol is extremely important. For example, you should know the accepted way of acknowledging your hosts and the other key people in your audience. In addition, you should adjust your pace. North and South Americans prefer a faster pace, while Europeans and Asians typically prefer more time to process information. In any case, slow down a bit and try to build comfort with the use of pauses.

When considering whether to use humor or not, you should use a conservative approach and exhibit caution. In many—if not most—cultures, there's a far greater risk that your humor will not be understood. Although cartoons and comic strips are the most universally accepted format for humor, be careful about your selection of cartoons, as many American cartoons would not be appropriate to use outside of the United States.

As a rule, applause is a universal sign of approval; however, be aware some exceptions do exist. In many parts of Germany and Austria, listeners seated around the table may signal their approval by knocking on the table instead of applauding. If you hear whistles in some European countries, it's a sign of disapproval. In some countries, like Australia, no one ever gets a standing ovation.

As with all situations, learn as much about your audience's culture as possible. Ask questions of your contacts in other countries and focus on possible areas of sensitivity.[9] When you have a better understanding of your audience, you can organize your presentation.

ORGANIZING THE PRESENTATION

Organize your presentation to provide purpose and direction. Examine your topic completely and organize the presentation into logical units. Do not cover too many points, because you often will have time constraints. A rule of thumb to keep in mind is to have only three main points, regardless of the length of your presentation. Each main point could then have three subpoints to add more depth to your presentation.

Develop a thesis, list your main points, gather material to support those points, and estimate your time and word constraints. Write your introduction and conclusion last, after you know what the content will be.

Developing a Thesis. Your thesis should be a clear, one-sentence statement presenting your central idea. The thesis names the main divisions or aspects you will develop and receives support from the main points.

---

[9]"What to Know When You're Speaking to an International Audience." Retrieved from *http://totalcommunicator.com/vol2_2/interaudience.*

Forming the Main Ideas.   Your main ideas should number from two to five, have equal importance, relate to each other, and be in logical order. There are several organizational patterns from which to choose. The *topical pattern,* the most widely used, arranges main points according to type or category. Another organizational pattern, the *spatial pattern,* arranges main ideas according to physical location and shows the relationships among them. You discuss points traditionally, for example, from east to west or from top to bottom. The *chronological pattern* progresses from one given point in time to another. A common way of using this process involves explaining steps. *Problem-solution* or *cause and effect,* a widely recognized form of organization, points out certain forces or causes and then discusses results or solutions. You can reverse the order of this pattern.

Determining the Support Material.   The support material clarifies the main ideas and makes interesting and memorable points to the audience. *Quotations,* as support material, help take advantage of someone else's memorable wording. Another form of support material, *analogies,* includes similes, direct comparisons (using *like* or *as*), metaphors, implied comparisons (not using *like* or *as*), and extended metaphors (comparing an unknown concept to a known one).

As support, *examples* demonstrate a general idea that can be factual, hypothetical, borrowed, or personal. *Statistics* show facts or principles. Statistics should be cited exactly as published and their sources identified in the presentation. *Explanations* typically describe the relationship between certain items, make clear the definition of a word, or give instructions on how to complete something or how to get somewhere. Presenters use *comparisons* to show the similarities or differences between two items. An *illustration* tells a story with such detail it paints a picture in the audience's mind. Illustrations can be factual, based on real incidents, or hypothetical, created for a particular situation or impact. *Expert opinion* refers to the thoughts or ideas of a noted expert in a certain discipline or field. To enhance the credibility of your expert's opinion, be sure to give the expert's name, qualifications, and where and when the individual reported the information.[10] Make sure you use several examples, illustrations, and visuals to support and reinforce your presentation.

Estimating Your Time and Word Constraints.   *Ask yourself the following question: "How much time do I have to present and how much can I say in that time?"* Once you find out approximately how much time you have for a presentation, you can begin to estimate how much you can say. Audiences tend to tune out if you go over the allotted time. One minute equals approximately 110 words spoken at a normal conversational speed. One sentence equals approximately 10 to 20 words. Keep in mind the following time and word constraints as you organize your material.[11]

- 1 minute = approximately 7 sentences or 110 words
- 2 minutes = approximately 14 sentences or 220 words
- 3 minutes = approximately 21 sentences or 330 words
- 4 minutes = approximately 28 sentences or 440 words
- 5 minutes = approximately 35 sentences or 550 words
- 10 minutes = approximately 70 sentences or 1,100 words
- 15 minutes = approximately 105 sentences or 1,650 words

[10] Cheryl Hamilton with Cordell Parker, *Communicating for Results: A Guide for Business and the Professions,* 4th ed. (Belmont, CA: Wadsworth, 1993), pp. 360–372.

[11] Tom Hajduk, "Interpersonal Communication: Moving Students Beyond Writing Assignments," 64th Annual Convention of the Association for Business Communication (Los Angeles, California, November 3–6, 1999).

- 20 minutes = approximately 140 sentences or 2,200 words
- 30 minutes = approximately 210 sentences or 3,300 words
- 60 minutes = approximately 420 sentences or 6,600 words

Constructing the Introduction. The introduction should include an attention-getter and a preview. The attention-getter captures the audience's attention so they will listen to your speech. Some attention-getters include referring to the audience, occasion, or date; reciting a quotation, startling fact, or rhetorical question; telling a joke or humorous story; describing a specific incident; or demonstrating your point. The introduction, as outlined in Box 9.2, should contain a preview of the main points to be discussed in the presentation. Your introduction should constitute about 25 percent of your speech.

According to Wicke Chambers and Spring Asher, communication consultants, presenters should learn from television. Television producers know they must capture their audience's attention during the first minute. All speakers must have an attention-getting introduction, no matter what position they hold or what type of presentation they make. Your opener should say, "Stay tuned." After you have hooked your audience, you can tell them you're glad to be with them and state the benefits of staying tuned.

Making the Conclusion. After the introduction, your next step involves preparing the conclusion. The conclusion reviews the thesis and main points as well as giving effective final remarks. The review simply restates the thesis and main points; in other words, it serves as a reinforcement for the audience. It should comprise approximately 10 percent of your presentation. The final remarks should complete the speech in a memorable way so the audience will remember the presentation. Methods for creating effective closings are the same as those used for developing attention-getting openings. When you have organized your presentation, formulate an outline.

OUTLINING THE PRESENTATION

An outline, as illustrated in Box 9.3, enables you to determine the order in which you will present your main points, arrange your support items, and specify what you will say in your introduction and conclusion. The outline unifies all the parts of your presentation.

You may need to revise your outline several times as you think of new points or research further information. Many presenters find it helpful to fully write out certain supporting details, such as statistics and quotes that must be exact. Others write out their introductions and conclusions to make sure they begin and end with an impact.[12]

Develop your outline on a single 8- by 11-inch sheet of paper, or place each major point on a single card in large, clear letters, enabling you to grasp the points on

> "Like the preacher said: 'Tell 'em what you're going to tell 'em. Tell 'em. Tell 'em what you told 'em.'"
>
> Source: Courtland L. Bovee and John V. Thill, *Business Communication Today,* 4th ed. (New York: McGraw-Hill, Inc., 1995), p. 592.

- Capture attention.
- Show benefit to listeners.
- State your qualifications.
- Preview purpose and main points.

BOX 9.2 〰 **The Introduction**

---

[12] Dalmar Fisher, *Communication in Organizations,* 2nd ed. (Minneapolis: West, 1993), p. 520.

I. **Introduction**
   A. **Attention-getter:** One of the largest and most expensive problems corporations face involves not hiring the right employee for the job.
   B. **Why audience should listen:** We will conduct interviews someday, if we have not already. Will you be able to hire the right person?
   C. **Credibility:** I am personally guilty of choosing the wrong candidate for a position.
   D. **Purpose:** Today you will learn about how to conduct an effective interview. You will learn to get accurate information during the job interview, fairly evaluate the information obtained, and set the stage for a successful career for the hiree.
   E. **Main Points:** (1) preparation before the interview, (2) the interview, and (3) follow-up after the interview.

II. **Body: Before the Interview**
   A. **Conduct a job analysis**
      1. Education
      2. Job experience
      3. Personality
   B. **Look for red flags**
   C. **Prepare a list of questions**
      1. Work experience/responsibilities at present job
      2. Behavior examples
      3. Strengths and weaknesses
      4. Short- and long-term goals

III. **Body: During the Interview**
   A. **Review résumé and ask questions**
   B. **Watch and listen**
      1. Hold interview away from office
      2. Watch body language
      3. Listen for what was not said
   C. **Be honest**
      1. Be specific about job requirements
      2. Answer questions honestly
      3. Be tactful to unlikely candidates

IV. **Body: After the interview**
   A. **Review notes again**
   B. **Call two or three references**
   C. **Compare candidates**

V. **Conclusion**
   A. **Review of purpose and main points**
   B. **Give effective final remarks—making new hire a part of the team**
      1. Inform staffers about new colleague
      2. Welcome and introduce person
      3. Help new hire get busy

BOX 9.3 🖝 **Basic Informative Outline Example**

each card quickly. Your outline, like a blueprint, helps you to assimilate the ideas in your talk more easily and helps draft the "speaker's notes" that you will take to the podium with you. In short, if you use your outline properly, you will deliver a better speech.

Toastmasters International recommends you use a *green* highlighter to mark those places you want to emphasize in your outline. Then they suggest

The argument draws on philosophy and philosophical anthropology to fix a notion of personhood consistent with this record of performance. Centrally, the distinctively human power of intelligibility-depends on the same kind of tolerance for mutual vulnerbility in collaboration that marks joint economic activity. In this realm understanding is always possible wherever it is advantageous, and if disagreements persist it is because the disputants disagree, mot because they do not understand what it would mean to come to an under-standing. Feyerabend's groups of scientists pursuing their conceptual projects in awareness of and even at the partial instigation of alternative conceptions

A recent *Wall Street Journal* article reported that Gen. Hugh Shelton, Chairman of the Joint Chiefs at the Pentagon, issued an order to skip the bells and whis-tles in PowerPoint and just get to the point.

Source: Gates Matthew Stoner, "Effectively Communicating Via the Web," 2001. Retrieved from *http://www.u.arizona.edu/~gstoner/effectiveweb.html.*

you photocopy your speech, because the green highlighter reproduces as a dis-tinctive gray, and you'll be able to read your copy clearly and easily.

DEVELOPING VISUAL AIDS

Visual aids should enhance your presentation, but not replace it. Research has shown that individuals retain more information when presenters incorporate vi-suals into their presentations (see Table 9.2).

A speaker's goals are met 34 percent more often when visuals are used than when they are not. In addition, group consensus occurs 21 percent more often in meetings with visuals than without. The time required to present a concept can be reduced up to 40 percent with the use of visuals. When visuals were used in teach-ing a course on vocabulary, learning improved 200 percent.[13] These statistics vali-date the importance of visual aids to your presentation.

Today's technology makes the task of creating visual aids quite simple. When choosing the correct visual aids, choose carefully; you do not want the visuals to de-tract from your presentation. The visuals should also be consistent with your objec-tives. You can choose from: transparencies, computer slide shows, flip charts, slides, flannel boards, easel pads, whiteboards, samples, maps, and videotapes. All of these reinforce your presentation. There are certain pitfalls, however, that you should avoid when using visuals. An online survey conducted in September of 2003 sought to find out how PowerPoint annoys audiences. The results of this survey are pre-sented in Table 9.3.

As you can see from the results of the previously discussed survey, you should use technology to support your message, but not replace you. Misuse of technol-

TABLE 9.2 🖙 **Retention of information.**

	Retaining Information	
	AFTER 3 HOURS	AFTER 3 DAYS
Heard Only	70%	10%
Seen Only	72%	20%
Heard and Seen	85%	65%

SOURCE: From Cheryl Hamilton, *Communicating for Results,* 3rd ed. (Belmont, CA: Wadsworth, 1992), p. 377.

[13] Bert Decker, *You've Got to Be Believed to Be Heard* (New York: St. Martin Press, 1992), p. 85.

Table 9.3 ☞ **Summary of the annoying PowerPoint.**

Question 1: What are the three most annoying things about the bad PowerPoint presentations you have seen?

The speaker read the slides to us	60.4%
Text so small I couldn't read it	50.9%
Full sentences instead of bullet points	47.8%
Slides hard to see because of color choice	37.1%
Moving/flying text or graphics	24.5%
Annoying use of sound	22.0%
Overly complex diagrams or charts	22.0%
No flow of ideas—jumped around too much	18.9%
No clear purpose of the presentation	18.2%
Too many fonts used	12.6%
Graphic images didn't fit the topic of the slide	6.3%
Poor quality video or audio segment	5.0%

(Total equals 325.7% because people were asked to select three options and some selected more than three.)

Question 2: What other things annoy you about PowerPoint presentations? (This was a free-form question and 94 of the 159 respondents (59.1%) added comments. Three common themes emerged from the comments:

1. **Poor Preparation of the Presentation.** People are very annoyed when the presenter does not even think about the structure of the presentation and simply copies the text of a report onto slides. PowerPoint slides should support the message, not substitute for the presenter or for a more detailed handout. Presenters need to connect with the audience instead of hiding behind the slides.
2. **Balance of Slide Elements.** People find too much text or too many fancy graphics and multimedia elements a big turn-off. These two extremes do not work well. A balanced approach is called for—text to give context for the audience's understanding of what the presenter will next be speaking about, and graphics and multimedia to touch the emotions of the audience.
3. **Not Knowing How to Use the Technology.** If presenters are going to use technology during a presentation, they should learn how to set it up, start it up so it looks professional, and smoothly move between the slides. Awkward usage of PowerPoint and presentation technology was mentioned a number of times as detracting from the message being delivered.

Question 3: In an average week, how many PowerPoint presentations do you see?

0–1	55.9%
2–4	35.2%
5–8	5.7%
9–15	1.9%
16 or more	1.3%

Question 4: Of those PowerPoint presentations that you see, what percentage are done poorly (suffer from one or more of the above problems)?

More than 50%	28.9%
41–50%	12.6%
31–40%	11.3%
26–30%	7.5%
21–25%	8.8%
16–20%	8.8%
11–15%	3.1%
6–10%	5.0%
0–5%	13.8%

SOURCE: Dave Pardi, "Summary of the Annoying PowerPoint Survey." Retrieved from *http://www.communicateusingtechnology. com/pptresults.htm.*

ogy can turn speakers into mere readers of captions for slides. A recent survey of captains at Fort Benning, Georgia, cited "the ubiquity of the PowerPoint Army" as a prime reason why the Army is losing too many bright young officers. "The idea behind most of these briefings," it said, "is for us to sit through 100 slides with our eyes glazed over." The term "PowerPoint Ranger" has even become a derogatory term, describing a desk-bound bureaucrat more adept at making slides than tossing grenades.[14]

"In preparing your visuals, you list only one point in each visual with no more than five lines of text and seven words per line."[15] A general rule is that every slide deserves at least 10 seconds, and none rate more than 100.[16] When developing your visuals, use phrases rather than sentences and upper- and lowercase type. Use a simple typeface. As can be noted from the survey in Table 9.3, the most annoying aspect of bad PowerPoint slides is the text and not the graphics or multimedia elements. Therefore, focus on presenting short, relevant, and readable text. Your reader will find serif typefaces easier to read than sans serif faces. (Serifs are the little lines on the ends of the letters.) To make items on a list show up, use bullets or symbols. Keep the lettering style for titles, legends, tables, and other illustrations consistent, and use no more than three type sizes in a single visual. For consistency, place the same amount of space at the top of each visual.

Audiences have visibly gone to their knees when a presenter flicks on the overhead switch to reveal a bulleted list. Chambers and Asher go on to say that television weather folks have learned how symbols or simple pictures grab their audience's attention. The same techniques seem to be emerging in corporate business today. Presenters choose pie charts and graphs to simplify concepts. *Businessweek, U.S. News & World Report,* and *Fortune* use more picture graphics than text. Newspapers such as *USA Today* use picture graphs that relate statistics to the subject and draw the eye to the data.

Visuals make information easy to grasp. The mind thinks and stores information visually. Maps, blueprints, machine diagrams, logos, dollar signs, and stock market arrows are parts of our visual memories. The right symbol brings the idea to life and tells the story. If you cannot picture your concept, you have not thought it out. Make it simple to make the listener feel smart. Audiences may forget your words 30 minutes after your presentation, but they can pass a test on your pictures a week later.

Grab your audience's attention by using color and short words and avoiding clutter. Do not use complicated typefaces, art techniques, or symbols.

Here are some guidelines to remember when using color:

1. Match color with the subject and audience. Consider the purpose of the visual aid and who will be viewing it. If you want a conservative presentation, use a blue background instead of yellow. Keep in mind the moods and themes colors can convey: Tranquillity can be conveyed by pale colors, grays, and pinks. Reds, oranges, pinks, or browns communicate warmth. Excitement can be shown by using reds and blacks together with some grays. Green represents growth; blue calms. Red signifies power, danger, loss, or energy; yellow creates dislike; and purple appears spiritual. Using color adds emphasis, interest, power, and focus.

2. Pick background colors first before choosing text or data colors. Text and data colors should contrast highly with the background for maximum legibility.

3. Colors should not clash—they should have a high degree of harmony.

4. Avoid the rainbow effect and use no more than three or four colors.

5. Generally, assign bright colors to the areas you want to receive the most attention.

[14] Patricia Fripp, "White Paper on Technology in Speaking Skills" and "A/V Technology: Necessity . . . or Nightmare? The Pentagon Declares War!" Retrieved from *http://www.fripp.com.*

[15] Norman B. Sigband and Arthur H. Bell, *Communication for Managers,* 6th ed. (Cincinnati: South-Western Publishing, 1994), p. 412.

[16] Art Fierman, "The Art of Communicating Effectively, Tips About All Aspects of Pulling Off a Successful Presentation!" Retrieved from *http://www.projectorsolution.com/effectivepresentations.asp?.*

In their book, *Wooing and Winning Business,* Spring Asher and Wicke Chambers state "Corporate America commits death by overheads daily."

Source: Spring Asher and Wicke Chamber, *Wooing and Winning Business* (New York: John Wiley & Sons, Inc., 1997), pp. 52–53.

You should plan your visuals to be consistent with your objectives.

SOURCE: Dorling Kindersley, Media Library.

6. If using slides or transparencies, keep the color theme consistent in all your slides.

7. Keep the contrast strong between the background and the text. Try to pick colors with high contrast, such as dark backgrounds with yellow or white text, to make your images more readable. Backgrounds with images can sometimes cause problems as the text seems to blend in the background instead of floating above it.[17]

    Again, keep in mind whether your presentation will have an international audience. If so, be careful about using certain colors in your visuals. For example, in the United States, white means purity, while in Asian countries and Japan, white is the color of death and red means luck and happiness. In Latin America, red illustrates passion and love and yellow has strong negative connotations.[18]

Most importantly, your visuals should emphasize the most important points and not impress or confuse your audience. Your visuals should focus attention, reinforce your verbal message, stimulate interest, and illustrate difficult concepts. Some experts recommend that you start creating your visuals by creating the last slide first. The idea is that your last slide should emphasize the most important points you plan to make.[19]

Make visuals large enough for your audience to view comfortably. If you do not, you have wasted your time making them and probably frustrated the audience, so they will resist your message. To magnify your visuals, move closer to your audience.

Prepare your visuals in advance as much as possible. For example, choosing to use a flip chart over a whiteboard allows you to prepare in advance. List your points on the flip chart before your presentation. Do not reveal the visuals until you present your points. Once you are finished, move on and don't leave that visual in view. If you choose to use the whiteboard, the audience will see your back. Wait to speak until you have eye contact with your audience.

Ask yourself the questions in Box 9.4 to make sure your visuals are appropriate.

USING A POINTER

If you use a pointer to refer to your visual aids, keep in mind that it should be used to make a quick visual reference. Do not use a pointer on word charts; refer to each point by an item or number. When using a pointer:

1. Keep your shoulders forward as much as possible and toward your audience. Do not cross your arm over your body to refer to something on the screen. Instead, hold the pointer in the hand closest to the screen. Do not play with your pointer. Either fold it up and put it away or put it down when it isn't needed.

2. Point at the screen, not the overhead projector. Standing at the projector often blocks somebody's view of the screen.

3. If you leave the pointer on the overhead projector, it can focus too much attention on the screen and detract from you.

[17] Dave Pardi, "HELP! My Presentation Display Looks Awful: Five Common Problems with Poor Display on Computer Presentations." Retrieved from *http://www.communicateusingtechnology.com/articles/poor_presn_display.htm.*

[18] "International Communication Is More Than Black and White." *Communication World,* Volume 12, Issue 9, October 1995, p. 11.

[19] Art Fierman, "The Art of Communicating Effectively," Tips About All Aspects of Pulling Off a Successful Presentation! Retrieved from: *http://www.projectorsolution.com/effectivepresentations.asp?.*

> "The final test for using a visual aid should always be: Will the visual aid (a table, pie chart, heading, or listing) help to clarify, reinforce, or explain an idea or concept? If you answer yes, it should be used. If it serves only as window dressing, it should be discarded."
>
> Source: Norman B. Sigband and Arthur H. Bell, *Communication for Management and Business,* 4th ed. (Glenview, IL: Scott, Foresman, 1986), p. 441.

When using a pointer, keep your shoulders forward as much as possible toward your audience.

SOURCE: Dorling Kindersley/Media Library.

BOX 9.4 📖 **Whether to Use Visuals or Not**

4. If you use a laser pointer, do not try to point with it. Instead, circle the part of the graph you are referring to. This helps prevent the trembling of your hands from showing![20]

Practice

Most people have anxiety about getting up in front of a group and making a presentation. To control your anxiety, know your sources of anxiety and get lots of practice before the actual presentation.

Taking a risk, such as speaking before a group, often makes you feel anxious. To a certain extent, being nervous can help you because it makes you alert, full of energy, and "up" for the presentation. By practicing, you can put this anxiety to work for you. In a study of fear conducted at the University of Wisconsin, researchers checked physiological signs of stress such as pulse rate and blood pressure in students who were taking a public speaking course. Results showed that the students

[20] Steve Mandel, *Effective Presentation Skills: A Practical Guide for Better Speaking* (Menlo Park, CA: Crisp Publications, 1993), p. 38.

were uniformly less fearful at the end of the course than at the beginning, and they remained less fearful even when they spoke later before an unfamiliar audience. Each speaking experience makes it likelier that the next will be less stressful.[21]

Practice to develop your self-confidence. Practice makes your presentation smoother and easier. You get better at speaking and feel more confident when you practice. Karen Horney did extensive work on the development of self-esteem and self-worth. She found that when an individual actually attempts something—intellectually or physically, be it a memory verse, an athletic event, going for a promotion, or even a speech—the great majority of the time the individual will succeed. Yet, when a person does not attempt, he or she has an impression of failure. The dramatic finding is that for most people, their self-impression is one of failure more than success, because most of the time they do not take a chance.[22] Bert Decker has traced this in himself and others. He found that about 95 percent of the time, individuals who attempt to speak—to communicate—succeed. Decker often asks this question of his seminar participants: "Why should you jeopardize every performance for the sake of that five percent?"[23]

Do not read your speech when practicing or presenting it. You will lose eye contact with your audience and speak too rapidly. Begin by practicing as though you were speaking to your audience. Do and say everything as you will for the actual presentation. Then conduct a dress rehearsal with a live audience. Dress and act the way you will on the day of the presentation. When practicing before this live audience, eliminate your introductory and summary slide. Find out what the audience found interesting, memorable, or confusing. Ask them to list what they thought was the most important point of your presentation and find out if they got your message. If they didn't, you may need to go back and make some changes.[24]

If you cannot practice before a live audience, tape record or videotape the speech (see Box 9.5). If audiotaping, stand in front of a mirror while taping the presentation so you can see yourself. Then watch or listen to your tape and ask yourself these questions:

If I were in the audience, would I like what I saw or heard?

Would I pay attention?

Would I learn something worthwhile?

When asked whether videotape would help a person's communicating ability, Dr. Norman Vincent Peale replied: "Yes, videotape could do that. When I see myself on a tape, I immediately ask myself, how could I have done that better? I have dropped out many personal adverse habits.

"I use to do this with my nose [as he put his right finger astride his right nostril], not picking my nose, just sort of rubbing it. But it looked like I was picking my nose and I have cut that out. If my finger goes up in that direction, I immediately take it down.

"I stopped a lot of nervous affectations that I didn't know I had even after years of speaking. Yes, video feedback has definitely helped me."

BOX 9.5 ✒ **Norman Vincent Peale on Video**

SOURCE: Bert Decker, *You've Got to Be Believed to Be Heard* (New York: St. Martin Press, 1992), p. 212.

---

[21] Diane Ulluis, "Crossing a Bridge of Shyness: Public Speaking for Communicators" (Alexandria, Virginia: EEI.Com, 1997), pp. 1–3 . Retrieved January 17, 2000, from *http://eeicom.com*.

[22] Karen Horney, *Neurosis and Human Growth: The Struggle Toward Self-Realization* (New York: W. W. Norton & Co., 1970).

[23] Bert Decker, *You've Got to Be Believed to Be Heard* (New York: St. Martin Press, 1992), p. 163.

[24] Art Fierman, "The Art of Communicating Effectively, Tips About All Aspects of Pulling Off a Successful Presentation!" Retrieved from: *http://www.projectorsolution.com/effectivepresentations.asp?*.

If you can say yes, give yourself a pat on the back. If not, pay attention to weak spots in the delivery. Jot down weak and strong spots on index cards to serve as a reference each time you prepare a speech. Then note needed changes, revise, and continue practicing!

Do not memorize your presentation, as you may get to the middle of your presentation and forget your place. Think through all your points, plan in detail, and use a yellow highlighter to note points where you fear your memory may fail. Use your speaker's notes for the opening, key transitional points, quotes, and the ending, but try not to rely too heavily on these aids.

Practice various phrasing by saying the same thing many different ways. This allows you to try different ways of saying the same thing to find the most comfortable way for your style. By practicing 15 minutes a day, you will improve pronunciation, articulation, and inflection.

In addition, practice also helps you to eliminate your non-words. The way for you to conquer your "ums," "ahs," and "you knows" is to replace them with pauses. Pausing for two to three seconds does more than just help you overcome using non-words. Here are just a few of the many benefits of the pause:

- A brief silence enables your listeners to absorb the point that you just made. It makes listening easy.
- Pausing gives you the opportunity to take a breath. The more air you have available, the greater the opportunity for your voice to project clearly and with variety.
- Framing your ideas in silence adds tremendous impact to your words.
- A pause gives your listeners the gift of silence and allows them to take in what you have said.

How do you begin to build more pauses into your spoken communication? Become aware of your favorite non-words by listening for them when you speak. You can also post a note that says "Pause" on your telephone to remind you to give yourself and your listener the gift of silence. When you record a voice-mail message, listen to it before you send it. Most voice messaging systems provide this option. If you hear non-words and not enough pauses, rerecord and listen again. This

Too many "ums" and "ahs" come from uncertainty.

Source: Mario Cuomo, "Stirring Words," *AARP*, May/June 2003, pp. 84–85.

1. Record your speech at least once while practicing and carefully evaluate it.
2. Develop an urge to communicate by selecting an interesting topic. If you do not find your topic interesting, your listeners will not be interested.
3. Speak informally and conversationally. Consider your talk an "enlarged conversation."
4. Be enthusiastic and sincere. If you do not appear convinced and comfortable with your presentation, nobody else will be either.
5. Vary the pace, pitch, and volume of your voice to emphasize main points.
6. Look at the audience; make eye contact to watch them to see how they respond.
7. Glance at, do not read, your notes.
8. Maintain erect posture. Do not slump or sway with the breeze.
9. Use gestures to help emphasize a point, not to draw attention away from what you need to say.
10. Speak loudly enough so all the members of the audience can hear, no matter where they are seated.
11. Avoid fillers such as *ah* and *um*. If you need a second to collect your thoughts, take it. Your audience will not find the sound of silence painful. Time yourself for one minute. If you use more than one *uh* or *um,* you have used too many!
12. Before approaching the podium, make sure you have everything in order.
13. Be friendly.
14. Lessen the distance between you and your listeners to break down barriers.

BOX 9.6 🖙 **Mastering Key Techniques and Skills**

SOURCE: Richard C. Huseman, James M. Lahiff, John M. Penrose, Jr., and John D. Hatfield, *Business Communication: Strategies and Skills,* 2nd ed. (Chicago: Dryden Press, 1985), p. 401.

exercise will build pausing into your speaking style. As you try to eliminate your non-words and replace them with pauses, make it fun! Ask a friend or colleague to keep track of your non-words and bill you 25 cents for each non-word you use.

Winston Churchill recognized the importance of rehearsing. One day while Churchill was bathing, his valet heard his voice over the splashing water. Entering the bathroom, the valet inquired, "Did you call, sir?" "No," shouted an angry Churchill, "I was just giving a speech to the House of Commons. And next time knock on the door before you come barging in."[25]

Without the ingredient of practice, even a great leader would not be an effective speaker. Many authorities choose practice as the most important element to a successful presentation. Use the key techniques and skills in Box 9.6 as a final test to enhance your oral speaking.

Presentation

You probably think your delivery will be the hardest part of the three *P*s. Before you get up to speak, review the information in Box 9.7.

You may experience nervousness when you give a presentation; most of us do. To feel less threatened, acknowledge and work through your natural shyness. Begin by recognizing how your fear affects you. Ask yourself the following questions to help identify your fear: Am I afraid of failure? Of exposure? Of judgment? Does your fear "save" you from having to put yourself out there? If you focus on the personal and

[25] Eugene Raudsepp, "When It's Your Turn to Speak at the Podium," in *Readings and Cases in Business Communications,* edited by C. Glenn Pearce (New York: Wiley, 1984), pp. 204–206.

- Know your audience's needs and concerns. Each member wants to know, "What's in it for me?"
- Know your subject. Fifty percent of confidence is preparation. Do not walk into a meeting, make a telephone call, or start a presentation without a plan.
- Know the questions the audience will ask. Plan ahead to answer objections.
- Know the turf. Check out the facilities and equipment before you speak, so you appear smooth and in control.
- Know when to quit. Franklin Roosevelt said it best: "Be sincere, be brief, and be seated."

BOX 9.7 🐾 **Jump Starts**

SOURCE: Wicke Chambers and Spring Asher, "Getting Ahead," *Atlanta Journal and Constitution*, December 16, 1990, p. B06.

professional benefits of speaking, you can help put fear in its place. Most speakers will tell you that their fear has not completely disappeared but they have learned to manage it. Others say that their fear gives them an edge that helps them succeed. For most individuals, just articulating fear in writing can help defuse it, and the worst blooper that can happen almost never does occur.

During an in-class exercise at Kennesaw State University, approximately 150 executive-MBA students and 35 Kroger store managers identified their "Top Ten Bloopers" for presentations. The following list reveals the results in the order of most to least frequent occurrence.

> Number 1: Distracting mannerisms—verbal (slang, cursing, *ums* and *ahs*) and physical (body language, gestures, and posture)
>
> Number 2: Poor intonation, inflection, volume, or rate
>
> Number 3: Not being prepared
>
> Number 4: Not connecting with audience
>
> Number 5: Poor visual aids or inappropriate use of, as well as not practicing with, the equipment
>
> Number 6: Poor structure or fragmented speech; weak openings and closings
>
> Number 7: Not practicing and managing the time
>
> Number 8: Lack of eye contact
>
> Number 9: Reading the presentation
>
> Number 10: Inappropriate humor

WAYS OF USING UP NERVOUS ENERGY

If you have too much nervous energy, do simple isometric exercises just before speaking. Clench your fists, hold them tight a few seconds, then relax. Repeat this activity two or three times. Another exercise involves pushing down on the arms of a chair for several seconds, then relaxing. Repeat this or other simple isometrics two or three times just before you speak. When muscles tighten and tense up, you use excess energy. The tighten-and-relax cycle helps to relax other muscles in your body.[26] To ease your nervousness, review the tips listed in Box 9.8.

ACTIONS DURING THE INTRODUCTION

As a way of dealing with your nerves, recognize that most, if not all, speakers experience some form of normal nervous anxiety. If you feel a little anxious, don't

Before and during your speech, your body goes through emotional and physical changes, perhaps including a rise in your blood pressure and pulse rate, a slowing down of the digestive system, an increase in perspiration, and irregular breathing. However, you can use your nervous energy to your advantage.

Source: Richard C. Huseman, James M. Lahiff, and John M. Penrose, Jr., *Business Communication* (Chicago: Dryden Press, 1992), p. 399.

"You've got to know your first three minutes cold. Have an opening you can get through perfectly, even if you're half asleep or sick as a dog. It frees you to focus on getting your rhythm and pacing and to build a rapport with the audience instead of worrying about content."

Source: Chip Bell, Performance Research Associates, Inc. Annually logs more than 150,000 air miles delivering 100-plus speeches to organizations and conferences.

[26] Anita Taylor, Teresa Rosegrant, Arthur Meyer, and B. Thomas Samples, *Communicating* (Englewood Cliffs, NJ: Prentice Hall, 1980), p. 381.

1. Learn as much as possible in advance about your audience and about the setting in which you will speak. The more advance knowledge you have, the less uncertainty you will feel.
2. Prepare your speech thoroughly. Stage fright happens because of lack of preparation.
3. Write your main points on a note card.
4. Practice, practice, practice—but do not memorize.
5. Space out your practice sessions. Rather than practicing for two hours the day before your presentation, practice for shorter periods for six or seven consecutive days.
6. Each time you practice go through the entire speech. In this way you will get a feel for the whole message.
7. Throughout your preparation, always keep your main purpose in mind.
8. While awaiting your turn to speak, sit in a relaxed, even limp, position.
9. While waiting your turn, breathe deeply.
10. Know your introduction especially well—this will ease you into your speech.
11. Refer to your note cards when necessary, but do not read to your listeners.
12. Focus your thoughts more on your message and the response you seek than on yourself.
13. Use gestures and movement to emphasize important points and your tension will be reduced.

BOX 9.8 🖙 **Guide for Reducing Stage Fright**

SOURCE: Richard C. Huseman, James M. Lahiff, John M. Penrose, Jr., and John D. Hatfield, *Business Communication: Strategies and Skills*, 2nd ed. (Chicago: Dryden Press, 1985), p. 400.

panic. Tell yourself you have normal nervous anxiety, which you can control—not eliminate.[27]

Smile and keep eye contact with your audience even before you begin to speak. Just smiling helps relax your muscles and sets the tone for the presentation. When people smile back at you, you will relax. To help your nerves, make eye contact with three or four people in different parts of the room. Making eye contact helps you relax by connecting you with the audience and reducing your feelings of isolation.[28] Maintain eye contact for approximately one to three seconds per person.

Finally, do something requiring movement. Typically, speakers tend to stand in one spot, as if glued to the floor. Take at least two steps toward your audience, but do not pace. Anything less than two steps makes you appear tentative and unsure. Use Decker Communications' ready position, which requires you to lean slightly forward with your knees flexed so that you can bounce lightly on the balls of your feet. This position directs your energy toward your listener. Step toward your audience; do not appear to be backing away from them.

If you have a podium, move to the side or the front to get closer to your audience. Your goal should be to remove any barriers between you and them. Most people tend to use the podium as a crutch. Without a podium, you will probably be more animated.

ACTIONS DURING THE REMAINDER OF THE PRESENTATION

Most individuals become more comfortable once they start presenting. Employ certain actions such as speak loudly, pay attention to articulation, use gestures,

[27] Myles Martel, "Combating Speech Anxiety," *Public Relations Journal,* Volume 37, Issue 7, July 1981, pp. 20–21.
[28] George Plimpton, *How to Make a Speech* (New York: International Paper Company, 1982), pp. 1–2.

"If people can't hear you, they often become inattentive and tune you out through daydreaming, doodling, or conversing with people around them."

Source: Toastmasters International, *Communication and Leadership Program* (Santa Ana, CA: 1987).

"A good speaking voice should be balanced between extremes of volume, pitch, and rate while having a pleasant sound quality."

Source: Eugene Raudsepp, "When It's Your Turn to Speak at the Podium" in Readings and Cases in Business Communication, edited by C. Glenn Pearce (New York: Wiley, 1984), p. 205.

Use gestures naturally to emphasize your points.

watch nonverbals signals and make your opening and closing statements count to help you stay focused and gain confidence.

During the speech, you want everyone to hear you. If possible, try the room with a listener stationed at various points to determine whether your voice will carry to the back without being too loud for the people seated up front.[29]

Pay close attention to articulation, use a conversational tone, and do not preach. Most importantly, speak at a rate that keeps your listeners interested.

Watch your audience's eyes, postures, and facial expressions to see whether they understand you. Based on what you see, either go back and repeat, or go on. Always check the audience. Don't feel uncomfortable about repeating a point to emphasize its clarity further.

Use gestures naturally to emphasize your points, just as you do when conversing one-to-one. Do not overdo your gestures so the audience watches your hands instead of listening to your words. Do not put your hands in your pockets, handcuff them behind your back, clasp them in front of you as though they were a fig leaf, put them on your hips, or wring your hands nervously. All these gestures, along with crossing your arms, can distract your audience. (See Box 9.9.) If you feel uncomfortable with your hands, keep them on the sides of the podium, but do not grip the sides and develop white knuckles! If your hands make you feel self-conscious, focus on your audience instead of yourself. If you concentrate on your message and your audience, your hands will probably take care of themselves.

When speaking with international audiences, you will need to watch your gestures. In some Asian cultures, audiences tend to find too many sweeping rapid gestures distracting. In Columbia, if you wanted to show the height of an animal, you would hold your arm out palm down and raise it to the appropriate height. If you are trying to show the height of a person you do the same thing, but your palm is on edge. So, if you meant to show the height of a person, but you did so palm down as we normally do in the United States, you would have either insulted the person by treating him or her like an animal. In addition, you would have confused your audience because they would think that you were actually talking about an animal that had the name of a person. In Hong Kong, Indonesia, and Australia, you would never beckon someone by putting your hand out and curling your index finger back and forth; for example, if you were inviting someone to come up on stage with you. This gesture is used to call animals and/or ladies of the night and could offend your audience.

Stance	Characteristics
The Bear Hug	Arms across your chest
Ten-Hut!	Arms stiff, waist firmly nailed to the pelvis
The Flesh Wound	One arm hangs useless at the side, while the other serves as a tourniquet above or below the elbow
Parade Rest	Legs slightly spread, hands held behind back
The Choir Boy or Girl	Hands clasped at waist level, every finger entwined
Supplicant	Same as above, but hands higher, at chest level
The Fig Leaf	Demurely crossed hands, strategically placed
Sisters of Mercy	Hands in praying position

BOX 9.9 🐾 **Gesture-Inhibiting Stances**

[29] Constance Courtney Staley and Robert Stephens Staley II, *Communicating in Business and the Professions: The Inside Word* (Belmont, CA: Wadsworth, 1992), p. 197.

When ending your presentation, if you wave goodbye you'll get a different response depending upon where you are. In some parts of Latin America, Argentina, and Europe, for example, a wave goodbye tells your audience to stay put, that there is more to come.

Follow the advice of Marjorie Brody in Box 9.10 for using gestures and watch the nonverbal communication of your audience. Yawns might signal a needed break, a change in your presentation, or a clue to shorten it. You might want to leave the audience a little ignorant rather than sound asleep, frustrated, or irritable! But keep in mind that international audiences might respond in different ways. For example, in Japan, listeners will show concentration and attentiveness by nodding the head up and down slightly—and even closing their eyes occasionally.

Your first and last statements can enhance or detract from your presentation, so make them count! Grab your audience's attention in the beginning and leave them wanting to hear you again. Your closing should be forceful, and should not just trail off. Additionally, you should not have to thank your audience. If you have done the job well, the audience will thank you through applause. Refer to Box 9.11 for errors to avoid in your conclusion, and Box 9.12 for the importance of knowing your material and not being dependent upon your visual aids.

Be sure to gesture when speaking. Gesturing can relax you, reinforce your message, and make your presentation more interesting to watch. *Some tips:*

- *Open up* your arms to embrace your audience. Keep your arms between your waist and shoulders.
- *Drop* your arms to your sides when not using them.
- *Avoid* quick and jerky gestures; they make you appear nervous. Hold gestures longer than you would in normal conversation.
- *Vary* gestures. Switch from hand to hand and at other times use both hands or no hands.

    Caution: Don't overuse gestures!

BOX 9.10   **How to Gesture When Speaking**

SOURCE: Marjorie Brody, President, Brody Communications, 1200 Melrose Ave., Melrose Park, PA 19126.

- Ending your speech with the words "thank you." Avoid ending any speech with these weak words. Just try to imagine Patrick Henry winding up his famous address like this: "As for me, Gentlemen, give me liberty or give me death! Thank you."
- Going on too long after you say, "In conclusion." One authority argues if you drag out your speech for more than a minute after you've said "In conclusion," you'll seriously compromise all the good you've accomplished up to that point.
- Pausing and then saying, "Well, I guess that's all I have to say." Instead of concluding, you are just ending or stopping.

BOX 9.11   **Avoid These Major Mistakes**

SOURCES: *Working Communicator,* Ragan Communications, 212 W. Superior Street, Suite 200, Chicago, IL 60610, 1-800-878-5331, Fax 312-335-9583; and Patricia Hayes Andrews and John E. Band, Jr., *Communication for Business and the Professions,* 6th ed. (Madison: Brown & Benchmark, Publishers, 1995).

An account executive with an ad agency had spent long hours and a great deal of money in an attempt to land a big account. Finally, after a year of frustrating attempts, she got approval to make a presentation to them. The stakes were big, not only to the personal career of the account executive, but to her agency. Billings would run into millions of dollars.

During the next few weeks, the account executive worked day and night to put together a presentation. She called in artists; sales graphs, research studies, demographic charts, and surveys were all done up on elaborate charts for visual support of her arguments.

Finally, the great day arrived. She was ushered into the luxuriously furnished boardroom of the company, where all the key people were seated around a huge table. She set up her easel at one end of the room and, just as she had rehearsed so carefully, began her pitch. As luck would have it, when she flipped the first chart, the easel collapsed, dumping the whole carefully arranged presentation on the floor.

Quickly she got it all picked up and back on the easel and, with profuse apologies, began again. But once more the thing collapsed. This time the president of the company, who was sitting directly in front, helped the harried account executive put the thing back together.

But it was not to be. Once more the easel collapsed, but the frustrated account executive would not admit defeat.

"Look," she said grimly, "just give me a few minutes of your time—just five minutes—and I'll tell you everything it would have taken me 45 minutes to explain on those charts."

"Shoot," said the corporation president, a faint smile on his face.

For the next five minutes the account executive poured out all her arguments, the gist of everything she had thought about and worked so hard to produce during the past year.

When she'd finished, the president said, "Mind waiting outside for a few minutes? We'll discuss your proposition and let you know."

A half hour later, she was summoned back into the conference room. "You've got the account," the president told the astonished account executive. "Cutting your presentation short gave us time to discuss your ideas. We like them."

The account executive managed to mumble her thanks.

The president smiled. "Frankly, if your easel hadn't collapsed, I doubt if you would have gotten it. The fact is we've had many presentations like the one you intended to give, and to tell you the truth, they bore me to tears. Ideas get lost in statistics. By cutting your pitch to a few minutes, your ideas—and they are good ones—came across loud and clear. Congratulations."

BOX 9.12 🖝 **Brevity Can Mean Victory**

SOURCE: Reprinted by permission. Copyright © 1984, *The Power of Little Words*, The Economics Press, Inc., 12 Daniel Rd., Fairfield, NJ 07004-2565, Phone: 1-800-526-2554. Fax: 973-227-9742. E-mail: info@epinc.com.

Team Presentations

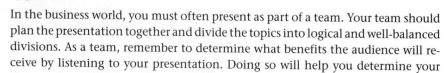

In the business world, you must often present as part of a team. Your team should plan the presentation together and divide the topics into logical and well-balanced divisions. As a team, remember to determine what benefits the audience will receive by listening to your presentation. Doing so will help you determine your three main points.

In planning your visuals, Asher and Chambers recommend following television's rules for visuals. These rules include using color, pictures, and graphics to excite the eye and invite curiosity. For example, if your team's presentation follows another presentation that made the audience sit through endless bulleted slides, think of how thankful they will be to have interesting pictures and imaginative graphics.[30]

In preparing your introduction, make sure the first team presenter hooks your audience, motivates the audience to listen, establishes credibility, states the purpose, and previews the three main points. In other words, you want to have the full attention of your audience before proceeding to the body of the presentation. Opening by just giving your team members' names does not really grab your audience's attention and motivate your audience to listen. Introduce your team members as experts in each of their topic areas to add credibility to your team's work.

To enhance the continuity of the team presentation, each presenter should refer to the previous speaker. Taking this action connects the individual parts of the presentation into a unified whole. In addition, it clearly demonstrates that the team has practiced together, and that each individual presenter is familiar with the material of the other presenters. In fact, if the team is truly working as a team, members could easily fill in for one another if an emergency arose.

When you present your section, talk to your audience, not to the other members of your team. You must stay within the time limits your group has set for each section. Your team members will become frustrated if they have too much or too little time to present their sections. Therefore, teams must practice before delivering the final presentation.

Establish a minimum three-hour rehearsal rule. Although most teams hate to practice, practicing will help your team's presentation appear unified. You do not want it to sound like five or six separate presentations, each with its own beginning and end. Therefore, your team must practice together to make the presentation flow and to transition from one speaker to the next.

Your team could videotape its presentation and then, together, analyze the team's performance. Look for mannerisms that could distract from your message. Ask the following questions: Did we work together well as a team? Did we honor each other's time? Did we show interest when our teammates spoke?[31] When you make your dry-run presentation, practice with all the visuals and with the proper equipment in the room where you will present. By videotaping and practicing together, each team member will have a sense of familiarity with the whole message and how the individual parts fit together. This presentation session will help cut out overlap and reduce logistical problems with presentation order, slides, and the closing.

Stay within Time Limits Given!

[30] Springer and Asher, pp. 159–160.

[31] "Skills for Success: Questions Anyone?" *Making the Spoken Connection,* Volume 1, Spring 1998, pp. 6–7. Retrieved January 17, 2000, from *http://www.novations.com/novations/go/nsdc/ 3373/en/DesktopDefault. aspx.*

Handling the Question-and-Answer Session

Question-and-answer sessions are often intimidating for new speakers because they don't know what to expect. One possibility is to consider a half dozen likely questions coming out of your 15-minute presentation and write out the answers. You can then massage your answers to fit whatever questions come your way. The process of thinking through the top likely questions and how you would answer them will help you prepare for the experience. Organize your answers in those always-helpful categories: Who, What, When, Where, Why, and How. If you get a question that stumps you, break it down into smaller parts and answer one of those parts, then another, and another until you start to flesh out the answer.

Anticipate that the audience will have questions to ask. You should encourage your audience to ask questions by using appropriate body language. If you step back from your audience, cross your arms, and appear to be challenging anyone to ask a question, you probably will not get any! Instead, step toward your audience, raise your hand, and ask, "Does anyone have questions for me?" or "What questions do you have?" You raise your hand to encourage others to raise their hands when asking questions. Having individuals raise their hands to ask a question helps keep order and encourages shy individuals to participate. You can even help start the questions by saying something like: "A question I'm often asked is. . . ." This simple act often helps your audience think of other questions to ask.

You should assume the audience will ask questions, so you need to give them time to ask them. Too often, speakers do not allow the audience time to formulate questions. When listening to questions, you should not interrupt: wait to respond. While listening, watch the speaker's body language to pick up clues about how the person feels about the question. You should also watch your body language as you listen to the question! Keep your hands in a neutral position with your arms at your sides and your fingers open to show openness and honesty. Americans and Canadians will usually ask questions; however, in most Asian cultures the audience is not likely to ask many questions, if any at all. When questions are asked, take extra time to make sure you fully understand them. Repeat the question if necessary. You can rephrase the question to assure the question's real meaning; this will also give you more time to think about your answer.

You should anticipate questions and determine how you will respond to them. Know as much about your subject and audience as possible. Practice your answers—you might even prepare backup visuals. Try not to preface your response with: "That's a good question." You may forget to preface other questions the same way, and those people asking may wonder why they did not ask a "good question."

Ordinarily you want to repeat the question so the entire audience can hear it. As you repeat the question, you will have some time to think about how you want to respond. Keep your answer short and do not volunteer extra information.

In the event that no one asks any questions after your presentation, you may want to review possible reasons presented by Asher and Chambers and shown in Box 9.13.

> "Many times, I see people try to answer impossibly broad questions and flounder when they could take a small piece of it and do just fine."
>
> Source: Deborah Levine, President, Communication Prose Ink, *http://www.proseink.com.*

1. You talked too long and they want lunch.
2. You offended someone and that person is punishing you.
3. They do not understand and are afraid to ask a dumb question.

BOX 9.13 ☛ Three Reasons No One Asked Any Questions

SOURCE: Spring Asher and Wicke Chambers, *Wooing and Winning Business* (New York: John Wiley & Sons, Inc., 1997), p. 71.

An audience member may try to trip you up. If this happens, remain calm, stay focused, and respond courteously. Use the question to reinforce your views, and use humor when possible to lighten the mood. If you cannot answer the question, simply say: "I don't know, but I will try to find out the answer." You can tell the person to leave a telephone number or business card so you can contact him or her. Then, to maintain your credibility, find out the answer and make the contact!

Do not ignore the rest of the audience when answering a question. Sometimes speakers direct their attention only to the person who asked the question. Instead, employ the 25- to 75-percent rule. Direct approximately 25 percent of your eye contact to the person who asked the question and 75 percent to the rest of the audience.[32]

If you receive a hostile question, begin by looking directly at the questioner, but finish your answer while looking at someone other than the person who asked you the question. This action will limit the exchange and make it less likely for the hostile questioner to fire off another unsettling question.[33] In most situations, you, as the speaker, determine when you would like to have questions asked. Some speakers prefer to take questions throughout their presentations; others want questions only after their presentation. Tell your audience when you prefer to address questions.

After your question-and-answer session, deliver a strong closing to your presentation. End with a statement that reinforces your point, emphasizes the actions you want your audience to take, and points out the benefits of taking those actions. That way, you control the final message your audience takes away.

Multimedia Presentations

The demand for high-quality presentation media, such as animation, audio, and video, is on the rise, according to the International Association of Presentation Professionals. Seventy-five percent of IAPP members are involved in some form of website development or online show-and-tell, compared to less than 20 percent three years ago.[34] These types of presentations combine text, graphics, animation, full-motion graphics, video, audio, and still pictures. Computers and multimedia software allow the complete automation of presentations in places such as airports and theme parks. Additionally, multimedia can be used for the development of sophisticated interactive training programs. Already, numerous multimedia functions can be added to standard computer applications to enhance their capabilities. If you think you might like to develop a multimedia presentation, you should keep the following four questions in mind:

1. **Which technology should I include?** Answer this question first. What combination of media will work best to deliver your messages to your targeted audiences?

2. **How will I deliver the message?** The location of the presentation can impose limitations on multimedia presentations. For example, will the auditorium or presentation hall accommodate this type of presentation? What about the quality of the sound system?

3. **What technical expertise will be required?** In the beginning, your organization will likely need to combine the skills of in-house personnel

---

[32] Mandel, *Op. cit.,* 1993, p. 82.

[33] "Skills for Success: Questions Anyone?" p. 6.

[34] Donna J. Abernathy, "Presentation Tips from the Pros," *Training and Development,* Volume 53, Issue 10, Alexandria, October 1999, pp. 19–26.

and outside experts. Animation, video, and interactive programming may require expertise beyond that available within your organization.

4. **How much will we have to pay?** The cost will depend on the sophistication of the content and programming. As with most technology, you can expect the prices to come down as the technology becomes more commonplace.[35]

Before you purchase any multimedia applications, seek advice from experts in the field. Remember, what you get depends on what you can pay. Weigh the cost of what you want against the cost of what you and your organization can afford.

Conclusion

Becoming an effective speaker requires work. You must develop your speaking skills and refine them through practice. Take advantage of opportunities to speak. The old

TABLE 9.4   **Presentation checklist.**

	YES	NO
1. Have I determined my general purpose?	❏	❏
2. Have I determined my specific purpose?	❏	❏
3. Have I analyzed my audience?	❏	❏
4. Is my thesis statement clear and concise?	❏	❏
5. Do I have at least one to three main ideas?	❏	❏
6. Did I use an organizational pattern?	❏	❏
7. Did I use a variety of supporting materials?	❏	❏
8. Does my introduction capture attention, show benefits, state my qualifications, and preview my purpose and main points?	❏	❏
9. Does my conclusion review the thesis and main points as well as give effective final remarks?	❏	❏
10. Did I outline my presentation?	❏	❏
11. Did I develop my visuals according to the guidelines given?	❏	❏
12. Did I practice using a pointer with my visuals?	❏	❏
13. Did I try to practice in the presentation room with the equipment I will use?	❏	❏
14. Did I practice as though I were speaking to a real audience?	❏	❏
15. Did I *not* memorize my presentation?	❏	❏
16. Did I videotape my practice session and review the tape?	❏	❏
17. Did I move to use up my nervous energy?	❏	❏
18. Did I smile and keep eye contact with my audience?	❏	❏
19. Did I avoid using a podium?	❏	❏
20. Did I use the ready position?	❏	❏
21. Did I speak loudly so all members of the audience could hear?	❏	❏
22. Did I avoid gesture-inhibiting stances?	❏	❏
23. Did I vary my pitch, volume, and intonation?	❏	❏
24. Did I gesture naturally?	❏	❏
25. Did I watch the nonverbal communication of my audience?	❏	❏
26. Did I anticipate questions that my audience would ask?	❏	❏
27. Did I repeat the question so the entire audience could hear it?	❏	❏
28. Did I direct 25 percent of my attention to the individual who asked the question and the other 75 percent to the rest of the audience?	❏	❏
29. Did I remember to stay within my time limit?	❏	❏
30. Did I conclude after the question-and-answer session to leave an impact on my audience?	❏	❏

[35] F. Stanford Wayne and David P. Dauwalder, *Communicating in Business: An Action-Oriented Approach* (Burr Ridge, IL: Irwin, 1994), pp. 379–381.

adage "practice makes perfect" applies to those who want to become polished speakers. For more help and guidance with your oral presentations, visit these websites:

http://www.ukans.edu/cwis/units/coms2/vpa/vpa.htm

http://www.toastmasters.org/

http://www.speech-works.com

http://www./en/DesktopDefault.aspx

Use Table 9.4 to make sure you have covered all aspects of preparation, practice, and presentation.

Exercises

EXERCISE 1   WATCHING SPEAKERS

Directions: Go to a campus lecture to note and analyze specific techniques used to engage and maintain the audience's attention. Which of the following techniques did the speaker use?

Beginning with a promise

Telling a story

Using eye contact to get attention

Moving away from the podium

Asking the audience questions

Using volunteers from the audience to make a demonstration

Giving away samples of products or promotional items

Using visuals (List the type used and discuss whether they were appropriate for the audience.)

EXERCISE 2   INTERVIEWING A SPEAKER

Directions: Interview someone who must make oral presentations. Ask how he or she developed his or her speaking skills. Ask the individual for advice on how to reduce stage fright. Then try to use that advice when you make your next presentation. Note which techniques worked for you.

EXERCISE 3   VIDEO FEEDBACK

Directions: Get video feedback of yourself to make you aware of your presentation skills. Practice one-on-one at every opportunity. Practice to a paper audience by drawing happy faces on pieces of paper and placing the faces on chairs.

EXERCISE 4   ELIMINATING NON-WORDS

Directions: Begin eliminating your non-words by placing reminder notes about non-words around your home or work. Place these notes next to your telephone, as individuals often employ these non-words when speaking on the telephone. Check your voice mail messages to see how many non-words you use. You can do this by copying yourself on outgoing messages or reviewing messages before you send them.

EXERCISE 5 TOYF (THINK ON YOUR FEET)—ACE (AFFIRM COMMENT EXPAND)

Adapted from Anne Bradstreet Grinols, Director MBA Communications, University of Illinois

Directions: At least twice during the course, you will be asked to make extemporaneous presentations. You will speak for one minute on a topic provided to you by your professor. You will receive evaluation from your classmates; your audience will send you their comments by e-mail. However, this feedback will not be used for grading purposes.

EXERCISE 6 CREATING VISUAL AIDS

Directions: Due to your outstanding presentation skills, the dean's office has selected your team to speak at the next student orientation. Your team will speak about the benefits of improving oral presentation skills. Create a visual aid for this presentation. Identify and list five things you will consider in developing your visual. Be prepared to discuss your visual with the class.

EXERCISE 7 SELF-ASSESSING YOUR COMMUNICATION STYLE

Directions: Answer the following questions to analyze your communication style:

Are you self-centered or other-oriented?

Do you try to dominate conversations?

Do you talk too much, overexplain, or lecture others?

Are you a complainer?

Do you draw other people out on topics they are clearly interested in discussing?

Are you a sympathetic listener?

Do you smile, laugh easily, and respond to others genuinely?

Do you have interesting things to say?

Can you discuss subjects besides your job or home life?

Do you occasionally use colorful language?

Do you avoid trite expressions?

Are you lively or dull?

Do you speak in a monotone and without enthusiasm?

Do you get to the point quickly and engagingly or do you belabor points?

Are you passive and nonresponsive, or active in the give-and-take of conversation?

Do you encourage monologues or dialogues?

Do you ask others open-ended questions that draw them out? Or are your questions closed-ended, prompting one-word responses?

Do you ask others how they feel about a subject, or do you talk about how you feel?

Are you open, candid, direct, and friendly, or tight-lipped, secretive, and aloof?

If you could improve a single thing about the way you communicate, what would it be?

SOURCE: Roger Ailes with Jon Kraushar, *You Are the Message: Secrets of the Master Communicators* (Homewood, IL: Dow-Jones-Irwin, 1988), pp. 8–9.

EXERCISE 8   POWERPOINT TAKE-HOME EXERCISE

Prepared by Steven J. Bell, Philadelphia University, bells@philau.edu/bells/
Tak%20Home%20PPT%20Exercise.doc. Reprinted with permission.

Directions: In this exercise you will practice developing a presentation from scratch and adding text, objects, and some animation to your slides. You will also practice different slide views and running the slide show. This exercise was developed for V.7 of PPT. You can try using it with an earlier or later version, and most of it should work well.

Create the First Slide in the Show

1. After you double-click on the PPT icon, the software will begin running. The first dialog box you see will be labeled **PowerPoint.** Choose **Blank Presentation** and click on OK.

2. The next dialog box will be labeled **New Slide.** Choose **Blank Slide,** which should be the far right slide on the third row, by clicking on it. It will be highlighted. Now, click OK. **NOTE:** Each type of Auto-Layout slide has a name that will show as you click on the box (so make sure the one you choose is labeled "blank").

3. Begin by adding the title, "Slide Show Introduction," to the new blank slide. Click on the text tool icon (shown below). This icon is found on the **drawing toolbar.** If you don't see this icon, go to the **View** menu, then **Toolbars**—look for "drawing" and make sure it is selected. When you click on the text tool icon, the cursor will become an inverted "t". Move the cursor to the upper region of the blank slide, and click once. You will now see the **Text box** on the screen, with the insert tool blinking inside. Begin typing the text.

4. After you have typed the text, paint it (click the insert tool at the first letter, and then drag over the text—it will be selected, and can now be edited). Change the font size to 40, and click on the bolding tool.

5. Position the text box so it is an inch from the top of the slide, and an inch from the left edge of the slide. (**NOTE:** If you click on **View** menu, you can select **Ruler** which may help you in lining up text.) To move the text box, make sure the object is selected. You will know it is selected because the "box" (either vertical lines or dotted) will surround the text, as pictured below. If you don't see this box, move the cursor (an arrow at this time) into the region of the text and click—that is how you select objects.

With the object selected, move the cursor to the box. When positioned correctly, you will see what looks like a cross with an arrow on each end. Click and hold down while you drag the text box to the proper slide position. When properly positioned, just unclick. To **Deselect** the text (that is, get rid of the box), just move the cursor away and click.

6. Repeat this process to create a second text box that will have three lines of text. However, this will be a list of bulleted text, so before you begin to type

anything, click on the **Bullet** button (shown below). Then type the following lines of text:

This is a practice slide show

It will demonstrate the basics of slide creation

Several techniques will be covered

Tip: You may want to leave a space between the bullet and first letter of text. Also, leave a space between each line of text. To do this without getting a bullet on each line, press SHIFT-ENTER, then ENTER again.

7. Again, reposition the text (select it, move it) so it is about an inch and a half from the left margin, and about two inches and a half from the top margin.

8. Change the font size of these three lines to 28.

Add a Design/Template to the Slide

In this section you can either add a preformatted template, or create your own simple design.

Template

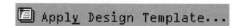

1. Go to the **Format** menu, and click on **Apply Design Template** (shown above). You will see the **Apply Design** dialog box. Click on any of the template names (e.g., "high voltage") to see a preview of the design. Click on one of the names, and then click on the "apply" button. Now your slide will have that design.

   Tip: If you decide you don't like this design, **Undo** the action by going to the **Edit** menu, and selecting "undo."

2. Once the design is applied, move on to the next section, duplicating the slide.

Original Design

1. Use the **Line Tool** from the **Drawing Toolbar** (**NOTE:** If the toolbar isn't showing on your screen, go to the **View** menu, click on **Toolbars,** then click on **Drawing**) to draw a line about a half inch under the title text. Click on the **Line Tool** (to the right of "autoshapes"). The cursor will become a cross. Go to the point where you want to begin the line, click, and then drag to the right, creating a line about 7 inches in length.

2. Now duplicate the line. First select the line by clicking on it. You will see a box appear on each end of the line, as shown below. Now click on the **Edit** menu. Click on **Duplicate.** A new line of the exact same length will appear. Now drag to a position directly under the first line. This is no different than moving any other object. When you move the cursor over the line and it becomes a cross with four arrow points, click and drag the line to its new position.

3. Now, make the upper line blue, and the lower line red. To do this, just select each line and, when you see the box on each end, click on the **Line Color** tool. It is the icon that resembles the tip of a paintbrush on the drawing

toolbar. Click on the arrow to see the color grid. Click on blue for the upper line, and then repeat and click on red for the lower line.

4. Now let's make the title text red, and the main text blue. Again, just paint each line of text (put the cursor at the first letter, and drag it over as much or as little of the text as you want to change). With the text painted, click on the **Text Color** tool on the drawing toolbar (to the right of the line color tool).

5. Your first slide should look something like this:

Slide Show Introduction

- This is a practice slide show

- It will demonstrate the basics of slide creation

- Several techniques will be covered

Note: Before you go to the next section, it is a good idea to save your work, using the **File** and **Save As** functions.

Duplicate the Slide and Use It as a Master

Now we want to create a second slide. As we want consistency in design between our slides, we will use the existing slide as a master, which we can duplicate and then copy to the second slide.

1. You are on your first slide at this point. Go to the **Insert** menu, and click on **New Slide.** This will bring up the **New Slide** dialog box. Once again, select **Blank Slide** and click OK.

2. You are now on the new slide, slide two. Go back to slide one. You can do this by clicking on the **Previous Slide** button, which is the double "up" arrow at the base of the vertical scroll bar, or simply use the **Page Up** key.

3. With the first slide on the screen, go to the **Edit Menu** and choose **Select All.** You will see that all the objects on the slide have been selected (have boxes around them). Note that another way to select all objects is to use the CTRL-A key combination.

4. With all objects selected, go to the **Edit Menu** and choose **Copy.** You can also copy by clicking on the copy icon on the standard toolbar, or using the CTRL-C key combination.

5. Click anywhere on the slide, away from the selected objects, to deselect them.

6. Now move to the blank slide (use the double "down" arrow or Page Down key).

7. Go to the **Edit Menu** and click on **Paste.** This will place all of the objects for the first slide on the new slide. Alternately, you can click on the **Clipboard** icon to copy, or use the CTRL-V key combination.

Add New Text to Slide Two

The next step is to modify the text on the second slide to create a new slide.

1. Place the **selection tool** (arrow shown below) in the region of the title text until you see it become an insertion tool, and then click to select the text box. Again, when selected the text will have a box around it.

2. There are several ways to replace the text. The easiest is probably just to paint the existing text, and then type in the new text. Change the slide title to "Presentation Objectives."

3. Next, change the main body of text. Again, use the **Selection Tool** to select the text.

4. Editing one bullet point at a time, change the text to:

   Demonstrate simplicity of PowerPoint

   Work with basic tools

   Be able to build a slide show efficiently

Add a Rectangle Around a Text Box

1. Begin by adding a new line of text about three spaces below the main text box. The text is: Time to experiment with special features

2. Select the box and move it to the center of the slide.

3. Click on the **Rectangle Tool** (also on the Drawing Toolbar; two to the left of the text tool). When the cursor is moved to the slide, it will become a cross. Place the cross where the upper left corner of the rectangle will be. Click and drag the cursor to where the lower right corner of the rectangle will be, and then release. It should look like this:

Time to experiment with special features

4. If the rectangle needs to be **Resized,** click on it. Boxes will appear at the corners. You can drag on the boxes to resize the rectangle.

5. Sometimes when you create a text box it automatically fills with a color. There are several ways to deal with this, but for simplicity's sake, we will just change the fill to "no fill." To do this, click on the **Fill Color** on the Drawing toolbar (the paint bucket icon). You will need to click on the small arrow to bring up the color options. Click on the "no fill" option.

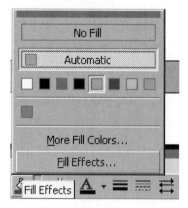

6. If you want to get fancy, you can attempt to keep the fill color in the rectangle, and **send the rectangle to the back.** To do this, first make sure the rectangle is selected. Then click on the button that says **Draw** on the drawing toolbar. From the pop-up menu, select **Order,** and then click on **Send to Back.** You should now see the text appear. Remember, when you have a text box and then place a rectangle over it, you are covering the first object with a second object. The **Order** functions allow you to reposition the objects, one in front of or behind another.

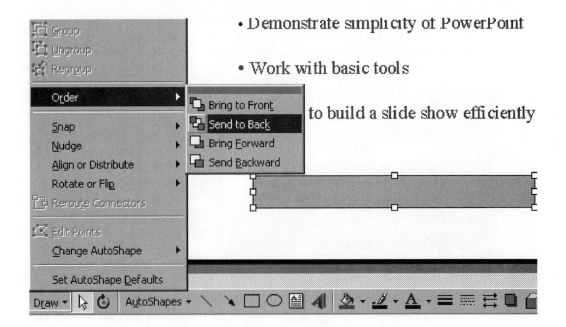

Animate the Slide Text

1. This will create a simple animation of two objects on slide two, the main body of text—which will come on to the screen one line at a time (and then dim). The rectangle will then stretch across the bottom.

2. Click on the **Slide Show** menu, and then click on **Custom Animation.** You will see the custom animation dialog box on the screen. On the **Order & Timing tab** select **Text 2** by placing a check in the box to the left. You will see a box pop up around the text on the small sample in the dialog box; this is to show you the text you are about to animate. You will also now see "on mouse click" selected. That is fine.

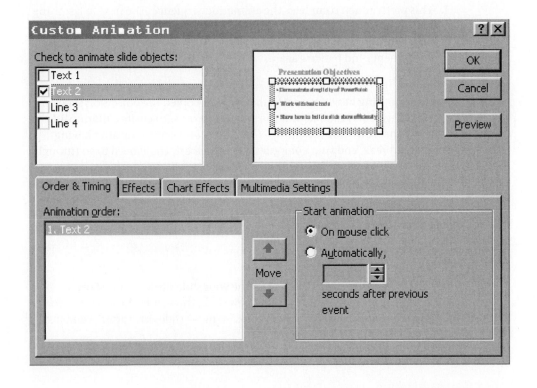

3. Next, click on the **Effects** tab. Under **Entry Animation and Sound** make sure that **Fly From Left** is selected. If it isn't already showing, drop the box to see all the different animations you can choose from. Most presenters do not add sounds.

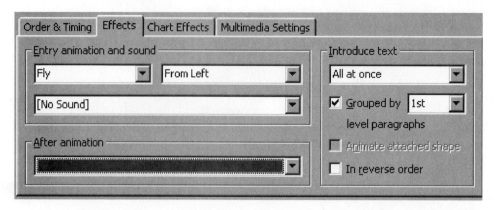

4. Next, proceed to the **After Animation** section. It will show "don't dim." We want each line to change to a dimmed color when the next line comes onto the screen. All you need to do is drop the box, and click on the dim color you want (e.g., if your text color is dark blue, select a contrast such as light blue).

5. Next, in the **Introduce Text** section of the dialog box click on **Grouped by Paragraph Levels**. Once you click there, the "1st" will appear. Grouping by level will make each line in the text box appear one at a time (if you want the whole box to animate together, just choose "all at once," and do not click on "grouped."

6. Now, go back to the **Order & Timing** tab, and click on **Text 5**. This will put a box around the next object to animate, the text in the rectangle. Again, click on the radio button next to **Animate** in the **Start Animation** area. Again, click on the **Effects** tab. Under **Entry Animation** drop the box and scroll down until you find **Stretch Across** and click on it.

7. This pretty much completes the animation sequence. The next to last thing to do is to click on **Preview**. This will show you what the animation will look like. If it is correct, then click on OK. If it is not correct, you can make adjustments and preview again.

Create the Third and Final Slide in the Show

1. Since nothing has been copied since we last copied the objects on slide one, we can use this again. Repeat the previous process to create a **Blank Slide** using the **New Slide** function. (**Note:** If you are continuing after having taken a break, and your computer was turned off, you'll need to go through the whole process of selecting and duplicating all of slide one).

2. Edit the title text to read: Finishing Up the Slide Show

3. Now, edit the body text to read:

   Check the different slide views

   Add a clip art

   Run the slide show

4. Click on the **View** menu and examine your slide show in **Slide Sorter** mode. Experiment by moving the new slide, three, into the number two position—and then move them back. To move slides in "sorter" view, just

click on a slide and drag it to the new position in the slide show. Now return to **Normal** view.

5. Next, for practice, add some notes where it says, "click to add text." Remember that you can print out a version of your slide show that shows these notes (you must set the "print what" section of the "print" dialog box to "notes"), but they will not show on the screen during your slide show.

6. Next, click on the **Insert** menu and place the cursor over **Picture** and then click on **Clip Art** from the **Insert ClipArt** dialog box. To get to individual clips, double-click on a category. Highlight any clip art by clicking on it, and a box will appear around it, along with a graphic menu box to the right (shown below the Clip Art dialog box). The top icon is an **insert** button; when clicked, it will insert the clip art into the slide. Then click on the insert button.

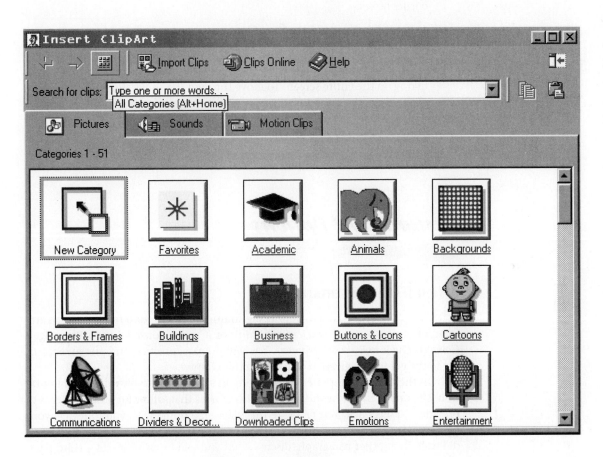

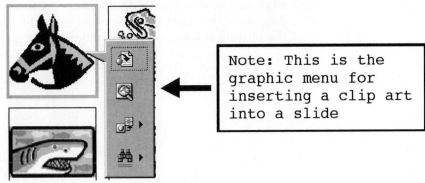

Note: This is the graphic menu for inserting a clip art into a slide

7. After the clip art is on the screen, practice moving it to different areas by dragging it with the mouse. If the clip art is not selected (you should see small boxes surrounding the clip art to show it is selected), just select it as you have selected other objects. Shown below is a "selected" clip art.

8. Also, practice **Resizing** the clip art by clicking and dragging. **Note:** To maintain the proper proportion of the graphic, only click and pull on the corner boxes.

Showing Your Slide Show in Slide Show Mode

1. Page up to return to slide one.

2. Go to the **View** menu and click on **Slide Show**. Now you will see slide one taking up the entire screen. To move through the show, simply left mouse click, or use the right directional key to move ahead.

3. You will return to slide mode when you move beyond the last slide, or simply press the **ESC** key.

That completes this exercise.

Assignment Options

OPTION 1: ORAL PRESENTATION

You will make a three- to five-minute oral training presentation to the class on any topic of your choice. If you cannot think of a topic, consult Letitia Baldridge's *Complete Guide to Executive Manners*. You will prepare, practice, and present according to the guidelines given in class and in this chapter.

On the day of your presentation, bring in a videotape to record your presentation. Use one of the presentation evaluation forms that follow for other students to provide you feedback. You will take this videotape home with you to review your presentation. Then you will write a memo. In one paragraph, detail what you felt you did well. In another paragraph, discuss what you will improve on. In a third paragraph, discuss what you will do differently the next time you give an oral presentation. In addition, make sure your memo has an introduction and a conclusion. Use the following self-diagnostic when critiquing your performance.

VIDEOTAPING MATERIALS

SELF-DIAGNOSTIC OF PRESENTATION

SPECIFIC OBSERVATIONS FOR CONTENT AND DELIVERY

	EFFECTIVE	OK	NEEDS IMPROVEMENT
Overall, my introduction was	_____	_____	_____
My stated message was	_____	_____	_____
My efforts to interest the audience were	_____	_____	_____
Overall, my main points were	_____	_____	_____
My information was sufficient	_____	_____	_____
My transitions were	_____	_____	_____
My concluding remarks were	_____	_____	_____
My audience could summarize my talk with little difficulty	_____	_____	_____
My delivery techniques enhanced my talk	_____	_____	_____
My bodily movements and facial expressions were	_____	_____	_____
My eye contact (focusing on camera and audience) was	_____	_____	_____
My voice was sufficiently loud	_____	_____	_____
My word pronunciations and sentences were	_____	_____	_____
My conversational style (standard English) was	_____	_____	_____
My talk was done without reading from notes	_____	_____	_____
My talk was within the time limit	_____	_____	_____

Overall Strengths and Weaknesses

My strengths are:

1.

2.

3.

My weaknesses are:

1.

2.

3.

My goals for improving are:

1.

2.

3.

Presentation Evaluation: Speaker's Name _____

Verbal Message

Gained Audience Attention and Involved Them	Yes	Somewhat	No
Clearly Stated the Purpose	Yes	Somewhat	No
Logical/Organized/Smooth Transitions	Yes	Somewhat	No
Used a Variety of Supports	Yes	Somewhat	No
Summarized and Provided a Memorable Ending	Yes	Somewhat	No
Interesting and Shows Preparation	Yes	Somewhat	No
Adapted and Related to the Audience	Yes	Somewhat	No
Stayed within Time Limit	Yes	Somewhat	No

Nonverbal Message

Speaker Notes:

Minimum Reliance on Notes

Reading

Occasional Reading

Eye Contact:

Looked to One Side

Looked Down

Looked Only at Instructor

Looked at Entire Audience

Voice:

Volume

Correct

Too Soft

Too Loud

Voice Expression

Monotone

Occasional Monotone

Conversational

Voice Rate

Pauses

Too Slow

Too Fast

Perfect

Voice Enunciation

Dropped Word Endings

Slurred Word Endings

Needed to Articulate

Crisp

Stance:

Swaying

Leaning

Tentative Movement

Slumped

Relied on Podium

Natural without Podium

Facial Expression:

Wooden

Serious

Relaxed

Pleasant and Smiling

Gestures:

Appropriate Gestures

No Gestures

Distracting Mannerisms: (List or Describe) _____

Composure:

Not Relaxed

Somewhat Relaxed

Relaxed

Enthusiasm:

No

Somewhat

Yes

Use of *Uhs* or Fillers:

None

Some

Several

Visual Aids:

Appearance

Clear and Simple

Cluttered

Visuals Aided Presentation

Yes

Somewhat

No

Visual Aid Quality

Not Professional

Adequate

Professional

Visual Aid Visibility

Poor

Somewhat

Great

Use of Visual Aid

Needs Practice—Awkward

Great

Overall Performance

Convincing

Interesting

Favorable

Unconvincing

Uninteresting

Unfavorable

Presentation Evaluation

Directions: Circle a number for each section, with 5 being high. Then place a number before each item within the section.

I. Introduction	1	2	3	4	5

_____ 1. Begins with an attention getter

_____ 2. Motivates audience to listen

_____ 3. Establishes credibility

_____ 4. States the purpose

_____ 5. Summarizes main points

II. Organization	1	2	3	4	5

_____ 1. Main ideas easy to follow

_____ 2. Main ideas easy to remember

_____ 3. Smooth transitions used

III. Supporting Materials	1	2	3	4	5

_____ 1. Ideas well supported with data

_____ 2. Data relevant to audience

_____ 3. Uses a variety of verbal supports (*Check those used:*)

    _____ Statistics   _____ Expert Opinion

    _____ Comparison   _____ Illustrations

    _____ Examples   _____ Explanations

_____ 4. Uses a variety of visual supports (*Use Y for yes and N for no:*)

    _____ Appropriate visuals or handouts

    _____ Lettering legible and easy to read

    _____ Simple (one idea for each visual)

    _____ Consistent in format

    _____ Professional looking

    _____ Handled in a professional manner

IV. Conclusion	1	2	3	4	5

_____ 1. Reviews the thesis

_____ 2. States the main points

_____ 3. Gives effective final remarks making an impact on the audience

V. Delivery	1	2	3	4	5

_____ 1. Relaxed, confident posture

_____ 2. Maintains eye contact

_____ 3. Sounds natural and conversational

_____ 4. Free of distracting mannerisms *(Check those used:)*

    Uh, Um, and *Uh, You know, Well, Okay,* or any other filler words

    Plays with pencil, clothes, hair, pointer, etc.

    Nervous laugh, cough, or clearing of throat

    Slouches, taps feet, paces, sways, switches weight on feet

    Other:

_____ 5. Refers to notes only briefly

_____ 6. Uses appropriate volume for the size of the audience and room

VI. Presentation as a Whole   1   2   3   4   5

Speech Critique Form

Name of Speaker _____

Time Start _____ Time End _____

Score _____

Instructions: Rate each speaker in the following area, using ratings of: 5 (Superior), 4 (Excellent), 3 (Average), 2 (Fair), and 1 (Poor)

1. Introduction   1   2   3   4   5

   (Used attention-getter, motivated audience to listen, and explained the purpose.)

2. Organization   1   2   3   4   5

   (Included significant facts clear to audience, used logical pattern, and connected points with good transition.)

3. Supporting Materials   1   2   3   4   5

   (Used a variety of supports that kept attention and clarified and convinced the audience; professional visuals followed guidelines given in class.)

4. Conclusion   1   2   3   4   5

   (Summarized; restimulated interest with a smooth ending and focus; made an impact on the audience.)

5. Delivery   1   2   3   4   5

   (Enthusiasm and conversational quality; no reading; eye contact; stance and appropriate gestures; dynamic; controlled nervous mannerisms; loud enough so that everyone could hear; and within time limit.)

Please give each speaker some written comments.

OPTION 2: GUEST SPEAKER

Invite a guest speaker to share his or her expertise with the class and please make sure your speaker's topic is relevant for class. Show them your text to see if they would feel comfortable speaking about a chapter topic. Check the class schedule to see the various topics covered throughout the course. The date of the presentation should correspond to the day that topic is covered in class. You may make this contact by telephone or letter. Usually, after you make the initial contact you should follow up the conversation with a letter.

In your letter, state the date, time, and location of the presentation. You also may include photocopies of the appropriate pages of the text. State the information you would like the speaker to share with the class. Please use proper letter format.

Submit a copy of the outline for your introductory speech one class period before your guest speaker presents. During the class before your guest speaker comes, distribute your speaker's résumé so the class can prepare questions.

On the day of the presentation, you will introduce the speaker to your instructor, then to the class. Please use the following guidelines to help you prepare your speech of introduction.

The Speech of Introduction of a Guest Speaker

1. Learn about the speaker. Study his or her background by asking for a résumé. If possible, arrange to have a personal talk with the speaker well ahead of time. Make certain you have accurate information. Also, be sure you have the individual's proper title and can pronounce his or her name correctly.

2. Include appropriate data. Make comments showing how the subject relates to the occasion or summarize the speaker's work; that is, the speaker's qualifications, educational background, and primary accomplishments. Use humor if you wish, but use care and good taste in doing so.

3. Organize your remarks. Like any other oral effort, the speech of introduction should be properly arranged.

4. Present the speaker. Make an appropriate statement that allows the speaker to know when to start the presentation. After your introduction, turn toward the speaker and lead the applause.

Speech of Introduction

_____ 1. Did the introducer present adequate information about the guest speaker?

_____ 2. Did the introducer relate the occasion to the speaker's field?

_____ 3. Did the introducer summarize the qualifications and educational background of the guest speaker?

_____ 4. Did the introducer dress appropriately?

_____ 5. Did the introducer appear enthusiastic, poised, and communicative?

_____ 6. Did the introducer speak loudly, clearly, and conversationally?

_____ 7. Did the introducer use appropriate body language?

_____ 8. Did the introducer maintain interest?

_____ 9. Did the introducer organize the speech properly?

_____ 10. Did the introducer fulfill the purpose of the assignment?

_____ 11. Did the introducer give an effective conclusion?

_____ 12. Did the introducer make an appropriate statement to tell the speaker the time had come to speak?

If you obtain and distribute your speaker's résumé, you may ask certain classmates to prepare questions to ask after your speaker's presentation. You do not want your speaker to ask for questions and then be embarrassed because no one has any. Other duties include keeping the speaker within a time limit and leading the applause once the speaker has concluded.

Within one week following the speaker's presentation, write a formal thank-you letter.

OPTION 3: THE SPEECH TO INSTRUCT

You will construct, rehearse, and present an instructional speech to the class. The presentation will be videotaped and you will be required to view the videotape with the instructor.

I. Time Limits:

Five minutes *maximum.* A penalty of two points will be assessed for every 15-second block of time in excess of the time limit.

II. Outline:

You will be required to present a speech outline to the instructor immediately prior to your presentation. (Refer to the sample outline for format requirements).

III. Descriptive Components:

The Speech to Instruct should involve a "telling/demonstrating" communication mode. You should select a specific, task-oriented, major-related subject for presentation to the class.

a. You should instruct the audience about how to perform a task and give directions pertaining to the sequential steps in the process.

b. During the presentation you should:

1. Use a visual aid.
2. Ensure that the information is organized.
3. Make clear the "knowing steps" and "doing steps."
4. Reinforce key points.
5. Use clear language.
6. Develop a clear relationship between the subject and the listener.
7. Use explanations of *what, why,* and *how.*
8. Highlight *association;* that is, link the new information to something the listeners already know.
9. Demonstrate command/knowledge of the subject matter.
10. Demonstrate good vocal and physical delivery skills.

Peer Assessment of Presentation

Presenter _____

Title _____

Peer Evaluator _____

As a member of the audience,	Plus	OK	Minus
the speaker made me feel involved	_____	_____	_____
the speaker told me what I wanted to know	_____	_____	_____
I was able to remember the key points	_____	_____	_____

The speaker's strengths are:

1.

2.

3.

The speaker's weaknesses are:

1.

2.

3.

OPTION 4: ORIENTATION PRESENTATION

You received an employment letter that stated you are to prepare an orientation session. At that session, you will be asked to briefly address an interview panel. Your presentation should include the following information:

Introduce yourself

Identify your hometown

Identify your college or university

Indicate your major and minors

Tell why you are interested in working for this corporation

Tell why you believe they should hire you

Due to time constraints, it is expected that you will only have *three minutes.*

Prepare your three-minute presentation. Assume the evaluation sheet below will be used by the interview panel.

PRACTICE ORAL PRESENTATION—INTERVIEW PANEL (name) _____

Evaluation Rating: 1 = Needs much improvement, 2 = Needs some improvement, 3 = Acceptable, 4 = Very Good, 5 = Excellent

Poise (self-confidence exhibited) _____

Voice (clear, projected to back of room, no annoying mannerisms) _____

Eye contact (included entire audience, not focused on notes) _____

Gestures, body language _____

Posture, moving to position to speak _____

Content of presentation _____

Time _____

OPTION 5: ORAL PRESENTATION OF FORMAL TEAM REPORT

Using the formal report your team developed in Chapter 8, make a team presentation.

STEP ONE

Your group will have complete control in making your oral team presentation. You may be as creative and innovative as you wish.

You will need to incorporate at least two *professional-looking* visual aids in your team presentation.

Each member of your team must participate in some area of the presentation. Limit your presentation to no more than 30 to 45 minutes. You will lose points if you exceed your time limit. Be sure to consider the following guidelines in preparing your team presentation:

1. Plan the team presentation as a group and divide the topics into logical and well-balanced segments.

2. Anticipate questions and prepare to respond to them.

3. Begin your speech by referring to the previous speaker (unless you speak first) to enhance the continuity of the team presentation.

4. Direct your speech to the audience, not to your team.

5. Stay within your time limit and do not infringe on the time of the other presenters.

6. Make sure team members can reach all materials. Arrange them in the order they will be used.

7. Check your visuals for typographical errors and make sure you followed the guidelines. If you make copies, make sure you copied your materials clearly. In addition, check for consistency of visuals among the team members (all the same format).

8. Remember the importance of an attention-getting opening and establishing the right tone.

STEP TWO

Your group will be required to conduct a videotaped dry-run of your oral presentation. During this dry-run, your group will perform as if it were the final presentation. You will need to set up the room, use the equipment, and present the report as if the entire class were present. You do not need an audience; however, if some friends want to listen, they can give you feedback on your team's volume level.

Following the dry-run, your group will review and discuss the videotape. Then, collaboratively, your group will prepare a two- to three-page memo critiquing each group member's performance and the performance of the entire group session. In the memo, include what the team did well, what the team could improve, and what the team should do differently for the final presentation. Please submit your group's video and your collaboratively written memo for feedback from the instructor.

Your memo should have a correct heading, one-inch margins, a current date, an appropriate subject line, and initials beside the senders' names. Your memo should open with the purpose and include a transition to the body of the memo. Within the body, your group should discuss what each member did correctly, what the group did correctly, what each member will improve on for the final presentation, and what the group will improve on for the final presentation. Use the following Self-Assessment of Dry-Run to critique your performance.

SELF-ASSESSMENT OF DRY-RUN VIDEOTAPE FOR FINAL PRESENTATION

SPECIFIC OBSERVATIONS ABOUT CONTENTS

INTRODUCTION	PLUS	OK	MINUS
Overall effectiveness	_____	_____	_____
Established speaker's credibility	_____	_____	_____
Involved audience (What do they want to know?)	_____	_____	_____
Stated the message	_____	_____	_____
Forecast the organization	_____	_____	_____

BODY	PLUS	OK	MINUS
Overall effectiveness	_____	_____	_____
Emphasized main points	_____	_____	_____
Provided sufficient detail	_____	_____	_____
Avoided information overload			
Indicated transitions	_____	_____	_____
Involved audience (What's in it for them?)	_____	_____	_____

CONCLUSION			
(ONE OR MORE OF THE FOLLOWING)	**PLUS**	**OK**	**MINUS**
Overall effectiveness	_____	_____	_____
Summarized the message	_____	_____	_____
Appealed for future action	_____	_____	_____
Stated expected results	_____	_____	_____
Involved audience (What do you want them to remember?)	_____	_____	_____

SPECIFIC OBSERVATIONS ABOUT DELIVERY				
NONVERBAL BEHAVIOR	**PLUS**	**OK**	**MINUS**	
Poised	_____	_____	_____	Nervous
Enthusiastic	_____	_____	_____	Uninvolved
Movements	_____	_____	_____	Distracting
Facial Expression	_____	_____	_____	Avoidance
Eye Contact	_____	_____	_____	Avoidance
VERBAL COMMUNICATION	**PLUS**	**OK**	**MINUS**	
Sufficiently Loud	_____	_____	_____	Too Soft
Varied Delivery	_____	_____	_____	Static
Spoke Fluently	_____	_____	_____	Spoke Haltingly
LANGUAGE AND USAGE	**PLUS**	**OK**	**MINUS**	
Standard English	_____	_____	_____	Nonstandard
Conversational	_____	_____	_____	Formal/Stiff
Concrete	_____	_____	_____	Abstract/Bureaucratic
Communicated with audience	_____	_____	_____	Static
GENERAL OBSERVATIONS	**PLUS**	**OK**	**MINUS**	
Designed for a business audience	_____	_____	_____	
Delivery techniques enhanced talk	_____	_____	_____	
Kept within the time limit	_____	_____	_____	
Visual aids, if relevant, integrated effectively	_____	_____	_____	
Spoke without reading from notes	_____	_____	_____	

STEP THREE

On the day of your oral presentation, try to get to the room early. You want to have plenty of time to set up. Keep the following in mind when preparing and practicing your presentation.

All presenters should:

Clearly state the purpose of the presentation in the introduction and explain the benefits of listening to the presentation.

Avoid reading notes and using non-words.

Vary rate, pitch, and volume to ensure everyone in the audience can hear the presentation.

Make eye contact with the entire audience and avoid just looking to certain parts of the room.

Use appropriate gestures; smile; be enthusiastic and sincere.

Appear well-rehearsed, with smooth transitions between speakers.

Mention research showing the importance of or basis for studying or attending the presentation. Facts and evidence presented should be credible and accurate.

Make a high-quality presentation.

Logically structure the presentation (e.g., the ordering of the material should lead to increased understanding and accomplishment of goals and be easy to follow).

Adapt the presentation to the audience. Presenters should appear knowledgeable of the audience.

Involve the audience in the presentation.

Provide a question-and-answer session.

Use media effectively. (Visuals should complement the verbal. Slides, tapes, or movies should present relevant information. Media should be appropriate for room size. The entire audience should have an unobstructed view and be easily able to read any written materials.)

Effectively control the presentation environment. (Arrange the room to optimize communication. Help interaction. Provide appropriate room size.)

Practice in the presentation room to know where to stand, where to seat the audience, and where to place visuals.

Use time effectively. (The presenters should not rush, drag on, or allow the audience to get bored.) No presenter should infringe on the time of other speakers.

The presentation should:

Contain an attention-getting introduction and an impacting conclusion.

Inspire audience participants to use what they have learned to be more effective on the job or in school.

Apply to a broad variety of business situations.

Use the following audience analysis form to help you plan for this presentation.

Who is the audience?

_____

Describe this audience in as much detail as you possibly can (think in terms of size, homogeneity, geographic dispersion, age, etc.):

_____

_____

_____

For this audience, what factors are at play that we should be aware of?

_____

_____

_____

Given the issues identified during the situational analysis/research phase of planning, what do you believe to be the most important communication needs with respect to this audience; which of your management objectives is of most importance to this audience?

_____

_____

What new attitudes, perceptions, behaviors, knowledge, and skills will the audience need to acquire to ensure your management objective is successfully implemented?

_____

_____

What media do you believe would be best used to communicate with this audience and why?

_____

_____

Other notes:

_____

_____

CHAPTER 10

Using Technology to Communicate Within Virtual Teams

*T*oday, virtual teams are established features of multisite and global companies such as Hewlett-Packard, Motorola, Bank of Boston, and Steelcase. Made possible by technologies like the Internet, intranets, and GroupWare, these teams are invaluable tools for organizations that need to bring together specialized groups of people to work on projects or comprise a spread-out business unit.[1]

Jessica Lipnack and Jeffrey Stamps,
Virtual Teams

[1] Jessica Lipnack and Jeffrey Stamps, *Virtual Teams Reaching Across Space, Time and Organizations with Technology* (New York: John Wiley & Sons, Inc., 1997), front flap.

LEARNING OBJECTIVES

After reading this chapter, you should be able to:

- Describe and list the advantages of virtual teams.

- Outline the stages of team development and how a Team Operating Agreement helps teams with the formation stage.

- Describe why team members should consider international team-building activities.

- Explain the role of technology within virtual teams.

- Explain collaborative writing and collaborative writing strategies.

The Virtual Team Movement

Recent research shows that by 2010, 70 percent of the United States population will spend 10 times longer per day interacting virtually.[2]

Many of today's organizations are made up of virtual teams and networks of teams. The network, not the pyramid, has become the conceptual model for how people work to achieve goals.[3]

These virtual teams work across space, time, and organizational boundaries with links strengthened by webs of communication technologies. Virtual teams rarely meet face-to-face and are supported by technology to collaborate.[4]

Often these teams are set up as temporary structures existing to accomplish a particular task, or they may be more permanent teams that address ongoing organizational issues. For example, at Georgia Power, 150 people, or 13 percent of the workers at headquarters, are teleworkers who work virtually. Two of every three Fortune 500 company employees also work virtually. Forty million employees telework on a global basis. In 2004, The Dieringer Research Group conducted the American Interactive Consumer Survey. Their survey revealed that the number of employed Americans who performed any kind of work from home, with a frequency range from as little as one day a year to full time, grew from 41.3 million in 2003 to 44.4 million in 2004, a 7.5 percent growth rate. Further, the study stated that teleworkers who worked at home during business hours at least one day each month increased in the past year from 23.5 million to 24.1 million, a 2.6 percent increase.[5]

Survey results indicate that employees want more opportunities for telework and that their top priority is to gain the flexibility to control their own time.[6]

Nortel has 80,000 employees located in 150 countries who work as members of virtual teams.[7] Often, membership in virtual teams is fluid and evolves according to changing task requirements.[8]

The primary difference between a team and a virtual team involves the dimension of physical space or distance between the team members. Distance significantly affects the way team members interact. The global expansion of electronic connections, particularly the new digital media, provides the link for virtual team members to interact. In all other ways, virtual teams emulate traditional teams.

Why Virtual Teams?

Fueled by the continuing advancement of the Internet, telecommunications, and the expansion of international business, many organizations have changed their organizational structure to include virtual teams. Global competition has also

[2] R. Emelo and L. M. Francis, "Virtual Team Interaction," *T + D*, Volume 56, Issue 10, 2002, pp. 17–19.

[3] Jessica Lipnack and Jeffrey Stamps, "Virtual Teams," *Executive Excellence*, Volume 16, Issue 5, May 1999, pp. 1–3.

[4] J. Lurey, *A Study of Best Practices in Designing and Supporting Effective Virtual Teams* (Los Angeles: California School of Professional Psychology, 1998).

[5] "Work at Home Grows in Past Year by 7.5% in U.S. Use of Broadband for Work at Home Grows by 84%." Results Presented by ITAC from The Dieringer Research Group's 2003–2004 American Interactive Consumer Survey. Retrieved from *http://www.telecommute.org/news/pr090204.htm*.

[6] W. F. Cascio, "Managing a Virtual Workplace," *The Academy of Management Executive*, Volume 14, Issue 3, 2000, pp. 81–90.

[7] C. Solomon, "Managing Virtual Teams," *Workforce*, 2001, pp. 60–65.

[8] A. Townsend, S. M. DeMarie, and A. R. Hendrick, "Virtual Teams: Technology and the Workplace of the Future," *The Academy of Management Executive*, Volume 12, Issue 3, 1998, pp. 17–29.

caused many organizations to move to the flat or horizontal structure. This flattening of structure pushes the decision-making authority down to lower levels within the organization and reduces the need for layers of management. With less centralized, hierarchical management, many organizations have restructured and distributed their workforces globally. For example, Aalborg Industries has reinvented manufacturing processes to meet the challenges of global competition. To reduce costs and shorten delivery time, the boilers and steam generators manufactured at the Erie, Pennsylvania, facility are now fabricated around the world through a chain of subsuppliers, subcontractors, and extended enterprise partners. Design activities are similarly dispersed to different locations, with about half of Aalborg's engineering work now done off-site by others. Their paper-based document procedures are being replaced with a "virtual office" where information in a central database can be accessed via a Web-based system anywhere, anytime, by employees, supply chain subsuppliers, subcontractors, strategic partners, and customers.[9]

Business environments are moving away from the competitive environment toward a nurturing cooperation that comes from synergistic teamwork. In the past, organizations had vertically integrated structures to maintain control of processes; but with diversification and specialization, this practice is no longer necessary. Now, organizations form strategic partnerships and outsource to allow for a more cooperative environment. These groups then become interdependent, with the success of each individual organization enhancing the success of the cooperative organizational system.

Today's employees expect organizational flexibility. They have grown up in an environment of personal computers, cellular telephones, and electronic classrooms.

As organizations move away from production and manufacturing into service and knowledge work, the work becomes more customer service oriented, requiring organizations to be able to respond quickly to customers' needs. Virtual teams enable this flexibility because they integrate traditional teamwork with advanced communication and information technologies.

The Virtual Organization (*http://www.seanet.com/~daveg*) provides a wealth of outstanding information on the virtual team movement. This website pays special attention to the reasons why dispersed teams have become so popular.

Advantages of Virtual Teams

Virtual teams respond to the challenges associated with downsized and lean organizations and the resulting geographical dispersion of essential employees.

Organizations can hire new employees without paying relocation expenses. These new employees can be located anywhere and may demand increasing technological sophistication and personal flexibility. For example, a team member in a Frankfurt office might initiate the first stage of a report and pass it on to headquarters in London for additional data. From London, it would go to the New York City office for the integration of customer data. From New York City, the report would go to the Sydney office for completion. By organizing the work in the correct sequence, members will only work an 8-hour day but the organization may gain the benefit of a 24-hour shift that never sleeps.[10] Additionally, the report generated by these organizational members would be more complete and comprehensive because input is received from all teams. Roger Rodriguez, an employee of BakBone Software, is a member of a virtual team that "follows the sun." Rodriquez may begin a day by dealing with customer support problems that were passed on to him

According to Julie Wilson, practice executive and principal for IBM Global Services and a director of the Project Management Institute in Newtown Square, Pennsylvania, "The advantage of being a virtual team member is that you don't have to move. You have to travel, but you don't have to move."

Source: K. Kiser, "Working on World Time," *Training*, Volume 36, Issue 3, 1999, pp. 28–34.

[9] H. Gunter, "Visiting a Virtual Office," *Computer-Aided Engineering*, Volume 20, Issue 7, 2001, p. 40.

[10] J. Willmore, "Managing Virtual Teams," *Training Journal*, 2000, pp. 18–21.

by colleagues in Lanham, Maryland, or in the city of Poole in the United Kingdom. A typical day for Rodriguez will end when he hands off support problems to team-mates in Tokyo. Rodriguez has never met most of his coworkers face-to-face and probably never will. Nevertheless, these individuals are his daily working companions on a virtual team who work from three continents to provide customer support for storage management.[11]

With virtual teams, organizations can build teams with optimum membership while retaining the advantages of the flat organizational structure. In addition, organizations benefit from virtual teams through access to previously unavailable expertise enhanced through cross-functional interaction, and the use of systems that improve the quality of the virtual team's work.[12] British Petroleum Amoco was one of the earliest corporations to fully embrace virtual teamwork on a company-wide basis. BPA used satellite videoconferencing technology to manage dozens of remote sites around the world. The videoconference enabled BPA to share critical data and accident prevention strategies among platform workers, construction contractors, structural engineers, and geologists.[13]

Many companies have instituted virtual workplaces and have reaped many benefits. By using virtual teams, organizations can assign the right person to the job, but that person does not have to be physically located at the company's headquarters. In addition, the best minds can be assigned to projects regardless of where they live. Finally, people who work virtually will not have to run to catch airplanes, sleep in hotels, or be away from their families.[14] IBM has saved 40 to 60 percent per site annually by eliminating physical offices. Northern Telecom has estimated the savings gained from not having to house an employee in a typical 64-square-foot space, considering only rent and annual operating costs, at $20,000 per person per year. Internal IBM studies show increased productivity gains of 15 to 40 percent for virtual team members, while US West reported that its virtual team members increased the company's productivity by 40 percent, and Hewlett-Packard doubled revenues per salesperson after moving its salespeople to a virtual workplace arrangement. Another important benefit is access to global markets. John Brown Engineers & Constructors, Ltd., a member of the engineering division of Trafalgar House, the world's third-largest engineering and construction organization with 21,000 employees around the globe, was able to access local pharmaceutical engineering talent at a project site in India. Using virtual work arrangements, the firm was able to traverse national boundaries, enabling the organization to work with and present a local face to its global clients, thus enhancing global competitiveness.[15]

Research has shown that virtual teams using GroupWare generate more ideas in brainstorming sessions than the same participants working face to face. In fact, research studies have indicated that geographically dispersed teams can often work as effectively as ones that are co-located.[16] Virtual interaction, especially e-mail or electronic chat, seems to be effective at reducing various kinds of discrimination within the team. With visual stimuli removed, there is more focus on content and less on the person generating the content.[17]

In addition, people who appear reserved in face-to-face activities seem to thrive in the virtual team, as they are more at ease in sharing their ideas by technology. Typically, dysfunctional team behaviors such as dominating, interrupting, arriving late, and carrying on side conversations simply do not exist. Similarly, individuals from

[11] S. Alexander, "Virtual Teams Going Global," *InfoWorld,* Volume 22, Issue 46, 2000, pp. 55–56.

[12] Jessica Lipnack, "The Organization of the Future: The Network," *Solutions: The Executive Magazine,* 2001. Retrieved August 10, 2001, from *http://www.virtualteams.com.*

[13] Success Stories. Retrieved August 28, 2001, from *http://www.virtualteamworks.com/12.htm.*

[14] A. Nucifora, "Build a Solid Roster for Your Virtual Team," *Shoestring Marketing,* August 27, 2001, pp. 1–4.

[15] W. F. Cascio, "Managing a Virtual Workplace," *The Academy of Management Executive,* Volume 14, Issue 3, 2000, pp. 81–90.

[16] C. Savage, *5th Generation Management* (Boston, MA: Butterworth-Heinemann, 1996).

[17] J. Willmore, "Managing Virtual Teams," *Training Journal,* 2000, pp. 18–21.

When your virtual team first forms, occasional face-to-face meetings can improve your team's processes and build more open, trusting relationships.

countries outside of the United States often find written communication easier to master than oral; therefore, they are apt to be more comfortable and productive in a virtual team. This environment also allows physically challenged people, retired individuals, and those with child or elder care obligations to contribute their expertise to companies looking for the most knowledgeable team members possible.[18]

Finally, virtual teaming allows team members to work from home rather than be on the road traveling.[19]

Antecedents of Effective Virtual Teaming

- Make the whole visible to everyone. Make sure to take a team picture and give everyone a copy or make a collage out of pictures of all individuals.
- Distribute a map showing where each team member is located.
- Create a graphic that shows the name of each team member "sitting" at a place around a table. This generates a feeling of the whole better than seeing the names of team members in a list.
- Create journalism-style (in contrast to "minutes") reports on meetings and publish to the rest of the team (including photos where possible).
- Encourage people to acknowledge who is missing in a room at the beginning of meetings and develop conscious strategies to connect disconnected members to the process.
- Create a "virtual water cooler," a space in the electronic communication system for informal swapping of stories and feelings about events as well as task-oriented messages.
- Hold periodic team telephone conferences described as "after dinner" talks—no administrative matters allowed.
- Rotate responsibility among team members to facilitate discussion on nonroutine topics in an online environment on the intranet.
- Invite experts (authors, consultants, essential people from other parts of the organization) to engage with the team.
- Find ways to "spotlight" individuals or parts of the team where something interesting is happening (initiate audio- and videoconferences from different places to feature different parts of the team).
- Develop a team norm of sending "hot news" bulletins to the team (and a norm to respond in order to provide reinforcement and support).
- Create ways to celebrate accomplishments as a whole team even when you are not together.
- Create a sign or team in-box or some other signifier of the team, even when there is only a single team member, so it is visible to everyone in that environment.
- Circulate team "output" with some kind of team-specific headings and formatting.

BOX 10.1 🖚 **How to Support the Virtual Team**

SOURCE: Lisa Kimball, "The Virtual Team: Strategies to Optimize Performance," *Health Forum Journal,* Volume 42, Issue 3, May/June 1999, pp. 58–62.

[18] Mark R. Hagen, "Teams Expand into Cyberspace," *Quality Progress,* Volume 32, Issue 6, June 1999, pp. 90–93.

[19] J. Katzenbach and D. Smith, "Virtual Teaming," *Forbes,* May 2001, pp. 48–51.

A virtual team should be visible to the entire organization. See Box 10.1 for ways to support your virtual team. When team members are not physically present, it is easy for others to forget about these virtual organizational members.

Further, senior management must support the virtual teams for them to be successful. As the vice-chair of American Express noted: "It's important to have a multi-function team of senior managers promoting and supporting a virtual-office initiative from the start. We had three departments involved in our effort: HR, technology, and real estate. The individuals must be enthusiastic and non-fettered by traditional approaches. And, they must be made knowledgeable about all the key issues."[20]

Stages of Virtual Team Development

Virtual teams typically follow the traditional stages of team development including forming, storming, norming, performing, and adjourning.[21]

In Stage 1, called **forming,** individuals get to know one another and establish ground rules. Members try to find out what interpersonal and task-related behaviors will be acceptable to the group. Often in this stage, members get confused and thus become uncertain about how to act in the team. They may question why and how belonging to this team will benefit them.

In Stage 2, called **storming,** there can be a period of high emotionality and tension.[22] Members may start to question certain actions of other team members or the team's leader. Members may show some hostility during this stage and conflict may arise. Team members may resist the control of the team's leader while other team members may withdraw. However, as conflicts are resolved and members begin to accept the team leader, the team moves through this stage to the third stage, norming.

During Stage 3, called **norming,** members start to work together and develop standard operating guidelines. Individuals begin to feel a sense of belonging, start to identify themselves as members of the team, and then develop close relationships with team members. Individuals begin to share feelings as well as a desire to find agreeable solutions.

In Stage 4, called **performing,** the team really starts to work together. By this stage, any questions about team relationships and leadership have been resolved and the team is ready to move forward and complete tasks. Because members have devoted energy to developing good relationships and have accepted the leader, the team can focus on meeting objectives and accomplishing tasks.

In Stage 5, called **adjourning,** the team ceases to exist. The team may disband after completing a project or meeting its goals. Some teams adjourn gradually as the team disintegrates, either because members leave or because the norms they have developed are no longer effective for the team.

"The adjourning stage of group development is especially important for the many temporary groups that are increasingly common in the new workplace." Virtual teams are definitely part of this new workplace.

Source: J. R. Schermerhorn, J. G. Hunt, and R. N. Osborn, *Organizational Behavior,* 7th ed. (New York: John Wiley & Sons, Inc. 2000), p. 180.

Launching the Virtual Team

How do you get a virtual team started? Current virtual teaming studies suggest they virtual teams can achieve the first two stages of *forming* and *storming* at the same

[20] M. Apgar, "The Alternative Workplace: Changing Where and How People Work," *Harvard Business Review,* 1998, pp. 121–136.

[21] J. Greenberg and R. A. Baron, *Behavior in Organizations, Understanding and Managing the Human Side of Work, 6th* ed. (Upper Saddle River, New Jersey: Prentice Hall, 1997), pp. 253–254.

[22] J. R. Schermerhorn, J. G. Hunt, and R. N. Osborn, *Organizational behavior, 7th* ed. (New York: John Wiley & Sons, Inc., 2000), p. 179.

time and in the same place, or at least at the same time in a different place, using technology such as videoconferencing. Glacel has stated: "I believe that a firm foundation of nonvirtual, face-to-face relationship building is an essential prerequisite for virtual teaming."[23] Therefore, the videoconference becomes vital for the startup of the virtual team. A real benefit of videoconferencing is not in the individual meeting outcome, but in the work process or social and relationship-building qualities of the medium. When you allow team members to meet through a videoconference, they learn idiosyncrasies, build friendships, start to trust one another, and create systems by learning common methodologies and a shared language to use in their work together. "It is especially important where the team members are interdependent."[24]

Videoconferencing can help facilitate the team's growth by allowing individuals to put faces to names and e-mail addresses.[25] When the students from Kennesaw State and the Institute of Business and Public Administration had their first video conference, they found this fact to be true.

At the first videoconference, a team needs to discuss the means of communication and the amount of personal communication that is expected. Unlike face-to-face settings where members can use nonverbal cues and physical proximity as a guide to clarify meaning, online interaction and even videoconferencing can make it easier to misread particular kinds of comments. Your members need to articulate their concerns in thoughtful and persistent ways and listen to each other. As team members view their world from their frame of reference or perception, they must work hard to understand the reality of their teammates.

Sirkka Jarvenpaa, a professor at the University of Texas, has stated that if team members cannot meet in person, they need to at least exchange get-acquainted messages.[26] Different personalities, cultures, and languages can make the communication much more difficult. When individuals begin working virtually, time should be spent getting to know each other and dialoging about such things as expectations in the area of time frames, what deadlines mean, best ways to communicate, and how individuals prefer to work. Taking time in the beginning to discuss such questions can help the team members develop respect and build trust for each other as well as prevent misunderstandings and conflict.

The Role of Trust and the Team Operating Agreement

GROVEWELL LLC is a worldwide consultancy delivering *Global Leadership Solutions* that have helped dozens of companies implement and improve the performance of their virtual teams. GROVEWELL's research review shows that about 50% of all virtual teams fail to obtain their goals. One of the key reasons for this high failure rate is the lack of trust and good working relationships among the team members. See Exhibit 10.1 on the following page, which illustrates the importance of addressing interpersonal and cross-cultural issues at the beginng of a team's life.[27]

[23] B. P. Glacel, "Virtual Teams Create New Challenges, *322304 Business Journal*, Volume 12, 1998, pp. 15–18.

[24] M. Kossler, "Leading Virtual Teams," *Virtual Organization*. Retrieved April 17, 2002, from *http://www.seanet.com/~daveg/ltv.html*.

[25] Martha Haywood, *Managing Virtual Teams* (Boston: Artech House, 1998), p. 26.

[26] C. Wardell, "The Art of Managing Virtual Teams: Eight Key Lessons," *Harvard Management Update*, 1998, pp. 3–4.

[27] C. Grove, "Why Is Virtual Team Facilitation Important?" Retrieved April 17, 2002, from *http://www.grovewell.com/virtual-team-facilitation.html*.

EXHIBIT 10.1

Effect of orientation on virtual team productivity.

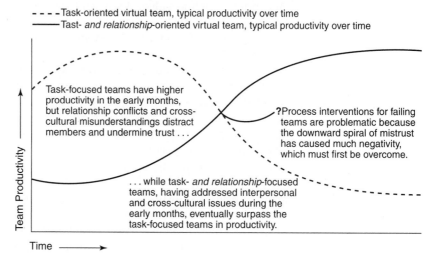

Effect of Orientation on Virtual Team Productivity

- - - - Task-oriented virtual team, typical productivity over time
——— Tast- *and relationship*-oriented virtual team, typical productivity over time

Team Productivity

Task-focused teams have higher productivity in the early months, but relationship conflicts and cross-cultural misunderstandings distract members and undermine trust . . .

?Process interventions for failing teams are problematic because the downward spiral of mistrust has caused much negativity, which must first be overcome.

. . . while task- *and relationship*-focused teams, having addressed interpersonal and cross-cultural issues during the early months, eventually surpass the task-focused teams in productivity.

Time

SOURCE: Reprinted with permission of Grovewell LLC (442 Forty-Seventh Street, Brooklyn, NY 11220; *www.grovewell.com*).

For virtual teams, the lack of physical contact may erode meaning and understanding. Therefore, a Team Operating Agreement can help the team build relationships while putting procedures in place regarding how the team will function. A Team Operating Agreement represents shared agreement on how to complete assigned tasks, attack problems, establish deadlines, and reward team members. "The team has to agree how to work together and how it will be managed."[28]

A team must prepare thoroughly and make assumptions, expectations, roles, procedures, standards, norms, and processes explicit. If team members make assumptions based on experience without a clear definition among teammates, they will waste time and effort. Once the team has developed a clear agreement, members will have a common language that minimizes misunderstandings. The more thought and time members invest initially in a Team Operating Agreement, the fewer difficulties the team will encounter later. As Eastman Chemical Company CEO Earnest Deavenport states: "I believe that you clearly expedite [team processes] by spending more time on the front end and getting consensus."[29]

Therefore, the clearer and more specific the Team Operating Agreement, the better your team will function. The common features of a team working agreement include a purpose statement, goals, and team norms.

PURPOSE OR MISSION

Your team should compose a clear, written purpose statement so that everyone understands the expectations and responsibilities. Make your written statement concise and focused, showing how you will work. According to Henry and Hartzler,[30] a team should collaboratively write its purpose statement in three sections:

1. Our purpose is to . . . (shows the work itself—mission)

According to Platt, team members should be concrete and specific in their expectations. She states that members should use concrete words to define measures and milestones.

Source: L. Platt, "Virtual Teaming: Where Is Everyone?" *The Journal for Quality and Participation,* Volume 22, Issue 5, 1999, pp. 41–43.

---

[28] A. Nucifora, "Build a Solid Roster for Your Virtual Team," *Shoestring Marketing,* August 27, 2001, pp. 1–4.

[29] J. Lipnack and J. Stamps, *Virtual Teams Reaching Across Space, Time and Organizations with Technology,* (New York: John Wiley & Sons, Inc., 1997).

[30] J. E. Henry and M. Hartzler, *Tools for Virtual Teams, A Team Fitness Companion* (Milwaukee: ASQ Quality Press, 1999), pp. 145–150.

S—Specific	When possible, list your goals in quantitative terms. Not all goals can be expressed in numerical terms, but vague goals and objectives have little motivating power.
M—Measurable	Provide your measurement steps and keep the steps small so you can measure them in increments and assign specific achievement on the way to the goal.
A—Assignable	Identify who should be responsible for completing this goal.
R—Realistic	Make the goal challenging but not unreasonably difficult. If a goal appears too difficult, individuals will give up; if too easy, individuals may not feel motivated.
T—Time Period	Set a time frame and stick to it. A time period provides a deadline for specifying the date on which goal attainment will be measured.

BOX 10.2 🖝 **SMART Goal**

SOURCE: Richard L. Daft, *Management,* 2nd ed. (Fort Worth: The Dryden Press, 1991), pp. 130–131.

2. In a way that . . . (shows how you will work—values)
3. So that . . . (shows the underlying results/payoff—strategic intent)

GOALS OR OBJECTIVES

Make your goals measurable and obtainable while spelling out the specific actions and activities needed to obtain results. Do not use general terms such as "To communicate effectively." Instead, be specific regarding how the team will communicate. For example, a specific goal might be: "Team members will communicate by e-mail at least twice weekly." This statement provides a specific, realistic, and measurable goal or action. Refer to Box 10.2 for elements of a SMART goal.

TEAM NORMS

Norms contribute to and reinforce team unity. According to Chris Newell, team norms can be anything team members feel is important for everyone to commit to doing. For instance, one item might be that all team members check the database once a day to monitor the progress of the project. Other norms might deal with the way the team will handle information. Other agreed-upon practices might cover ways to deal with conflict. Teams sometimes enforce a rule that if one team member has a conflict with another and it can't be dealt with electronically, then they must telephone or meet in person.[31]

Establishing team norms helps clarify expectations about acceptable and unacceptable behaviors for team members. Team norms guide participation, communication, conflict management, meeting management, problem solving, and

[31] Jane E. Henry and Meg Hartzler, *Tools for Virtual Teams, A Team Fitness Companion* (Milwaukee: ASQ Quality Press, 1998), p. 58.

decision making. Because virtual teams have little face-to-face interaction, they may require more unique and detailed process norms. Virtual team norms may include telephone, audioconference, and videoconference etiquette and meeting management. These norms may specifically address how to ensure participation from all team members and protocols for virtual team meetings, such as: saying your name before speaking, using the mute button when you do not talk, giving people who are using a second language time to collect their thoughts, using a meeting agenda, taking and distributing minutes, and rotating time zones. Other team norms might include guidelines for:

- acceptable time frames for returning telephone calls and the uses of voice mail and pagers;

- e-mail usage: when it should be used, when it should not be used, and how e-mail messages should be constructed, including when to flag messages as "urgent" and as "important";

- face-to-face meetings, teleconferences, and videoconferences;

- how the team will review and approve each other's work, including which team members will review work and which ones can approve deliverables;

- procedures for scheduling meetings using group scheduling systems; and

- the types of technological applications the team will use and the policies regarding upgrades.

Box 10.3 provides sample team norms and questions that team members might answer to evaluate and measure their team's functioning and performance.

Keep in Touch with Other Team Members
Did you:
    Check your voice mail every day and return calls within 24 hours?
    Check your e-mail every day and respond to messages within 24 hours?
    Exchange documents using _____ (type of software)?
    Attend all mandatory meetings?
    Let other people know when you were going to be out of the office and leave a message on your voice mail—an "out of the office alert"?
    Use e-mail for updating and exchanging information?
    Use the telephone or hold a face-to-face meeting to resolve interpersonal problems instead of e-mail?
    Communicate with those outside the team using the team's established communication plan?

Meeting Management
Did you:
    Show up on time and stay for the entire videoconference, teleconference, or face-to-face meeting?
    Rotate time zones for meetings in order to be equitable and fair?
    Link times and dates to distance locations?
    In videoconferences or teleconferences, keep the mute button on when not speaking?

BOX 10.3 🖝 **Sample Team Norms and Evaluation Questions**

SOURCE: Deborah L. Duarte and Nancy Tennant Snyder, *Mastering Virtual Teams* (San Francisco: Jossey-Bass Publishers, 1999), pp. 103–105.

Take breaks every 60 or 90 minutes during teleconferences and videoconferences.

Not interrupt others in meetings?

Respect the facilitator's attempts to foster participation from all team members?

Respect and follow the agenda?

As meeting leader, send out the agenda by e-mail 48 hours in advance of every meeting?

As scribe, send out minutes by e-mail 48 hours after every meeting?

Rotate taking minutes?

Allow those participants who speak another language time to think and time to speak?

Provide "think breaks" so that people can gather their thoughts?

At the end of each meeting, evaluate how well your team performed in terms of abiding by the team norms?

Decision Making and Problem Solving

Did you:

Strive for consensus but realize that consensus takes time and is not always necessary?

Go with the expert team's opinion, if your team could not reach consensus?

Use a specific approach to problem solving and decision making?

Keep the interests and goals of the team in the forefront of all decisions?

Balance the local interests of team members with those of the entire team?

First call the team member you consider an expert in a particular area, before you went outside the team?

Conflict Management

Did you:

Resolve differences as to ways of doing business using the team's code of conduct?

Use the telephone to settle differences instead of e-mail?

Seek to resolve the conflict with the other individual before involving other team members to settle the dispute?

Use an established conflict management process?

Realize that conflict happens as a normal part of the team's life cycle?

Focus on the task and not on another person to keep the conflict healthy and productive?

Recognize that unproductive conflict is more difficult to detect in a virtual setting and take the pulse of the team frequently to ensure that conflict produces positive tension?

Prevent tensions from building?

Working Together to Produce or Review Documents

Did you:

Edit and review documents individually before meetings?

Move the document through the team review process in a timely manner?

Give one another feedback when promised?

Keep confidential documents within the core team?

Review the team's progress for one hour by audioconference every Monday morning?

Attend all meetings without exception?

Send your agenda items and updates to the facilitator by time set by team?

Abide by the rule that the team leader is the only person who has the authority to release documents to the client?

BOX 10.3 ☞ (continued)

Continuing the Virtual Team's Growth

Your team may have to learn how to go through the *storming* stage without face-to-face meetings. Because team members may not have worked with each other before, they may not know each other's work standards and cannot scrutinize the differences in work ethic as consistently as traditional teams. In the beginning, virtual teams often do not realize that this drawback exists, but when team members begin to dismiss e-mail messages, forego team cyberchats, and do not meet deadlines, the importance of understanding work habits becomes clear.[32] To help facilitate your team's growth through this stage, your members will require basic teamwork training and development. However, if a team can have occasional face-to-face meetings, the team will improve processes and build more open, trusting relationships. At Deloitt and Touche, practice leaders and client service partners meet in person several times a year at conferences to assure understanding, establish new goals, and further develop relationships.[33]

Team members must choose to communicate completely with each other for the virtual team to succeed. Because each individual makes an important contribution to the team, members should seek input from all members. Some individuals share easily, while others experience more difficulty. A team needs the ideas and thoughts of all members.

Virtual team members often find messages difficult to interpret, especially if someone is being sarcastic or facetious. Light or constructive criticisms sometimes are judged more harshly than intended. Conflict seems to escalate when no opportunities occur to stop someone in the hallway and clear up a misunderstanding shortly after it occurs. In a virtual team, miscommunication can simmer and erupt at an unforeseen time, causing consternation and surprise. Team members cannot take for granted the exchange of information in cyberspace.

A team must communicate to share critical information, to leave nothing to chance, and to have personal contact. Team members should make special efforts to create fun, to celebrate progress and successes, and to show personality. Good virtual communication is difficult and requires even more accountability, trust, and adaptability.[34]

Often communication issues are the most voiced complaint among virtual team members. One such example follows. "[It's frustrating] not being able to get a response from people as soon as you like. Weeks can slip by and we are all doing other jobs. You send out a question and in some cases, an answer never comes back. You do not know how to interpret it. They don't want to answer or what?"

Source: D. Gould, "Leading Virtual Teams." Retrieved August 28, 2004, from *http://www.seanet.com/~daveg/ltv.htm.*

Understanding and Appreciating Cultural Differences

If your team members come from other countries, an understanding of intercultural differences will allow your team to *norm* and *perform*. For example, when your team represents a variety of national or cultural groups, your members need to learn about each other's respective cultures, how they may differ, how to overcome these differences, and how to use them to the team's advantage. Your virtual team should embrace the diversity among its members. When your team is composed of individuals residing in different countries, your members must realize that the quality of ideas is important, not the quality of the grammar used

---

[32] J. Gundry, "Working by Wire." Retrieved August 8, 2000, from *http://www.knowab.co.uk/wbw2c.html.*

[33] C. Solomon, "Managing Virtual Teams," *Workforce,* 2001, pp. 60–65.

[34] "Creating Successful Virtual Organizations," *Harvard Management Communication Letter,* Harvard Business School Publishing, 2000, p. 3.

to express the ideas. If your members are not completely sure they understand a message, they should be encouraged to restate the idea to make sure they interpreted the message correctly. According to Tim Miller from BakBone Software, "Communication needs to be carefully managed to take into account the cultural differences among team members."[35] Virtual team members need to be careful in how they ask questions and make requests. "These communication skills are the key to making the virtual team work across cultural boundaries," says Craig Gardiner, BakBone's UK support manager in Poole. Gardiner works with Rodriguez on Miller's geographically dispersed team. "The rule of thumb is to be precise in what you want and how you ask for it. Due to the time zone differences, if you do not ask for the right information at the right time, you could be a day behind in getting something done," Gardiner says.[36] Ori Eizenberg, executive vice president and chief operating officer of ItemField, a New York-based business-to-business software developer, has a 15-person IT shop in Israel. His virtual teams face a seven-hour time difference and cultural issues. The company tries to overcome obstacles by e-mail, a shared Web server, conference calls, and videoconferencing.[37] (Any individual whose entire team is located in another country may want to obtain a translator if language differences hamper communication between members.[38])

Many global virtual teams make it a point to avoid online humor because it is rarely universal and is so prone to confusion. Metaphors offer similar challenges. Because metaphors and symbols are often unique to a particular culture, they are more likely to confuse than to communicate. For instance, an e-mail reference to a "sticky wicket" on a project would be clear to UK professionals but not U.S. staff. During a chat session within one global team, the representative from the Mexico City office remarked that the upcoming client meeting should be a "superclassico." The home office representatives from Toronto took the statement to mean it should be a pleasant client meeting. What the Mexican reference actually meant was symbolic of a long-standing and bitter sports rivalry—a grudge match, quite the opposite of a nice, productive session. Examples such as these are why Chevron is encouraging its international virtual teams to avoid references to humor or metaphors as a means of improving communication.[39]

Time differences sometimes make it difficult to pull off live discussions. Some organizations allow their virtual team members to work at home to meet these challenges. On days that team members need to have a "night" meeting, they stay home and may even take a nap during the day because they will put in their time during the night. Most of the time, you will be able to use e-mail to address the time differences. However, be aware that it does take longer to make decisions with the lag in response time.

You may want to visit the websites at *http://www.a-zoftourism.com/travel-tips-Etiquette-in-London.htm* and *http://www.cyborlink.com/besite/resource.htm* as they offer etiquette tips for business travelers who must travel internationally. Many business and social etiquette tips are provided as well as fun facts about many countries.

Keep in mind that such cultural differences can cause the team to experience another period of *storming*. Reviewing Box 10.4 may help you understand these cultural differences.

In 1998, Kennesaw State University and the Helsinki School of Business and Economics located in Helsinki, Finland, formed an educational partnership to pro-

Understanding cultural differences will help you communicate better with your international virtual team.

[35] S. Alexander, "Virtual Teams Going Global," *InfoWorld,* Volume 22, Issue 46, 2000, p. 56.

[36] Alexander, p. 56.

[37] Alexander, p. 56.

[38] "Practical Advice for Global Virtual Teamwork." Retrieved August 26, 2004, from *http://www.cs.tcd.ie/courses/ism/sism/resource/papers/knoll/advice.htm.*

[39] J. Willmore, "Managing Virtual Teams," *Training Journal,* 2000, pp. 18–21.

Individualism/Collectivism is the tendency of a culture's members to emphasize individual self-interests or group relationships.
If your team has a high concentration of individuals from individualistic cultures: Use team-building activities and instruments that allow individuals to talk about themselves first, then move to how the team members will work together.

If your team has a high concentration of individuals from collective cultures: Use team-building activities and instruments that allow individuals to talk about the team first, then move to how each individual contributes. Avoid activities or instruments that call too much attention to the individual apart from the team.

Uncertainty avoidance is the cultural tendency to be uncomfortable with uncertainty and risk in everyday life.
If your team has a high concentration of individuals from high-uncertainty-avoidance cultures: Use team-building activities and instruments that allow individuals to discuss very concretely how the team members will work together.

If your team has a high concentration of individuals from low-uncertainty-avoidance cultures: Use team-building activities and instruments that allow individuals to discuss generally how the team will work together; discuss specifics later.

Power distance is the willingness of a culture to accept status and power differences among its members.
If your team has a high concentration of individuals from high-power-distance cultures: Use team-building activities and instruments that allow individuals to discuss their backgrounds in relation to others in the organization. Use team-building activities that do not disrupt power differences in the team.

If your team has a high concentration of individuals from low-power-distance cultures: Use team-building activities and instruments that allow individuals to discuss their backgrounds in relation to the team. Feel free to use competitive team-building activities in which any team can win. Be certain to discuss the pros and cons of competition.

High or low context is in relationship to the ways language is used. In a low-context culture, messages are expressed mainly by the spoken and written word. In a high-context culture, words convey only part of a message, while the rest of the message must be inferred from body language and additional contextual cues.
If your team has a high concentration of individuals from high-context cultures: Use team-building activities and instruments that allow individuals to discuss their backgrounds and preferences in detail.

If your team has a high concentration of individuals from low-context cultures: Use team-building activities and instruments that allow individuals to discuss their backgrounds and preferences in general terms.

BOX 10.4 ☛ **International Team-Building Considerations**

SOURCES: Jane E. Henry, Ph.D., and Meg Hartzler; by *Tools for Virtual Teams* Deborah L. Duarte and Nancy Tennant Synder; by *Mastering Virtual Teams* John R. Schermerhorn, Jr., James G. Hunt, and Richard N. Osborn; *Organizational Behavior*, 6th ed. (New York: John Wiley & Sons, Inc., 1997).

vide students with an opportunity to experience international virtual teaming. The international virtual teaming project began with a teleconference that allowed the students to begin the *forming* stage of team development. Following the teleconference, the teams were asked to create Team Operating Agreements. As the teams came to finalize their agreements, many of the Finnish students became uncomfortable and even offended. The Finnish students felt that their American teammates did not trust them because they were asking them to sign the Team Operating Agreement. The Finnish students perceived their word should be enough without creating what they perceived was a legal document. The American students just thought they were getting commitment from the team members by asking them to sign the document. This was a source of conflict and storming for these teams until they were able to meet face-to-face to work through this cultural difference. This example illustrates that individuals cannot make assumptions and must work hard to understand cultural differences to operate effectively in a virtual environment.

Simons points out six specific areas of virtual teaming that should be carefully managed. Those areas include:

1. **Mismatch of cultural context in virtual communication.** The ways of expressing meanings differs from country to country. In individualistic cultures, where the tendency of a culture is to emphasize individual self-interests, the messages are usually shorter and more straightforward in nature than in collective countries. In collective countries, the tendency of a culture is to emphasize group relationships, so the messages are formulated differently.

2. **Difference in action orientation affecting communication styles.** In many Western cultures the facts, data, and deadlines are important. In some other cultures the contacts, relationships, and roles serve the more important role.

3. **Time in cyber work.** The different understanding of time may also create new challenges. In individualistic cultures, time is money, while in collective cultures, relationships are considered more important than money. In virtual working, such differences are not so visible and could even help the collaboration.

4. **Cultural preferences for certain technologies.** People from different cultures may prefer or resist the use of certain media or technology. One obvious reason is the individual language skills that can reinforce the imbalance between the native language speakers and others.

5. **Conflict management.** Problem-solving techniques are very much dependent on the cultural background. Losing face has very different meanings in different cultures.

6. **Differing understandings of authority and who is in charge.** Difficulties may also occur due to the different values and use of authority.[40]

Since the fall of 2002, Kennesaw State University executive-MBA students have been working with Romanian students from the Institute for Business and Public Administration in Bucharest, Romania. Working with the Romanian students gives the Kennesaw State students another cultural perspective. The Romanian-American teams faced some of the same challenges that had occurred with the American-Finnish teams. It seems that often in the beginning, the American students dismiss the cultural aspects. But by the end of the project, culture is often noted as one issue they experienced. For example, one team stated the following: "If we were to make two recommendations to future executive-MBA students, we would recommend that you get the cultural piece and be patient. You should take the time to enjoy the company of your fellow teammates. Try not to be so focused on the task that you miss out on the journey along the way." It seems

> Relationships will go a long way if handled properly. Americans can definitely be arrogant and this does not bode well for international business and interpersonal relationships.
>
> Source: Kennesaw State University and the Institute of Business and Public Administration in Romania, Joint Virtual Team Number 13.

---

[40] George F. Simons, "Meeting the Intercultural Challenges of Virtual Work," *Language and Intercultural Training*, Volume 16, No. 1, 1998.

- Host a team member dinner party for a face-to-face setting.
- Ask each individual to describe his or her expertise and background as well as his or her best practices collected from other team experiences.
- Ask each team member to tell the team something interesting about his or her culture or function and its way of doing business that the team may want to adopt.
- Ask each team member to explain how he or she plans to facilitate boundary-management activities with his or her function, region, or organization.
- Ask each team member to describe how the team can best use his or her particular expertise.
- Use a whiteboard or other presentation software to share interesting information about previous projects or best practices.
- Examine best-practice documents from other teams and apply them to the team. Subteams of people from different cultures can work together on this activity.
- Use GroupWare functions, such as anonymity, to vote or poll in the early part of the team's activities so that team members from collective or high-power-distance cultures feel comfortable stating their opinions.

BOX 10.5 ☛ **Intercultural Team-Building Activities**

SOURCE: Deborah L. Duarte and Nancy Tennant Snyder, *Mastering Virtual Teams* (San Francisco: Jossey-Bass Publishers, 1999), p. 115.

that getting to know each other is an important element of making these international virtual teams function. Box 10.5 offers some suggestions and ways to help this process along.

Research has shown that the last two stages of team development, *norming* and *performing,* can occur in different times and places if properly supported by technology. Technical training will be necessary to empower team members to function in the virtual environment.

The Role of Technology and Collaborative Software

When selecting the type of technology for a meeting, team members should consider the amount of interaction required. If members simply need to share information, voice mail and e-mail can be used.

If the team needs to brainstorm and make some decisions, they may want to set up a chat room, hold a videoconference, or use an electronic bulletin board. Another alternative is group support systems, which provide team members with a variety of support tools to poll participants and assemble statistical information relevant to decisions. These systems even allow team members to "turn off" their individual identities during a brainstorming session and interact with relative anonymity.

Another type of collaborative software provides support for project management, product design, document creation, and information analysis. These collaborative software applications facilitate multiple authorship of your documents and presentations as well as allow you to share databases, spreadsheets, and other information resources. One collaborative software product, Lotus Notes, provides asynchronous teamwork. *Asynchronous* means that your team members can share data and communicate at different times. This software combines scheduling, electronic messaging, and data sharing into one common product. By combining a number of collaborative applications and communication systems into an integrated framework, products like Lotus Notes facilitate both the production and communication necessary for effective teamwork.

Regardless of the technological applications, your team members should agree on which groupware products to use. In addition, you should make sure all software and systems are compatible so members can share information easily.

At the conclusion of each year's international virtual teaming experience between the American and Romanian students, the teams are asked to provide their insights into their international virtual teaming experiences. Each team collaborates together to respond to questions considering what they have learned, what behaviors have helped or hindered their teaming, how technology has facilitated their communication, and challenges they have faced. Table 10.1 presents the insights gleaned from some of these teams.

The Role of Collaborative Writing Within the Virtual Team

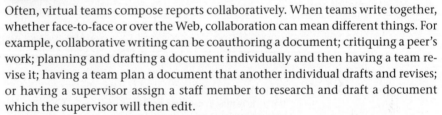

Often, virtual teams compose reports collaboratively. When teams write together, whether face-to-face or over the Web, collaboration can mean different things. For example, collaborative writing can be coauthoring a document; critiquing a peer's work; planning and drafting a document individually and then having a team revise it; having a team plan a document that another individual drafts and revises; or having a supervisor assign a staff member to research and draft a document which the supervisor will then edit.

As you can see, many forms of collaborative writing exist. As the name implies, collaborative writing involves working with others. This section gives guidelines for working within a team setting.

ALLOW TIME TO GET ACQUAINTED

When working with others, allow time to get acquainted. When you begin working on a project, you may find it difficult to start until you know the other members. When you work within a team, each member brings certain strengths. If you take the time to get to know one another, you can draw on these strengths.

DRAW OUT SILENT PARTNERS

Because each individual makes an important contribution to the project, you should seek input from all members. As you probably know, some individuals share easily while others experience more difficulty. As a team, you need the ideas and thoughts of all members.

ALLOW AND ENCOURAGE DISAGREEMENTS

Sometimes individuals think they should not disagree. Yet if individuals never disagree, they might not come up with the best solution. Costly mistakes have occurred because people were afraid to disagree. When you disagree, you look objectively at all the alternatives.

TABLE 10.1 🖙 **Lessons learned from international virtual teaming.**

Question 1. Now that you are nearing the completion of this project, if your companies were considering implementing virtual or distance project management in their operations, what "lessons learned" and "Do's and Don'ts" would you recommend?

DO'S

Meet to get to know one another before starting on tasks
Build the relationship
Have more face-to-face meetings
Take advantage of the videoconferencing that is provided
Agree on roles and responsibilities of each member
Work and follow Team Operating Agreement
Understand the approaches used by different cultures in managing a business

DON'TS

Do not rely too much on technology
Do not hold back from sharing ideas, thoughts, questions, or concerns
Do not let one person be in charge of the whole team
Do not let a conversation pass with "we'll take care of it" or no response
Do not go for extended periods of time without checking on people's work
Do not allow the team to sway from the operating agreement
Do not be rigid in decision making; remain flexible and allow for change

Question 2. In looking at team behaviors, what are the five most important attributes that contributed to the success of your team's activities and assignments?

Understanding of differences as well as similarities	Consistent and useful communication
Commitment	Organization
Responsibility	Flexibility
Trust and Honesty	Shared leadership
Patience	

Question 3. In looking at team member behaviors, what are the three most important behaviors that detracted from the success of your team's activities and assignments?

Not doing work on time
Not being accountable
Not participating in meetings or discussions
Not communicating

Question 4. If you were to make two recommendations to future executive MBA groups planning to engage in international virtual or distance project management, what would they be?

Get to know your teammates
Start on the project early
Establish meeting times and dates
Establish a framework and plan each step/make deadlines, assign tasks
Use chat rooms/course room
Communicate frequently

Question 5. Recognizing technology can support or detract from virtual or distance project management and problem solving, what alternative approaches would you suggest to enhance team performance? What are the aspects in which technology has been more useful for managing the project? (Please be specific in terms of software, vendor providers, or other issues)

Video teleconferencing
Instant messenger program—MSN, Yahoo
E-mail
Telephone conferencing

Question 6. What were the main challenges / difficulties faced during the project?

Document management
Communication
Time management

AVOID SETTLING ON QUICK AND EASY ANSWERS

Sometimes, especially when you are in school, you find yourself under time constraints. These constraints may prevent you from taking the time to analyze all the alternatives to a solution. However, you need to take time to analyze all solutions because doing so may save you time in the end.

AVOID LOOKING FOR THE ONE RIGHT ANSWER

Individuals tend to look for one right answer when, in reality, many answers may be appropriate. When working with others, you must seek the best answer for the team.

WORK TOWARD ACHIEVING CONSENSUS

Seeking the best answer for the team means working toward consensus. When all members agree to the solution and will support it, consensus occurs. The final choice may not have been the first choice of all, but after discussing the alternatives, the team feels the final choice meets the particular situation best.

DEVELOP A WORK PLAN

When working with others, you need to develop a strategy for attacking your problem. Your team needs to develop deadlines for completing aspects of the project and deadlines for duties. Develop agendas for meetings and stick to them. In addition, appoint a leader to keep discussions on task. Appoint a recorder for each meeting to take notes and develop progress reports. The team should develop a system of rewards and punishments for not completing tasks or meeting deadlines. In Box 10.6, Maki and Schilling suggest doing the following when writing collaboratively.

1. Brainstorm to discover a general theme or idea, a presentation strategy, and an outline of the contents.

2. Delegate authority.

3. Research and write in isolation. Writers compose individual versions of an entire document or section; or they each work on different sections, which will be pooled with sections written by other group members.

4. Convene for progress meetings to discuss progress and to establish new responsibilities for the next meeting.

5. Write a test draft.

6. Review and revise a test draft.
   - Send drafts to specialists within the organization, such as lawyers, who are not members of the writing group.
   - Further writing in isolation.
   - Hold progress meetings to review and revise.

7. Write a complete and nearly final draft.

8. Review and edit the nearly final draft.

9. Have a third party review the draft.

10. Review the effectiveness of the document design.

11. Type and proofread.

12. Evaluate the effectiveness of the document based on the action the reader takes.

BOX 10.6 🖙 **An Example of a Collaborative Writing Strategy**

SOURCE: Peggy Maki and Carol Schilling, *Writing in Organizations* (New York: McGraw-Hill, 1987), pp. 355–362.

Conclusion

As a virtual team member, you will need to be prepared to adapt to a changing variety of assignments and tasks during the life of any particular team. You will have little time to learn how to work together. Because your team membership will be somewhat fluid, you will need to quickly assimilate into the team. You will probably be asked repeatedly to change membership without losing productivity. Your membership in virtual teams will be substantially more dynamic and will likely include team members from locations that you would not have traditionally worked with in the past. Thus, effective virtual team members will have to be adept at fitting into a variety of team situations.

For your virtual team to be successful, your members must be firmly committed to the team's purpose and to each team member. They must want their collaborative work to be successful and be willing to go the "extra mile" to make sure it is successful. Team members must be persistent in overcoming technical challenges, because they will occur. They must be patient with other team members who may not be as comfortable communicating in this medium. Capitalizing on the resources that virtual team members bring requires more than just investing in technology. An investment must be made in training the team. Human aspects such as diversity and communication that are so necessary for the success of a virtual team must be addressed. Effective communication depends on much more than just developing writing strategies and technology tools. At the root of effective communication lies the importance of strong interpersonal relationships and support systems. Your team members must choose to communicate completely with each other for the virtual team to succeed. Once these virtual team characteristics are

TABLE 10.2 🖙 **Virtual team checklist.**

	YES	NO
1. Do we know our goal? The outcome of our work?	❏	❏
2. Can everyone state the vision, mission, and objectives of our team?	❏	❏
3. Does every member understand his or her accountability for output and the time frame?	❏	❏
4. Do we have the training and resources necessary to accomplish our mission?	❏	❏
5. Have we established a set of operating agreements based on our values and our organization's culture?	❏	❏
6. Does everyone know how to use the technologies and processes necessary to do the work? Is training necessary?	❏	❏
7. Are our decisions and meeting minutes documented and distributed within 24 hours of the action?	❏	❏
8. Do we know something personal about how each team member prefers to work together?	❏	❏
9. Do we deal with incompetence and broken agreements in a timely and effective manner?	❏	❏
10. Do we deliberately build in some fun and celebration of milestones?	❏	❏
11. Do we communicate progress, changes, and problems up, down, and across the chain of command?	❏	❏
12. Do we check in with each member on a regular basis formally and informally?	❏	❏
13. Do any members lack expected communication skills? Is training necessary?	❏	❏
14. Do all team members understand the concepts, data, and projects?	❏	❏
15. Is anyone's message offensive to another team member?	❏	❏
16. Are there any members who consistently misunderstand messages?	❏	❏
17. Are all team members upholding communication-operating agreements?	❏	❏
18. Do team members need a new operating agreement? Should existing ones be revised?	❏	❏
19. Are my communication skills effective as a virtual team member?	❏	❏

SOURCE: Jane E. Henry, and Meg Hartzler, *Tools for Virtual Teams, A Team Fitness Companion* (Milwaukee: ASQ Quality Press, 1999), pp. 135–136.

mastered, you will be ready to face whatever the new wave of teaming technology offers. To learn more about virtual and self-directed teams, visit the websites at *http://www.teambuildinginc.com* and *http://www.workteams.unt.edu*.

Use the checklist in Table 10.2 to evaluate your virtual team's performance.

Exercises

EXERCISE 1   GETTING TO KNOW YOU!

Directions: At the beginning of your team's life, each member should learn something about each other's values, beliefs, and cultures. Taking the time in the beginning to discuss the following questions can help your team members develop respect for each other as well as prevent misunderstandings and conflict. Answering the questions provides a simple way to understand each other better. The questions represent areas where cross-cultural differences may occur between people. By learning how each team member likes to work, you can gain respect for each person's preferred methods of working with others.

What are your expectations in the area of time frames?

Do people in your culture believe that deadlines are requirements, options, or moving targets?

Do you usually think about long-term, immediate, or short-term goals?

Would you describe yourself as more action oriented, or thoughtful and reflective?

How is it best to communicate to you? Written, verbal, or other?

Are suggestions viewed as calls for actions, food for thought, or directives?

What is your philosophy toward people in positions of power?

How do you tend to behave when working with people who have more power than you do? Less power than you have?

What is the role of the individual in your culture?

Do you tend to work alone, or prefer to work collectively?

Do you find the people in your culture to be competitive, or do they avoid competition? Is competition considered rude?

Do you generally follow a hierarchical structure? Do you prefer to "go through the channels?" Alternatively, do you prefer to work with whoever you believe will help to accomplish the work?

How do you prefer to work with others?

Do you like to be more formal and polite? or do you like to be casual and informal? Can you give an example of rudeness or impropriety in this area?

EXERCISE 2   TRADING POST

Directions: This exercise works well with virtual teams that do not meet or talk face-to-face. It allows members to share what they need and what they have to offer.

Individually answer the following questions:

How do I like to work?

What do I have to offer?

What areas do I believe we need to collaborate on to get the job done?

What do I need from my teammates?

After completing these questions individually, share your responses with your team. Then, as a team answer the following questions:

What does the team need from its members?

What are team members willing to offer?

EXERCISE 3 BIOSKETCH

Directions: Use this exercise to reenergize your team and learn more about each other. Begin the exercise by providing as much information as you can in the time given by your professor. When your professor signals, pass your answers around to the other members of your team. Once everyone has had a chance to review all team member responses, discuss what team members learned and what they have in common.

What is my greatest extravagance?

What is my pet peeve?

Something I am proud of:

How do I like to work?

My career highlight to date:

Things guaranteed to turn me off at work:

My most embarrassing moment:

My most treasured possession:

If not working for my current company, I would most want to:

My greatest fear:

Five words that best describe me are:

My poison is:

Characteristics I think I have inherited from my parents:

The most important lesson life has taught me is:

Best thing about working in this team is:

My motto is:

EXERCISE 4 BON VOYAGE

Directions: Use this exercise to start thinking about visiting another country. Begin with Step One. You are to pack your suitcase with items in response to the four questions that follow. Choose items that will help you adapt to the category, based upon your own travel experiences or other sources. You will have 15 minutes to complete this exercise.

Step One

Pack your bags! Your boss has just told you that you're going on a three-week trip to the company's location in the country of _____ (your instructor will fill in the blank for you).

What things or objects will you take?

Pack some things you'll say (expressions).

Figuratively speaking, pack some ways you'll act or behave.

Finally, pack the emotions or feelings that you'll take.

Step Two

You packed your bags for a three-week trip to your company's location in _____.
On second thought, after remembering what you learned in that orientation session on cultural adaptation and on your own characteristics, you think you'd better take a look at what you packed. Do you really have what's needed to work effectively there? Repack, thinking specifically about characteristics of the other culture and of yourself.

Assignment Options

OPTION 1: ANALYZING YOUR VIRTUAL TEAM PERFORMANCE

For your virtual team to function well, you must contribute in many different ways. Reflect upon the following questions as you think about your participation in your virtual team. Then write a memo about your reflections. Make sure your memo has an introduction, body, and conclusion.

Did you initiate discussion? How?

Did you request more information from a particular team member? How?

Were you active in clarifying any confusing points? How?

Did you actively encourage and respond to others? How?

Were there disagreements about how to approach the project? If so, did you contribute to recognizing the different opinions and work to reconcile the disagreements?

Did anyone in your group use humor to create a comfortable atmosphere? Did the use of humor make you feel uncomfortable?

After reflecting upon these questions, write a memo reporting your role within the virtual team.

OPTION 2: VIRTUAL TEAM REPORT

Your virtual team should study the importance of effective written and oral communication skills for career advancement. You will interact with your virtual team electronically to establish your plan of how to complete your report. Each team member will consult at least three Internet sites and conduct a face-to-face interview with a key person in an organization. Each team member will send his or her interviewee a thank-you letter within one week of the interview. Team members will compile their research findings into a formal report. Review Chapter 8 for the steps in writing a formal business report.

CHAPTER 11

Communicating in Meetings and by Telephone

Lots of people think that virtual or electronic meetings just involve e-mail or discussion groups. In fact, the telephone system is an extraordinarily complex technological marvel that is getting more flexible all the time. Good Enough Information Systems, as a completely virtual company, uses the phone for serious conversations, team meetings, and brainstorming. We also use e-mail, instant messaging, and other technologies, but phone calls give a feeling of immediacy and personal connection that most people don't get through computers. In fact, research on virtual meetings rates telephone calls as being more intimate than videoconferencing.[1]

Gillian Kerr, Ph.D., C.Psych

[1] Gillian Kerr, "Virtual Meetings and Teleconferences—the Internet and the Telephone," Retrieved from Charity Village at http://www.charityvillage.com/cv/research/rtech3.html.

LEARNING OBJECTIVES

After reading this chapter, you should be able to:

- Define a meeting, present the questions you should ask before calling a meeting, and discuss why one might fail.

- List the types of meetings.

- Identify ways of problem solving and making decisions.

- Describe the task and people duties of the chair.

- Prepare a leader's orientation speech and summarize the parts of an agenda.

- Differentiate between room arrangements.

- Relate the guidelines for preparing minutes and the summary of meeting results.

- Identify when you would use videoconferencing, Web collaboration, or streaming.

- Explain the differences between a face-to-face meeting and technology-enabled meetings.

- Understand the important role of the telephone and what it means to have a voice with a smile.

- Identify guidelines for improving your telephone etiquette.

- List the steps for handling incoming calls and placing outgoing calls effectively.

- Define voice mail.

- Identify the role of cellular telephones, personal digital assistants, pagers, and fax machines.

- Define techno-etiquette.

Meetings occur daily in most organizations.

As you've learned thus far, technology plays a significant role in your world of communication. Technology enables you to communicate with individuals from around the globe, thus making your world truly boundaryless. In this chapter, you focus specifically on some standards of work such as meetings, telephones, facsimiles, and pagers.

The Necessity of Meetings

Haynes defined a *meeting* as a gathering of three or more people sharing common objectives where communication (verbal or written) serves as the primary means of achieving those objectives.[2]

Technology continues to play an increasingly sophisticated role in both face-to-face and electronic meetings. According to Janis Cannon, Director of the Georgia Department of Industry, Trade and Tourism, "Wireless is the biggest recent change in meeting technology. Even when individuals come together face-to-face to attend meetings, they want to be able to virtually communicate with their colleagues back at work."[3]

Meetings have become a regular part of business life for most individuals. If you involve your employees in having a meeting, you will probably have more employee commitment, better decisions, and quicker completion of projects. However, you must weigh the advantages of meetings against the disadvantages since meetings take a great deal of time and cost money.

Based upon the research by MCI WorldCom Conferencing, people now spend nearly three hours a day in business meetings. More than a third say meetings are unproductive, and many employees are so tired of all of the meetings they are skipping them. According to the research, more than 90 percent of workers have missed all or part of a meeting, while 73 percent admit to having done other work when they're supposed to be paying attention.

Based on another survey done in 1998 by A. T. Cross, other meeting participation problems include: daydreaming—9 out of 10 employees have daydreamed during a meeting; catnaps—41 percent of men have dozed, compared with 31 percent of

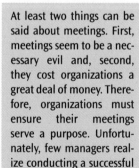

At least two things can be said about meetings. First, meetings seem to be a necessary evil and, second, they cost organizations a great deal of money. Therefore, organizations must ensure their meetings serve a purpose. Unfortunately, few managers realize conducting a successful meeting entails skill.

Source: Larry G. McDougle, "Conducting a Successful Meeting," *Personnel Journal,* Volume 60, Issue 1, January 1981, pp. 49–50.

[2] Marion E. Haynes, *Effective Meeting Skills* (Los Altos, CA: Crisp Publications, 1988), p. 2.

[3] "What's New in Meeting," *TechLinks,* January/February 2004, p. 56.

women; and faking—6 percent of executives take notes to make it look as if they're listening. "I carry a folder with me that I keep stuff in from other meetings. I spend time in meetings preparing for other meetings," says Dean McKay, 36, a Sears store manager in Ashland, Kentucky. "One woman I saw cleaned out her briefcase. She took everything out right there."

Other meeting participants use technology as an excuse. As described by Stephanie Armour in *USA Today*, pagers, portable computers, and other gadgets are proving to be invaluable meeting survival tools. Individuals page themselves and sneak out while others doodle on their handheld organizers. Laptop-toting employees send e-mail instead of passing notes while others i-page back and forth. "We stretch the truth, we say I've got a production problem," says Dianne Packer, 34, an Atlanta computer programmer analyst. "Anything to get you out."

These meeting participation problems result from meetings that are too long, too unfocused, and irrelevant to day-to-day tasks, experts say. "Our attention span is not much better than a school child's," says Michael Begeman, a meeting expert and manager with 3M Meeting Network. "After a half hour, our mind wanders."[4]

To avoid these disruptive behaviors and improper uses of technology during meetings, the leader must ensure that he or she does not run the meeting poorly or invite the wrong people. See Box 11.1 for 20 common causes of failed meetings.

- Too many people invited.
- Wrong people attended.
- Leader created a long agenda.
- Leader chose a bad location—inhospitable environment (e.g., too cold, too hot, poor lighting, bad acoustics, or insufficient ventilation).
- The only person who wanted the meeting called it.
- A few people dominated the discussion (showing favoritism—surefire way to kill a meeting).
- Meeting ran over time limit.
- Meeting contained no structure and ran all over the place.
- Outcomes were predetermined. (Do not play at being democratic and do not ask for ideas unless you really want them.)
- The interaction happened only one way, usually top-down.
- The meeting dealt with superficial issues, not the real ones.
- Too many meetings have been held close together.
- Too many surprises and last-minute items that no one was prepared to address.
- The meeting had a hidden agenda. (Never call a meeting as a ruse for manipulating the group.)
- Participants were not honest (no trust).
- Suggestions and new ideas were unwelcome.
- People created too many distractions by coming late and leaving early.
- Participants were not nice (argumentative and disrespectful) or were too nice (skirted the rough issues).
- Nothing was decided and no closure occurred.
- The meeting did not follow the agenda. (It was not about what it was supposed to be about.)

BOX 11.1 ☛ **20 Common Causes of Failed Meetings**

SOURCE: Charlotte L. Stuart, "A Meeting a Day Keeps Team Problems at Bay," *Training and Development*, Volume 46, Issue 10, October 1992, p. 19. Reprinted from *Training and Development*. Copyright © 1992, American Society for Training and Development.

[4] Stephanie Armour, "Meetings Inspire High-Tech Survival Skills," *USA Today*, Section B, January 22, 1999.

John S. Deutsch, vice president of SMART Technologies, Inc., a Canadian company that designs and sells services and high-tech equipment to improve meetings, states: "First, if you don't need it, don't have it. About half of all meetings aren't necessary. If you're the one calling the meeting, ask yourself if there's another way to accomplish your goals, be it e-mail, a company memo or a phone call."

Source: Mary Ethridge, "Workplace Expert Offers Advice on Conducting Meetings," *Knight Ridder Tribune*, Business News, January 12, 2004.

An effective meeting, however, can achieve its objectives to the satisfaction of the participants in a short time. However, most meetings should not be held. You might accomplish the task in personal interactions or through the judicious use of memos. Before you call a meeting, ask yourself these questions:

Have we done our homework?

Have we prepared for the meeting?

Have the discussion ideas been fully developed?

Can a meeting speed up my work?

Do I need input from others?

Will enough information be presented to make a decision?

Can a decision be made immediately after receiving the information?

Types of Meetings

The reasons for having meetings can be best understood by examining the different types of meetings. When you call a meeting, you may develop ideas, elicit information, make plans, or make decisions.

TO DEVELOP IDEAS

This meeting should take place when you need to expand present activities of the participants. Do not allow this meeting to turn into a "bull session" by specifying the areas to be discussed and constrainting the topics.

TO ELICIT INFORMATION

Hold this type of meeting if individuals need to know information and need to interact about it. Participants should write a summary of their information before they meet and submit it to the meeting leader.

TO MAKE PLANS

Hold this type of meeting after you have developed your ideas and elicited information. Here, you and the participants combine ideas and information to create functional programs for implementation. During such a meeting, discuss resources, people, time table, and alternatives.

TO MAKE DECISIONS

Hold this meeting when you need approval of your plans from a higher authority. All the previously discussed meetings should have already been held, as this meeting will be reserved for presenting proposals, answering specific questions relevant to the proposal, and moving to a decision.

The chairperson decides how the group will discuss each issue. The leader chooses from three commonly used problem-solving methods: **reflective thinking, nominal group,** and **brainstorming approaches.**

Reflective Thinking Model. This method starts with defining the problem. Often what we believe to be the problem is, in reality, just a symptom of something else. Therefore, the problem must be accurately defined. After the group has defined the problem, they can analyze and discuss it. The group determines a standard or set of criteria to measure the problem and develops possible solutions. They must evaluate each solution and pick the best one. After the team chooses the solution, they must decide how to implement it. An important final step involves evaluating the implementation and getting feedback from the individuals involved.

Nominal Group Model. When individuals use this method, they begin by listing ideas independently, without talking to other members. Then, as a group, the participants compile a list, recording at least one item from each person's list until they have included all items. As a group, they revise this list of ideas—rewording, combining, and avoiding duplicates. Next, each person independently orders the master list. The last step requires that the group collate these orderings. This method allows all individuals to participate in the decision, because each team member must first generate a written list.

Brainstorming Model. To conduct an effective brainstorming session, the chairperson must divide the session into two distinct stages. **Stage one** allows participants simply to record their ideas without evaluations or reactions. Listing ideas helps individuals to feel more comfortable sharing. A team recorder lists every item, as stated, on a flip chart. **Stage two** allows the group to review, list, and group related items, and to strike irrelevancies. From the more organized list, the group can work on reaching a decision.

The chairperson ultimately decides how to resolve or decide the issues the team has discussed. The chairperson can choose from a decision by a single individual, a decision by a minority, a decision by majority, or a decision by consensus. The value of a given decision-making mechanism depends upon the situation, the participants, and the task.

For example, the Japanese have a unique decision-making style, and you must have patience to get a reply. Your communication will be routed horizontally and vertically in the organization before a reply is crafted and sent. Getting a decision in a business meeting with a Japanese group differs from the Western style. The leader of the group often remains silent. The person who does the talking is just the spokesperson. Someone has to watch for the facial reaction of the group's leader to get an idea of the decision.[5] The decision-making mechanism truly depends upon the situation, the participants, and the task.

Chairpersons should take care not to base their choices on a method, ideology, or habit. After reaching the decision, the chairperson finalizes how to implement the decision. The chairperson formulates a specific list, stating action items, who will perform them, and deadlines for completion.

The group has now explored the problem and must make a decision. The chair chooses from four decision-making mechanisms.

Decision by a Single Individual.   The chair can make the final decision, with the group serving as a sounding board. This strategy works best when the individual has the competence to make a decision or time is critical.

Decision by a Minority.   Often one or two people who are more vocal can make the decision for the group, although they are a small minority. Often the more vocal members carry along other members who believe, because other members have remained silent, the minority represents the majority. This method may be inefficient if the minority members are not competent. Additionally, the other members may not support the decision.

Decision by Majority.   The most popular decision-making mechanism is majority rule. After a thorough discussion of the issue, the chair calls for a vote. A shortcoming of this mechanism is that the losers may not support the decision and may feel left out.

Decision by Consensus.   This is one of the most effective decision-making mechanisms. When using the consensus method, the team may reach a final decision that may not have been anyone's first choice. However, each person willingly agrees to support and implement the decision after exploring all other alternatives. Consensus decision making requires time to explore the advantages and disadvantages of the alternatives, but it eventually provides a decision agreeable to all. The team reaches this type of decision by agreement, not by voting.[6]

Task Duties of the Chairperson

When you serve as the leader of a meeting, you must develop the agenda.

When acting as chairperson, you have multiple roles to play. You must manage both the task duties and the people duties. Before your meeting begins, you must do some work: develop an agenda, select the participants, and decide where and when to hold the meeting.

DEVELOPING AN AGENDA

Every meeting should have an agenda. (See Box 11.2.) Agendas formalize the activities to take place during the time allotted to accomplish the objectives. Too often,

---

[5] "International Communication: Beyond Words," *Communication World,* Volume 13, Issue 7, September 1996, pp. 33–35.

[6] Dalmar Fisher, *Communication in Organizations,* 2nd ed. (Minneapolis: West Publishing Co., 1993), pp. 340–341.

TO: Sue Brown, Lorie Smith, Joan London, and Jane Benson

FROM: Hillary Medford *hm*

DATE: April 3, 20XX

SUBJECT: Meeting to discuss establishing a Training Division

AGENDA

DATE OF MEETING: April 15, 20XX

PLACE AND TIME OF MEETING: BB 225
                                2:00 P.M. until 3:00 P.M.

For Discussion:

2:00–2:15 P.M.   1. Debate the advantages of a training unit for salaried and hourly personnel.

2:15–2:30 P.M.   2. Discuss the disadvantages of a training unit for salaried personnel.

2:30–2:45 P.M.   3. Establish the training staff required and cost.

For Decision:

2:45–2:50 P.M.   1. Determine whether the group wants to have a training unit.

2:50–2:55 P.M.   2. Decide time and place of next meeting.

For Announcement:

2:55–3:00 P.M.   Present the winner of bean-counting contest.

Before our meeting, please review materials regarding the establishment of a Training Division. Come prepared to discuss this issue!

BOX 11.2 ☞ **Sample Agenda**

individuals do not distribute a complete agenda that will allow individuals to prepare for the meeting. The complete agenda should guide the discussion and provide the meeting with a sense of direction. Deliver your written agenda at least two days before the meeting, if possible, so participants have enough time to prepare. When sending your agenda by e-mail, provide it at least 24 hours before the scheduled meeting. If possible, include the names of people in charge, also called the "PPR" (primary person responsible), of certain aspects of the meeting. Participants can volunteer information to those people before the meeting. You can include references to source materials or reports so participants can read them before the meeting or bring them to the meeting.

Meetings and Conferences.   Experts agree that meetings should not run over two hours. You need to include start and stop times on your agenda and budget tentative times for agenda items. Include only those items consistent with the tasks you are trying to accomplish. Solicit agenda items from other people in advance. Label agenda items with headings such as: *For Discussion, For Your Information, For Announcement, For Decision,* or any other relevant heading. Be careful not to use the heading *Any Other Business.* This heading invites participants to waste time and get off track.

SELECTING PARTICIPANTS

The most important decision you will make about a meeting involves whom *not* to invite. Having too many people at a meeting causes confusion, congestion, and discontentment. Refer to Box 11.3 for the recommended number of participants for your meeting type. Invite only those people who need to attend.

When *developing ideas,* include individuals who have the technical knowledge to determine the feasibility or practicality of your ideas. You may want to invite people from other departments (a limited number, of course) who can tell you about the soundness of your ideas.

When *eliciting information,* ask individuals for information to cover at the meeting. Ask them this question: "Does this information need to be given out in person or can I communicate it through e-mail or a written memo?" If they feel it must be presented orally, then include it in your agenda.

In a *planning meeting,* be sure to invite those people who will carry out the plans. Supervisors and top employees can tell you the problem areas of a plan before you go into action. This can save you time, money, and embarrassment.

In *decision-making meetings,* remember that the real decision-making power lies in the hands of a select few. Invite only those individuals who have the power to give the green light. Gauge the level of authority needed to decide and stop. The president of your organization probably will not be interested in a decision affecting only your department. But your president would want to know about a major reorganization of your division. If you do not know whom to invite, ask your boss.

Meeting Type	Maximum Number of Participants
Problem Solving	5
Decision Making	10
Problem Identification or Brainstorming	10
Training Seminar	15
Informational	30
Review or Presentational	30
Motivational	No Limit

BOX 11.3 ☞ **Maximum Number of Participants per Meeting Type**

SOURCE: 3M's "Mastering Meetings."

DECIDING WHERE AND WHEN TO HOLD A MEETING

Where and when you should hold a meeting becomes almost as important as what will happen during the meeting. Observe the following basic rules for selecting and arranging the location and choosing the time.

Selecting and Arranging the Location. The meeting location and its setup contribute significantly to an effective meeting. When you choose proper facilities, they go unnoticed; but if the facilities appear inadequate, they detract from your meeting.

Allow more space than necessary for the number of people who will attend. You never know who might decide to attend, and you want your participants to be comfortable.

Choose a convenient location. An on-site meeting room is attractive; however, interruptions frequently occur. If possible, try to eliminate telephones in the meeting room and ask participants to turn off cellular telephones and pagers.

Keep in mind that seating arrangements affect the participants' listening, viewing, and learning.

If you plan to use visuals, make sure the room will accommodate audiovisual equipment. Make sure you can control the lighting to adjust for slides or other types of visuals. When you set up the room, be guided by the communication needs for the type of meeting. You usually want those talking with each other to maintain eye contact. Therefore, in meetings where individuals must discuss items together, have them face one another. If the meeting involves formal presentations, you can have the participants face the front of the room. Research on the nonverbal dimension of meetings suggests the seating shapes the dynamics of the interpersonal communication at the meeting. Your goal as meeting leader should be to create easy interpersonal contact among all the participants of the meeting.

Seating formations impact visibility, contact, interaction, networking, and bonding between participants as well as safety, access, and special effects. Seating arrangements affect participants' listening, viewing, and learning as well as their comfort level. The next time you sit in a straight row, look at and talk with the second person to your right or left. Someone has to lean back just to make eye contact. Lengthen the row, and you increase the difficulty of seeing everyone on it.[7]

Exhibit 11.1 provides examples of different room arrangements. The Quality Circle and Personal arrangements invite equal participation. The Boardroom sitting style is the most common arrangement in many meeting rooms, but is the least effective for discussion and equality, especially when the leader sits at one end or the other. In this arrangement, people who sit directly across from you probably are individuals who tend to oppose or wish to confront proposals, but you should not view them as the enemy. People who choose to sit on either side of you probably are your allies—those who, consciously or unconsciously, wish to align themselves with you. To control interaction, seat people who tend to talk to each other on either side of you. People who tend to sit at the corners of the table often symbolically reflect their marginal attitude about the topic or the group.[8]

Merck & Co. in Rahway, New Jersey, uses stand-up meetings with a 20-minute time limit for peer review of proposed projects. To emphasize that you do not want long-winded presentations, consider an occasional stand-up meeting.

Choosing the Day and Time. When choosing the meeting date, make sure you give any individuals who will be presenting adequate time to prepare. Check with

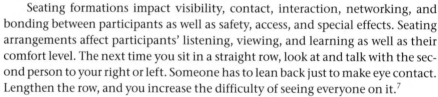

---

[7] Joseph Conlin, "Park It Here: Small Meetings," *Successful Meetings*, Volume 41, Issue 12 (part 1), November 1992, pp. 87–95.

[8] *Interpersonal Communication, Managing the Language of Leadership,* Course Packet at Carnegie Mellon University—Course 70–343.

EXHIBIT 11.1

Room arrangements.

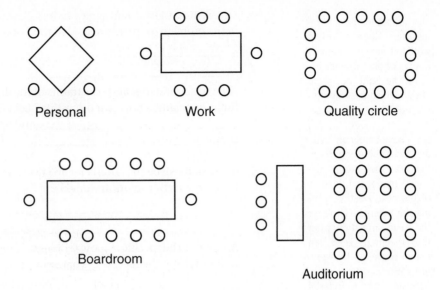

Personal   Work   Quality circle

Boardroom

Auditorium

them to determine their schedules and get their input as to when they feel they can be ready to present.

Certain times of the day should be off-limits for meetings. Avoid any meetings before 9:00 A.M. because most individuals need the first hour of the day to get their workday organized. On the other side, avoid scheduling meetings after 4:30 P.M. because people will be more interested in the time than in accomplishing the objectives. Having a meeting just before lunch can also prove dangerous, as you may compete with growling stomachs.

You should also consider vacations, holidays, and other time factors in setting up meetings. Do not waste anyone's time by not having the necessary people present. Avoid a late-afternoon meeting before a holiday or a weekend. If you must have a meeting before work or during lunch, consider providing food; your attendance will be greater.

PREPARING THE LEADER'S ORIENTATION SPEECH

As the leader, you should help your participants focus by beginning the meeting with an explanation of the meeting's purpose and the expected outcomes. Tom Hajduk calls this opening the Leader's Orientation Speech.[9] Use the following model to help you prepare this opening.

1. Explain the purpose of the meeting by concisely stating the problems, objectives, expected outcomes, and procedures. Ask the audience this question: Why is this meeting necessary?

   The basic problem/issue on the table today is _____.

   The general objectives today are _____.

   The procedure or format we'll use is _____.

2. Provide the information base to promote informed listening and discussion. Ask the audience this question: What key facts surround this problem or issue? Most of you are aware of the history of this problem/issue and understand our need to resolve/address it. Briefly, we _____.

   The present status is critical for us. Right now the problem or issue is

   _____.

[9] Tom Hajduk, "Interpersonal Communication: Moving Students Beyond Writing Assignments," 64th Annual Convention of the Association for Business Communication (Los Angeles, California, November 3–6, 1999).

I think most of us would agree on the following three or four basic causes of the problem (or points related to this issue).

_____   _____

_____   _____

Note the boundaries and constraints of the discussion. Should we put limits or parameters on our discussion? Let's focus mainly on _____. And let us agree we will not talk about _____, because _____. Another constraint on our discussion will be the criteria for an effective solution. For our problem or issue, an effective solution would be

_____   _____

_____   _____

Announce the specific responsibilities or duties of participants. Who is responsible for the mechanics of the meeting?

[name]   has agreed

to _____.

Review the agenda and note any revisions. Then ask: How shall we proceed?

People Duties of the Chairperson

Once you have completed the task duties for your meeting, put your people skills into action. Traditionally, leaders have had to lead and facilitate interaction. Now, many experts recommend using a *facilitator* to accommodate the people issues. This individual helps keep the meeting on track and is concerned only with keeping things running smoothly.

Whether you use a facilitator or decide to handle all aspects of the meeting yourself, you must encourage, support, and listen to your participants. You must remember that by supporting others' right to speak, you do not show agreement. Instead, you show your respect for them, accept them, and allow them to express their opinions. For example, you could say: "That idea shows much thought. What do the rest of you think?" Or, "Let's consider what Kathy has just recommended."

Ask open-ended questions—questions not answerable with a yes or no. You want to encourage all to provide input to make your meeting more effective.

Do not let yourself or anyone else dominate the meeting. To control yourself, avoid interrupting, don't talk for more than a couple of minutes, keep asking other people to contribute, allow someone else to present background information, and hold your opinions until the end.

To control others—especially those with high status or authority who tend to talk too much and interrupt more often—avoid a direct confrontation in front of the group. Instead, try talking to the person outside of the meeting. If that does not work, try nonverbal signs, such as giving attention and providing visible signs of approval to other people trying to speak. As a next step, try a tactful but firm interruption, such as, "Excuse me, Nancy, but we need to keep our remarks brief so everyone has a chance to talk."

You may have to place the disrupter at your side, rather than across from you, and call on him or her minimally. You can try giving the disrupter a job to do—keeping the minutes or chairing a subcommittee. Often these people need some kind of status or recognition. You can channel their energy for the welfare of the group.

To encourage participation and stimulate discussion, sit opposites across from each other. People generally do not communicate with people sitting next to them as much as they do with the people sitting across from them. If you need to encourage a particular individual to speak and participate, sit that individual directly across from you.

When leading your meeting, try to avoid hostile conflict. When individuals conflict over ideas, they avoid the "groupthink trap" of just going along. Nevertheless, conflict of personality can be destructive to the group. If the latter kind of conflict arises, summarize or paraphrase the different viewpoints and emphasize the places where people agree. Try to keep the discussion centered on ideas, not on attacking people. Instead of asking other participants to choose sides, try to work toward a solution allowing all sides to win and maintain their pride.

Suppose that, as the leader, you have closely followed your agenda, and the time has just about run out. To bring the meeting to closure, indicate your intention to end the meeting on time. Briefly review the problem, summarize the progress made, emphasize major agreements, inform the team of developments, and thank the group for participating. You may need to send the participants a summary sheet of what you accomplished or complete other necessary follow-up activities. In effect, as the leader you must monitor yourself and the progress of the members. Effective, thorough follow-up contributes to the continuation of the progress the group meeting began.

To analyze your success as leader, ask yourself the following questions:

Did I meet my goals?

Did the people participate?

Did the participants seem comfortable?

Could I have done anything better?

What should I do differently?

What actions must be taken?

Did I plan and therefore meet my goals?

Did people participate and know the purpose of the meeting?

Did I start and end according to my agenda?

Did I stick to my agenda?

Did I choose an appropriate meeting room for the participants and audiovisual needs?

Did I project my voice so all participants could hear?

Did I involve everyone in the discussion?

What should I do differently next time?

What follow-up needs to take place?[10]

Minutes of a Meeting or Summary of Meeting Results

On some occasions, you will keep a record of your meeting. Minutes of a meeting serve as a written record of what took place. They serve as a permanent, official record of those who attended the meeting, significant discussions taking place during the

---

[10] Edward E. Scannell, "We've Got to Stop Meeting Like This," *Training and Development,* Volume 46, Issue 1, pp. 70–71.

meeting, any decisions made, and follow-up actions to be taken. The recorder distributes copies of the minutes to all individuals who attended the meeting.

Minutes vary in the degree of formality required. An informal meeting may require only a simple, concise record; a more formal meeting requires a detailed account of actions taken and the exact wording of motions and resolutions.

If the leader of the meeting asked you to be responsible for preparing the minutes, become familiar with the agenda items before the meeting and review minutes of previous meetings. You may decide to tape record the meeting to make sure you have gotten every detail.[11]

If you must prepare the minutes for a meeting, use an appropriate writing style, be accurate and complete in preparing the minutes, and use an acceptable format.

USE AN APPROPRIATE WRITING STYLE

Follow the 7 *C*s of effective business writing to make sure you write a concise, factual, and objective report of the meeting. Use complete sentences to describe occurrences and write in the past tense.

BE ACCURATE AND COMPLETE

Record the name of the organization, location of the meeting, and the time the presiding officer started the meeting. You should list the members present as well as those absent.

Then summarize the actions taken to approve the previous meeting's minutes and the treasurer's report, if given. Briefly state important points in the discussion and record who made motions, who provided seconds to the motions, and whether the motions passed or failed. Make sure you include the date, time, and place of the next meeting, if given, and end the minutes by recording the time of adjournment.

USE AN ACCEPTABLE FORMAT

Formats differ depending on the organization; however, the format shown in Box 11.4 has been widely adopted. Headings introduce the parts of the minutes and guide their order. A signature line concludes the minutes. Boxes 11.5 and Box 11.6 provide examples of alternative formats.

Rolling Hills Saddle Club

January 5, 20XX Minutes

President Bruce Fitzmore called the regular monthly meeting of Rolling Hills Saddle Club to order on Tuesday, January 5, 20XX, at 7:45 P.M. at Midway Restaurant.

Attendance

The members present were: Samantha Baubz; Robin Ceaty; Laura and William Terman; Doris Frog; Sam Cans; Jonathan Chap; Bryan Coke; Janet Corn; Karen Hood; Randy, Russell, and Teresa Ford; Don Lester; Rob and Debby Roebuck; and Stephanie Than.

BOX 11.4 ☞ **Minutes of a Meeting**

---

[11] Eleanor J. Davidson, *Business Writing at Work* (Burr Ridge, IL: Irwin Mirror Press, 1994), p. 184.

Minutes

Debby Roebuck read the minutes, and they were approved as read.

Treasurer's Report

Robin Ceaty gave the Treasurer's Report. Currently the treasury has a balance of $8,905.60.

Old Business

Bruce brought the first item of old business to the floor. He stated the club needed to define some unclear terms. These terms were *novice rider, novice horse, beginner rider,* and *green horse.* After considerable discussion the following actions were taken:

Robin Ceaty made a motion that *novice rider* be defined as: a rider in the first year of showing at Rolling Hills Saddle Club in a specific event in a particular discipline. Teresa Ford seconded the motion. After debate, the motion was withdrawn and Robin Ceaty made a new motion defining *novice rider* as any rider showing in his or her first year at Rolling Hills Saddle Club shows who has not shown in more than four shows the previous show season in a particular discipline. Janet Corn seconded the motion. Motion voted on and passed. Jonathan Chap made a motion that *novice horse* be defined the same as *novice rider.* Bill Terman seconded the motion. Motion voted on and approved. Bryan Coke moved that *beginner rider* be defined as any rider in his or her first two years of showing. Stephanie Than seconded the motion. Motion voted on and passed. Bill Terman moved that *green horse* be defined as any horse in his or her first two years of showing over fences. Laura Terman seconded the motion. Motion voted on and approved.

New Business

President Bruce stated the running ring needed more panels for safety. Don Lester made a motion that six more panels be bought. Rob Roebuck seconded and the motion passed.

Doris Frog made a motion that a tape recorder, batteries, and tapes be purchased for the corresponding secretary. Don Lester seconded the motion and the motion passed.

Announcement

Karen Hood stated her telephone number would be removed from the show sheet.

Bruce encouraged everyone to bring a door prize to the End-of-Year Awards Banquet Saturday night. Doris Frog stated she would bring her boom box and tapes if anyone wanted to stay and dance.

Bruce announced the February meeting would again be held at Midway Restaurant on the first Tuesday of the month at 7:30 P.M.

A motion to adjourn was made by Don Lester and seconded by Rob Roebuck. Motion carried and meeting adjourned at 9:00 P.M.

Respectfully submitted,

Debby Roebuck
Debby Roebuck, Corresponding Secretary

BOX 11.4 ☛ (continued)

TO: gselden@coles2.kennesaw.edu,
gmanners@coles2.kennesaw.edu

FROM: Deborah Roebuck < droebuck@coles2.kennesaw.edu >

SUBJECT: Boss/Subordinate Relationships

DATE: November 12, 20XX

I appreciate your attending our November 10 meeting on "Managing Your Boss." I hope you found it not only interesting but helpful. Doug and TP gave tremendous presentations that provided pertinent information. We now have some important information not only to use in our department, but with our associates.

Doug discussed the importance of a boss—he or she can both improve your career and improve your performance. On the other side, though, a boss could also bring your career to a screeching halt if you do not perform to his or her expectations. While playing the "game," you need to understand office politics. We should note the perceptions of those around us. If we understand these perceptions, we will encounter few barriers to a successful working relationship with our bosses. Finally, Doug talked about how to improve your relationship with your boss. Attitude plays a large role in this. In other words, we should not criticize the boss behind his or her back, but try to understand the situation from the boss's perspective if a disagreement arises.

TP provided a wealth of information. He gave some characteristics of outstanding leaders as well as characteristics of incompetent leaders. He stressed the need of the boss to share information. When a boss does share information, he or she gains the trust and respect of his or her subordinates. In addition, information sharing gives follower's responsibility, which they definitely enjoy. TP ended his portion of the meeting by discussing performance appraisals. He encouraged individuals to separate the performance review from a reward or punishment. He also noted that the expectations for performance should be jointly determined by both the boss and the subordinate.

TP and Doug's presentations complemented each other quite well. Doug presented how a subordinate should act toward a superior, and TP reversed the situation and illustrated how a superior should act toward a subordinate. No matter where you work, you will always have to relate to a boss or a subordinate. By following TP and Doug's advice, we can overcome many of the potential communication obstacles found in the workplace.

Thank you again for attending the meeting and enjoy your weekend!

BOX 11.5 **Written Summary of Meeting Results**

Meeting Types and Formats

With increasing frequency, individuals from different geographical locations are being asked to meet. Technology serves as the great enabler as it allows people to meet without actually traveling away from their offices. A group of individuals in distant locations can talk and exchange ideas without the fatigue and disruption caused by travel. These meetings still require the leaders to complete many of the basic tasks and people duties, however, in addition, they may require some additional

MEETING TEMPLATE			
DISTRIBUTION OF ROLES		**DATE** *(insert mm/dd/yy)*	12/15/04
Team Leader	Diane	**TIME** *(start/stop)*	7:00am - 8:00am
Team Facilitator	Gavin	Time Keeper	Gavin
Process Observer	Bryan	Location:	Con Call Bridge
Scribe	Jean	Other :	800-743-7560 ID#44698293

ATTENDEES			
Name	**Check If Present**	**Name**	**Check If Present**
Diane	X	Bryan	X
Tim	X	Joe	X
Jean	X	Gavin	X
Deborah		Other: L. R., Energy	X

AGENDA ITEMS			
ITEM		**OWNER(S)**	**TIME ALLOCATED**
Agenda Review & Opening Comments		Diane	5 minutes
Team Check-in		Entire Team (Optional)	5 minutes
Feedback/Review/Offer Feedback		Entire Team	5 minutes
Review status update on the Team Charter. Due 12/19	What is outstanding? Set deadlines for completion for final review.	Gavin	10 minutes
Personal & Professional Development Plan—Final Check in—Any questions? Due 12/19		Entire Team	10 minutes
360 Degree Evaluations - Any questions? Due 12/19		Entire Team	10 minutes
Revise Meeting Schedule for replacement dates for Saturday, Dec 25 and Saturday, Jan 1.		Entire Team	10 minutes
Closing/Action Items		Diane	5 minutes

MEETING PREPARATION REQUIRED	
PREP ITEM	**OWNER(S)**

MEETING MINUTES	
ITEM	**CONCLUSION**
1 Team charter discussion. Discussion of final revisions.	Final charter will be complete and placed in Lotus Notes by Saturday, 12/18/04.
2 Discussion of PPDP, memo report 1 due 12/19.	Most team members are complete. All team members will complete and place final documents in his or her journal by 12/19.
3 Discussion of the 7005 360 feedback assignment.	Team members that have started the assignment suggest we allocate more time to ensure quality feedback. Team members agree to take the feedback constructively and avoid being defensive.
4 Discussion of dates/times for next 3 meetings in Dec.	1) Sat, 12/18 9-11 am teleconference 2) Thurs, 12/23 7-9 pm face to face meeting 3) Thurs, 12/30 7-9 pm teleconference No meetings 12/25/04 or 1/1/05

FOLLOW-UP	OWNER(S)
1 Capture meeting minutes and share with team.	Jean
2 Develop stakeholder revision for the team charter and send to Gavin.	Joe and Bryan
3 Develop 7010 assignment list and place in Yahoo groups.	Joe

Lessons Learned
1 We learned from a previous mid-week one hour meeting to limit the agenda and be realistic with the one hour available for discussion. It appears we had a more productive meeting. Bryan, as the observer, do you agree with this statement?
2 Reminder: Residency evaluation due 12/17/04. Thank you Bryan.

EFFECTIVE MEETING GUIDELINES			
Planning	**Organizing**	**Conducting**	**Concluding**
1. Determine Purpose 2. Write Objectives Targeting What to Accomplish 3. Determine Agenda Items, List in Logical Sequence Prior to meeting 4. Set Approximate Time Limits on Specific Agenda Items Based on Complexity and Importance to Objectives 5. Determine Overall Length of Meeting	1. Decide Who Should Attend and Why 2. Select Someone to Take Minutes, a Timekeeper, and a Facilitator 3. Schedule the Best Meeting Date, Time, and Location to Accomplish Objectives 4. Send Memos to the Appropriate People, Inviting Them, Outlining the Purpose, Objectives, and Advance Preparation Needed	1. Start the Meeting ON TIME 2. Agree on What Should Be Accomplished 3. Define Specific Problems to Be Resolved as a Group to Reveal Possibly Conflicting Perspectives 4. Generate a Number of Alternate Solutions to Each Issue by Encouraging Active Participation 5. Refer to the Agenda to Keep on Course 6. Move the Group toward Decisions on Key Issues	1. If Consensus Cannot Be Reached on Certain Issues, Confirm What Has Been Agreed upon and Schedule Another Meeting 2. Agree on Action Steps to Be Taken to Ensure That Each Decision Will Be Properly Implemented 3. Delegate Responsibility and Set Deadlines for Specific Tasks and Overall Plan 4. Determine How and When to Evaluate the Effectiveness of Actions Discussed 5. Have Participants Critique the Meeting

BOX 11.6 ☞ **V6 Alliance**   305

technology tasks. Some examples of technology-enabled meetings include: audioconferences, videoconferences, Web collaboration, electronic or computer-mediated meetings, and streaming.

AUDIOCONFERENCES

One of the best-known extensions of the business telephone is the audioconference. Multipoint conferencing products known as *bridges* connect two or more people through a voice call. Today's technology makes placing conference calls as easy as placing an ordinary telephone call. Companies often use audioconferencing for brainstorming and making decisions when they do not have the time or funds to bring people together for a face-to-face meeting.

Leadership duties for this type of meeting are similar to those for any face-to-face meeting: define the purpose, determine the best time for the conference, and decide who should participate. Because the audioconference does not offer the advantage of sight, you should limit participation to no more than seven or eight active participants. More individuals can listen in, if desired. Remember to distribute your agenda and any prework before the meeting.[12]

Some additional duties you may have for this type of meeting include:

- Testing the bridge before the call and determining how many callers you can connect.
- Being aware of the volume and mute features of your equipment.
- Having a backup phone available.

Before the conference begins, print out the agenda notice so that you have the telephone number and access codes available in case you lose the telephone link. Once the meeting begins, check to see who is on the call and wait no more than five minutes for individuals to join the meeting. At the beginning of the conference, ask participants to introduce themselves. After the introductions, establish any ground rules, such as using the mute button when you are not speaking, declaring an intent when you must leave the meeting, acknowledging when an individual rejoins the conference, and stating that conversation segments inappropriate for speakerphones will be prefaced by a statement such as "We will continue this in private." After establishing the rules, review the agenda and facilitate the discussion. Before concluding the audioconference, ask each participant what he or she heard and what he or she perceived were the decisions made. Taking this action will help eliminate any misunderstanding. At the end, summarize the conversation, review the actions to be taken, and evaluate the effectiveness of the meeting. Try to distribute the minutes within two days.

VIDEOCONFERENCING

As equipment costs continue to decline and travel budgets are reduced, many companies have begun using videoconferencing to replace face-to-face meetings. Videoconferencing is becoming more of a business norm than an exception.[13]

Nearly half of Fortune 500 companies now use videoconferencing. The strongest focus has been to deliver corporate training programs. Some companies have begun testing videoconference job interviewing for campus recruiting. Employers like the application's potential for reducing travel costs associated with interviewing.[14]

---

[12] Deborah L. Duarte and Nancy Tennant Synder, *Mastering Virtual Teams* (San Francisco: Jossey-Bass Publishers, 1999), p. 176.

[13] Thomas C. Hayes, "Doing Business Screen to Screen," *New York Times,* Sec. D, Col. 3, February 21, 1991, p. l.

[14] Karl O. Magnusen and K. Galen Kroeck, "Videoconferencing Maximizes Recruiting," *HR Magazine,* Volume 40, Issue 8, pp. 70–72.

Video is no longer a high-cost luxury for only the most important meeting; rather, it is a friendly medium to help span distances and make internal business decisions faster, or to enhance closer contacts with customers at all levels of the organization.[15]

Traditional videoconferences usually take place in specially designed rooms where long-distance telephone companies have installed fiber-optic networks to transmit the digital signals. However, you can use a direct connection between IP addresses through the Internet or you can use a gateway provided by one of the large online portals, such as Yahoo or MSN. There are even special videoconference websites that help you make easy connections for a cost.

Videoconferencing formats span a range from *still motion* to *delayed motion* to *full motion*. *Still motion* means you simply see a picture of the individuals, while *delayed motion* makes the participants appear as if moving in slow motion. *Full motion* videoconferencing provides a "live meeting," just as if the participants were sitting across from one another in the same room.

More and more individuals are now participating in desktop videoconferencing systems (DVCS). These systems run on desktop workstations or personal computers and re-create face-to-face interactions. You can add DVCS to virtually any new generation of personal computer, and you do not need outside facilitation, as in traditional videoconferencing systems. The combination of affordability and operational simplicity make DVCS an affordable organizational communication solution.[16]

DVCS systems have smaller screens than their bigger counterparts and provide a lower quality of video because they operate at slower speeds. A small camera is mounted atop a computer monitor to provide the video feed to the system. Voice transmissions operate through an earpiece and microphone combination or speakerphone. Connection to other individuals is managed through software on the user's computer; to ensure user familiarity, the software uses an on-screen version of a traditional telephone to control the system. The final component of the system is a high-speed data connection, which may be accomplished through local area network connections or specialized digital telephone lines. DVCS creates the potential for two primary types of group communication: all members actively connected in a session, or a face-to-face group with an absent member or outside resource. What this means is that a local group can connect with up to 15 different individuals or groups.

With DVCS, individuals can simultaneously work on documents, analyze data, or sketch out ideas on shared whiteboards. In many respects, the DVCS creates a work environment in which users have more options available to help them collaborate and share data than would be possible working around a conference table. You will not even have to get up out of your chair to have a meeting. Technology becomes as convenient as using your telephone!

The latest emerging technology is wireless. Wireless videoconferencing systems connect to a local area network without being directly wired to a computer or network. These systems promise to bring great mobility as people transport the systems, set them up, and can begin transmitting without being physically connected to a network. No longer is space dedicated to videoconferencing. The system travels to the event and is stored away afterward.[17]

Videoconferencing Guidelines. In preparing for your videoconference, in addition to the normal tasks you must do as the meeting leader, you may want to consider whether or not to use name cards. If the videoconference involves several people, name cards will help direct people to ask questions of the correct person.

---

[15] Becky Waring, "Ready or Not," *Presentations,* Volume 13, Issue 10, October 1999, pp. 34–40.

[16] C. Brookshaw, "Virtual Meeting Solutions," *Infoworld,* Volume 19, Issue 22, pp. 96–108.

[17] "Emerging Collaborative Technologies," *Videoconferencing Cookbook,* Version 4. Retrieved from *http://www.videonet.gatech.edu/cookbook/.*

You should make sure the cards are cream-colored instead of white as white may reflect too much light and not appear well on the screen. When preparing these cards, use a bold font such as Times New Roman or Arial and make sure the font is large enough so that people can read the name cards while viewing the screen.

Since you may be videoconferencing with individuals from other countries or different parts of the United States, you should keep in mind the different time zones. When setting up a conference, be sure to specify in what time zone the meeting time will occur. It is usually best to use Greenwich Mean Time as the standard when having a conference with individuals from other countries. Some executive MBA students from Kennesaw State University learned the importance of this task "after the fact." They had forgotten to take into consideration daylight savings time when setting up their videoconference and thus had to wait an hour before they could start their conference.

Once you start the conference, you should properly introduce the participants to help people feel more at ease. If the conference is being held with any new participants, it is important to introduce yourself and everyone else that is there.[18]

Videoconferencing Etiquette. Videoconferencing has certain behaviors that help to make it successful. Keeping in mind the following will help improve your videoconferencing experience.

Do a dry-run. Before the actual videoconference, you should explore how others will be seeing and hearing you as much of the experience at one end is affected by conditions at the other. Most videoconferencing packages include a "self-view" window that lets you see how you appear to the other end (called remote end). You can determine whether or not you are completely viewable on camera, if there are distractions in the background, and whether you are looking toward the remote caller and not "gazing down from above" or "peering up from below." Even if the self-view window is not going to be kept up during the call, you should preview your image in the window and make adjustments before the call begins. Unfortunately, you cannot adjust your audio because the local audio is almost always suppressed from "feeding back" to you in local mode or even in most test modes. Therefore, you should test and adjust with a live call before a meeting begins or take a few minutes to test and adjust at the start of a call. Once a call is in progress, many people seem to tolerate poor audio or video conditions as they do not want to interrupt the conversational flow or simply think it must be something "at their end." A short audio/video "rehearsal" is well worth the time spent as it contributes to making the technology as transparent as possible and enables comfortable, effective, and rich communication.

Make minor adjustments. Once adjustments have been made, try to just talk naturally and make as few additional adjustments as possible once the conference begins. Some adjustments, though, may still be required in response to environmental changes (lights are turned on/off, background noise increases). However, unnecessary "twiddling" of audio or video can have distracting results. For example, if you lean forward and adjust a desktop camera at your end, you may produce the dreaded "giant palm monster" effect: All your colleague will see is all or parts of your hand. If limited range or unidirectional microphones are being used, excessive movement or position shifting can produce audio break-up, swells and fades at the receiving end.

Eye contact and body language. Once you have correctly positioned your camera and incoming view window, you should remain focused in that direction. As you know, real eye contact is not possible as individuals are really looking at a camera. However, individuals can note shifts in attention such as looking out a window, looking at other applications on the computer screen, or "multitasking" with

---

[18] Source: "Video Conferencing Etiquette," *E-Mail Etiquette*, pp. 8–11. Retrieved from *http://web.csuchico.edu/~ar68/web.htm.*

other work in your office, which can have the same effect as not looking someone in the eye when talking to him or her in person. Videoconferencing is much more like an in-person exchange than a telephone call; therefore, you should be careful of your facial expressions and gestures. In addition, arrange and organize your papers before the conference begins; any paper rustling noise could be a distraction, as microphones can magnify any noise.

Watch side conversations and speaking.   As with any in-person meeting, stray noises and side conversations can distract from the primary conversation. Sometimes, individuals may forget that they are part of a group conversation since the meeting room is virtual rather than physical. Side conversations seem to spring up more readily than they would if everyone were seated in the same room. In addition, the microphones and speakers complicate matters further as they pick up these conversations as well as background noises. Given these "imperfections" with technology, you should mute your own audio when you are not speaking. Ensure you know how to do this before your conference begins. In a one-to-one conversation, you probably should not mute your audio as it can result in unnatural pauses in the conversation.

Be careful that you do not speak over other people, as this can create confusion or make the person who is speaking feel offended. You should notice verbal clues or body language to know when a person is finished. Many times the person talking will pause in anticipation of a question or comment, so this pause presents an ideal time to say whatever you have on your mind. You must keep in mind that the meeting is not at real time and there can be a time delay of five to ten seconds. Therefore, when talking, pause once in a while to allow for comments or questions and to give time for people at other sites to receive your message and reply to it.

Dress and room set-up.   Now that you have minimized the audio distractions, you should focus your attention on minimizing video distractions. Traditional videoconferencing has paid significant attention to proper lighting, room aesthetics, and attire. However, as videoconferencing becomes more of a daily norm that occurs from desktops located in individuals' offices or homes, some of these details may not be as important. However, you should employ common sense and make sure that your setup and dress is professional.

One team at the meeting.   Most of the meeting tips previously shared still apply to videoconferences. For example, "you should be on time," "you should pay attention," "you should make sure everyone has the same information going into the meeting," and "you should bring enough materials for everyone." If you are conducting a multipoint meeting, make sure hard copy materials are sent to all locations ahead of time. If printouts will be made from electronic material presented during the meeting, make sure that all sites have the capability to print the materials. If flip charts or room locations will be shown during a meeting, you should ensure that the camera views these before the meeting begins.

Information sharing.   In multipoint meetings, some information may be specific to each local site, but not relevant to the remote sites, such as where the restrooms are. That type of information should be shared before the videoconference begins.[19]

You can use the tips in Box 11.7 to make your videoconferencing meetings even more effective.

WEB COLLABORATION

Web-based collaboration allows multiple people to work on a document at the same time during meetings. The current Web collaboration tools allow you to work

The expanding mobile workforce and need for virtual teams make collaboration more difficult but more important. Web-based collaboration provides a cost-effective solution without the headaches inherent with supporting complex in-house systems.

Source: Greg Alwang, "Web Collaboration," *PC Magazine,* October 30, 2001. Retrieved from *http://www.pcmag.com/article2/0,4149,71267,00.asp.*

---

[19] "Best Practices and Etiquette," *Videoconferencing Cookbook,* Version 4. Retrieved from *http://www.videonet.gatech.edu/cookbook/.*

- Send out the agenda and supplemental reading ahead of time.
- Agree ahead of time about how to handle absences.
- Start on time.
- Begin with a roll call.
- Review agenda and ask for comments.
- Use a facilitator or timekeeper to keep things moving.
- Ask questions to get participation.
- Pause long enough for answers. There may be a slight delay in the transfer of images. Allow the on-screen site to finish speaking before you respond.
- Use graphics. Keep them large and simple.
- Be yourself. Speak naturally as if you were all in a room together.
- Be aware of which camera you are using.
- Tell people when you will be using a graphic.
- Record important comments and decisions for each agenda item. Use this summary to check for agreement and understanding before moving to the next item.
- Rotate the order in which you poll members.
- End with a process check of meeting effectiveness.
- Ask members to summarize discussions and decisions.
- Set a time for the next conference and check for agenda items that are already known.
- Follow-up immediately with written minutes.

BOX 11.7 🖙 **Tips for Videoconference Meetings**

SOURCE: Jane E. Henry, and Meg Hartzler, *Tools for Virtual Teams, A Team Fitness Companion* (Milwaukee: ASQ Quality Press, 1998), p. 93.

the way you are accustomed to working, but to use electronic media to do your work faster and to reach more people efficiently. Remote meeting locations work well with this technology, as most meetings include at least one presentation with a meeting leader showing visual aids while talking through major points. With Web collaboration, meetings have a similar structure, but the participants are all connected over two separate but linked networks. Voice communication occurs by a conference call over the telephone, thus providing the level of audio quality and interactivity people are accustomed to experiencing in business meetings. Participants view the visual aids over the Web. Any authorized participant with a Web browser can go to the designated Web location (URL) and see the slides. Typically, a server computer or service provider keeps the audio and graphics synchronized. You can even record the entire audio or graphics presentation for anyone who missed your meeting.[20]

ELECTRONIC OR COMPUTER-MEDIATED MEETINGS

In this meeting format, participants sit side-by-side without talking while communicating through their computers. You may be wondering why an organization would fly team members great distances to meet using PCs. According to Douglas S. Griffen, managing partner of D. S. Griffen & Associates, this type of meeting

[20] Janet G. Caswell, "Web-Based Collaboration Tools: Solutions for Today's Business," *Ohio CPA Journal,* Volume 58, Issue 2, April–June 1999, pp. 8–10.

produces high performance. In a traditional face-to-face meeting, only one participant can speak at a time. In a computer-mediated meeting, numerous individuals can "talk" simultaneously and do it anonymously. In a computer-mediated meeting, participants type comments into a dialogue box. These comments are sent to the server, and a moment later they appear back on each participant's computer screen, identified only by a number that corresponds to the order of submission. According to Maryann Alivi, chairperson of information systems at Robert H. Smith School of Business at the University of Maryland, anonymity is a powerful feature. People get brutally honest and provide negative feedback more freely and frequently through this technology. She states further that in traditional meetings, ideas are tied to the person who voiced them.

Typically, a minority of the participants actually contribute ideas in face-to-face meetings. Contributors are the individuals who feel comfortable in a group setting and who are natural leaders. However, they may not have the best ideas.

Another advantage of the computer-mediated meeting is that when no one talks, individuals do not politick, grandstand, or entertain. Typically, the electronic meeting stays on-task better and maintains focus. Often in 15 minutes or less, a group can brainstorm a topic that would take all morning in a traditional meeting. In addition, a complete record of an electronic meeting that includes graphs and tables can be printed and distributed immediately or e-mailed to participants after the meeting. Everyone works from the same easily accessible notes, which allows organizational learning.[21]

STREAMING

Streaming began in 1995 as a way to deliver audio messages in real time over the Internet. Streaming can take place on the Internet as well as on a corporate intranet. The corporate network provides higher bandwidth and limited access, and hence higher levels of performance and reliability than are possible on the public Internet.

Streaming is also a meeting and corporate communication tool, enabling hundreds or thousands of "listeners" to attend an event at low cost. Senior executives can broadcast speeches or announcements to all employees or customers on the network, and the sessions are readily archived for reply later over the network or the Internet.

The latest enhancement to streaming is its integration with videoconferencing. While two videoconferencing sites may be connected over a telephone call, either one of them may be connected simultaneously to a streaming server so that the meeting is "broadcast" over the corporate network for anyone to watch.[22]

With streaming technology, when you click on a file, the audio or video session begins after just a few seconds' delay. You do not need to download and store the file on your own system, a task that can take from minutes to hours with today's multimedia files, depending on the speed of the network connection. Streaming provides instant gratification. Just about any network-attached computer capable of running a Web browser can receive a streaming file; no special hardware is needed.

With streaming media, you can access training videos directly from your office or from any authorized computer at any time of the day or night. You do not have to duplicate, distribute, or update libraries, CD-ROMS, or videotapes.

Because technology-enabled meetings are a bit different, they may require different roles. Szerdy and McCall present four roles that they perceive as important for any electronic meeting: owner, participant, facilitator, and technology.[23]

[21] John Grossman, "The Sounds of Silence," *Sky,* June 1998, pp. 28–32.

[22] "The Next Generation Business Phone," pp. 185–186.

[23] Deborah L. Duarte and Nancy Tennant Synder, *Mastering Virtual Teams* (San Francisco: Jossey-Bass Publishers, 1999), pp. 158–159.

EXHIBIT 11.2

Meeting interaction continuum.

Information Sharing	Brainstorming and Decision Making	Collaborative Work
Low Interaction	Moderate Interaction	High Interaction
Voice mail	Electronic bulletin board	Real-time data conference with audio/video and text/graphic
E-mail	Chat rooms	Whiteboards with audio/video link
	Video conference	Electronic meeting system (EMS) with audio/video and text and graphic support
	Real-time data conference	Collaborative writing tools with audio/video links

SOURCE: Deborah L. Duarte and Nancy Tennant Snyder, *Mastering Virtual Teams* (San Francisco: Jossey-Bass Publishers, 1999), p. 160.

The **owner** defines the objectives and outcomes of the meeting. If you serve in this role, you will determine who participates and the background information needed. You will work with the facilitator to develop the agenda, select the technology, and conduct the meeting. During the virtual meeting, you will interact with the facilitator to ensure that the objectives are met and that necessary decisions are made. You will also decide the best way to follow-up on the next steps and action items.

As a **participant,** you will need to take responsibility for preparing for the meeting, including reading the background material and becoming familiar with the technology. During the meeting, you should speak out, listen, and discuss all ideas. You must actively take responsibility for making suggestions and decisions as well as following up on meeting actions.

If you serve as **facilitator,** you will conduct the process of the meeting. In a virtual meeting, this role involves more technology than in a face-to-face meeting. You must match the technology to the goals of the meeting and to the items on the agenda. You will need to test the technology before the meeting and check the technology throughout the meeting. You will also need to manage the process of the meeting. Keep the group focused and moving through the agenda, keep the communication open, make sure the participants stay focused, and summarize the decisions and actions to be taken.

Technology will enable your virtual team to meet and accomplish what would be impossible otherwise. Technology should increase productivity and serve the meeting, but not dominate it. When you select the technology for your meeting, consider the amount of interaction required. See Exhibit 11.2 above.

The old adage "practice makes perfect" applies to managing meetings. You now know how to make meetings more effective. Use the meeting checklist in Table 11.1 to guide you in developing your meeting. Then view each meeting you conduct as a learning experience. Always analyze how you can improve and solicit feedback to conduct better meetings.

The telephone continues to be an important part of your business day.

The Telephone

The telephone still dominates business communication. It is often the first sound you hear in the morning, as well as the last sound of the day. It may be one of the most powerful, efficient, and cost-effective business tools you have at your disposal. Telephone calls provide the most immediate, personal response. However, when a telephone call transfers to voice mail, it becomes less personal and immediate. According to a July 2, 1997, Dallas Morning News article entitled: "Message

TABLE 11.1 ☞ **Meeting checklist.**

			YES	NO

I. Planning

			YES	NO
The First Step	A.	*Do you need to call a meeting?* To give or obtain information To assure understanding To analyze and solve a problem To obtain acceptance To provoke or speed up action To reconcile differences	☐	☐
When Not to Call a Meeting	B.	*Does your meeting fall under the following situations?* *If so, you do not need a meeting!* You must act fast. You must interact with a large audience. You do not need reactions or want them. The problem appears to be between individuals.	☐	☐
Alternatives	C.	*Have you considered the alternatives to calling a meeting?* Personal action Telephone Written communication	☐	☐
Objectives	D.	*Have you set specific objectives for your meeting?* Does it answer the question: "Why am I calling this meeting?" Does it complete the statement: "I want the following to happen as a result of this meeting. . . . "	☐	☐

Participant Analysis	E.	*Have you justified the participation of each member?*
		Do you need the individual's approval?
		Can the individual make strategic contributions?
		Does the individual have unique information to offer?
		Does the individual have responsibility for implementing any decisions?
		Have you considered the following about each participant?
		    Knowledge of subject
		    Level or status in organization
		    Vocabulary and understanding
		    Information and techniques likely to gain attention
		    Opinions and open-mindedness about subject
		What are the advantages and disadvantages of any decision?
		Which information or techniques are likely to get negative reactions?
		What is the group mix: departments, conflicts?
			☐	☐

II. Preparing

			YES	NO
The Agenda	A.	*Have you worked up an agenda as a personal planning aid and as a means of communicating with participants?* If necessary, have you called participants before sending out an agenda to briefly explain the meeting's purpose? Have you allowed sufficient time for participants to prepare? Have you made personal notes in the margins (e.g., questions to initiate discussion, starting statements, names, etc.)?	☐	☐
How Long	B.	*Have you allowed sufficient time for participants to speak and discuss agenda items?*	☐	☐
Rooms and Arrangements	C.	*Have you checked the meeting room arrangements?* Does the size of the room match the number of participants? Does the room accommodate visual and audio aids? Is the room satisfactory from the standpoint of acoustics, ventilation, entrances and exits, and supplies? Do you feel you have selected the best arrangements for the size of your group and for your objectives? ___Classroom ___Center table ___U-table ___Circle ___Clustering ___Semicircle	☐	☐

TABLE 11.1 📨 (continued)

		YES	NO
Visual Aids	D. **Have you followed the general principles for preparing visual aids?**	☐	☐
	Have I made appropriate visuals for the size of the room?		
	Do the participants need copies?		
	Have I checked the equipment to make sure it works?		
III. Conducting			
Group Behavior	A. **Have you observed the dynamics of your group?**	☐	☐
	Emotional or work modes of fight, flight, dependency, support, or work?		
	Hidden agendas?		
	Invisible committees?		
	Who talks to whom?		
	Who talks most often? Least often?		
Leadership Skills	B. **Have you taken care of the basic leadership responsibilities?**	☐	☐
	Have you assured all is in order before beginning your meeting?		
	Will you open and close your meeting promptly?		
	Will you close the meeting with a summary of decisions made and plans for implementation?		
Effective Leadership Principles	C. **Do you possess the principles of an effective person?**	☐	☐
	Are you **proactive**?		
	Do you begin with the **end in mind**?		
	Do you put **first things first**?		
	Do you seek **first to understand**, then **to be understood**?		
Task and Maintenance Skills	D. **Have you made sure you and others use the basic task and maintenance skills?**	☐	☐
	Initiating		
	Information or opinion-seeking		
	Information or opinion-giving		
	Clarifying or elaborating		
	Summarizing		
	Consensus testing		
	Encouraging		
	Expressing group feelings		
	Harmonizing		
	Compromising		
	Gatekeeping		
	Setting standards		
Diagnosing Work Teams	E. **Have you attempted to set the climate for changing your team's behavior?**	☐	☐
	Have you avoided rejecting ideas and instead reworked them to make them acceptable?		
	Have you set up a means for obtaining feedback on your team's behavior?		
	Observer record?		
	Member reaction sheets?		
	Videotaping and discussion?		

Madness," new technology is adding to the volume of communication. This is because people tend to "bundle" or send the same message in more than one form to ensure its arrival. The results are a potential productivity drain caused by improper use of technologies that were designed to make tasks easier.[24]

This channel of communication does not allow you to see the other person's nonverbal communication. Because you lose the visual dimension, you may have

---

[24] Cyndi Maxey, CSP, "Your Telecommunication Image." Retrieved from *http://www. bremercommunications.com/Your_Telecommunications_Image.htm.*

difficulty knowing what the listener is thinking or feeling. How you come across on the telephone reflects the image of your company. You have about 4 to 10 seconds to make a first impression and get the listener's attention.[25]

Playing telephone tag frustrates individuals, as they lose productive work time by being put on hold, getting busy signals, or placing calls that do not reach the intended receiver. According to Dibble and Langford, only about 25 percent of all business calls reach their intended recipient on the first try. As a result, managers and staff spend 30 minutes a day, or almost 13 days a year, on hold, getting a busy signal or no answer, and playing telephone tag.[26]

Probe Research found that 75 percent of all callers do not complete their business calls on the first attempt; 50 percent of calls comprise one-way transfers of information; and 67 percent of calls are less critical than the tasks they interrupt.[27]

Still, communicating by telephone can be as important as face-to-face communication. Knowing how to use the telephone correctly can have a significant impact on your effectiveness and the image of your organization. Learning to use the telephone effectively can be easy, because you can incorporate several communication skills you have already learned. Smiling plays a significant role in effective telephone communication.

THE VOICE WITH A SMILE

Remember to smile when you speak on the telephone as your voice reflects your personality.

Your voice reflects your personality. Always have a smiling voice when you speak on the telephone. Mary Ann McKenney recommends keeping a small mirror by the telephone so that you can watch yourself smile. She states, "You really can hear the difference." When you say hello, imagine shaking hands with the caller and smiling. Show your enthusiasm and warmth in your greeting. If you sound abrupt, rushed, or indifferent, you may get negative feedback.[28]

According to Jeffrey Jacobi, 37 percent of a person's first impression (in face-to-face encounters) is based upon the sound of the voice. Appearance counts for 55 percent, and what you say only 8 percent. On the telephone, the importance of the voice jumps to 80 to 90 percent.[29] Apply the six rules in Box 11.8 to develop a pleasant telephone voice.

GUIDELINES FOR IMPROVING YOUR TELEPHONE ETIQUETTE

Apply the rules of face-to-face conversations to the telephone. Take the Telephone Test in Table 11.2 to determine how well you now handle the telephone. Then, employ the guidelines that follow the test to improve your telephone etiquette.

Over the telephone, you must listen harder than you would in person because you cannot see the individual. You must be more alert for cues. You can ask questions and use encouragers such as *yes* or *I see.* Follow-up to make sure you have heard correctly. Effective listening skills pay off in your telephone conversations.

Remember to sound alert and positive. You do not want your listeners to feel they have intruded on your time. Sprinkle your conversations with "Thank you" and "I'll get it to you today." Manners and consideration can go a long way toward winning customers and clients.

[25] Shelly Friedman, "Skill on Telephone Builds Good Image," *Atlanta Journal and Constitution,* Sec. F, Col. 1, February 28, 1993, p. 3.

[26] Jerry A. Dibble and Beverly Y. Langford, *Communication Skills and Strategies* (Cincinnati, OH: South-Western Publishing, 1994), p. 93.

[27] M. Bransby, "Voice Mail Makes a Difference," *Journal of Business Strategy,* Volume 11, Issue 1, January/February 1990, pp. 7–10.

[28] Estelle L. Popham, Rita Sloan Tilton, J. Howard Jackson, and J. Marshall Hanna, *Secretarial Procedures and Administration* (Cincinnati, OH: South-Western Publishing, 1994), pp. 271–277.

[29] Gail Dutton, "Gaining a Vocal Edge," *Management Review,* Volume 85, Issue 7, July 1996, p. 9.

- To avoid monotony, speak at a normal speed with rising and falling inflections. Try not to yell or fade away at the end of sentences. Pause to give your listener time to comprehend and ask questions. When presenting dates, names, and other important information, take more time.
- Use a tone suitable for face-to-face communication. Your pitch can rise during the greeting to show interest, but mostly you converse in a low pitch for the comfort of the listener. To ensure that you do not speak in a monotone, you may want to record yourself and listen to how you sound.
- Speak directly into the transmitter, which should be from half an inch to an inch from your lips. Enunciate your words when you speak. Many letters sound alike over the telephone, so you need to make certain you include the last sound in the word. You can open your mouth more to create a clear, open sound. Practice in front of a mirror.
- Try to visualize and speak directly to the person calling.
- Convey a friendly, intelligent interest and articulate carefully.
- Use simple, nontechnical language and avoid slang. Do not end the conversation by saying "Bye-bye."

BOX 11.8 🖝 **Telephone Voice Tips**

Follow through with your call and do not leave the caller stranded. Get the information, transfer the call, or arrange for someone to call back, and then make sure someone does so. A promise must be carried out.

Try to keep telephone calls short, as all individuals have limited time to waste. Get to the point; be specific; use short, easy, and uncomplicated words; stick with the facts; and utilize positive action words.

INCOMING CALLS

Use specific techniques when receiving incoming telephone calls. The following guidelines can improve your technique.

Answer Promptly and Identify Yourself. Try to answer your telephone by the third ring. If you identify yourself when you answer, you save time because you avoid the unnecessary, time-consuming question-and-answer period involved in wrong numbers or strangers calling.

Take the time to clearly state your name, title, and company. Then give the caller your full attention and do not complete other work while on the telephone. If you try to do two things at once, you cannot listen effectively. Study the following examples:

Marketing Department, Jane Daily.

Rockin R Ranch. Rob Roebuck speaking. May I help you?

Jane Daily speaking; how may I help you?

If you state your name, department, or organization, callers should have no doubt about what number they have reached.

Get the Caller's Name Immediately. Often you recognize the voice on the other end of the line; in other situations, callers identify themselves immediately. However, occasionally, callers do not say their names. If that happens, simply ask:

May I ask your name, please?

TABLE 11.2 🖙 **Telephone checklist.**

Directions: *Check the best answer.*

	ALWAYS DO	USUALLY DO	SELDOM DO
1. Before leaving my phone, I leave word where I am going and when I plan to return.	☐	☐	☐
2. I answer my own phone whenever possible. I answer promptly before the third ring.	☐	☐	☐
3. I identify myself at the beginning of the conversation, whether I am taking or placing the call.	☐	☐	☐
4. I take care to speak directly into the telephone clearly, naturally, and pleasantly.	☐	☐	☐
5. I try to personalize my conversation by using the caller's name at every opportunity.	☐	☐	☐
6. I try to be informative when taking calls for others.	☐	☐	☐
7. I offer my help and assistance to the caller.	☐	☐	☐
8. When taking messages, I note all essential information and, if necessary, double-check.	☐	☐	☐
9. If the caller must wait longer than a minute while I leave the line, I offer to return the call.	☐	☐	☐
10. I thank the party for calling and allow the caller to hang up first.	☐	☐	☐
11. I return all calls promptly.	☐	☐	☐
12. I treat all kinds of messages as important calls.	☐	☐	☐
13. I place my own calls and I stay on the line.	☐	☐	☐
14. I explain why I am transferring the call and to whom.	☐	☐	☐
15. I explain the call briefly to the person taking over so the caller does not have to repeat the entire story.	☐	☐	☐

SOURCE: Southern Bell Telephone & Telegraph Company, 5340 Roswell Road, NW, Atlanta, Georgia.

Take Messages Accurately. If you are taking a call for someone else, record the telephone message accurately. The telephone message pad can be one of your handiest pieces of office equipment. Always complete the following:

Name of caller

Telephone number

Date

Time

Message

Your name or initials

Repeat the information to the caller to be sure you have noted it correctly. Pay special attention to the name and telephone number.

Do Not Make the Caller Wait for You. No one likes to be put on hold. Try to avoid leaving your callers on hold for more than 30 seconds without checking back. The caller may choose to call back later. If the caller waits for you, apologize when you get back on the line. If you have to locate more information, offer to call people back immediately rather than have them wait.

Transfer Calls Effectively. Individuals sometimes are transferred from person to person, and they become annoyed! Several techniques show them you want to be helpful.

- Make sure the person to whom you transfer the call can give the information sought.
- Tell the caller you will transfer the call, but give your extension in case you get disconnected. Stay on the line to make sure the transfer went through.
- Consider the possibility of getting the information for the caller and then returning the call.

OUTGOING CALLS

One secret to successful telephone skills is planning. Plan what you hope to accomplish before placing the call. As the caller, guide the conversation to make sure you achieve your objective. Apply the rules that follow to place outgoing calls effectively.

Write Out Key Words or Phrases Before You Place the Call. Just as with written communication, you need to plan your call. Target the main points you want to emphasize and know how you will say them. Keep your call focused so you reach your desired outcome.

Identify Yourself Immediately. Open your call by stating your name and the reason for your call. Be courteous and establish a positive rapport. If you need to speak to someone other than the individual who answered, pause before asking for a specific person. If the person cannot take your call, repeat your name and number to ensure the person will be able to call you back.

Take Notes During the Call. While you converse with the individual, jot down the main points to keep a record of the call. Keeping notes allows you to follow-up on the telephone meeting with specific action.

Make Your Closing Positive. End your telephone call when you have achieved your objective. Be careful not to get drawn into an unproductive conversation. Take your time to say good-bye and do not hang up abruptly. Since you placed the call, you should end it. Be pleasant and thank the person for the time and information.

OTHER USEFUL TIPS

To enhance your image, you should return all telephone calls promptly. If you delay returning calls, individuals get the message that you do not care or do not want their business. No one should have to leave multiple messages before you return a call. If the caller doesn't answer when you call back, leave a voice message that you returned the call and suggest times when you can be reached.

The website *http://vm.cfsan.fda.gov/* provides a wealth of useful information such as airline toll-free numbers; residential and business telephone directories; AT&T 800 directory on the Web; area code lookup (United States); and city and zip code lookup (with geography information). To reach this information, click on the link entitled "Reference Shelf."

The general rule of thumb regarding answering your telephone has been to answer by the third ring. However, with today's voice mail messages, it often requires four or more rings for the system to respond. It seems designers have unwittingly rewritten the rules (not necessarily for the better), as your callers are still likely to be upset by long delays. If you can, try and adjust your voice mail system to let the telephone ring only three times before the message begins. Because some people still resent being relegated to voice mail, give callers the option of speaking to someone immediately.

Source: Chir Holin, "Mastering Business Etiquette and Protocol," *National Institute of Business Management,* Special Report N107A, Nolin, McLean, VA 2001.

As a manager, you may spend up to 70 percent of your time in communication activities. Therefore, you need an effective mechanism for reaching individuals. Voice mail may be the solution to the time-consuming inefficiencies of telephone tag.

Voice mail links a telephone system to a computer system that stores and digitizes incoming messages. Some systems allow you to reach any extensions by pushing specific buttons on a touch-tone telephone. Interactive systems allow you to receive verbal information from a computer database.

Today, voice mail has become an increasingly popular communication channel chosen by small and large firms alike for their internal office communication. Voice mail provides faster communication, extended office boundaries, and enhanced communication across time zones, and it saves money.[30] *Voice mail makes the business environment "radically different."*[31]

Voice mail allows messages to be stored. Incoming information can be delivered without interrupting potential receivers. Voice mail also allows you to call at any hour of the day, across any time zone.

Your greeting to voice mail callers should sound warm and friendly. Identify yourself and your company so your callers know they have reached the correct number. Thank callers for calling and tell them you cannot answer their call. Invite them to leave a message or to call back, and state when you might be available to talk. Make sure you test your message before setting it up to receive calls. Change your message frequently to show you listen to your messages.

When you reach an individual's voice mail, keep your message short. Briefly tell the person why you called and the action you want taken.

Voice mail can increase your time and abilities, but it can stretch people's patience if you do not use it correctly. Follow the tips in Box 11.9 to enhance your voice mail.

You can find additional helpful hints for preparing your messages for voice mail online at *http://www.ohms.com/guide.htm.*

Communication Breakdown

International Communications Research said men talk on their cell phones for an average of 455 minutes a month, while women talk slightly less, an average of 391 minutes a month.

Source: Kristi E. Swartx, "Men Average More Cell Phone Minutes, Study Shows," *The Palm Beach Post,* Florida. July 19, 2004.

[30] J. Mann, "The Business of Phone Tag," *Datamation* (International Edition), Volume 37, Issue 17, September 1, 1991, pp. 89–90.

[31] D. W. Straub, "Validating Instruments in MIS Research," *MIS Quarterly,* Volume 13, Issue 2, June 1989, pp. 147–170.

When leaving a message on voice mail:

Instead of saying, "Please call," leave a detailed, concise, and complete message.

Offer a convenient time for the person to call you back or state when you plan to call again.

When using your own voice mail:

Always provide an option to get out of voice mail and talk to a live person.

When you leave for lunch or an appointment, forward your calls directly to the telephone mail system so it will answer after only one ring.

Change your message when you go on vacation or plan to be away from your desk more than a few hours.

Let callers know when you will be back and whom else they can talk to in the meantime.

Call your own voice mail and listen to your greeting. Do you sound inviting or monotonous? Practice until your message sounds relaxed and comfortable.

Follow the "sundown rule." Whenever possible, return calls the same business day.

BOX 11.9 🖙 **Voice Mail Tips**

SOURCE: *California Banker,* First Interstate Bank of California, 633 W. Fifth St., Los Angeles, CA 90071.

Cellular telephones allow you to send and receive calls from anywhere.

"Sprint survey finds nearly two-thirds of Americans are uncomfortable overhearing wireless conversations in public." According to the Sprint survey (Sprint calls it the "2004 Sprint Wireless Courtesy Report"), 73 percent of the 723 U.S. adults surveyed said people are less courteous in general today than five years ago, while 80 percent said they felt people were less courteous when using a wireless phone today than five years ago. But like the AT&T Wireless survey, 97 percent said they classified themselves as "very courteous" or "somewhat courteous" in their use of a cell phone.

Source: Keith Shaw, "Got Any Rude Cell Phone User Stories?" *Network World Wireless Computing Devices Newsletter,* July 13, 2004. Retrieved from: *http://www.nwfusion.com/ newsletters/mobile/2004/ 0712mobile1.html.*

Cellular Telephones

Cellular telephones have become an accepted part of our personal and business lives, as they allow individuals to place and receive calls from anywhere. In fact, in many countries, cellular telephones are more popular than traditional land-line telephones.

Cellular telephones continue to grow smaller and lighter. For example, the Motorola v3668 weighs in at 83 grams and compares in size to a candy bar. Being small does not limit the features of this telephone, however, as it includes dual band, 9,600 bps data transmission, as well as standard features such as integrated paging, caller ID, and data connectivity.[32]

In addition, as digital technology has replaced analog, cellular calls now have better quality. Therefore, most subscribers have switched to digital cell phones.

Siemens Mobile conducted a survey on consumer likes and dislikes concerning cellular telephones. An overwhelming 85 percent of respondents admitted that mobile phones were a necessity to their lifestyles, while 57 percent stated that they call their family first, with work and friends second and third (22 percent and 21 percent). Eighty-five percent of the respondents stated that it was unacceptable to leave your telephone on in meetings and during appointments, and that people should not use them in elevators or on busses or trains, especially if they talk loudly. Seventy-five percent thought the telephone should never be turned on at the movies, theaters, or sporting events, and 5 percent thought people should leave their telephones at home during a date. Sixty percent shared they would pull over to answer the telephone rather than talk and drive. Other questions asked the

[32] Christy Hong, "The New Motorola V-Series: Small in Size, Big on Features," *PhoneChoice,* September 4, 1999. Retrieved January 23, 2000, from *http:www.phonechoice.com.au/.*

respondents about features of the cellular telephone. Sixty percent believed that storage and talk time were the most important and that bad reception and drop-out were the most annoying aspects of using a cellular telephone.[33]

Cellular telephones still cost more to use than traditional telephones, but these costs are plummeting. However, keep in mind that whether you place the call or receive it, you will be charged for each minute you talk.

Mr. Jormalainen of Nokia has stated: "The development of multimedia applications for digital phones will culminate in them being used widely for electronic commerce, navigation services and tourist guides, the transport of electronic postcards and the receipts of news services."[34]

Cellular telephones have certainly influenced the way we do business. Whether you use a cellular telephone or the tried-and-true land-line, you should plan your conversation, say it, and close promptly.[35]

Judith Martin has spent almost 25 years writing etiquette columns under the pen name "Miss Manners." According to Miss Manners, you should be aware that cell phones can bleed across the open airwares. Therefore, you should keep your conversations clear, concise, and professional, as you never know who might be able to listen to your conversation. In addition, Miss Manners states that it is rude to carry on a lengthy phone conversation when in someone's company regardless of whether it is a business or social situation. She goes on to say that you can forget about securing employment if you get and answer a call during the interview. The quickest way to alienate yourself is to put the interviewer "on hold" while you "take a call" in the middle of answering the question, "What can you tell me about yourself?" Your actions may well tell the interviewer more than you intend![36]

According to Jacqueline Whitmore, one of the nation's foremost experts on etiquette and protocol, when using your wireless phone you should take these steps to avoid offending others:

- Let your voice mail take your calls when you're in meetings, courtrooms, restaurants, and other busy areas. If you must speak to the caller, excuse yourself and find a secluded area where you can talk.

- Speak in your regular conversational tone. People tend to speak more loudly than normal on a wireless phone and often don't recognize how distracting they can be to others.

- Do not display anger during a public call. Conversations that are likely to be emotional should be held where they will not embarrass or intrude on others.

- Set the ringer on vibrate or turn off your phone in public places such as movie theaters, religious services, restaurants, and so on. Many wireless phones now have environmental settings that automatically adjust the phone and its features so you do not disrupt your surroundings.

- If you are expecting a call that cannot be postponed, alert your companions in advance and excuse yourself when the call comes in; the people you are with should take precedence over calls you want to make or receive.

- Avoid interrupting meetings, social gatherings, or personal conversations by answering your wireless phone or checking your voice mail. Discreetly excuse yourself if you must take the call.

[33] Judy Davie, "Mobile Mania—A Life Necessity or Pain in the ≡?" *PhoneChoice,* March 3, 1999. Retrieved January 23, 2000, from *http:www.phonechoice.com.au/.*

[34] Judy Davie, "Video Mobiles from Nokia," *PhoneChoice,* September 15, 1998. Retrieved January 23, 2000, from *http:www.phonechoice.com.au/.*

[35] "Talk Is Cheaper," *Fortune 1 Technology Buyer's Guide Supplement,* Winter 1996, pp. 128–134.

[36] "Business Etiquette," *A & S Career Programs.* The University of Akron, Butchel College of Arts and Sciences. Retrieved from *http://www.wzip.uakron.edu/ascareer/businessetiquette.html.*

- Use discretion when discussing private matters or certain business topics in front of others. You never know who is within hearing range.

- Practice wireless responsibility while you are driving. Place calls when your vehicle is not moving. Don't make or answer calls while in heavy traffic or in hazardous driving conditions. Use a hands-free device to help focus attention on safety. Always make safety your most important call.[37]

Speakerphones

If you have a speakerphone, use it only when necessary; that is, if more than one person must hear the conversation. Otherwise, using it may give the caller the impression that you are not listening, but doing something else. Sometimes background noise on a speakerphone can make it difficult for your caller to hear you well.

Kristin Anderson, who provides telephone etiquette training, has stated you should keep the following tips in mind when using a speakerphone:

- Consider the people around you. Speakerphones can be loud. If you are talking into yours from across the office, you may be loud, too. So make sure you shut your door (if you have one) and are sensitive to the needs of those who have offices around you.

- Always advise a caller when you are placing him or her on a speakerphone or using a recording device.

- Indicate whether others will be listening in on the conversation. And if so, introduce that person at the start—even if he or she won't be taking an active role in the discussion.

- Some callers are uncomfortable with the sound quality of speakerphones. Before using it, ask the caller if he or she minds.[38]

Choosing Between the Telephone and E-Mail

Sometimes you must choose whether to send an e-mail message or to pick up the telephone. Because the telephone provides a voice, most individuals perceive it to be more personal and to provide more give and take in a negotiation situation. However, more and more negotiations are taking place over e-mail rather than over the telephone or in personal meetings. It seems that with e-mail, negotiations often degenerate into an unpleasant exchange. According to Kathleen Valley, when the interaction is purely electronic, people are more willing to escalate conflict and get downright rude. She states further that the e-mail dynamic makes it much more difficult to reach an agreement. In a recent study comparing e-mail, telephone, and face-to-face negotiations, she found that when people meet face-to-face, the most frequent outcome is a mutually beneficial agreement. When people talk over the telephone, the most frequent

[37] Jacqueline Whitmore, "Learn About Wireless Etiquette" *Consumer Tips*. Retrieved from *http://www2.sprint.com/as_scope/values/consumer_info/topics.do?topic=1111617*.

[38] Kristin Anderson, "Speakerphones and Recording Devices," *E-mail Etiquette*. Retrieved from *http://web.csuchico.edu/~ar68/web.htm*, p. 14.

outcome is that one party takes the greater share of the profits. With e-mail, the most common outcome is impasse. She found that more than 50 percent of e-mail negotiations end in impasse; only 19 percent end that way in face-to-face negotiations.[39]

However, the reality is that more and more negotiations will occur electronically, because it can be much more efficient; individuals do not have to travel, organize meetings, or play telephone tag. So how can you make your negotiations effective? First, establish a rapport with the other person. Try to meet with the individual face-to-face or at least talk with the individual over the telephone. If you must negotiate strictly by e-mail, spend some time in social information exchange to get to know the other individual. As you negotiate, watch for signs of an impasse. If you ask a question and get a response that seems defensive, do not respond back defensively. Try not to get personal or angry; focus on information or facts.

In his article, "Getting More Mileage from E-Mail," Frank Grazian shared that he and a colleague sent each other six e-mail messages trying to solve a problem, and that one five-minute telephone call cleared it up.[40]

This illustrates that sometimes you should choose to use the telephone instead of e-mail. After your telephone discussion, you can follow-up with an e-mail message to confirm your understanding of the conversation. To make sure your next telephone call is successful, review the checklist in Box 11.10 before making that call.

Pagers

For many of you, pagers are a part of your life. These little devices allow companies to stay in contact during and after business hours as well as inside and outside of the organization. They seem to have experienced a rebirth with the addition of text and two-way paging.

Two BellSouth employees, Matthew Barnett and Foster Halley, offer the following advice when using pagers. First, when sending messages, make sure your message is clear and concise as tone and sarcasm can be lost in text messaging. When waiting for a response, you should be patient if you do not get an immediate response, as the other person could be driving down the highway or fighting another battle. Foster and Matthew have stated that some basic etiquette principles apply to pagers, such as never sending anything you would not say in person and not paging when you are talking with another individual to show respect to the person who is physically present. They recommend if you must respond or send a page that you obtain the permission of the individual you are speaking with to do so. If you find you must reply to a page, you should excuse yourself so as not to ignore the other person or persons to type in a message. Typically, during meetings, you should wait to reply or remove yourself from the meeting if the situation requires your immediate attention. However, on some occasions, you might find it necessary to use your pager during the meeting to get an immediate answer to a question. For example, a question may arise that you did not know would be asked, so using your pager can allow you to send a message, receive an answer, and provide that answer during the meeting and thus save time for everyone. Finally, Matthew and Foster recommend that you "mute" your pager during meetings. Pagers are usually equipped with a number of alerting signals and a vibrating mechanism. You should use the less-disruptive vibration option or mute when in a meeting or any other well-populated place.

---

[39] Kathleen Valley, "The Electronic Negotiator," *Harvard Business Review,* Reprint F00103.

[40] Frank Grazian, "Getting More Mileage from E-Mail," *Public Relations Quarterly,* Volume 41, Issue 4 Winter 1996–1997, pp. 40–41.

You do not have a choice whether you will make an impression. Why not make it a winning one?

How to Be More Professional on the Telephone

When Your Telephone Rings:

Answer promptly.	Give callers your immediate attention by responding after the first ring, if possible.
Identify yourself.	Let the caller know your name.
Offer a pleasant greeting.	Open a conversation by saying, "Jim Robert's office, may I help you?" Show that you intend to be courteous.
Treat every call as important.	Never treat a call as routine. Building confidence in you and your organization starts with showing personal consideration for the caller. Focus on the caller's needs and wants.
Be an active listener.	Give the caller your undivided attention. Never make callers think they are in competition with someone in your office.
Use common courtesy words.	*Please, thank you,* and *you're welcome* powerfully communicate a positive attitude and build a reputation for you and your organization.
Use the caller's name.	People like to hear the sound of their names.
Take time for a proper ending.	Know when and how to end the conversation to create a win–win situation.

When the Caller Needs Information:

Be helpful.	Offer what information you can. If you leave the line to obtain information, explain what you intend to do, and ask, "Will you wait?" or, "When should I call you back?"
Never leave a caller hanging.	If the caller chooses to stay on the line, use the hold button if your telephone has one, or lay the handset down quietly. Give progress reports every 30 seconds or so to assure the caller you are working on the request. Leaving people on hold offends them.
Be tactful.	If the caller must be refused the requested information because of organizational policy, give a straightforward and sympathetic explanation. Say, "If you'll come in, we'll be happy to check for you," rather than, "You'll have to come in."
Thank the caller for waiting.	Show your appreciation for the caller's patience. Saying "Thank you for waiting" helps you *smile* over the telephone.

BOX 11.10 ☛ **Enhancing Your Image**

When You Must Transfer a Call:

Transfer calls only when necessary.	Handle the call yourself if you can.
Explain yourself.	When you need to transfer an incoming call, say politely, "Will you hold the line, please? I'll transfer you to Dick Green." Stay with the caller until you complete the transfer.
Check your instructions.	If the caller agrees to be transferred, make certain you know how to complete the transfer successfully. If in doubt, check your organization's telephone manual, guide, or directory.

When Answering for Someone Else:

Always identify yourself.	For example, say, "Jane Irwin's office." Never use the words *line* or *desk*. Tell the caller when you expect your coworker to return, or whether the person can be reached elsewhere.
Be discreet.	You can create the wrong impression with the statement, "He's still on his coffee break," or "I don't think she has come in yet." Instead, say, "May I take a message and have Mr. Jones return your call?"

When You Take a Message:

Be prepared.	Any telephone you answer should have beside it a pad of paper or telephone message forms and a pencil or pen.
Be thorough.	When you take a message, be certain to include:

1. The caller's name (do not hesitate to ask the individual to spell it).
2. The caller's telephone number (include the area code if different from your own, and repeat the number to the caller).
3. The caller's firm or department.
4. Date and time the message was taken.
5. A message, if the caller chooses to leave one.
6. Your name or initials.

BOX 11.10 ☞ **(continued)**

Miss Manners states that if you are "on call" after official office hours, you should take precautionary measures when attending public functions and know how to exit in the least disruptive way. In addition, she states you should inform any host or hostess if you think you might have to leave early to attend to business.[41]

Robert Weiss, Sales Manager for American Paging of Minnesota, offers these tips for effective pager use:

☞ If a pager is being used for emergencies only, define what an emergency is and do not use the number for nonemergency situations.

[41] Eve Tushnet, "Miss Manners and the Language of Tradition," *Jewish World Review,* December 4, 2002, 29 Kisleve, 5763. Retrieved from *http://www.jewishworldreview.com/1202/tushnet120402.asp.*

- If you have a pager, carry it with you at all times. Pagers cannot connect you when they are left on your car visor or on top of your dresser.

- Wear or carry your pager as intended, usually on a belt or attached to a purse. Pagers get lost or are easily stolen when people do not attach them as recommended.

- Let the people who will be calling you on your pager know how long it usually takes you to return a call. This is professional and courteous, and it will help eliminate unnecessary duplicate pages.

- Before you give a pager number, explain the type of message the pager will accept. Different types of pagers can take different types of messages. Some only allow you to send a phone number. Others will accept a voice message. The newest pagers will accept a text message that is transmitted by the sender.

- Check for messages frequently.

- Do not leave confidential information on voice pages.

- Always leave adequate callback information including your area code and extension.[42]

Personal Digital Assistants or Palm Pilots

Handheld computers have become increasingly more popular. These small computers allow you to synchronize your key organizational elements with your desktop computer, and make your address book, your calendar, and your to-do list portable. Today, most of these devices also allow you to send and receive e-mail. Some basic rules of etiquette include:

- Make sure not to bring up games or e-mail during meetings or conferences.

- Try not to get distracted by organizing your palm pilot or playing with its features.

- If you need to exchange data with a coworker using your palm pilot, do it before or after the meeting. Even if the data pertains to the information in the meeting, exchanging data could cause a distraction and appear rude.[43]

Fax Machines

Fax machines provide the easiest and quickest way to send a document that exists only in hard-copy form.

SOURCE: Corbis/Stock Market/ Jon Feingersh.

Faxing remains a popular means of communication and has kept up with the changes in the technological world by merging old-style fax-to-fax with e-mail. Today you can find a fax number printed on virtually every business card and letterhead. The practical side of the fax machine makes it a viable communication medium. Doing business over the Internet is a growing trend, but when it comes to transmitting printed forms and signed documents, the fax remains the technology of choice. The fax also provides an easy and quick way to transmit a document existing only in hard-copy form or that isn't in your system.

An advantage of faxing is that you know your receiver received the fax because you receive a confirmation. Remember that faxed messages usually do not carry

---

[42] "Pagers and Beepers," *E-mail Etiquette*. Retrieved from *http://web.csuchico.edu/~ar68/web.htm*, pp. 15–16.

[43] "Pagers and Beepers," *E-mail Etiquette*. Retrieved from *http://web.csuchico.edu/~ar68/web.htm*, pp. 15–16.

the expectation of a quick response, unless you notify the receiver up front. For example, you may be asking for a signature or completion of a form with a deadline.[44]

According to Miss Manners, a faxed letter is slightly more formal than an e-mail, but is still not as official as an engraved or hand written message or those typed on company letterhead. In business, letters and other miscellaneous information are generally faxed because of expediency. She states that you should make sure the information you are sending is truly sought by the addressee before sending it. You can use the smaller Fax Note cover post-its if you have just had a telephone or personal conversation regarding a specific transmission and really do not need to attach a detailed explanation. Be sure that you verify the fax number, as you're defeating expediencey if your message doesn't reach the right individual.[45]

Relay broadcasting lets you send a fax to another fax machine, which broadcasts multiple copies. For example, if you wanted to send a fax to different cities in another country, you could send one international fax to the relay broadcast facility. Then that facility would transmit your document to the other cities at the local rate, thus saving you time and money.

Network faxing has become increasingly popular and allows employees to send and receive faxes from their desktops. You can choose to route the fax to a particular desktop or straight to a fax machine, where it will be printed in hard copy. Brother, one manufacturer of fax machines, found that 90 percent of users still prefer to have a hard copy.[46]

Some new fax machines now include built-in speakerphones and digital answering systems for offices that want to use a single line for voice and fax. If a call comes in while you are away from your desk, the machine automatically senses whether the caller is a human or a fax machine and then switches to the appropriate receiving mode.[47]

Eventually, Internet technology will totally replace faxes. But that won't happen, analysts say, until online authentication and authorization technologies such as digital certificates are developed for widespread, low-cost use as legal verification of the sender's identity. For now, "Fax is still the only way to transmit legal documents with signatures," says Sean Ford, a product manager for Softlinx.[48]

Techno-Etiquette

In this information age, you rely on technology to communicate. This reliance brings a new battery of challenges. One of the most notable challenges is determining what is proper techno-etiquette. We know the rules for some communication situations. For example, we would not send a letter with misspelled words, or clutter conversations or memos with rambling verbiage or tasteless jokes. We use tact with confronting individuals face-to-face. Yet when it comes to technological communication, we tend to overlook otherwise unacceptable and unprofessional behaviors. In a 1999 survey of 1,281 business professionals across the United States conducted by ETICON, Inc., etiquette consultants for business, 80 percent of respondents reported an increase in rudeness in business and 62 percent felt they experienced telephone rudeness through long, abrupt holds, unreturned telephone calls, and voice mail mazes.[49]

---

[44] Cyndi Maxey, "Your Telecommunication Image." Retrieved from *http://www.bremercommunications.com.*

[45] Judith Martin, *Miss Manners' Basic Training: Communication,* (New York: Crown Publishers, Inc., 1997).

[46] Beth Corning, "Be Aware of the Fax," *Accountancy,* Volume 123, Issue 1270, June 1999, p. 50.

[47] Susan Breidenbach, "The Faithful Fax," *Forbes,* Fall 1998, pp. 50–51.

[48] Aisha N. Williams, "The Fax Advantage," *Informationweek,* Volume 694, August 3, 1998, pp. 65–66.

[49] "What Are the Costs of Rudeness to Business?" Retrieved from *http://www.eticon.com/statistics.html.*

It seems more rude behavior is being exhibited today, and with the growing concern comes hope for heightened awareness of all users of technologies. Emily Post and others have published articles and dedicated websites in a valiant attempt to form a specific set of etiquette guidelines.

According to Lorraine Behnan, a communications consultant and speaker, the fallout from the abuse and misuse of telephones, voice messages, and faxes is causing high levels of frustration and stress in the workplace. Therefore, to maintain a positive working environment, you should avoid making these mistakes:

- Calling or faxing after hours on purpose to avoid personal contact.
- Leaving long-winded rambling messages with irrelevant information.
- Using voice messages that have "funky" background music or little ditties chirped by pet canaries.
- Using a voice message that does not include the date or accessibility of the person you are trying to contact. The recording, however, does not have to include a minute-to-minute action plan.
- Leaving unclear messages that do not include your name, number, and the nature of your message. If you have a unique name, spell it. Be considerate and always leave your number. This small gesture will be greatly appreciated by the listener.
- Having illegible or poor handwriting and spacing on faxes.
- Sending personal faxes without notice, thus putting your most intimate details out for the viewing pleasure of the whole office.
- Sending lengthy faxes during peak hours.
- Sending unsolicited faxes. Even if you consider it important, the fact that it arrived unannounced may irritate the recipient. Call ahead, and ask if you may send the fax.
- Making sure if you send confidential information by fax, have the recipient waiting at the machine.
- Remembering to not use fax machines for communications such as invitations, thank-you notes, and so forth.[50]

Conclusion

Technology has transformed the way we do business. However, the future of communication depends on the continued development of an organization's most valuable resource—its people. In today's world of work, you will deliver your messages to increasingly splintered and diverse audiences. You live in an environment in which signals bounce off satellites around the world. As a communicator, you need to be careful not to let the technology take over and become the end rather than the means. You should know that it is predicted that by the year 2010, face-to-face interaction in business may be largely unnecessary.[51]

The ability to see each other through our telephones and send documents from anywhere could easily render face-to-face meetings and business travel unnecessary. However, there are still times when the newest technology may not be the best means

---

[50] Lorraine Benham, "Are You Techno Etiquette Impaired?" Retrieved from *http://www.lorrainebenham.com/technet.html.*

[51] Christopher Bunting, "International Communication toward 2010," *Communication World,* Volume 11, Issue 1, January/February 1994, pp. 44–45.

of communication due to the complexity of a question or the need to meet for face-to-face to dialogue. Sometimes, you just have to pick up the telephone, call a meeting, or talk to someone in person. As an effective communicator, you will learn the art of recognizing those times. Knowing when to communicate using technology and when to communicate in person can save you time and make you more productive. So even when e-mail is the most expedient way of communicating, don't be afraid to pick up the telephone if a specific task can be handled more effectively in that manner. Although technology continues to change, people will determine the future. The written word, judgment, and common sense will never be replaced by hardware.

Exercises

EXERCISE 1   KEEPING A DIARY

Directions: For one week, keep a pad and pencil next to your telephone. Keep track of your successes and failures as you try to incorporate all the rules for effective telephone communication into your phone technique.

EXERCISE 2   WORKING DEFINITION OF TELECOMMUNICATIONS

Directions: Obtain definitions of *telecommunications* from four or more current newspaper or magazine articles. Develop your own definition of telecommunications from your research and bring it to class. Attach copies of the articles to your definition.

EXERCISE 3   ONLINE DISCUSSION

Directions: In your team's chat room, discuss this topic:
A human being and an E-rater, an electronic robot, are now scoring the Graduate Management Admissions Test. Until now, two experts have graded each essay. If scores differed by more than a point, a third reviewer was assigned to determine a final score. Now the E-rater will serve as the second reader. If the electronic score differs from the human reviewer's score by more than a point, a second expert will judge the essay. Critics argue that a computer cannot judge creativity, but supporters claim that a computer can evaluate the true measurements of a well-written essay: structure and the organization of ideas. What do you think? Should computers grade business letters, memos, or reports?

SOURCE: William H. Honen, "High Tech Comes to the Classroom: Machines That Grade Essays," *New York Times,* 27, January 1999, p. A22.

EXERCISE 4   MEETING QUESTIONNAIRE

Directions: Think about the last meeting you attended as you answer the following questions.

Yes No

❏   ❏   Did the meeting start on time?

❏   ❏   Did everyone know specifically what was to be accomplished in the meeting?

❏   ❏   Were the right people, rather than extraneous people, invited?

❏	❏	Was there a timed agenda?
❏	❏	Did the meeting stay on track?
❏	❏	Did the participants make concise reports?
❏	❏	Did they get buy-in for their ideas?
❏	❏	Were visuals used effectively in the meeting?
❏	❏	Did the meeting end on time?
❏	❏	Did the group leave with a sense of purpose and a clear understanding of their responsibilities?

Scoring: Score one point for each yes answer and two points for each no.

_____ + _____ = Total

Be a perfect 10. If your meeting rates 13 or above, you may be spending unprofitable time and not getting the results you want to achieve.

SOURCE: Spring Asher and Wicke Chamber, *Wooing and Winning Business* (New York: John Wiley & Sons, Inc., 1997) p. 193.

EXERCISE 5   BRAINSTORMING SESSION

Directions: During an in-class team meeting, apply brainstorming to a problem your team faces that calls for creativity.

Assignment Options

OPTION 1: MEMO REPORT

Using the information from the diary you compiled in Exercise 1, write a memo to your instructor detailing your communication strengths, areas needing improvement, and goals you will set to improve your telephone communications.

OPTION 2: TOPIC PRESENTATION ABOUT ORGANIZATIONAL COMMUNICATION TECHNOLOGY

Prepare and deliver an oral presentation discussing a current article related to some aspect of organizational communication technology. The minimum requirements for the oral presentation are:

1. A length of at least 10 minutes, but not more than 20 minutes.
2. A minimum of one visual aid.
3. *No reading:* People do not enjoy or glean information from a presentation that is read to them.
4. An outline of your presentation submitted to the instructor before beginning your presentation.
5. Critiquing by yourself, your peers, and your instructor.
6. One blank videotape brought to class on the day of your presentation.

OPTION 3: COMPANY VISIT AND RECOMMENDATION REPORT

Assess the telecommunication capabilities of a local business. Choose an organization employing at least 200 individuals. Contact the company, visit the company, take pictures of the technology in place, and interview personnel about their systems. Following your interviews, write a thank-you letter and submit a copy of that letter for evaluation.

Using the information you acquired on your visits, write a recommendation report. Describe the technology in use, discuss whether you feel the technology meets the company's needs, and offer any recommendations for change. Your report should include an introduction, a body, and a conclusion.

Please use the following headings for your report:

Introduction and Background

In this section, introduce your reader to the company. Provide some historical background as well as current information. Specific company information should include the name of the company, location, and description of business (including product or services provided, company size, organizational structure, organizational mission, and other similar information). Also, include the names, titles, and telephone numbers of the individuals you interviewed. Following the background information, state the purpose of your report and provide transition to the rest of your report.

Body

Within each section of the body, provide an overview of the company's telecommunications system. Discuss advantages as well as perceived problems with the company's present telecommunications system. Offer suggestions as to what could be done to improve the telecommunications system. Be sure to address the questions you asked in the interviews.

Use the Following Actual Headings Within the Body of Your Report:

> Long-distance carriers
>
> Teleconferencing
>
> Facsimiles
>
> Mobile communications
>
> Computer system and networks
>
> Electronic mail
>
> Voice processing
>
> Videotext and teletext
>
> Teleconferences
>
> Multimedia
>
> Other applications of technology

Conclusion

Do not confuse a conclusion with a summary. A conclusion requires you to draw an inference from conducting your research.

OPTION 4: VISIT TO LOCAL POLICE OR FIRE DEPARTMENT

Visit your local police or fire department to find out what kind of 911 emergency services they use and the features offered by these services. What kind of equipment do they use? Does the equipment connect to the central office switch? What geographical areas do the services cover? How much do the services cost? How helpful have the services been? Do the services have any limitations? Prepare a one- to two-page memo of your findings for the instructor.

OPTION 5: WEEKLY PROGRESS REPORT

Provide a weekly e-mail report to your professor informing him or her of concepts you have learned from this chapter.

OPTION 6: GROUP MEETING PROJECT

To provide you exposure to the process of planning, conducting, and following up on a meeting, your group will be given responsibility for such an event.

As a group, you will experience the entire process, including leading meetings, recording meetings, brainstorming for possible topics, developing a needs assessment, planning a team oral presentation meeting, making the presentation, and following up on your presentation through a written assessment.

The following section explains some general guidelines regarding certain aspects of the project. Then, more specific step-by-step directions will guide you through the various stages of the process.

Each member of your group should chair and record at least one meeting. Some of you naturally enjoy leading; you like being in charge. Others have never had the opportunity to experience leadership. By enforcing this rule, you will have the opportunity to play both a task and a maintenance role. After each member has chaired and recorded one meeting, your team can organize any additional meetings.

Group Leader's Duties

When you lead, you will:

> Develop an agenda and decide who should attend.
>
> Determine when and where the meeting should be held.
>
> Decide the purpose of the meeting.

Then you will need to ask yourself some questions:

> Does the proposed meeting date allow ample time for group members and the group leader to prepare for the meeting?
>
> Did I choose a properly equipped and furnished meeting room?
>
> What materials, other than the agenda, do group members need to review before the meeting?
>
> What meeting procedures should be followed?
>
> What questions should be asked to maximize the group members' participation?
>
> How can group members' similarities and points of agreement be emphasized?
>
> How can a group decision be reached without forcing conformity?

Distribute your agenda at least two days before your meeting. Make sure you submit a copy to the professor.

During the meeting, make sure you facilitate as well as lead. Then, before adjourning your meeting, recap major discussion points and assist the group in reaching a decision on debated issues. Check to make sure people have completed the tasks they said they would do.

Following your meeting, ask the group to examine its proceedings and evaluate how effective the meeting was. Such evaluation can be done after the meeting by asking the participants to take a moment to express their thoughts on the evaluation form and discuss briefly how well they thought the meeting went. Following this discussion, the leader will collect the evaluation forms and use the feedback to prepare a self-evaluation memo of his or her effectiveness. Please attach your self-evaluation memo and your peers' evaluation forms.

Group Recorder's Actions

Actions of the meeting should be reported to those who need to be advised. The recorder should prepare a copy of the minutes for each meeting participant and for the professor.

Group Members' Responsibilities

Before coming to a meeting, you should ask yourself several important questions, such as:

What should be the purposes and objectives of this meeting?

What can I learn from this meeting?

What questions should I ask during the meeting?

What can I contribute to this meeting?

What do I need to do to prepare for this meeting?

After a meeting has ended, you should complete any meeting-related assignments and evaluate your performance as a group member.

Steps Involved in Meeting Project

This section gives you step-by-step directions regarding the different phases of the group project. These steps will help you organize your group more effectively.

STEP ONE

At your first organizational meeting, your group should establish a schedule of leaders and recorders. The leader sets the agenda, makes sure all members know about the meeting, and leads the discussion. The recorder takes minutes and keeps track of who does what.

STEP TWO

At one of your beginning meetings, brainstorm for possible communication topics for your group project. Try to come up with two or three different possibilities. Search the Internet for topics that might interest your fellow classmates.

STEP THREE

In another meeting, develop a needs assessment of your audience. A needs assessment identifies topics or issues needing to be addressed in an organization. Try to get as many views as feasible within the constraints of time, money, and the scope of the problem. A variety of methods can be used to do a needs assessment and each method has its own impact on different groups. Methods must be chosen based on what will be most effective for each group. Key ways to conduct a needs assessment include questionnaires, interviews, polls, discussions, and observations.

Schedule a time with the instructor to administer your needs assessment to the class.

STEP FOUR

Your group will formulate a proposal to submit to the professor. Your proposal should follow the guidelines presented in Chapter 7.

STEP FIVE

This step involves planning your team presentation. Begin by developing a clear written statement of the purpose of your meetings. Some additional questions you should ask include:

Why do participants need to be here?

What exactly will be completed by the end?

How will we go about accomplishing our task?

What specific activities will best achieve our purposes?

What objectives will be accomplished?

What outcomes should emerge?

What should the people be told?

When and where will the meeting be held? (Consider convenience and suitability. Did you choose a room large enough for the number of participants selected, along with the necessary tables, chairs, and audiovisual equipment required? Other factors to consider include noise level outside the room, physical appearance, and control over temperature.)

How much time will the presentation take?

What materials, equipment, refreshments, and room layout will be required?

- Notepads and pencils for each participant?
- Name or place cards?
- Handouts?
- Flip charts?
- Overhead projector?
- Proxima or lite pro?
- Slide projector?
- VCR?
- Lectern for speakers?
- Refreshments?
- Water and glasses?
- How should we lay out the room?

STEP SIX

Your group will have complete control in conducting your presentation. Some questions to ask include:

Have you placed all materials within easy reach? Did you arrange them in the order they will be used?

Did you check to make sure the written materials are clearly copied and have no distracting typographical errors?

Will we start on time?

Will we end on time?

What will we say when we begin?

How will we establish the right tone?

Should we review the objectives?

How will we get people to participate?

How will we signal the completion of the presentation?

STEP SEVEN

After your team's presentation, write a memo report addressing the following questions about the presentation and project:

Was the presentation what you hoped it would be?

What verbal and nonverbal reactions did the group have? Were they consistent or did nonverbal actions seem to imply underlying problems or disagreements not voiced?

How could your presentation, selection of audiovisual materials, or general management of the group have been improved? What would you do differently next time?

What did you learn from this project?

What could be done to make this assignment more beneficial for future students?

CONDUCTING PRODUCTIVE MEETINGS EVALUATION FORM

(Make copies for your peers.)

Leader's Name

Rate all the items using the following scale:

0	1	2	3	4
Absolutely Not	No	Unsure	Yes	Definitely Yes

1. The purpose of meeting was apparent.	0 1 2 3 4
2. The participants seemed to know what was expected of them.	0 1 2 3 4
3. The participants did not argue with each other.	0 1 2 3 4
4. The participants seemed to express their real thoughts and feelings.	0 1 2 3 4
5. The leader provided all roles, such as initiating, orienting, clarifying, informing, coordinating, and summarizing. If the leader lacked any role, which one?	0 1 2 3 4
6. The location of the meeting was appropriate.	0 1 2 3 4
7. The agenda was complete and effective.	0 1 2 3 4
8. The leader established a friendly atmosphere.	0 1 2 3 4
9. The leader started on time.	0 1 2 3 4
10. The leader opened the meeting with an attention-getter, then brought everyone up-to-date.	0 1 2 3 4
11. The leader introduced the current topic, stated the purpose of the meeting, and established a method for attacking the problem.	0 1 2 3 4
12. The leader involved members of the group in the discussions.	0 1 2 3 4
13. The leader promoted an open atmosphere.	0 1 2 3 4
14. The leader tested possible solutions and avoided turning down ideas solely on the basis of past experience.	0 1 2 3 4
15. The leader kept the group aware they were making progress and worked for consensus.	0 1 2 3 4
16. The leader used questions to open discussions.	0 1 2 3 4
17. The leader helped clarify thinking, reach agreements, spark the nonparticipants, and guide the course of discussion.	0 1 2 3 4

18. The leader listened actively and remained objective.	0	1	2	3	4
19. The leader avoided evaluating and listened for what was not said.	0	1	2	3	4
20. The leader concluded the meeting on time.	0	1	2	3	4
21. The leader reviewed the problem and summarized the progress.	0	1	2	3	4
22. The leader emphasized major agreements.	0	1	2	3	4
23. The leader asked for any questions.	0	1	2	3	4
24. The leader clarified follow-up duties.	0	1	2	3	4
25. The leader used the meeting time wisely.	0	1	2	3	4

Total Points Earned _____

CHAPTER 12

Searching for Your Career

LEARNING OBJECTIVES

After reading this chapter, you should be able to:

- Understand the importance of knowing yourself.

- List the steps for knowing yourself.

- Compare and contrast interpersonal skills and technical skills.

- Define networking.

- State where to obtain company information.

- Describe an informational interview.

- Detail the way to conduct an informational interview.

- Develop your job search plan.

- Use websites for career guidance.

Each year millions of people graduate from colleges and universities, and you will soon join them. As you graduate, you should have the following:

- A specific career objective or job target. This requires that you know youself.

- A clear understanding of your profession and the options within it that are available to you. This involves knowing the job market.

- A comprehensive job search plan. This requires that you know the employment process.

The Importance of Knowing Yourself

To develop a specific career objective or job target, you must first know yourself. As can be seen from Box 12.1, the better you know yourself, the better chances you have of finding the right job. Knowing yourself involves defining who you are and what is important to you. It begins by assessing your vision, values, skills, qualities, and interests. Doing so helps to establish what functional role you desire and what level of responsibility may interest you. This step also helps you understand the relationship between work and personal satisfaction.

To help you analyze your personality and personal attitudes, visit *http://www.keirsey.com* and complete the online assessment. It will give you immediate feedback.

The Keirsey website provides information about your preferences and tendencies in relation to where you get your energy, how you gather information, how you make decisions, and how you take actions. The website provides detailed descriptions of four temperaments. Knowing your preferences and tendencies will allow you to match your personality to a particular occupation.

You will likely succeed in a job you truly enjoy. James M. Citrin and Richard A. Smith propose in their book, *The 5 Patterns of Extraordinary Careers,* that an extraordinary career is not about getting top dollar for a top position. They say extraordinary career success requires that individuals play to their strengths, set their passions free, and fit into their work culture naturally and comfortably.[2]

To find your ideal job, you must ask yourself, "What kind of job will I enjoy?" To help you answer that question, complete the following steps honestly and keep in mind that your assessment should be expressed in job-related terms. Later, when you begin to develop your résumé, you may refer to some of these questions. As you

---

Sticking with It!
Jobs last an average of 4.2 years.
2 of 14 workers are basically unemployed.
6 of the 14 are employed, but worried about losing their jobs.
1 of 12 employed voluntarily changes careers.

*The better you know your talents, gifts, and skills, and in priority,
the better your chances of finding a job!*

BOX 12.1 **Importance of Knowing Yourself**

SOURCE: Richard Nelson Bolles, *What Color Is Your Parachute?* (Berkeley, CA: Ten Speed Press, 1995), p. xi. Retrieved from *http://www.career-intelligence.com.*

---

[2] James M. Citrin and Richard A. Smith, *The 5 Patterns of Extraordinary Careers* (New York: Crown Business, 2003), pp. 148–149.

answer the following questions, be imaginative, farsighted, and realistic—and don't sell yourself short.

Take stock of your underlying personal qualities and attributes to help determine your level of effectiveness, your job satisfaction, and your ultimate value in the job market.

These steps start with generalities about yourself and then let you narrow your focus to more specific functional areas. As you begin to focus on the specifics, give examples as evidence of your positive qualities and state how they can be used effectively in the workplace. Interviewers want to glean specific information about you, not generalizations such as, "I am well organized and good with people."

STEP ONE: IDENTIFY YOUR GENERAL LIKES AND DISLIKES

Begin step one by listing your general interests. Think of the day-to-day activities and environments you enjoy and specify particular projects or experiences. Then give a brief reason why you enjoy each activity. List the activities you especially dislike, and briefly note why.

STEP TWO: ASSEMBLE YOUR ACCOMPLISHMENTS

Next, analyze what you do best. Think of how your accomplishments relate to future job-oriented activities—even if those accomplishments were not specifically achieved in a paid environment. State your accomplishments briefly and crisply. If you helped an organization obtain a specific outcome, discuss how you contributed to this achievement. Whenever possible, include measurements in numerical terms. Whether school- or job-related, describe at least five of your most significant accomplishments. This will also help you to articulate your value to a potential employer by knowing what sets you apart from others who will be seeking a similar position.

STEP THREE: LIST YOUR INTERPERSONAL SKILLS

If you have limited work experience, your "people" skills may be your most important job-related asset during the early stages of your career. Almost every employer puts considerable emphasis on a candidate's ability to communicate and work well with other people. List the skills you feel you can put to work for someone else (e.g., communicating, organizing, training, teaching, and speaking). Then list the skills you feel need further development.

STEP FOUR: LIST YOUR TECHNICAL SKILLS

Having several highly technical skills greatly improves your job-hunting chances. Skills such as programming, mathematics, science, and foreign languages, as well as extensive travel experience, may be equally useful in your job search. List the technical skills you have and those you feel should be developed further. You may want to visit the website at *http://www.ed.gov/databases/ERIC_Digests/ ed399484.html*. This website provides a list of skills classified into three main categories: academic skills, personal management skills, and teamwork skills.

STEP FIVE: RATE YOUR JOB VALUES

Identify and rank the job values most important to you. These include salary, benefits, travel, growth opportunity, chance to help people, and type of company. Also, consider whether you prefer to work with data or people. Taking the Keisey Temperment Sorter can help you understand why you prefer to work with people or data. Once you understand yourself, it becomes much easier to understand others. Check with your on-campus placement office for types of assessments to complete so that you can learn more about yourself. Then describe your hypothetical "perfect" job. Don't forget to assess your personal values. It is important that you understand how the career you have chosen will fit in with the other important aspects of your life.

STEP SIX: MATCH YOUR ATTRIBUTES WITH FUNCTIONAL ROLES

Now merge your personal attributes and preferences into a selection of functional roles that best matches your personality. Try to look for a common thread in your previous answers to establish an appropriate job target. Choose at least five job possibilities, including the one for which you will develop an effective résumé.

Completing these steps should produce a career objective and some job targets for you. Additionally, computerized programs may be available to guide you through a self-assessment of what you want and what you enjoy doing. For example, **SIGI PLUS**[3] (System of Interactive Guidance and Information—Plus More) covers all the major aspects of career decision making and planning. **SIGI PLUS** provides answers to questions about 27 different occupations and gives alternate job titles within an occupation. Check with your school's placement office and ask if they have **SIGI PLUS** or a similar program. Once you have completed these steps, you should learn about various career possibilities.

You may find that your self-assessment suggests that you pursue self-employment and entrepreneurship. According to Ben Graham, a career coach with Punta Gorda, "Job seekers have just about lost their faith in corporate America, and it's easy to see why. We can all recite company names and even point our fingers at specific people who have been responsible for the change in how we perceive once-respected companies. . . . The industry giants that have fallen have made all companies suspect. Many people now are actively deciding to be their own boss."

You should research this career path extensively and make sure that your self-assessment definitely supports this career decision. It is only through self-knowledge that you will be able to adequately accomplish this goal.[4]

Once you have analyzed your personal characteristics and interests, your accomplishments, your skills and competencies, and your values, you are ready to write your career objective. This objective should be a brief phrase or statement that clearly articulates the type of work and the level of responsibility that you desire. It should be clearly stated and easy to understand. This objective will give you a sense of direction in your career search and give you a focus for your job search plan. Your career objective will serve as a springboard from which to draft your résumé and cover letters. The good news is that it doesn't have to be set in stone and can evolve as your job search progresses. Some examples of career objectives are as follows:

Entry Level Real Estate Industry Professional providing property management, leasing, market, and tenant relations expertise.

Mid-Level Transportation Industry Manager in the shipping and freight consolidation industries with focus on marketing, business development, and key account management.

Health Care Industry Executive providing strategic planning, development, and leadership of health care practice organizations.

To prepare yourself fully for your job search, you will need to understand more about the job search process. You need to understand what is happening on the other side of the résumé review. You need to understand what is happening on the other side of the job fair booth. You need to understand what is happening on the other side of the interview desk. You need to understand what is happening on the other side of the telephone. You need to understand what is happening as the job offer is being put together. You need to understand the process.

Source: "Job Search Prep." Retrieved from: *http://www.collegegrad.com/jobsearch/1–0.shtml.*

---

[3] Educational Testing Service, *SIGI PLUS,* New Jersey, 1991.

[4] George Collins, "Coach Helps Job-Seekers Improve Careers, Nurtures Success," KnightRidder/Tribune Business News, Washington, Sept. 1, 2003, *The Sun,* Port Charlotte, Fla., Punta Gorda, Fla.

Knowing Your Career Possibilities

The next step in your job search is understanding the job market and exploring available opportunities. To begin, look in the Occupational Outlook Handbook for information about the job duties, working conditions, and training requirements of many occupations. The Handbook is available online at: *http://www.bls.gov/oco/* and can also be found in most libraries and career centers.

Visit the counselors at your school, career center, or state employment office. They have resources and advice to help you choose an occupation and develop a job search strategy. State employment offices offer free advice and computer access to people who are unemployed. To find your state office, call (202) 219-5257, or write to the address below:

U.S. Employment Service
200 Constitution Ave., NW
Washington, DC 20212

This link: *http://www.job-hunt.org/state_unemployment_offices.shtml*, will provide links to each state's employment office and to other state resources.

Each day, read the business section of your local newspaper and browse *The Wall Street Journal* or similar types of newspapers for more information. You want to identify the latest trends, challenges, and problems facing particular careers or industries. You can also go online to assess career trends and look at online occupational handbooks that give specific information on everything from working conditions to education and training requirements. After you have an overview of industries, you need to research information regarding specific organizations that are in need of your services and that meet the personal criteria you have established in your self-analysis.

LEARNING ABOUT SPECIFIC COMPANIES

You can usually obtain a wealth of information from your on-campus placement office. These offices have files or references on many organizations. Also, check with your on-campus reference librarian and search the World Wide Web.

Most companies now have their own websites, which offer valuable information to prospective candidates. Many websites also include lists of available job opportunities. To find a link to a particular firm, try accessing an online business directory such as Hoover's Online (*http://www.hoovers.com*), or enter the company's name in a search engine such as Altavista (*altavista.digital.com*). Visit the sites of companies that interest you and investigate the values and mission of each organization. Take note of what products or services the company provides. Also, review the corporate history and executive profiles, if available, to familiarize yourself with the professional achievements of the company and its decision makers.

If an online version of the annual report is available, download a copy for further study. If an online version is not available, write or telephone corporate headquarters; companies make these reports available free of charge to their stockholders and interested parties. However, remember that only publicly held companies have annual reports.

Once you have an annual report, examine the firm's financial strengths and weaknesses. Note whether you see opportunities for growth and expansion. All of this research will be useful in preparing for an informational interview.

Once you have gained insight into each organization, develop a "big picture view" by reviewing pertinent articles and reports. This will help you to be "in the know" relative to trends and happenings within your target industry or organization and will help to lead you to the insiders who may be able to offer you a job.

Most media websites maintain archived files of stories that can offer valuable information. If you are interested in a large, well-established corporation, read what analysts and leading business journalists consider its strengths and weaknesses. For researching smaller or private firms, explore the online versions of your favorite major magazines and trade publications for industry-related news items and financial forecasts. Some sources may require a fee for access to or downloading particular reports, but many other articles are available free. This information may generate some questions that you can answer through additional research or in an interview.[5]

You can also check directories in particular fields to obtain company and financial information. Table 12.1 lists a few of the directories you may find in your library.

If you still need insight into possible careers, you may need to network and conduct an informational interview or job shadow an industry manager. In these experiences, your objective is to find out as much information as you can about an organization or job. These types of "real" job experiences provide an opportunity to gain more detailed information about your target profession and industry.

You can network with anyone you come in contact with. You will find that everyone you meet will not have the capacity to help your career. However, many will know someone who may lead you to someone who can help your career. So, do not make prejudgments or feel like you are wasting your time.

Source: "Career Article 149: Make Networking Work For You." Retrieved from *http://www.seekingsuccess.com/articles/art149.php3*.

TABLE 12.1 ☞ **Where to get company information.**

General Directories

Directory of Corporate Affiliations
Million Dollar Directory
Standard & Poors; Register of Corporations, Directors, and Executives
Standard & Poors Corporation Records
Thomas Register of American Manufacturers and Thomas Register Catalog File
Ward's Business Directory

Specialized Directories and Resource Books

Accounting Firms and Practitioners
America's Corporate Families
Annual Statement Studies
California Manufacturers Register
Compact Disclosure
Directory of American Firms Operating in Foreign Countries
Directory of Foreign Manufacturers in United States
Directory of Hotel and Motel Systems
Directory of Management Consultants
Directory of New England Manufacturers
Dun's Business Rankings
Industry Norms & Key Business Ratios
Industry Surveys
Investext
Market Share Reporter
Moody's Investor Service
O'Dwyer's Directory of Public Relations Firms
One Source
Predicasts F. & S. Index United States
Principal International Businesses
PROMT
The Rand McNally Banker's Directory
Thomas Grocery Register
SECFILE
Standard Directory of Advertisers ("Red Book")
Television Factbook
Value Line Investment Survey
Who's Who in Direct Marketing Creative Services
Who's Who in Finance and Industry

[5] Max Messmer, "Net-Savvy Job Searching," *Strategic Finance,* Volume 80, Issue 12, June 1999, pp. 10–12.

NETWORKING AND INFORMATIONAL INTERVIEWING

The old saying is: "It's not what you know, but who you know!" To be successful in your job search, you must network and develop contacts.

Begin by making a list of friends, relatives, family friends, and anyone working. Then contact as many as possible and ask them if you may "job shadow" them for a day. Explain that you want to observe and learn more about their jobs and organizations. If they agree, spend as much time with them as they will allow. Before you leave, ask this question: "If you were me, whom else would you talk with?"

In addition, check the Internet for networking opportunities. Visit the sites of associations and investigate local chapter activities. Many organizations offer online registration for seminars and events that can enhance your skills while increasing your visibility with potential employers and key contacts. In addition, explore forums and chat rooms to get to know others and exchange career tips and advice. Two websites to review are: the Institute of Management Accountants (IMA) at *http://www.imanet.org* and the Society for Human Resource Management (SHRM) at *http://www.shrm.org*. See Box 12.2 for additional ideas for building and maintaining relationships.

Building a contact chain takes time, but you will find it time well invested. Conducting informational interviews can be another avenue to help you decide on a career. People typically enjoy talking about their chosen field and how they managed to climb to the position they now hold. If you plan your interview and ask thoughtful questions, these types of experiences can provide a wealth of useful information.

Job shadow or conduct informational interviews early in your educational career. You never know when this opportunity may pave the way for an internship, co-op job, summer job, or employment offer after graduation.

To gain the most from the experience, you must do your homework. Go to your library and research the company and the industry. If you can obtain a company's annual report, read it to seek general information about the company and industry. Once you have completed your homework, make an appointment with an individual.

Join a professional organization to network with potential employers.

Karen Susman, a speaker, author, and presentation skills coach, offers these suggestions to build and maintain relationships:

- Write a note. Handwritten notes are opened more quickly and aren't as easily thrown away. Keep the message brief and mention something about your encounter with the person to trigger his or her memory.

- Send a tip sheet with 10 ideas that demonstrate your expertise, with a "thought you'd like to see this" note. Be sure to include your contact information.

- Refer to a website related to the conversation you had with the contact. When talking to the contact, make a note on the back of his or her business card for any areas of interest he or she may bring up in the conversation.

- Find three unusual quotes from business leaders and send them to the contact.

- Send a handwritten note or printed postcard, or e-mail the contact with news of your receiving an award or certification.

- Send a note or small gift for referrals and update the contact on the outcome.

- Never leave a contact dangling. Make note of when and how you will follow-up next with each person.

BOX 12.2 🖝 **Building Relationships**

SOURCE: Reprinted with permission of Karen Susman. Speaker, Remarkable Association. *www.karensusman.com*.

If you do not know whom to contact, then network. This means you ask your friends, classmates, or relatives about individuals they know who might be willing to talk about their jobs. Most individuals are willing to help college students.

After you have the name of an individual, contact the person to set up an interview. Begin your telephone conversation by stating your name and reason for calling. Be sure to make it clear that you seek only information, not a job—at least, not at this point.

Once you have obtained an appointment, make a list of pertinent questions. A suggested plan follows:

Begin by thanking the person and explaining the purpose for your visit.

Ask how this person chose this field and how he or she got started.

Ask follow-up questions, such as:

- How did you get your first job after college?
- What should I do to prepare for this career?
- What career progression can I expect?
- What do you like most or least about this position?

On the day of the interview, arrive 10 to 15 minutes early and dress professionally. Do not overstay your welcome and be respectful of the individual's time. If you are job shadowing, be a "fly on the wall" and do not interfere with the individual's job tasks. You are not there to participate, but to listen and learn.

Follow-up by writing a thank-you letter. When you send a letter of appreciation, you show respect. Not only does this practice show you have manners, but it provides an opportunity to practice your business writing skills. Your letter should briefly express your appreciation for the individual's time and the information provided. Compose the letter immediately and mail it after your interview. In addition, you should keep a record of your meeting. You may wish to call upon this person again when graduation time comes around.

Prolonged unemployment, as a result of an unsuccessful job search, is most often caused for the the following reasons:

- 80 percent cannot identify skills
- 90 percent cannot answer questions
- 40 percent have poor appearance
- 85 percent don't spend enough time on the job search

Source: "Career Planning." Retrieved from: *http://www.soicc. state.nc.us/soicc/planning/c3.htm.*

Developing Your Job Search Plan

As you know from your studies, when your goal is to sell something, you must have a plan to market your product or service. In this case that is you. Developing your job search plan will give you a structure around which to build your daily job search activities, such as marketing yourself to potential employers. Your job search plan should include:

- **A statement of your career objective.** You have already completed this.

- **A brief statement of the value you will bring to your potential employer.** What sets you apart from other candidates? What are your strengths? Tap into your list of accomplishments created in step two of your self-analysis to include a list of bullet points of your competencies as exhibited through your accomplishments. Having solidified your value to a prospective employer will help you in writing your résumé and in the interview process.

- **A statement of your target industry and list of target companies.** Use the research and analysis you performed in getting to know your career opportunities to define your target industry and the 40 to 50 specific companies you would like to target first in your job search process. Refer back to your self-analysis to make sure you take into account your preferences for work environment, work culture, and job values. You will also take into consideration the geographic area in which you wish to work.

- **A specific plan that states how you will communicate with the target companies you have identified.** Flying by the seat of your pants in your job search process will not get you where you want to go. Further, inactivity is your worst enemy in conducting your job search. Establish specific, measurable daily and weekly productivity goals so that you make progress every day in your job search. How many phone calls will you have each week with prospective employers you have targeted? Flowing out of these prospective employer contacts, how many informational interviews will you set up to learn more about how the company selects and hires its employees? How much time will you spend on the Internet researching information about these companies that may lead you to individuals with whom to speak about potential openings? How many job search boards will you search for job listings for your target companies? What method and time frame will you use to follow-up on the contacts you have made? How many networking meetings will you attend each month?

- **A measurement system that gauges your productivity toward your communication goals.** Develop a spreadsheet and track your progress toward your daily and weekly goals. Identify areas where you are successful and areas where you need to concentrate more efforts. Analyze what factors may be inhibiting your job search. Does your productivity fall off after a company rejects your efforts to gain information about its hiring processes and job openings? If so, remember that marketing yourself is not unlike marketing any product or service; it is all a matter of number of contacts. Turn each "no" into "on" and move on to the next company.

- **A plan for interviewing and soliciting job offers.** This will be covered in depth in Chapter 14.

Searching the Net for Career Information and Opportunities

You should search the World Wide Web for career guidance and job postings.

SOURCE: Pearson Education/PH/Frank La Bua.

The proliferation of online resources and services has dramatically impacted the job search process for both job seeker and employer. A Web application from Hire.com has made it even easier for job seekers and companies to meet. This application lets companies gather information at their websites about what kinds of jobs visitors would consider, at what salary range, and in what regions. The software matches those requirements with available positions and notifies registrants by e-mail when a job listing that fits their criteria comes up.

Candidates then fill out a questionnaire to further narrow their qualifications. A scoring system determines whether candidates move to the next step, which would be an interview. The **e-recruiter** helps companies create an interactive relationship with would-be candidates who may not be actively job hunting.[6]

Individuals seeking advertising and newspaper industry jobs can regularly check *Editor & Publisher's* printed and online job listings for new employment. The new Ad Alert feature, developed and managed by Thomson Interactive, allows website users to input specific job types and requirements to the *Editor & Publisher*

---

[6] Ramin P. Jaleshgari, "Web Sites as Tools for Recruiting," *InformationWeek*, 746, August 2, 1999, p. 82.

website, *http://www.mediainfo.com*, and have specific job listings e-mailed to them in the future. Criteria used in searches can include a general category of position, such as editorial, promotion, advertising, or circulation, along with more defined elements, such as level of job, geographic location, and type of publication sought.

Ads that are e-mailed to prospective employees may also include links to the potential employer's website or reply e-mail links. The new feature is free of charge to anyone accessing the *Editor & Publisher* website. *Editor & Publisher* has been the premier source for advertising and newspaper industry jobs for more than 100 years.[7]

As you can see, you can gain important career information by searching the World Wide Web. In addition to accessing numerous job-posting sites, you can also go online to research companies, network with other professionals, and communicate with potential employers.[8] Initially, most of the job-related Internet resources were sites listing employment openings. Today, in addition to job postings, you can find websites that offer advice on how to sell yourself to a prospective employer and that offer expert advice on how to plan and conduct a job search.[9]

WEBSITES PROVIDING CAREER GUIDANCE

The following list provides a sampling of career guidance sites. These sites offer guidance on creating cover letters, tips on putting together résumés, and helpful hints on handling several other aspects of your career.

http://www.dbm.com/jobguide
> This site provides one of the most well-known guides on the Internet. It provides advice and links to a variety of job-hunting resources and includes a list of résumé databases.

http://www.jobhuntersbible.com
> Richard Bolles, author of *What Color Is Your Parachute?,* provides advice on how to write résumés and where to find career resources on the Web. He provides a list of the most well-used résumé banks and some critical information about their effectiveness.

http://www.careermag.com
> *Career Magazine* provides a résumé bank, job listings, current feature articles and columns, and an archive of advice on interviewing, résumé writing, networking, diversity, finding a job after college, and many other topics. You can search the archive with key words or browse it by category. To find information anywhere on the site, use the search engine at the bottom of the home page.
>
> *Career Magazine* also offers separate message boards for job search tips, workplace issues, internships, and general discussions. Moderated boards include Online Résumé Writing Help and Career Coach.
>
> The site's other features include information on job fairs, directories of recruiters and consultants, and a selection of relocation resources (e.g., calculators for determining moving costs and the salary you'll need to make in a new city to maintain your current lifestyle). Also available is an extensive list of links to other sites.

http://www.jobweb.org
> JobWeb is sponsored by the National Association of Colleges and Employers. JobWeb includes a digital publication called *Job Choices Online Magazine,* which publishes articles with advice from career counselors and recruiters. You can post your own questions in a section called Ask the Job-Search Experts.

---

[7] "Newspaper Jobs Sent Via E-mail," *Editor & Publisher,* Volume 132, Issue 17, April 24, 1999, p. 82.

[8] Jaleshgari, p. 82.

[9] Messmer, p. 12.

JobWeb's discussion forums let students and recent graduates share information on various topics.

JobWeb also offers a section on résumés and interviews at *http://www.jobweb.com/Resumes_Interviews/default.htm*. It contains a wealth of information on résumés, interviews, cover letters, and other documents, as well as tests to take before you interview.

The JobWeb Career Library provides, among others, links for *Job Outlook* to find out who's hiring and where the jobs are; *Salary Information,* which offers previews of average salaries and benefits for various fields; and *General References,* which provides links to reference material helpful in the job search including online directories, business reports, money management, and professional associations.

http://www.garywill.com/worksearch

Worksearch bills itself as "the Web's most comprehensive guide to resources that will help you sell yourself to an employer." To live up to that slogan, Worksearch provides a list of career guidance articles and gives a one- to five-star rating for each article.

In addition, Worksearch offers tips on selecting a résumé-writing service and details on "ridiculous questions and awkward situations from actual interviews." Other resources include information on such topics as networking, making effective use of the telephone, maintaining a customer-focused approach, and career-related books.

http://www.CareerShop.com

CareerShop provides candidate resources such as career resource and training sections along with a tips section entitled "Ask the Career Dr.," a free service that offers answers from Dr. Randall S. Hansen, an associate professor of marketing at the School of Business Administration, Stetson University.

http://www.fortune.com/fortune/careers/

This website includes articles from *Fortune* magazine that address career topics. It also has interactive quizzes to help you answer such questions as "Could you make it to CEO?" "What's the right work-life strategy for you?" "What's your EQ at work?" "Do you have a fear of success?" "What kind of manager are you?" Another feature of this website is rankings of companies including the Fortune 500, Fortune 1000, the Global 500, 100 Best Companies to Work For, American Most Admired Companies, Global Most Admired Companies, and 100 Fastest Growing Companies, among others.

http://www.careercity.com

Want to know why building relationships at work is important to your career? Head over to TrueCareers at the above link and click on the career section, then move to the career articles. Included in this section are also subsections with advice and articles on résumés, cover letters, and interviewing. There's also a salary calculator and a Diversity Center. The Career Blog is where you "get the real scoop on how to get the job you want faster. No big formal articles to weed through, just quick insider tips from people in the business." TrueCareers is a leading source for career data and has been quoted by CNN, CBS MarketWatch, *USA Today, BusinessWeek,* and other media organizations.

WEBSITES COMBINING JOB POSTINGS, RÉSUMÉ POSTINGS, AND CAREER GUIDANCE

The Internet provides access to thousands of jobs, from entry-level to CEO, around the world. So you should use the Internet as another tool in your job search. However, the Web is not the only job lead source. Usenet groups also offer databases of job listings, and most of these services are free. Start your search by using search engines like Google, Yahoo, or Altavista to find career-related websites. Some

A career search site should:

- Be user-friendly.
- Be updated regularly with new job leads.
- Contain a large database of positions.
- Sort job leads by geographical location.
- Allow the job seeker to update and change personal information within a specified time.

BOX 12.3 ☛ **Characteristics of a Career Search Site**

SOURCE: Society for Human Resource Management.

search engines even provide reviews of sites. Use key words, such as "high-tech jobs" or "medical job," to fine-tune and accelerate your search. The point of the Internet is to make it easier than the newspaper classifieds, says Sue Weiner, director of marketing for TMP Worldwide Interactive, which created the Monster Board. See Box 12.3 for the characteristics of an effective career search site.

Career management websites are gaining momentum on newspaper classified ads. According to a preview of a Newspaper Association of America/Scarborough report, local newspapers and the Web are neck-and-neck in importance when it comes to readers gathering job information. Overall, 36 percent of the respondents said local newspapers were a primary source of employment information, while 31 percent said the Internet was. Perceptive newspapers can count themselves in both categories if they run robust online job sites.[10]

Many Internet job seekers look for more than just position listings. They want tools to help them manage their careers as well as review job listings. In response to this demand, many career-related sites now combine their job-search and résumé-posting services with a variety of other career development resources. If you register with a handful of sites, you can get your résumé in front of hundreds of employers with minimal effort. Most job seekers are employed and want to keep their identities secret from their employers. Most websites, like Monster, Career-Builder, and HotJobs, have a feature to keep résumés private from selected individuals. "The issue that is so quintessential is privacy," says Robert Liu of HotJobs. He explains that its HotBlock feature allows people who post résumés to control who sees them.[11] As most sites are free, you can try several different ones to find those that meet your needs. The following websites provide these combined services:

http://www.careerbuilder.com/

> With more than 900,000 jobs, this site boasts that it is the Internet's largest job search site. You can post your résumé online and, if you see a job you are interested in, you can apply directly from CareerBuilder. You can search by industry, company, or job category and can search geographically within each of these categories. You can create a personal search agent to e-mail you when new positions are posted meeting your specified criteria. Free e-mail is also available so that those e-mail messages can be sent to a non-work account. This site also offers career advice, business opportunities, relocation services, a job seeker toolkit, and 401(k) rollover centers.

http://www.monster.com

> Monster.com boasts that it is the "1 choice of job seekers in every ranked local market from coast to coast." Along with job search tools, a résumé-posting service, and regular e-mail updates of appropriate positions similar to those

[10] Martha L. Stone, editor and publisher, "Help Wanted!" *Mediainfo.com Supplement,* September 1999, p. 14.

[11] Stone, p. 14.

offered by careerbuilder.com, the site offers specialized job search and career advice by industry and by special interest group such as contract, temporary, entry level, management, military, career changes, and so forth. It also has an online networking resource community of professionals.

http://www.hotjobs.com

This site has hundreds of listings in various job categories and operates in much the same way as careerbuilder.com and monster.com. It too has excellent career tools in categories such as résumé writing, salary and benefits, job search, interview, diversity center, assessments, and industry news. In addition it offers advice on furthering your education and training and provides links for obtaining your own background check and credit report so that you will be aware of what is on these reports before your potential employer sees them. Finally, the site offers newsletters and a networking community.

http://www.brilliantpeople.com

In addition to its job bank and résumé bank, this site offers information on hiring trends across the nation and within specific fields. Tips for writing a resume, developing interviewing skills, and building a long-term career plan are also available.

A highlight of this website is its extensive set of relocation tools. These include resources for helping job seekers determine how much they would need to earn in a new city to maintain their current lifestyle, what it would cost to move, how much they can afford to pay for a house, and the type of mortgage that would best meet their needs. Users can also compare crime statistics in cities across the United States and create a timeline for planning relocation.

http://www.computerjobs.com, www.dice.com, and www.Techies.com

These sites specialize in technical jobs and list more permanent, contract, and consulting jobs nationwide for programmers, systems administrators, and other information technology (IT) professionals.

http://www.blackenterprise.com

The online version of the popular business magazine for black professionals offers a Career Center, including a directory of executive recruiters; a career-related message board; a job bank; and a personal search agent similar to that on careerbuilder.com, in which registered job seekers are automatically e-mailed when new positions are posted that meet their criteria.

This website also dispenses valuable career guidance through features from past issues of *Black Enterprise*. These articles provide general business and career management advice, as well as information targeted specifically to black Americans, such as a list of the top 50 colleges for black students and success stories from top black executives.

http://www.hire-quality.com

Hire-Quality offers a unique service for honorably discharged military personnel. They have created a network of 60,000 people that helps honorably discharged and transitioning military service members by referring them to Hire-Quality. Hire-Quality has a database of 200,000 people seeking jobs in the civilian workforce. Hire-Quality also offers job seekers free e-mail as well as a chat room and links to the websites of the various branches of the armed forces and a few military interest sites.

In addition to these sources, you can look to local professional associations and alumni associations for guidance. Many of these organizations offer online job banks and career-related services that are specialized to your local area.

When seeking a job or career development resources on the Internet, make sure the information comes from a trustworthy source. Seek recommendations from other Internet users. The Internet offers a seemingly infinite variety of tools to help you manage your career. You just need to know how to find them and the best way to use them.[12]

Using the Internet Versus Traditional Job Search Tools

With the recent downturn in the economy, many firms have begun to do Internet recruiting as opposed to hiring an executive search firm. However, the Internet will not totally dominate recruitment efforts by organizations. Executive search specialists will still best fill senior positions. And, "There will always be a segment of the population that likes to draw a circle around a print ad," says Peter Weddle, the Connecticut-based author of *Weddles,* the newsletter for successful online recruiting. "Many people take comfort in the fact that in the newspaper, they know just where to find a certain category of work."[13]

Conclusion

Developing your job search skills not only helps you find your first full-time job, but also aids you later with career changes. On average, college and university graduates stay only five years with the company they first join.[14] Finding a new job has always required a skillful combination of initiative and ingenuity. Today's applicants can take advantage of a wealth of online information available through corporate websites, electronic media, and recruiting and staffing firms. By augmenting traditional job search techniques with Internet research and communication, you will save both time and energy. Take control of your job search process by evaluating your likes and dislikes, studying the job market, reviewing company information, and conducting informational interviews.

Career coach Susan Zitron runs her own coaching business, *http://www. zitroncareerservices.com/career_tips.html*, to help clients minimize mistakes while job hunting. She offers the following tips: Always have one eye on the market and one eye on your job. Your job is your company's responsibility, but your career is your own responsibility. You can expect to be in a job no longer than three years, given the constant changes in the industry. Even if you have been with one company for a long time, that company will have gone through changes. Balance your current job with your job search. Shopping for a new job while you already have one can be tricky, but staying connected can ease the anxiety. You must commit yourself to meeting the goals at your present company and continuing to do a great job. But, at the same time, you should join and attend professional associations where you can meet people, as great opportunities often are filled by referral. Although it may be tempting to let your coworkers know you are job hunting, it probably is not a wise decision. Sometimes people resent other people getting a new job. Staying on top of job trends can be hard work, but it pays off. If you know your goals, you will be better able to manage the stress of job seeking.[15] Use the Checklist in Table 12.2 to make sure you have covered all the bases.

[12] Julie Nilson Chyna, "Career Resources on the Web," *Healthcare Executive,* Volume 14, Issue 6, November/December 1999, pp. 46–47.

[13] Lee Murphy, "Top Job Sites," *Marketing News,* Volume 33, Issue 16, August 2, 1999, p. 13.

[14] Sterling Institute, Washington, D.C., cited in Sandra E. La Marre and David M. Hopkins, "The New Employee of the Eighties," *Journal of College Placement,* Fall 1982, p. 31.

[15] Karen Gerencher, "Managing the Stress of Looking for a Job," *InfoWorld,* Volume 21, Issue 32, August 9, 1999, p. 7.

TABLE 12.2 ☞ **Checklist for career search.**

YES	NO		
☐	☐	1.	Have I taken a personality assessment to understand myself better?
☐	☐	2.	Have I taken an inventory of my likes and dislikes?
☐	☐	3.	Have I identified my accomplishments, my interpersonal skills, and my technical skills?
☐	☐	4.	Have I identified what I value in life and in a job?
☐	☐	5.	Have I reviewed the Occupational Outlook Handbook?
☐	☐	6.	Have I researched potential companies?
☐	☐	7.	Have I joined some professional organizations to network?
☐	☐	8.	Have I conducted any informational interviews?
☐	☐	9.	Have I written thank-you letters to the interviewees of those informational interviews?
☐	☐	10.	Have I gone online to search for career information and opportunities?

Exercises

EXERCISE 1 TAKE A PERSONAL INVENTORY AND DISCOVER YOUR HIDDEN TALENTS

Directions: What positive qualities and skills do you offer a prospective employer? Which ones do you need to work on? Rate yourself on each quality, then emphasize your strong points in your résumé.

Always	**Sometimes**	**Rarely**	
_____	_____	_____	1. **Direction:** I know the field I want to be in and the type of work I want to do. I have definite career goals.
_____	_____	_____	2. **Communication:** I can organize and express my thoughts logically, clearly, and concisely, both orally and in writing. I use correct pronunciation, grammar, spelling, and punctuation.
_____	_____	_____	3. **Practical skills:** I work hard to develop my vocational skills, such as keyboarding, graphic design, data processing, drafting, accounting, nursing, or engineering.
_____	_____	_____	4. **Harmony with others:** I like people and get along well with those of other backgrounds, beliefs, cultures, and points of view.
_____	_____	_____	5. **Positiveness:** I look forward to the work I want to do and give it my best. I tend to have a positive outlook and usually say "I will" or "I'll try" rather than "I can't."

_____ _____ _____   6. **Flexibility:** I adapt easily and readily to new work tasks, methods, and responsibilities.

_____ _____ _____   7. **Initiative:** I am a self-starter. I recognize what needs to be done and do it without being told or supervised.

_____ _____ _____   8. **Competitiveness:** I try to do things better and faster than others because I want to gain recognition and get ahead.

_____ _____ _____   9. **Organization:** I plan, organize, and schedule my work, then carry it out step by step according to the plan.

_____ _____ _____   10. **Integrity:** I try to be honest. I respect the confidences of others. I do not gossip.

_____ _____ _____   11. **Performance:** I try hard to meet every deadline. I am an energetic worker and proud of my work.

_____ _____ _____   12. **Inventiveness:** I enjoy devising new ways to do tasks faster and more easily and to achieve better results.

_____ _____ _____   13. **Problem solving:** I like challenges. I can foresee and analyze problems, then solve them quickly and effectively by thinking them through.

_____ _____ _____   14. **Grooming:** I prepare what I am going to wear ahead of time and try to look neat, clean, and professional.

_____ _____ _____   15. **Mobility:** I am willing to relocate to another area, city, or state if my work requires it.

_____ _____ _____   16. **Enthusiasm:** I like to work. I am eager to learn all I can. I am willing to do more than my boss expects.

_____ _____ _____   17. **Motivation:** I have the drive to get things done. I stick to the job, overcoming every obstacle until I finish it.

_____ _____ _____   18. **Leadership:** I like to take charge. I know how to direct and motivate others to do their best. I am willing to accept responsibility for the decisions I make.

_____ _____ _____ 19. **Self-confidence:** I prepare ahead for situations so I will be confident to meet them. I respond effectively to people, problems, and challenges.

_____ _____ _____ 20. **Responsibility:** I can be counted on to get the job done. I try to be on time, comply with regulations, and meet deadlines.

_____ _____ _____ 21. **Self-awareness:** I know my limitations and areas of weakness. I try hard to improve on them.

EXERCISE 2   ONLINE NETWORKING

Directions: Go to the World Wide Web and communicate with other professionals in your field. You can probably find a Usernet bulletin board devoted to a career or profession in which you are interested. Bring to class the names of three professionals you meet and come prepared to share your interactions.

EXERCISE 3   LEARNING ABOUT A COMPANY ONLINE

Directions: Pull up a company's home page and contact some online financial research sites to find out about the financial strength of a company in which you are interested. Come prepared to share the results of your research and share what analysts think about the financial future of your chosen company.

EXERCISE 4   ONLINE JOB FAIR

Directions: Here is an opportunity to meet with potential employers without ever leaving home. In most cases, you will be able to converse online with an interviewer privately and in real time. Usually these fairs are free. Come to class and share the results of your interview.

EXERCISE 5   ONLINE ASSESSMENT

Directions: Go to the following web address: _http://www.collegegrad.com/careers/index.shtml._

Then, complete the following: _Free Career Analysis_ using the MAPP (Motivational Appraisal of Personal Potential). This career analysis will show you the top 11 to 20 jobs with your greatest potential for success, including five free job matches.

Take the _Keirsey Temperament Sorter,_ the most popular personality test in the world. The Temperament Sorter is used by major universities and career counselors worldwide as a tool for helping graduates select a career.

Assignment Options

OPTION 1: USING YOUR CAREER PLANNING OR PLACEMENT OFFICE

Preparing for the job search process requires careful thought and preparation. Deciding what major to study and what type of career to pursue means hours of consideration and soul-searching.

Much of this process has been condensed onto computer software packages, which may be available on your college campus. If available, check with your Career Planning or Placement Center to set up an appointment. When you set up your appointment, plan to make several trips. You will answer questions posed by the program and change your answers as you reconsider them. The program will give you a list of jobs suitable for people with your unique combination of interests and ambitions. Additionally, you can get computerized information regarding career outlooks for the next decade, education requirements, likely income, and much more.

No one knows the results of your profile but you, and you may take home a copy of the printouts. After you have completed the exercise, narrow down the career choices to fewer than six and write a memo to your instructor.

In the opening paragraph, state the purpose of your memo and provide transition to the body. In the body, describe what you learned and what careers might suit you. Be sure to include a conclusion and attach a printout of the program listing possible positions for you.

OPTION 2: STUDENT INTERVIEWER

Locate a person (not a friend, relative, or boss) who currently holds a job you might want to hold sometime. Schedule a 30- to 45-minute interview with this person. You will be the interviewer and the professional will evaluate your interviewing skills. Conduct an informational interview in which you hope to find out everything possible about a particular position. Some typical questions to ask include:

- What do you do on your job?
- What do you find difficult about your job?
- What do you enjoy doing the most?
- What do you find interesting about your job?
- What skills does this job require?
- What educational background did you need for this job?
- What does it take to be successful at this job?
- What do you recommend I do to prepare myself for this type of position?
- Tell me about your company? Your industry? Your profession?
- How did you get your job?

You may have additional questions to ask, but these questions should spark your thinking as you prepare for the interview.

After the interview, ask the interviewee to evaluate your performance as an interviewer, using the Interview Evaluation Form on page 355. The interviewee should mail the interview form, with a business card attached, to your professor. You should provide a stamped, addressed envelope for your interviewee.

Following the interview, write a self-evaluation memo and send a thank-you letter to the interviewer. In your memo, devote a paragraph to the following: your interviewing strengths, your interviewing areas needing improvement, what you learned about being the interviewer, what you learned about the position, and whether you would like to hold a similar position. In your thank-you letter, express your appreciation to the interviewee.

INTERVIEW EVALUATION FORM

Student's Name _____

Instructions: Please respond to the following questions concerning the interview in which you have participated. Your responses will provide the student with valuable feedback regarding his or her progress in developing effective interviewing skills.

    Please rate the student on the following six questions. Circle the number that most closely reflects the student's overall performance in that area.

    After completing the evaluation, please sign the form, attach a business card, and mail the evaluation in the envelope provided.

		Low				High

1. **Initial Impressions:**   1   2   3   4   5

    How favorable were your initial impressions of the interviewer?

2. **Introduction and Conclusion:**   1   2   3   4   5

    Did the opening comments establish rapport?

    Did the statement of purpose give you a clear idea of what to expect during the interview?

    Did the interviewer close the interview effectively?

3. **Questions Asked:**   1   2   3   4   5

    Were the questions asked appropriate?

    Were the questions asked clear?

    Were the questions organized in a logical sequence?

    Were the more private or embarrassing questions placed near the middle of the interview?

    Were good transition statements used between question areas?

4. **Communication Ability:**   1   2   3   4   5

    Was the interviewer's verbal communication (voice and articulation, fluency, volume, vocabulary) effective?

    Was the interviewer's nonverbal communication (eye contact, posture, showing interest, dress) effective?

    Did the interviewer really listen effectively?

5. **Composure and Control:**   1   2   3   4   5

    Did the interviewer seem composed and relaxed?

    Did the interviewer control the interview effectively?

6. **Overall Reactions:**   1   2   3   4   5

    Taken as a whole, how would you evaluate this interview?

    What did the student do well? Please use the back to provide your comments.

    What does the student need to continue to practice? Please use the back to provide your comments.

Please provide the student with some written comments on the back of this form.

Please attach business card here.

    Evaluator's Signature _____

    Name of Company _____

    Date _____

CHAPTER 13

Composing Cover Letters and Résumés

*O*ver the past decade as the U.S. economy has undergone dramatic and long-lasting changes, the business world globalized and the employment market has become more competitive, résumé writing has evolved into a much more complex and more sophisticated process. Today résumé writing is a competition among often very well-qualified candidates vying for a limited number of opportunities.[1]

Wendy S. Enelow

[1] Wendy S. Enelow, *Best Résumés for $100,000+ Jobs,* Rev. ed. of *100 Winning Résumés for $100,000+ Jobs: Résumés That Change Your Life* (Manassas: Impact Publications, 2001), p. 1.

LEARNING OBJECTIVES

After reading this chapter, you should be able to:

- Explain why you should put yourself in the reader's shoes when developing your job search tools.

- Describe the role of a cover letter.

- Identify the purpose of the four paragraphs in a cover letter.

- Debate the importance of the final, action-taking paragraph of a cover letter.

- List examples of action verbs.

- Discuss the purpose of the résumé.

- Itemize the basic parts of a résumé.

- Differentiate between the required parts of a résumé and the optional ones.

- Distinguish between the three traditional résumé formats.

- Understand electronic résumé formats.

- Become aware of using Personal Web Sites and Blogs for posting cover letters and résumés.

- Differentiate between plain-text résumés and scannable résumés.

- List the guidelines for making sure your documents get read.

- Outline the reasons for completing a job application completely.

The Importance of Developing Effective Job Search Tools

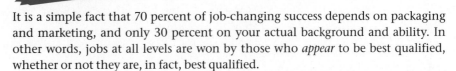

It is a simple fact that 70 percent of job-changing success depends on packaging and marketing, and only 30 percent on your actual background and ability. In other words, jobs at all levels are won by those who *appear* to be best qualified, whether or not they are, in fact, best qualified.

"A lot is changing in the way companies are soliciting candidates, and the way people are submitting résumés," said Jennifer DeHaven, executive vice president of Millennium Staffing & Management Services, a Las Vegas executive search firm. "But we continue to see the résumé as the most important tool in the job search. Always has been, always will be."[2]

Your résumé has approximately 15 seconds to tell the reader what has happened in your career, what actions you took to make those things happen, and what personal qualities and strengths allowed you to succeed in the job. Today's résumé is a targeted sales document designed to convey information through nuances that few job seekers even think about. If it fails, you are out of the game. That is why the most important business documents you will create are your cover letter and résumé. Because you know what you want and what you have to offer, no one can write them the way you can.

Writing cover letters and résumés that get results takes time. As you develop these tools, put yourself in your reader's shoes and ask yourself these questions:

Do I like the way these documents look? Do they grab my attention?

How do they sound? Can I easily read and understand them?

Have I included all information and omitted all unnecessary details?

Will they achieve my goal of getting an interview?

As you develop your job search tools, you may follow examples or templates, but your documents will be unique. No two résumés look exactly alike because no two people have the same education and experience. Still, recruiters and human resources professionals expect to see certain items. The following sections provide guidelines for developing your cover letter.

> Employers say they want to hire people who can communicate clearly, handle personal interactions, and analyze complex situations. Use your application package to demonstrate these qualities.
>
> Source: Dr. Margaret Procter, "Application Letters and Résumés." Retrieved from *http://www.utoronto.ca/writing/applic.html*.

Cover Letters

You use your cover or application letter to obtain an interview. You may use one of two types of cover letters. If you respond to an advertisement, you have written a

[2] Matt Crowley, "Format of Résumés Moves to E-Mail, But Same Principles Still Apply," *Knight Ridder Tribune Business News*, Washington, Aug. 10, 2003.

According to Wendy Enelow, author of *Best Cover Letters for $100,000+ Jobs*, a cover letter is defined as:

- A marketing document that is a "teaser," designed to entice someone to read your résumé and extend you the opportunity for a personal interview.
- A tool designed to sell the high points of your career—your successes, achievements, and most notable and relevant qualifications.
- A document that demonstrates the value you bring to a prospective employer.
- A document that is fairly quick to read and easy to peruse.
- A visual presentation that communicates an executive image.

A cover letter is not:

- A transmittal letter that simply states "Enclosed is my résumé . . . may we meet for an interview?"
- A document containing lengthy text and long paragraphs that is slow to read.
- A passive, low energy, and narrative summary of your work history.

BOX 13.1 📌 **Learning What a Cover Letter Is and Is Not**

SOURCE: Wendy S. Enelow, *Best Cover Letters for $100,000+ Jobs,* Rev. ed. of *201 Winning Cover Letters for $100,000+ Jobs: Cover Letters That Change Your Life* (Manassas Park: Impact Publications, 2001), p. 3.

solicited application letter. In contrast, an *unsolicited* letter is used as a "feeler" to find out about vacancies in a company.

Regardless of how you send your résumé, you should include a cover letter. Sending a résumé without a cover letter is like starting an interview without shaking hands. N. Jane Diggs, president of Career Connections Inc. in Charleston, West Virginia, has stated: "It's surprising how many applicants don't send a cover letter, even though most prospective employers expect one."[3]

In order to understand the value of your cover letter, read Box 13.1 to understand what a cover letter is and what it is not.

> "The point is if I can plug in someone else's name above your opening sentence, then it (your cover letter) can't be very unique. It's a tough market. You need to tell us what makes you special. And you have about two sentences to do it."
>
> Source: Ed Tazzia, "It All Starts with One Sentence," *Brandweek*, Volume 44, Issue 9, March 3, 2003, p. 38.

The best cover letters spark the employer's interest and create an impression of competence. Cover letters provide an opportunity to convey your focus and energy. "If you don't have a lot of experience, use the cover letter to show you have enthusiasm," says Sharon Swann, manager of administrative services for a management consulting firm in Menlo Park, California. "Writing a strong cover letter and then calling to follow up shows the employer you have drive and interest." Although you should feel free to consult references and models, use your own words when writing a cover letter; do not mimic another person's writing style.

Some employers go immediately to the résumé before reading the cover letter, while others review the cover letter first. Since you never know the preference of the employer, you need to make sure that your letter and your résumé grab the attention of your reader and sell your top skills so that employers will call.[4]

Some authorities suggest combining the major points of your résumé into your cover letter and having only one document describing your qualifications. If

[3] Robyn D. Clarke, "Since You Asked . . . Cover Story," *Black Enterprise*, Volume 29, Issue 11, June 1999, p. 83.

[4] Regina Pontow, "Cover Letters That Generate Higher Salaries and More Interviews," *ProvenResumes.com*, 1999, pp. 1–6.

this combination document does its job, you will be called for an interview. Then, you can carry a traditional résumé to your interview.

Whichever approach you choose, your letter should be perfect in every detail. Never direct your letter to the Human Resources Department; if you do, it probably will be filed somewhere and never read by anyone. Instead, make every effort to identify the name of the appropriate individual. Call the organization for the correct spelling and complete address. Make sure you spell the receiver's name correctly and use the correct title. Pay close attention to the Mr. or Ms. before gender-neutral names. Finally, use a colon after the name, not a comma.

The personal touch distinguishes you from the crowd. Keep in mind that your letter will be just one of many received by a prospective employer; be unique and use the persuasive approach.

Your cover letter should sell you. Grab the readers' attention, get their interest, create a desire, and make a call for action (AIDA). Write your cover letters in standard business format; however, do note that e-mailed letters do not include mailing addresses.

THE ALL-IMPORTANT, ATTENTION-GETTING FIRST PARAGRAPH

When you develop your first paragraph, you must make your cover letter stand out. If you write a solicited cover letter, you may refer to the name of an employee in the company who told you about the job, to the source of your information, or to the job title. Then describe how your qualifications fit the requirements.

If you have written a cover letter for an unsolicited job, you must be more creative. Present your special skills and experience that will benefit the organization by using key words from the job posting. Show your accomplishments, your skills, your experience, and your qualifications in terms of reader benefit. You must get the reader's attention up front or your letter will never be read.

THE SECOND PARAGRAPH—INTEREST

The second paragraph states your interest in the company and industry, as well as the purpose of your letter. Show you have done your homework by quoting information about the organization from annual reports or other sources. Briefly describe your experience with company products, cite a recent company success, or refer to an article written about the company. Then tie your qualities and experiences to the company to stress what you can do for them. Do not simply repeat your résumé; instead summarize your most relevant qualifications or provide additional details about a noteworthy accomplishment. If you have work experience, emphasize it. If you have little work experience, highlight your education and its practical applications. You want to pique the readers' interest so they will keep reading. Address the employer's requirements directly and do not be afraid to use special formatting to your advantage. "One of the best cover letters I've ever received," says Tom Harris, a manager at a Minneapolis marketing firm, "included a chart with my requirements on the left and the applicant's matching qualifications on the right."

THE THIRD PARAGRAPH—DESIRE

The third paragraph builds desire. It answers the question, "Why should I hire you?" Here you highlight your educational background and personal traits. Many organizations look for individuals who take responsibility, show initiative, and consider themselves team players. Use action verbs (see Table 13.1) to paint a picture of your skills and always maintain a positive, confident tone. Finally, refer to your attached résumé.

TABLE 13.1 🖝 Action verbs.

accelerated	accomplished	accounted for
achieved	acquired	added
adjusted	administrated	advised
aided	alphabetized	analyzed
anticipated	applied	appointed
appraised	arbitrated	argued
arranged	assessed	assisted
attended	authored	authorized
bolstered	boosted	briefed
budgeted	built	calculated
cataloged	caused	debated
chaired	critiqued	counseled
corrected	contracted	crafted
demonstrated	devised	dramatized
elected	enlisted	excelled
foresaw	found	fostered
grossed	innovated	interpreted
persuaded	pioneered	policed
prepared	presented	prevailed
scrutinized	smoothed	sought
spearheaded	specified	stated
defined	delegated	designed
earned	edited	educated
familiarized	filed	financed
gained	gathered	guided
handled	helped	highlighted
identified	implemented	improved
joined	judged	labored
launched	lectured	led
maintained	managed	maximized
negotiated	netted	observed
opened	operated	ordered
painted	participated	performed
qualified	rated	received
recognized	recommended	reduced
saved	scouted	screened
sent	served	shipped
suggested	straightened	suggested
trained	transcribed	verified

THE FOURTH PARAGRAPH—TAKING ACTION

In the fourth paragraph, you take control of the situation and request action. Ask for an interview, suggest a time to meet, or tell the employer you will call to make sure he or she received your résumé and to answer any questions. Whatever you do, sound sincere and appreciative. Remember to make any action easy for your reader by supplying your telephone number or suggesting best times to call you.

The closing is your chance to show commitment to the job. If you tell the reviewer you plan to call, make sure you follow through. "It really impresses me when someone takes the step to call and follow up," says Vin Vu, former Director of Sales and Marketing for a company in Spokane, Washington. "You have to be aggressive and continue to keep your name in the interviewer's mind." See Boxes 13.2 and 13.3 for examples of cover letters.

Karen A. Frazer
4904 Hawk Trail
Columbia, GA 30066
(404) 713-3932

May 10, 20XX

Mr. John Dickson
President
BellSouth Telecommunications
1500 West Peachtree
Atlanta, GA 30303

Dear Mr. Dickson:

Attention-getting first paragraph →

With more than 10 years' experience in the Telecommunications Industry, I will bring to BellSouth Telecommunications unique expertise in Government Affairs. Currently, as the Director of Government Relations and External Affairs for Alltel Wireless, I am leading a highly visible drive to win the support of local municipalities to facilitate our CARE project and further establish our public relations position within the city of Warner Robbins.

Interest paragraph →

Previously during my tenure as Public Relations Manager, I led the public relations team that established a positive presence in the southeastern Georgia region. This position also required extensive government liaison efforts to meet immediate and long-term goals. One of my greatest strengths lies in building consensus. As detailed in my attached résumé, I have been recognized throughout my career for building a sense of teamwork with the local municipalities within my area of responsibility. I have also been commended throughout my career for departmental team building and project success.

Desire paragraph →

Although my years at Alltel have been a wonderful experience, I am now ready to pursue new professional challenges such as your open position for Vice President of External Affairs. There is no other telecommunications firm in the southeast I would rather be associated with than BellSouth Telecommunications.

Action paragraph →

I would welcome the chance to spend some time with you—either in person or over the telephone—to discuss how my proven governmental relations and team building skills can benefit BellSouth Telecommunications. I will follow up with you early next week to schedule an appointment.

Sincerely,

Karen Frazer
Karen Frazer

BOX 13.2 ☛ **Sample Cover Letter**

Linda Lee
943 Trail Lane
Arlington Heights, IL 60065

November 18, 20XX

Ms. Peggy S. Weldon, Senior Designer
Drawford Interactive Publishing
9089 Piedmont Road, Suite 123
Atlanta, GA 30305

Dear Ms. Weldon:

Attention-getting first paragraph →

I have spent the past 11 months in college preparing to meet the needs of a publishing company such as yours. I know your organization requires its employees to demonstrate superb communication skills, attention to detail, and versatility. I have these abilities because I have worked hard to develop them through education, training, and real-world experience.

Interest paragraph →

Drawford Interactive Publishing leads the communication field, and I want to work for a leader. My desktop publishing, communication, and organizational skills would complement the high-quality publications, presentations, and programs you produce. Please consider me a candidate for the position of Project Coordinator.

Desire paragraph →

As the enclosed résumé indicates, my past work experience in arts administration, retail, and the service industry has helped me develop my ability to deal with customers effectively, keep accurate records, pay attention to details, and prioritize my time. I have learned being gracious can be more important than being right.

Action paragraph →

I will contact you next week to make sure you have received my letter and to answer any questions you may have.

Sincerely,

Linda Lee
Linda Lee
Enclosure: résumé

BOX 13.3 🖙 **Sample Cover Letter**

Electronic Cover Letters

If you are sending your application package electronically by file transfer or e-mail, make sure you have the recipient's name and details correct. Nothing creates more frustration than receiving an e-mail error due to an improper e-mail address. Your e-mail cover letter should follow the same format as a hard copy cover letter except that you should try to be more concise and succinct to allow for ease in file trans-

"You get about one or two sentences to give a recruiter or hiring manager a reason to read on. It's like a great direct mail piece or the best print ad you've ever seen. You get one chance to stop me from turning the page."

Source: Ed Tazzia, "It All Starts with One Sentence," *Brandweek*, Volume 44, Issue 9, March 3, 2003, p. 38.

fer. Be sure, however, to include enough information to grab the prospective employer's interest and ensure that your value and contribution to the organization is clearly stated. When sending your cover letter in this way, avoid bold print, italics, underlining, and other type enhancements. Use all caps to make specific words or titles stand out. Don't center, justify, or use columns, as they usually do not survive the file transfer intact.

Résumés

In an article in the *Atlanta Journal and Constitution,* Joyce Wessel stated: "Pity the poor résumé. They have such a rotten reputation. Job seekers hate to write them. Employers hate to read them. Everyone knows they don't land jobs, and worse yet, they cost money to print and mail."[5]

Ms. Wessel goes on to quote résumé authority Tom Jackson, who refers to résumés as simply junk mail to those receiving them. Unfortunately, you have to write one.

Despite the views of Ms. Wessel and Mr. Jackson, résumés are an important part of the job application process. Potential employers will ask for one, as your résumé advertises you on paper. It helps an employer decide whether to pursue a business relationship with you.

Résumés may not be the best screening device, but right now, they seem to be the best show in town. Your résumé should not be a razzle-dazzle document or a biographical sketch of your life and work. However, it should stress your previous accomplishments.

If you provide a run-of-the mill résumé, you will not get an interview. Employers across the country complain about the hundreds of unwanted, unclear résumés received each week. Because they receive so many, recruiters spend little time reviewing poor ones. In fact, a résumé gets only 10 to 40 seconds of attention when read by a reviewer.

Your résumé communicates your ability to perform meaningful work and creates interest in you. In short, your résumé opens doors. Your résumé should clearly prove your ability to produce valuable results and motivate potential employers to want to meet you.

Because your résumé serves as both a vehicle of communication and a demonstration of how you communicate, you must make sure the reader gets the right message. Refer to Box 13.4 to avoid making résumé-writing mistakes.

A résumé should contain three basic sections: heading, experience, and education. The following paragraphs discuss these three parts and other items you might choose to include or not include. The final section discusses different résumé formats.

HEADING

The heading appears at the top of the page and should contain your name, address, e-mail address, area code, and telephone number. Include the position you seek to fill. Notice you can vary the placement of the information within the heading. See Box 13.5.

[5] Joyce Wessel, "Cold Hard Truth About Résumés and What to Do About It," *Atlanta Journal and Constitution,* April 13, 1986, p. 9–S.

People summarize, water down, and oversimplify their responsibilities and accomplishments. The result is that the potential employer thinks, "This person is lazy and doesn't do much."

People write about themselves, creating an autobiographical document. The résumé should be an advertisement addressing the needs of the potential employer reading the résumé. Employers should be thinking, "Wow, this person has exactly what I am looking for," as they read the résumé.

People use hard-to-read and confusing formats. A potential employer will spend approximately 20 seconds scanning each of the 50 to 100 résumés in front of him or her. An easy-to-read format enables this individual to read your whole résumé in that 20 seconds.

People provide more detail and depth in the job description of older jobs than in the description of their present jobs. The employer who thinks your career peaked and is declining will interview other candidates.

People submit résumés with spelling errors, grammatical errors, and formatting inconsistencies. The potential employer will think, "A person representing himself or herself this poorly on paper will not hesitate to represent the company poorly as well."

The writer buries important information in the text or layout. Prioritize the information the employer seeks and simplify or omit information of minimal interest to the employer.

Visit the website **www.accent-resume-writing.com** to see résumés that illustrate these typical mistakes.

BOX 13.4 🖝 **Typical Résumé-Writing Mistakes**

SOURCE: Accent Résumé Writing, 1998.

EDWIN R. COULTER
225 Normany Village
Shreveport, Louisiana 71104
(381) 865-7544
ecoulter@aol.com

Position applied for: Director of Publicity

Qualifications of
JANET LEE FELDER
Old Lyme Road
Northbrook, VT 05663
(820) 264-5911
jfelder@yahoo.com

for the position of SYSTEMS ANALYST

Brighton Industries, Inc.

BOX 13.5 🖝 **Résumé Heading**

EXPERIENCE

The two most important parts of your résumé are the education and experience sections. If you have five years or more of full-time work experience, the experience section becomes more important than your education. If you have gone back to school to advance within your current organization, emphasize your recent education. If you have worked only part-time while pursuing your degree, emphasize your education. Within this section, include the name and location of past employers, dates of employment, job title, responsibilities, and accomplishments. When presenting your work experience, concentrate on descriptions convincing the employer of your ability to do the job. Ask yourself these questions as you prepare this section of your résumé: What have you done or accomplished? What accomplishments indicate that you will perform in the future? Be confident but truthful. Again, use action verbs to describe your duties and accomplishments as you want your accomplishments to "jump out" at the reader, so make them apparent.

EDUCATION

After you have attended college, do not list your high school diploma. However, make the most of your college education on your résumé. List degrees, training certificates, and your major. Use chronological order, listing your most recent education first. If you have not graduated yet, give your anticipated date of graduation and include your grade point average if it is 3.0 or above. Recruiters may ask about your grade point average if you recently graduated from college. Typically, after you have become a full-time employee, your grade point average becomes less important.

If you have little work experience, consider putting the education background section before your work experience. When making this strategic move, add more details about your studies to show your preparation for the job you want.

ITEMS YOU MAY INCLUDE OR LEAVE OUT

You may use such items as personal information, job objectives, activities and interests, military experience, professional organizations, licenses, and references on your résumé. Obviously, you should use only those relating to you and enhancing your résumé.

Personal Information.   Most authorities feel personal information should be omitted. Federal law prohibits employers from asking about your height, weight, health, marital status, or religious preference.

Job Objective.   The job objective (also called a professional objective, goal, or personal statement) states how you will use your skills and knowledge for the organization in which you seek employment. Focus your job objective on what you can do for the prospective employer. When you use a job objective, try not to be too specific, because you may eliminate related jobs. If your goal seems too lofty, the employer may decide you have unrealistic goals. Be sure it is precise, consise, and active. If your objective appears vague, the employer may not know what you want.

Activities, Military Experience, and Professional Organizations.   New college graduates should list awards (including academic honors such as Dean's list), special skills, and outside activities. The bottom line is that while you are in college you should join something, do something, or volunteer for something, because employers like active, engaged people. Today's organizations emphasize teamwork. By listing team-related activities, you demonstrate your ability to interact and work with others. Military experience and membership in professional organizations can also show your leadership abilities.

References. Many authorities suggest leaving references off your résumé. They perceive that employers should only contact references after the interview. Therefore, they recommend you carry a copy of your references to the interview. Many human resources managers see little reason for including the statement: References furnished upon request. "It's like saying the sun comes up every morning," remarked one human resources professional.[6]

If you choose to list references, seek out three or four individuals and ask permission to use their names as references. When selecting your references, use supervisors, managers, and executives. If you have little experience, list the names of major professors and be sure they will say positive things about you.

On your résumé, include the complete names and titles, company names, and addresses including e-mail and work telephone numbers of individuals who have agreed to serve as references for you. When you learn a potential employer has contacted them, send a thank-you note; they have provided you a service.

Traditional Résumé Formats

The three most widely recognized traditional résumé formats are chronological, functional, and targeted. You may even see some combinations of these formats.

CHRONOLOGICAL

The chronological résumé starts with the most recent job experience and goes back several years to provide evidence of a work record. For example, you may want to include only the last five years of employment. Review this résumé format in Boxes 13.6 and 13.7. Many job recruiters prefer this format because they find it easy to read and understand. Employers widely accept the chronological format, and some job counselors recommend it.

FUNCTIONAL

The functional résumé format organizes information under functional or topical headings. See Box 13.8 for an example of the functional résumé. Each paragraph contains statements related to your experience. This format highlights major areas of accomplishment and allows you to organize them to support your work objectives and job targets. In this format, your actual job titles and work history become secondary.

The functional résumé gives you considerable flexibility. It also helps to eliminate repetition and often de-emphasizes a broken work history record. The functional résumé can be used when you seek to change careers, when you first enter the job market, or after a period of unemployment.

TARGETED

The targeted résumé focuses on a clear, specific job target. An example can be found in Box 13.9. Because this style focuses on a specific job target, you must write a different résumé for each of your targets (or jobs). Fortunately, job seekers find this résumé style easy to write.

---

[6] Mary Ellen Guffey, *Essentials of Business Communication* (Cincinnati, OH: South-Western College Publishing, 1994), p. 293.

John W. Glenn
650 Kamblin Road, Morrow, Georgia 30297
Home: (770) 914-8654, Mobile: (404) 917-6909
JohnGlenn@bellsouth.net

Information technology expert with an emphasis on design, development, and implementation of client IT systems. Results-oriented manager with strong interpersonal skills, leadership qualities, and a focus on the bottom line with highly transferable technical skills and business savvy.

PROFESSIONAL EXPERIENCE

SIX CONTINENTS HOTELS—Atlanta, Georgia　　　　　　**1996–Present**
(Parent Company of Intercontinental Hotels, Crown Plaza, Staybridge Suites, and Holiday Inn.)

Technical Advisor
October 2000–Present

- Provide guidance and expertise to senior management for NT engineering and operations on a daily basis.
- Develop global network and messaging system designs to support business initiatives.
- Lead project teams in implementing network designs.
- Prepare project plans, estimates, and assignments for team.
- Serve as U.S. representative to parent company's global planning group.
- Develop global desktop and server strategies.
- Develop documentation standards guide of planned architecture.
- Lead team in review and selection of key software components.
- Guide Windows NT team in disaster recovery planning.
- Manage internal projects with budgets of $500,000 to over $1.0 million.

Senior Systems Engineer
September 1999–October 2000

- Engineered the desktop, server, and messaging infrastructure for upgrade from Novell and Windows 3.11 to Windows NT and Windows 95, reducing support calls by 50 percent.
- Tested and implemented hardware and software monitoring tools, resulting in 99.9 percent uptime on NT servers.
- Designed the enterprise NT domain structure with cooperation from all divisions.
- Developed and implemented capacity planning for new and existing production systems.
- Provided level 3 support throughout 12-month project.
- Trained level 1 and 2 support team on troubleshooting new infrastructure.
- Developed best practices for evaluation of new hardware and software platforms.

Systems Engineer (London, England)
January 1999–September 1999

- Fulfilled lead engineer obligations in relocation of corporate headquarters.
- Managed all aspects of global desktop, server, and application deployment.
- Wrote and evaluated vendor responses to RFP (Request for Pricing) for desktop and server hardware purchases and support services within the United Kingdom.
- Selected vendors for hardware, software, and support services.

BOX 13.6 ☛ **Chronological Résumé**

Systems Engineer
October 1996–January 1999

- Guided team decision on choosing server hardware vendor.
- Evaluated and implemented software to meet project requirements.
- Provided level 3 and 4 support for desktop and server environments.

TROUTMAN SANDERS LLP—Atlanta, Georgia
(One of the southeast's largest law firms with offices in eight cities including London and Hong Kong.)

Systems Engineer
May 1996–October 1996

- Migrated 700 users from Novell and DOS to the Microsoft Application Suite in one of the first such standardizations for law firms in Atlanta.
- Designed and implemented Exchange messaging environment.

HOWARD SYSTEMS INTERNATIONAL—Atlanta, Georgia
(An industry leader in Information Services and Management Consulting.)

Consultant (AT&T Global Information Services)
September 1995–May 1996

- Designed and implemented Windows NT systems.
- Migrated 800 users from Banyan Vines and Windows 3.11 to Windows NT and Windows 95.

COMMAND DATA—Birmingham, Alabama
(A global leader in providing business solutions and support to the construction materials industry.)

Account Representative
September 1993–September 1995

- Managed company's largest customer.
- Designed and configured client networks to meet business needs.
- Trained in-house and client staff on company software packages.

EDUCATION

Kennesaw State University—Kennesaw, Georgia
Masters of Business Administration, May 2003

Jacksonville State University—Jacksonville, Alabama
Bachelor of Science in Computer Science, August 1992

MCSE Microsoft Certified Systems Engineer Windows NT 4.0

Omicron "Transition to IS Management"

Omicron "Creative Problem Solving Skills"

BOX 13.6 ☞ (continued)

Hillary Grace Roebuck

Current Address	**Permanent Address**
802 Burnt Pottery Lane	**1356 Hendon Road**
Statesboro, GA 30460	**Woodstock, GA 30188**
(404) 668-1941	(770) 591-2007
hroebuck@georgiasouthern.edu	

Objective
To obtain an entry-level marketing position with an organization seeking an individual with outstanding communication skills and leadership abilities who has the knowledge and education to contribute to the organization's profitability and success

Education
Georgia Southern University, Statesboro, Georgia
Bachelor of Business Administration in Marketing
May 2005 GPA: *3.58*

Work Experience
Taco Mac, Roswell, Georgia
Wait staff, November 2000–August 2001
- Provided excellent customer service resulting in average tips each night of $100
- Assisted in training ten new employees
- Thrived in the fast paced environment and managed on average six tables and served over 50 customers each night
- Asked to move into a management position

Leadership Experience
Georgia Southern University Equestrian Team
Georgia Southern University, Statesboro, Georgia
Show Judge Manager, August 2002–May 2003
- Contacted and hired judges for intercollegiate horse shows
- Constructed and mailed out contracts to judges
- Lead monthly meetings

Volunteer Experience
Old Indian Trail Homeowner's Association, Statesboro, Georgia
Secretary, November 2002–present
- Create, edit and distribute subdivision monthly newsletters
- Create and maintain resident data base
- Take minutes at monthly meetings
- Mail minutes of all meetings to homeowners

Activities
Gamma Beta Phi Honors Society, 2002–present
Golden Key Honors Society, 2003–present
Delta Epsilon Iota Academic Honor Society, 2004–present
Georgia Southern Equestrian Team, 2001–2004

Honors
Presidents List Recipient, 2004
Deans List Recipient, 2001–2004
Hope Scholarship Recipient, 2001–present

Computer Skills
Microsoft Word, Excel and PowerPoint

Class Project
Georgia Southern University Marketing Plan for Russell Union
Marketing Research Class Project, Fall Semester 2004
- Conducted personal interviews
- Handed out surveys
- Entered data into SPSS for analysis

BOX 13.7 ☞ **Chronological Résumé**

Sara Dee Roebuck
792 Cliff Court
Marietta, Georgia 30066

Objective: General management position in carpet production or related field. Willing to travel or relocate.

Experience

General Management:	Have supervised more than 300 hourly employees in two carpet plants. Scheduled all workers and handled all employee-relations issues.
Quality Assurance:	Met or exceeded quality standards 95 percent of the time. Helped establish quality standards for new carpets.
Production:	Assisted in introduction, setup, and operation of new machines. Extensive knowledge of Corrland and Weighlight equipment.
Motivation:	Used management by objectives (MBO), goal setting, quality circles, and piece-rate systems.

Work History

1989 to Present:	Production Manager, Royal Mills, Dalton, Georgia
1986 to 1989:	Production Supervisor, Quality Carpets, Calhoun, Georgia

Education

June 1985:	Graduated from Kennesaw State University, Kennesaw, Georgia, with a Bachelor of Business Administration concentrating in Production Management.

Community Activities

1984 to Present:	Toastmasters International, served as president of local chapter
1990 to Present:	Big Sister Program

References

Available upon Request

BOX 13.8 ☛ **Functional Résumé**

REBECCA BRITT
145 South Seventh Street
Canton, GA 30114
770-975-1234 Office 404-379-2424 Mobile

EXECUTIVE PROFILE:

Seventeen-year professional career highlighted by rapid advancement and consistent achievement in development and management of wireless corporate real estate assets. Organizational driver and consummate business leader with a strong track record of performance in start-up and high-growth organizations. Accustomed to overcoming market, technical, financial, and competitive challenges to drive system development, customer growth, financial profitability, and performance improvement. Expertise includes:

Management and Leadership Qualifications

- Strategic Planning and Corporate Development
- Finance, Fixed Assets, and Accounting
- Budgeting and Cost Management
- Profit and Loss Management
- Organizational Design and Development
- Quality, Efficiency, and Performance Improvement
- Multi-Site Operating Management
- Problem Solving and Decision Making
- Human Resource Affairs and Teaming

- Marketing, Sales, and New Business Development
- Key Account Development
- Client Relationship Management
- Corporate Policy and Best Practices Establishment and Compliance
- Corporate Staff to Field Coordination and Liaison
- IT Tool Development for Consolidated Corporate Reporting

Industry Experience

- Turn Key Project Management
- Site Acquisition
- Zoning and Permitting
- Title Clearance
- Lease and Contract Negotiations and Compliance
- Property Management

- Site Design
- Tower Site Construction
- Switch Site Construction
- Equipment Purchase
- Equipment Installation
- Vendor Qualification and Selection

- Equipment Inventory Control
- FCC Compliance
- FAA Compliance
- Hazardous Material Reporting
- Tower Co-location Management
- Co-location Pricing
- Site Maintenance

- Warehouse Management
- Budget Modeling and Development
- Budget Variance to Actual Tracking and Reporting
- Project Tracking and Control
- Asset Management

Featured in Who's Who in the South and Southeast and Who's Who among Women

PROFESSIONAL EXPERIENCE:

Crown Castle USA: **January 2003 to Present**

Vice President and General Manager—Atlanta Region
Recruited to provide leadership and direction for start-up and complete operation of the Georgia Region of Crown Castle USA. Responsible for managing wireless network sales, operations, and maintenance to create growth and increase market profitability. Developed strategic plans and procedures, business goals, and objectives for the regional market. Sourced new business, developed and managed opportunities, and provided leadership in creating innovative responses to customer requests for service and new business. Evaluated business opportunity and business plan information for profitability. Established professional credibility as an industry expert and represented the region in the market to assure government and community leaders were aware of the organization and responded favorably to its stated purpose. Created new executive relationships with wireless carriers and maintained existing relationships in order to have access to information that enabled the company to respond to the changing business environment and to

BOX 13.9   📧   **Targeted Résumé**

outperform the competition. Managed and evaluated projects to determine if intervention was needed with carriers and company employees to assure that projects were completed within budget, on time, and to complete customer satisfaction.
- From start-up, staffed and trained 38 employee and 11 in-house contractor organizations
- Achieved 1st year annual EBITDA of $10 million
- Achieved 1st year annual service revenue of $8.8 million
- Achieved 1st year end monthly tower revenue of $1.3 million
- Executed 203 site license agreements during first operating year

BellSouth Cellular Corporate (BSCC)   **Dec. 1998 to Dec. 2002**

Director Corporate Real Estate and Development
Provided leadership and direction to integrating and coordinating all aspects of corporate real estate and infrastructure build-out among various BSCC markets and with BSCC corporate departments. Responsible for the identification of strategic issues, the development of the company's short-term and long-term strategic plans, and the development of specific tactical actions to meet corporate goals for revenue enhancement and increasing shareholder value related to its wireless real estate assets. Acted as strategic team member in negotiations and closure of sale of BellSouth towers to Crown Castle USA.
- Developed integrated reporting tool to measure co-location activity and revenue from all BSCC markets.
- Developed real estate database for management of contractual obligations related to cellular properties nationwide.

BellSouth Mobility Inc. (Cingular Wireless)   **June 1984 to Nov. 1998**

Director—Engineering Implementation   **Dec. 1995 to Nov. 1998**
Selected by Senior Management to provide the overall management effectiveness and results of BellSouth Mobility Region II engineering implementation department. Responsible for engineering and operations required to provide cellular mobile service. Directed departmental managers responsible for: land acquisition, zoning, co-location issues, and property management; building design and construction; switch and cell site equipment engineering and installation; project tracking, asset accounting, and inventory management; FCC and FAA compliance; network administration; and engineering and operational expense budget development and performance. Assessed complex situations and developed strategy and tactics for successfully achieving acquisition and zoning goals in the face of changing parameters and complicated competitor, community, and political relationships. Directed development and implementation of creative solutions to the requirement for cellular facilities in highly residential metropolitan areas.
- Directed build for 1996 Summer Olympic Games of 101 cell sites that provided cellular coverage for 19 venue locations; 3 Olympic Park sites; 4 in building hotel locations; 10 Airport micro cells, and 28 Marta stations and 9 Marta tunnels.

Sr. Manager of Real Estate and Construction   **Dec. 1991 to Nov. 1995**
Increased responsibility for the direction of the real estate and building construction program within a regional area in all phases of site acquisition, zoning, design, construction, and maintenance. Developed and managed an annual acquisition and construction capital budget of $30 million and an annual rental expense budget of $4.5 million.
- Built some of the first "stealth" site church bell towers in the industry
- Designed and constructed creative solution to equipment engineering installation in small equipment areas

Manager of Real Estate and Construction   **Sept. 1987 to Nov. 1991**
Provided management of all phases of the real estate and construction build program within BellSouth Mobility Region II.
- Built first cellular buried geothermal controlled environmental vault in the Southeast
- Pioneered use of first concrete monopole for cellular in the nation

---

Education:

Bachelor of Business Administration **(Summa Cum Laude)** / Major in Management and Organizational Communications,
Kennesaw State University, 1992

BOX 13.9 ☛ (continued)

Electronic Résumé Formats

Often, you need to format your résumé for e-mailing, posting to Internet sites, or scanning. These digital résumés include the same information that other résumés do, and they come in the same varieties—chronological, functional, or combination.

E-MAILED RÉSUMÉS

Even though e-mail is a less formal medium than print, disregard this fact when sending your résumé in this way. A professional looking résumé is still your goal. First, be sure your e-mail name is professional. Cute or funny e-mail names are fine among friends, but not appropriate for job applications. Next, format the body of your e-mail like a cover letter, with a proper business salutation and closing. Include your name and the position you are applying for in the subject line. Once you have achieved a professional format you must decide whether to include the résumé in the body of the e-mail or to send it as an attachment. Whichever way you choose to go, avoid excessive formatting.

If you decide to include your résumé in the body of the e-mail message, send it as text-only. It may be less attractive without formatting, but it will be neat and readable, which is what matters. Using HTML code is not advisable either as many e-mail systems cannot read HTML e-mail and your résumé may be converted to hundreds of lines of squiggles and code.

If you decide to send your résumé as an attachment, limit the formatting. Since there are a great many kinds of e-mail software, your perfectly professional-looking résumé can become an unreadable mess on someone else's computer with misalignments, line breaks, and unnecessary tabs.

ONLINE RÉSUMÉS

Typically, you can enter your résumé online in two ways. The first way is to create your résumé by choosing items from a series of menus. The second type of résumé entry requires that you cut and paste your résumé into a plain-text field.

When using a form-based résumé entry system, be sure to choose selections that clearly define your job experience. Be sure the items you choose describe your actual job duties and use every opportunity to type in additional information that will set you apart from others seeking similar job opportunities.

Employers search for key words in résumés that are cut and pasted into plain-text fields. One way to identify key words is to underline all skills listed in advertisements and job descriptions. You want your résumé to be found in many types of searches, so try to vary the key words that you use to allow for the widest possibility that your résumé will be found. See Box 13.10 for a sample list of key words.

To add key words to your résumé, study the job announcement, and where appropriate, copy the exact words from the job announcement to describe your skills. That way, when a manager enters key words, your résumé will be selected. Fill your résumé with important nouns the computer will recognize, such as the names of professional organizations and industry jargon. Follow each abbreviation with the phrase it stands for, with the exception of B.S. and B.A. for Bachelor of Science and Bachelor of Arts.

List every key word that applies to you; do not expect the computer to infer. For example, do not simply write "word processing: Microsoft Office." Instead, write "word processing: Microsoft Office, Microsoft Word, Excel, and PowerPoint." Rules about length are relaxed for digital résumés. Some career counselors even suggest adding a key word paragraph to the top of your résumé, but others do not believe such paragraphs are useful.

CLERICAL

Front Desk, Data Entry, Reception, Multiple Telephones, Word Processing, Database Management, Filing, Customer Service, Time Management, Document Management

OFFICE MANAGER

Problem-Solving Abilities, Multitask Management, Detail-Minded, Human Relations Skills, Spreadsheet Development, Contract Review, Travel and Meeting Planning, Vendor Coordination, Written Communication Skills, Small Business Environment

TEACHER

Adult Education, Adult Learning Theory, GED, Instructional TV, Special Education Group Training, Group Facilitator, Needs Assessment, Curriculum Designer, Bilingual

PERSONAL KEY WORDS

Ability to Delegate, Analytical, Dependable, Flexible, High-Energy, Leadership, Problem Solving, Results Oriented, Self-Directing, Takes Iniatitive

BOX 13.10 ☞ **Sample Key Words**

SOURCE: Rebecca M. Smith, "Electronic Résumés and Online Networking: How to Use the Internet to Do a Better Job Search," *Career Press*, 1999, *http://www.eresume.com.*

Today's new reality—eloquently discussed in the book *Free Agent Nation: The Future of Working for Yourself*—is that *everyone* is a small business owner . . . of their own career. Retrieved from *http://www.resumeblog.blogspot.com/* "Why a Résumé Blog™?"

Be aware that when résumé searches are conducted online, most employers ask for the most recently posted résumés. Therefore, it is wise to go into the job site where your résumé is posted and make small changes at least weekly. You can do something as simple as changing a single word. This adjusts the date associated with your résumé to the most recent update date and causes your résumé to continue to appear as a recent résumé listing.

PERSONAL WEBSITES AND BLOGS

Although e-mailed résumés and cover letters dominate electronic job hunting, they're not the only e-method. You can now also demonstrate your technical expertise by creating your own website that will allow, at the click of a mouse, your cover letter and résumé to be displayed in their original quality and format. You can refer recruiters and potential employers to your website by including the URL in an e-mail. Wendy Enelow, president of the Lynchburg, Va.-based Career Masters Institute, and author of *Expert Résumés for Computer and Web Jobs,* has shared that some Web-savvy job hunters use personal Web page résumés to restore any design edge lost in plain-text e-mail versions. "It's the latest and greatest," Enelow said. "What Web-based résumés have done is allow you to use the latest technology but also create sharp visual presentation. Now you have the best of both worlds, you have the aesthetic presence combined with state-of-the-art technology."[7]

In addition to creating personal websites, you can also create a blog. According to Blogger.com, a blog can be a personal diary, a collection of links, your own private thoughts, or memos to the world. It is a place where you can share infor-

[7] Matt Crowley, "Format of Résumés Moves to E-Mail, But Same Principles Still Apply," *Knight Ridder Tribune Business News,* Washington, Aug 10, 2003.

mation such as your résumé with others.[8] You can visit this website *http://resumeblog. blogspot.com/#instructions* to learn how to create a special résumé blog. Begin by taking the quiz and then creating your own résumé blog.

Plain-Text and Scannable Résumés

This section describes two types of digital résumés: plain-text résumés that you e-mail to employers or post to databases, and scannable paper résumés that you format for reading by computer optics.

PLAIN-TEXT RÉSUMÉS

To e-mail or post your résumé to the Internet, you must write your résumé using the American Standard Code for Information Interchange (ASCII), also known as plain text. Plain text contains no special formatting codes, so every computer can understand it.

To create a plain-text résumé, open your existing résumé document with a word processing program, and save it as a text or ASCII file. Taking this action will eliminate any formatting codes. You can use the computer's built-in text editor application, such as Notepad for Windows or Simpletext for Macintosh, to edit the résumé. The success of your electronic résumé depends, in part, on the number of key words it contains.

Writers of plain-text résumés should not use any characters or formatting not found on a standard keyboard. Boldface, italics, and underlining are unavailable, as are tabs, bullets, and multiple font sizes. Nevertheless, alternative attention-getting devices are still useful; asterisks and plus signs can replace bullets, rows of dashes can separate sections, and all-capital letters can emphasize headings.

When you write in ASCII, you disable the word wrap function. Words will not automatically move from one line to the next. Instead, you must hit the enter key at the end of every line. A line should hold only 65 characters, or it may not fit on the reviewer's screen. To be certain your line lengths are correct, count characters and use a standard-width typeface, such as Courier. Times New Roman is not a standard-width typeface, so 65 of its characters will not always translate to 65 of the reviewer's characters. See Box 13.11 for a sample plain-text résumé.

You can also post your plain-text résumé to Internet databases and apply instantly to thousands of companies. When you do this, the posted résumé becomes public information. Take precautions, such as omitting your home address and the address of your current employer. Also, do your homework; read several industry magazines and books to determine which sites are reputable. "If you're going to market your résumé, you don't want it to fall into just anyone's hands," says Gary Wright, executive recruiter with the Dallas-based McClane Co., an executive search firm. "Ask for references, a list of participating employers and how long the company has been in business. The company should also give a disclaimer that they will not sell your name and address."

Another issue you should weigh is the possibility that your current employer may see your résumé on the Internet. One individual reported that he had put his résumé online before he had accepted his current job. A few months passed and his boss called him into his office and asked him why he was seeking a new job. The individual was dumbfounded. The résumé that he had posted several months before was still floating out in cyberspace. He was able to calm his boss down, but

---

[8]"What Is a Blog?" Retrieved from *http://www.blogger.com/tour_start.g.*

```
THOMAS B. SEEKER
1234 Circle Drive
Chicago, IL 12345
H: (410) 555-1212; W: (410) 555-2121
E-mail: seeker@mingspring.com

OBJECTIVE

Client Server Systems Architect for a high technology firm.

QUALIFICATIONS SUMMARY

Nine years of experience in designing, installing, and
troubleshooting computing systems; a proven track record in
identifying problems and developing innovative solutions.

TECHNICAL SKILLS

* PROGRAMMING: C, C++, Visual BASIC, FORTRAN, Pascal, SQL,
OSF/Motif, UNIX Shell Script (sh, ksh, csh), BASIC, Clipper,
Algol 68, and 80X86 Assembler.

* OPERATING SYSTEMS: UNIX (bsd & SVr3/r4), MS Windows, MS DOS, MS
Windows NT, Solaris, HP-UX, Ultrix, AIX, VAX/VMS, and Macintosh
System 7.

* NETWORKING: TCP/IP, OSI, Microsoft LAN Manager, Novell Netware,
DDN, Internet, Ethernet, Token Ring, SNA, X.25, LAN-WAN
interconnection.

* APPLICATIONS: Microsoft Office, Microsoft Access, Microsoft
Visual C++, Microsoft Project, Microsoft Publisher, Lotus 123,
Lotus Freelance, System Architect, and others.

PROFESSIONAL EXPERIENCE

Systems Engineer
Computer Engineering Corporation, Los Angeles, CA, 1993-Present

* Provided systems engineering, software engineering, technical
consulting, and marketing services as a member of the Systems
Integration Division of a software engineering consulting
company.

* Designed and managed the development of an enterprise-level
client/server automated auditing application for a major financial
management company migrating from mainframe computers, db2, and
FOCUS to a workgroup oriented, client/server architecture involving
Windows for Workgroups, Windows NT Advanced Server, Microsoft SQL
Server, Oracle7, and UNIX.

* Designed an enterprise-level, high-performance, mission-
critical, client/server database system incorporating symmetric
multiprocessing computers (SMP), Oracle7's Parallel Server,
Tuxedo's online transaction processing (OLTP) monitor, and
redundant array of inexpensive disks (RAID) technology.

* Conducted extensive trade studies of a large number of vendors
that offer leading-edge technologies; these studies identified
proven (low-risk) implementations of SMP and RDBMS systems that
met stringent performance and availability criteria.
```

BOX 13.11 ☞ **Sample Plain-Text Résumé**

SOURCE: Rebecca M. Smith maintains the award-winning Résumés & Resources website (*http://www.eresumes.com*) and is the author of *Electronic Résumés & Online Networking: How to Use the Internet to Do a Better Job Search, Including a Complete, Up-to-Date Resource Guide* (Career Press, 1999) and *The Unofficial Guide to Getting a Job at Microsoft* (McGraw-Hill, 2000). She has been monitoring technology and its impact on employment for the past 10 years. E-mail to: rsmith@eresumes.com.

Systems Analyst
Business Consultants, Inc., Washington, DC 1990-1993

* Provided technical consulting services to the Smithsonian
Institute's Information Technology Services Group, Amnesty
International, and internal research and development initiatives.

* Consolidated and documented the Smithsonian Laboratory's
Testing, Demonstration, and Training databases onto a single
server, maximizing the use of the laboratory's computing
resources.

* Brought the Smithsonian Laboratory online with the Internet.

* Successfully integrated and delivered to Amnesty International
an $80,000 HP 9000/750 Server consisting of 8 Gigabytes of disk
space and 9 software systems that required extensive porting work
and documentation.

Automated Data Processor
US Army Infantry, Germany 1986-1990

* Analyzed problems and ADP processes; designed, tested, and
implemented software and hardware systems for an organizational
operations center.

* Supervised the maintenance, deployment, installation, and
operation of a battalion's personnel system that monitored and
controlled up to 12 platoons in a fast-paced, technically
demanding environment.

* Designed a maintenance reporting program that converted the
labor-intensive task of producing weekly status reports from a
4-day to a 2-hour process.

* Developed a departmental computer literacy training program,
teaching classes on microcomputer operating systems, office
automation software, and introductory programming.

* Taught a "Structured Programming and Problem Solving" course
for the Community Education Center after work hours.

EDUCATION

* Computer Systems Technology Program, Air Force Institute of
Technology (AFIT), Graduate Courses in Software Engineering and
Computer Communications (24 quarter units); GPA: 3.43

* BS, Mathematics/Computer Science, University of California, Los
Angeles (UCLA), GPA: 3.57; Major GPA: 3.62

SPECIALIZED TRAINING

* Database Administration, Performance Tuning, and Benchmarking
with Oracle7; Oracle Corporation.

* Software Requirements Engineering and Management Course;
Computer Applications International Corporation.

* X.400 Messaging and Allied Communications Procedures-123
Profile; ComTechnologies, Inc.

BOX 13.11 ☞ (continued)

```
   * GOSIP LAN Operating System Network Administration; ETC, Inc.

   * Interactive UNIX System V r4 (POSIX) System Administration; ETC,
   Inc.

   * Effective Briefing Techniques and Technical Presentations;
   William French and Associates, Inc.

   * Transmission Control Protocol/Internet Protocol (TCP/IP);
   Technology Systems Institute.

   * LAN Interconnection Using Bridges, Routers, and Gateways;
   Information Systems Institute.

   * OSI X.400/X.500 Messaging and Directory Service Protocols;
   Communication Technologies, Inc.
   * US Army Signal Officer Advanced Course, US Army Signal Center,
   Georgia; Honor Graduate.

   CERTIFICATION, HONORS, & PROFESSIONAL AFFILIATIONS

   * MCP Trainer, DCS.
   * MCP Trainer, SDD.
   * MCP Certified Systems Engineer.
   * MCP Certified Product Specialist, Networking, MS TCP/IP,
   and MS Mail 3.2 for PC Networks.
   * Member, Armed Forces Communications and Electronics
   Association (AFCEA).
   * Recipient, Department of Defense Meritorious Service
   Medal, Defense Information Systems Agency (DISA).
```

BOX 13.11 🖝 **(continued)**

it certainly was an embarrassing situation. To keep a situation like this from happening to you, review the guidelines in Box 13.12 to safeguard your online résumé.

Gerry Crispin recommends evaluating sites based on their level of confidentiality. A private database should seek permission from the candidate before releasing a résumé to an employer.[9]

- At a minimum, date your résumé— just in case it lands on your boss' desk two years from now.
- Include a legend that forbids unauthorized transmission by headhunters. It may not work, but you never know.
- Call a job site's administrator before posting to it. Ask these questions: Are résumés ever traded or sold to other databases? Is a firewall up to protect them from being cherry-picked by "spidering" programs? In addition, who has access to the database? Only corporate recruiters? Headhunters too? Anybody at all?
- Keep your résumé off Usenet news groups, the most exposed posting spots.
- If possible, cloak your identity with a "power résumé"—one that lists your capabilities but not your name or employer—and with an anonymous e-mail account to receive inquiries.

BOX 13.12 🖝 **Safeguarding Your Online Résumé**

SOURCE: Jerry Useem, "Read This Before You Put a Résumé Online," *Fortune,* Volume 139, Issue 10, May 24, 1999, pp. 290–292, .

[9] Audrey Arthur, "Take Your Job Search Online," *Black Enterprise,* Volume 27, Issue 8, March 1997, p. 56.

The Internet can be part of a complete job search effort, but it should not be your sole job searching technique. Some companies may not use Internet recruiting.

SCANNABLE RÉSUMÉS

Many large companies, and a growing number of small ones, use computers to sort the hundreds of résumés they receive. These companies scan paper résumés into a computer database. See Box 13.13 for an example of a scannable résumé. According to Brett Warner, president of Atlanta-based JobBank USA, which archives 125,000 résumés, you should include a separate line of key words related to your occupation at the bottom of your résumé.

This technology helps job seekers. When companies put your résumé on file, your qualifications are ready and waiting to be electronically retrieved. Before you submit your résumé to a company, however, call to find out if it scans. If it does, you will need to make sure your résumé's design is computer-friendly.

Stylistic touches that you use on a traditional résumé may not be so easy on a computer scanner. Again, make sure your résumé has no graphics or formatting that a computer might misinterpret.[10] The following steps will increase a scanner's ability to read your résumé:

- Use nontextured white or off-white paper with black letters.
- Choose a well-known font such as Helvetica, Arial, or Courier.
- Pick a font size of 10 to 14 points and do not condense spacing between letters.
- Do not underline or italicize text and do not use asterisks or parentheses. Modern systems can understand bold, but older systems might not. You can still distinguish headings by using capital letters.
- Avoid boxes, graphics, columns, and horizontal or vertical lines.
- Put your name on its own line at the top of each page. Also, put telephone numbers on their own lines.
- Do not staple or fold your résumé.

You can easily identify how electronic résumés differ from traditional ones. First, you have separate lines for name and address information. Second, you only use capital letters and hyphens as visual cues. Finally, the margins of your electronic documents are wider.

Guidelines for Making Sure Your Documents Get Read

If you remember to write for your reader, chances are better that he or she will spend more time reviewing your documents. Before you send out a résumé, review the job announcement and fine-tune your résumé to meet the employer's specific criteria. Sprinkle your résumé with language found in the position description. You will create a positive first impression if your reader finds your cover letter and résumé attractive and easy to read. An inviting style draws attention to your qualifications.

---

[10] Olivia Crosby, "Résumés, Applications, and Cover Letters," *Occupational Outlook Quarterly,* Volume 43, Issue 2, Summer 1999, pp. 2–14.

```
JOB L. SEEKER

1234 Circle Drive
Chicago, IL 12345
H: (410) 555-1212; W: (410) 555-2121
E-mail: seeker@mindspring.com

OBJECTIVE

Client Server Systems Architect for a high-technology firm.

QUALIFICATIONS SUMMARY

Twelve years of experience in designing, installing, and
troubleshooting computing systems; a proven track record in
identifying problems and developing innovative solutions.

TECHNICAL SKILLS

- PROGRAMMING: C, C++, Visual BASIC, FORTRAN, Pascal, SQL,
  OSF/Motif, UNIX Shell Script (sh, ksh, csh), BASIC, Clipper,
  Algol 68, and 80X86 Assembler.

- OPERATING SYSTEMS: UNIX (bsd & SVr3/r4), MS Windows, MS DOS, MS
  Windows NT, Solaris, HP-UX, Ultrix, AIX, VAX/VMS, and Macintosh
  System 7.

- NETWORKING: TCP/IP, OSI, Microsoft LAN Manager, Novell Netware,
  DDN, Internet, Ethernet, Token Ring, SNA, X.25, LAN-WAN
  interconnection.

- APPLICATIONS: Microsoft Office, Microsoft Access, Microsoft
  Visual C++, Microsoft Project, Microsoft Publisher, Lotus 123,
  Lotus Notes, Lotus Freelance, System Architect, and others.

PROFESSIONAL EXPERIENCE

Systems Engineer

Computer Engineering Corporation, Chicago, IL, Present

- Provided systems engineering, software engineering, technical
  consulting, and marketing services as a member of the Systems
  Integration Division of a software engineering consulting company.

- Designed and managed the development of an enterprise-level
  client/server automated auditing application for a major
  financial management company migrating from mainframe computers,
  db2, and FOCUS to a workgroup oriented, client/server
  architecture involving Windows for Workgroups, Windows NT
  Advanced Server, Microsoft SQL Server, Oracle7, and UNIX.

- Designed an enterprise-level, high-performance, mission-
  critical, client/server database system incorporating symmetric
  multiprocessing computers (SMP), Oracle7's Parallel Server,
  Tuxedo's online transaction processing (OLTP) monitor, and
  redundant array of inexpensive disks (RAID) technology.

- Conducted extensive trade studies of a large number of vendors
  that offer leading-edge technologies; these studies identified
  proven (low-risk) implementations of SMP and RDBMS systems that
  met stringent performance and availability criteria.
```

BOX 13.13 🖙 Scannable Résumé

SOURCE: Rebecca M. Smith maintains the award-winning Résumés & Resources website (*http://www.eresumes.com*) and is the author of *Electronic Résumés & Online Networking: How to Use the Internet to Do a Better Job Search, Including a Complete, Up-to-Date Resource Guide* (Career Press, 1999) and *The Unofficial Guide to Getting a Job at Microsoft* (McGraw-Hill, 2000). She has been monitoring technology and its impact on employment for the past 10 years. E-mail to: rsmith@eresumes.com.

JOB L. SEEKER

Systems Analyst

Business Consultants, Inc., Detroit, MA, 1993

- Provided technical consulting services to the Smithsonian
  Institute's Information Technology Services Group, Amnesty
  International, and internal research and development
  initiatives.

- Consolidated and documented the Smithsonian Laboratory's
  Testing, Demonstration, and Training databases onto a single
  server, maximizing the use of the laboratory's computing
  resources.

- Brought the Smithsonian Laboratory online with the Internet.

- Successfully integrated and delivered to Amnesty International
  an $80,000 HP 9000/750 Server consisting of 8 Gigabytes of disk
  space and 9 software systems that required extensive porting
  work and documentation.

Automated Data Processor

US Army Infantry, 1990

- Analyzed problems and ADP processes; designed, tested, and
  implemented software and hardware systems for an organizational
  operations center.

- Supervised the maintenance, deployment, installation, and
  operation of a battalion's personnel system that monitored and
  controlled up to 12 platoons in a fast-paced, technically
  demanding environment.

- Designed a maintenance reporting program that converted the
  labor intensive task of producing weekly status reports from a
  4-day to a 2-hour process.

- Developed a departmental computer literacy training program,
  teaching classes on microcomputer operating systems, office
  automation software, and introductory programming.

- Taught a "Structured Programming and Problem Solving" course
  for the Community Education Center after work hours.

EDUCATION

- Computer Systems Technology Program, Air Force Institute of
  Technology (AFIT), Graduate Courses in Software Engineering and
  Computer Communications (24 quarter units); GPA: 3.43

- BS, Mathematics/Computer Science, University of California, Los
  Angeles (UCLA), GPA: 3.57; Major GPA: 3.62

SPECIALIZED TRAINING

- Database Administration, Performance Tuning, and Benchmarking
  with Oracle7; Oracle Corporation.

- Software Requirements Engineering and Management Course;
  Computer Applications International Corporation.

- X.400 Messaging and Allied Communications Procedures-123
  Profile; ComTechnologies, Inc.

BOX 13.13 ☛ (continued)

```
JOB L. SEEKER

- GOSIP LAN Operating System Network Administration; ETC, Inc.

- Interactive UNIX System V r4 (POSIX) System Administration;
  ETC, Inc.

- Effective Briefing Techniques and Technical Presentations;
  William French and Associates, Inc.

- Transmission Control Protocol/Internet Protocol (TCP/IP);
  Technology Systems Institute.

- LAN Interconnection Using Bridges, Routers, and Gateways;
  Information Systems Institute.

- OSI X.400/X.500 Messaging and Directory Service Protocols;
  Communication Technologies, Inc.

- US Army Signal Officer Advanced Course, US Army Signal Center,
  Georgia; Honor Graduate.

CERTIFICATION, HONORS, & PROFESSIONAL AFFILIATIONS

- MCP Trainer, DCS.

- MCP Trainer, SDD.

- MCP Certified Systems Engineer.

- MCP Certified Product Specialist, Networking, MS TCP/IP, and MS
  Mail 3.2 for PC Networks.

- Member, Armed Forces Communications and Electronics Association
  (AFCEA).

- Recipient, Department of Defense Meritorious Service Medal,
  Defense Information Systems Agency (DISA).

KEY WORDS

Troubleshooting, Programming, Engineering, Design Database
Administration, Supervise, Lead, Analye
```

BOX 13.13 ☞ **(continued)**

The following sections discuss how to design your documents, how long you should make your résumé, the importance of proofreading your work, and how to properly send your documents.

DESIGN PRINCIPLES

To make your résumé easier to read and copy, print it on white or lightly colored paper. Loud, bright colors may attract attention, but they risk creating an unprofessional impression. Also, use a laser printer and keep the font size at 10 point or above. The reviewer should not have to struggle to read your words.

Remember to use design elements strategically. Boldface, large type, capital letters, centering, or horizontal lines can make headings stand out on the page. Bullets or italics can draw attention to essential accomplishments. Using one-inch margins around the page and blank lines between sections will make all the information easier to see.

Any graphics you use should be consistent with your occupation's standards. Graphics appropriate for one occupation might be inappropriate for another.

To give your documents consistent flow, maintain the same style from beginning to end. Every section should have the same design elements. For example, if your education heading is bold and centered, every heading should be bold and centered. In the same way, chose one typeface, such as Arial, Courier, or Times New Roman, and use it throughout.

When you have finished, hold your documents at arm's length and examine them. Make sure that the type is easy to read and that the material lays out evenly on the page. You may need to experiment with different styles before deciding which you like best.

LENGTH OF THE RÉSUMÉ

A long résumé takes longer for your reviewer to digest and retain. Given the volume of résumés many reviewers receive, a long résumé may not get read. Although rules about length are more flexible than they once were, general guidelines still exist. Most students and recent graduates use a one-page résumé; other workers use one or two pages; and the most experienced individual uses two or three pages. If you have a lot of experience, limiting yourself to one page is not a good idea. In fact, it would only hurt you if you left out experience that may help qualify you for a job.[11]

If your résumé does not match this pattern, it probably contains unnecessary words or irrelevant information. Eliminate anything that does not help prove you are qualified for the job.

PROOFREADING

Take time to prepare the best documents you can. You might not be the most qualified candidate for every job, but your cover letter and résumé might be better than the competition's. The most common mistakes in résumés are simple typographical and spelling errors. Computer spelling checkers do not catch correctly spelled words used incorrectly—"of" for "on," for example, or "their" for "there." You want your documents to stand out, but not for the wrong reasons. Avoid mistakes by having several people proofread for you.

HOW TO SEND YOUR DOCUMENTS

Finally, consider how your cover letter and résumé will look when they arrive on a reviewer's desk. Hastily stuffed, illegibly addressed, and sloppily sealed envelopes do nothing to enhance your image.

If you are faxing your résumé, set the fax machine to fine printing mode and always fax an original. Your résumé may have to withstand several trips through a copy machine, so you want it to transmit as clearly as possible.

Before e-mailing your résumé to an employer, call the firm's human resources department or appropriate representative and inquire about the organization's policy on electronic résumés. If e-mailing materials is appropriate, be sure to confirm any style guidelines, such as acceptable file types (e-mail or attachment) and page formatting.[12]

Before e-mailing to the company, e-mail your documents to yourself and a friend to see how the document transmits. That way, you may be able to uncover some formatting errors. When an employer asks for an e-mailed résumé, never attach a word-processed document unless specifically requested to do so. Employers may not be able to open a word-processed document. Even if they can, they may not want to risk receiving a computer virus. Always send your cover letter and résumé as text in a single message. If you are responding to an advertisement or job posting, use that posting as the subject line of your message.[13]

[11] Kristen Gerencher, "Finding the Path to Your Next Job," *InfoWorld*, Volume 21, Issue 31, August 2, 1999, p. 75.

[12] Max Messmer, "E-Mail Etiquette," *Strategic Finance*, Volume 80, Issue 12, June 1999, pp. 10–12.

[13] Crosby, pp. 2–14.

Completing the Job Application

Many jobs require you to complete an application. If you think about it, an application provides similar information as a résumé but in a different format. Some companies use application forms to screen potential job candidates. If an individual does not completely fill out the form, the company may not consider that individual for a job. Therefore, to make this process easy, keep a file folder with the following information to help you quickly and completely fill out all application forms, whether on paper or on the computer.

IDENTIFICATION

Make sure you fill in your address and telephone number completely. Be prepared to provide your Social Security number as well. You may also need to bring proof of identification when you pick up and drop off the application.

EMPLOYMENT HISTORY

List the month and year you started and ended each job. Also, include your supervisor's name, address, and telephone number; your job title, location, salary, and major duties; and your reason for leaving.

EDUCATION AND CERTIFICATIONS

Make sure you have the complete addresses for any colleges or universities you attended. List the years you received your degrees. The same guidelines apply to certifications: List the complete name, level, award, and renewal dates of certification.

SPECIAL SKILLS

List any special skills you have that are closely related to the job, such as computer applications or equipment operation.

REFERENCES

Provide the names, telephone numbers, and addresses of three or four people who have agreed to recommend you.

When you pick up an application, do not miss an opportunity to make a good first impression. Dress as you would for the job interview. Politely request two copies of the form, or make your own copies of the original before you start filling it out. Read the entire application before you begin. Then, use one copy as a rough draft and the other as the final product. Use a typewriter or write neatly with black ink.[14]

Answer every question on the application and write "Not applicable" or "None" if a question does not apply to you. Some reviewers suggest answering "Will discuss in interview" if asked for information that might disqualify you.

Make a copy of your completed application. If you go back for an interview, take this record with you. Having a completed form will also make it easier to fill out the next one.

[14] Crosby, pp. 2–14.

Although forms do not offer the same flexibility as a résumé, you can still find ways to highlight your best qualifications. For example, use strong action verbs to describe your duties. If you do not have paid experience, give job titles to your volunteer work or list relevant academic experience, substituting student for job titles.

If you are filling out an application for a computer database, use key words and simple formatting—no boldface or bullets. Put the most important information first. Include as much information as you can for each question without becoming wordy or repetitive. The more relevant details you provide, the better your chances of using a key word that matches an employer's requirements. Before submitting the form, copy and paste your answers into a word processing program so you can check the spelling.

Keep Updated on Changes

Some of the basic principles, such as, "Write for your reader" and "Proofread your work," will never change. Nevertheless, technological advances keep changing the way we work and interact with others. Continue to learn about writing résumés and cover letters by consulting the many sources of information available on both subjects. Some of the best places to go are your local library and the World Wide Web, where you can read a variety of sources that match your needs and preferences. Some sources give general advice and instruction, some address specific problems or occupations, and others provide examples of résumés and cover letters. Be careful to choose recently published sources, as résumé standards change over time.[15]

The Internet is full of résumé-writing advice. But remember, websites are not filtered for accuracy or timeliness. Some established sites are:

- JobSmart: Résumés and Cover Letters, *http://www.jobsmart.org/tools/résumé*
- The Riley Guide, *http://www.rileyguide.com*
- Rebecca Smith's Electronic Résumés, *http://www.erésumés.com*
- The Quintessential Guide to Career Resources, *http://www.quintcareers.com*

Conclusion

In summary, technology in the twenty-first century allows many ways to get your application package into the hands of potential employers. Whatever means you choose to do this, make sure your cover letter and résumé are *your* original creations, because no one knows you as well as you do. Emphasize your strengths and what you can do for the company. Remember to follow the AIDA approach, and your documents will help you land that important job interview. Check your cover letter and résumé against Tables 13.2 and 13.3 to help you prepare the best documents to reflect you.

[15] Crosby, pp. 2–14.

TABLE 13.2 📄 **Checklist for writing a cover letter.**

	YES	NO
1. Did I print it clearly on quality, bond paper? (Remember: The cover letter and résumé should be on the same quality paper.)	❑	❑
2. Did I include my telephone number with the return address, e-mail address, or signature?	❑	❑
3. Did I use a courtesy title and the receiver's name on the inside address *and* the salutation (not *Human Resources Department*)?	❑	❑
4. Did I include an enclosure statement for the résumé?	❑	❑
5. Have I used the word "I" carefully? (Hint: You can reduce the overuse of "I" by making activities and outcomes the subjects of sentences. For example, instead of "I took classes in Business Communication," say, "Business Communication prepared me.")	❑	❑
6. Does the first paragraph capture my reader's attention? Does it emphasize my qualifications in terms of reader benefit? Does it note my skills, experience, and accomplishments?	❑	❑
7. Does the second paragraph gain the reader's interest? Does the letter state my interest in the company? The industry? Does the letter indicate I have researched the company and industry?	❑	❑
8. Does the third paragraph convince the reader of my ability and suitability for the opening? Do I create desire? Does the third paragraph refer to the enclosed résumé?	❑	❑
9. Does the last paragraph state the action I will take? Does the letter end appropriately, with a quiet tone of confidence, showing no egotism or presumption?	❑	❑
10. Do I feel this document appears absolutely perfect? Did I use a quality laser printer?	❑	❑
11. Did I carefully proofread it several times?	❑	❑
12. Did I have someone else proofread it as well?	❑	❑

TABLE 13.3 📄 **Checklist for résumés.**

	YES	NO
1. Did I keep my résumé brief?	❑	❑
2. Did I stick to the facts? *Never make up information about employment or education.* Many interviewers do check such things. Be honest.	❑	❑
3. Did I use plain English?	❑	❑
4. Did I use smooth-reading phrases instead of complete sentences?	❑	❑
5. Did I keep an eye on the goal?	❑	❑
6. Did I emphasize my education and experience best matching me to the job?	❑	❑
7. Did I speak the reader's language by using the industry's vocabulary?	❑	❑
8. Did I show that I know what the employer needs and that I can fill that need?	❑	❑
9. Did I start phrases or sentences with action verbs such as *organized, managed,* or *designed,* rather than with lead-ins (I was the person responsible for . . .)?	❑	❑
10. Do I think my résumé invites someone to read it?	❑	❑
11. Did I use correct margins with a clear, easy-to-read layout?	❑	❑
12. Did I use a quality bond paper matching my cover letter in color and weight?	❑	❑
13. Did I use a top-quality printer?	❑	❑
14. Did I eliminate extraneous information, such as my high school diploma?	❑	❑
15. Did I proofread to make sure my résumé was free of spelling, punctuation, and grammatical errors?	❑	❑

16.	Did someone else proofread it?	❏	❏
17.	Have I composed a résumé absolutely perfect in appearance and correctness?	❏	❏
18.	Did I include a complete heading with daytime telephone number and e-mail address?	❏	❏
19.	Did I put the information in reverse chronological order?	❏	❏
20.	Under education, did I list the dates attended, name and location of school, and degrees earned or anticipated?	❏	❏
21.	Did I note special projects, activities, or honors?	❏	❏
22.	Under experience, did I list dates, names of employers, titles, and accomplishments, as well as duties?	❏	❏
23.	Did I use action verbs?	❏	❏
24.	Did I list skills adding to the overall impression of the résumé?	❏	❏

Exercises

EXERCISE 1   RATE YOUR RÉSUMÉ

Directions: Take the quiz at *http://www.provenresumes.com* to rate your résumé.

EXERCISE 2   COMPLETE CAREER WORKSHOPS

Directions: Complete the Top 12 Workshops at *http://www.provenresumes.com*:

Before and After Examples

Learn to Control Your Image

Critique and Graph Your Résumé

Design Content

6 Easy Steps to Create Résumés

2 Popular Styles

Identify Your Skills

Marketing the 10 Hottest Skills

Selling Benefits of Your Skills

Solving Employers' Needs

Creating Targeted Résumés

Confidence-Building Strategies

EXERCISE 3   TAKE THE "ELECTRONIC RÉSUMÉ THAT GETS RESULTS" WORKSHOP

Directions: Complete the workshop "Electronic Résumés That Get Results" at *http://www.provenresumes.com*.

EXERCISE 4   TAKE THE "COVER LETTERS THAT LAND INTERVIEWS" WORKSHOP

Directions: Complete the workshop "Cover Letters That Land Interviews" at *http://www.provenresumes.com*.

Assignment Options

OPTION 1: COVER LETTER

Compose a cover letter responding to an advertisement in the newspaper or to an individual who currently employs you. Do not pretend you have graduated. In these economic times, you never know when you will be job hunting. After you develop this document, you can use it as a model for updating your résumé.

OPTION 2: RÉSUMÉ

Develop a résumé using one of the formats discussed in this chapter. Do not make up information, but report honestly what you have done.

Use the following heading to guide you as you develop your résumé.

Name:

Address:

Telephone:

Job objective: (Your work direction—not a necessity—but helpful if you can target.)

Capabilities: (Describe what you can do here. Use action words and list six to eight things you know you can do, even if you have not yet had the opportunity to prove them on a job.)

Accomplishments: (Things you have accomplished related to your target. Be sure your accomplishments support the capabilities you asserted in the first part of the résumé. List six or eight specific things you have accomplished in past work and nonwork activities. To be most powerful, these statements should start with action verbs.)

Work experience:
Period employed:
Activities:
Title:
Employer:
Education:
Dates attended:
School:
Degree:
Major:

[Do not list high school or high school activities.]

Activities and interests: (List and describe relevant activities and interests, including dates when appropriate.)

Now transfer this information into a formal-looking résumé and submit it for grading.

CHAPTER 14

Preparing for and Surviving the Interview

According to an old saying, "Your education, experience, and preparation will get you the interview, but it is your performance in the interview that will get you the job."[1]

Dan O'Hair, Gustav W. Friedrich, and
Lynda Dixon Shaver

LEARNING OBJECTIVES

After reading this chapter, you should be able to:

- Understand the importance of the interviewing process.

- List the steps in preparing for an interview.

- Recall dress items that make a bad first impression.

- Recount questions you will probably be asked and questions you should not ask.

- Answer behavioral-based interviewing questions.

- Explain the purpose of knowing where you will go and what you should take.

- Describe your behavior during an interview.

- Detail how to close the interview.

[1] Dan O'Hair, Gustav W. Friedrich, and Lynda Dixon Shaver, *Strategic Communication in Business and the Professions,* 2nd ed. (Boston: Houghton Mifflin, 1995), p. 251.

- Explain the purpose of the thank-you letter following the interview.

- Describe how to prepare for an online and luncheon interview.

- Understand the importance of business etiquette.

- List the steps in the resignation process.

- Write a resignation letter.

Preparing for the Interview

You succeeded—your cover letter and résumé got you an interview! The interview will be a two-way process whereby both you and the interviewer will learn and evaluate. The employer wants to determine whether you have the necessary qualifications for the position and how well you would fit into the organization. Companies, like individuals, develop unique personalities and look for candidates who fit those characteristics. Finally, the employer wants to know what you expect. You, in contrast, want to know if the organizational culture matches your personality and if the job provides the challenges and opportunities you desire.

During the interview, you must put your best foot forward and prove yourself to the interviewer. Make sure you do not commit any of the three deadly sins:

- answering a question that was not asked (a failure to listen);

- providing superfluous information (not being brief, thorough, and to the point); and

- not knowing anything about the company (not preparing for the interview).[2]

To avoid these deadly sins, do your homework. You must think about questions you should ask prior to the interview, research the company, decide the appropriate dress, practice probable questions, including traditional interview questions and behavioral description interviewing questions, know the questions not to ask and the things not to say during an interview, prepare questions you will ask, and know where you must go and what you should take with you.

TEN QUESTIONS YOU SHOULD ASK PRIOR TO THE INTERVIEW

In Colleen Sabatino's book, *The Play of Your Life: Your Program for Finding the Career of Your Dreams—And a Step-by-Step Guide to Making It a Reality,* she states that "the world is your stage and you are the star of your own life." She compares networking and interviewing to "auditioning" and goes on to say that good acting "is not just reading lines from a script. It requires a performance that ignites the producers' imagination and lets that person know you are capable of implementing a vision." To provide that great performance during your interview, she recommends that you ask some questions before the interview.

- Could you please give me an indication as to the amount of time I can expect to spend at your organization?

- Who will I be interviewing with?

- Will I be interviewing with each person separately or as part of a panel?

- What are the names and titles of each person I will be meeting?

- In what capacity would I be interacting with each of these people if offered the position?

---

[2] Executive Résumé, 1040 N. Kings Highway, Suite 600, Cherry Hill, New Jersey 08034, 800-563-6359, 856-875-3008, Fax: 856-875-8618, E-mail: *jobcoach@juno.com.*

- Is there an organizational chart I could review prior to the interview?
- How long has the present director been with the organization?
- How many candidates have been selected for this round of interviews?
- Will there be any particular tests or additional forms I will need to fill out when I arrive or during the interview process?
- Though I have the description of the position from the newspaper (or wherever you learned about the position), is there any additional information on file about the position, the performance criteria, and the organization that I could request for review in preparation for the upcoming interview?[3]

RESEARCH THE COMPANY

Find out all you can about the company, industry, and product or service to determine how well it matches your qualifications and personal interests. You must judge how comfortable you will feel with the corporate environment and the managerial styles.

For example, locate the official name and corporate headquarters to see how long the organization has existed. Note what current market share the organization holds and identify any trends in its stock.

Find out about the particular job by investigating the exact job title, job functions, job qualifications, and career path. Of course, you want to know the salary range the organization offers in comparison to the industry and the geographic area.

Locate information in annual reports, in-house magazines or newsletters, product brochures, stock research reports, business and financial pages of local newspapers, and periodical indexes. Consider visiting the Better Business Bureau, Chamber of Commerce, and your college placement office. If time allows, talk with former and current employees of the company.

Just as you prepared for the information-seeking interview, you must prepare for the job-seeking interview. The employer will expect you to be knowledgeable about the company and position. You also need to know what employers do not want. Review Box 14.1 to find out the six most frequent reasons for dismissing job applicants.

APPEARANCE

An old adage states: You only get one chance to make a good first impression. The way you look speaks about you before you utter a word, and your appearance may

Beginning with the most common, here are six frequent reasons for dismissing job applicants (cited by 360 companies in a survey conducted for the National Association of Manufacturers):

1. Applicant will adapt poorly to work environment.
2. Applicant has inadequate reading and writing skills.
3. Applicant has no work experience.
4. Applicant has deficient calculation skills.
5. Applicant has poor verbal skills.
6. Applicant failed medical or drug test.

BOX 14.1 ☛ **A Shortage of Basic Skills**

SOURCE: Reprinted from January 13, 1992, issue of *Business Week*. Copyright © 1992 by the McGraw-Hill Companies, p. 1.

[3] Colleen Sabatino, *The Play of Your Life: Your Program for Finding the Career of Your Dreams—And a Step-by-Step Guide to Making It a Reality* (Emmaus, PA: Rodale Books, 2004), pp. 193–194.

TABLE 14.1 🖙 **Before you go on the interview . . . What to wear.**

SELECT AN APPROPRIATE OUTFIT AND CHECK YOUR APPEARANCE.

Make sure:

Shoes are clean. No flip-flops.
Clothes are pressed and stain-free. A business suit is always acceptable. Don't wear loud-colored clothing.
Accessories are minimal. Same goes for perfume and after-shave. Remember: Less is more.
Nails are clean.
Hair is neat.

SOURCE: *http://www.youngmoney.com/careers/job_hunt/041203.*

determine whether you have a successful interview. Treat yourself well in the days before the interview by getting plenty of sleep and eating right. Review Table 14.1 for some basics about how to dress for interview success.

You have approximately 30 seconds to make a first impression. Dress appropriately for your targeted job level. If you have little information about the company's style, dress conservatively.[4]

Kathi Whitley and Cara Stevens, in their article "Does It Take a Gimmick to Get a Job?," state that "If you are still not sure how to dress for the interview, you should call them and ask!" You should say: "I have an interview with _____ in the _____ department for a position as an _____. Could you please tell me what would be appropriate dress for this interview?"[5]

When *The Wall Street Journal* surveyed 351 chief executive officers for their preferred suit color, no one was surprised that 53 percent of the respondents favored blue, dark blue, or navy blue, and 39 percent opted for gray, charcoal, or dark gray. For both men and women, dark suits spell formality, conservatism, and authority. Dark ties, too, contribute to the image; and for a man, the tie can be the single most important denominator of respectability and responsibility. The tie should have minuscule geometric patterns to convey the proper image of respect. Also, this dark-is-beautiful look is not appropriate for shirts. The general rule is that the darker the color of suit and tie, the lighter the color of the shirt. White was still the preferred color of 53 percent of the CEOs surveyed by *The Wall Street Journal* and blue came in second with 35 percent.[6]

Therefore, men should favor dark gray or blue suits or navy blazers and gray slacks. Shirts should be light blue, yellow, or white. Add a dash of pizzazz with your tie, if you like, but keep the pattern conservative. There is only one acceptable material for ties—silk. The tie should not be wider than your suit lapels or long enough to cover your belt buckle. Socks should be dark, and long enough to cover your calf when you cross your legs. Shoes should be dark and polished. If you have a beard or mustache, make sure it is neatly trimmed. Be careful about a ponytail or earrings as they can send the message, "I am not going to fit in." Males should opt for a simple, short haircut.[7]

Likewise, women should wear conservative business attire. Females can wear the colors navy, medium gray, charcoal, and camel. Accessories such as scarves,

---

[4] Courtland L. Bovee and John V. Thill, *Business Communication Today* (New York: McGraw Hill, 1992), p. 391.

[5] Kathi Whitley and Cara Steven, "Does It Take a Gimmick to Get a Job?" Retrieved from *http://www. collegegrad.com/jobsearch/15-5.shtml*

[6] "Dressing For Interview Success. Retrieved from *http://www.jobfairy.com/articles01/ DressingFor InterviewSucce.html.*

[7] Norma Carr-Ruffino, *The Promotable Woman: Becoming a Successful Manager,* revised ed. (Belmont, CA: Wadsworth, 1985), p. 87.

pearls, and jewelry can be worn if they add to, rather than dominate, the overall appearance. A simple hairstyle eliminates the necessity of having to fuss with it throughout the interview. Makeup and perfume should be used sparingly. Otherwise, your fashion statement may conflict with your professional image.[8]

The casual dress trend is reversing, and workplace dress codes are becoming more formal. The result is that many young adults start from scratch when creating a professional appearance. Women can get by with two basic nonpatterned suits in neutral colors that go together, another skirt, a pair of pants (or another pair if one of the suits is a pantsuit), another subtle patterned jacket, four to six shirts, and two pairs of nice black shoes. Men need two suits, one gray and one navy (the navy suit should have a jacket that can double as a blazer), gabardine pants, another sport coat if possible, three dress shirts for each suit, six ties, two pairs of shoes, and belts to match. Any leftover money should go into accessories: scarves, socks, ties, jewelry, sandals, and handbags. "Keep the basics of the pieces pattern-neutral—you can dress up all kinds of outfits with accessories so your outfits go further," said Heather Bradley of Flourishing Co. of Washington, a corporate training and coaching firm.[9]

Your personality should shine through in the interview. Your enthusiasm and positive attitude can make you an interesting candidate. Smile and present a positive image. Holiday Inn was looking for 500 people to fill positions for a new facility. Managers interviewed 5,000 candidates, and they chose to exclude all candidates who smiled fewer than four times during the interview. This ruling applied to people competing for jobs in all categories.[10]

Your professional look, according to *Careers* magazine, provides "that extra something you bring to an interview." Your professionalism comes through in your personal expressions, saying you care about your job and career. According to Christy Zahm, the Southwestern Regional Director of Golden Key, knowing you look professional helps build your confidence. You feel better, you stand straighter, you control the situation, and you win!

PRACTICE FOR PROBABLE QUESTIONS

Research has suggested that, when answering questions, successful job applicants refer to technical jargon common to the position; use active, positive, and concrete

Remember, you only get one chance to make a good first impression.

Mary Pike, president of the executive coaching firm Inside Job, Inc., says some women spend so much effort rehearsing the answers to possible interview questions that they fail to grasp what's really happening. "Women aren't trained to 'speak into the listening,'" she says. "They're trained to answer the questions."

Source: Terri Thorton, "Create a Knockout Presentation," *Atlanta Woman*, Volume 1, Issue 4, September/October 2002.

---

[8] Sue Cejka, "How to Ace a Job Interview," *Medical Economics,* Volume 74, Issue 12, June 9, 1997, pp. 213–214.

[9] "What to Wear 101," *Atlanta Journal/Constitution*— AJC Jobs, R1, Sunday, March 21, 2004.

[10] "A Smile Will Get That Job," *Newsday,* 235 Pinelawn Road, Long Island, NY 11747. Quote came from *Communication Briefings,* Vol. XII, No. VI, 700 Black Horse Pike, Suite 100, Blackwood, NJ 08012, (609) 232-6380, Fax: (609) 232-8245, p. 4.

language; support answers with specific examples, comparisons, illustrations, and statistics taken from personal experience, coworkers, company publications, and supervisors; use humor when appropriate; and describe job weaknesses or physical disabilities in a positive manner.[11]

Traditional interview questions center on education, qualifications, opinions, and experience. If an applicant meets the educational requirements, appears to have the experience and personal characteristics, and responds as expected to traditional interview questions, the candidate is perceived to be qualified for the position. The problem with traditional interview questions is that the candidate rarely tells the interviewer about actual performance on the job or about job experiences and accomplishments in specific situations. A recent review of all published research (over 150 studies) on interviews found that one-to-one unstructured interviews averaged only 19 percent predictive accuracy.[12]

Therefore, many organizations have moved to employing **behavior description** questions to increase their probability of hiring the best candidate for the job. The basic principle underlying a behavior description interviewing system is that the best predictor of future performance is past performance in similar circumstances. By focusing on past performance, these interviews greatly increase the organization's ability to predict whether a person will be a "top performer" within the organization. In fact, research-based behavioral interviews achieved an accuracy of over 80 percent.

As an interviewee, you should prepare for traditional interview questions and behavioral-based questions as well. In addition, there are some questions you should not ask and some statements you should avoid making.

TRADITIONAL INTERVIEWING QUESTIONS

Recruiters frequently ask the following questions. If you prepare your answers to these questions, you can handle any other questions. Keep in mind that the interviewer can ask only job-related questions and must ask the same basic questions of all applicants for the position.

Tell Me About Yourself.   When answering this question, be on guard against the interviewer who gives you free rein. Do not spend too much time answering, avoid details, and do not ramble. Limit your answer to approximately two minutes. Practice answering this question on videotape, so you can time your answer and view your nonverbal signals.

What Do You Know About Our Organization?   Now you can shine and prove you have done your homework. Discuss their products, services, revenue, problems, people, and history.

What Would You Do for Us?   What Can You Do For Us That Someone Else Cannot? Answer these questions by relating any experiences representing your success in solving problems similar to those of the prospective employer. You can emphasize what new knowledge you bring with your educational background.

Why Should We Hire You?   Again, this is a chance for you to sell yourself. Relate your strengths and what you can do for the organization.

Please Give Me Your Definition of (the Interview Position).   Do your homework and be sure you can answer this one. You should know what duties would be expected of you.

---

[11] Auren Uris, *Action Guide for Executive Job Seekers and Employers* (New York: Arco, 1971), pp. 186–187.

[12] Tom Janz and Greg B. Monney, *Behavior Description Interviewing, Trainer's Guide* (Amherst, MA: HRD Press, 1991).

How Long Will You Stay with Us?   Whatever you do, do not say one year or two! Organizations will invest time and energy into training you for the position, but they do not want to waste their time on you if you will not reciprocate.

In What School Activities Have You Participated? Why? Which Did You Enjoy Most?   The recruiter wants to know about your leadership skills and team spirit. Especially in today's organization, individuals who show they have performed well in school and have developed interpersonal communication skills will be sought. You want your answer to reflect these attributes.

How Do You Spend Your Spare Time? What Do You Do in Your Spare Time? Interviewers use these questions to discover whether you enjoy working with others. Your hobbies also reflect whether you enjoy being by yourself or with people. As organizations emphasize teams, be sure you include some people-oriented activities in your answer.

What Do You Expect Regarding Salary?   You have some negotiating power, but you must know the salary range of the job. Use your networking sources to prepare for this question. Also, check with your on-campus placement office.

What Do You Consider Your Strengths? Your Weaknesses?   You can be sure these two questions will be asked. When the interviewer asks you these questions, focus on your work-related strengths impacting your performance. Give examples of how you led teams or communicated effectively. For the weaknesses side of the question, take a strength and turn it into a weakness. For example, you might say you never quit until you "dot the last *i.*" This weakness, in reality, shows perseverance.

Tell Me About Your Education and Work Experience.   Provide strong, positive answers to these questions. You must realize the interviewer probably will ask about your grades when you have just graduated from college. When the interviewer asks you about extracurricular activities such as clubs, church, community involvement, and volunteer work, describe your activities. Present yourself as a well-rounded individual.

If you have worked full time, raised a family, and gone to school, they will not expect to see as many activities. However, if you attend school full time, they will look for some type of activity besides school.

If you lack specific work experience, try to relate the experience you do have and show how this experience will be valuable. Don't forget to include any volunteer work, as this type of work most definitely counts.

What Goals and Ambitions Do You Have?   When asked, "What do you plan to be doing five years from now?" do not give a vague answer or say, "I don't know." Show you have realistic goals. If you state you want to make unreasonably large sums of money or to "own the company in five years," your expectations might exceed what the position can ultimately offer. The recruiter may then decide the position does not match your expectations.

All interviewers prefer employees who have ambition—who seek to advance in the company by learning more than what their specific jobs require. Companies also want team players, so you may be asked about former work experience to assess your level of team spirit. During the interview, express your desire to advance, but clearly state this advancement will occur only if you work hard.

BEHAVIORAL DESCRIPTION INTERVIEWING QUESTIONS

The following are examples of behavior description questions you might be asked. These kinds of questions may be a little more difficult to answer quickly. Take the time that you need to answer them completely.

- Thinking back over your recent job positions, in which job position did you make the best use of your technical or problem-solving skills? At that position, please describe the specific technical challenge that brought out the best in your technical skills.
- Describe a time when, despite your best efforts, you were unable to meet a technical challenge or solve a technical problem.
- In which job position did you make the best use of your communication skills?
- Describe the time when it was most challenging to communicate effectively.
- In which job position were you the best at motivating yourself or others?
- Tell me about the most difficult client interview you faced last year. How did you prepare? How did you respond to the client's concerns?
- Catching major problems early can save a lot of money. Think about a time when you noticed the early warning signs of a problem that would have been costly if not detected. When did you first notice the problem? What was the first thing you did to correct the problem?

The information that comes from these types of questions allows the interviewer to more objectively assess your qualifications and yields more accurate hiring decisions. The interviewer gains an understanding of how you perform in the workplace.

QUESTIONS NOT TO ASK AND THINGS NOT TO SAY DURING AN INTERVIEW

Preparing for an interview also means knowing what not to say or do. Jennifer Atkins offers the following tips regarding some things you should never say in an interview.

1. "What does your company do?"

   If you ask this question, it will show that you've not adequately prepared for your interview.

2. "My salary requirements are very flexible."

   You should come prepared with a salary range and know approximately what the company will pay. In addition, you shouldn't pretend to be flexible when you aren't. If you're worried that your salary requirements are too high for the job, you may need to do some serious thinking about how low you're willing to go. Don't sell yourself short, but ask yourself how much you honestly think you're worth. Do research about what similar jobs pay and what salaries are like in the region. If a company comes back with too low an offer, you can always try and negotiate up.

3. "It would be really cool to have this job."

   Avoid using slang, as it is a serious turnoff to interviewers.

4. "Bill Gates himself offered me a $100,000 bonus."

   Don't lie! You'll be found out, and you'll regret it. Someday when you least expect it, someone somewhere will discover that you didn't really increase sales by 99 percent in six months.

5. "In five years, I see myself on a boat in the Caribbean."

   When interviewers ask you about long-term goals, they want an answer that relates to the company. Even if you don't plan to stick around long, say something that reflects a commitment to the position and the company. This may seem to contradict the previous exhortation about lying, but try to think of it as a rhetorical question. It is possible you might still be at the same company in five years.

6. "Sorry, I don't know how to do that."

Rather than admitting that you don't have a specific skill, stress that you're a fast learner and are excited about the possibility of acquiring new skills. Most companies would rather hire an enthusiastic, smart person who needs to be trained than someone who already has the required skills but isn't as eager to learn.

7. "You see, I just went through a painful divorce. . . . "

Even if an interviewer starts getting personal, don't follow suit. Keep it businesslike and polite.

8. "What can your company do for me?"

Interviewers hate arrogance and selfishness. They want to know why they should hire you, so stress the contributions you can make, and how you helped your previous employers. Don't start asking about raises, bonuses, and promotions right away.

Remember, you're the one being interviewed, and while you should use the opportunity to get your questions answered, you shouldn't make it seem as if you'll be doing them a favor if they hire you.

9. "I left my last job because my boss was a real jerk."

Bad-mouthing your previous employer is possibly the dumbest thing you can do during an interview. Even if your last company was too chaotic or your boss was difficult, say that you left because you were looking for more responsibility, greater opportunity, for advancement, or that you just needed a change.[13]

On the day of your interview, allow at least 15 minutes more than you think it should take to get to your interview.

PREPARE QUESTIONS YOU WILL ASK

As previously noted, the interviewer will expect you to ask questions. Having some questions about the organization demonstrates your preparation for the interview, your knowledge of the firm, and your interest in the company and its business. Keep in mind that interviewers do not expect you to ask about salary and benefits at the first interview. Some questions to ask are:

1. Whom would I be reporting to?
2. What would be my duties and responsibilities on the job?
3. Will any opportunities for advancement occur?
4. What would be my job title?
5. What new areas of responsibility will open up in this job?
6. How will I be evaluated or reviewed on the job?
7. What kind of working environment can I expect?
8. Do you like working here? Why?
9. What comprises a typical day?
10. Why did this position become available?

KNOW WHERE TO GO AND WHAT TO TAKE

You have completed some important steps to prepare for the interview, but you need to be familiar with the interview site. The day before your interview, make a

---

[13] Jennifer Rae Atkins, "9 Things You Should Never Say in an Interview," and "Avoid the Following Interview Pitfalls as Part of a Strategy That Sells Your Strengths and Assets." Retrieved from *CareerBuilder.com*.

trial run to gauge how long it will take you to get there. Try pulling into the parking area and see if you will be allowed to park in the visitor parking section.

Take a small notebook, pen, and extra copies of your résumé with you. Make sure you have company information and the questions you want to ask. Try to organize these materials neatly in a small briefcase or folder, so you do not appear unorganized or messy.

Then, on the day of the interview, allow at least 15 more minutes than you think it should take. The impression you create will be more favorable if you arrive early rather than late. Remember that your interview really begins when you enter the reception area of the company. Greet the receptionist pleasantly and respectfully. You never know whether he or she might be asked to give input about you to the interviewer. Then state your name and the interviewer's name. While waiting for the interviewer, do not chew gum, smoke, or drink coffee.

The Interview

Your behavior during an interview can literally make or break your chances of getting hired. Show up with a notepad and a rehearsed strategy for highlighting your abilities.

Most people have some nervous energy; use that energy to make sure you appear engaged, but not hyperactive. Avoid tapping your foot excessively, fidgeting in your seat, or darting your eyes around the room.

Another interview pitfall that frequently entraps eager job applicants is dominating the conversation. Most interviewers are not only looking for information, but also for someone who can listen and respond in a way that encourages dialogue. Although it's both advisable and necessary to sell yourself in an interview, the pitch can quickly become too one-sided, says Jim Slattery, vice president of recruiting at Whittman-Hart, a Chicago-based IT consultancy firm.[14]

Note the ways to strike out during an interview in Box 14.2. Take these 34 negatives and make them positive. Then go to an interview and make a positive impression on the interviewer.

[14] Kristen Gerencher, "Finding the Path to Your Next Job," *InfoWorld,* Volume 21, Issue 31, August 2, 1999, p. 75.

1. Poor personal appearance
2. Lack of interest and enthusiasm (passive and indifferent)
3. Overemphasis on money
4. Condemnation of past employers
5. Failure to look at interviewer when conversing
6. Limp, fishy handshake
7. Unwillingness to go where sent
8. Late for interview
9. Failure to express appreciation for interviewer's time
10. Asks no questions about position
11. Vague responses to questions
12. Overaggressive, conceited, with superiority or know-it-all complex
13. Inability to express self clearly (poor voice, diction, grammar)
14. Lack of planning for career (no purpose or goals)
15. Lack of confidence and poise (ill at ease, nervous)
16. Failure to participate in activities
17. Unwilling to start at the bottom, expects too much too soon
18. Makes excuses, evasive, hedges on unfavorable factors in record
19. Lack of tact
20. Lack of courtesy, ill-mannered
21. Lack of maturity
22. Lack of vitality
23. Indecisive
24. Sloppy application form
25. Merely shopping around
26. Wants job only for short time
27. No interest in company or industry
28. Cynical
29. Low moral standards
30. Lazy
31. Intolerant (strong prejudices)
32. Narrow interests
33. Inability to take criticism
34. High-pressure type

BOX 14.2 ✏ **34 Ways People Strike Out During an Interview**

At the start of the interview, introduce yourself while giving a firm, confident handshake. When asked to be seated, sit in an attentive position. Display a positive attitude, use correct communication skills, and take appropriate closing actions.

DISPLAYING A POSITIVE ATTITUDE

Go into the interview with the mind-set that this is the job you want—even if you are just window shopping. Companies want to hire people with an obvious passion for the job. "This is just as important at the CIO level as it was when you interviewed for your first job out of college," says Dudley Brown—Managing Director of Bridge Gate UC, a recruiting firm in Irvine, California.[15]

During the interview, sell yourself. Confidently and enthusiastically answer all questions while directing your eye contact to the interviewer. Exhibit your ability to be in control and maintain composure. Your friendly smile and enthusiasm can go a long way.

Your attitude should show self-assurance, but not arrogance. List prior accomplishments comfortably, while giving recognition to others who helped you succeed.

Don't discount the important role that the receptionist plays. Often, the receptionist is asked to share his or her impressions of you.

[15] Jennifer Mateyaschuk, "References Really Matter," *InformationWeek,* no. 715, January 4, 1999, p. 80.

USING STRONG COMMUNICATION SKILLS

Most interviewers say that when an applicant cannot talk to them in an interview, they doubt that the applicant can talk with customers and clients. In a study of successful and unsuccessful interviewees, successful interviewees spoke rapidly and forcefully, gestured and smiled often, looked directly at the interviewer, nodded their heads in a positive manner, and leaned forward while maintaining natural, comfortable postures.[16]

Listen carefully and thoughtfully before responding to questions. Answer all questions thoroughly, using proper English. When you answer, avoid using slang such as "you know," and "like." Make sure you do not exhibit any of the behaviors discussed in Box 14.3 if you want to land that job.

Based on a nationwide survey of executives by Accountemps, the interview behavior of some job seekers can be described as bizarre, unconventional, humorous, and counterproductive. Executives were asked: "What is the most unusual thing you have ever witnessed or heard of happening during a job interview?" Below are some of the more exceptional responses:

- Said if he was hired, he would teach me ballroom dancing at no charge, and started demonstrating.
- She returned that afternoon, asking if we could redo the entire interview.
- Apologized for being late, said he accidentally locked his clothes in his closet.
- Took three cellular telephone calls. Said she had a similar business on the side.
- After a difficult question, she wanted to leave the room momentarily to meditate.
- Candidate was told to take his time answering, so he began writing down each of his answers before speaking.
- Shortly after sitting down, she brought out a line of cosmetics and started a strong sales pitch.
- Man brought in his five children and cat.
- Said that if I hired him, I would soon regret it.
- Applicant indicated that if he were not hired, the future of the company would be jeopardized for confidential reasons.
- Arrived with a snake around her neck. Said she took her pet everywhere.
- Brought a mini tape recorder and said he always taped his job interviews.
- Left his dry cleaner tag on his jacket and said he wanted to show he was a clean individual.
- Applicant handed me an employment contract and said I would have to sign it if he was going to be hired.
- When asked about loyalty, showed a tattoo of his girlfriend's name.
- Woman brought a large shopping bag of canceled checks and thumbed through them during the interview.
- After a very long interview, he casually said he had already accepted another position.

BOX 14.3 🖝 **Job Seekers Give Bizarre Interviews**

SOURCE: Accountemps, 2884 Sand Hill Road, Menlo Park, CA 94025.

[16] Cheryl Hamilton with Cordell Parker, *Communicating for Results,* 4th ed. (Belmont, CA: Wadsworth, 1993), p. 241.

CLOSING THE INTERVIEW

The interviewer will usually signal the end of the interview by asking you if you have any questions. Now, ask the questions you have prepared. Asking the following questions before you leave will ease the after-interview stress.

- When do they intend to have the position filled?
- Are any internal candidates being considered?
- Have they extended an offer to anyone yet?
- Is there any reason why I would not be considered a top candidate for this position?

The interviewer will close the session by telling you when a decision will be made and how the decision will be communicated to you. If the interviewer does not give you this information, you should feel free to ask for it. If you really want the position, make a strong concluding statement of interest.

Allow for a gracious end to the interview by thanking the interviewer and shaking hands. The next day, write to thank the interviewer and reiterate what you think you can do for the company.

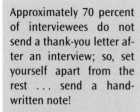

A handshake communicates much about your self-confidence.

After the Interview

The best interviewees always take time to prepare a thank-you letter. Many a recruiter has stated that the person who took the time to write a thank-you letter got the job. The thank-you letter lets your name pass by the interviewer one more time. Begin composing the letter as soon after the interview as you can and mail it immediately.

The letter does not have to be lengthy. Simply express your appreciation for the interviewer's time and indicate your interest in the job. Again, highlight your qualifications and tie them into the desired position. Mention something you found interesting about the job and mention the names of others you met during your interview. Close your letter with another thank-you and state that you look forward to hearing the firm's decision. In Box 14.4, you will see a sample thank-you letter

184 Dogwood Lane
Athens, Georgia 30609
June 1, 20XX

Mr. Ralph Holler
Director of Personnel
Dow Chemical U.S.A.
Post Office Box 1713-C
Midland, MI 55101

Dear Mr. Holler:

Thank you for talking with me yesterday about the vacancy in your Finance Department. You gave me a vivid picture of what would be expected from the person who fills the position.

BOX 14.4 Sample Thank-You Letter and Sample Thank-You E-mail

Mr. Ralph Holler
Page 2
June 1, 20XX

I want to reaffirm my strong interest in this exciting and challenging opportunity. I feel my outstanding performance on the summer internship with Arthur Anderson and my BBA degree in Accounting demonstrate my ability. I feel I would contribute greatly to this department.

Again, Mr. Holler, thank you for meeting with me. I appreciate your hospitality and look forward to hearing from you concerning the outcome of our discussions.

Sincerely,

Thomas Agnew
Thomas Agnew

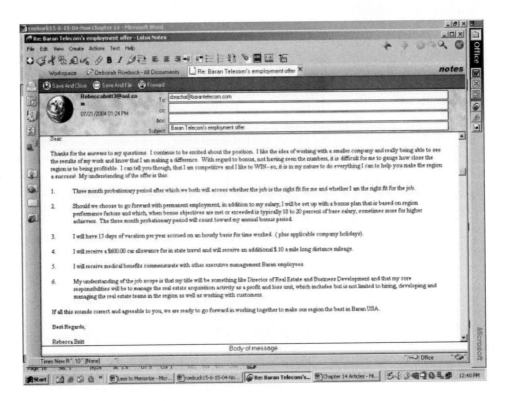

BOX 14.4 (continued)

and a thank you e-mail message. As the sender, you would know whether it was appropriate or not to use e-mail.

Be persistent about following up after your interview. If you have not heard back from the interviewer after a week, call. Sometimes things can happen. If it turns out you did not get the job, briefly mourn. Give yourself 15 minutes to be really disappointed or 30 minutes if it is a really great job. Then, get on with it! Trust that you will find the right job for your career goals. Use the checklist in Table 14.2 to make sure you completed all before-, during-, and after-interview activities.

TABLE 14.2 🖙 **Checklist for effective interviewing.**

YES	NO	

Before the Interview

☐	☐	1. Did I research the company?
☐	☐	2. Did I make sure that my appearance was appropriate for that organization?
☐	☐	3. Did I practice for traditional interview questions?
☐	☐	4. Did I prepare for behavioral-based interview questions?
☐	☐	5. Did I prepare questions that I should ask and remember which ones not to ask?
☐	☐	6. Did I know where to go for my interview?
☐	☐	7. Did I take extra copies of my résumé, my references, and information that might be needed?

During the Interview

☐	☐	8. Did I control my nervous energy?
☐	☐	9. Did I display a positive attitude?
☐	☐	10. Did I use strong communication skills? Did I listen carefully and respond thoughtfully?
☐	☐	11. Did I ask the questions I prepared?
☐	☐	12. Did I thank the interviewer and shake his or her hand?

After the Interview

☐	☐	13. Did I write a thank-you letter?
☐	☐	14. Did the letter reiterate what I can do for the company?
☐	☐	15. Did I express appreciation for the interviewer's time and indicate my interest in the job?
☐	☐	16. Did I highlight my qualifications and tie them to the desired position?
☐	☐	17. Did I mention an interesting aspect of the job or someone I met?
☐	☐	18. Did I close by stating that I looked forward to hearing from them?
☐	☐	19. Was I persistent about following up after the interview?
☐	☐	20. Did I call if I had not heard from the company within a week?

Two Special Types of Interviews

Preliminary telephone or online interviews appear to be a new trend for many organizations as they save the company and the candidate time. In addition, as a final test, many employers will ask you to attend a luncheon interview.

ONLINE AND TELEPHONE INTERVIEWS

Myles Weissleder, Director of Marketing at I-traffic Inc., a New York–based direct marketing firm whose clients include Walt Disney, ESPN, and Beyond.com, does 60 percent of his recruiting online. Interesting candidates are queried by e-mail by CEO Scott Heiferman, who follows up with more questions via e-mail. "In our company, most of what we do is performed by e-mail. By doing some of the interview on-line, we are able to determine if the person can spell and communicate well in cyberspace. That's important to us," Weissleder explains.[17]

Some job candidates err by not realizing the importance of these initial screening interviews, which can open the door to a face-to-face interview. Telephone screens are increasingly used by companies to avoid wasting a manager's time on a candidate who is not right for the company. Typically, if you do not get through that telephone screen, you are not going to get in the door.

The mistakes most often made in telephone screening interviews are bringing up money too soon, whispering so that coworkers cannot hear, and exhibiting

Teleconferencing has become a common interviewing tool, especially in the preliminary stages, providing an economical way to take advantage of not only the national talent pool but even international talent. Job candidates can be anywhere.

Source: Mary Ellen Slayter, "Phone Interviews Gain Favor in Job Searches. The Process Saves Money, but Follow a Few Valuable Tips to Help It Click." *Washington Post,* February 28, 2005.

[17] H. Lee Murphy, "Top Job Sites," *Marketing News,* Volume 33, Issue 16, August 2, 1999, p. 13.

disinterest by typing on a keyboard. You should not ask about money until interviewers bring it up. Once they do, however, the candidate should name a price on the spot. An applicant who waits until an on-location interview may risk not getting a target salary, says Laura Johnson, a senior technical recruiter at T. Rowe Price Investment Technologies. "If I need to get approval for a special salary increase, that takes a while," Johnson says. "If the candidate waits until the face-to-face interview, I can't move the machine fast enough to ask for more dollars—even though I don't mind asking for more if it's the right candidate."[18]

When you're in the job market, you should follow the tips presented here for telephone interviews.

1. Schedule the telephone interview for a quiet time. You should give the interviewer your full attention. Try to eliminate any background noises or distractions. Of course, you might not know when the interviewer is going to call, so do your homework and always be prepared.

2. Have your résumé next to the telephone. If you have different versions of your résumé, make sure you have the right one for that employer. In all likelihood, the interviewer will use your résumé to guide him or her in the questions asked. By having your résumé in front of you, you'll have some idea of what the next question might be.

3. Prepare notes. As in all interviewing situations, think about the potential questions you might be asked and have your answers prepared. Having written notes will help to ensure that you say what you want to say.

4. Research the company. This is true of any interviewing situation as it allows the organization to know that you've done your homework.

5. Have questions ready. To make the interview a bit more personal, ask a question every now and then.

6. Know your schedule. Be prepared by having your calendar available. The interviewer may want to immediately set up a face-to-face interview.

7. Plan a closing. Think about how you want to end the interview and jot down some notes.[19]

LUNCHEON INTERVIEWS

Often employers will request a "luncheon" interview as a final test. If you are not prepared for this type of interview, it could cause you to appear less confident. Typically the dialogue is more free flowing; you and the interviewer may discuss such items as workplace challenges, business goals, and operations. The setting is meant to ease the communication flow.

Because the luncheon interview is often your second interview, you should dress professionally. It is always safe to wear a traditional dark suit, white cotton shirt, and silk tie or a skirted navy, black, or gray suit and professional blouse. Remember, as with all interviews, to limit your jewelry and makeup and to forego cologne and perfumes. Handbags should be placed inside your briefcase or left in the car. Remember to polish your shoes as well as your knowledge of the company to enhance this dining experience.

Dining with individuals you do not know and who will determine whether you are the "right fit" for their organization can be rather nerve-wracking. Therefore, understanding dining etiquette and practicing will alleviate your fears. Butchel College of Arts and Sciences of The University of Akron suggests following the business etiquette guidelines below for luncheon interviews.[20]

[18] Steve Alexander, "The Interview Spotlight," *InfoWorld*, Volume 21, Issue 19, May 10, 1999, pp. 111–112.

[19] Mike Worthington, "Tips on How to Handle Phone Interviews." Retrieved from: *http://www.net-temps.com*.

[20] "Business Etiquette." A & S Careers Program, The Univesity of Akron, Butchel College of Arts and Sciences. Retrieved from *http://www.wzip.uakron.edu/ascareer/businessetiquette.html*.

Remember also, the more comfortable you are in your clothes, the more relaxed you will be during the meal. The more relaxed you are during the meal, the better you will be at marketing your skills.

Source: "Business Etiquette." A & S Careers Program, The Univesity of Akron, Butchel College of Arts and Sciences. Retrieved from *http://www.wzip.uakron.edu/ascareer/businessetiquette.html*.

Bill Mahoney recalls the exact moment he decided to hire an etiquette expert. He was hosting a business dinner for a client, the CEO of a billion-dollar company, and noticed an employee eating in a less-than-professional manner. "She was chewing with her mouth open, not using the appropriate utensils and literally attacking her food," said Mahoney, who runs Mahoney & Associates, an employee benefits management and consulting firm in Fort Lauderdale. "I noticed my client watching her. I was mortified."

Source: Robyn A. Friedman, "Mind Your Manners: Proper Etiquette Can Make a Deal, Get You a Job," *Sun Sentinel*, March 2004. Retrieved from *http://www.etiquetteexpert.com/news_article_march_04.htm*.

Dining.   Often, the interviewer is seeking clues from your behavior regarding how you will conduct business. When dining, you should display manners, courtesy, respect, and trust. Begin by arriving on time; in fact, arrive early.

Arrival.   Make sure you arrive at least 10 minutes early to check your appearance, to remove your coat, and to prepare to greet your host with a smile and firm handshake. Typically your host will introduce you to the others at the table, if any. You should not sit until your host has indicated you should or until he or she is seated.

Napkins.   Your host will signal the beginning of the meal when he or she opens his or her napkin. Try to open your napkin below the table without great fanfare. You should keep your napkin in your lap throughout the meal. If you must leave the table, place the napkin, soiled side down, on your chair or to the LEFT of your plate to signal the server that you will be returning soon.

If you discover you have ingested a bone or something similar, discreetly remove it from your mouth between two fingers and place it on the edge of your plate instead of in your napkin. If the sight of it will be displeasing, excuse yourself from the table and visit the rest room for disposal. Remember, if you place something inside of your napkin, it may accidentally be displayed by the server at the end of your meal.

When you are officially finished with your meal and are leaving the table, place your unfolded napkin on the table to the RIGHT of your plate. This signals you are finished with your meal.

Ordering.   Your host will provide the direction concerning foods to order. If the host orders first, follow his/her lead. If she/he defers to you to place your order first, ask for his or her recommendations. If the host has not previously eaten in the restaurant and cannot make a recommendation, use your common sense when ordering. If your menu carries prices, stay in the middle of the offered price range. Generally the company will pay for your meal, but you should ensure you have enough cash to cover your meal and tip just in case it might be needed.

Avoid "saucy" foods that may drip on your clothing, such as spaghetti, and stay with the standards such as a fruit or vegetable plate, chicken breast, or steak and baked potato. You should not order an alcoholic drink even if your host does or if you believe it would help "relax" you.

Table Setting.   When you first sit down, take a few minutes to look over your table setting. Exhibit 14.1 features an example of a formal place setting that you might encounter.

SOURCE: SM Publications, http://www.smpub.com/setable.html.

EXHIBIT 14.1

Table setting. Above the plate. Left to right: salt & pepper, dessert fork & spoon, water/wine glasses. Plate row. Left to Right: fish fork, dinner fork, salad fork, napkin, rim soup plate, plate, salad knife, dinner knife, fish knife, soup spoon.

When in doubt, watch your host and table mates to determine what to do.

- Always use utensils from the outside inward to plate: forks = left, knives/spoons = right, dessert = above.
- Keep blades of knives turned toward the plate and the bread knife blade turned downward toward yourself.
- Cups are above your plate; glassware sets to the top *right* of the plate positioned by height, beginning with the water goblet.
- Bread plate/butter knife is to the top *left* of the plate: each bite is to be torn, buttered individually on the plate, and then eaten.
- Salad plates are sometimes found immediately to the left of plate/silverware, below the bread plate.
- If your napkin slips to the floor, leave it and signal the server for a clean one.
- Once the meal begins, elbows are forbidden on the table at least in the United States; wrists can rest on the table, although idle hands should be in one's lap.
- NEVER, EVER insult an establishment's cook by seasoning food before tasting!
- Do NOT reach for an item on the table—ask the nearest person to pass it.
- Pass the bread basket, salad dressing, salt and pepper together, and so forth, to the right; pass food to the left.
- Pass gravy/syrup/creamer conveyances with handles turned toward the recipient.
- Fill the soup spoon with soup from the cooler sides of the bowl using a circular motion away from you, then tip soup into your mouth.
- Remember to say "Please" and "Thank you" to your server AND your host!

Eating Tip. Typically, you should wait until everyone has been served to eat. However, if it appears that there will be an extended wait for one or more of the meals and you are encouraged to begin eating by your host, please do so. The polite behavior would be to eat slowly while you wait for the others to be served. If the group is extremely large [eight or more], there is no mandate to wait. You begin as the meal arrives.

There are two basic styles of using your utensils during a meal. It would be beneficial to practice both to see which is easier for you to master.

The American standard style. Using the hand with which you write, hold the fork tines up and balanced between the first knuckle of the middle finger and the tip of the index finger with your thumb steadying the handle. While most of your meal can be cut and eaten using only the fork, some foods will demand a knife. When cutting into a steak, for example, place your fork in the hand with which you do not write, tines down, and grasp the knife with your opposite hand. Cut only one or two bites at a time. Place your knife on the top of your plate with the sharp edge toward you [avoid touching the table please] and transfer your fork back to your writing hand. Continue with your meal. Remember that you will use the fork without help from your knife for even the most difficult foods, such as peas.

European or "Continental" style. Many individuals prefer this style because it seems more sensible. The fork remains in the left hand and the knife remains in the right throughout the meal. The fork, however, is held with the tines down. Because it is already on the fork tines, once food is cut it can be popped directly into the mouth. The fork and knife also work in unison against such stubborn foods as peas.[21]

---

[21] "Dining Etiquette," Career Center. Retrieved from: *http://www.bsu.edu/students/careers/students/interviewing/dining.*

TABLE 14.3 ☛ **Types of food, as well as food to avoid during luncheon interviews.**

FINGER FOODS	FORK FOODS	SPOON FOODS
Stemmed berries	Stemless berries	Berries with sauces
Caviar on toast	Cake	Ice cream
Cheese on crackers	Clams/Oysters/Shrimp	Melon
Corn on the cob	Fish/Sushi	Peas
French fries [informal]	French fries [formal]	Soup
Crisp bacon	Fruit	
Hamburgers/Hot dogs	Ice cream on cake/pie	
Hors d'oeuvres	Large chicken pieces	
Olives	Pastry	
Pizza [informal]	Pizza [formal]	
Onion rings	Shish kabob	
Tacos	Steak	

And what foods to avoid altogether . . .

Unfamiliar foods
Spaghetti
French onion soup
Buffalo wings
Ribs
Bony fish
Shellfish
Big sandwiches
Cheesy food
Foods requiring special utensils

Used Utensils.   Once you use your utensil, no part (even a clean handle) should ever touch the table surface. If merely pausing during a meal, place the fork with tines down over the knife, forming an inverted V on your plate. Second servings necessitate placing both the knife and fork on the right side of plate to allow serving room. When you have completed your meal, the knife (blade toward you) and fork (tines up or down and to the left of the knife) should be paired together diagonally or horizontally across the plate. Make certain that all other utensils are placed on flat-surface dishes to avoid accidents during bussing. You should not stack your plates or push them away from you—leave them as you found them.

Table 14.3 provides examples of foods that require fingers, forks, or spoons as well as what food to avoid during luncheon interviews.

How to Handle the Job Offer

In one corner: the prospective employer, who wants to hire you at the lowest reasonable salary. In the other corner: you, wanting to be hired at the highest reasonable salary. In between is the negotiable area, which, according to HR managers we spoke to, ranges anywhere from 10 to 30 percent.

Source: Kate Lorenz, "10 Tricks for Negotiating a Higher Starting Salary," Retrieved from *CareerBuilder.com*.

You may be wondering if you should accept the offer the interviewer gives. According to human resources expert Lori Kocon, "The level of salary is a predictor of the level of responsibility you will have within the company." And since future salary increases and bonuses are based on this amount, an increase of just $1,000 in the negotiated salary may represent $15,000 to $30,000 over the next 10 to 15 years. Therefore, she states that you should definitely negotiate your salary, as most employers expect you to do this. She offers the following tips to ensure your success.

1. Dress and act the part. You communicate a great deal nonverbally when you first enter the interviewing room based upon your image and bearing. Make sure you are communicating the right message.

2. Be patient. Make sure you get the offer before starting to negotiate.

3. Research the normal salary range for this type of position. If you know someone who already works for the company, ask for his or her guidance. If you don't have inside contacts, you can find out what other companies are paying individuals with your skills and education by checking out third-party salary research.

4. Don't be the first to give a definitive figure. In negotiating, you want it to be a win-win for both of you. Therefore, begin by asking for a salary range before giving a specific figure.

5. Keep your full attention on the person you are negotiating with. Listen and watch for all verbal and behavioral cues that will give you a better idea of the real needs, values, and aspirations of the other party. Eye contact and body language communicate a great deal if you pay attention.

6. Be comfortable with silence. In a negotiation situation, the person who has the least tolerance of silence will fill the void by speaking—often with a concession.

7. Never downplay your strengths or overemphasize your weaknesses. Be friendly, but firm. If you're going for a higher-level position, have a pleasant air of confidence.

8. Do not put pressure on yourself to make a decision or grant concessions on the spot. Never think you have to accept their offer immediately. You should always ask for and be granted a day or so to think their offer through.

9. Negotiate for the future as well as the present. If you are told the salary isn't flexible, perhaps there's something else you can negotiate such as an extra week of vacation or a car allowance. You should try to increase the total value of your compensation package, which as a general rule should be worth approximately 25 to 30 percent of the offered salary.

10. Be sure. Never say "no" or turn down an offer until you are absolutely certain you must do so.

Your negotiation skills will also give the prospective employer an idea how you will negotiate for the company. The key is to do it in a way that gains you not only a higher salary, but also the employer's trust and respect.[22]

Resigning from Your Current Job

Congratulations! Your interview got you the job. Now you must take a deep breath and prepare yourself for the next challenge. Although you may be floating on cloud nine now, you must go through a lot of emotional and logistical hurdles.[23]

Changing your job arouses all sorts of feelings. During the transitional phase that begins with your acceptance of an offer and ends a month or two after you have started your new position, the emotional turmoil you will experience will be especially acute. Focus on the positive aspects of this challenge and the benefits of taking this new career opportunity.

---

[22] Kate Lorenz, "10 Tricks for Negotiating a Higher Starting Salary." Retrieved from *CareerBuilder.com.*

[23] Bill Radin, "The Proper Way to Resign," *Career Development Reports,* Innovative Consulting, Inc., 1998. Retrieved from http://www.radinassociates.com/resignation-proper.htm, January 28, 2000.

Keep in mind that in today's working environment, people change jobs more often. Moving forward to better opportunities is a normal career transition. As you move on from your current job, remember to be gracious and tactful.

Resigning from your current job can be a difficult task. To ease the transition, give at least two weeks' notice unless you are under written contract to offer longer notice. Let your boss know that should anyone in the firm need information from you after the two weeks, you are available for calls. Also, let your boss know that if the two weeks' notice is not needed, your new employer is ready for you to start immediately. Any exceptions to the two weeks' notice rule should be discussed with your recruiter or your new employer as soon as possible.

Do not resign until you are ready to leave your firm. Your company does not have to accept your notice, and they can end your employment immediately and choose to withhold any future bonus, paid vacation days, and other cash benefits.

Your written and verbal notice should be short and positive and provide only basic information. Normally, you do not provide reasons why you are quitting or information on your next employer. The only exception is if you are going to work for a customer or supplier of your current company. Be careful and never, never burn bridges, as you may cross paths with your employer again. Refer to the following steps for making this transition as smooth as possible and visit the following websites for further guidance: *http://www.i-resign.com, http://www.quintcareers.com,* and *http://www.jobstar.org/electra/question/resign.htm.*

STEP ONE

Make sure you have a firm offer with a start date. The offer does not have to be in writing, but you may wish to ask for written confirmation. An offer of employment is a binding contract, whether verbal or written.

STEP TWO

Write your resignation letter before talking with your boss. While it may be an unpleasant task, the letter is simple and direct. Date the letter, say when and what you are resigning, and sign it. Do not write much more if you wish to use your employer as a reference. In most cases, you do not need to explain your reasons for resigning. For example, if you write that you have found a challenging career opportunity, you may be perceived as implying that you are bored with your current job.

Keep your reasons and other unnecessary statements out of print, especially if you are leaving under less than desirable circumstances. While you may feel compelled to defend yourself, voice opinions, or settle scores, do not take these actions, particularly in writing. A simple, "I resign . . ." statement is powerful enough in itself. You do not want to jeopardize termination benefits and any hope of a decent reference just to blow off steam. If you think you have a legal case, then take it to court; but do not first turn the tables against you by making slanderous accusations. Tell it to an attorney instead. Remember, your employer requires and files your letter of resignation for exactly that reason: in case there is a legal problem down the road. Never commit to writing what you may later regret!

If you are leaving under good circumstances and feel that you owe more than just a one-liner, keep it short, simple, and positive. Resist the temptation to write too much and keep the intended audience in mind. It is nice to express your gratitude to your colleagues, but typically only your manager and the human resources department will see your letter. If you wish to thank management for the opportunities they gave you, include it in your letter. If you wish to thank your colleagues, take them to lunch. In all cases, resign with class and walk away clean. Do not mail or fax this letter until you have completed step three.

STEP THREE

Make an appointment for a personal meeting with your immediate supervisor or manager. You should resign in person, not by letter. Resigning orally may place you in the compromising position of having to explain your decision on the spot, so choose your words carefully. Your boss may want to probe for factors that led to your decision. You may be asked who or what is the reason for your leaving or may be invited to offer suggestions to help make the organization more effective. Be careful in how you respond to such questions because your interrogator is still your boss. Whatever you say may be viewed as biased and could eventually be used against you. Offer sincere praise for the firm and those with whom you worked. Prepare yourself beforehand by focusing on several positive aspects of your workplace, and mention them liberally when the opportunity arises.

STEP FOUR

Mail or fax a copy of your resignation letter to payroll or human resources. Make sure your permanent file shows you resigned and were not let go. Do not send copies to others in the company. If you feel compelled to talk with subordinates, coworkers, or others, do so informally and in a personal setting such as at lunch.

STEP FIVE

Keep a positive attitude throughout the experience. You want to leave your former employer smiling and having positive thoughts about you. You may even choose to do some special things during this transition phase, such as arrive a little earlier, send flowers to the administrative staff, or bring in cookies for the break room.

If your company conducts an exit interview, do not succumb to the temptation to "tell it like it is." While your soon-to-be-former company may say they want constructive criticism, you do not know how the information will really be used. Remember, with all the acquisitions and mergers, your soon-to-be-former employer could become a business partner in the future.

Before leaving the firm, take time to speak with each of your support staff, peers, executive personnel, and others with whom you have worked. To the extent practical, clear up any unfinished business. Be sensitive to others' reactions and keep your conversations positive and constructive. Some people may naturally express their own discontentment and may try to get you to agree with them. Instead of agreeing with them, express your appreciation for the opportunities the company has given you and tell your colleagues you will miss them.[24]

See the sample resignation letters in Boxes 14.5, 14.6, and 14.7.

---

[24] "How to Resign with Class," *SoftSearch Executive Recruiters Inc.,* PO Box 8416, Turnersville, NJ 08012, E-mail: *info@jobpros.com.*

Ms. Mary Brown
125 Stone Street
Bevier, MO 63344

July 25, 20XX

Mr. Stuart Boling
ABC Company
1234 East Union
Macon, MO 63552

Dear Mr. Boling:

Please accept my resignation from ABC Company effective August 12, 20XX. I would like to offer my full cooperation in making this a smooth transition, so that my departure will not have any impact upon you, my teammates, or our customers.

I have accepted another opportunity, which I believe to be the next step in my professional development. My resignation is certainly not a reflection upon ABC Company. I enjoyed my work and feel that I have learned and grown during my time here. Working with you and your team has been a pleasant and rewarding experience.

I am grateful for the professional opportunities and friendships I have enjoyed over the past five years. Please extend this appreciation to the management team. I hope our paths cross again in the future. I wish you and ABC much success in your endeavors.

Sincerely,

Mary Brown
Mary Brown
495-62-4567

C: Corporate Payroll/Human Resources

BOX 14.5 🐾 **Sample Resignation Letter**

1234 Pear Creek Road
Jacksonville, FL 32224
January 2, 20XX

Mrs. Sara Brown
Brooke Company
1456 Wilson Street
Jacksonville, FL 32225

Dear Mrs. Brown:

I have accepted a new position. I would like to express my gratitude for a rewarding professional association during my employment here.

This decision was not an easy one and involved many hours of thoughtful consideration, particularly with respect to my own plans for my future. I am confident, however, that this new position represents a positive move toward fulfilling my career goals.

I plan to work hard to wrap up my projects here and turn over my responsibilities as quickly and smoothly as possible. Therefore, if convenient, I would like to request that you waive my termination notice.

I am giving you two weeks' notice of my resignation from Brooke Company. My last day of work will be January 16, 20XX.

I have found my work challenging and enjoyable during my three years here. However, I have obtained a position that will provide higher levels of responsibility and career advancement.

Again, I thank you for your support and guidance during my employment. Best wishes for continued success.

Sincerely,

Wally Smith
Wally Smith

BOX 14.6 🖝 **Sample Resignation Letter**

Mr. Tom Rogers
2505 Bayridge Drive
Kennesaw, GA 30152

January 28, 20XX

Ms. Katie Cammack
Human Resources Director
Stephen Fuller, Inc.
6971 Peachtree Industrial Boulevard
Norcross, GA 30039

Dear Ms. Cammack:

During my six years at Stephen Fuller, Inc., I have gained considerable knowledge about residential design. I have enjoyed working with the people associated with Stephen Fuller, Inc., and I am quite sure that the success of the company will continue.

Unfortunately, at this time my family is faced with a child care issue that we must remedy. Presently, the only child care solution is for me to be home on Tuesdays. Stephen Fuller, Inc. offered me several alternatives, which I appreciate. Nevertheless, at this time, those alternatives are not feasible for my family.

Therefore, I must offer my resignation effective Monday, February 15. I do hope to continue my relationship with Stephen Fuller, Inc. as an independent contractor in whatever capacity you might need me.

Thank you for your understanding. I wish you continued success.

Sincerely,

Tom Rogers
Tom Rogers
Portfolio Studio Director

c: Tim Call Gary T. Fuller
     Stephen Fuller Debbie Linton

BOX 14.7 🖝 **Sample Resignation Letter**

Conclusion

Every job seeker must develop successful strategies for interviewing. If you do your homework before and after the interview, your chances of succeeding will increase. Additionally, the more you prepare, the more confident you will be during the interview. Review the following "ABCs of Job Hunting" from Robert Calvert Jr., editor of *Career Opportunities News,* as you seek that ideal job.

🖝 **A**lways assume a job hunt will take months, not days or weeks, and plan accordingly.

- **B**e punctual for all appointments, but arrive no earlier than five minutes before the scheduled time.

- **C**areer counselors can be helpful, but do not necessarily limit yourself to using only one.

- **D**o not relax just because you have just learned of a dream job. Keep researching; you might find one even better.

- **E**xpect far more rejections than acceptances. One job expert says you are lucky if you get one "maybe" after following up on your first 20 leads.

- **F**ollow-up every interview with a thank-you letter, expressing interest in the job and highlighting one or two of your best qualifications.

- **G**ive feedback from your job contacts to career counselors and people in your network so they know about your status—and will think of you often.

- **H**andshakes are important. Act like you have a high level of energy and look the interviewer in the eye.

- **I**nformation interviews are a great way of making contacts and learning more about your chosen field, and possibly discovering new job leads.

- **J**ob hunting is a 40-plus-hour-a-week process. Start early; work late and intelligently.

- **K**now exactly how to read interview questions and respond as clearly as possible.

- **L**everage the Internet for your job search, but don't limit yourself only to that resource.

- **M**emorize the name of the interviewer and use it once or twice in the conversation.

- **N**etwork using your best contacts and be prepared to share leads with others, just as they may share with you.

- **O**bserve the way employees dress in an organization and appear for an interview in slightly more formal attire.

- **P**ositive reactions you express about your school, former employers, and other organizations will help create a more positive impression for you.

- **Q**uit worrying every time you receive a rejection. Make each an excuse to develop three more leads.

- **R**ésumés should be slanted to the job in question, even if you have to create a number of different versions.

- **S**it alertly during the interview. Ron and Carly Krannich recommend leaning slightly forward, toward the interviewer.

- **T**aking a temporary job may help pay the bills and keep up your morale during a long job search. Over 1.3 million Americans are "temping."

- **U**se all possible sources of job leads: employment services, classified want ads, family, friends, and so forth.

- **V**ary your job approach, if necessary. If your letters or résumés are not getting results, try new formats.

- **W**rite down notes on all contacts and follow-up as soon as you leave an interview.

- e**X**amine your job progress each week. Sit down and think over what you did. What mistakes did you make? What seems to work for you?

- **Y**our family and friends can be the best sources of job leads. Even though they may not be in the mainstream of your career field, seek their help.

- **Z**ero in on potential employers. Research their activities and, during the interview, show that you have studied.

Exercises

EXERCISE 1 TESTING YOUR KNOWLEDGE

Directions: Circle the numbers of the questions you may legally be asked during a job interview.

1. Are you age 18 or over?
2. What languages can you write or speak fluently?
3. Are you a native-born citizen?
4. Do you have any relatives already employed in this company?
5. Is English your second language?
6. When were you born?
7. Can you work on Sundays?
8. Do you have a valid driver's license?
9. What are your children's names?
10. Do you have a legal right to be employed in the United States?
11. What is your religion?
12. Are you married?
13. Do you plan to have children?
14. Have you ever been arrested?
15. What country are you a citizen of?
16. What type of work does your father do?

EXERCISE 2 PREPARING RESPONSES TO INTERVIEWING QUESTIONS

Directions: Select three traditional interviewing questions and three behaviorial-based interviewing questions presented in this chapter. Write your answers to each of these questions and send your answers to your instructor as an e-mail attachment.

Assignment Options

OPTION 1: MOCK INTERVIEW

Interviewing requires careful preparation and practice. Your placement center on campus may offer opportunities for you to get interview coaching, practice, and immediate feedback.

Usually the Director of Career Placement conducts a mock job interview with you. Carefully prepare for your mock interview as you would for a real interview. The Director of Career Services will interview you for the position of your choice at a particular company or within a certain industry.

Bring a videotape so you can study your verbal and nonverbal messages later. Also, bring a current copy of your résumé to the interview.

After your interviewing session, ask the director to complete the Interview Rating Sheet you have provided (see next page). Submit this form and a self-evaluation memo to your instructor. In your memo, devote a paragraph to each of the following: what you did to prepare for the interview, what strengths you exhibited during the interview, what interviewing areas you will improve, and what you will do differently the next time you are interviewed. Be sure your memo has an introduction and a conclusion.

INTERVIEW RATING SHEET

Applicant's Name: _____

Date: _____

Position Applied for: _____

Low				**High**		
1	2	3	4	5	6	Technical Qualifications
1	2	3	4	5	6	Knowledge of the Field
1	2	3	4	5	6	Experience Level
1	2	3	4	5	6	Personality Factors
1	2	3	4	5	6	Appearance

Outstanding Strengths:

Opportunities for Improvement:

OPTION 2: ADVICE AND COUNSEL INTERVIEW

Contact an individual who presently holds a job in your major area or works for a company you might like to work for some day. Ask the individual to provide advice and counsel concerning your cover letter and résumé.

Take or mail your documents to the individual and schedule an appointment to review your work. If you choose your reviewer carefully, you will gain valuable information.

Ask the interviewer these questions:

- How do you feel about me after reading my documents? (You can evaluate each separately.)
- What three adjectives would you use to describe me based on these documents?
- Would my cover letter make you want to see my résumé or arrange an interview with me?
- What strengths do you see in my documents?
- What areas of weakness in the letter and résumé need to be addressed?
- How might these documents be improved?

After the appointment, collect your documents and ask for a business card or some form of identification. Within one week, send the reviewer a thank-you letter. Then write a memo about what you learned from the interview and include the interviewer's responses to the questions above. Make sure your memo has an introduction, body, and conclusion. With your memo, submit the business card, a copy of your thank-you letter, and your critiqued cover letter and résumé.

OPTION 3: DECLINE LETTER

You passed the test and landed the job. However, the only problem is that you landed two jobs. Now you must tactfully and graciously decline one position. Write your letter, employing the principles of presenting bad news.

OPTION 4: RESIGNATION LETTER

Write a letter to your highly incompetent boss, Ms. Slave Driver. Inform her you will be leaving your job as Marketing Representative with Sham, Inc., effective (your professor will supply a date). You have accepted a job with the Up and Coming Organization as Marketing Director. Be sure to give proper notice.

CHAPTER 15

Understanding the Challenge of Ethical Communication

The Enron scandal is the most significant corporate collapse in the United States since the failure of many savings and loan banks during the 1980s. This scandal demonstrates the need for significant reforms in accounting and corporate governance in the United States, as well as for a close look at the ethical quality of the culture of business generally and of business corporations in the United States.[1]

Kirk Hanson

[1] Kirk Hanson, executive director of the Markkula Center for Applied Ethics at Santa Clara University, March 5, 2002.

LEARNING OBJECTIVES

After reading this chapter, you should be able to:

- Define business ethics.
- List the ethical considerations in communicating.
- List the steps to building ethical communication systems.
- Relate the recommendations for improving on-the-job ethical behavior.
- Describe an ethical outline.
- Discuss the parts of an ethical outline.
- Understand the important role of global issues and ethics.
- Discuss ethical issues involving technology.
- Outline how to train for ethics.

The Importance of Ethical Communication

A young boy returns home from school one day and tells his father that his teacher was discussing ethics. "Dad," he says, "what is ethics?" The father, a co-owner of a small hardware store, ponders the question. "What is ethics?" he says aloud. "Alright, I'll tell you son. Let's say I am working in the store and a customer buys some tools. The tools cost $10 and the customer takes a crisp ten-dollar bill out of her wallet to pay me. I take her $10 and she begins to walk away. I discover, however, that the customer has given me *two* ten-dollar bills by accident. These new bills were stuck together so that she thought she was giving me only one ten.

"Ethics, son, is about this one question: Should I or should I not tell my partner about the extra $10?"[2] This story reveals the challenges of dealing with ethics.

In the last three years, the U.S. government has been battling corporate corruption and just recently sent the message that truthfulness will be expected when corporate executives communicate with shareholders. The demands now are for frank, honest communication, which is a significant departure from the practices of the late 1990s when relentlessly upbeat statements on corporate performance were often the products of rationalizations that trimmed away the uncomfortable or the unpleasant. Many corporations relied on the wiggle room created by the law to keep things upbeat. Facts that were considered immaterial were often not reported. Opinions, under a Supreme Court ruling, were not actionable absent direct positive proof that the speaker had knowledge of their falsity. Puffery, which is known to put a positive spin on facts for the purpose of making them seem as good as possible, was just an accepted part of doing business. Now Congress has stepped in with legislation that requires senior officials to certify the accuracy of their books or risk severe penalties. New regulatory restrictions on accounting firms require that companies spend more time and effort assuring that internal financial controls are adequate. The government is showing no tolerance for statements that served to deceive, even if they might have been allowed in the past.[3] The indictments of Kenneth L. Lay, John J. Rigas, Martha Stewart, and others clearly illustrate the important role of ethical behavior and communication.

Supreme Court Justice Potter Stewart defines ethics as knowing the difference between what you have the right to do and what is the right thing to do.

Within the field of ethics, there are two areas: descriptive and normative ethics. *Descriptive ethics* reflects facts about the moral judgment of a person or a group. For example, a manager might determine that John, an employee, appears honest because he returned a misplaced gold pen to its rightful owner. *Normative ethics,* however, involves formulating and defining moral principles. In other words, it means deciding appropriate actions to perform.[4] Berko, Wolvin, and Curtis define business ethics as how people should act within given business structures.[5] However, business *ethics* means different things to different people. The increasing number of multinational corporations, the internationalization of the workforce, and the

---

[2] Alan Zaremba, "Issues in Ethics," Proceedings of the 1990 Southeast Regional Conference of the Association for Business Communication, pp. 58–59.

[3] Kurt Eicehenwald, "Warning to Executives: Honesty Is the Best Policy," *The New York Times, Business Section,* July 10, 2004.

[4] Betsy Stevens, "Communicating Ethical Values: A Study of Employee Perceptions," *Journal of Business Ethics,* Volume 20, Issue 2, June 1999, pp. 113–120.

[5] Roy M. Berko, Andrew P. Wolvin, and Ray Curtis, *This Business of Communicating,* 5th ed. (Madison, IA: WCB Brown and Benchmark, 1993), p. 191.

information explosion make attention to the ethical dimension of business communication more critical than ever.

According to Boone and Kurtz,[6] you face the following ethical considerations in communicating:

Ethics influences what a candidate tells a prospective employer at a job interview and the questions that the employer asks the candidate in return.

Ethics influences the information a company reveals about goods and services and the information it holds back.

Ethics influences how companies handle consumer complaints.

Ethics influences the use of confidential information.

Ethics influences respect for individual privacy.

Ethics influences how people respond to business pressures.

Today, more than 15 percent of American companies with more than 50,000 employees have ethics offices empowered to examine reports of misconduct, and 37 percent of American companies with more than 100 employees offer ethics training. Since the General Dynamics' program started in 1985, the office has received more than 30,000 employee contacts resulting in 1,419 sanctions, including 165 terminations, 58 cases requiring financial reimbursement, 26 demotions, and 10 cases referred to lawyers for civil action or criminal prosecution. Among the complaints regularly reported are falsified résumés.[7]

Organizations now realize that actively promoting ethical behavior and practices not only makes sense from a customer relations standpoint, but also represents a better way to run a business. Clients are pleased and employees are satisfied when they view their organization as acting in an ethical manner. Because of free market forces that drive organizations to perform at optimum efficiency and cus-

Code of Ethics

[6] Louis E. Boone and David L. Kurtz, *Contemporary Business Communication* (Englewood Cliffs, NJ: Prentice Hall, 1994), pp. 22–24.

[7] Barnaby J. Feder, "Helping Corporate America Hew to the Straight and Narrow," *New York Times*, November 3, 1991, p. F5; and Chris Lee, "Who Gets Trained in What," *Training*, October 1991, p. 55.

A recent ethics survey by the Society for Human Resources Management found that 59 percent of human resources professionals said they personally observed employees lying about the number of hours they worked; some 53 percent reported that they saw employees lying to a supervisor, a jump of 8 percentage points in six years.

Source: Jane Spencer, "Shirk Ethic: How to Fake a Hard Day at the Office—White-Collar Slackers Get Help from New Gadgets; The Faux 4 A.M. E-Mail," *Wall Street Journal*, Print Media Edition: Eastern edition, New York, N.Y., May 15, 2003, Pagination: D.1, ISSN: 00999660.

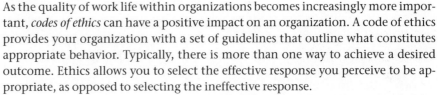

1. Consider others' well-being and avoid actions that will hurt others.
2. Think of yourself as a member of a community, not an isolated individual.
3. Obey—but don't depend only on—the law. An action may be legal yet unethical.
4. Think of yourself and your organization as part of society.
5. Obey moral guidelines. Consider them "categorical imperatives" with no exceptions.
6. Think objectively to be sure your action is truly ethical and not rationalized self-interest.
7. Ask, "What sort of person would do such a thing?" Or, as Peter Drucker has said, "Can you look at your face in the mirror in the morning?"
8. Respect others' customers—but not at the expense of your own ethics.

BOX 15.1 🖙 **Eight Rules of Ethical Thinking**

SOURCE: Robert C. Solomon and Kristine Hanson, *It's Good Business* (New York: Harper & Row, 1985).

tomer satisfaction, ethics plays a large role in how successful the organization will be.[8] Successful organizations follow the Eight Rules of Ethical Thinking presented in Box 15.1.

Creating an Ethical Organization

As the quality of work life within organizations becomes increasingly more important, *codes of ethics* can have a positive impact on an organization. A code of ethics provides your organization with a set of guidelines that outline what constitutes appropriate behavior. Typically, there is more than one way to achieve a desired outcome. Ethics allows you to select the effective response you perceive to be appropriate, as opposed to selecting the ineffective response.

Once a code of ethics is developed and made public, you must be totally and unavoidably responsible for your own actions. You cannot use the excuse, "I didn't know." Having a clearly stated code of ethics supports the concept of dignity as the central factor that drives all human interaction in the workplace. Most codes set boundaries for what constitutes ethical behavior as determined by professional organizational values. Organizational codes of ethics clearly identify behaviors that demand people treat each other with respect and dignity.

A clear code of ethics provides a safe environment to all organizational members. Once you have a clear understanding of what does and does not constitute ethical behavior in the organization, you can stop looking over your shoulders and constantly wondering, "Is what I am presently doing okay?" A code provides a commonly held set of guidelines that form a consistent value-driven basis for judging what is right or wrong in any given situation. The code defines the organization's uniqueness as much as its mission statement and objectives. The code should speak clearly to what this system values in terms of how its members should or should not be treated and how they should or should not respond.[9]

Creating a code of ethics is the first step to creating the **ethical office.** When you have an ethical office, the culture fosters mutual respect, trust, and honest

Many organizations solicit the input from their employees in developing an organizational code of ethics.

[8] Arthur Gross Schaefer and Anthony J. Zaller, "Why Ethics Tools Don't Work," *Nonprofit World,* Volume 17, Issue 2, March/April 1999, pp. 42–50.

[9] H. B. Karp, Ph.D., "Why a Code of Ethics." *Ethical Management,* April 1992, p. 6.

communication among coworkers, customers, and vendors. Your code of ethics provides a "big picture" statement of your principles and values, and then allows you to set a personal example. People want to trust the people they work with every day. Those who work around you will mirror your conduct and attitude. Ethical companies enjoy five long-term advantages.

1. **Productivity.**   Ethical workers outperform all others. They sell more products, receive fewer service calls, and post superior profit margins. The "personality" of an ethical office is healthy, energized, forward-looking, confident, creative, and resourceful. In this environment, people are not confused about the expectations for them.

2. **Accountability.**   With a clear understanding of expectations, employees take responsibility and feel accountable for their personal behavior and performance, regardless of their position. They take responsibility to resolve ethical dilemmas. They place high value on personal integrity. They communicate loudly, clearly, and often about doing things right and doing the right things.

3. **Communication.**   People want to talk about ethical dilemmas as they arise. This leads to earlier resolution and less confusion, which always saves money.

4. **Confidentiality.**   Information is power, and a lot of it leaks out. Individuals should treat everything as confidential unless told differently. Erring on the safe side will result in buttoned-up information about deadlines, prices, budgets, performance reviews, and product services.

5. **Predictability.**   Nasty surprises like harassment lawsuits and compromised security are expensive. In an ethical culture, employees address ethical dilemmas as they surface. Employees nip potential ethical dilemmas in the bud.

When you stick with an ethical policy, you will see the advantages. Simple statements of principles and values inspire employees to change their behavior and make their next decision the right decision.[10]

Can consumers actually make informed decisions if they can't understand the information because the documents are written in an incomprehensible writing style? Is it ethical to give consumers information they can't understand?

Source: Mark Hochhauser, Ph. D., Readability Consultant, "Plain Language Is Ethical Language," April 2004, 3344 Scott Avenue North, Golden Valley, MN 55422, Phone: 763-521-4672, Fax: 763-521-5069, E-mail: *MarkH38514@aol.com*.

Building Ethical Communication Systems

An organization should strive to build credibility and trust with its employees, customers, and clients. If the organization has communication that is two-way, relevant to needs, understandable, useful, timely, and mature (does not talk down), that organization will build credibility and trust with its stakeholders. Box 15.2 presents ethical communication practices.

Building a communication system around these principles reinforces positive relationships with employees. Further, communication systems based on these principles and practices will help ensure that the communication process contributes to the ultimate success of the organization. How do you, as a leader within an organization, put it all together?

Begin by creating a communication planning and delivery process in collaboration with your employees. Involving your employees ensures the relevance that the communication processes meet the needs of the "consumers." You must make this effort genuine; token involvement will end up reinforcing old messages to the workforce.

---

[10] Nan Demars, "The Ethical Office," *Executive Excellence,* Volume 15, Issue 11, November 1998, p. 12.

- The communication is central to the business and the performance of the business. It does not focus on topics and issues at the fringe (e.g., bowling scores, classified ads).

- Communication comes out regularly rather than on an intermittent basis.

- Communication is congruent with actions. It does not send mixed signals to employees.

- Communication activities and content are coordinated; that is, they fit together versus being a random pattern of disbursing information.

- Communication is courageous rather than timid and safe.

- Communication is collaborative. Collaborative communication allows employees to participate with top leaders rather than be controlled by them.

- Stakeholders view communication as credible rather than self-serving to the needs of the owners or the people at the top of the organization.

BOX 15.2 👉 **Ethical Communication Practices**

SOURCE: Ellen F. Harshman and Carl L. Harshman, "Communicating with Employees: Building on an Ethical Foundation," *Journal of Business Ethics*, Volume 19, Issue 1, March 1999, pp. 3–19.

Another action you can take involves creating a communication oversight committee composed of employees who have authority to identify issues and create communication processes. Involving your employees ensures that the communication has integrity in design and delivery. Such a committee should exist independent of the organization's formal communication entity, as the roles are significantly different.

Have this committee conduct a communication audit to help your organization understand where you are. Understanding where you are is the first step to getting to where you want to be. This audit will create a baseline against which your organization can measure change over time. Second, it provides a tool for planning. From the audit, the communication oversight committee can get a clear picture of the strengths, weaknesses, pockets of problems, and employees' needs. Finally, the audit will provide the data for discussion with leaders about the discrepancies in how various levels and constituencies perceive communication in the organization.

Be clear about the values, principles, and practices that serve as the foundation of the communication process. Putting them down on paper and committing to them go a long way toward making the communication process a reality. The first place to use stated values is in the creation of a communication plan. The communication plan allows you to check day-to-day actions against commitments. If your organization openly shares the values and reinforces the existence of an open, honest, two-way communication system, employees will be encouraged to give leadership feedback when they think leaders are straying from the values path. When creating this communication plan and process, make sure it supports the stated values. If the organization stops with the statement of values and goes no further, probably no substantive change will occur in the communication. The Communication Oversight Committee should develop the initial plan and get it approved by the leadership. Then, the committee should oversee the implementation of the plan and monitor its effectiveness in achieving stated goals and living up to stated values.

You and the organization should be willing to learn. Creating new, open, two-way communication processes can produce anxiety, but you and your organization must have courage. Understand that your organization will probably not be able to "get it right" the first time. As with all new endeavors, you face a learning curve to high performance. If you willingly take the risk, and if the communication process keeps employees informed of the successes and setbacks, an organizational climate supporting learning will occur.[11]

As you communicate with others, be aware of the ethical implications of your actions.

USING AN ETHICAL OUTLINE

As a communicator, whether speaking, writing, or interacting with others, you must develop a heightened consciousness of the ethical implications of your actions and the actions of your colleagues.

Brownell and Fitzgerald[12] provide an *Ethical Outline* requiring you to consider the various aspects of a particular communication event. By using the Ethical Outline, you discover that answers to ethical questions often depend on how information or strategies are applied in a particular context. The outline encourages you to think about your subject within an ethical and effective framework. Paralleling the concerns of effective speaking and writing, it addresses your purpose, research methods, selection of material, development of ideas, use of language, and audience analysis. Review the Ethical Outline in Table 15.1 to check your communication.

MAKING ETHICAL DECISIONS

You must measure the decisions you make against your standards of right and wrong while considering what character traits you believe are necessary to be an ethical person. Begin by getting the facts and thinking about these questions.

- What are the relevant facts?
- What individuals and groups have an important stake in the outcome? What is at stake for each? Do some have a greater stake because they have a special need or because you have special obligations to them? Are there other important stakeholders in addition to those directly involved?
- What are the options for acting? Have all the relevant persons and groups been consulted? If you showed your list of options to someone you respect, what would that person say?

Then you must evaluate your alternative actions by answering the following questions:

- Which option will produce the most good and do the least harm?
- Which option respects the rights and dignity of all stakeholders? Even if individuals do not get all they want, will all individuals still be treated fairly?
- Which option would promote the common good and help all participate more fully in the goods we share as a society? As a community? As a company? As a family?
- Which option would enable the deepening or development of those virtues or character traits that we value as individuals? As a profession? As a society?

---

[11] Ellen F. Harshman and Carl L. Harshman, "Communicating with Employees: Building on an Ethical Foundation," *Journal of Business Ethics,* Volume 19, Issue 1, March 1999, pp. 3–19.

[12] Judi Brownell and Michael Fitzgerald, "Teaching Ethics in Business Communication: The Effective/Ethical Balancing Scale," *Bulletin of the Association for Business Communication,* LV (3), September 1992, pp. 15–19.

TABLE 15.1 🖝 **Check your communication using the Ethical Outline.**

	YES	NO
Message Purpose:		
If my purpose is accomplished, will it be in the best interests of my listeners?	☐	☐
Will a small group benefit or will the larger organization or society be served?	☐	☐
Do I have any hidden agendas affecting my purpose or thesis?	☐	☐
Research Methods:		
Are my sources recent, reliable, and unbiased?	☐	☐
Was my research thorough?	☐	☐
Have I explored all avenues in gathering information pertinent to my subject and purpose?	☐	☐
Have I given credit where due?	☐	☐
Selection of Material:		
Have I chosen information communicating my ideas fairly and accurately?	☐	☐
Are my sources representative of the information available on my topic?	☐	☐
Development of Ideas:		
Have I relied too heavily on emotional appeals?	☐	☐
Are my logic and reasoning sound?	☐	☐
Have I avoided propaganda techniques that omit, exaggerate, or otherwise distort information?	☐	☐
Is my information accurate and relevant?	☐	☐
Use of Language:		
Am I easily understood by my listeners?	☐	☐
Is my language appropriately concrete and specific?	☐	☐
Have I relied on ambiguities, abstractions, and loaded words?	☐	☐
Does my language show respect for my listeners? Have I used plain English?	☐	☐
Ethical Context:		
Have I considered my listeners' values, feelings, and attitudes in designing my presentation?	☐	☐
Have I avoided using communication strategies that take advantage of their roles, status, or background?	☐	☐
Self-Analysis:		
Do I feel comfortable with the purpose and development of my presentation?	☐	☐
Do I sincerely believe what I have to communicate is important and true?	☐	☐
Have I done everything possible to prepare a message within my ethical comfort zone?	☐	☐

Pierre de Charentenay said that Europe should and can become a global leader with high moral and ethical values. It should promote multilateralism. The unification should create a strong partnership between member states and ultimately serve their citizens' best interests. Despite the daunting challenges that absorbing another 10 members poses in the years ahead, Europe has been cautiously moving toward integration since 1952—and it is not about to stop now.

Source: Roundtable Discussion with Pierre de Charentenay, S.J., May 13, 2004. Retrieved from *http://www.scu.edu/ethics/practicing/focusareas/global_ethics/european_union.htm.*

After you have considered the alternatives, you must then decide which of the options is the right thing to do. After you have made your decision, you should go back and evaluate if, in fact, you did make the right, ethical decision. As you evaluate your decision, you should determine if you had to do it all over again, whether you would make the same decision or do things differently.[13]

[13] "Framework for Ethical Decision Making," Markkula Center for Applied Ethics, Santa Clara University. Retrieved from *http://www.scu.edu/ethics/practicing/decision/framework.html.*

Understanding Global Issues and Ethics

Practicing global ethics requires work and effort.

SOURCE: Aurora & Quanta Productions/Maggie Steber.

One definition of *global ethics* refers to "any form of communication, written or spoken, that applies to providing a service or product to a different culture or country in exchange for compensation or intangible reward." In this era of rapid change and globalization, you should expect the best from yourselves and others. In fact, you should deliver more than is required or expected. If you take these actions, you will provide a positive direction, improved expectations, increased accountability, and greater growth toward achieving global standards.

Seven practical reasons show why global ethics and standards should be important to you. First, you demonstrate a willingness to play by international rules; at the same time, you raise standards. Second, you become accountable and predictable during your engagements. Third, you exhibit a willingness to develop your professional potential. Fourth, your character and reputation appear sound and marketable. Fifth, you show a desire to develop long-term relationships. Sixth, you become a leader in the global community. Seventh, you project uniformity in your professional life, which one rarely finds in a changing world.

Practicing global ethics requires work and effort. You must learn about the ethics of other nations and see how sometimes these ethics may be contradictory to yours. Learning global ethics and standards allows you to move from the old way of doing business to success in the global arena. If you desire to become an ethical global communicator, keep the following tips in mind.

LEARN THE HISTORY OF A COUNTRY'S CULTURE

A consulting company was working for an organization in Singapore to develop a logo. Their plan called for using a black square with one of its corners highlighted by a vibrant aquamarine sphere. One member of the team, who had grown up in Singapore, remembered small black squares were worn on the sleeves of traditional Chinese Singaporeans as a sign of mourning for the death of a close family member. Before proceeding with the design, the consulting company chose instead to find out how using black in the logo would be perceived in Singapore. They contacted another person who owned a Singapore agency and found out that this design, and not a plain black square, would work because the color black is used in different ways. In this example, the team considered the effect of the design, colors, and format. If they had not done so, unintended implications might have undermined their work.

Lesson to Learn. Check with local experts to save yourself time and money. Doing so can potentially make the difference between success and failure in a local market.

TAKE INTO ACCOUNT LOCAL HOLIDAYS AND LOCAL TRAFFIC CONDITIONS

One consultant was asked to visit a Bangkok office. He had not visited Bangkok for 20 years and did not realize how bad the traffic had become. Though the location was 10 to 15 miles from where he was staying, getting there and back was a full-day affair. He did not prepare for local conditions and blithely made arrangements assuming he would be able to keep them.

Lesson to Learn. Global ethics is having an appreciation for what you take for granted in your country the majority of the time.

BE SENSITIVE TO THE NEEDS OF OTHERS AND GO BEYOND WHAT IS ASKED

One individual shared his experience with Mexican and Native American clients. His clients often bought computers and accompanying software, but did not know how to use them or how to apply the applications in their everyday work settings. For no extra charge, he offered assistance and made referrals to other more competent consultants when he did not have a particular expertise. By taking these actions, he received many positive intangibles such as respect, appreciation, and a sense of satisfaction. By being sensitive to their needs and going beyond what was asked, he engaged in ethical practices readily accepted by others of a different culture.

Lesson to Learn.   Give assistance beyond the written contract. In every culture, kindness and sincerity will earn you respect and a sense of professional satisfaction. Many times this kind of behavior can help you extend or obtain additional business.

STOP BRIBES BY OFFERING POSITIVE MUTUAL OUTCOMES

In Korea, an individual experienced a situation in which a client attempted to engage in bribery. The client tried to stop the consultant from completing his assignment and wanted money to get the job completed for the consultant. Instead of paying the client, the consultant made a counteroffer. He offered to teach some of their employees how to use their computers and how to apply them to their work setting. In this instance, a conflict over values arose; the two parties had to find a compromise to meet both parties' goals.

Lesson to Learn.   Work on tasks benefiting both parties and do not reward bribery. Each party must search for common ground and values so that assignments can be completed in a satisfactory manner.[14]

> Although employees might be surprised their e-mail is monitored, companies have that right because they own the e-mail accounts. However, civil liberties groups say there are limits. "Ethically, we suggest employers use the technology only when necessary," says Kevin Bankston, a lawyer at the nonprofit Electronic Frontier Foundation. "People should get used to the idea their e-mail at work is just for work."
>
> Source: Jon Swartz, "More Firms Keep an Eye on Outgoing E-mail," *USA Today*, Money, Section B, Wednesday, July 14, 2004, page 1B.

Understanding Technology and Ethical Issues

While technological advances enhance organizational productivity, the real possibility exists that information technology can be used in ways that raise ethical questions. For example, the latest generation of office accessories, from cell phones to the RIM BlackBerry, has brought a new level of sophistication and a way to manipulate perceptions. The new options allow people to do far more than send e-mails from the beach. Services like GoToMyPC.com let you operate your office computer by remote control. You can even move the cursor on your screen, opening documents and printing them out on the shared office printer. Other strategies involve using existing technology in new ways. E-mail timers, a standard feature in Microsoft Outlook, let you send e-mails hours after you have gone to bed—a painless way to suggest to the boss that you are burning the midnight oil. Instant Message programs, a more-immediate form of e-mail now used by millions of employees, can also be reconfigured. Typically, if you haven't touched your computer in a while, the people you chat with online see an "idle" message next to

---

[14] Thomas J. Venardos and Mei Lin Fung, "Seven Reasons Why Global Ethics Should Be Part of the Way You Communicate," *Communication World*, Volume 15, Issue 7, August/September 1998, pp. 16–17.

your name. Diehard slackers can crack into the program settings to make themselves appear perpetually available. Psychologists call these games "impression management," a field whose rules have been transformed now that so many people communicate through technology rather than a handshake and a conversation. In some ways, the e-mail that arrives at 11 P.M. is the modern sign of a dedicated worker. But others see it as yet another legitimate technology that has been hijacked by people with skewed ethics. "If you're out playing golf, and you look like you've spent four hours in the office. . . . If everybody does that, the company goes bankrupt," says Stuart Gilman, director of the Ethics Resource Center in Washington.[15]

Another difficulty that technology has created is high-tech crime. Technologies such as e-mail, cellular telephones, and the Internet have fostered new types of organizational problems, from employees using their computers to snoop through confidential computer files to criminal theft of trade secrets. In a recent mail survey of 500 corporate security directors, 98.6 percent reported that their companies had been victims of computer-related crimes. Of those, 43.3 percent said they had been victims at least 25 times. The most common crimes reported were credit card fraud, telecommunications fraud, employee use of computers for personal reasons, unauthorized access to confidential files, and unlawful copying of copyrighted or licensed software.[16] Organizations have grappled with problems related to computer-based sexual harassment, pornography, copyright infringement, obscenities, software piracy, and the communication of trade secrets to external audiences.

People can also be victims of unethical behavior. For instance, in 1993, Jack Szwergold's survey found that an overwhelming number of individuals reported uneasy feelings and concerns about technology-related problems. In his study, he found 89 percent of the respondents perceived that computers made it easier for someone to improperly obtain personal and confidential information. Seventy-six percent felt people have lost all control over how personal information is circulated because of computers. Sixty-nine percent noted that computers represent a threat to their personal privacy. Sixty-six percent indicated a lack of adequate safeguards to protect the privacy of personal information stored in computers.[17]

A 1995 study conducted by Louis Harris & Associates for Equifax found similar results that paralleled Szwergold's earlier study. Eighty percent of those respondents reported they felt they had lost all control of the personal information collected and tracked by computers. The survey also found that individuals were becoming increasingly concerned about protecting their privacy, and 60 percent said they refused to provide information to businesses they felt were being too "nosy." Eighty percent stated they would be willing to put their medical records in a computerized system if a piracy code were in place and they could be guaranteed that records would not be used for marketing purposes. Forty-three percent expressed concern about marketers who collect information, while 54 percent reported being more worried about the government. Finally, Yankelovich Partners reported that of the 4,000 people they polled, 90 percent favored legislation to protect them from organizations that invade their privacy.[18]

Maria Perotin recently provided an example of how a thief can pirate your résumé. She wrote that thieves will post ads for fictitious job vacancies and then follow-up with eager applicants. Just like real recruiters, they may even exchange e-mail, conduct telephone interviews, or offer to fly candidates to company headquarters for a face-to-face meeting. The catch is that they ask applicants to reveal

---

[15] Jane Spencer, "Shirk Ethic: How to Fake a Hard Day at the Office—White-Collar Slackers Get Help From New Gadgets; The Faux 4 A.M. E-Mail," *Wall Street Journal,* Print Media Edition: Eastern edition, New York, N.Y., May 15, 2003. Pagination: D.1, ISSN: 00999660.

[16] "Computer Crimes Plague Businesses, New Survey Finds," *Greensboro News & Record,* October 25, 1995, p. B7.

[17] Jack Szwergold, "The Great Hi-Tech Threat," *Management Review,* 82, April 1993, p. 9.

[18] Bernard Horovitz, "80% Fear Loss of Privacy to Computers," *USA Today,* October 31, 1995, p. A1.

their Social Security number and date of birth so that they can basically steal people's identities. Some job boards and résumé-writing services have sold résumés at prices from 10 cents to 50 cents a piece, while others lack written privacy policies and may even claim ownership of individuals' résumés in order to keep the document indefinitely.[19]

CRITICAL ETHICAL ISSUES INVOLVING TECHNOLOGY

Technology becomes associated with ethical issues because it serves as the medium through which many problematic transactions occur. Technology may mistakenly be identified as the culprit simply because it acts as a conduit through which unethical behavior can be demonstrated at accelerated speeds, on potentially vast audiences, and often without the ability to identify the perpetrator. While ethical concerns are not inherent in technological advances, several over-arching issues may present ethical dilemmas for those who use computer technologies.

Issue One: Privacy. Mason argues that individuals may use technology to threaten our privacy in two ways. First, technology offers vast capabilities in terms of enhancing the capacity for surveillance, communication, computation, storage, and retrieval. In addition, information has become increasingly valuable in decision making.[20] Some decision makers may covet information to such an extent that they will invade another's privacy. For example, when Alana Shoars arrived for work at Epson America, Inc. one morning in January 1990, she discovered her supervisor reading and printing out electronic mail messages between other employees. As electronic mail administrator, Ms. Shoars was appalled. When she had trained employees to use the computerized system, Ms. Shoars had told them their mail was private. Now a company manager was violating that trust. When she questioned the practice, Ms. Shoars was told to mind her own business. A day later she said she was fired for insubordination. She filed a $1 million wrongful termination suit.[21] Similarly, confidentiality may also be at risk, even though protecting confidences that grow from professional interactions is the hallmark of professionalism in virtually every kind of business organization. Communicating private or confidential information over the Internet could be extremely damaging, since the potential for widespread information dissemination is so great.[22]

Issue Two: Accuracy. Because technology captures and stores such vast amounts of information, individuals or organizations could create, store, manipulate, or alter data in such a way as to cause harm to others. For instance, on a Prodigy bulletin board, a Prodigy member accused an investment firm of fraud. In a libel case, *Straton Oakmont vs. Prodigy,* the investment firm sued Prodigy, seeking $200 million.[23] In a 15-page ruling that put Prodigy on a moral and financial hot-seat, New York State Judge Stuart L. Ain argued that Prodigy Services Company, as a publisher, is fully responsible for the content of its subscribers' electronic postings.[24] The compelling need to ask who is responsible for the authenticity,

[19] Maria M. Perotin, "Job Seekers Should Be Cautious When Posting Resumes Online," *Knight Ridder Tribune Business News,* March 10, 2003.

[20] Richard Mason, "Four Ethical Issues of the Information Age." In Roy Dejoie, George Fowler, and David Paradice (Eds.), *Ethical Issues in Information Systems* (Boston: Boyd & Fraser 1991) pp. 46–55.

[21] Glenn Rifkin, "Do Employees Have a Right to Electronic Privacy?" *New York Times,* December 8, 1991, pp. 3, 8.

[22] Robert Hauptman and Susan Motin, "The Internet, Cyberethics, and Virtual Morality," *Online,* Volume 18, Issue 2, March 1994, pp. 8–9.

[23] Michael Snider, "E-Mail Isn't as Private as You Think," *USA Today,* October 10, 1995, p. 6D.

[24] Sebastian Rupley, "On-Line Services: Publishers or Service Providers?" *PC Magazine,* May 26, 1995.

fidelity, and accuracy of information should be obvious. Other questions arise regarding the identification of those responsible for errors in information and the development of procedures to ensure the injured party will receive fair compensation.

Issue Three: Ownership.   Technology increases the bandwidth of communication channels. Computers and networks carry vast amounts of information (data, voice, video, and message transmissions), and these technologies allow information to be stored, copied, and forwarded quite easily. This capability raises new concerns over the protection of intellectual copyrights regarding software, text, images, sound, and video, causing many organizations to become more active in protecting themselves. For example, at Chicago's Davy-McKee Corporation, a battery of federal marshals and computer experts barged into the construction engineering firm's office on a raid. The Software Publishers Association lawyer flashed a court order permitting the search of the company's computers for illegally copied software. Surprise drop-ins by the software industry's trade association have become a staple in the anti-piracy battle, as courts dole out search warrants and the software association increases its piracy police.[25]

Issue Four: Accessibility.   Because computers can store vast amounts of information, it becomes important to consider what information organizations can keep, the conditions under which they might obtain it, and safeguards to protect all individuals' rights. Access to databases, whether internal or external to the organization, must be protected to prevent access by information hijackers or software viruses. In the past, intruders have broken into the giant Internet computer network, and users were advised to protect themselves by changing their passwords. In particular, intruders can delete or remove other users' files.[26] Computer hardware and software are oftentimes not fully secure; thus, other accessibility issues arise. For example, should employees be able to use the company computer for personal benefit, or during "off" hours, or to access other employees' computer files that are not password protected? Finally, accessibility is clearly related to cost.[27] Organizations and individuals pay substantial fees for Internet access and computer equipment. The Internet provides equal access only for those who can afford for it, or for those whose work requires it.

Issue Five: Digital Signatures.   A signature on a paper document makes it legal and completes a contract. The downside to a signed contract is that it takes time to prepare and deliver original copies. Fortunately, technology has come to the rescue to speed up this process. When the facsimile was invented, the reports or contract could be delivered quickly from one office to another over a telephone line. Technology improved to the point that you could electronically fax a document, once again speeding up the process of getting a signed, legal document from one location to another. Your signature could be stored electronically and inserted into the document just before the document was sent. The next technological advancement was PDFs (portable document format). With PDFs and the convenience of e-mail, you can place your signature into the report or Word document, print it to PDF, and attach it to an e-mail. But, "What people don't realize is that, unlike faxes, which are one digital image, a PDF is a digital document that can be broken down and altered. Data can be taken out of the document, altered or imported into other applications. Your digital signature could be placed

[25] John Hendren, "Software Police Crack Down on Piracy," *Greensboro News and Record,* January 10, 1993, p. E3.

[26] "Computer Net Intruders Threaten Work of Users," *Greensboro News & Record,* February 5, 1994, p. A4.

[27] Hauptman and Motin, pp. 8–9.

on a check or used to sign another document. It's not secure at all," said Mr. James Hea, President of DataWorks, an Ottawa-based software development company that has been working with the real estate appraisal industry for the last 10 years. "What's worse is if that document is attached to an e-mail, it can be sent all over the world. . . without you knowing," he added. Digital signatures (essentially digital copies of your manual signature) are easily manipulated. So too are digital documents. PDFs are a convenient way to send supposedly non-editable documents for reading from one person to another. However, PDFs are editable with the full version of Adobe Acrobat or with the use of many OCR (optical character recognition) programs available on the market. That means numbers can be changed, signatures added, and reports altered—all of which is untraceable.[28]

Issue Six: Data Loss. According to Alexander Drobik, vice-president of Gartner Research, as e-mail has evolved into a business critical technology and has become the primary medium of business communication, businesses do not understand the risk/obligations of e-mail. Gartner suggests that as the value of e-mail data increases, it will become increasingly more important that the e-mail service always be available, reliable, and protected from data loss. As privacy and confidentiality legislation take on the force of law, organizations will be increasingly challenged to adhere carefully to regulations. The difficulty will be to ensure employee compliance.[29] Instant messages are an easy way to send confidential information outside an organization through the Internet. Employees sometimes treat it so casually that they send messages others find harassing. Some regulated industries, such as financial firms regulated by the United States Securities and Exchange Commission are required to preserve their instant messages just as they do other business records. "In case of lawsuits or a regulatory investigation, your instant messages are going to be subpoenaed," said Nancy Flynn, executive director of the ePolicy Institute in Columbus, Ohio and author of the upcoming book *Instant Messaging Rules*. If workers have been using the free consumer versions of the software, they may not have records of the messages—but the person suing the company could.[30]

Options for Managing Ethical Concerns

Substantial debate is going on in Washington, across the country, and on the Internet concerning whether the remedies to ethical abuses should, in fact, be legislated. On February 1, 1996, Congress passed the Communications Decency Act (CDA) as a part of the Telecommunications Act of 1996. According to this legislation, it is currently illegal to knowingly use an interactive computer service to send or display to a person under 18 years of age information with sexual content that is offensive as measured by contemporary community standards. As presently articulated, violations can result in fines under Title 18 of the United States Code and two years in prison. Even so, the ACLU announced on February 7, 1996, that it would file suit to challenge the constitutionality of the CDA.

Open discussion is viewed as another means of managing ethical concerns. The Internet has become a catalyst for promoting and facilitating the discussion of the relationship between computer technology and ethics.

---

[28] Leonard Carty, "Members Express Views on Electronic Delivery of Documents—I Need That Report Now!" *The Canadian Appraiser,* Winnipeg, Volume 46, Issue 2, Fall 2002, p. 26.

[29] Parveen Bansal, "E-mail Menace Must Be Tamed," *The Banker* , London, Volume 153, Issue 925, March 2003, ISSN: 00055395, pp. 142–143.

[30] Margaret Steen, "Instant Messaging Becoming a Workplace Tool," *Knight Ridder Tribune Business News,* Washington, February 16, 2004, p. 1.

1. *Information rights and obligations*—covering topics such as employee e-mail privacy, workplace monitoring, treatment of corporate information, and policies on customer information.

2. *Property rights and obligations*—addressing topics such as software licenses, ownership of firm data and facilities, ownership of software created by employees on company hardware, and software copyrights. Specific guidelines for contractual relationships with third parties should be covered as well.

3. *Accountability and control*—specifying a single individual responsible for all information systems, and underneath this individual others who are responsible for individual rights, the protection of property rights, systems quality, and quality of life (job design, ergonomics, employee satisfaction). Responsibilities for control of systems, audits, and management should be clearly defined. The potential liabilities of systems officers and the corporation should be detailed in a separate document.

4. *System quality*—describing the general levels of data quality and system error that can be tolerated, with detailed specifications left to specific projects. The code should require that all systems attempt to estimate data quality and system error probabilities.

5. *Quality of life*—stating that the purpose of systems is to improve the quality of life for customers and for employees by achieving high levels of product quality, customer service, employee satisfaction, and human dignity through proper ergonomics, job and workflow design, and human resources development.

BOX 15.3 📎 **Five Moral Dimensions of Ethical Standards**

SOURCE: Richard Herschel and Patricia Hayes Andrews, "Ethical Implications of Technological Advances in Business Communication," *Journal of Business Communication*, Volume 34, Issue 2, April 1997, pp. 160–170.

A third possibility asks businesses to enact codes of ethics specifically addressing the uses of technology. A number of individuals and organizations have drafted and circulated standards for ethical behavior. These standards should be grounded in the five moral dimensions presented in Box 15.3.

Such codes of ethics convey organizational expectations and offer guidance on how to behave. Individuals may not automatically see the need to examine their use of technology (communication behaviors and choices made) by using the same ethical criteria they would typically apply elsewhere. For instance, a so-called "flaming" response to another's expressed opinions or actions is more likely to be sent through e-mail than through a traditional memo. Writers must pause to recall that sending insults, obscenities, or threats is usually not regarded as particularly ethical or professional, whether one engages in such acts through e-mail, letter, memo, or face-to-face encounters.

Certainly, a code of ethics standing alone cannot have a profound impact on ethical business communication involving the use of technology. As an official clarifying statement, however, it can be part of the process of establishing an organizational climate in which ethical behavior is taken seriously and is actively encouraged. The code will only be taken seriously if those in positions of leadership abide by the code and take notice when violations occur.

The final means of managing or encouraging ethical behavior in business contexts resides in technology itself. Companies can develop technology-based solutions to technology-related problems. For example, the V-chip (the "V" stands for violence) is an electronic circuit whose purpose is to block violent programs from an individual's television. The technology empowers the viewer to control the types of television programming received in the home. The V-chip mandate is part of the sweeping telecommunications legislation passed by Congress. It requires TV manufacturers to include a chip in every new TV set. Another way technology manages potential ethical concerns is the development of the "firewall," computer network security software allowing an organization to access the Internet's vast resources without compromising internal network security. Such software gives organizations the ability to build their own customized electronic security policies. Finally, encryption and authentication software enable secure commercial transactions over the Internet.

As you can see, technology has profoundly impacted business communication. E-mail, voice mail, fax, GroupWare, cellular phones, pagers, and the Internet provide a vast array of new channels that you, as an employee, can use to communicate with others inside and outside your organization. Technology is a powerful tool you can use either to share information and ideas or to exclude and alienate. You can use it to wield power or to empower. You can use it ethically or unethically. As Hyde noted, "The danger is not technology; rather, the danger is us—we who do not question, we who do not understand, we who do not communicate beyond the rhetoric of either–or."[31]

How you choose to use technology and the ends you seek through its use will depend upon your values. You will use your values to evaluate the words and actions of one another. As Medhurst observed, "Between technology as miracle and technology as mirage lies the gray area of human choice making, human valuing."[32] Your ethical standards will be critical determinants of whether you choose to use technology in ways that serve to enhance the general well-being of the organizations of which you are a part.

Training for Ethics

What can you do to make ethics come alive in your organization? Begin by employing realism, making a commitment, using your imagination, and communicating effectively.

EMPLOYING REALISM

You must give rewards for long-term results such as quality, product development, process improvement, and customer retention, and not just based on the bottom line. Give promotions to those individuals who consider how results will be achieved in addition to just getting the results.

How you act sends a powerful message. If you set unrealistic deadlines or expectations, you may be encouraging your employees to behave unethically. If you put too much pressure on people to get results, they may perceive that you do not care how they get those results. If you ask for too much, your workers may think the only way to achieve the results desired is to cut corners.

MAKING A COMMITMENT

You and your workers want to do what is right. Your employees will strive to act ethically if they believe you, as their manager, are willing to pay the short-term

[31] M. J. Hyde, "Introduction: The Debate Concerning Technology." In M. J. Hyde (Ed.), *Communication Philosophy and the Technological Age* (Tuscaloosa, AL: University of Alabama, 1982), p. 4.

[32] M. J. Medhurst, "Human Values and the Culture of Technology." In M. J. Medhurst, A. Gonzalez, and T. R. Peterson (Eds.), *Communication and the Culture of Technology* (Pullman: Washington State University Press, 1990), pp. ix–xvi.

price, on occasion, for the long-term benefits. The message you convey through your actions can speak volumes. Acting ethically cannot be something you do only occasionally, such as when the cost seems unimportant or when your reputation depends on it. Ethical behavior must be the way things are done every day. When employees are unsure of what to do, they revert to the usual way of doing things.

When you serve in the role of middle managers, you often face conflicting pressures from the top, from your customers, and from your employees. Having realistic goals, receiving proper coaching, and making ethical conduct part of the goals (not only bottom-line performance) can help ensure you know what is expected and what it takes to achieve it.

USING YOUR IMAGINATION

Years of doing things a certain way, of trying to stay out of trouble, and of conforming to office politics have seriously stifled most people's imagination. When faced with difficult ethical choices, many freeze and take the easy way out. You cannot expect ethical conduct in situations of uncertainty or greater risk if ethical behavior is not practiced. "It will cost too much," and "It will take too much time" are typical excuses to avoid taking the ethical path. Creative juices seem to stop flowing. Preconceived ideas and self-imposed limitations jump right in. No one said ethics was easy. But then, neither are staying ahead in technology, getting the best people on your payroll, or finding new ways to sell products.

Being ethical does not mean that you forego the consideration of profit, but it does mean profit is not your only priority. Being ethical means that you add ethical elements to the results you expect from people and to what you reward. Reward those who help keep your clients' trust and loyalty, instead of only rewarding new sales.

COMMUNICATING EFFECTIVELY

Ethical leaders must set the standard of truth each and every day. The moment you become a leader, you have an opportunity to place the highest premium on truthfulness. The recent cases at Enron, WorldCom, and Arthur Andersen illustrate the need for every form of communication that a leader puts forth to be an accurate representation.[33]

When communicating your expectations, you must go beyond general and abstract statements. You must translate values and principles into concrete ways of thinking and doing. You must consistently enforce the standards you set, since this communicates just how serious you are about them. Your people must know you will hold them accountable for their actions. However, communication on ethical issues involves more than just setting the rules and enforcing them. Efficient communication must include listening to what your employees go through in their jobs, understanding what their ethical issues are, and hearing what they would like to see happen to have a more ethical workplace. To have effective communication, you must instill trust and gain respect. People will talk to you about problematic issues if they respect you. Managers who report to you will not bring up sensitive issues or concerns if they do not perceive they can trust you, are afraid of retribution, or believe nothing will be done about a problem. As a manager, you should be accessible to your employees and talk to them. They will find it easier to talk about sensitive issues with someone they know.[34]

---

[33] "Five Standards of Excellence Practiced by Ethical Leaders." Retrieved from: *http://www.workforce.com/section/09/article/23/55/60.html.*

[34] Dianne Girard, "Where Do Ethics Fit In?" *Executive Excellence,* Volume 15, Issue 11, November 1998, pp. 11–12.

Conclusion

How can you encourage ethical behavior? Researchers have recommended the following actions:

- ➤ Behave ethically yourself. Serve as a role model for others and initiate discussions about ethical values. Your actions send a clear message, so you must take the lead.
- ➤ Screen potential employees. Be diligent when you check references, credentials, transcripts, and other applicant information.
- ➤ Develop a meaningful written code of ethics. Putting something in writing often gives it more weight. These codes must be given to all employees and must be specific, concrete, supported, and enforced.
- ➤ Provide ethics training. As part of employee orientation, identify and deal with ethical issues.
- ➤ Reinforce ethical behavior. Employees should be rewarded for ethical conduct. You must clearly communicate managerial expectations.
- ➤ Create positions, units, and other structural mechanisms to deal with ethics. Ethics needs to be a regular part of organizational life.[35]
- ➤ James F. Lincoln, founder of the highly successful Lincoln Electric Company, said: "Do unto others as you would have them do unto you. This is not just a Sunday school idea, but a proper labor-management policy."[36]

As an ethical communicator, you should desire to treat others fairly. To help you stay current with ethical issues, visit the website at *http://onlineethics.org.*

Exercises

EXERCISE 1 ORGANIZATIONAL VALUES

Directions: The list below provides values found in organizational value statements. Choose and circle a value most relevant to you. You will be asked to share your response with a group of other students. Then brainstorm a list of some common inappropriate behaviors that can or do occur as a result of attempting to conform to this value.

Openness	Respect for the individual	Trust
Honesty	Low-level decision making	Support
Fairness	Teamwork	Achievement

EXERCISE 2 CREATING A STATEMENT

Directions: Use the following criteria to help you create an ethical statement to guide future behavior. Then answer the questions that follow.

---

[35] Robert Kreitner and Angelo Kinicki, *Organization Behavior,* 3rd ed. (Chicago: Irwin, 1995), pp. 101–102.

[36] C. Roland Christensen, Norman A. Berg, and Malcolm S. Salter, *Policy Formulation and Administration,* 8th ed. (Homewood, IL: Irwin, 1980), p. 591.

Criteria:

1. Visible (brief, clear, simply stated)
2. Reflects group value (the value you circled)
3. Supports individual values (your personal values)
4. Behaviorally focused (The purpose is to guide an action, not change an attitude.)
5. Responsive to day-to-day conditions (Focus on what is happening, not what "should be" happening.)

ETHICAL STATEMENT:

_____

_____

What exceptions would be appropriate for your ethical statement?

What kinds of resistance can you expect?

EXERCISE 3 CLASS DEBATE

Directions: Come to class prepared to discuss and debate the following questions:

1a. What constitutes ethical communication?

1b. What constitutes unethical communication?

2a. Is it ever ethical to lie?

2b. Is it ethical to tell a "white lie" to spare the feelings of a friend?

3. Is it ethical to tell a lie if someone else gave you permission to? For example, if the phone rings, you pick it up, and your dad tells you, "If it's for me, tell them I'm not home," or your boss instructs you, "Tell the customer it's been backordered" when in reality, he forgot to order the part.

4. Is it ethical for a salesperson to tell you the price is $500 when s/he knows that s/he can sell it to you for $430?

5. Is it ethical to use racial, ethnic, or religious slurs when a member of the insulted group is not present?

6. Sam meets an old friend and says, "I'll have you over for dinner sometime." As happens so often, Sam does not really intend to invite the friend over. Are these phrases such as "I'll call you" (at the end of a relationship) and "We'll do lunch" ethical?

7. To what degree is the use of sexist language, such as "girl," "chick," "gal," "humankind," vs. "mankind," or "salesperson" vs. "salesman," unethical?

8. When does the public's right to know go too far in violating an individual's right to privacy? For example, is it our right to know that Magic Johnson has AIDS, Kathy Lee Gifford's husband had an affair, and whether President Clinton acted inappropriately with Monica Lewinsky?

9. Is it ethical to conduct an experiment on someone without that person's full knowledge and consent of the experiment?

10. Is it ethical for advertisers to use persuasive sales tactics on an unsuspecting public?

11. Is it morally correct to advertise to young children? For example, is it ethical to use cartoons to promote a product or to target children who are too young to understand that they are being targeted?

12. Is it ethical for presidential candidates to make exaggerated promises to get elected?

13. Is a communicator unethical when utilizing ghostwriting? Can a speaker ethically use another to write a speech and then present it as his or her own?[37]

EXERCISE 4 ETHICS CHECKLIST

Directions: For each of the statements below, determine whether the described action is ethical, unethical, or both and then make a brief statement on why you chose what you did. Note, if the answer is "Both," cite an example for both the ethical and unethical situation. Try to identify the value guiding your decision.

1. Sending a small gift to a client.

   Ethical   Unethical   Both

   _____

   _____

2. Reducing the price of your service or product at the request of one customer, but not offering the reduction to the next one.

   Ethical   Unethical   Both

   _____

   _____

3. Disclosing information you heard in confidence that could damage your client or boss.

   Ethical   Unethical   Both

   _____

   _____

EXERCISE 5 ETHICS CASE

Directions: Completely review all aspects of the Challenger case on the website at: *http://onlineethics.org/moral/boisjoly/RB1–0.html*. Come to class prepared to discuss key events of this case and key learnings.

Assignment Options

OPTION 1: ETHICAL DILEMMAS MEMO

(Questions taken from Judi Brownell and Michael Fitzgerald's article entitled "Teaching Ethics in Business Communication: The Effective/Ethical Balancing Scale," published in the September 1992 issue of the *Bulletin of the Association for Business Communication*.)

   Directions: Answer the following questions and then summarize your responses in a memo to your professor.

1. What values do you believe to be important in a manager? In an employee? In an organization?

2. What businessperson do you respect a great deal?

---

[37] *http://lynn_meade.tripod.com/id115.htm.*

3. What recent business-related event has generated a significant ethical dilemma? What are the various sides of the issue? What position do you hold and why?

4. What ethical dilemmas have you experienced within your family? How were they resolved?

5. What ethical dilemmas have you experienced in a business environment? How were they resolved?

OPTION 2: CURRENT BUSINESS ETHICS MEMO

Directions: Find two current articles about business ethics. Compare and contrast those articles in a memo to your professor. Identify what you learned from the articles and how they apply to your class.

OPTION 3: ETHICS INTERVIEW

Directions: Interview an individual about ethical behavior at his or her organization. If possible, obtain a copy of the organization's code of ethics. Write a memo discussing your findings.

OPTION 4: DISCIPLINE INQUIRY: A TOOL FOR DEALING WITH BUSINESS DILEMMAS

(Used with permission from Mary E. Vielhaber, Eastern Michigan University.)

Directions: For every manager, issues and situations pose a dilemma. According to *Webster's Dictionary,* a dilemma is defined as "a choice between two equally undesirable alternatives." Please take a few moments to reflect upon a current business dilemma that you would be willing to share with colleagues. If you are not sure it is a dilemma, but it is an issue or a decision that continues to bother you, then consider how you would describe that issue or decision. Write a paragraph or two describing the dilemma as specifically and concisely as you can. Please include a complete description of the dilemma. If you choose to share it, you will be asked to read it to a group of colleagues. Limit your description to no more than one page.

Process:

Steps to Prepare for the Questioning Process

1. Identify the person who will present his or her dilemma and ask the person to read the written dilemma.

2. Ask for a few minutes of reflection.

3. During the reflection time, group members are invited to write down questions they may choose to ask the presenter.

4. Ask one of the group members to be a scribe and to record all of the questions asked.

The Questioning Process

5. After a few minutes to prepare, one of the group members begins by asking a question.

6. The presenter may respond to the question or simply say "Thank you," which is an acknowledgment that the question has been heard.

7. The scribe should record all questions.

8. No discussion will occur among the group members nor should statements be hidden in the guise of questions.

Post-Questioning Process

9. After _____ minutes, the group takes time to reflect.

10. The presenter is invited to make some comments describing his or her experience. The intent is not to resolve the dilemma, but to describe what the person is thinking or feeling.

11. The scribe gives the questions to the presenter, who is encouraged to "hold" the questions for at least 24 hours. The presenter then discusses the dilemma with a trusted person to review shifts in understanding and new insights.

OPTION 5: ETHICS PROJECT: SUMMARY OF RESEARCH MEMO AND PERSUASIVE MEMO

(Contributed by Jeanne Blum, Indiana University and Purdue University at Fort Wayne.)

Directions: Assume your supervisor at work or a former supervisor has asked you to research the issue of ethics and propose an action plan as it applies to his or her organization. If you like, you can assume you have been hired as a consultant to the organization. You could also assume that you have decided to propose some action on your own on the issue of ethics. Create the context of this project.

Make this project as real-world as possible to have a clear sense of your audience and the action you want taken when you compose the persuasive memo. A large part of the assignment is clarifying the context of the situation. If you are somewhat unclear about the needs of your audience and what action you want taken, your correspondence will not be effective.

Think about answers to the following questions:

- What do you want people to do?

- What objectives, if any, will the audience have?

- How strong a case can you make?

- What kind of persuasion is best for the organization and the culture?

Learn more about ethics as it relates to your organization through research or observation at the company before you decide what action you want taken in the persuasive memo.

Writing the summary of research memo will give you an opportunity to learn even more about ethics and how it relates to the field or industry of your organization. Write a memo (at least two pages) summarizing your research on ethics and the specific industry, using the proper APA documentation. Use articles from at least four scholarly or professional journals on ethics in general or ethics in the particular field of the organization.

Also attach an actual code of ethics to this memo. Make sure you mention this attachment in the memo. You could use a code that a particular professional association or society uses, but it should be somehow related to the organization that will receive your memo. Some of these codes are published. Write or call a company to ask if they will send you a copy.

Your memo should also discuss how you will use the information you found to persuade your supervisor to take some action on the issue of ethics. Of course, you will discuss this with a real audience and why the persuasive tactics will be effective. Think of the summary of research memo as a way for you to clarify the context of this project to help you write the persuasive memo, which will be fairly complex. The issue of ethics and how it applies to a real organization is a sensitive situation.

Also, write a persuasive memo (at least one page) to your supervisor. In this memo, use the information from the memo to the professor to persuade your supervisor to take some action on the issue of ethics. You might suggest that the company adopt or improve its code of ethics, hold training sessions to discuss an existing code, or take some other action related to ethics.

The audience for your memo is not an academic one, so you don't need to use APA documentation. However, you will need to informally document the information you used from your research. Your audience will be interested in the author and publication, so use an informal style such as the following: In an article in *Business Ethics,* Jane Smith reports: "Make sure you put quotation marks around direct quotes." *You must use some of the information you found from the articles in your persuasive memo.*

You will need to use the persuasive tactics you mentioned in the summary of research memo to your professor. Again, remember how sensitive this issue can be. Think about what objections your reader may have to the action you want taken. How can you refute those objections? How can you make it easier for the reader to take this action? Think carefully about your audience and their needs and attitudes. How will your taking this action help them?

Your summary of research memo and persuasive memo will be handed in at the same time, in a folder with photocopies of the articles you used.

APPENDIX A

Checklist of Common Problems That Occur

Completeness

Completeness means including only the necessary details and excluding the unnecessary. Answer the following questions: Who? What? Why? How? Where? When?

1. **Too much, too little, misplaced, omitted information or words**
    You included either too much information, too little information, or information altering the meaning of the message. Some examples of altered meanings include: generalizations, misleading statements, and contradictions.

2. **Incorrect writing strategy is employed**
    Given the anticipated audience's reaction to your message, you did not use the correct direct, indirect, or persuasive writing strategy.

Clearness

Clearness involves using familiar words, avoiding technical jargon, and checking for readability.

3. **Simpler, shorter, more familiar words**
    Much of the time, big words distance you from your audience and increase the risk of miscommunication. Therefore, you should use simpler, more familiar words.

4. **Technical jargon, cliché, and business slang**
    Use technical jargon sparingly and eliminate business slang. Jargon creates a sense of unity among the in-group, but distances people in other units. Some business slang (as per your request, enclosed please find, please do not hesitate, task at hand) was common years ago, but no longer. Only business writers used these expressions. Writers had the impression they ought to use a specialized terminology. Today writers call these terms "dead wood" because they are no longer living words. A cliché is an expression that has been used for so long that it is no longer useful. If you use clichés, it may give the impression that you have not thought much about what you are writing.

5. **Awkward sentence structure, organization, or difficult readability**

   Awkward sentences seem difficult to read and require rereading. Remember, long words and long sentences make the reading difficult.

Concreteness

Skillful business writers avoid words that are vague in meaning, create disagreeable mental pictures, or express general ideas.

6. **Word choice**

   Avoid using abstract or vague words. Words like "very," "good," "nice," "important," "bad," "thing," and "fine" encompass such broad meanings that they are vague in most contexts. Use specific words to paint pictures in the mind.

7. **Nonsexist language**

   People have become sensitive to sexism expressed in language. The old terms and titles have become illogical and incorrect. Use generic pronouns that refer to groups of persons. When you use plural pronouns such as "they" or "their," you do not indicate the sex of the group members. Alternatives you can use include:

   a. Eliminating the pronoun.

   b. Changing from singular to plural.

   c. Using words that do not indicate gender ("you," "individual," "person," "one").

   d. Using job titles instead of the pronoun.

   e. Changing the pronoun to an article.

   f. Changing to passive voice.

   g. Adding names to eliminate generic usage.

   h. Repeating the noun instead of using the pronoun.

Correctness

Correct writing involves using proper format, spelling, grammar, and punctuation. It also involves writing actively and allowing the doer to do the action.

8. **Ending in a preposition (in, on, of, for, into)**

   Prepositions indicate relationships. The end of a sentence (like the beginning) emphasizes, and a preposition may not be worth emphasizing. When readers see a preposition, they expect something to follow it. At the end of a sentence, nothing follows. In job application letters, reports, and important presentations, avoid ending sentences with prepositions.

9. **Misspelled word or lack of proofreading**

   Always remember to proofread. Read your work aloud to help avoid costly mistakes. The *i* before *e* except after *c* rule applies to 1,000 words in the English language. Doubling the final consonant rule governs 3,000 words. "Offered" does not double the *r* because the accent falls on the first syllable; do not double the last consonant before adding the ending. "Referred," with the accent on the second syllable, does double the final *r*.

10. **Subject and verb agreement**

    Subject–verb agreement errors often occur when other words come between the subject and the verb. Edit your drafts by finding the subject and the verb of each sentence. Subjects and verbs must both be singular or plural. Compound subjects require plural verbs. Example: *The president, as well as his staff, was able to attend;* or, *The president and his staff were able to attend.* Don't be confused by words that come between the subject and its verb. For example: The price of the computers keeps some businesses from having access to the Internet.

    Indefinite pronouns such as "anybody," "everybody," "everyone," "everything," "somebody," "each," and "no one" use singular verbs.

11. **Faulty parallelism**

    Parallel construction requires using the same parts of speech for items in a series. Compare like nouns and avoid shifts in tense.

12. **Dangling modifiers**

    Modifiers give more information about the subject, verb, or object in a clause. Your modifiers dangle when the words they modify are not in the sentence. Whenever you use a verb or adjective ending in *-ing,* check to see what word in the main clause it modifies. Modifiers used as introductory phrases must modify the grammatical subject of your sentence. Use adjectives to modify nouns and pronouns. Use adverbs to modify verbs, adjectives, and other adverbs. Examples: *The flowers look beautiful;* not, *The flowers look beautifully. She filed the reports quickly;* not, *She filed the reports quick.*

13. **Incomplete thoughts and sentence fragments**

    You must have a subject and a verb for a sentence to be complete. To fix the problem of an incomplete sentence, add whatever parts of the sentence you need.

    A sentence fragment occurs when a piece of a sentence, such as a phrase or dependent clause, is erroneously punctuated as if it were a complete sentence. When you discover a fragment in your writing, either (1) attach the fragment to an independent clause, or (2) rewrite the fragment to form a sentence by itself. Even a statement with a subject and a predicate can be a fragment if it follows a subordinate conjunction, such as "if," "when," or "because."

14. **Paragraphing and coherence**

    A typical paragraph has these elements: the topic sentence, details, and words binding paragraphs together. The topic sentence contains the central idea, details support the main idea, and binding words provide coherence. Coherence ties the thoughts together smoothly. Transitional expressions and repetition aid coherence. Your paragraphs should have organization and not seem like scattered ideas.

    Paragraphs should usually have at least two sentences, although you may have just one sentence in a closing paragraph. Generally, business documents have more than just one paragraph. Using only one paragraph makes the document look unbalanced.

15. **Effective sentences**

    A well-written sentence reflects clear thinking. If your sentence appears clumsy, you have not thought through your ideas. Consider not only what you want to say, but how you can best say it. A well-written sentence has unity, coherence, and emphasis. Unity and coherence make it logical and clear; emphasis makes it forceful.

Always edit sentences for tightness. Even a 17-word sentence can be wordy. When you use a long sentence, keep the subject and verb close together.

16. **Pronoun–antecedent agreement**

The pronoun must agree with the antecedent—the noun, noun phrase, or other pronoun to which the pronoun refers. Pronouns must correspond to their antecedents in number (singular or plural). Errors in noun–pronoun agreement occur when the pronoun reflects a different number or person than the word to which it refers. When antecedents are joined by "or" or "nor," the pronoun must agree with the antecedent closest to it, if one is singular and the other is plural.

17. **Numbers**

Use the same form (figures, words, or combined figures and words) within each set of numbers. Sets of numbers relate to one another.

Write the numbers 1 to 9 in words; express larger numbers in figures.

If the month follows the day or if the writer does not state the month, use ordinal numbers (1st, 2nd, 3rd, etc.) or ordinal words (first, second, third, etc.).

If a sentence begins with a figure, spell it out, even if figures are used later in the sentence.

Write approximate amounts in words.

Write amounts of money and percentages as figures.

Use figures with nouns.

Use figures with distances of more than one mile.

Use figures to express numbers in a series.

Write house numbers and building numbers in figures, except for the number one.

Use figures for quantities and measurements.

18. **a.m., p.m.**

Typewritten times of day should be written as "a.m." or "p.m." in lowercase letters.

Use "o'clock" with spelled-out numbers (it adds formality) and "a.m." or "p.m." with numerals.

19. **Spacing**

Follow the spacing guidelines given in your text. Remember to double-space between paragraphs.

20. **Pronouns cannot be interchanged**

Person	Singular	Plural
First [person(s) speaking]	I, my, mine, me	we, our, ours, us
Second [person(s) spoken to]	you, your, yours	you, your, yours
Third [person(s) spoken about]	he, his, him, she, her, hers, it, its	they, their, theirs, them

The case of a pronoun refers to the form it takes in a particular use in a sentence (subject, direct object, etc.). English has three cases: nominative, possessive, and objective. Pronouns with different nominative and objective forms cause the most confusion: I/me, he/him, she/her, we/us, they/them, who/whom.

	Nominative Case (Subject forms)	Possessive Case (Possessive forms)	Objective Case (Object forms)
Singular	I, he, she, it	my, mine, his, her	me, him, her, it hers, its
Plural	we, they	our, ours, their, theirs	us, them
Singular and Plural	you, who	your, yours, whose	you, whom

Use the possessive case before a gerund.

Example: The professor objected to Hillary's arriving late for every class. Reflexive pronouns typically function as an object of the verb, a verbal, or a preposition. It indicates that its antecedent is acting upon itself.

Example: She practiced it over and over to herself.

21. **Who, whom, which, that (relative pronouns)**

Use "who," not "which," when referring to people. "Who" replaces the noun, or "he," "she," or "they," as the subject of a sentence. "Whom" takes the place of a noun, or "him," "her," or "them," as the object in a sentence. "Which" refers to things. "That" can refer to people or things. "Who" may introduce either a restrictive or nonrestrictive clause. "That" introduces restrictive clauses.

22. **Capitalization**

The first word of each item in a formal outline and in a sentence should be capitalized.

The first and last words in the salutation of a letter and the first word in the complimentary close should be capitalized.

Do not capitalize points of the compass, seasons, words denoting a family relationship, names of academic disciplines, and common nouns.

All personal names should be capitalized.

Days of the week, months of the year, personal titles, abbreviations, acronyms, languages, and nationalities should all be capitalized.

23. **Commas**

Use a comma in the following situations:

Parenthetical—word or phrase not necessary to complete a sentence but gives emphasis.

Example: Furthermore, the report did not meet the guidelines.

Apposition—word, phrase, or clause that explains other terms.

Example: Our representative, Mr. Black, attended the meeting.

Introductory Subordinate Clause—Main clause follows introductory subordinate clause, which may begin with the words "as," "if," "when," "while," "after," "although," or "because."

Example: As you know, the meeting started at noon.

Long Introductory Phrases—Use a comma after a long introductory phrase, but not after a short one.

Example: During the last two months of every year, executives search for ways to decrease company taxes.

Introductory Verb Phrase—Use a comma to lead your reader after an introductory verb phrase.

Example: After checking the numbers for accuracy, the manager handed the report to her superior.

Conjunctions—Use a comma to separate two independent clauses joined by one of the following conjunctions: "and," "but," "or," "for," "nor."
Example: We have no record of a school by that name in Woodstock, nor do we have a record of anyone by the name of Heart in our files.

Series—When the last member of a series of three or more items comes before "and" or "or," place a comma before the connective as well as between the other items.
Example: The shipment included a large selection of combs, brushes, and hair supplies.

Omission of and Between Consecutive Adjectives—When two or more adjectives modify the same noun, separate them by a comma.
Example: Our well-trained, efficient staff will do a top-notch job for you.

Use a Comma If the Sentence Would Be Confusing Without It.
Example: The day before, I borrowed George's calculator; not, The day before I borrowed George's calculator.

Do not use a comma to separate a subject and verb or verb and complement. Also, do not use a comma to join two independent clauses in place of a coordinate conjunction ("and," "but," "or," "nor," "for," "yet," "so"). If you use a comma this way, you create a comma splice.

Always use "which" (instead of "that") to introduce nonessential clauses: *The bay, which was full of small sailing craft, was rough.* A comma should precede "which."

In a month-day-year date, place the year within commas. Do the same with the state or country in an address.

24. **Apostrophe**
Use an apostrophe to form the possessive case of nouns. Almost all singular nouns require an apostrophe, then *s*. Plurals ending in *s* require only the apostrophe. An apostrophe with *s* (*'s*) should never be used to form plurals except to avoid confusion (*CPAs,* not *CPA's;* but, *dot your i's.*) Use an apostrophe to form contractions (when one or more letters have been intentionally omitted).
Do not use an apostrophe to form the plurals of nouns, including acronyms (example: "PCs")
Do not use an apostrophe to form the possessive of personal pronouns ("his," "hers," "ours").

25. **Percent**
Express percentages in figures and spell out the word "percent" in text. In tables, you may use the percent sign. Spell out a number that begins a sentence or reword the sentence.

26. **Comma splices and fused sentences**
A comma splice occurs when you erroneously join independent clauses with a comma rather than a conjunction or semicolon.
A fused sentence occurs when you join independent clauses with no conjunction punctuation at all.
To avoid such errors (called run-ons or run-togethers) be sure you can recognize an independent clause. Use the following four ways to correct run-ons. Choose the solution best fitting your purpose and your paragraph.

a. Separate the clauses into two sentences.

b. Join the clauses with a coordinating conjunction.

c. Join the clauses with a semicolon.

d. Join the clauses by making one of them a dependent (subordinate) clause. Join them with a subordinate conjunction such as "because," "if," "when," "since," "after," "although," and "unless;" or with relative pronouns: "who(m)," "which," "that." Subordinating can be the best way to eliminate run-ons, since the kinds of words listed here show the precise relationship between ideas.

27. **"Its" versus "it's"**
The possessive form of "its" does not include an apostrophe. The apostrophe indicates the contraction of "it is."

28. **Words with similar meanings**
Writers often misuse these words. Although the differences may be subtle, you should use these words correctly to make sure your message conveys the meaning you intend.
Among is used for relationships involving more than two people or things.
Between is used for relationships involving two people or things.

anxious	fearful, worried
eager	enthusiastic
disinterested	impartial, detached
uninterested	indifferent, not interested
fewer	refers to items individually counted
less	refers to bulk or volume
good	desired or right qualities
well	satisfactory manner
than	used in making comparisons
then	at that time (when)
conscience	inner sense of right and wrong
conscious	knowing, aware
human	people
humane	having the best qualities of human beings
incidence	degree of occurrence
incidents	events

29. **Words sounding alike**
Writers use many words incorrectly because they sound alike. The incorrect use of the following words may make a negative impression on your reader. The most commonly confused pairs of words are listed and defined here.

accept	(v) to receive
except	(v) to exclude or leave out
	(prep) other than
adapt	(v) to adjust or alter, to make suitable
adept	(adj) skilled
adopt	(v) to take as one's own
advice	(n) suggestions, recommendations
advise	(v) to give advice or make suggestions
affect	(v) to influence
effect	(n) result
	(v) to bring about

all ready	(adj) prepared
already	(adj) previously
capital	(n) money
capitol	(n) government building
compliment	(v) to praise or flatter
complement	(n) that which completes or makes whole
council	(n) a group
counsel	(n, v) advice, advise
ensure	(v) to make certain
insure	(v) to protect against financial loss
everyday	(adj) commonplace, usual
every day	(adj and n) two separate words
farther	(adj) at a greater distance (measurable)
further	(adj) additional, extending beyond
	(adv) additional, a greater extent
	(v) to promote or advance
later	(adj) after the proper time
latter	(adj) the second of two things mentioned
loose	(adj) not fastened
lose	(v) to fail to keep or to misplace
moral	(n, adj) generally accepted principle of right or wrong
morale	(n) mental and emotional condition
overdo	(v) to exaggerate
overdue	(adj) delayed beyond an appointed time
passed	(v) to go by
past	(n) time gone by or time ended
personal	(adj) of a particular person
personnel	(n) persons employed
perspective	(n) point of view
prospective	(adj) likely
principal	(adj) main, most important
	(n) a sum of money, administrator
principle	(n) rule, law
rational	(adj) in possession of one's reason
rationale	(n) explanation of reasons
respectively	(adv) in order named
respectfully	(adv) with due regard
sight	(v) to see or to take aim
	(n) a view
site	(n) a location
stationery	(n) letterhead or writing materials
stationary	(n) permanent, not movable
their	(pron) possessive of "they," in the predicate
there	(adv) in, at, or to that place
too	(adv) excess and also
to	(prep, adv) toward
two	(n, adj) number

| your | (pron) possessive pronoun |
| you're | (contraction) contraction for "you are" |

30. Gerunds (verb 1-ing), used as noun:

Whenever a noun or a pronoun comes before a gerund, the possessive form should be used.

Example: I am concerned about your taking the job. (Common error: I am concerned about you taking the job.)

Example: Did you find any record of the customers' being notified? (Common error: Did you find any record of the customer being notified?)

31. Hyphens

A compound adjective should be hyphenated when used immediately before a noun.

Hyphenate fractions and the numbers 21 through 99 when spelled out.

32. Format errors

A problem that occurs with the standard format for letters, memos, or reports. See your professor if uncertain where the problem occurred.

33. Semicolons and colons

A semicolon may be used to replace a coordinating conjunction between independent clauses. (Coordinating conjunctions are "and," "but," "for," "or," "nor," and "so." Independent clauses have a subject and verb and can stand alone as sentences.)

Example: The sun rises earlier and the days are warmer.
The sun rises earlier; the days are warmer.

Use a semicolon between independent clauses joined by a conjunctive adverb ("therefore," "however," "nevertheless," "thus," "moreover," "also," "besides," "consequently," "meanwhile," "otherwise," "then," "also," "furthermore," "likewise," "in fact," "still").

Example: On weekdays we close at eleven; however, on weekends we stay open until one.

Use a semicolon between independent clauses joined by a coordinate conjunction when commas occur within the clauses.

Example: Today, people can buy what they need from department stores, supermarkets, and discount stores; but in colonial days, when such conveniences did not exist, people depended on general stores and peddlers.

Use a semicolon between items in a series when commas occur within the items.

Example: At the high school alumni dinner, I sat with the school's best-known graduate, Harper White; the editor of the school paper; two stars of the school play, a fellow and a girl who later married each other; and Tad Trump, the class clown.

Use a colon to separate independent clauses when the second clause explains or amplifies the first.

Example: Carl seemed proud of his wife: She had been promoted to manager.

Use a colon before a list, a long quotation, or an explanation.

Example: The things we need are: staples, pencils, pens, and disks.

34. Verb tense

The first principal part of the verb (the present tense) expresses present time, makes true statements, and uses "shall" or "will" to express future time.

Example: *We fill all orders promptly.* (present time)
Water seeks its own level. (true statement at all times)
We will order new stock next week. (future time)

The second principal part of the verb (the past tense) expresses past time. (No auxiliary verb is used with this form.)

Example: *We filled the order yesterday.*

The third principal part of the verb (the past participle) can be used:

a. To form the present perfect tense. This tense indicates action starting in the past that has recently been completed or will continue up to the present time. It has the verb "have" or "has" plus the past participle.

Example: We have filled the order.

b. To form the past perfect tense. This tense shows action that will be completed before a certain time in the future. It has the verb "shall have" or "will have" plus the past participle.

Example: We will have filled the orders by that time.

The fourth principal part of the verb (the present participle) is used:

a. To form the present progressive tense. This tense indicates action still in progress. It takes the verb "am," "is," or "are" plus the present participle.

Example: We are filling all orders as fast as we can.

b. To form the past progressive tense. This tense indicates action in progress sometime in the past. It consists of the verb "was" or "were" plus the present participle.

Example: We were waiting for new stock at the time your order came to the store.

c. To form the future progressive tense. This tense indicates action that will be in progress in the future. It consists of the verb "shall be" or "will be" plus the present participle.

Example: We will be working overtime for the next two weeks.

d. To form the present perfect progressive, the past perfect progressive, and the future perfect progressive tenses. These tenses appear like the simple perfect tenses, except the progressive element suggests continuous action. These tenses consist of the verbs "has been," "have been," "had been," "shall have been," and "will have been" plus the present participle.

Example: *We have been filling these orders with Model 212A instead of 212.* (present perfect progressive) *We had been filling these orders with Model 212A until we saw your directive.* (past perfect progressive) *By next Friday, we will have been working overtime for two straight weeks.* (future perfect progressive)

35. **Terminal punctuation: periods, question marks, and exclamation points**

Use a period at the end of a sentence. Many abbreviations have periods following each letter or word. Do not space after periods within an abbreviation. Space after the final period, as though the abbreviation were a word and the period were the final letter in that word.

Use a question mark to end a sentence that is a direct question.

Use an exclamation point to indicate strong emotion or urgency at the end of your sentence.

36. **Delayers and false starts**

Some examples include: "there is," "there are," "it is," "this is," or "this will." You want your writing to be active. Delayers encourage passive writing that creates longer sentences.

37. **Helping verbs and passive writing**

Some examples include: "is," "are," "can," "will be," "had," "has," "was," "were." Try to replace helping verbs with an active verb. An active verb does the action the verb describes. To change a passive verb to an active verb, you must make the agent (that is, the person taking action) the new subject. If you do not specify an agent, you must apply one to make the sentence active.

Active: The plant manager approved the request.

Passive: The request was approved by the plant manager.

38. Italics

Words to be defined in a sentence are usually set in italics. Italicize foreign expressions.

Italicize words when you are calling attention to them as words. Don't underline; use italics.

Use italics for titles of books, newspapers, magazines, and periodicals.

39. Quotation marks

Use quotation marks to enclose an exact repetition of someone else's spoken or written words.

Use quotation marks to set off a word used in a special sense.

40. Abbreviations

Abbreviations, such as "etc.," are generally not used in business writing. When you cannot list all items, use "and so on" or "and the like" rather than "etc." Or begin the list with "for example."

Conciseness

A concise writer avoids wordy expression, trite phrases, and useless repetition.

41. Wordiness

Avoid filler words that add nothing to the meaning of the sentence. Use gerunds (the *-ing* form of verbs) and infinitives to make sentences shorter and smoother. Combine sentences to eliminate unnecessary words. Reword sentences to cut the number of words. When you eliminate unnecessary words, you save time for your reader.

(If you included information the reader did not need to know, omit the unnecessary information.)

42. Redundancy or inflated wording

Redundancy means needless repetition. Remember, careful planning can help eliminate rambling and repeating ideas.

You inflate words when you use elaborate modifiers and unnecessary Latinate diction (words with endings such as *-tion, -ity, -ize,* or *-ify*). Avoid useless suffixes (as in "zealousness" for "zeal"); unfamiliar foreign phrases; and needless, unexplained jargon.

Express your ideas in clear, direct language. Try to increase your vocabulary, but use words with accuracy and intent to convey meaning, not merely to impress your reader. Otherwise, your writing may appear affected, and you may even obscure your ideas.

Courtesy

When you write with courtesy, you express an attitude of friendliness and goodwill. Focus on the positive, not the negative. Use the "you-attitude," and avoid negative words such as "delay," "can't," "impossible," "inconvenience," or "trouble."

43. Expressing the "you-attitude"

Focus on what the receiver receives or can do. Using second-person pronouns ("you") rather than third-person ("he," "she," "one," "they") gives your writing more impact. You can refer to a single person or to every member of your organization.

44. Starting some sentences with "I" and others with "We"

Using "I" too often can make your writing sound self-centered. Using it unnecessarily makes your ideas seem tentative. If you write, "I think we should adopt this plan," you imply that it's really only your idea. When you write, "We should adopt this plan," you sound more confident.

When you write about things you've done, said, or seen, use "I". Don't resort to awkward phrases such as "this writer" or "the undersigned" or to using the third person.

Your writing should be consistent from sentence to sentence or paragraph to paragraph. One paragraph should not be all "I" sentences and the next paragraph all "we" sentences. Ask yourself this question: "Am I writing for myself or the company?" When you answer that question, you will know when to use "I" or "we."

However when you write a document such as a self-improvement memo or a review of your performance you use first person "I" instead of the more formal third person.

45. Positive rather than negative

Eliminate negative words and words with negative connotations. Focus on what the reader can do instead of what you won't or can't let the reader do.

Character

Character combines all the principles of effective business writing. You give your document character when you avoid all stereotyped words and worn-out clichés. You gain character when your document shines with courtesy and clear writing.

APPENDIX B

Websites

Active writing: *http://fisher.osu.edu/~ryan_3/ugd/active_writing.htm*

Allyn and Bacon's Compsite: *http://www.abacon.com/compsite/*

American Psychological Associations (APA) Guide to Style: *http://www.apastyle.org/*

APA Publication Manual Crib Sheet: *http://www.sv.uit.no/seksjon/psyk/apacrib.htm*

Attribution: *http://www.lib.berkeley.edu/TeachingLib/Guides/Internet/Style.html*

BGSU Online Writing Lab: *http://www.bgsu.edu/departments/writing-lab/*

Business Communication World Wide Web Resource Center:
http://college.hmco.com/communication/resources/students/speech/speechcom_res_links.html

Capitalization: *http://owl.english.purdue.edu/handouts/grammar/g_caps.html*

Career and Job Search:

http://www.dbm.com/jobguide

http://www.jobhuntersbible.com

http://www.garywill.com/worksearch

http://www.hotjobs.com

http://www.joboptions.com

http://www.careermag.com

http://www.jobweb.org

http://www.CareerShop.com

http://www.fortune.com/fortune/careers/

http://www.careercity.com

http://www.zitroncareerservices.com/

http://www.dice.com

http://www.Techies.com

http://www.spherion.com/corporate/careercenter/home.jsp

http://www.monster.com

http://www.careerbuilder.com

http://www.brilliantpeople.com

http://www.blackenterprise.com

http://www.imanet.org/ima/index.asp

http://www.shrm.org

http://www.hire-quality.com

Computer Virus Myths: *http://www.kumite.com/myths/*

Dakota State University Online Writing Lab (OWL):
http://www.departments.dsu.edu/OWL/

DeVry Online Writing Support Center:
http://www.orl.devry.edu/academics_asc_lab.html

Dictionaries: *http://www.dictionary.com/*

E-Mail Decoding: *http://www.ust.hk/itsc/email/tips/decode.html*

E-Mail EQ Test: *http://www.ewriteonline.com/index.php?display=ShowPage&id=213*

E-Mail Guide: *http://www.webfoot.com/advice/email.top.html*

Electronic Greeting Cards: *http://www.bluemountain.com*

Elementary Grammar:
http://www.xtec.es/~dpermany/creditvirt/students/unit2/task2/hiway.htm

Elements of Style: *http://www.bartleby.com/strunk/*

English as a Second Language:
http://www.english.uiuc.edu/cws/wworkshop/eslresources.htm

English Grammar FAQ as Posted to alt.usage.english: *http://alt-usage-english.org/*

Ethics: *http://onlineethics.org*

FAQ: How to Find People's E-mail Addresses:
http://www.cis.ohio-state.edu/hypertext/faq/usenet/finding-addresses/faq.html

Finding Zip Codes: *http://www.zipcode.com*

Format for Citing Online Sources:
http://www.columbia.edu/cu/cup/cgos/idx_basic.html

Grammar and Style Notes: *http://andromeda.rutgers.edu/~jlynch/Writing/*

Grammar Tips: *http://www.chompchomp.com/*

Graphics:

http://info.med.yale.edu/library/ref/writing.html

http://www.boutell.com/newfaq/

http://www.adobe.com

http://www.agocg.ac.uk/graphics.htm

Hoovers: *http://www.hoovers.com*

Humorous Quotes: *http://www.lhup.edu/~dsimanek/neverwrk.htm*

Impact of Color: *http://www.colorize.com*

Interactive Grammar Exercises: *http://www.chompchomp.com/menu.htm*

Internet Fax Services: *http://www.ntfax-faq.com*

"It's" vs. "Its" Page: *http://englishplus.com/grammar/00000227.htm*

LEO Literacy Education Online: *http://leo.stcloudstate.edu/*

Main Writing Guide: *http://www.english.uiuc.edu/cws/wworkshop/*

Modern Language Association (MLA) Guide to Style: *http://www.mla.org/*

Networking Opportunities: *http://www.imanet.org*

Nonsexist Language:

http://owl.english.purdue.edu/handouts/general/gl_nonsex.html

http://www.stetson.edu/artsci/history/nongenderlang.html

http://www.towson.edu/~loiselle/genderedterms.html

Occupational Outlook Handbook: *http://www.bls.gov/oco/home.htm*

Online English Grammar: *http://www.edufind.com/*

Oral Presentation Skills:

http://www.duc.auburn.edu/~burnsma/oralpres.html

http://www.toastmasters.org/

http://www.novations.com

http://www.speech-works.com

Paradigm: Online Writing Assistant: *http://www.powa.org*

Punctuation: *http://www.grammarbook.com/*

Purdue Online Writing Lab: *http://owl.english.purdue.edu/*

Rensselaer Writing Center Handouts:
http://www.rpi.edu/dept/llc/writecenter/web/handouts.html

Research: *http://www.prenhall.com/english/3explore/3explore.htm#style*

Researchpaper.com: *http://www.researchpaper.com*

Resigning from Job:

http://www.jobstar.org/electra/question/resign.htm

http://www.unf.edu/dept/cdc/publications

Résumé Help:

http://www.accent-resume-writing.com/

http://www.absolutely-write.com/

http://www.jobsmart.org/tools/resume

http://www.rileyguide.com

http://www.eresumes.com

http://www.quintcareers.com

Spamming: *http://spam.abuse.net*

Teaming Websites:

http://www.teambuildinginc.com

http://www.workteams.unt.edu

Telecommuting:

http://www.gilgordon.com

http://www.att.com/telework

Telephone Directory: *http://www.loc.gov/rr/askalib/virtualref.html*

Tips and Resources for Writers:

This website provides a listing of all university OWLS:
http://owl.english.purdue.edu/internet/owls/writing-labs.html

Travel Etiquette: *http://www.traveletiquette.com*

Virtual Teaming: *http://www.seanet.com/~daveg/ltv.htm*

Voice Mail: *http://www.ohms.com/index.shtml*

Web Resources for Writers:

http://www.internet-resources.com/writers/

http://www.bedfordstmartins.com/lunsford/weblinks/toc.htm

Writer's Block: *http://www.writersblock.ca/summer2004/notice.htm*

Writing Centers Online:
http://owl.english.purdue.edu/internet/owls/writing-labs.html

Writing Information: *http://www.eeicommunications.com/eye/eyeindex.html*

APPENDIX C

Checklists

INDEX

Modified block style, 163, 164
Multimedia presentations, 243–244

N

Nervous energy, using up your, 236
Netiquette, 5
Networking, importance of, 343–344
Neutral statement, using a, 88
"No," saying, 87
Noise, and, 18
Nominal group model, 294
Nonverbal messages, and, 17–18
Normative ethics, 419
Normative perception, 16
Norming, 272

O

Online documents
    chunking, 171–172
    format principles, 170, 173
Online interviews, 403–404
Openings
    sample direct, 78
    sample indirect, 90
Oral presentations
    actions and gestures, 236–237, 237–240
    audience, analysis of your, 223–224
    determining the general purpose, 222
    fear of public speaking, 220
    importance of, 220–221
    mistakes in presentations, common, 239
    nervous energy, using up your, 236
    organizing the presentation, 224–226

outlining the presentation, 226–227
    pointer, using a, 231–232
    practice, importance of, 232–235
    retention of information, 228
    stage fright, 237
    support material, determining the, 225
    team presentations (*See* Team presentations)
    thesis, developing a, 224
    time and word constraints, estimating, 225–226
    visual aids, 228–231, 232
Orientation speech, preparing the, 299–300
Outgoing calls, 318
Outlines, 33–34, 226–227, 424, 425
Owner, 312

P

Pagers, use of, 4, 323, 324
Paragraphs, 180–181
Parallel structure, using correct, 126–127
Participants, 297, 312
Partner system, 58
Passive writing, 47–49
PDAs, use of, 3, 326
Perceptions, based upon differing, 15–16
Performers, 20
Performing, 272
Periodic reports, 135–136, 137–138
Personality differences, 19–21
Personal websites and blogs, 374–375
Persuasive writing
    action, persuading to take, 104–105
    attention, techniques for gaining, 103
    checklist for, 115

collection letters, 108–110
    desire to act, building up the readers, 104
    discussion or inquiry letter, 109–110
    effective writing strategies, 112–113
    e-mail sales messages, 108
    emphasizing your ideas, 113–114
    friendly reminder letter, 108–109
    importance of, 102–103
    interest, maintaining the readers, 104
    international audiences, for, 115
    logical appeal, using the, 104
    samples, 106–107, 110–111
    superior/subordinate messages, 111
    urgent appeal letters, 110
Pie charts, 185
Plain-text résumés, 375–379
Pleasers, 20
Pointer, using a, 231–232
Policies and procedures, writing company, 142–145
Positive attitude, presenting a, 399
Positive note, ending on a, 89
Post-interview, 401–402
Postscripts, 161
Presentations, oral. *See* Oral presentations
Progress reports, 135
Proofreading, 56–59, 383
Proposals, 136, 140–142
Public speaking. *See* Oral presentations
Punctuation style, 161

Q

Question-and-answer sessions, 242–243

R

Readability, checking for, 39–40
Realism, employing, 433
Receiver, 10
Reference initials, 160
Reflective thinking model, 294
Refusal and offer an alternative, presenting the, 88–89
Relay broadcasting, 327
Reports, short
    checklist, 146
    executive memo reports, 136, 139
    feasibility reports, 136
    guidelines, 145
    importance of, 135
    justification reports, 136
    periodic reports, 135–136, 137–138
    policies and procedures, writing company, 142–145
    progress reports, 135
    proposals, 136, 140–142
Repurposing, 165
Researching the company, 391
Resigning from your current position, 408–413
Responses, sample direct, 79
Résumés
    checklist, 386–387
    chronological résumés, 366, 367, 368
    design principles, 382–383
    educational accomplish-ments, 365
    electronic formats, 373–374
    experience, 364–365
    functional résumés, 366, 370
    heading, 363–364
    importance of, 363